Civilizing Habits

Civilizing Habits

*Women Missionaries and the Revival
of French Empire*

SARAH A. CURTIS

OXFORD
UNIVERSITY PRESS

OXFORD
UNIVERSITY PRESS

Oxford University Press, Inc., publishes works that further
Oxford University's objective of excellence
in research, scholarship, and education.

Oxford   New York
Auckland   Cape Town   Dar es Salaam   Hong Kong   Karachi
Kuala Lumpur   Madrid   Melbourne   Mexico City   Nairobi
New Delhi   Shanghai   Taipei   Toronto

With offices in
Argentina   Austria   Brazil   Chile   Czech Republic   France   Greece
Guatemala   Hungary   Italy   Japan   Poland   Portugal   Singapore
South Korea   Switzerland   Thailand   Turkey   Ukraine   Vietnam

Published by Oxford University Press, Inc.
198 Madison Avenue, New York, New York 10016
www.oup.com

First issued as an Oxford University Press paperback, 2012.

Oxford is a registered trademark of Oxford University Press.

Library of Congress Cataloging-in-Publication Data
Curtis, Sarah Ann.
Civilizing habits: women missionaries and the revival of French empire / Sarah A. Curtis.
p.   cm.
Includes bibliographical references (p.).
ISBN 978-0-19-539418-4 (hardcover); 978-0-19-992284-0 (paperback)
1. Women missionaries—France—History—19th century. 2. Missions, French—History—19th century.
3. Duchesne, Philippine, Saint, 1769–1852. 4. Vialar, Emilie de. 5. Javouhey, Anne Marie, 1779–1851. I. Title.
BV3703.C87 2010
266.0092'341—dc22   2009040631

Photo credits: Philippine Duchesne: Archives Society of the Sacred Heart; Emilie de Vialar: Archives
St-Joseph de l'Apparition; Anne-Marie Javouhey: Archives St-Joseph de Cluny

Chapter 4 is adapted from "Emilie de Vialar and the Religious Reconquest of Algeria," in *French Historical
Studies*, Vol. 29, pp. 261–292. © 2006, Society for French Historical Studies. All rights reserved. Reprinted
by permission of the publisher, Duke University Press.

Chapter 8 is adapted from *Views from the Margins: Creating Identities in Modern France*, edited by Kevin
J. Callahan and Sarah A. Curtis, published by the University of Nebraska Press. © 2008 by the Board of
Regents of the University of Nebraska.

Printed in the United States of America
on acid-free paper

In memory of Minna L. Jensen

Acknowledgments

Writing a book about three individuals who traveled to three very different parts of the world sometimes felt like multiple personality disorder as I struggled to cross into new territories of knowledge beyond metropolitan France. Many individuals helped in the journey, each adding particular expertise from his or her own field. Phil Kilroy, Virginia Meacham Gould, and Eva Sheppard Wolf read drafts of the section on Philippine Duchesne and provided valuable feedback on the RSCJ and antebellum America. For Emilie de Vialar, I could have asked for no better guide to the nineteenth-century Mediterranean world than Julia Clancy-Smith, who was particularly generous with her own research-in-progress. I first met J. P. Daughton in the archives of the Soeurs de St-Joseph de Cluny, where I also discovered Anne-Marie Javouhey, and he has been a strong supporter of the project ever since, always encouraging me to make larger claims than I dared myself. Trevor Getz vetted the section on Africa. Naomi Andrews read large parts of the manuscript and shared her expertise on nineteenth-century Romantic socialism. Rebecca Rogers, Stephen Harp, and Karen Offen read the entire manuscript, parts of it more than once, and brought valuable insights to every chapter. Jo Burr Margadant, Karen Offen, Rebecca Rogers, and Thomas Kselman have written many, many letters of support that have advanced this project over the years.

This book would have been impossible without the cooperation and generosity of archivists, particularly those within the religious orders themselves. Sister Margaret Phelan of the Religious of the Sacred Heart welcomed me to the archives in St. Louis and has retained a lively interest in this project from her current post as RSCJ general archivist in Rome. At the Soeurs de St-Joseph de l'Apparition, then-Superior General Bernadette Galea and then-Secretary General Thérèse Armouet facilitated my access to the archives from Rome, and Soeur Marie-Agnès Cavasino helped me navigate them in Paris. At the Soeurs de St-Joseph de Cluny in Paris, an entire cohort of researchers, including me, are indebted to the late Soeur Yves Le Goff, who welcomed us to the archives and shared her vast knowledge of the sisters' work. Since the private papers of each of these women were essential to this book, I am especially grateful that all of these individuals and their communities were willing to share them with an outside researcher.

Research and writing runs on money, and I have benefited from many funding sources. Early on, the Spencer Foundation provided a research grant for a semester in France when I was still rummaging around the archives looking for the perfect next project. In subsequent years, I received funding to support research and foreign travel from the Fulbright Commission, St. Louis University, the American Association for University Women, and San Francisco State University. The Institute for Research on Women and Gender at Stanford University provided a community of scholars and valuable library access during a critical year. The book finally got finished due to a fellowship from the National Endowment for the Humanities and the financial support of Dean Joel Kassiola at San Francisco State University.

In Paris, I am always grateful for the warm interest and logistical support of Philippe Boutry at the Ecole des Hautes Etudes des Sciences Sociales, as well as the expertise of Claude Langlois. Ginger Gould seems to have appointed herself my housing fairy, lending me her Paris apartment at several critical junctures. Maitane Ostolaza Esnal has been a good friend and colleague for many years since we first met at the Ecole Française de Rome and discovered we shared many research interests. Dorothée Chifflot acts as my makeshift translator and all-around booster, and Bernadette Angleraud and Jean-Marc Dinten are always ready to welcome me to back to Lyon, my French home away from home.

I have the great fortune to be a member of one of the most collegial and intellectually stimulating history departments in America, at San Francisco State University, where I am inspired by the scholarly work of my colleagues and grateful to those who took time to read parts of this project at our faculty research colloquium, especially Julyan Peard, Mary Felstiner, and Eva Sheppard Wolf. Before my return to SFSU, Hal Parker, Elisabeth and Lewis Perry, and Annie Smart at St. Louis University were model colleagues, and I am especially grateful for the friendship and good humor of John Carroll, whose arrival at SLU improved my working life considerably. At Oxford University Press, I am delighted to have benefited from the sharp editing skills and consummate professionalism of Nancy Toff, author and scholar in her own right. My thanks also to her assistant, Sonia Tycko, for finding the cover image for this book.

Finally, I dedicate this book to the memory of my grandmother Minna L. Jensen, who was neither French nor Catholic but, sharing the spirit of adventure of the women in this volume, made her own journey across the seas almost one hundred years ago to make a new home in a foreign land.

Contents

Introduction, 1

PART I   The Limits of Enclosure: Philippine Duchesne

1. From Old Worlds to New, 23

2. Foothold on the Frontier, 47

3. "We Shall Need Jesuits to Bring Them to Us," 75

PART II   SAVING SOULS: EMILIE DE VIALAR

4. Rehearsal in Algeria, 101

5. Refuge in Tunisia and Malta, 131

6. Expansion in the Ottoman Empire, 151

PART III   MISSIONARY UTOPIAS: ANNE-MARIE JAVOUHEY

7. French Origins and African Experiments, 177

8. The Mana Colony, 209

9. Catholics and Abolitionists, 233

Conclusion, 263

Notes, 273

Bibliography, 333

Index, 361

Introduction

After an eight-day river and overland trek west from St. Louis, a seventy-two-year-old Frenchwoman stands in a field shaking the hands of seven hundred Potawatomi Indian men and embracing their wives and children. In distant Tunis, a much younger woman, also French, receives permission from the bey to open a pharmacy, clinic, and hospital in the center of the medina, previously off limits to non-Muslim inhabitants of the city. And finally, in the same year, 1841, a woman whom the French king had called a "great man" and who feeds, clothes, shelters, and educates approximately five hundred semifree Africans in an experimental colony on the edge of the Amazon forest writes to the colonial minister offering—no, insisting—to take in an additional four thousand slave children in view of their eventual emancipation. Catholic nuns all, intrepid, determined, and not a little daring, these three women had transgressed boundaries both real and imagined to arrive in these diverse and somewhat surprising places. However individual their journeys and divergent their sites of evangelization, their stories, taken collectively, have much to tell us about the role both religion and women played in the project of constructing French empire in the nineteenth century.

This book began its own journey in the archives of the Soeurs de St-Joseph de Cluny, where I discovered the life of Anne-Marie Javouhey, founder of the order and an early missionary to West Africa and the French slave colonies. In the 1830s Javouhey initiated an unusual colony in the wilds of French Guiana, where sisters from her order oversaw the communal work of more than five hundred Africans seized in the now illegal slave trade. As a result, she became an advocate for the gradual emancipation of slaves in France's empire, all the while building up a religious order that numbered in the thousands and was present in most of France's colonies at the time of her death in 1851. Javouhey's story—familiar in some ways and surprising in others—was one I wanted to tell. Yet I did not want to write a traditional biography of Javouhey; instead I was interested in the ways in which her life intersected with important developments in religious, gender, and French colonial history in the first half of the nineteenth century. Javouhey was among hundreds of women who founded new, active, and apostolic religious orders in the wake of the French Revolution, revitalizing the French Catholic church from the ground up. Her independence and power as the head of an important religious order defied the emerging ideology of domesticity that trapped women in a set of gender expectations and laws in the early nineteenth century. Moreover, her interest in founding missions in French colonies just at the moment that France was redefining its empire brought women missionaries into the colonial realm for virtually the first time and had important repercussions for both church and state.

Javouhey was not the only woman missionary of this type, though she may have been the most audacious. Through a fortuitous combination of scholarly sleuthing and serendipity, I chose two more women to include in this study, Philippine Duchesne and Emilie de Vialar. Like Javouhey, they were born before or during the Revolution; all three women died in the 1850s. Duchesne was a founding member of the Religious of the Sacred Heart, an important post-Revolutionary religious order, and Vialar founded the Soeurs de St-Joseph de l'Apparition, an order that, like the (unrelated) Soeurs de St-Joseph de Cluny, expanded rapidly. Until the Second Empire, these three orders were the most important suppliers of French women missionaries overseas.[1] Through the collective lives of all three women, then, this book explores the rise of female missionary orders from their origins in the religious chaos of the French Revolution to their dominance under the Second Empire in ways previously invisible to most historians.

As missionaries, however, these women chose vastly different imperial arenas that bring to light the often-forgotten revival of French empire in the early nineteenth century. Duchesne, the oldest of the three and the only one to have entered religion before the Revolution, established the first overseas Sacred Heart mission in St. Louis, Missouri, in 1818, a territory she imagined as part of a lost French empire in North America. Her primary interest, like the Jesuits of seventeenth-century New France, was in evangelizing Indians. Vialar, the youngest of the three, decamped to Algeria a mere five years after the French conquest in order to (re)establish a Catholic presence in North Africa. Forced out of Algeria within a decade because of a dispute with the new bishop, Vialar nonetheless founded missions around the Mediterranean, footholds for the Catholic church in

Muslim lands, and outposts of informal French empire in Ottoman territory. Javouhey, for her part, concentrated on the French empire as it existed at the time of the Restoration, almost entirely slave colonies located in West Africa, the Caribbean, French Guiana, and the Indian Ocean. Often eclipsed by the better-known empires of the seventeenth and eighteenth centuries, on the one hand, and the post-1870 "new imperialism" on the other, the first half of the nineteenth century was formative in reestablishing France as a colonial power, and women missionaries like Duchesne, Vialar, and Javouhey were an important part of this process.

Historians have usually imagined imperial agents as either male and secular—explorers, merchants, soldiers—or, less often, male and clerical—the priest in the wilderness. But by 1850 these archetypes had been joined by thousands of religious women who displaced the traditional male missionary as educators, nurses, and evangelists to natives and French settlers alike. Because their work was ordinary and everyday and because it was done by individuals schooled in habits of self-abnegation and humility, it often fell under the radar of both contemporaries and subsequent historians. Nonetheless, it is the central contention of this book that precisely because it appeared benevolent and uncontroversial, this work was vital to the cultural construction of empire in the nineteenth century. In promoting Catholicism as universally applicable to peoples of all races and backgrounds, women missionaries like Duchesne, Vialar, and Javouhey laid the groundwork for the expansion of French Catholic culture, whether or not it was tied to institutions of state power.

The ability of women missionaries to participate in the ideological and practical work of empire depended, paradoxically, on religious institutions designed to shield their femininity. Few, if any, laywomen in the early nineteenth century had the freedom that Duchesne, Vialar, and Javouhey exercised as Catholic nuns to travel outside of France, negotiate with colonial agents and indigenous leaders alike, challenge church power, and evangelize among non-Christians, all roles more commonly ascribed to men. This freedom, in turn, was facilitated by changes in the nineteenth-century Catholic church, which became increasingly shaped by the evangelical energy of women. The female religious order of the nineteenth century underwent a radical transformation that allowed women religious to take up new roles in France and overseas. The innovative nature of this transformation, however, was camouflaged by the traditional nature of their calling. The very structure of female religious life and the respect it engendered in lay society allowed scope for experimentation not experienced elsewhere. Within the framework of one of the oldest institutions in French history, nuns carved out a space to pursue new and often controversial agendas, including evangelization on a global scale.

This book is conceived as a collective, contextualized biography. By focusing on three specific missionaries, I show how individual life stories crosscut the French imperial enterprise, as well as how women experienced the resurgence in French religious life after the Revolution. Their journeys are compelling in and of themselves. However, my primary interest is not in chronicling the lives of these women from cradle to grave—or baptism to canonization, in these cases—but in using their experiences as means to examine how they used the protection and opportunities offered to them by religious habits to spread Catholicism and French culture into global spheres of influence. In their evangelical enthusiasm, their leadership abilities, their skill in exploiting resources and networks to achieve their goals, their facility in adapting to changing circumstances, and, above all, their fierce determination not to compromise their sense of mission even when confronted by opposition in their own church, these three women had much in common. However, North America, the Mediterranean basin, and the French slave colonies presented different problems and challenges. Because Duchesne, Vialar, and Javouhey worked in three very different colonial contexts, juxtaposing their experiences allows us to understand the range of cultural adaptations necessary to successful missionary and imperial work in the early nineteenth century, as well as the limitations of the religious "civilizing" mission as disseminated by Catholic missionaries. Recovering the history of these three women opens up a new perspective on imperial history just as it does on gender and religious history.

Inventing the Modern Nun

The missionary experiences of Philippine Duchesne, Emilie de Vialar, and Anne-Marie Javouhey are incomprehensible without the revolution in active religious orders that marked female religious life after the French Revolution. Before the revolution, the vast majority of French nuns belonged to cloistered convents whose primary purpose was prayer and contemplation.[2] Some female orders, especially those founded during the Catholic Reformation, such as the Ursulines or the Visitation, also provided educational services to girls who boarded at the convent. Each convent, although it might belong to a religious family sharing the same purpose, charism, and rules, was self-governing and lived under the jurisdiction of the local bishop. The exception to the contemplative cloistered order were the so-called third orders or associations such as the Filles de la Charité, whose members ran hospitals, visited the poor and the sick in their homes, operated soup kitchens, and taught girls needlework, basic literacy skills, and the catechism. Drawn from a significantly lower-class milieu, these women took only annual vows and were not, in fact, considered true nuns but simply pious women dedicated to the service of others. With the exception of the Filles de la Charité, most such orders were small and operated locally. They survived not only because of their utility to local communities but also because they did not claim a higher status in the church. Attempts by religious women at the time of the Catholic Reformation to create active and apostolic orders—modeled on the Jesuits—that would work in the world failed due to clerical anxiety over the role of women religious in active ministry. Fledgling initiatives were forced into cloister. Only Vincent de Paul, founder of the Filles de la Charité, practicing what he called "holy cunning," got around these restrictions by denying that he was creating a religious order at all, eschewing perpetual vows, and recruiting among lower-class women who were, in fact, better prepared to take on the heavy work of nursing, visiting, and teaching among the popular classes.[3]

In post-Revolutionary France, however, the active and apostolic model became the predominant one while contemplative orders languished.[4] The new orders were distinguished from older ones in two important ways. First, they took up the active work of nursing, teaching, and serving the poor, which required that they leave their convents, breaking with traditions of cloister. Time devoted to these activities reduced the amount of time that nuns in traditional convents had devoted to prayer and contemplation. Second, they had a very different organizational structure. Instead of each convent being self-governing, the order was centralized under the direction of a *supérieure générale* (usually the founder of the order until her death) and an elected council. Members, who were trained in a common novitiate, joined the order with the understanding that they could be moved to any one of its establishments at any time—under the vow of obedience—to undertake whatever work was most needed. No longer would a young woman enter a convent knowing she would live and die within its walls. The superior general had responsibility for the personnel and the finances of the entire order. In admittedly anachronistic modern-day corporate terms, women's religious orders ceased being franchises and became national—or multinational—corporations run by the latter-day equivalent of a CEO. This centralized structure allowed for a far greater reach geographically and more unity of purpose.

Frenchwomen pioneered in the creation of the active and centralized religious order in part because French religious structures had been destroyed by the Revolution, giving them a new field on which to work. During the Enlightenment, the convent and the nun became widely used metaphors to discuss the tyranny of the monarchy and the calcified structures of the Old Regime.[5] In 1790 revolutionaries challenged the authority and wealth of the Catholic church, nationalizing its property, requiring priests to take oaths of loyalty to the nation, and transforming clerics into servants paid by the state and elected by parishioners. Reflecting the polemic against regular clergy—that is, nuns and monks—during the previous decades, most legislators felt that they did no useful work in society.[6] Nuns, furthermore, were believed to have been incarcerated in convents against their will; freeing them therefore was an act of revolutionary liberty. As a result, in February 1790 law-makers abolished monastic vows, providing small pensions to compensate for the loss of dowries and inheritance. By the fall of 1792, when the national government seized convents as properties of the state, it was no longer possible, legally at least, to be a nun in France.[7]

Although the Catholic church in general and women religious in particular experienced—and often resisted—these changes as unparalleled calamities, the destruction of cloistered religious life made way for the new apostolic model of the nineteenth century. Catholic women were at the forefront of a grassroots religious revival in France in the late 1790s. Energized by the persecution of priests who refused to take the loyalty oath, the de-Christianization campaign during the Terror, and the closure and ransacking of churches, Frenchwomen hid priests in their homes, sponsored clandestine religious rites, and mobilized to protect churches, sometimes with violence.[8] In short, they supported an underground church that predated the more formal reestablishment of religious liberty, first under the Directory and then under Napoleon, whose concordat with the pope finally established religious peace in 1801. With these initiatives came also the first stirrings of a return to religious life. The Filles de la Charité had regrouped by 1800, as had various branches of the St-Joseph order in central France.[9] New initiatives, like Sophie Barat's Religious of the Sacred Heart (which counted Philippine Duchesne as an early member), the Soeurs de la Charité of Besançon (where Javouhey was briefly a member), and Javouhey's own Soeurs de St-Joseph de Cluny, were founded between 1799 and 1808. Active orders were favored because they were more likely to receive authorization from Napoleon, whose vision of the church was utilitarian. Women religious were useful to the extent that they could teach the illiterate, heal the sick, and care for the poor. But women who founded and joined religious orders were not merely responding to leadership at the top. Instead, they saw in the apos-tolic model a means to re-Christianize France after the religious chaos of the Revolution. Even after the Restoration of the French monarchy in 1815, active orders flourished, whereas contemplative orders languished. For every ten cloistered nuns in 1790, only one remained in 1808, but for every ten apostolic nuns, eight remained.[10] The new orders were built, literally, on the remains of the old orders, as many of the new founders bought or rented former religious buildings that had become prop-erty of the state. More significant, they responded to the new religious challenge of rebuilding a church whose weaknesses had been unveiled during the Revolution in a France where religious life had to be reimagined from scratch.[11] By and large, they were new—and younger—women. Of the approximately 30,000–55,000 nuns who were forced out of religious life during the Revolution, only 6,700 returned.[12]

The numerical dimensions of this phenomenon are impressive. In 1808 there were 12,300 nuns in France, of whom just under half lived in the new kind of active, centralized order, both those apostolic orders founded during the Catholic Reformation and new foundations. Between 1800 and 1880, however, almost four hundred new active orders were founded in France, peaking between 1820 and 1860, with an average of six new foundations a year. By 1880, their membership had also multiplied tenfold, counting more than 130,000 sisters and outnumbering male clergy (priests and brothers) three to two. Here, too, the most intense growth phase was before 1860, when French nuns numbered at least 100,000.[13] In their rapid expansion, the new active orders clearly fulfilled a certain demand for low-cost, devoted workers in fields such as health care, education, and social services. In part, this demand can be traced to the emerging needs of what we now call the welfare state in a century of profound socioeconomic change. However, the supply of women religious met and sometimes precipitated demand. Nineteenth-century Frenchwomen found in the active religious order a model that served their spiritual and secular needs. In a century of increased focus on the role of women within the family, a large number of women escaped the confines of domesticity by joining religious orders. In religion, they did useful and respectable work while ensuring their personal salvation, as well as, they hoped, the salvation of others. Although confined by vows of chastity, obedience, and poverty, they found community and personal security and often acceded to positions of real responsibility.

Those who founded religious orders—as exemplified by the three women in this book—had particular latitude to exercise qualities of leadership and autonomy that were denied most laywomen. This sense of forging new religious identities was strongest for women in the first generation of foundations, especially the leaders of the new active orders. Indeed, the early nineteenth century was arguably the most creative period for French women religious—before the orders they invented became large and institutionalized. During this period, women founders adapted old rules to new purposes, experimented with new roles, and challenged existing notions of acceptable work and behavior. In so doing, they created a powerful model of women's religious organization that spread throughout Europe either through new houses in other countries or through imitation. Both for the useful work they did and for the otherwise "redundant" women they employed in female-led organizations, Catholic nuns earned the admiration—or envy—of Protestant women in Europe and America, some of whom set up parallel institutions such as Anglican sisterhoods or Lutheran deaconnesses.[14] Even Florence Nightingale's pioneering, and secular, nurses worked within an institutional framework closely derived from Catholic religious life without the permanent vows or, of course, the theology.[15]

The new kind of nun—active, uncloistered, seemingly responsible only to female leaders—produced a certain amount of anxiety in the nineteenth-century church even as it reshaped it. On the one hand, parish priests, bishops, and the church hierarchy in

Rome could not afford to ignore or squander the tremendous religious energy and opportunity for spiritual renewal that these women represented. Indeed, many women religious worked closely with male clerics as partners in new evangelization efforts. Nonetheless, conflicts, especially between female superiors and diocesan bishops, were also legion.[16] No longer confined to a single diocese, these orders controlled their own membership, finances, and choice of establishments. Many leaders had networks of friends, relatives, and allies on whom to draw in case of disputes. Their trump card was to appeal to Rome for formal recognition of their status as religious orders that crossed dioceses and were therefore independent of any single bishop. Growing ultramontanism in the church opened a space that gave women religious increased room for maneuver.[17] Yet, in the past, papal orders of women had always been cloistered orders, and the Roman hierarchy responded to these requests with a certain ambiguity that could result in years, even decades, of prolonged uncertainty and conflict. Yet over time, the new model became both acceptable and dominant, representing the main form of religious life for Catholic women, finally officially accepted by the church in 1900.[18] Frenchwomen were its pioneers.

In telling the stories of Philippine Duchesne, Emilie de Vialar, and Anne-Marie Javouhey, this book returns religious women to modern women's history. Despite the large numbers of women who joined religious orders in the nineteenth century and a growing body of historical scholarship on the "feminization of Catholicism," women religious sit uneasily in the dominant narratives of modern French and European women's history, which are primarily concerned with the growth of domesticity, as well as the attempts to resist it. The lives of hundreds of thousands of nuns who lived outside of marriage and the domestic model—all the while upholding domesticity as the pinnacle of womanhood—simply do not figure in this picture. Not invested in marriage themselves, they did not seek to reform it and therefore did not participate in the century's most prominent set of struggles for women's rights. Historians of women have sought instead the feminist heroes of the past—women like Olympe de Gouges or Suzanne Voilquin or Flora Tristan—who wrote explicitly about the rights of women and who sought legal, political, and economic equality with men. Catholic nuns, by contrast, overtly challenged authority only within the structures of the church; otherwise, they appeared to accept both male power and male discourses about power. Indeed, in France, where the Catholic church was a strong supporter of monarchy throughout the nineteenth century, women religious could usually be placed on the conservative side of the political spectrum. I would argue, however, that the ability of Catholic nuns to transgress certain gender norms was intimately linked to their participation in an old and respected institution, the female religious order, which appeared to embody traditional values. If women religious were subversive, then, their subversion is to be found outside the usual categories of analysis.

Although historians now acknowledge that a significant religious revival took place in the nineteenth century, women's disproportionately high participation in this revival is often treated as embarrassing evidence of their failure to modernize—or, more generously, of the second-class status to which they were relegated. Women religious also confound the categories of public and private spheres, which have long served as organizing tropes for understanding the roles of nineteenth-century women. Heirs to a tradition of enclosure and distance from society, as private a sphere as one can imagine, they nevertheless acted as active, visible, and very public agents of social change. Indeed, in a pathbreaking article on Quaker women, Phyllis Mack claims that "in the history of Western culture, it was devout Christian women who demonstrated the greatest degree of agency, particularly that element of agency that involves activity in the public sphere." In order to imagine this agency, however, Mack argues that it cannot be defined merely as "acts of will" but also as "acts of obedience" and "the freedom to do what is right."[19] Like the women in Mack's article, the three missionaries in this book sometimes acted in ways that modern feminists would recognize—traveling widely, exercising authority, speaking out—while seeking simultaneously to subjugate themselves to what they saw as God's will. In their minds, these were not contradictory impulses, and they were not fundamentally antimodern.[20] Indeed, this book argues that through their missionary work French Catholic nuns were integral to the process of transforming France into both a modern state and a global empire in the nineteenth century.

Between Empires

The early nineteenth century, while representing an unusually creative period in female religious life, was an anomalous moment in the history of French empire.[21] The first French empire, represented above all by the vast territories claimed by France in North America and the valuable sugar colonies in the Caribbean, was reduced first by France's defeat in the Seven Years' War in the mid-eighteenth century and then the Napoleonic defeats in the early nineteenth. Yet the second French empire, based primarily in Africa and secondarily in Asia, did not really come into being until the second half of the nineteenth century. The period in between those two empires was a transitional period, during which France's empire was made up of old colonies like Martinique and Guadeloupe, as well as emerging colonies like Algeria, and overshadowed by the memory of France's earlier imperial dominance. During the Restoration (1814–30) and the July Monarchy (1830–48), those French officials interested in the revival of French power overseas pursued their objectives in somewhat haphazard, accidental, and experimental ways, from the military adventure in Algeria to the shoring up of French commercial interests in the Middle East to plans for settlement and agricultural plantations in Senegal and Guiana. Out of these projects and plans, many of them failures, came experience that helped establish the more extensive empire later in the century. However, relatively little has been written about this imperial moment, compared to others. French Canada and Louisiana have been of longstanding historical interest; St-Domingue is now an integral part of French Old Regime and revolutionary history, and the post-1870 French empire (in West Africa, Madagascar, Oceania, Indochina, and the Middle East, among other places) is the object of innovative historical studies. Even Algeria, which has come under increasing historical scrutiny by French historians as a part of greater France, is examined more extensively during the period after 1850 (when, among other reasons, the sources get remarkably better) than in the first two decades after its conquest.[22] Neither has much light been shed on lost, imagined, or informal empire, arguably as important to France as actual colonies, in the first half of the nineteenth century.[23]

This book concerns itself with three separate arenas of French overseas expansion, each identified with one of the women missionaries under discussion. The first is the lost empire of New France in North America, still surprisingly alive in the French imagination, especially the imagination of French Catholics. When Philippine Duchesne sailed for America in 1818, at the request of the new French bishop of Louisiana, she entered territory that, for her, was still marked as French. Docking in New Orleans and traveling up the Mississippi River to St. Louis, she journeyed through lands that had been controlled by France and settled, however sparsely, by people of French descent until the late eighteenth century. Both upper and lower Louisiana remained French in language, culture, and religion for some time after their transfer to Spain in 1764 and their subsequent sale to the United States in 1803. Although French migration to the United States in the nineteenth century was negligible in comparison to other immigrant groups, French clerics and women religious like Duchesne formed a significant part of the early nineteenth-century Catholic establishment. Revolutionary clerical refugees from France and St-Domingue found new homes in the United States. Before 1850, the bishops of major American cities, including Boston, Baltimore, New York, New Orleans, Louisville, Indianapolis, Mobile, Galveston, and, of course, St. Louis, were French. More than fifty women's religious orders that established houses in the United States (which the Catholic church designated as mission territory up until 1908) also originated in France, beginning with the Ursulines of Rouen, who arrived in New Orleans in 1727.[24] These orders established convent schools that spread French culture through their use of the French language and French pedagogical models.[25] French missionaries, led by the Jesuits, also reprised work among Native American Indian tribes, evoking an almost mythic connection to the work of seventeenth-century Jesuits in particular, the legendary "black robes" whom, missionaries like

Duchesne claimed, Indians still revered in their historical memory. Back in France, public interest in Indian-American relations was high, whether viewed through missionary accounts, newspaper reports, or popular novels and plays.[26]

Clearly, American territory in the nineteenth century cannot be construed in any formal way as French. Nonetheless, Harry Liebersohn has traced continuing elite French interest in North America, arguing that French travelers "came to a site of colonial ruins" that "continued to inhabit the imagination of visitors from the metropolis, who followed the trail of former French glory from New Orleans to St. Louis, from the battlefields of upstate New York to the towns and villages of Canada, dreaming of a New France that had but recently flourished, its remnants still scattered across the gray skies and vast forest of the interior."[27] Travelers, exemplified above all by Alexis de Tocqueville, also came to the United States to compare the new world, especially its emerging democratic structure, to the old. By the 1830s and 1840s, utopian socialists also found in the United States a more promising site for experimentation than France.[28] Of the three missionaries in this book, Duchesne was the least dependent on either formal or informal structures of French power, but the past French presence in North America and its potential as an outpost of French culture remained surprisingly relevant for her and other French exiles.

The second empire under consideration comprised the actual French colonies at the time of the Restoration: St-Pierre and Miquelon off the coast of Newfoundland, Martinique and Guadeloupe in the Caribbean, French Guiana on the coast of South America, St-Louis and Gorée in West Africa (now Senegal), Bourbon (later Réunion) in the Indian Ocean, and five trading outposts on the coast of India, the most important of which was Pondicherry. By 1827, Anne-Marie Javouhey had established missions in all of these places. These colonies formed an archipelago of French power overseas that was a shadow of its former self. During the Napoleonic period most had been controlled by the British, who now dominated the great trading routes that had enriched French Atlantic cities during the eighteenth century. At the time of the Restoration, these colonies were put under the centralized control of the ministry of the navy and colonies, which increased France's naval budget and reorganized the system of colonial administration. Excepting St-Pierre and Miquelon and the Indian ports, they were all slave colonies dependent on Napoleon's 1802 restoration of slavery for their livelihood. Only Martinique and Guadeloupe could be considered prosperous, though they were pale imitations of the great wealth brought in by that other Caribbean island, St-Domingue, which liberated itself in 1804 as Haiti and still hung over the remaining colonies as a specter of all that could go wrong in a slave colony.[29] With the outlawing of the slave trade—nominally in 1817 and enforced after 1830—and anticipating the abolition (again) of slavery itself, especially after its abolition in the British Empire in 1834, colonial officials eagerly sought alternatives to economic dependence on slavery. These schemes, in which

Anne-Marie Javouhey participated, largely consisted of agricultural projects for yet unexploited land in the interior of West Africa or Guiana. Unable to coerce local labor, they also encouraged—by and large unsuccessfully—the emigration of French settlers to these distant outposts. With the collapse of slavery in 1848, these projects were abandoned as plantation economies faltered or failed. French Guiana, for which officials had the most grandiose plans, became a penal colony. Only West Africa figured prominently in the next imperial surge.

The third empire represented here was that emerging in the Mediterranean basin. European powers had never lost interest in the Mediterranean world, which was the site of considerable traffic in goods and captives throughout the early modern period. In 1798, a French army commanded by Napoleon Bonaparte invaded and held Egypt, remaining until 1801, when it was driven out by the British. The Egyptian expedition, however brief, whetted France's appetite for Middle Eastern and North African conquest. Napoleon took with him a veritable battalion of scientists and intellectuals whose role was to disseminate French civilization, as well as amass knowledge about the East. State-sponsored Orientalism of this kind prefigured the nineteenth-century empire in its focus on cultural appropriation as much as the control of resources.[30] In 1830, France invaded Algeria on a flimsy diplomatic pretext and spent the next two decades bringing it under full French control. At first, public and colonial opinion was divided over the extent to which France should settle or develop Algeria, but by 1848 Algeria had become three French departments, nominally integral parts of the home country, although virtually all of its residents lacked citizenship rights.

From one perspective, Algeria returned France to the colonial game and foreshadowed the successful African empire of the late nineteenth and early twentieth century. From another, however, it was France's first permanent colony in territories controlled by the Ottoman Empire. As Ottoman power weakened around the eastern and southern Mediterranean, European powers eagerly moved in to assert their alleged rights. Yet before 1870, the direct control that the French established in Algeria was the exception in this region rather than the rule. Instead, France and other European powers used indirect methods to increase their influence in places like Tunisia, Malta, Greece, Palestine, and even Turkey itself. Foreign consuls asserted their rights over foreign nationals. Business interests increased their activity. Christians went on pilgrimage to the Holy Land. Progressives heralded the liberation of subject peoples like the Greeks from the Ottoman yoke. However, missionaries like Emilie de Vialar, who set up establishments first in Algeria and then in Tunisia, Malta, Greece, Palestine, and Armenia, were also potential agents of French influence. Indeed, the Catholic church became an active player in these lands, claiming a revival of the early Christian empire, seeking to edge out Protestant and Orthodox competitors, and squabbling over control over Christian holy sites in

Palestine. European governments, for their part, sought to co-opt religious initiatives as reasons—or pretexts—for increased control. France, in particular, claimed special powers in Ottoman territories based on sixteenth-century treaties that gave French clerics oversight over Catholic practice and practitioners. Church and state here jostled for power and influence in ways that would help determine the extent of European mandates over the defunct Ottoman Empire after World War I.

Empire of Faith

These three "empires" of the early nineteenth century are by no means the only way of conceptualizing empire in this period or even the only places where France began to exert power before 1850. There is nothing in this book about East Asia or Indochina, for example, and only passing mentions of Oceania, Burma, and Australia, places where Javouhey and Vialar did send missionaries. Nonetheless, the disparity in experiences represented by these three case studies provides an opportunity to examine the relationship between missionaries and the French state in three very different imperial contexts. That relationship was complex. In the first half of the nineteenth century, it was not primarily marked by church-state conflict, as J. P. Daughton has shown for the Third Republic.[31] Instead, state actors saw missionaries as agents of "civilization" who could be harnessed to their own ends, and by and large the two groups cooperated. In the first half of the nineteenth century, French officials still saw conversion to Christianity, as Robert W. Hefner has called it, as a necessary first step in the "march toward human enlightenment,"[32] an attitude they would lose later in the century, when a purely secular version of the civilizing mission took hold.[33] Until then, however, the "civilization" that the French promoted overseas was still—at least nominally—a Christian one. Missionaries could also be useful auxiliaries to the state, especially as imperial interests turned toward holding and settling colonial lands rather than merely exploiting their resources through trade arrangements. The future inevitability of permanent slave emancipation in the French colonies also encouraged a positive attitude toward religious conversion. Even secular liberals believed that Christianity was good for fostering obedience and docility in subaltern groups from women to blacks.

Still, the fact that church and state were often partners in colonization does not mean that their objectives, methods, or impact always coincided. French clerics, including the three missionary women in this volume, saw themselves first and foremost as agents of God rather than agents of the French state. Although willing to exploit French power and protection for their purposes, their goal was the expansion of Catholicism under any flag. Like the British Protestant missionary societies discussed in Andrew Porter's *Religion versus empire?*, French Catholic missionaries had an ambivalent attitude to state power.[34] Because Catholicism, in their view, was a universal creed and the Catholic church a global institution, it transcended national interests. In addition, often "the missionary frontier ran ahead of empire," as missionaries chose new locations irrespective of their political allegiance.[35] In this volume, only Anne-Marie Javouhey consistently opened missions in actual French colonies of the time, a choice that was determined more by financial considerations than by any particular patriotic impulse. Home ties for missionaries were important but not absolute. Furthermore, in some places, especially Muslim lands, state power stood in direct opposition to Catholic interest in conversion. Colonial officials often desired the "civilizing" benefits of religion without the actual religious content or at least without the overt appearance of proselytization where it might be deemed inflammatory.[36] Missionaries, for their part, had to balance their "universalist Christian religious values and the imperial context of those values," as Jeffrey Cox has put it in his book on missionary work in the Punjab.[37] Opposing slavery, for example, was a position taken by some (but by no means all) Catholic missionaries like Javouhey in direct contradiction to French policy. The dictates of faith did not always match the needs of empire.

In the early nineteenth century the Catholic church was undergoing a significant spiritual and institutional revival that fueled the missionary drive. Like the last great missionary push in the sixteenth and seventeenth centuries, in the aftermath of the Protestant Reformation, the impulse to combat religious ignorance and effect conversions overseas was directly related to the same impulse at home, this time the re-Christianization campaign in the aftermath of the French Revolution.[38] The new female religious orders in France were at base evangelizing institutions that sought to restore religious faith and practice through example and good works. During the early years of the Restoration, domestic missionaries from male religious orders like the Jesuits traveled the length and breadth of the country, preaching in revival meetings that sought to reanimate French faith after the dislocations of the revolutionary and Napoleonic periods.[39] At least one of the women in this volume, Emilie de Vialar, participated in such a mission before her entry into religious life. On an institutional level, Pope Pius VII reopened the church's missionary arm, Propaganda Fide, in 1817. Although Propaganda Fide had few funds with which to support missions, it did play a critical role in defining mission territory and adjudicating conflicts between religious orders and national interests overseas.

Overseas missionary work also captured the imagination of the public. Following his successful novellas about American Indians, Romantic thinker and writer François-René de Chateaubriand published *Genius of Christianity* in 1802, which discusses French missions at length. His *Itinéraire de Paris à Jérusalem*, published in 1811, rekindled interest in the Holy Land. The next decade witnessed a flurry of publications or republications of other missionary books, from a new edition of the well-known *Lettres édifiantes et curieuses des Jésuites du Paraguay, des Indes, et de la Chine* in 1815–16, to a new version, *Nouvelles lettres édifiantes* published by the Société des Missions Etrangères in 1818–21.[40] In 1822, a pious laywoman in Lyon, Pauline Jaricot, founded Propagation de la Foi, which became a fund-raising organization for Catholic missions abroad, collecting the proverbial "petit sou" for the missions, and redistributing the funds to needy missionaries. Beginning in 1825, it also published an influential journal, *Annales de la Propagation de la Foi*, which kept Catholic subscribers up to date on missionary developments abroad, often publishing missionary letters verbatim. By 1835, Propagation de la Foi was active in nine out of ten French dioceses and collecting a half million francs per year, increasing to two million by 1845.[41] In 1843, the bishop of Nancy founded l'Oeuvre de la Sainte Enfance (the Holy Childhood Association) in order to support indigenous children in mission areas.[42] All of these organizations saw tremendous growth in the nineteenth century as public interest in missionary work soared. At the same time, interest in missions built support for empire.

The shock troops of the nineteenth-century missionary movement were new and old religious orders, among which French orders predominated. At the death of Pius IX in 1878 three-quarters of Catholic male and female missionaries in the world were French.[43] Napoleon reauthorized three important French male missionary orders from the Old Regime: the Congrégation de la Mission (Lazarists), the Société des Missions Etrangères de Paris, and the Congrégation du Saint-Esprit (Spiritains), who reprised their missionary work in the Ottoman Empire, Asia, and the French colonies. New male orders, many of them originating in the pious and prosperous Lyon region joined them in expanding all over the world.[44]

Nonetheless, the novel development in the missionary movement was the entry of female religious orders. Traditionally, in both Catholic and Protestant discourse, Christian missionaries were assumed to be men.[45] The term *missionnaire* was gendered male in French, and throughout the nineteenth century when statistics were collected on clerics abroad, *soeurs* or *religieuses* were counted separately (if they were counted at all) from *missionnaires*. The model missionary remained the Jesuit or Lazarist priest of the sixteenth or seventeenth centuries, venturing into unknown and often unmapped spaces, confronting indigenous peoples, often at risk to his own life. His goal was the conversion of these peoples as measured by, first, baptisms and then regular practice of the Christian sacraments. The vocabulary was martial: the missionary as a soldier of God, ready to die for the cause. His exploits were publicized and his relics venerated. By contrast, only a handful of women missionaries traveled to French colonies before the nineteenth century. In Canada, under the influence of the Catholic Reformation, a few orders established missions whose work anticipated their nineteenth-century descendants. Exceptionally, Ursuline nun Marie de l'Incarnation became the most celebrated woman missionary, a role model for Duchesne in particular. The Soeurs de St-Paul de Chartres, also an Old Regime foundation, had small establishments on the

Indian Ocean islands of Ile de Bourbon (Réunion) and Ile de France (Mauritius). In Louisiana the Ursulines established a convent in 1727.[46] But few in number and limited, by and large, from both travel and martyrdom, early modern women missionaries did not challenge the dominant model.

The introduction of uncloistered women into the missionary environment in the nineteenth century changed the nature of missionary work. Catholic nuns could not, under normal circumstances, baptize converts; for these and other sacraments, they were dependent on priests.[47] They could, however, provide instruction in Christian faith and practice, whether that was formally in schools or catechism classes or informally in soup kitchens and pharmacies or at the bedsides of the ill and dying. For the first time, women and children became the focus of Catholic missionary efforts, in keeping with an emerging domestic ideology that argued that the home was the key to acculturation. The feminization of missionary work put a heavier emphasis on assimilation of non-Europeans to European standards of education, cleanliness, and housekeeping whether or not formal conversion was achieved. Just as Catholic sisters in France provided vital services in education, nursing, and welfare, these same skills in the missionary context gave them new methods for evangelization that Catholic priests lacked. Schools were obvious places to inculcate the faith, but care of the sick and dying, as well as the indigent, runaway wives, prostitutes, and other marginal individuals, provided opportunities to speak of one's faith and urge others to embrace it. Women missionaries did not preach, but they could convert in more subtle ways. Even priests recognized that women religious were now essential partners in their work, citing their usefulness again and again in the sources.

For the French government, eager to tout its "civilizing mission" as a pretext for colonization, women missionaries were the perfect cover. Not only did missionary work in health, education, and welfare make credible the claim that the French were improving local conditions, but the work of women religious was often less confrontational and threatening as well because they lacked the public authority of Catholic priests. There were also, after the rapid expansion of female religious orders in the nineteenth century, more of them to draw upon. By 1900, there were more than ten thousand women missionaries, in comparison to just over seven thousand men.[48] Unlike Protestant missionary women, also an expanding group in this period, especially in the British Empire, Catholic sisters had the advantage of strong, female-led institutions in the form of the religious order itself, although within the overall structure of a patriarchal church.[49] Freedom from enclosure allowed them to travel and work in public spaces, yet their habits and rules made such work acceptable for unmarried women, a significant advantage over laywomen.

There is good reason to argue that, by the end of the century, missionary work had become "feminized" not just in the makeup of its personnel but also in its image, even when practiced by men, as domesticated and nurturing.[50] The importance of domestic ideology to nineteenth-century empire has been noted by numerous historians, as is suggested by the title of the best-known essay collection on the subject, *Domesticating the Empire*. That collection, like other work on gender and empire, however, contains no information on women missionaries and little evidence before 1870.[51] Influenced by postmodern discourse analysis, much of the recent work on nineteenth-century French empire and gender, in fact, looks less at actual women than at the ways in which imperial lands and peoples were constructed as feminine, which leaves the focus on the men, who did most of the framing. If Anne McClintock is right when she writes that "colonialism took shape around the Victorian invention of domesticity and the idea of the home,"[52] then the contributions of women missionaries like the three under study here—even if they were celibate Catholic nuns—to this ideology is central to the shaping of modern colonialism.

Until recently, missionaries—of either gender—have been marginal to the history of French empire. Secular histories of empire mention them only in passing, if at all, or assume that their work was simply a pretext for French expansion and cultural appropriation. Catholic historians tend toward the celebratory, lauding the sacrifice made by European clerics in the goal of universal salvation.[53] If nothing else, however, the timing—the simultaneous revival of overseas missionary work and that of French colonialism in the aftermath of the French Revolution—suggests that missionaries, especially women missionaries, were important players in the imperial game. Their expansion into missionary work just as the French came to reinvent their empire gave them an opportunity to shape both imperial discourse and imperial reality. At the same time, French expansion provided both opportunities and limitations to the work of French missionaries. Close examination of their work suggests that they were neither villains nor heroes, although, unsurprisingly, they carried with them not only absolute faith in their creed but also assumptions about the superiority of European culture, though not always about Europeans themselves. The three women in this book never doubted that Christianity could bring salvation to all peoples, but they did sometimes doubt that Europeans were the best embodiment of faithful Christians. Yet their view of non-Europeans contained an essential paradox: All people were equal in the sight of God but could express that equality only by embracing a religion that remained bounded by European cultural assumptions.

Writing the Lives of Saints

Finally, this book not only addresses historical and historiographical questions about empire, gender, and religion but also does so through the prism of three individual lives. Biography, like empire, is enjoying a scholarly renaissance, but today's biographies often use methodological tools that are very different from those of the past. This book has been influenced by the "new biography," which seeks to locate individual lives in larger cultural patterns. After decades of analyzing social forces as abstract entities, historians have come back to biography, as well as narrative, in order to understand the play of those forces on individual lives or to use one life—often obscure—as a prism through which to examine larger forces. These biographies are seldom heroic as their subjects do not so much change reality as reflect it. Their biographers are less likely to make sweeping generalizations about character or personality, and they often employ innovative narrative strategies. Instead of reconstructing the interior life, as psychobiographers tried to do, new biographers, influenced by postmodern theory, are especially interested in the construction of identity and self.[54] Indeed, historian Joan Wallach Scott goes so far as to argue that traditional biography is fundamentally flawed because it assumes that "agency is an expression of autonomous individual will, rather than the effect of a historically defined process which forms subjects." The four women that she profiles in *Only Paradoxes to Offer* she claims are not "heroines" but "sites—historical locations or markers—where crucial political and cultural contests are enacted."[55]

Although I do not agree with Scott's epistemological premise that the "personal lives" of biographical subjects are insignificant compared to the "complex determinations of language,"[56] in this book I am primarily concerned with the interplay between the experiences of Philippine Duchesne, Emilie de Vialar, and Anne-Marie Javouhey and the larger political, social, and cultural world in which they acted out their lives. To borrow from the vocabulary if not all of the theory of postmodernists, if we conceive of their lives as "texts," then it is the relationship between "text" and "context" that I seek to establish. Placing three similar, yet not identical, lives in the same book, in fact, suggests that there are bigger themes and forces to explore beyond a narration of their activities or an examination of their personal motives, virtues, and vices. Structurally, this book most resembles Natalie Zemon Davis's *Women on the Margins* in juxtaposing the lives of three women who were neither ordinary nor representative but whose life stories can illuminate both each other and the larger culture. Methodologically, I have been inspired as much by microhistory as by biography, two genres that now often overlap but are not identical. Microhistorians take an individual event or life and use it to examine broader issues, whereas biographers are most interested in the singularity of the person under study—what indeed makes that person unique.[57] Often microhistorians study lives for which source material is lacking, resulting in substantial gaps in the life story. Understanding the larger context provides one way of hazarding guesses as to what might have filled in those gaps. This methodology transcends the problem of inadequate sources, which is not the case in this book. Biography cum microhistory ties the individual with the global, the intimate with the impersonal. Just as the context can explain the individual life, so the lives of individuals can illuminate the larger historical forces. Duchesne, Vialar, and Javouhey participated in the reshaping of both the French church and the French empire; their stories can in turn reshape our understanding of those processes.

That premise also distinguishes this book from previous biographies of these women.[58] Mostly written by clerics or members of the religious orders that they founded, their biographers, unsurprisingly, were interested first and foremost in understanding the unique qualities of their founders—those that might explain their success and their sanctity. Although they did not shy away from discussing the faults, lapses, and contradictions of these women, previous biographers focused first on personality and works and only secondarily on context. Furthermore, sharing the religious beliefs of their subjects, some were willing to consider "providence" or the hand of God as a motivating force in history, a perspective that secular historians reject. Their biographies were meant to explain but also to inspire. Anne-Marie Javouhey is even the subject of a French comic book whose target audience is children.[59] All three women, in fact, have had their lives vetted by Catholic theologians as exemplary in view of their beatification or canonization. Vialar was made a saint in 1951 (beatified 1939), Duchesne in 1988 (beatified 1940), and Javouhey was beatified in 1950. Several of the extant biographies were written specifically as a part of this process. This does not make them hagiographic (except in the literal sense) or uncritical by any means—several of the more recent biographers had advanced historical training—but they brought a particular point of view and purpose to their writing. Only Anne-Marie Javouhey has been the subject of a lay biography, an excellent recent work by historian Geneviève Lecuir-Nemo. Although Lecuir-Nemo is sensitive to the religious and imperial context of Javouhey's life and work, her goal and method remain that of the traditional biographer, who accounts for Javouhey's activities and actions from birth to death in chronological fashion.[60]

Besides my position as a professional historian and an outsider (American and non-Catholic to boot—all of which presuppose certain biases of my own), my purpose in this book is quite different. I am interested in these women's lives for their own sakes—indeed, I cannot imagine taking on a project of this magnitude without a basic sympathy for my subjects—but I am more drawn by what we can learn about the interplay of their experiences with the larger changes in opportunities for women, the nineteenth-century French church, and the role of missionaries in French expansion. Although the stories of these women are told in a more or less chronological fashion, my narrative relies more on themes than on chronology, and I do not feel obliged to account for every year in their lives or every movement in their journeys. Instead, I feel free to pick and chose the themes that I find most revealing of the time and context in which they lived. Writing about three women rather than a single one also allows me to look for commonalities indicative of broader trends and issues. Since these three women chose different destinations, however, I am able to take a more comprehensive (if not complete) view of empire.

Because these three women have been objects of veneration and study from the time of their deaths, I have benefited from abundant source material. As traveling women, often distant from their families—both birth and religious—they left behind literally thousands of letters that have been carefully preserved, catalogued, transcribed, and even published.[61] Indeed, one of the most valuable characteristics of the insider biographies is their unparalleled access to archival sources and an oral tradition within the congregations themselves. Fortunately, these sources are now largely available to outside researchers. The letters written by Duchesne, Vialar, and Javouhey, however, do not always answer the questions that twenty-first-century historians, at least, would most like answered. The sights and sounds of foreign lands and cultures are not consistently described. Although these women's life work was the evangelization of non-Christians, it is striking how few of those individuals made it into their correspondence, almost none of them by name. Instead, these women wrote most often about administrative concerns and issues: the recruitment and placement of nuns, the raising of funds, relations with bishops and other clerics, plans for expansion, and so forth. They also retained a lively interest in the welfare of their birth families and, of course, their spiritual sisters. Only by finding and reading other available sources, especially in the archives of the French colonial and foreign affairs ministries and those of the church, can a more balanced "big picture" be assembled. Silent still, however, are indigenous voices, who seldom made it into the written record, especially the records of the colonizers.

This book remains, for better or worse, a story told from the point of view of the three women who embarked on their own personal journeys to convert souls and "civilize" peoples that they only dimly understood. Their worldview, however, is well worth exploring for what it teaches us about the global reach—and the limitations—of French Catholic evangelization in the nineteenth century. At a moment when we are reminded daily of the power of religion in world events, understanding its historical relationship with imperialism and globalization is both important and timely.

PART I

The Limits of Enclosure
Philippine Duchesne

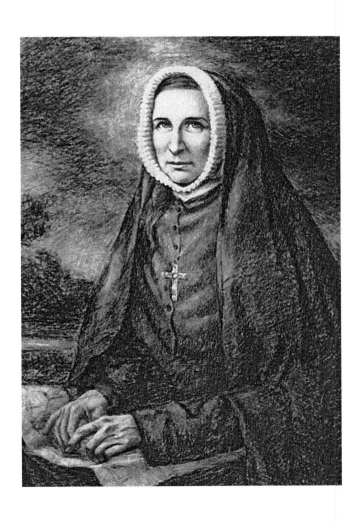

1

From Old Worlds to New

On the tenth of September 1788, in the presence of her family and friends, nineteen-year-old Philippine Duchesne took the habit as a novice in the convent of the Visitation, which is perched on the hill overlooking the old town of Grenoble and the parish of St-Louis, where Duchesne was born and baptized in 1769. Dressed in her best clothes and jewels, she knelt in the center of the convent chapel, a Baroque masterpiece, to declare her desire to join the Visitation order and to request admittance to the community for the remainder of her life. After withdrawing to change from the elaborate and ostentatious clothing of a bourgeois bride into the austere black habit and white veil of the novice, the choir grille, located at a right angle from the chapel (affording a view of the altar but not the public) was slammed shut, and Duchesne gave the kiss of peace to the members of her new religious family, seated on the polished wood benches of the nuns' choir. Several days earlier she had made a public confession of faults in front of these forty or so women with whom she had already lived for about a year as a postulant and heard the convent superior, Mère Marie-Anne Félicité de Murinais, instruct her on the religious engagement she was about to make. When the ceremony was over, she, the superior, the officiating priest, and the male witnesses (including her father, brother, uncles, and cousins) signed the convent register, now preserved in the municipal archives of Grenoble. Hers would be the second-to-last vesture ceremony recorded in the small community.[1]

If we are able to reconstruct this day, it is thanks not so much to the surviving documentation, which is meager, but to the predictability of women's religious life in the Old Regime. Since the Visitation was a cloistered religious order founded in 1610 under a fixed rule, on the day she became a novice it would have been easy for Duchesne—as it is for us—to envision her long-term future, as well as her everyday activities.[2] She had already spent two years there as a boarding pupil and another year as a postulant in preparation for this day, so the personalities and ways of life of Ste-Marie-d'en-Haut, as the Grenoble Visitation convent was known, were already familiar to her. During her novitiate she would train, intellectually and spiritually, for the life ahead of her, as well as perform some of the menial labor of the convent. After her profession ceremony—which her father insisted would not happen before her twenty-fifth birthday—her veil would become black and her vows permanent, but her life would continue on the same structured religious path she had chosen when becoming a novice. Of course, there would always be unknowable elements: the dimensions and quality of her spiritual life; her relationships with other Visitation sisters in the community, particularly those who had not yet entered; the leadership positions she might fill. However, the very essence of monastic life was its regularity and the belief that religious perfection, at least for women, could best be found within the physical and spiritual confines of convent walls. As she changed her clothing and signed the register, what kind of life awaited Philippine Duchesne?

It would be, first of all, a life of prayer. François de Sales and Jeanne de Chantal founded the Visitation order in the early seventeenth century in order to ensure the salvation of its members through contemplation and common worship. Although in order to accommodate women whose health would not allow the rigors of the round-the-clock "great" divine service, Visitation nuns recited instead the "little office" of Our Lady, their day was nevertheless dominated by fixed religious services, five times a day, beginning at half past six in the morning and ending just before nine in the evening. When not attending services, nuns used all but two hours a day to deepen their own spirituality through individual prayer and study of religious works available in the convent library. Religious colloquia, special sermons, pious readings at mealtimes, and spiritual retreats punctuated the otherwise unvarying and minutely planned routine.[3] In contrast with many medieval monasteries or the reformed Carmelites of Teresa of Avila, however, the Visitation emphasized interior mortification over physical rigor. Visitation nuns were allowed meat and wine at their meals, as well as furniture in their cells and mattresses and blankets on their beds. Although those at Ste-Marie-d'en-Haut sewed their habits themselves, every year they received a new pair of shoes made by a Grenoble artisan.[4] Their life was not ostentatious—the most luxurious purchases and goods were reserved for chapel decorations and altar linens—but extended fasts, physical deprivations, and corporal mortifications were forbidden or discouraged. Visitation spirituality was based on the daily practice of humility and charity, the interior struggle against self will and pride, and consistent, deep, and thoughtful religious study rather than extreme physical austerity.[5]

When not engaged in services or study, Philippine Duchesne would most likely spend her time teaching boarders—young, elite Grenoble girls like herself preparing their first communion. Although the Visitation was not a teaching order per se, by the end of the eighteenth century, the education of the daughters of the upper and professional classes had become an important part of its identity. Boarding pupils provided an important source of income for the convent, and families were assured their daughters would receive an appropriate education among their social peers. Choir sisters of the Visitation, who paid a substantial dowry to enter, were drawn from the nobility, as well as the liberal and professional bourgeoisie.[6] At Ste-Marie-d'en-Haut, seventeen of the twenty-nine professed sisters came from noble families at the time of Duchesne's entrance into the novitiate; others presumably came from rising bourgeois families like her own.[7] Traditionally, Visitation nuns provided instruction in Latin, French, arithmetic, spelling, needlework, and of course religion; some convents might add singing, dancing, acting, and other accomplishments useful to their charges once they entered society. By the end of the eighteenth century, however, many well-off families found convent education old fashioned and preferred to educate their daughters at home, boarding them for only one or two years in preparation for their first communion. This, in fact, was how Duchesne herself, after having been tutored at home with her siblings and cousins, first entered Ste-Marie-d'en-Haut at the age of ten. By her own account, she made the decision to enter the Visitation order two years later, on the day of her first communion, although she did not return to the convent—against her parents' will—until she was seventeen years old. This was not an atypical trajectory. Although most girls educated by the Visitation did not enter religious orders, almost two out of three nuns had spent some time in its boarding school, one of whose purposes was to identify promising new recruits.[8] Once she became a professed nun, it is more than likely that Duchesne in turn would have taught the daughters of Grenoble's elite.

Finally, and probably most important of all, the Visitation life, including its school, was cloistered. Once Philippine Duchesne put on a religious habit and moved to the Visitation side of the chapel, behind the heavy double grille, her physical existence was circumscribed by the convent walls, and contact with the outside took place only in the convent parlor behind another grille, with a second Visitation sister in attendance to monitor her conversation and behavior. Although not part of the original Visitation concept, François de Sales and Jeanne de Chantal quickly accepted clausura as part of the church's conditions for allowing a new form of women's monastic life in the seventeenth century.[9] Established in 1618, the same year cloister was imposed on the Visitation order by papal bull, the convent of

Ste-Marie-d'en-Haut was always enclosed. Yet full enclosure did not necessarily mean full withdrawal from the world. Novices and nuns continued, despite the grille, to converse and exchange news with visiting family members and friends. Some nuns, though not Duchesne, had sisters, aunts, and nieces who had also entered the convent.[10] Local Grenoble inhabitants attended religious services held in the Visitation chapel, and once a year the faithful processed along the road to the convent, where a Calvary cross had been erected in 1723, to hear the bishop say Mass.[11]

Like most convents in Old Regime France, Ste-Marie-d'en-Haut was also an economic unit. Grouped around several courtyards, the three-story building included a parlor, chapter room, refectory, infirmary, pharmacy, kitchen, oven room, laundry room, linen room, storage rooms for church vestments and ornaments, library, dormitory, bedroom for the superior, individual cells (whose windows faced away from the city) for each choir sister, and of course the chapel. The property also included a terrace, gardens, and an orchard located within the convent walls and additional pieces of land, including vineyards, just beyond the walls. The gardens and orchards allowed space for walking and meditation by the nuns and provided foodstuffs for their table. By the mid-eighteenth century, the vineyards at Ste-Marie-d'en-Haut produced eighty barrels of wine per year, most of which the nuns sold; they also raised silkworms, fabricated artificial flowers, and packaged apothecary herbs. On the eve of the Revolution their annual revenues from the property they rented to peasants, as well as various investments, totaled about twenty thousand livres.[12] Like many Old Regime convents, the Visitation community at Ste-Marie-d'en-Haut also served as a private lender to individuals and groups both near and far.[13] These loans were a means by which the convent transformed the dowries of its members into an annual revenue stream; through them, it participated actively in the Old Regime economy.

Although Philippine Duchesne, once she took her final vows as a Visitation nun, would cease to have a legal identity in Old Regime France, which would have allowed her to own or inherit property, the same was not true of the convent itself. From within the convent walls, its mother superior conducted business on both a small and a large scale. One day, perhaps, the superior might even be Duchesne herself, though humility would have certainly prevented her from imagining such a possibility as a novice. What was absolutely certain on the day she put on the Visitation habit, however, was that the rest of her life would be played out within the walls of the convent and its gardens; she would never again walk the half mile to her family home across the Isère river, much less die in a place as unimaginably far away as St. Charles, Missouri.

This was the life that Philippine Duchesne did not live, however predictable it appeared in 1788. One year later, the Revolution fundamentally changed the relationship of church and state and the nature of religious life, and Duchesne, like thousands of men and women religious across France, was forced to adapt to radically new circumstances. Rather than spending the remainder of her eighty-three years as a Visitation nun in Grenoble, she spent only three more there, leaving the convent by government decree on 1 October 1792. Yet the Visitation experience was formative in her own life just as the Old Regime monastic model weighed heavily on the new women's religious orders that women like Duchesne founded and joined in the wake of the Revolution. She was already thirty-five years old when she joined the Religious of the Sacred Heart and forty-nine when she sailed for America. Like many Old Regime nuns, she had already proven her ability to adapt to adverse circumstances. The destruction of religious life during the Revolution inspired in her a missionary impulse to restore Catholic practice through education, first in France and then outside of France. Moreover, like many nineteenth-century women religious, this new, peripatetic missionary life was essentially made possible by the Revolution itself. Once freed from the bonds of enclosure, she was able to pursue a new religious goal, the evangelization of American Indians. Yet this life also had roots in the Old Regime, as Duchesne modeled her missionary work on the seventeenth-century Jesuits and Ursulines, whose exploits among Native Americans were legendary among nineteenth-century Catholics. On the rapidly changing frontier, however, Duchesne's real impact was less the work among Indians than the establishment of French-style convent schools that educated the daughters of the American republic. Transitional in many respects, Duchesne merged the religious traditions of the Old Regime with the innovations of the new and brought French religion and culture to a rapidly homogenizing borderland in her chosen land of Missouri.

The Revolution and After: Adaptation and Resistance

That Philippine Duchesne entered a religious order in 1788 was, if not surprising, not entirely predictable, either. The oldest daughter of Pierre-François Duchesne and Rose-Euphrosine Périer, her father was an up-and-coming lawyer to the Parlement de Grenoble, and her mother the sister of Claude Périer, who was rapidly becoming one of the most important industrialists and traders in the Grenoble region. The Duchesne family lived next door to the Périer family, and the families were close.[14] In many ways they were the quintessential late eighteenth-century bourgeois family, whose members had moved from the land to the liberal professions, trade, and industry. In 1769, the year of Philippine Duchesne's birth, her father's legal office brought in 582 livres a year; by 1782 his annual income was 6,176 livres. He also founded the Grenoble public library and was admitted to the

Académie Delphinale, a local learned society. Duchesne's maternal grandfather, Jacques Périer, became a textile merchant in Grenoble and married the daughter of another merchant family, whose dowry brought the family 50,000 livres. Duchesne's uncle, Claude Périer, used the growing family wealth not only to invest in new technology—the family château (purchased from the Duc de Villeroy) now housed a modern factory for textile printing—but also to branch into banking; by 1781 he had loaned the French monarchy more than half a million livres.[15] His brother Augustin joined the Company of the Indies in 1786, hoping to make an equivalent fortune. With growing wealth and influence, the Duchesne and Périer families were at the forefront of the challenge to the monarchy and the nobility on the eve of the French Revolution; the first meeting of the provincial Estates of the Dauphiné in the Grenoble region, which established the principle of the doubling of the Third Estate, was held at the Périer estate at Vizille on 21 July 1788, shortly before Philippine Duchesne became a Visitation novice. This act was their entrance into an influential political career that continued until the Second Empire.

Like many Old Regime parents, Duchesne's parents initially opposed her becoming a nun. For the most part, they had educated her at home; because she shared tutors with her male cousins, she received a more substantial education than might have been expected for a girl of her class. Yet two years of "finishing" education at the Visitation convent not only prepared her for her first communion but also trained her in the modest and serious demeanor expected of a well-brought-up bourgeois girl. According to one biographer, her mother and her aunt were also "convinced Christians,"[16] reflecting the gender divide in religious belief that was already emerging in France by the late eighteenth century. When she stated her intentions to become a nun at the time of her first communion, her parents promptly withdrew her from the convent, and Duchesne attended the social events expected of a teenaged girl looking to make a good marriage. Five years later, however, she returned to Ste-Marie-d'en-Haut and refused to leave until her parents gave their consent, speaking to them from behind the grille.[17] This was a far cry from the view of forced religious vocations sensationalized in Diderot's The Nun and other Enlightenment writings; indeed, parents' objecting to a daughter's religious vocation was probably more common than their obliging her to enter.[18] In Grenoble, support for the church appears to have declined in the eighteenth century, particularly among the professional classes that the Duchesne and Périer families represented.[19] Yet, although the Visitation convent had been more populated a generation earlier at seventy inhabitants, its forty members at the time of Duchesne's entrance was a respectable number for an establishment of its kind. Between 1775 and 1787, nine novices had taken their final vows; all but two were twenty-five years of age or younger.[20] There was no reason to think that the convent did not have a stable future, and, faced with his daughter's determination, Pierre

Duchesne gave her permission to enter, first as a postulant and then as a novice in 1788, when he, along with the rest of the family, witnessed her vesture ceremony.

The outbreak of the Revolution on 14 July 1789 did not have an immediate impact on the cloistered community, though it is likely that Duchesne, whose family was at the center of events in Grenoble, had frequent news of its progress.[21] Dismantling the wealth and institutional power of the Catholic Church was an early priority of the revolutionaries, who nationalized church property in November, though no practical steps to confiscate it were taken. By February 1790, however, responding to a long-held Enlightenment belief that they performed no useful function, the National Assembly outlawed all monastic orders with solemn vows, which included, of course, the Visitation. Members who wished to leave their orders were now free to do so; their dowries were compensated by means of a pension provided by the state, 700 livres for an upper-class choir nun and 350 for a lower-class converse nun. Monks were obliged to leave their monasteries, but nuns allowed to stay, if they chose, until the convents became national property.

At Ste-Marie-d'en-Haut, not a soul budged. This resistance was typical of other Visitation communities, indeed of the vast majority of cloistered nuns throughout France, who not only refused to leave their convents but often petitioned the government protesting their eventual dispersal as well.[22] By early 1791, nuns who wished to remain in their convents were required to declare so officially to government agents and elect a superior and financial agent. At Ste-Marie-d'en-Haut two municipal officers arrived at three in the afternoon on the first of February to meet with the nuns assembled in the chapter room. Each signed a statement of intent to stay. Six days later another city official supervised the reelection of the current superior for a two-year term.[23] Although these steps suggested continuity and survival, by 1791 the requirement that clergy take an oath to the constitution had radicalized religious relations in Grenoble, as elsewhere. Priests who refused to swear the oath needed sanctuary at the same time that the vast majority of nuns refused to receive the sacraments from those priests who had; as a result, convent chapels became sites of refuge and clandestine worship. By summer the municipal council of Grenoble had locked and sealed the outside doors of the chapel at Ste-Marie-d'en-Haut, preventing the public from entering; now only the Visitation nuns could hold services there.[24]

When war broke out in April 1792, the frontier location of Grenoble increased concern over supposed enemies, clerical and otherwise, of the Revolution. In May the public cross at the center of town was torn down, and churches began to close. Finally, on 18 August 1792, the national government ordered the closure of all convents and monasteries and the seizure of their property by 1 October. The Visitation nuns of Ste-Marie-d'en-Haut, including twenty-three-year-old Philippine Duchesne, still a novice, were finally obliged to leave, taking with them only their personal effects. The remainder of the convent's possessions now belonged to the nation. Duchesne returned to her parents' home on Place St-André, recently renamed Place de la Constitution. By December, her father had moved them to the countryside; for the next five years Duchesne lived either with family members around Grenoble or on her own in the increasingly violent city.

What were her options? Many nuns, like her, returned to families who had never expected them back; by Old Regime law professed nuns had given up their legal identity and inheritance rights in exchange for the dowry that paid their entrance into the convent. After 1793, to receive the small compensatory pensions promised them by the French state, ex-nuns were required to take the Liberté-Egalité oath; those who refused found their state support cut off.[25] Nuns without family sometimes lived together in small groups under the protection of refractory clergy or sympathetic supporters. About a dozen former nuns from the Visitation convent on Rue St-Jacques in Paris, for example, moved to a country house outside the city limits, where they were imprisoned for five months after the arrest of the local priest. Moving back to Paris, they lived on the proceeds of their needlework. Another way of making ends meet was by opening a small school, as did a Visitation sister from the Paris convent on Rue St-Antoine.[26] Such a step responded to one of the key anticlerical critiques that nuns were social parasites who performed no social functions, but it also carried the danger that such a school would be perceived, usually with reason, as a front for clandestine Catholic instruction. Persecution of nuns was very intense in some places, while in others they were left alone provided they behaved with discretion. In April 1791, for example, when the rumor spread in the radical Faubourg St-Antoine in Paris that the Visitandines were hiding priests who had refused the oath in their chapel, the crowd stormed the convent, seized the nuns, and subjected some of them to public whippings. In Nantes, a center of Catholic resistance to the Revolution where the Terror was particularly virulent, 26 out of 39 Visitandines were imprisoned.[27] In many cities in France, including Grenoble, former convents were transformed into prisons, and some recalcitrant nuns were held within the very walls they had never intended to breach.

For those Old Regime nuns who refused to live outside of their vows, there remained two additional possibilities, external and internal exile, exemplified by two existing memoirs of former Visitation sisters. One chronicles the transfer of the Lyon (Bellecour) convent to Mantua, Italy, a voyage made more dangerous by the transport of the heart of founder François de Sales, a relic of critical importance to the entire network of Visitation communities.[28] Led by local sympathizers and in secular dress, the Lyon sisters traveled on foot or on horseback across the border in small groups, passing through numerous checkpoints, sometimes without passports. Both the preparations to emigrate and the journey itself entailed considerable risk; in 1794, with France at war, emigration was tantamount to treason. Once outside of France, they took refuge in local monasteries, where one of their first concerns was "to be clothed once again in the livery of their Divine Spouse."[29] Once established in Mantua, they also reestablished cloister and established a boarding school, which local Italian elites were eager to patronize. However promising its future, exile abroad proved a precarious solution; two years later, when the French army invaded northern Italy, this Visitation community fled to Bohemia, finally settling in Venice in 1801.

Another kind of exile, this one internal, was exemplified by Gabrielle Gauchet, a Visitandine in Langres in eastern France.[30] She and another sister decided to re-create enclosed life within the small room they rented in town after leaving the convent. The room, she explained, "faces the back, is surrounded by high walls...the doors are always carefully closed...we avoid with the greatest of care, all ordinary visits."[31] In this small space, they placed pious objects and observed as much as possible the Visitation rule, notwithstanding the crucial problem of finding a reliable local priest (one who had not taken the oath to the constitution) to bring them the sacraments. Their self-imposed cloister was violated by municipal authorities who searched their lodgings for arms and compromising religious material, which the two nuns hastily hid. Unwilling to take any loyalty oaths at all to the new French state, Gauchat lost her pension in 1793; several years later it was reinstated when she acquired a "civic certificate" that conceded that she had never made a public statement against the Revolution. Her memoir is dominated by the problem of maintaining a state of grace while outside of the convent and focuses largely on spiritual issues. In 1804 she made her cloister absolute by entering a Trappist monastery.

Like Gauchat, Philippine Duchesne wrote of the outside world as "a land of exile, a foreign country" in which she had lost the "sanctuary of religion."[32] Yet she had neither the option of fleeing abroad nor that of re-creating the cloistered life within. Although her novice mistress became the superior of a convent in Italy, Duchesne's family refused to let her follow. In the family country home in Grâne, Duchesne and a cousin, a former Visitation nun from a different convent, attempted to follow a religious schedule on their own but found it difficult in the midst of the family responsibilities expected of young bourgeois women. In July 1797, when her mother died, Duchesne was at her bedside. According to her youngest sister, Mélanie, only eleven years old and later a Visitation nun herself, the daughters "went almost every day to pray at her tomb" and to "recite the service of the dead."[33] After her mother's death, Duchesne was dispatched to Romans to live with her paternal grandmother, whose bad temper she fled for the nearby village of St-Marcellin, where a group of former Visitation nuns, headed by Duchesne's aunt, were living a clandestine religious life. She seems, however, not to have intended to join the St-Marcellin community, referring to it instead as a retreat, nor did she consider it her duty to remain in permanent residence with her grandmother, who "refused to have me around" and "moreover, with three daughters near her—all quite as free as I—and two house-servants, there was not the least anxiety as to the manner in which she would be cared for."[34]

Deprived of a "life of security in religion" and considering herself superfluous at home, Duchesne chose instead a life of celibate charity in Grenoble, setting up housekeeping with "a companion somewhat older than I and free like myself."[35] This unusual decision was not her first such stay, having returned to Grenoble for a period between her departure from Ste-Marie-d'en-Haut and her mother's last illness, leaving the confines of the home of her maternal grandmother, still resident in Grenoble, "in order to be more free" in her own apartment with several other young women.[36] During her absence, the religious landscape in Grenoble had been dramatically transformed. The French government had prohibited religious symbols, imposed a new calendar, and transformed church properties for revolutionary uses. The cathedral had become a temple of reason, the church St-Louis a leather warehouse, the Carmelite convent a sword factory, the chapel St-Nicolas a bayonet factory, the convent of Ste-Marie-d'en-Bas an armory, the church St-André the seat of the Comité révolutionnaire, and the former convent of Ste-Claire the headquarters for the Société populaire. Its precious objects sent off to the Lyon mint and its books transferred to the public library, Ste-Marie-d'en-Haut had been transformed into a prison in April 1793. Between April and July 1793, at the height of the Terror, it held approximately 120 individuals from a wide variety of professions, including former nobles, priests, and men and women religious. Three women superiors from Grenoble convents were among this group: that of the Ursulines, that of the Carmelites, and Marie-Anne Félicité de Murinais, former head of the Visitation, now incarcerated in her own convent.[37] In June 1794 two priests were executed for treason. During her first stay in Grenoble, Duchesne began visiting prisoners, particularly refractory priests, as well as the ill, trying to get them last rites.[38] In this, she typified the solidarity between imprisoned clerics and former women religious during the Revolution. In 1797 the municipal authorities in Grenoble transformed Ste-Marie-d'en-Haut into a prison for beggars, though it still housed refractory priests.

By this time, Grenoble was undergoing a charitable crisis caused by economic hardship and the effects of the war, which had greatly increased the numbers of indigent people. Early Republican efforts to provide aid ceased after Thermidor, and the city fathers struggled to find new models of philanthropy and reestablish older institutions.[39] In such an environment, the person-to-person, small-scale charity—visiting the sick, distributing alms, and so forth—practiced by Duchesne and her companion filled in some of the gaps. This kind of charity also held the potential for reintroducing religious practice and belief, which began tentatively to reappear.[40] Women, especially former nuns like Duchesne, were instrumental in this religious revival all over France. Evangelization, however, was not without risks. Grenoble experienced another brief period of religious persecution in 1798 (the "Fructidor Terror"), and former nuns teaching school were accused of "inspiring the principles of fanaticism" by using Catholic textbooks, refusing to be addressed as "citizen," and failing to acknowledge the *décadi*, which had replaced Sunday in the Republican calendar.[41]

Duchesne herself turned to teaching in 1800, when she opened a school for poor boys. Her inspiration in this appears to have come from a pilgrimage she made to the tomb of St. François Régis in La Louvesc, not far from her grandmother's home in Romans. A Jesuit saint of the Catholic Reformation, François Régis abandoned a dream for missionary work in Canada to work with the poor and criminal in France; Duchesne had wished to visit his tomb since 1797 but had considered it too dangerous to travel. At La Louvesc, although the church was in ruins, the crowd attending mass was large and enthusiastic, and Duchesne reported that she "left very taken by the desire to bring instruction to the poor, in imitation of St. François Régis." Since other former nuns had already established girls' schools, she set about rounding up poor boys "abandoned and living like animals" by promising them meals and clothes she bought out of her own pocket. Though they were "unbearably fickle" and "noisy" and embarrassed her by greeting her constantly on the streets, Duchesne took pride in having taught them prayers, hymns, and the catechism that allowed them to confess and take first communion.[42]

What Duchesne set as her ultimate goal, however, was much more daring than opening a school for Grenoble street urchins; she wanted to reestablish Ste-Marie-d'en-Haut as a Visitation convent.[43] The property still belonged to the municipality but had been abandoned and needed repairs. Duchesne's ability to possess it depended largely on family money and family connections. Overall, the Duchesne-Périer clan had done well in the Revolution. Although their generally moderate stance drew some hostility during the Terror, it stood them in good stead after 1795. Pierre Duchesne, Philippine's father, was elected to the national Council of 500 in 1796 and then to the Tribunat from 1799 to 1802, as was her cousin Camille Jordan. Her uncle Claude Périer, already wealthy in 1789, participated in the development of arms manufacturing during the war, bought former church property in Grenoble in 1794, and in 1795 invested in the Anzin mines, which ensured the family fortune for the nineteenth century. In December 1799 he was one of the bankers who provided a twelve-million-franc loan to Napoleon, in exchange for which he was elected deputy to the Corps Législative and became one of the founders of the Banque de France. Her cousin's husband, Jacques Savoye-de-Rollin, was one of the authors of the Napoleonic Code.[44] It was Rollin who approached the local prefect about renting Ste-Marie-d'en-Haut after Duchesne's initial inquiries had gone unanswered. For an annual rent of eight hundred francs and the cost of repairs, Duchesne came into possession of the house in December 1801.[45] After her mother's death in 1797, she had forfeited her share in the family property to her sisters and brother in exchange for an annual income, which went toward her charitable projects, which, without an independent means of support, would have been nearly impossible to execute. Throughout her life, Duchesne relied heavily on the financial largesse of her large, close-knit, and generous family.

At Ste-Marie-d'en-Haut, Duchesne's purpose was twofold: the reestablishment of Visitation life and the education of girls. By 1801, the year Napoleon concluded a concordat with the pope that reestablished Catholic structures in France, religious orders were beginning tentatively to reemerge. The same year, her aunt, also a former Visitation nun, rented her former convent in Romans in order to open a boarding school, and Duchesne spent a few days with her during the summer. Whereas the Visitation convent in Romans was reconstituted "in little time" with the "rule in force," Duchesne experienced problems from the outset. Although most of her former sisters still lived in the Grenoble region, more than ten years after their departure from the convent, they clearly did not share her enthusiasm for rebuilding either Visitandine life or the convent itself. The former superior, whom Duchesne had wished to sign the rental agreement on behalf of the community, responded that she could not leave her present home without consulting the nephew who supported her. Others complained that Duchesne had been rash in renting a building—however symbolic—that was in such bad repair without considering how the community would support itself. Duchesne quoted them as stating, "We do not want to die of hunger, we took vows of poverty, not of begging; we will not return to our houses until we can exist there on the same footing as before."

When she returned to Ste-Marie-d'en-Haut on 14 December, a cold, rainy night, Duchesne was accompanied only by a single former sister and a twelve-year-old boarder, both of whom took up residence with her, and the boys from her Grenoble class, who carried her baggage. By Christmas, however, she had sewed improvised black Visitation habits and claimed "all the satisfaction of St. Teresa [of Avila] sweeping in her monastery," as well as praying in the chapel "that lacked three windows and a door." On the feast of St-François-de-Sales, 29 January 1802, the convent chapel was reconsecrated, but most of the former Visitandines celebrated mass elsewhere "to protest against what they called the measures taken by Madame Duchesne." Grenoble inhabitants, on the other hand, "came in crowds by the interior of the monastery" for the first Catholic service "in all its splendor after the revolution."[46]

Thérèse de Murinais, former superior of Ste-Marie-d'en-Haut, now seventy-nine, finally returned to the convent during Holy Week 1802, accompanied by several other sisters. The experiment was not a success. The former Visitandines criticized the rule, which Duchesne had devised with a sympathetic priest for the transition period, for its variations from former Visitation practice but simultaneously objected to common ownership of belongings, always a hallmark of Old Regime orders. Duchesne in turn thought that their attempts to write a new rule were "very vague" without "common property, nor enclosure" and that "the order could not exist as long as everyone had a pocketbook and worked for herself." The superior, she felt, "in order to attract her daughters…yielded to everyone." By summer, Duchesne's hopes of returning to cloistered life had been dashed: "[W]e kept only services in common and prayer, of the rest no silence, no religious practice, no reading at table, no blessings and graces in common, nor enclosure, nor uniformity in dress." Besides the lack of commitment (Duchesne reprimanded them for having come with only enough baggage "to pass a month in the countryside"), issues of authority and initiative undoubtedly also came into play, with several Visitandines accusing her of having "sacrificed all to her pride." Unlike her aunt, Duchesne had never been a professed Visitation nun but only a novice. Now, although Duchesne proclaimed obedience to the former superior, she came constantly into conflict with those whose vision was less developed than her own. By the feast day of the Visitation, on 2 July, when all the former Visitandines attended a mass in the convent, Duchesne claimed that she "found the spirit so different from what I had formerly known, and the will to return to the cloister so undecided" that she decided to "make the sacrifice of the order," the stress of which brought on a nosebleed. Finally, on 26 August de Murinais herself decided to leave, telling Duchesne that she did not have the "youth and strength" for the project.

Although Duchesne's narrative does not mention it, political considerations undoubtedly also came into play in this failed reestablishment of Visitation life. In 1802, religious orders had not yet been officially relegalized in France, and reconstituting an order entailed some risk. By 1806, the Visitation order was formally reauthorized by Napoleon, but following his view that religious orders should have a social function, their ostensible purpose was no longer prayer but educating girls and providing homes for women who wanted to live in religious retreat. At this time, twenty-three former sisters from both former Grenoble Visitation convents reincorporated in a rented house with a new rule.[47] When Napoleon fell from power in 1814, however, the new Visitation community immediately petitioned the much more sympathetic Bourbon regime for the return of Ste-Marie-d'en-Haut. Claiming a sentimental connection to the property personally chosen by François de Sales and Jeanne de Chantal, these nuns argued that they had been cheated of it by the persecution of the Revolution. As for the current occupants, "Mme Duchesne, one of our novices, by means of her protectors, despite our protest at the time, received its use" from Napoleon. If the king restored the Visitation monastery, he could be assured that "nothing would interrupt our prayers and the vows we would address to Heaven for the preservation of the Bourbons who are inseparable from the Happiness of France."[48] Duchesne did not own the property outright, but because the Visitandines had refused to participate in 1801, the lease was in her name. Now a member of the Religious of the Sacred Heart, she protested vigorously that the Visitation sisters had not wanted the convent earlier, only now that it was repaired, expanded, and housed a flourishing school. Local authorities and the bishop of Grenoble also wanted to leave matters as they stood. Both the boarding (40 pupils) and the free school (140 pupils) were of real social use and self-supporting, whereas the former Visitandines were elderly, most still living isolated from one another.[49] The moment for the reestablishment of the Visitation order at Ste-Marie-d' en-Haut had passed.

Despite her ardent desire to re-create her past religious experience, Philippine Duchesne instead pioneered in a new kind of women's religious congregation of the nineteenth century by joining with another energetic religious woman, Madeleine Sophie Barat. Ten years younger than Duchesne, Barat was the leader of a fledgling women's religious order dedicated to the Sacred Heart. Coming of age immediately after the Terror, Barat's initial religious impulse was to enter a cloistered and rigorous Carmelite convent, an impossible aspiration after their destruction during the Revolution. Instead, she joined a project championed by her brother Louis Barat and his friend Joseph Varin, both members of the Fathers of the Faith, an association that sought to reestablish the Jesuits in France, as one of the first four French members of its women's branch, the Dilette di Gesù (the Beloved of Jesus). In 1801, they merged with a similar group in Amiens, and Barat, at the young age of twenty-three, was appointed local superior. Meanwhile, in Grenoble, after the departure of the Visitation sisters, Duchesne was left in charge of a small community that had taken the name of Filles de la Propagation de la Foi in March 1803 and that continued to board and educate young girls. Interested in affiliating with the Dilette di Gesù, she made a favorable impression on Joseph Varin, who was invited to inspect the community by Pierre Rivet, the priest who served as her confessor. By the time Barat arrived to effect the merger, in December 1804, she and the sisters at Amiens had broken with the Dilette for political reasons but were eager to absorb the Grenoble house as part of a new French religious order.[50] At Ste-Marie-d'en-Haut, she found six committed nuns (including Duchesne), a former Ursuline nun who participated in religious exercises informally, two widows, twenty boarders, and five servants. Duchesne simultaneously ran the school and the convent.[51] For the rest of her life, Duchesne celebrated the anniversary of the arrival of Sophie Barat in 1804 with a special religious ceremony.

Without a written rule and no longer part of a larger order, Barat and Duchesne set about inventing a new form of religious life. The new religious order, known at first as the Dames de l'Instruction chrétienne and after 1815 as the Religieuses du Sacré-Coeur de Jésus, differed from Old Regime orders in several key ways. Although it had houses in several locations, it remained under the control of Sophie Barat as superior general, unlike the Visitation order, for example, where each house was self-governing and independent although following a common rule. It was also much more explicitly focused on active work rather than contemplation. Recitation of the divine office was replaced by silent prayer, and the grilles at Ste-Marie-d'en-Haut, to Duchesne's lasting regret, were removed. Religious of the Sacred Heart spent too much time in the classroom to strain their voices during religious services, and grilles impeded their contact with the community.

Above all, the main purpose of the congregation was the re-Christianization of French society through the education of girls and women. A year after the association was approved by Napoleon in 1807 and four years after Barat and Duchesne met, Ste-Marie-d'en-Haut enrolled 92 boarders and 250 free pupils, and both municipal and church authorities praised the quality of its education.[52] These enrollments far outnumbered the handful of elite pupils the former Visitation convent had accepted in a single year. This ministry dovetailed with growing societal expectations of the role of women as the most important religious educators of children, fueling both active teaching orders and the increased education of girls. These modifications in religious life also paralleled the great shift at the beginning of the nineteenth century toward centralized, active religious congregations over independent, contemplative religious houses. Although at the time of the Revolution the vast majority of cloistered nuns, like the Visitandines of Ste-Marie-d'en-Haut, first rejected dispersal and then marriage, only a minority returned to religious life after the concordat. Indeed, most new recruits to religious life after the Revolution were not former nuns.[53] In the Society of the Sacred Heart, Sophie Barat herself preferred young subjects who would not seek to reestablish "the customs of the former monasteries." Barat saw Duchesne's Grenoble vocation as too restrained: "She did not understand that in order to attract more souls to Our Lord, we needed a more extensive enclosure," meaning that Sacred Heart sisters needed more freedom.[54] Barat, far from being cloistered, traveled constantly, establishing new houses and solidifying her own authority within the congregation. The model Barat most consistently embraced was that of a female branch of the Jesuits, active evangelizers par excellence, asking Duchesne in 1828, "Is this possible for women?"[55]

Women's religious life in general and the Society of the Sacred Heart in particular, however, were "haunted" by the convent model and the idea of religious perfection it was thought to provide.[56] This was particularly true since, largely due to the prestige of its fashionable Parisian boarding school, the society achieved a social status that many contemporaries associated with cloistered rather than active nuns. After the Catholic Reformation, the only women religious who successfully evaded papal strictures on cloister belonged to lower-class orders such as the Filles de la Charité, and some of the social stigma attached to apostolic work still lingered in the early nineteenth century. Throughout its first decades of existence, the Society of the Sacred Heart attempted somewhat imperfectly to balance an active apostolate with religious retreat from the world. The middle way proved hard to achieve. Through three general councils (in 1815, 1820, and 1826–27) to write and revise the constitutions of the society and the negotiations for papal approval, which lasted until 1827, the Religious of the Sacred Heart struggled to define their exact status somewhere in between strictly cloistered nuns and "filles seculières" dedicated to good works. They retained daily periods of prayer despite the demands of providing care to the ever-growing numbers of young girls enrolled in their schools. Corporal austerities were prohibited, but most sisters practiced at least interior mortification, especially during Lent. They provided advanced education for girls based on the model of elite Old Regime convents, as well as classes for poor children to teach basic literacy and religion.

But the most difficult issue was that of cloister. At issue in the long and complex negotiations with the Holy See over this question was nothing less than the definition of the modern nun in the wake of the French Revolution. Unlike many of the new teaching orders multiplying throughout France, Sacred Heart sisters did not leave the convent to teach and visited their families only when voyages between houses took them near home (a loophole rather frequently exploited by Sophie Barat herself, who had significant family responsibilities). On the other hand, they welcomed visitors to the convent and traveled on business on behalf of the society without hesitation. In a centralized order, members had to have, at the very least, freedom to travel between houses. When Duchesne later left for Louisiana, Barat gave her and her companions specific permission to leave the convent grounds "if the superiors judge it useful for the glory of God."[57] Her vision was one of a sort of "open cloister" that would depend on circumstances. Papal approval of their statutes, however, which the society ardently sought, required that they bend to the requirement of papal cloister, which would have stopped both visits and visiting. In France, where traditional cloister had been discredited during the Enlightenment and religious life outlawed during the Revolution, many women religious were experimenting with new models; in Rome, church officials were eager to reestablish order by sticking to the letter of the law. Could an order of women religious with solemn vows under the authority of the pope dispense with full cloister as had male orders such as the Jesuits? In order to become "true nuns" the Religious of the Sacred Heart accepted specific papal rules regarding travel and contact with outsiders to replace the vaguer language of their early constitutions. Nonetheless, they did not become a fully enclosed order on the Roman model and retained far more flexibility than, for example, Old Regime orders such as the Visitation. When the final rule was adopted in 1826, Sophie Barat wrote Duchesne, "Our approbation is similar to that of the Jesuits; it is unique for an order of non-cloistered women."[58]

Despite the removal of the grilles, Duchesne herself remained cloistered at Ste-Marie-d'en-Haut for the ten years between 1805 and 1815 and left only once with special permission to visit her dying father. Her life in this period was dominated by community and school activities, the comings and goings of Barat and various priests, pupils, illnesses, entries to the order, the taking of vows, and religious retreats. The most exciting break in this routine was the sojourn of Pope Pius VII in Grenoble (as a hostage of Napoleon), whose procession Duchesne first watched from the windows of the convent before pulling strings to get a private audience for the Sacred Heart community and permission to care for his linen and vestments during his stay.[59] She also persuaded Barat to allow her to spend part of her nights in the convent chapel in adoration of the Holy Sacrament, an activity Barat found dangerous because of the potential effects lack of sleep might have on Duchesne's health, "with the unremitting work you have." Finally Barat worked out a system where three nuns at Ste-Marie-d'en-Haut shared the nighttime adoration for about three hours each. Yet she kept such activities secret from other Sacred Heart sisters because not all members believed that Eucharistic adoration was an appropriate undertaking for an active religious order.[60] Trained in Visitation spirituality, Duchesne especially embraced the mystic life that found its outward expression in long periods of prayer, devotion, and solitude. Such moments were harder to find in a convent whose educational mission now took center stage.

The devotion to the Sacred Heart also spanned Duchesne's pre- and postrevolutionary religious experiences. During the seventeenth century, the heart of Jesus became an increasingly popular object of religious devotion and veneration. Its worship became more widespread, however, after a Visitation nun in Paray-le-Monial, in central France, Marguerite-Marie Alacoque, had a series of intimate visions of the Sacred Heart. The tradition of reflection, intimacy, and divine love fostered by Visitation spirituality provided a fertile environment for Alacoque's divine visions, and over time, the Visitation order became one of the primary propagandists for this cult.[61] Although Grenoble, unlike many other Visitation convents, did not dedicate its chapel to the Sacred Heart, surely Philippine Duchesne had been introduced to this devotion during her years as pupil, postulant, and novice at Ste-Marie-d'en-Haut. In 1765, following the centenary of Alacoque's visions, the Visitation order was authorized to celebrate the Feast of the Sacred Heart, and in 1787, a year before Duchesne became a novice, all of the houses were informed of new revelations made to an anonymous Visitandine in Nantes.[62]

Because Alacoque's original visions commanded the king of France to dedicate the nation to the Sacred Heart in order to achieve national redemption, the cult became politically charged during the Revolution. As convents were threatened with closure, nuns, led by Visitandines, began to fabricate images of the Sacred Heart by the hundreds for distribution among the faithful. The geography of this production and distribution was highly political, taking place largely in the west of France, where armed resistance to the Revolution, particularly its religious reforms, had resulted in civil war by 1793. Nuns stitched the insignia, clergy distributed them, and insurgents carried them into battle against revolutionary soldiers.[63] There is no evidence that the sisters at Ste-Marie-d'en-Haut, in relatively moderate and peaceful (by revolutionary standards) Grenoble took up this work. However, the Sacred Heart remained a potent symbol of religious and political reconstruction after the Revolution for Catholics and monarchists alike. Joseph Varin, who urged Sophie Barat to join the female branch of the Society of the Sacred Heart, had served as a counterrevolutionary soldier in the Vendée before returning to the priesthood as one of the early members of a men's order modeled on the Jesuits yet dedicated to the Sacred Heart.[64] Her brother, Louis Barat, had preached Sacred Heart devotion in clandestine church services in Paris before he was imprisoned during the Terror. The name itself was considered so seditious that both the male and the female branches used pseudonyms, Pères and Dames de la Foi, until the Restoration. In her new religious order, Sophie Barat took on the Sacred Heart theology of a loving, redeeming God as first developed by the Visitation order, as well as its monarchical associations; the Society of the Sacred Heart, through the education of girls, particularly elite girls, could redeem France.[65] Joining with Philippine Duchesne in the former Visitation convent in Grenoble, therefore, was a link of some significance for both women. If the form of evangelization had changed, its essence remained intact; Sacred Heart theology not only survived the Revolution but also grew stronger in the face of religious persecution.

The Missionary Impulse

Above all, Duchesne and Barat saw themselves as missionaries seeking to restore Catholic France. To the church, the violence of the Revolution against religious personnel and symbols made a renewal of Catholic belief and practice imperative. After the Restoration, male missionaries conducted religious revival meetings throughout France and exhorted the faithful to repent for past sins and return to Catholic practice. Mission crosses were often erected to replace the "liberty trees" of the Revolution, and many of these missions were dedicated to the Sacred Heart.[66] The foundation of active women's orders, by contrast to the traveling male preachers, was a more sustained, lower-key, and grassroots response to the crisis facing the Catholic Church in France. However, women like Barat and Duchesne were equally committed to the revival of French Catholicism by placing service to others and evangelization of the faith through education at its core. The saint to whom Duchesne became most devoted during this period of her life was François Régis, the seventeenth-century Jesuit missionary whose conversion work in remote regions of France ravaged by Protestantism and the wars of religion was legendary.[67] Duchesne clearly saw her own work, though within convent walls, as following in this tradition. At some point, however, she developed another ambition modeled on François Régis, a desire to travel overseas to evangelize among non-Christian populations.

Just when and how Philippine Duchesne decided that her destiny was outside of the walls of Ste-Marie-d'en-Haut, Grenoble, and France is hard to determine. By her own account, written retrospectively in 1818, the year of her departure for America, she was first inspired as a young pupil at Ste-Marie-d'en-Haut by her Jesuit confessor, who related tales of the Indians he had encountered as a missionary in Louisiana. The convent library also provided plenty of reading material on past Jesuit missionaries, whose voyages were the stuff of legend. Duchesne was drawn not only to the work of evangelizing among non-Christians but also to "the life of the martyrs" that such evangelization often implied. She also claimed to have chosen to enter the Visitation rather than the Carmelite order because of the possibility of missionary work.[68] Nonetheless, if Duchesne was harboring missionary dreams when she entered the Visitation in 1788, they seemed unlikely to come true. Although Visitation monasteries did spin off other houses on occasion, Ste-Marie-d'en-Haut had made only three foundations in its history, in the nearby Alpine and Provençal towns of Embrun, Sisteron, and Apt.[69] Duchesne's decision to enter the Visitation was undoubtedly more strongly conditioned by her familial connections and sojourn there as a boarder, while her missionary ambitions were nurtured by her revolutionary and Restoration experiences.

Indeed, from the time of her forced departure from Ste-Marie-d'en-Haut, various religious orders and countries "focused my thoughts and were the object of my prayers," she also wrote.[70] The same village church near her grandmother's country home, where she became devoted to St. François Régis, had an altar dedicated to St. François Xavier, with whose missionary works she was already familiar. Upon returning to Ste-Marie-d'en-Haut, she painted the walls of the cloister with scenes representing his life and death.[71] In early 1806, the convent hosted Dom Augustin de Lestrange, Trappist monk and Catholic resistance hero of the Revolution, who had just returned from a visit to American missions. Soon after this, Duchesne wrote about her spiritual life in missionary terms: "All night long [which she spent in adoration of the Holy Sacrament] I was in the New World, but I traveled in good company…St. François Xavier is still concerned to make this precious seed bear fruit and from the foot of the throne of God he asked for the opening of new lands to enlighten."[72] Which new lands, however, was not immediately clear. Like François Xavier, Duchesne apparently dreamed of going to China, but, she wrote, "this was impractical because women could not appear in public."[73] Cloister apparently went only so far. In 1810, she accused Sophie Barat of keeping from her an opportunity to join a group of priests setting off for the Middle East during a break in the continental blockade, and in 1811 there was some discussion of establishing a Sacred Heart community in Italy. By 1816 she was writing one of her cousins about missions in the far-flung French colonies of Pondicherry, Cayenne, and Senegal.[74]

Although by all contemporary accounts, Barat was hesitant about Duchesne's ambitions before her departure for America, at the time of Duchesne's death in 1852, Barat reclaimed the missionary initiative for herself, telling a group of novices that as a child she had read the letters of François Xavier and had developed a desire for missionary work, which she set aside upon deciding that her destiny was in France. According to this telling, Barat actively sought a "soul who could replace me, who would sacrifice herself for the foreign missions," and a month after confiding this longing in Duchesne, the latter returned to declare that "she believed herself to be this soul."[75]

Duchesne's—and perhaps Barat's—growing attraction to these opportunities was emblematic of a rekindling of interest in Catholic missions among the French public after 1800. In his *Genius of Christianity*, published in 1802, Chateaubriand devoted an entire section to French missions to the Middle East, Asia, the Antilles, and the Americas, concluding that scholars who were "dispatched to faraway countries with the instruments and programs of an academy, could never do as much as a poor monk, leaving on foot from his convent, with his rosary and breviary."[76] Two novellas, *Atala* (1801) and *René* (1802), reimagined French encounters with the Natchez tribe on the lower Mississippi from the historical reality of violence and failure to a kind of nostalgia for French empire.[77] Multiple editions of *Lettres édifiantes et curieuses*, which related Jesuit missionary experiences from around the world, appeared after 1803, inflaming the imaginations of romantic Catholics. The Catholic Church reestablished and reorganized its missionary branch, Propaganda Fide, in 1817, and in France the Restoration government encouraged French missions as it scrambled to reestablish influence abroad after the loss of the Napoleonic empire.

Missionary vocations also resulted from the religious experience of individuals like Duchesne, who had fought to preserve the Catholic faith in France during the Revolution. If Enlightenment rationality had failed—in their view—to create the ideal society, then Christianity could become the basis of a universal civilization.[78] Accustomed to total engagement, martyrdom, and the abandoning of their lives to God's will, to some Catholics "civilizing the savages" became the next great evangelical challenge and one that evoked the last great struggle in French Catholic history, the Reformation. The school of French spirituality originating in the seventeenth century also emphasized the mystical self-denial and mortification that could be found in missionary endeavors.[79] Initially, too, French missionaries turned their attention to North America, the land of now mythical past conversion activity, when Jesuit "black robes" proselytized among Indian tribes in New France and often lost their lives in the process. Not only did the exiled Dom Augustin de Lestrange and Chateaubriand travel to North America in the first decades of the nineteenth century and return to relate their adventures among French Catholics, but about a hundred and fifty emigrant priests also ended up in the United States or Canada during the Revolution, and thirteen Catholic bishops in the United States appointed before 1850 were French, who in turn recruited French clergy. One of these was Louis Guillaume Dubourg, who became bishop of Louisiana in 1815.[80]

Was there a model for women religious like Philippine Duchesne in the new missionary revival of the early nineteenth century? In *Genius of Christianity* Chateaubriand recounted a chance meeting with a white-bearded "Louisiana missionary" living "in the middle of American solitude…where he directed a little flock of French and of Christian savages."[81] This almost mythical figure, whom Chateaubriand compared to a hermit living in the deserts of Egypt, was explicitly gendered male; he described no female counterpart living alone and uncloistered in the forests of the new world. Still, women had already participated in the Christianization of New France, both in Quebec and Louisiana. Upon her arrival in North America, Duchesne would lodge in the Ursuline convent in New Orleans, established in 1727. However, her view of North America and of her own personal role in missionary work was undoubtedly most shaped by the life and writings of Ursuline sister Marie Guyart—Marie de l'Incarnation in religion—who founded the first convent in North America, in Quebec in 1639.[82] Near the end of her life, Duchesne wrote, "From my first vows to go to America, I thought only of Canada and placed in it all my hope, admiring Mère de l'Incarnation."[83] She would have most likely read Marie de l'Incarnation's substantial writings in the Visitation convent library, and other individuals, knowing of her missionary longings, held her up as an example.[84] Among women missionaries, who were few and mainly anonymous, Marie de l'Incarnation was a celebrity and a role model.

Although the details of Marie de l'Incarnation's personal life did not resemble those of Philippine Duchesne (the former was from an artisan family and entered the Ursuline order as a widow, leaving behind an eleven-year-old son), her Canadian mission provided a model of a cloistered nun exercising a vibrant ministry among the natives of New France. Soon after arriving in Quebec, the five Ursuline sisters built a convent and enclosed their large yard with cedar fences; except during a fire in 1650, Marie de l'Incarnation never again left this enclosed space.[85] From this base, however, she daily ministered to Indian women and girls (Algonquin, Huron, Nipissing, Montagnais, and Iroquois, among other tribes) who came to the convent for food, clothing, and instruction. The Ursulines opened a boarding school for Indian girls, where they taught Christian belief, as well as the French language, reading and writing, music, and needle and decorative work. Meanwhile, Marie de l'Incarnation herself mastered four Indian languages, into which she translated and composed catechisms, prayer books, and dictionaries. A constant hub of activity for settlers and natives alike, the Ursuline convent sponsored baptisms and religious processions, and Indian men consulted the nuns through the grille in the parlor and collected food from the convent kitchen.

The mixed vocation of the Ursuline order, founded in the wake of the Reformation, combining teaching with cloister, proved adaptable to this particular location, where Jesuits had already established a residence, chapel, school, and seminary and traveled constantly between Quebec proper and various Indian tribes living in the woodlands. Except for summer, when they were busy in the fields, native women and girls, having learned of the Ursuline mission from the Jesuits, came to them; the nuns hoped that, once Christianized, they would return to their villages as emissaries of Christian belief and culture. Despite their fixed locale, however, the Ursuline mission was not without the frisson of danger that characterized Catholic evangelization in the Americas and that sustained many missionaries. War between Indian tribes and against the French was always imminent, and the Ursuline convent was briefly evacuated in 1660 due to the threat of an Iroquois attack. In seventeenth-century France, martyrdom among foreign "savages" represented the highest level of religious heroism to which a devout Catholic could aspire. More than any other Catholic settlement, New France appeared to offer opportunities for self-annihilation and sacrifice.[86] Although blocked from the kind of martyrdom that often awaited men religious isolated in hostile native communities, Marie de l'Incarnation nevertheless had far more scope for religious hardship in Canada than she would have had by remaining in France. Her Quebec mission provided an opportunity to universalize the Christian message while simultaneously allowing her to seek mystical union with God. Philippine Duchesne was drawn to a similar dual spiritual experience—the conversion of non-Christians while abandoning her life and soul to the workings of providence on the frontier. "Those who have the courage to stay and to work there," Sophie Barat wrote to her after reading a book on Catholic missionaries Duchesne had sent her, "soon discover the treasures that make them perfectly happy, the possession of God alone."[87] Like Marie de l'Incarnation, Duchesne was originally drawn to a purely contemplative convent and then entered one with a mixed vocation. The example of her seventeenth-century predecessor suggested that cloister, conversion of the Indians, and a deeper mystical relationship with God were mutually achievable goals.

When the new bishop of Louisiana arrived in Paris in January 1817 at the tail end of a well-publicized tour of France and Italy in order to recruit new missionaries, Philippine Duchesne knew her moment had arrived. A Sulpician priest born in St-Domingue before the Revolution but educated in France, Bishop Dubourg had fled France in 1792, first to Spain and then two years later to the United States. He spent the following two decades administrating Catholic educational institutions in the diocese of Baltimore (under the legendary Bishop John Carroll), serving as president of Georgetown College, and founding St. Mary's College in Baltimore and Mount St. Mary's Seminary in Emmitsburg. He also brought a group of Poor Clares from Cuba to Washington, D.C., and helped establish Elizabeth Seton's Sisters of Charity. By the time he was appointed apostolic administrator of Louisiana in 1812 and bishop in 1815, Dubourg was experienced in building the kind of infrastructure Catholics hoped to establish throughout the United States, and he saw women religious as a key element of this expansion.[88] Persuasive and enthusiastic, he had preached in Lyon, where among his receptive audience was Duchesne's sister, and he had heard of Duchesne from Louis Barat, who had recommended her for the St. Louis mission. After some hesitation about the feasibility of establishing an overseas branch of a religious order barely established in France, as well as losing one of her most capable and devoted disciples, Sophie Barat finally ceded to the intense lobbying of Duchesne, Dubourg, and her brother and agreed to send Duchesne and four companions to open an American house. Duchesne was named local superior and delegated special decision-making authority due to the great distance between France and Louisiana.[89] The other participants in this pathbreaking mission were Octavie Berthold and Eugénie Audé, both choir sisters who had entered the society in Grenoble and who took their vows shortly before leaving for Louisiana, and Catherine Lamarre and Marguerite Manteau, converse sisters who had slightly longer and more practical experience in the society.

The months that followed were ones of intense preparation. In the Paris house, which buzzed with the comings and goings of workers and merchants, Duchesne's Sacred Heart sisters witnessed her joy "in the midst of the greatest confusion, but [it was] a calm, deliberate, intrinsic joy, not forgetting anything, packing all the trunks, crates, and packages herself without worry, without trouble." Characteristically, Duchesne enlisted the help, advice, and expertise of her wealthy and well-connected family, asking them to collect donations in kind—particularly to outfit a new convent and chapel in such a way as "to catch the eyes of the savages whom we want to attract by the trappings of the ceremonies"—and in money since Dubourg had already warned her, she said, that he did not have sufficient funds to underwrite the entire enterprise, and her companions "brought with them nothing but their good will." Duchesne personally raised seven thousand francs for the voyage and new establishment. The little group of missionaries finally embarked from Bordeaux on 19 March 1818, and Philippine Duchesne, aged forty-nine, stood, by her own account, at the threshold of a "new career" in which she could fulfill her "desires to instruct the infidels, desires long fought by my superiors and my confessors" but which "finally Providence had all arranged for their realization."[90]

2

Foothold on the Frontier

After 71 days at sea, 52 of them without sight of land and often seasick, Duchesne kissed the ground at New Orleans on 29 May 1818, the feast of the Sacred Heart, a day, not surprisingly, that she found providential. Sweltering in her heavy winter habit (the summer ones having been safely packed away for the sea voyage), she was welcomed to Louisiana by the French-speaking Ursuline sisters, who had been resident in New Orleans for nearly one hundred years and who were prepared to offer advice and perspectives on the New World.[1] For all her energy and commitment to missionary work, Duchesne had no real-world experience with other cultures—until she arrived in Bordeaux to embark for America, she had never even tasted saltwater fish. Relieved both by the familiarity of a city where, even fifteen years after annexation by the United States, "the language and the customs make one believe we are in France," and by the comforts of the Ursuline convent, social and cultural differences nevertheless became apparent within a matter of days.[2] From behind the Ursuline grille, Duchesne "was charmed" by her first sight of American Indians, who came to the convent to sell handcrafted baskets. "Absolutely covered up as Our Lord is represented at the moment of *ecce homo*," she wrote to Sacred Heart pupils back in France, "one of them who came to put his head in the door of the church on Sunday, had the air of a devil who wanted to put his head in the door of heaven." Even more visible, however, were Africans and their descendants, enslaved and free, including the three hundred girls and women whom the Ursulines instructed on Sundays. "The condition of these slaves," she opined, "is not always unhappy, they have two or three hours to themselves during the day that they use to cultivate the little land that is given to them....They each have their little house....They are all clothed." After calculating the great wealth slaves brought their owners, she concluded, however, "I would rather instruct one Indian woman and eat like she does than to see myself in such a great abundance with responsibility over so many people, for whose salvation they are so indifferent that they leave them without instruction and without religious practice."[3] Like many new arrivals in New Orleans, Duchesne and her companions were also struck by the apparent immorality and avarice of its inhabitants, both white and black. However, "the inhabitants of Saint Louis and Sainte-Geneviève," one of them suggested hopefully, "are simple people whose hearts are well disposed, without ambition; they know how to be content with little and not introduce among themselves this such dangerous luxuriousness that has penetrated here into the lowest classes of society."[4]

The forty-day journey up the Mississippi confirmed Duchesne's sense of destiny. On the banks of the river, she wrote, "I saw Savages of all kinds...all clothed, good, and some, half-civilized, speaking French or English,"[5] attracted no doubt by the sight of one of the first steamboats to travel upriver. This was old French missionary territory, dotted with villages and military outposts—New Bourbon, Ste-Genevieve, Kaskaskia, Fort de Chartres, and Cahokia—settled by French or French Canadian colonists and once served by Catholic priests belonging to orders like the French Society of the Foreign Missions, who founded the first mission at Cahokia, across from St. Louis, in 1699 and by the Jesuits, who established the second at Kaskaskia, farther downriver, in 1703.[6] Although Jesuit penetration of the Mississippi never matched that of the St. Lawrence River in Canada, much less their extensive colony among the Guaraní tribe in Paraguay, Duchesne reported enduring Indian loyalty to the "black robes," whose departure in 1763 (at the time of the suppression of the Jesuit order in France) left the Illinois tribe "inconsolable."[7] At a stop in Ste-Genevieve, founded in the mid-seventeenth century by French settlers from Kaskaskia, just across the Mississippi, the enthusiastic parish priest tried to convince Duchesne to stay. The offer was tempting. Besides the emotional attraction of Jesuit roots, the twin villages of Kaskaskia and Ste-Genevieve offered the most concentrated settlement of French-speaking settlers in a rapidly Americanizing region; it had a recently established seminary and a large church to provide confessors and regular religious services; the Indians were nearby; schools lacking, and the inhabitants eager. It was not the only offer that Duchesne entertained as she arrived in St. Louis. On the sea voyage to New Orleans, a wealthy French merchant embarking in Havana suggested that they settle there if the St. Louis project did not work out, and Duchesne, intrigued, wrote Sophie Barat that Cuba was "an earthly paradise," healthier and wealthier than the southern United States and also populated by Indians; the only problem she foresaw was the sisters' lack of Spanish.[8]

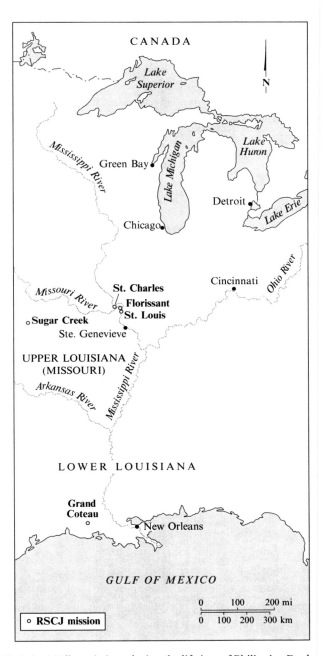

CANADA

Lake Superior

Mississippi River

Green Bay

Lake Michigan

Lake Huron

Detroit

Lake Erie

Chicago

Cincinnati

Ohio River

Missouri River

St. Charles
Florissant
St. Louis

Sugar Creek

Ste. Genevieve

UPPER LOUISIANA
(MISSOURI)

Arkansas River

Mississippi River

LOWER LOUISIANA

Grand
Coteau

New Orleans

GULF OF MEXICO

N

0   100   200 mi
0   100   200   300 km

○ RSCJ mission

Mississippi Valley missions during the lifetime of Philippine Duchesne

The Ursulines, on the other hand, who had lost sixteen of their number to Havana when Louisiana reverted from Spanish (to French and then to American) control, urged the Religious of the Sacred Heart to stay in New Orleans, where each order could run a separate convent and boarding school. To Duchesne's response that her mission was among Indians, they responded that New Orleans "lacked nei-ther Indians, nor blacks, nor colored." Ste-Genevieve, Havana, or New Orleans remained options for the future, however, unlike Detroit, whose Catholic priest also paid Duchesne a visit once they had settled in Missouri to request that she send a superior to train nuns for his mission. Despite his being "a Jesuit of the heart and a zealous missionary in every sense of the word," she quickly decided the trip north was too far, the country too cold and too poor, and the settlement offered too few paying pupils.[9] For the moment, Missouri was martyrdom enough.

In 1818 St. Louis was a city undergoing rapid change. Founded by French set-tlers who resisted acculturation during forty years of Spanish rule, it began to Americanize after the acquisition of Louisiana by the United States in 1803. An influx of American immigrants in the late 1790s was followed by a "tidal wave" of settlers moving west after 1815, doubling the population of the city from 1,500 in 1815 to 3,000 in 1818 and tripling it to 4,500 in 1820.[10] English, as Duchesne was immediately to note, was quickly replacing French as the area's lingua franca. The growing population put an enormous demand on land and skilled labor; land was expensive and rents were high. The territory also suffered from financial and economic instability. The Bank of St. Louis failed in 1819, and was followed by the Bank of Missouri in 1821. Prices were higher in St. Louis than in Paris. Bishop Dubourg himself lived in an episcopal "palace" that "resembles one of our poor farmhouses" in France, and his promised cathedral was not yet built, Duchesne reported to correspondents back home upon her arrival.[11] Under these circum-stances, to Duchesne's dismay, Dubourg placed them not in St. Louis, where acquiring or building a house was prohibitively expensive, but in a small rented house in St. Charles, the trading outpost across the Missouri River. A rough frontier town, Duchesne claimed that, until a few years earlier, "one would have thought to see there the Bacchanales of the pagans: half-naked girls, a bottle of whisky in one hand, hanging onto a man with the other, running around night and day without working, dancing every day of the year." Here Indian contact had resulted in "half breeds" who shared the Indian "hatred for work and their love of drink." Her only consolation was the fanciful expectation that St. Charles would become a commercial hub between North America and China, believing that the Missouri River emptied into the Pacific, affording a two-week passage to Asia.[12]

Conditions for Duchesne and her companions were harsh. The first winter they went two weeks without bread or corn and had difficulty procuring water. The winters were bitterly cold—Duchesne suggested in 1821 that if priests serving in

Siberia were "looking for a mission field with the same climate," they might relocate to Missouri[13]—and summers oppressively hot. A year after their arrival, Dubourg moved them to the tamer village of Florissant, fourteen miles north of St. Louis— Duchesne bouncing in the back of a wagon with the reliquaries and the chickens— where they hoped to attract a larger number of paying pupils than they had in St. Charles. Building a convent there, however, was extremely expensive; Duchesne estimated the cost at 30,000 francs ($6,000), of which she was able to pay 10,000 herself; another 10,000 came from an advance from Bishop Dubourg, and the final 10,000 she borrowed at 10 percent interest for two years. Money problems were constantly on her mind. "The situation," she wrote to Louis Barat, "is very different from the one we faced at Grenoble, where we never had a feeling of debts piling up."[14] The Sacred Heart sisters remained reliant on donations of books, clothing, and religious ornaments from France and the occasional barrels of food sent up from New Orleans by the generous Ursulines.

Unlike most French or American laywomen, who withdrew from active partic- ipation in business affairs during the nineteenth century, Duchesne engaged in continual financial management. For decades, she continued to draw on her por- tion of the family trust and solicited her generous relatives for small and large sums to keep the Missouri establishments afloat. As the minority religion, all Catholic missions in the United States were having difficulty, she admitted in 1824, "whereas in Societies established by Protestants in New York, Boston, etc., they have an annual fund of 1,250,000 francs in order to send their missionaries all the way to the East and they maintain Indian schools in those areas…Without the help of France, the [Catholic] missionaries would accomplish little here." A year later she lamented that Catholics benefited from no state aid, unlike past missionaries in the Spanish empires of California and Paraguay, where the king of Spain provided funds for the maintenance of missionaries and churches.[15] Bishop Dubourg diverted most of his discretionary funds to the establishment and maintenance of his seminary and his men's college in St. Louis, leaving the Sacred Heart sisters to fend for themselves. Donations from the Association de la Propagation de la Foi in France, which took a great interest in the American missions, were also apportioned unequally: In 1829, out of the 25,000 francs sent to the dioceses of St. Louis and New Orleans, more than 6,000 francs went to the Jesuit superior in St. Louis and only 1,000 francs to Duchesne.[16]

In order to survive, the Sacred Heart mission had to pay for itself, and decisions about where to live and what establishments to open on the frontier were inti- mately linked to the practical problems of financing them. The Society of the Sacred Heart, like many nineteenth-century French teaching orders, used the profits from boarding and day schools for wealthier girls to subsidize institutions for poorer pupils. This meant, however, that they needed to find a location where such a boarding school could flourish. In St. Charles, most of their pupils attended the free school. In Florissant, their establishment nearly collapsed after the financial panic of 1819, when all but four paying boarders left, and day pupils brought in only nine dollars a year.[17] It was saved by the opening of a new establishment in rural Louisiana, at Grand Coteau, where a rich widow endowed land, house, and furnishings and paid the salaries and travel expenses of the Sacred Heart sisters. Although Duchesne initially found a rural location problematic—"I still regret that we do not have a foothold in New Orleans," she wrote in 1820[18]—she quickly saw the advantages of such a generous donation. Grand Coteau offered adequate space for a flourishing boarding school patronized by the daughters of elite Louisiana families, who were wealthier than their Missouri counterparts. "Lower Louisiana," she wrote to Sophie Barat, "is necessary to make Upper exist....Two establishments, far from burdening us with debt, will in part liquidate us. We will be able to double the number of new religious, pupils, and poor children, extend devotion to the Sacred Heart, multiplying His altars." Three years later, running a surplus, Grand Coteau paid the $250 necessary to keep Duchesne's beloved Indian school open in Florissant. By the end of the decade, when each location had three establishments, those in Louisiana were "quite flourishing," while those in Missouri remained "very poor."[19] On balance, however, the society made ends meet.

In making these decisions, Duchesne had to negotiate with Bishop Dubourg, whose energetic vision for the future of Catholicism in his diocese did not always square with her own, and with Sophie Barat, far removed from the realities of frontier life, whose instructions took months to arrive. "Why doesn't your pious bishop place you in St. Louis?" Barat wrote, exasperated, to Duchesne at the time of the move to Florissant. "[W]ill not all these sacrifices become almost useless in a village where you will be without boarding pupils?" More important, how was she expected to contribute additional funds and members until the American mission was on a firm financial footing? "You will vegetate in that corner of the world, by being unable to work among the Indians," Barat fretted from France.[20]

While reassuring Barat and explaining American realities to her, Duchesne used her obedience to her superior general as a negotiating tool with Bishop Dubourg, who saw the small band of nuns he had recruited as an extension of his own authority. However, the Society of the Sacred Heart was a centralized religious order with an established rule whose ultimate decision maker was the superior general, Sophie Barat, in France. Although Duchesne's instinct was to defer to male ecclesiastical authority, this status offered her some protection from episcopal interference. "He speaks of some changes in our rules to which we do not consent," Duchesne reported after a contentious visit with Dubourg in 1819, "and we told him frankly that when a bishop allows us in his diocese, he leaves to us the choice of location."[21] Sacred Heart houses in the United States had to follow the same rules as those in France, also located in a variety of different dioceses. Although most women's congregations of this type came under the purview of the local bishop, the Society of the Sacred Heart had attempted to avoid this diocesan control by obtaining papal approval of its statutes. The final compromise, hammered out in 1826, put them under papal authority but with episcopal control over the travel arrangements of individual members.[22] This arrangement gave them some small measure of independence, unlike, for example, Elizabeth Seton, foundress of the American Sisters of Charity, who spent much of her time fighting against the control of her (French) clerical superior, John B. David.[23] Although Duchesne and Dubourg shared a European model of Catholicism (which Seton and David did not), Duchesne never intended that the Sacred Heart would become a mere tool in the hands of the local bishop. In America, the Religious of the Sacred Heart would remain one of the few religious orders of European origin that never separated from its founding congregation. Duchesne could not afford to offend the bishop who had made her missionary dream possible—indeed, she found his advice and support invaluable—but she would not allow him to "crush us under the weight of authority," either.[24] The final responsibility for the success of the Religious of the Sacred Heart in America belonged to her, and her ultimate loyalty was to the order itself.

Race and Class on the Frontier

Besides money, the most formidable obstacle facing the transplanted Sisters of the Sacred Heart was finding adequate personnel to open and maintain establishments and schools. The five original sisters from France were joined by seven others by 1831, but, unlike the Soeurs de St-Joseph de l'Apparition or the Soeurs de St-Joseph de Cluny, the Society of the Sacred Heart in France never became a missionary congregation in the sense that nuns were recruited and trained specifically for missionary work or expected to do regular tours of duty abroad. Sophie Barat excused her inability to send new recruits on the demands made of her in France, writing to Duchesne in 1821, "Many of ours burn with the desire to leave, but in addition to their vocation not being tested enough, their removal would create too much of a vacuum....We are so pressed for [new] establishments, and we refuse many."[25] Harsh frontier conditions were also undoubtedly discouraging to new recruits. Even after a decade in Missouri, Duchesne presented missionary work to French novices for its sacrificial qualities, suggesting that they exchange the "sweetness of the novitiate" for "misery, harshness, fickleness, ingratitude, [and] poverty" in order to experience the "pure love of Jesus's cross." After experiencing the voyage to America in 1822, Lucile Mathévon declared that the majority of French sisters "would not be able to live here; I think they would die before arriving."[26] By 1831, though the Religious of the

Sacred Heart in America had grown to sixty nuns, forty-eight of them were American recruits. "But how difficult to make religious life understood by people with a different language who have no idea about our customs, with completely different habits for food and clothing," Duchesne wrote about American postulant Mary Layton in 1820, to whom she could not herself give religious instruction due to the language barrier. She was more optimistic about the entrance of two sisters, Mathilde and Eulalie Hamilton, bilingual, whom "I regard as the foundation of the Society in the American nation," and one of whom, at least, had the character traits to make a "good superior."[27] Local novices were not only essential to the growth of the Society of the Sacred Heart in America but also contributed skills, like English, that the French nuns did not have. However, they also brought attitudes that clashed with European cultural norms and the very structure of a French religious order.

The most important of these attitudes was the question of social class. Like all contemporaneous European religious orders, the Society of the Sacred Heart admitted two classes of nuns, converse sisters to do manual labor and choir sisters to teach, who were further distinguished by slightly different habits. The original group of five religious who left France included three choir sisters and two converse, which in theory allowed for a balance of roles and responsibilities. In fact, given the primitive conditions in which the group initially lived, the choir sisters also participated in the heavy housekeeping chores, without which the establishment could not have survived. Among the new skills that choir nuns Duchesne, Audé, and Berthold acquired were spading the garden, spreading manure, leading the cow to water, and cleaning its stable, tasks common to pioneer women but ones they never could have imagined doing in France. As their schools expanded, Duchesne's goal was to free up choir sisters to teach while recruiting new sisters of both types into the society. Here, however, she ran up against American hostility to overt class segregation. In the United States, Duchesne wrote to Sophie Barat, "everyone wants to be equal," and the American women who have inquired about joining as converse sisters expected that the cooking would be done "each in turn." The spirit of equality had even infected Soeur Catherine Lamarre, one of the French converse sisters, who "wants to be an apostle" and wear the habit of the choir sisters. "To appease this fever of desire, she has a slave mulatress to instruct," Duchesne admitted.[28] The Ursulines in New Orleans, she had discovered, though maintaining two classes of sisters, had virtually no sartorial distinction between them. Bishop Dubourg also weighed in against converse sisters, "saying that this system was worthless in this country" and arguing for a single rank and a single habit.[29] Duchesne saw nothing but dangers in this erasure of status:

> With difficulty I imagine equality, obstacle to many vocations; even with a
> single rank, because merit, etc. will always make a difference and pride

will always find means of complaint. Those who know nothing will want to be schoolmistresses. And if teachers also do manual labor, where will they find time? And their personal cleanliness? And if they don't do it, there is immediately a distinction. All things considered, it would perhaps be better to stay as we are and risk not recruiting very much, expanding less here, and doing it later in those countries where the spirit of subordination has less of a hold than reflections of pride. When the superior takes a turn cooking, many will want to be superiors in their turn.

Sophie Barat's response was in full agreement: "Keep two ranks among you, well distinguished."[30]

An alternative solution to the problem of converse sisters was hired servants. In European convents, outsiders were uncommon; among other reasons the comings and goings of lay individuals posed a threat to enclosure. In the frontier context, however, lack of outside help threatened cloister—and survival—even more. "I expected deprivations," Duchesne wrote soon after her arrival in St. Charles, "but I did not imagine that on the banks of the Missouri [river], we could, while seeing flow its abundant water, lack it ourselves...no one is willing to fetch it regularly for us." White servants, she soon discovered, were impossible to hire. Duchesne placed the blame on the American character rather than the local labor market. The same spirit of equality that encouraged converse sisters to think that all convent work would be shared by turns ran rampant, in Duchesne's view, throughout American society: "French servants who have come to this country, have forgotten kind deeds and gratitude, and have taken up an independent life, or a lazy one."[31] Few frontier residents were interested in working as servants for low wages when more lucrative and self-sufficient opportunities were available. Once the sisters moved to Florissant, the problem was initially solved, in part, by a manservant belonging to a religious order attached to the bishop and loaned to the sisters to help with the heaviest work. In 1821, they hired a Flemish man to whom they provided a house, wood, and one thousand francs a year in exchange for farming their land.[32] Much of the everyday manual labor continued, however, to be done by the sisters themselves.

The flip side of American class equality was racial inequality, as Duchesne remarked within days of her arrival at the Ursuline convent in New Orleans. "Witnessing my astonishment that there were only blacks available for service in this country, while so many people die of hunger in France," she wrote, "they told me that, despite the vices of negroes, they preferred them. Whites are spoiled here for work and by *equality*. With these words: *We have the same skin as you* [emphasis hers], they all acquire the right to be gentlemen." The "equality" that seemed so much a part of the American character did not include people of color. Duchesne, however, was prepared to accept nonwhites on equal terms under God, scolding a converse sister who balked at doing the laundry with black servants: "I answered her that they had the same soul as she, that they were redeemed by the same holy Blood, received into the same Church, and that if she did not want to associate with them, she should avail herself of the ship that was about to return, because we had come for the blacks."[33]

Duchesne had not, in fact, come to America for blacks, and her interest in working with those of African descent never matched her interest in evangelizing Indians. Nonetheless, the racial realities of antebellum Louisiana and Missouri could not be ignored. Louisiana's wealth was based in large part on slave labor, and the Ursulines actively ministered to both blacks and whites, as well as employing black domestics and owning slaves.[34] Missouri's immigration boom, particularly from the Southern states, was fueled in part by the lack of antislavery restrictions, and most of its white population made the issue of statehood dependent on the continuation of slavery, resulting in the "Missouri crisis" when it requested admission to the Union as a slave state in 1821.[35] Arriving in the midst of this impassioned debate, Duchesne stated that the small Sacred Heart community did not "want any" slaves, nor could it afford any, but then "we do not know what to do for service especially without going out; no one hires out as a servant—all want to be equal." In 1822 she declared that "despite my repugnance for Negroes, we might be obliged to get to the point of taking them on" due to the servant shortage.[36]

Judging by the number of times that it came up in her letters, the expense was more significant than the moral problem of owning slaves. In Louisiana, the Society of the Sacred Heart accepted slaves as part of the Grand Coteau establishment and purchased others.[37] In 1826, with the help of Bishop Dubourg and with the permission of Sophie Barat, Duchesne purchased a black woman named Rachel as a cook. Money concerns remained paramount: "[T]hey have told me that in Kentucky the choice will be easier and cheaper," she wrote to Bishop Rosati in 1827, and in 1839 she wrote to her cousin that "often a bad enough negro costs three or four thousand francs." In 1831, the St. Louis establishment acquired a slave given in exchange for tuition.[38] Ten years later, when Duchesne and three sisters of the Sacred Heart traveled west into Kansas to establish an Indian mission, her colleague Soeur Lucile Mathévon praised the work of "our negro Edmond," "a completely important man here" who "was almost as respected as we," largely because of his carpentry skills. Still, "I am careful not to tell him that he is free here, because however happy he is and perhaps too pious to take advantage of it, it is nevertheless surer to leave him if possible in ignorance."[39]

In their willingness to own slaves and unwillingness to denounce slavery, the sisters of the Sacred Heart followed the example of their church. Pope Gregory XVI did not condemn the slave trade until 1839, and slavery itself was proscribed only in 1888. Slavery was first introduced into the Illinois country by Jesuit priests in

Kaskaskia evangelizing among Indians in the early eighteenth century, a seemingly moral contradiction not unlike that of Duchesne's a century later. The first Catholic bishop in the United States, John Carroll, owned slaves, and the Catholic Church in Maryland, a significant landowner, relied on slave labor that it rationalized both by economic necessity and by a sense of paternal responsibility toward the slaves under its control. When the Maryland Jesuits decided to divest themselves of their slaves in the 1830s rather than emancipating them, however, they sold them to other, often non-Catholic, slaveholders and reaped the profits.[40] In Missouri, Bishop Dubourg (born into a slaveholding family in St-Domingue and a slaveowner himself) supplied the new Vincentian seminary with slaves as domestic and agricultural workers; he also raised a series of questions with Rome—whose answers are unrecorded—regarding the ethics of slaveholding, including whether it was permissible when no other domestic servants could be found.[41] The Jesuits who came to Missouri in 1823 to become the neighbors, collaborators, and confessors of the Sacred Heart community arrived with "three Negros and their wives."[42] Contemporaneous women's religious orders also owned slaves in some locations; besides the Ursulines in New Orleans, these included the Carmelites in Maryland, the Visitandines in Washington, D.C., the Daughters of the Cross in Louisiana, the Dominican Sisters, and the Sisters of Charity in Kentucky.[43]

Enmeshed as they were in the slaveholding economy, neither the Catholic episcopal hierarchy nor religious orders in the colonial and antebellum United States became involved in any significant way in the antislavery cause. Not only did religious orders often need the labor that slaves provided, but as the minority religion Catholic survival also often depended on assimilating to the values of their neighbors rather than challenging them. Until the migration of large numbers of European Catholics to northern cities beginning in the 1830s, more than half of American Catholics lived in the South, and Southern culture helped mold American Catholicism.[44] Alliance with northern evangelicals, who formed the backbone of the abolitionist movement, was also impossible due to the hostility between Catholics and Protestants in antebellum America. From the available evidence, it appears that Philippine Duchesne shared most of the tenets of "white racialism" as defined by historian George M. Fredrickson, especially a belief that blacks were different from and inferior to whites and that those differences could only be overcome, if at all, by a slow process of black assimilation to white norms.[45]

What did interest some Catholic clerics, including Duchesne, was the conversion and Christian education of blacks, both slave and free. The French Code Noir, promulgated in Louisiana in 1724, focused on the responsibilities of slaveowners, requiring, for example, baptism and the religious education of slaves, and this emphasis still marked some French clergy, like Bishop Flaget of Kentucky, who threatened Catholic slaveholders with excommunication for inhumane treatment of slaves.[46] For some American Catholic bishops, like John Carroll of Maryland, the numbers of black Catholics (in this case, 20 percent of his diocese) made them a significant pastoral responsibility.[47] In 1827, the first religious order of black women, the Oblate Sisters of Providence, was founded among the Haitian refugee community in Baltimore under the spiritual direction of a French priest.[48] The Ursulines of New Orleans were the first American women's order to concern themselves with black education. Soon after their arrival in 1727, they enrolled black girls in both the boarding and day divisions of their convent school and, in conformity with the provisions of the Code Noir, helped prepare slaves for baptism. They also founded a confraternity of laywomen, the Enfants de Marie, whose members included women of color. In the 1830s, a group of free black women in New Orleans spun off from that tradition to form a congregation of black religious women, the Sisters of the Holy Family.[49] One of the three founders, Henriette Delille, received novitiate training in a Sacred Heart convent and took vows shortly before Philippine Duchesne's death.[50]

Admitting black women into the American branch of the Society of the Sacred Heart was a possible solution to the servant crisis that Duchesne considered. In late 1819, Duchesne proposed to Bishop Dubourg and Sophie Barat that "a few girls of color, desiring a religious life," join the society as "Soeurs commissionnaires" and that "with this title they would be able to help as much as the converse sisters, who will be hard to have among the whites, all being equal here." On the one hand, these sisters would be third-class citizens, ranking below converse sisters in the pecking order; on the other, Duchesne conceded that they would be given the same habit due to the "spirit of the country." The admission of black sisters (and pupils) "would degrade us greatly," she admitted at one point, "but I cherish this degradation," seeing it as part of her apostolic mission. Dubourg, for his part, suggested that some women of mixed blood (Indian or African) whose lack of marriage prospects made them susceptible to prostitution could be "admitted to a sort of subaltern profession, with a different habit than converse sisters."[51] In this, he adapted well-established European models of allowing repentant prostitutes to live out their lives in convents. Barat, in turn, gave permission for Duchesne to admit women of color as sisters, "provided that it is not known that they are members of the Society."[52]

Both Barat and Dubourg expressed concern that the Society of the Sacred Heart, new to the American racial landscape, do nothing that would alienate white parents, whose school fees would enable it to establish itself on a firm financial footing and whose daughters would provide new recruits into the order. "Do not make the foolish mistake of mixing the whites with the blacks," Barat wrote categorically from France. "[Y]ou will have no more pupils. The same for your novices; no one would join if you were to receive black novices. We will see later what we can do for them." Dubourg gave Duchesne the same advice, based on his experience in

Baltimore, where the bishop there had upheld segregation as a "prejudice that had to be kept as the last safeguard of morals." Duchesne's Paris confessor even weighed in, assuring her not only that he would prefer the "exercise of her zeal for these unfortunates whose very abjection made them more precious to the heart of Jesus Christ" but also that she must bend to local prejudice by segregating black and colored pupils. As far as their entering the society, "that seems to me too delicate in the beginning."[53] The plan to admit women of color as associate sisters came to nothing, although Duchesne was still writing about it in 1831, this time proposing a secondary order, modeled on one run by the Dames de St-Michel in Paris for delinquent girls, "under the same enclosure, in a separate location, and with a special rule." "Could we not also bring together the girls of color who want to leave the world and consecrate to it one or two of ours?" she asked Bishop Rosati.[54] If women of color were to be admitted to Catholic religious life in America, they would not do so on equal terms with white women but be segregated into orders or secondary orders of their own.[55] Significantly, however, the two founding orders of women of color in the United States, the Oblate Sisters of Providence and the Sisters of the Holy Family, identified themselves as French in language, culture, and religious tradition.

Educating Girls

Class and race also remained important parameters in the education of girls, which in America, as in France, constituted the primary work of the Religious of the Sacred Heart, overshadowing for at least two decades Duchesne's desire to minister to American Indians. The society sought to open at least two different types of establishments in each location where they set up shop: a boarding school for upper-class girls and a "free" school for the poor. Besides the financial advantages of such segregation—fees paid in boarding school subsidized the more populous free school—it followed the French educational model, where children of different social classes seldom sat side by side in the same classroom or received the same lessons. Catholic educators, particularly those of European origin, justified expending the greatest number of resources on the fewest pupils by what they saw as their disproportionate influence on society. The education of elite girls was expected to have a trickle-down effect on all levels of society, as Bishop Dubourg reminded Duchesne, "'through the influence of the rich on the poor.'" Even among the wealthiest Missouri families, he claimed, few women knew how to read, and even fewer how to write. Literacy, however, was not the only goal of their education; it was equally important that these girls became dedicated Catholics and serious women who were turned away from "vain and dangerous amusements" and "once mothers" would seek a more refined culture for their daughters.[56]

The curriculum and organization of the boarding school was based on the Sacred Heart *plan d'études*, written in 1804 and modified in 1810, 1820, and 1833, itself based on the famous Jesuit curriculum, *Radio studiorum*. This document enforced uniformity by specifying not only the subjects taught but also the times of day for each lesson throughout the school year, the organization of daily life (rising times, meals, recess, outings, and so forth), and the rules of conduct, including rewards, punishments, and prizes. Based on the concept of a religious rule, where every hour of the day was accounted for, the *plan d'études* guaranteed a standardized product throughout the network of Sacred Heart schools and ensured that girls were well supervised. It also linked them with sisters and pupils in France. "*Cor unum et anima una*," Octavie Berthold wrote in 1820, "Florissant, Paris, Grenoble, Amiens, Saint-Acheul are all included in this dear motto." Although Duchesne apologized to Sophie Barat in 1822 for having made some modifications to the rule regarding timing compared to Paris or Grenoble—on Sundays the hour of the mass upset the order of other activities, for example—her preoccupation with such details only proved how determined the Sacred Heart sisters in America were to remain one with France.[57] In this, they differed from other religious orders of European origin, who more readily adapted to American customs. The uniform Sacred Heart rule "frightened," in the words of Eugénie Audé, the Ursulines of New Orleans, an Old Regime order where every house was governed independently, who advised them to become more adaptable: Ursuline education "was not at all [like] ours, but it pleases parents who give their children a lot of freedom."[58] The Sacred Heart boarding schools in Florissant, Grand Coteau, and St. Louis, on the other hand, were conceived as distant echoes of the elite institutions the society ran at the Hôtel de Biron in Paris (established in 1820, the same year as the school in Florissant) and at the Trinità dei Monti in Rome (established in 1828). If neither the clientele nor the conditions were quite as grand, the essential concept remained the same.

However modest the circumstances of frontier life, Philippine Duchesne believed that societal corruption of young women was as strong in the New World as in the Old, if not stronger. "Who would have expected to find on the wild banks of the Missouri, a Paris for luxury, laxness, laziness, corruption, and ignorance," she wrote Mère Josephine Bigeu, her successor in Grenoble, from St. Charles in 1819. Despite the poverty of the inhabitants, day pupils arrived at school in flimsy linen dresses and cheap fashionable shoes, brightly colored rather than serviceable black, "pride hiding misery." Boarders brought with them more fancy dresses than handkerchiefs, using instead their sleeves to wipe their noses. Besides vanity, many pupils disdained "the docility of French girls," having "sucked independence with their milk" and associating obedience with racial subordination. The schoolyard taunt to excessively servile behavior, Duchesne reported, was " 'You obey like a Negress.' "[59] Their parents were not much better, seduced by many of the same superficial values and allowing their children to dominate. Even more important, American parents did not respect the enclosed space of the convent, withdrawing their daughters on the slightest pretext and lobbying for longer vacations and more frequent visits home. "It is the American spirit," she wrote, exasperated, "to poke their noses everywhere." Duchesne argued that the advantage of the Florissant convent over a site in St. Louis was precisely its distance from meddling parents, who "for a hurt finger, take their children home."[60] Attendance at balls was a particular point of contention. "Two pupils," the St. Louis house journal reported in 1830, "went out without our approval for a society party and spent two nights dancing." "I consider St. Louis like Malacca [Malaysia] at the time of St. Xavier," Duchesne wrote in 1823. "[A] moment of zealousness or turmoil is followed by the greatest indifference toward religion, resulting from a frenzy for pleasure. Our children are dragged to balls, spectacles, [Protestant] sermons, have bad books put in their hands, live in idleness."[61]

Into this sartorial and behavioral chaos, the Sacred Heart nuns attempted to establish French-style convent norms. Once they moved to Florissant, Duchesne reported with satisfaction that the girls were now properly clothed, "as in Grenoble" in dark red-purple ("amaranth") dresses edged with black velvet, having banned feathers, flowers, and lace trimmings.[62] In order to encourage appropriate behavior, they honored the best-behaved students (eight or nine out of twenty-one) with the designation of Enfants de Marie (Children of Mary). As soon as the number of pupils allowed, the full panoply of rewards and prizes, consisting primarily of ribbons and medals, was imported from France, and girls demonstrated their musical and artistic skills at end-of-year examinations and prize distributions. Just before the school moved from St. Charles to Florissant in 1819, for example, Bishop Dubourg bestowed the "prix de sagesse" and the "ruban de mérite" on Mlle Odile de Lassus, after hearing several boarding pupils recite verse and fables that Duchesne had prepared; this inaugural event was deemed a great success. The school year lasted virtually twelve months, from 1 October until the following 8 or 10 September, and girls were encouraged to stay in school during vacations "because even that time, though granted for relaxation, may be very usefully improved."[63]

The five-year curriculum of the boarding school, like other convent academies in the United States and France, was designed to prepare upper-class girls for a life of marriage and motherhood in elite social circles: a solid humanities-based education (reading, writing, arithmetic, French grammar, spelling, history, literature, mythology), religious training (catechism, Bible history, lives of the saints), the skills necessary to run a household (domestic economy, needlework), and socially expected *arts d'agrément* (drawing, music, and singing). One of Duchesne's "first necessities" upon arrival was to acquire a piano, which was finally donated by the nuns at Ste-Marie-d'en-Haut and shipped to Missouri.[64] The advertised curriculum for the boarding school opened in the city of St. Louis proper in 1833 added serious subjects such as geography, poetry, rhetoric, and natural philosophy, as well as ornamental skills like "Lace, Muslin, Tapestry and Bead work, Painting on Velvet and Satin, drawing, painting in water colors and crayons, Shell and Chenille work, Artificial Flower making, Filagree, Hair work and crystallized Parlor Ornaments."[65] Scientific subjects such as astronomy and chemistry were introduced into the curriculum in the 1830s. Duchesne constantly supplicated her Sacred Heart sisters and her relatives in France for various items she considered essential for teaching and virtually impossible to find on the frontier, from textbooks to globes and maps to examples of handwriting and embroidery. Duchesne even hand-copied essential texts for use in the schools. Just as American girls were to behave like their French counterparts, they were to learn the same lessons with, as far as possible, the same materials. In fact, the international network of schools, particularly boarding schools, developed by the Society of the Sacred Heart, shared customs and vocabulary derived from French school practice that were often foreign to the schoolgirls enrolled there.[66]

Although in Missouri and Louisiana, additional instruction was offered in English grammar, spelling, literature, and American history, it was precisely the Frenchness of the curriculum that remained one of its most important selling points. Especially in the 1820s, many of the girls who enrolled in Sacred Heart boarding schools were daughters of the old French elite and therefore native speakers of French.[67] Even for American families, however, a French education for their daughters remained a marker of social status. A number of private academies in St. Louis added French to their curriculum in the 1830s in order to attract new pupils just at the time that Sacred Heart schools were switching over to English as their lingua franca as the proportion of native French speakers diminished. Yet the curriculum, methods, and style of its education remained French because they followed lesson plans developed in France for French girls, as well as French methods of discipline. In the nineteenth century, as Rebecca Rogers has convincingly argued, upper-class education in boarding schools run by religious orders of French origin, like those founded by the Society of the Sacred Heart, were particularly prized for their ability to turn out polite, refined, and well-brought-up young women,[68] precisely the attributes that Duchesne so energetically tried to put in place. In addition, the private academy itself, as a recent collection of essays has argued, was the "dominant institution of higher schooling" in this period,[69] particularly for girls, putting Sacred Heart on the cutting edge of American education.

Pupils in the day and free schools received an education with the same emphasis on behavior and comportment, though without the twenty-four-hour supervision that boarding school allowed. They, too, were expected to learn modest and polite manners, but classes were larger and lessons more rudimentary, consisting simply of religious instruction, reading and writing in English and French, arithmetic, and basic needlework (sewing, knitting, darning). After 1830, pupils at the St. Louis school could pay an additional fee to learn grammar and geography.[70] Teachers and parents alike assumed that lower-class girls would not need the fancier subjects offered to better-off boarding pupils. Physically segregated into different class-rooms, they also often got less-experienced teachers: In 1821, the youngest novice, aged fifteen, with "little ability but much devotion," taught one of the day classes.[71] As Sacred Heart schools began to produce new vocations, the educational social structure reproduced itself with former day pupils, although accepted as choir sis-ters, trained to teach only those of their own social class. Day classes were also much larger, and the mix of abilities and languages, as well as the lack of materials, often created a challenging teaching environment. "How will we manage with the Plan of Studies from France," Duchesne asked, when some sixteen-year-old girls "know neither how to read nor how to pray to God," while "others at eight speak their two languages perfectly?"[72]

Duchesne believed that all girls should have access to an education but not that they should all be educated in the same way. As late as 1846, she expressed her dis-approval of a day pupil who wanted to learn algebra; "they want to know all about the movements of the heavens and the stars, yet don't know Bible history or how to cultivate a garden." Educational opportunity did not erase social distinctions even if "riches are the idol substituted for titles." Americans, however, she reported, became offended if those pupils in the tuition-free classes were labeled "poor," as was commonplace in France.[73] Both to soothe the feelings of some better-off par-ents and to raise badly needed revenue, some Sacred Heart schools in the United States broke with French tradition by adding a separate, fee-based class of day pupils (tuition in St. Charles was $3/month).

Nomenclature aside, the girls' school that Duchesne and her companions opened in September 1818 in St. Charles was the first such school west of the Mississippi, an achievement that has ensured Duchesne pioneer status in Missouri to this day. At the time of statehood, Missouri had a weak educational record. During the Spanish period, educational efforts were ephemeral and casual. Occasional classes were run by parish priests (most of whom deserted the territory when their government stipends dried up at the time of the American takeover) or lay teachers, who might well abandon the classroom for the more lucrative fur trade. Only Ste-Genevieve maintained a regular primary school during most of this period, but the attempt of three self-styled nuns to open a class for girls in 1794 was stopped by Governor Carondelet, who sent them to the Ursuline convent in New Orleans. The cost of schooling, in any event, was assumed to be the financial respon-sibility of parents, and most educational initiatives floundered for lack of funds.[74] Following a Southern rather than a Northern pattern of education, Missouri's municipalities offered few schools. Not until 1838 did the city of St. Louis open public schools that enrolled girls, and not until 1850 did it establish a school tax.[75] In this environment, the French convent model, by providing both trained personnel and funding, however precarious, vastly expanded the educational opportunities for girls on the Missouri frontier. Its popularity—the St. Louis free school reached an apex of ninety-three pupils in 1832[76]—reflected a demand for such instruction.

The Society of the Sacred Heart also raised and educated orphans at first informally and later by establishing an orphanage in St. Louis, funded by local businessman and Catholic philanthropist John Mullamphy in 1827, who provided a house for their use in exchange for taking in twenty orphans a year. Duchesne explicitly compared this plan to her experience in Grenoble: "I have been to see this house whose location, [though] less attractive and poorer than that of Ste-Marie-d'en-Haut, is still similar: elevated, isolated, with healthy air, overlooking the Mississippi and having a view of the city on one side."[77] And, as in France, in exchange for care and education, the orphans were expected to perform manual labor, especially valuable in America, where servants and converse sisters were lacking. Class issues, however, remained somewhat delicate; the Sisters of Charity in Maryland, Duchesne pointed out to Barat, put their orphans "on the same footing as the boarders." In 1830, Barat tried to segregate the orphans in Florissant away from the recently consolidated St. Louis boarding school because "our experience is that the poor, living in the same house as the rich, envy their lot, want to imitate them, and become bad subjects." Mullamphy, however, would not agree, and the orphans stayed where they were, rubbing shoulders with the daughters of St. Louis's elite.[78] Both Duchesne and Barat's class assumptions found little support in St. Louis.

The Protestant Challenge

The main goal of Sacred Heart education, on all levels, in the United States as in France, was the Catholicization of society through the religious instruction of girls. Duchesne's correspondence is littered with references to the poor religious practice and education of American Catholics. "How schoolhouses need to multiply in this country!" she wrote on arrival in 1818. "[O]ne sees young people of eighteen years" who "have learned so little how to pray that they do not know how to make the sign of the cross nor how to kneel."[79] Religious instruction, attendance at Mass, celebration of church holidays, and preparation for first communion were all important aspects of a Sacred Heart education, which their teachers hoped would last a lifetime. The lack of Catholic clergy throughout the region meant that few children had been exposed to catechism or first communion instruction, and the Sisters of the Sacred Heart constantly ran across girls and young women totally ignorant of

Catholic doctrine and practice. The mission of the society was precisely to fill this gap in knowledge—considered particularly critical for girls, given their future role as mothers who could transmit the faith—in order to strengthen the Catholic church in upper and lower Louisiana. It was, in Duchesne's view, an uphill battle, given the frontier context. "We recommend to your prayers this little flock and their companions who have left school," she wrote to Eugénie de Gramont. "Their pliant and inconstant character cannot withstand the dangers of the worldliness, which is at its peak here as a result of extravagance in dress and food, balls, comedies, indolence, and bad books."[80]

Headmistress of the society's flagship boarding school in Paris, Eugénie de Gramont probably sympathized with the dangers to innocence and faith lurking in the social world outside school and convent walls. Nonetheless, she did not have to contend with the competition of other religious beliefs, namely the bewildering variety of Protestants that Duchesne encountered on the American frontier. "One counts more than ninety sects in these United States," she reported. "[T]here are those where one does not marry, others where one turns about in meetings until one falls over and then the minister goes to listen to the inspiring words that one spouts."[81] Traveling down the Mississippi in 1822, she found sixty to eighty Catholic families in New Madrid whose children had learned the Methodist catechism because only Methodist missionaries had opened schools. Americans were fickle in this, too, she complained: "In this country of tolerance, one thinks of nothing to be one religion or another. There are those who have changed up to twenty times."[82]

The relationship of the Society of the Sacred Heart with Protestantism in America, however, was complicated by its dependence on the daughters of the Protestant elite as pupils. As the first institutions to provide advanced education for girls on the Missouri frontier, both Protestant and Catholic parents enrolled their daughters in Sacred Heart boarding schools. Duchesne boasted in 1820 that the twenty boarders at the Florissant school "were the most remarkable of the area by the age of the families and their influence in the area.... Protestants, like Catholics, look on our establishment with pleasure."[83] In 1830, only two other girls' "seminaries" existed in addition to two coeducational schools, serving a population of 3,744 whites in St. Louis proper.[84] Even as educational opportunities multiplied, however, Catholic convent academies remained popular among families of all faiths; Duchesne complained in 1846 that it was difficult to recruit new members of the society from the St. Louis academy because two-thirds of its enrollment of around eighty pupils were Protestant girls.[85]

This development was not limited to the Society of the Sacred Heart. Between 1820 and 1850, convent academies in the United States increased from ten to one hundred, especially in the West, fueled by lack of alternatives and the positive publicity generated by prominent academies such as the one run by Visitation nuns in

Georgetown, where presidents attended their commencement ceremonies.[86] Parents liked the attention and security provided by Catholic boarding schools, and those run by French nuns in particular had a certain intellectual reputation and social cachet. Catholic clergy claimed that as soon as parents saw the good order of a convent boarding school, they became staunch supporters, overcoming their prejudices and enrolling their daughters. Historian Nikola Baumgarten has argued that the high number of Protestant girls enrolled in the academy run by the Society of the Sacred Heart in St. Louis, in particular, depended on the quality of the education it offered, the feminine values it reinforced, and the tolerance it extended to religious beliefs.[87]

The extent of the curriculum, the training of its teachers, and the pedagogical sophistication provided by the *plan d'études* distinguished Sacred Heart education from that of the other private academies that sprung up on the frontier. Its focus on mothers as educators of their children and guardians of domestic morality reflected the growing consensus not only about women's roles within the Catholic church in France but also about their role in American society in the nineteenth century.[88] Religious education in particular provided the kind of training in feminine virtue and discipline that resonated with St. Louis parents, both Catholic and Protestant. Furthermore, the nuns assured the latter that their daughters would not be pressured to convert despite mandatory attendance at religious services "for the sake of order."[89] When St. Louis mayor William Carr Lane, who had enrolled his two daughters in the school, complained about the omnipresence of Catholic ritual and doctrine, Duchesne reassured him that "As to faith in no way do we intend to influence in it for their change [*sic*]; they are to submit to the outward discipline of the school, you are aware that this is the way of acting in all institutions where order should prevail."[90] This outward tolerance was echoed by Elisabeth Galitzine during her inspections in 1840 and 1843, when she warned the American sisters not to make disparaging remarks about Protestants or to speak to Protestant children directly on religious subjects.[91]

As Lane and other parents undoubtedly noticed, however, Catholicism was impossible to escape in Sacred Heart spaces, particularly for boarding pupils. Even Protestant girls were exposed not only to religious services but also to religious symbols and instruction, the rites of passage of their Catholic schoolmates, and of course the powerful spiritual example of the nuns themselves. Not surprisingly, a certain number of them expressed a desire to convert, and some even proposed joining the society. However, aware that their survival as educators depended to a large degree on keeping the goodwill of the Protestant elite, Baumgarten argues that the Sisters of the Sacred Heart carefully balanced the essential Catholic nature of their education with "non-interference" in religious matters, counting instead on the power of emulation to "pass on the essential message of their religion."[92]

Indeed, during the decades preceding the Civil War, the United States was in the midst of a significant Protestant revival, which was readily apparent to Duchesne from her position on the Missouri frontier. In St. Louis, Presbyterian missionaries established a church in 1817, Baptists in 1818, and Episcopalians in 1819.[93] In St. Charles in 1828, she promoted the reopening of a Sacred Heart school in order to combat the influence of "three heretical temples" serving four Protestant sects, whose disputes indirectly helped "our holy religion." As late as 1851, she still described it as "the only resource, in this area, for Catholic education, while Protestant schools abound on all sides."[94] After the cholera epidemic of 1832, Protestant women competed in the care of orphans, establishing the St. Louis Association of Ladies for the Relief of Orphans in 1834.[95] Catholic clergy in the large diocese of St. Louis continually lamented the inadequacy of their resources to combat the growing influence of Protestants, who were protected, they believed, by the U.S. government. Anti-Catholic feeling was strong in the United States in the antebellum period and was symbolized perhaps most vividly for Duchesne by the burning and pillage of the Ursuline convent in Charlestown, Massachusetts, by Protestant mobs in 1834. "The religious and their boarders," she wrote, "escaped by a back door."[96] Like the Sacred Heart sisters, the Ursulines offered a French-style boarding education whose main clients were upper-class Protestant families. "In Missouri," Duchesne wrote to a cousin in France a year later, "there are among the prejudiced Presbyterians many people hostile to us. In their newspapers they speak of convents as devil-houses which should be burned."[97] Convent education was criticized both as superficial because of its emphasis on external behavior and piety and as abnormal because it separated children from their parents. Nuns, in particular, were often targets of bigotry due to their "unnatural" status as unmarried women, and some women religious who appeared in public, like the local Sisters of St. Joseph, experienced harassment.[98] Although St. Louis never saw the level of anti-Catholic violence experienced by some other American cities, Duchesne had good reason to placate Protestant elites.

Yet the potential of persecution notwithstanding, Duchesne saw her educational mission as one not only of shaping and strengthening the faith of Catholic pupils but also of attracting as many individuals as possible to Catholicism. Whatever Duchesne's practical compromises with Protestants in order to further her educational mission, there was no doubt that she saw them as religious heretics, whose conversion to the "true faith" was to be encouraged. When possible, she effected conversions with the permission of Protestant parents and reported in 1822 that she had become the godmother to Governor William Clark's stepdaughter, who was baptized along with some of her classmates in a public ceremony. Protestant orphans were usually admitted to the care of the Sacred Heart with the proviso that they be free to become Catholics—and even nuns—if they desired. When living parents objected, however, Duchesne was faced with a trickier problem, especially when the most enthusiastic converts wanted to embrace religious life as well. Publicly she discouraged such vocations, while privately she lamented that her hands were tied. In 1822, boarding pupil Sara Benton, niece of Thomas Hart Benton, one of Missouri's most prominent senators, decided she wanted to convert to Catholicism against the express wishes of her family. Duchesne wrote, "How angry I am that we cannot baptize her without the consent of [our] superiors....She wants to be a nun and is educated." On the advice of several priests, Duchesne allowed the baptism, which was held secretly at midnight, provoking the fury of the Benton family, who immediately pulled their daughter out of the school.[99]

Sara Benton was not the only Protestant pupil whose secret baptism Duchesne facilitated. Two others were baptized at the same time as she, and the Florissant boarding school, she wrote, "abounds in spiritual graces: spiritual retreats every year, confessions whenever one wishes, instructions of every kind in the two languages, nothing is lacking, not Masses nor salvation nor expositions. All the children become Catholics there, but the majority in secret." And in a letter to Bishop Rosati, "We have a number of children who have been secretly baptized in our house in St. Ferdinand [Florissant]." However, she acknowledged, keeping these converts true to the faith once they had returned to their Protestant families was difficult: "Many will not have the strength; others expose themselves to violent persecutions; others also do not declare themselves and by attending [Protestant] sermons, considerably risk their faith."[100] Sara Benton, in fact, did not follow through on her youthful enthusiasm for Catholicism; far from becoming a nun, she married in the Presbyterian church in 1830. One of the roles Catholic schools could play, Duchesne believed, was to provide "an asylum" for converts to practice their faith, but she remained pessimistic about the dangers just beyond the convent walls. She wrote at length on this problem to Louise de Videau, Sacred Heart sister in France, citing numerous examples of seemingly enthusiastic Catholic converts who wavered once they left the sacred space of the convent and were "all alone to fight against error." She went on to regret the lack of "houses of retreat," which provided refuge and honest work for "exposed innocence." Ultimately, the only role Sacred Heart nuns could play was to provide as good a Catholic education as possible, hoping that once married and an adult, the converted woman "could follow the religion that she had tasted, or even make her choice at death."[101]

To Protestant women educators, the powerful attraction of Catholic convents and convent schools like those of the Sacred Heart presented a serious challenge in the nineteenth century. The West, in particular, became a battleground for Protestant and Catholic activism, with Protestants like preacher Lyman Beecher exhorting his coreligionists "to save the West from the Pope."[102] Critics like his daughter Catharine Beecher, the most prominent advocate of the expansion of women's education in the antebellum United States, argued that Protestants had to attract the same high-quality educators as had Catholics, while simultaneously denouncing nuns for having renounced marriage and motherhood and providing a too ornamental and domestic education in their convents. One historical study estimates that about 10 percent of the membership of Catholic religious orders for women between 1790 and 1860 were Protestant converts, attracted, perhaps, by the opportunity to participate actively in society through education, nursing, and charity work. Grudgingly admiring of the "active, useful life" of Catholic sisters, as Protestants Elizabeth Blackwell and Emily Blackwell, the first women doctors in the United States put it, the existence of convent academies was a spur to the development of equivalent Protestant institutions.[103] East Coast Protestant academies began training teachers to migrate West and open schools on the frontier, which in turn helped feminize the teaching profession in the United States.[104]

In St. Charles, local resident and staunch Presbyterian Mary Easton Sibley opened a school for girls in 1832 in direct response to the Sacred Heart academy Duchesne had established there, criticizing Catholic schools for turning out alumnae who were "very pretty to hold in the Drawing room or Ball room but of no manner of use either to ourselves or their fellow creatures, when called upon to take their station in society as wives, mothers, and heads of families."[105] Had they ever overcome their denominational hostility, however, Duchesne and Sibley would most likely have agreed on the necessity to educate strong, accomplished, intelligent women of faith who could serve their families, communities, and church.

Like the legendary founders of new Protestant women's academies, whose names are now well known (Catharine Beecher, Emma Willard, Mary Lyon, Zilpah Grant), one of Philippine Duchesne's primary legacies was to provide new generations of American women teachers.[106] The growth in the Society of the Sacred Heart in the United States, almost entirely from local recruits, was a testament to the emulatory power of the teaching sisters. "We have forty-three [day pupils]," Lucile Mathévon reported from Florissant in 1822, and "most of them want to be nuns and torment me every day to let them enter the society."[107] The Society of the Sacred Heart, like women's religious orders in general, reproduced itself primarily through encouraging new vocations within their schools. After a "novena for this intention, three vocations have been decided within the pensionnat," Duchesne wrote to Sophie Barat, detailing the qualities of the three new novices.[108] The ceremonial taking of vows of new novices, a rite in which the entire school participated, further inflamed the ardor of many of their former classmates. Emilie Chouteau, from one of the wealthiest and most influential families in St. Louis, defied her parents to return to the Sacred Heart convent "in the handcart of a Negro." Only sixteen years old, she was reluctantly sent back home by the nuns, who hoped she would return when she came of age.[109] Attracting girls from good families, educated and trained in Sacred Heart pedagogy and spirituality, was essential to the survival of the small band of immigrants in the early years. Over time the training of new generations of teachers, in America as in France, was also an important contribution to the educational advancement of women, both Catholic and Protestant.

The Limits of Expansion

The Sisters of the Sacred Heart also extended their mission to adults, boys, and people of color (adults and children) within the range of their convents, usually by improving the level of worship at services and by providing Sunday catechism classes. In churches attached to Sacred Heart convents—which served the community, as well as the school—the sisters put up religious images, decorated the altar, provided music, and led their pupils in blessings and hymns during the services. "Already the Sacred Heart shines in several churches," Duchesne wrote Sophie Barat proudly from St. Charles, "as I have resuscitated my talents in painting and flowers."[110] The new church next to the Florissant convent—where the nuns attended services in a chapel at right angles to the congregation, in the model of Ste-Marie-d'en-Haut—was consecrated, at Duchesne's express request, to St. Jean François Regis in 1821. When Sophie Barat considered closing the Sacred Heart convent in Florissant in 1836, the Jesuit chaplain protested vigorously to the bishop: "Who will keep up the church as neatly as they do? And what will their house be used for if they go? A tavern?"[111] Here Duchesne assigned the Sunday catechism class to Sister Lucile Mathévon, who reported high levels of religious ignorance and more enthusiasm among children than adults. "The little boys come with pleasure," she wrote, in terms that evoked Duchesne's experience teaching boys during the Revolution in Grenoble. "[A]s soon as they see me, they begin to run to be the first, they listen with all ears and don't take their eyes off of me. But they are so ignorant!"[112]

After an initial enrollment of a few mixed-race children to the day school in St. Charles in 1818, Duchesne acceded to the request of both Bishop Dubourg and Sophie Barat not to admit black or mixed-race children to the same classrooms as whites—for fear of local hostility—but she did not give up on educating them entirely. As early as January 1819 she reported to Sophie Barat that "two intelligent slave Negresses have come of their own accord to receive instruction; you would be touched by their manner, by their admiration before the holy Virgin in the chapel."[113] In Grand Coteau in 1823, Sister Anna Murphy included black men and women in her catechism classes, and they made their first communion the following Easter. "I hope," she wrote, "that for Pentecost, I'll have another group."[114] The first historical account of the Sisters of the Holy Family, the order founded for women of African descent in New Orleans, reported of its early members, "Many were also instructed by the Ladies of the Sacred Heart," suggesting that in Louisiana such instruction was commonplace, if generally unrecorded.[115] When the Sacred Heart sisters returned to St. Charles in 1828, the question of admitting mixed-race girls as boarders was reopened, though the Jesuit superior admitted that "If the colored girls come, there will be no question of getting any white girls. The house would be exclusively for the former. However, the school for day pupils could be kept up separately. Moreover, they say you can scarcely notice anything peculiar about these girls, as mulattoes have very little color." The idea went nowhere, but in the same year Duchesne quietly opened up a Sunday school in St. Louis "for mulatto women after the parish service, in order to instruct them in their religion."[116] This school was closed in 1847, when the state of Missouri outlawed the education of blacks.[117]

These schools—boarding school, day classes, orphanage, Sunday classes—did not exhaust the educational opportunities in Missouri or Louisiana, as Duchesne was well aware. From the time of her arrival in the United States, she wrote about the need for "petites écoles" in smaller towns and villages that would serve the growing population of children on the frontier and proposed various schemes to create them. Her plans were hampered, however, by lack of personnel and the enclosed nature of Sacred Heart life. Spread very thin already, the Sisters of the Sacred Heart could initially barely staff two establishments (Florissant and Grand Coteau) until American recruitment added to their numbers. Even with more teachers available, however, the model of religious life that the society proposed, codified in its constitutions, was one in which nuns lived communally in cloistered convents, not alone or virtually alone in isolated local parishes.

Cloister, in fact, remained a nagging problem in the open society of the frontier, especially for Duchesne, whose religious life had begun in clausura. Unable to build the stone walls that would have traditionally surrounded an enclosed convent in France, Duchesne made do with "boards and shrubs," following the advice of her Paris confessor, who reassured her: "I think that you must content yourself at present with a small enclosure that surrounds your house, in a way that one cannot immediately knock at your door or surprise you in your rooms and your cells…the essential is to hold always to what draws you to the spirit of your state."[118] Although the Sacred Heart sisters avoided mixing with local society, the necessities of housekeeping and teaching required contact with merchants, workers, doctors, and parents, who were admitted to the convent grounds in the modified form of cloister long familiar to French nuns. Duchesne traveled alone to inspect the new Sacred Heart establishment in Grand Coteau, but she also lauded "with great joy" the strengthening of cloister in the wake of papal approval of the new constitutions in 1827, planting hedges around the new convent in St. Louis and recommending the building of a new fence to enclose the prairie and woods adjacent to the one in Grand Coteau.[119]

If the Sacred Heart sisters were not, in theory, to leave the buildings and grounds of their convents, they could not embark into the villages and towns of the frontier or even the neighborhoods of St. Louis to provide education to the children unable to come to them. Duchesne acknowledged these limitations by proposing the creation of a third order of "nuns integrated into the greater world," who would staff parish schools, perhaps under the rule of the Filles de la Charité, the legendary French religious congregation that provided educational and welfare services to the poor. Bishop Dubourg argued instead that the missionary context justified adapting the Sacred Heart model in a way that would allow for the recruitment and training of teachers for schools throughout the diocese, yet under "a uniform plan and spirit."[120] When Sophie Barat failed to acknowledge either request, in 1823 Dubourg recruited twelve nuns from a Kentucky religious order, the Friends of Mary at the Foot of the Cross (more commonly known as Filles de la Croix, or Lorettines), founded in Loretto in 1812, to live in the Barrens, Missouri, and expand into smaller parishes from there. These sisters, whom Duchesne described as "very austere," went "barefooted, do all the heavy labor: they sow, scythe, cut wood, take care of the horses," as well as "teach the poor." Semienclosed, respected for their piety, and capable of doing everything from teaching poor children to growing their own food, these "Kentucky sisters take away the whole idea of the small establishments. They will fulfill that need."[121]

Other women's religious orders also began to fill the gap. Four Sisters of Charity from the Maryland congregation founded by Elizabeth Seton in 1809, following the rule of the French Filles de la Charité, opened a hospital in St. Louis in 1828, which they supported in part by founding an academy for girls.[122] Well known to Philippine Duchesne since they were cofounded by Bishop Dubourg when he worked in Maryland, she reported to Sophie Barat that they "were favored among the clergy and the people" because of their various good works, including hospitals and schools. Sensing competition, however, she worried: "If we give them room, they will soon eclipse us."[123] Their hospital was funded by the same John Mullamphy who had provided the Sacred Heart sisters with their St. Louis house. They also opened schools and educated foundlings and orphans. In 1833 a Visitation convent was opened across the river in Kaskaskia, Illinois, followed by one in St. Louis in 1843, attracting to its school many daughters of elite families, a clientele similar to that of the Sacred Heart pensionnats. In 1834 these four orders (Sacred Heart, the Cross, Charity, and Visitation) together provided the diocese of St. Louis with sixty nuns dedicated to various good works, chiefly educational.[124] In 1836 the Sisters of St. Joseph of Lyon sent a group of six missionary nuns to St. Louis, where they settled in the neighboring villages of Carondelet, Missouri, and Cahokia, Illinois, and opened a day school, an orphanage, and a boarding school, as well as trained themselves to teach deaf children. In five years, the total number of women religious in the diocese had increased to 121, dispersed in twelve communities and five orders, serving a Catholic population of seventy thousand. They outnumbered the male clergy, estimated at seventy-five priests, plus thirty-eight novices. The bishop acknowledged that the efforts to provide a Catholic education for girls had out-paced that of boys, especially poor boys who could not attend the "colleges" at the Barrens and St. Louis; he hoped to bring in the Clercs de St-Viateur, a French order that specialized in small parish schools.[125]

The Religious of the Sacred Heart continued to expand, opening a new estab-lishment, St. Michael's, sixty miles north of New Orleans, in 1825 on land donated by a local resident. They also established communities and schools in New York in 1841, McSherrytown, Pennsylvania, and Montreal in 1842, Philadelphia and Natchitoches, Louisiana, in 1847, Buffalo in 1849, Detroit and Baton Rouge in 1851, and Albany and Sandwich, Ontario, in 1852, the year of Philippine Duchesne's death. By 1850 they counted 227 North American nuns, fourteen schools, and 1,360 pupils.[126] However, they occupied a specialized niche that reflected both their French origins and the particular opportunities available to them in the United States. Dedicated to educa-tion, they did not branch into hospital or generalized charity work except in extreme emergencies such as the cholera epidemic that devastated St. Louis in 1849. As in France, the Sacred Heart ran several high-profile and well-regarded boarding schools for upper-middle-class and wealthy girls. Attached to these establishments, also following a common French model, were schools for girls of more modest means, offering a more basic education, as well as free schools for the poor and Sunday instruction for the community, including, on occasion, people of color.[127] The schools in Missouri emphasized education for the poor more than those in Louisiana, a result of the different socioeconomic environments—there was simply more wealth in the South—as well as Duchesne's particular bent for charity education.

Notwithstanding the American context, Duchesne's model remained that of Ste-Marie-d'en-Haut, with its flourishing pensionnat and adjacent free school, as it had developed during the period from 1801 to her departure in 1818.[128] This model proved, in fact, adaptable to the American frontier, furthering, as historian Nikola Baumgarten has argued, republican democracy through the ideal of universal school-ing.[129] Ironically, perhaps, it was Sophie Barat in France more than Philippine Duchesne in America who encouraged adaptation to the more flexible American mores. In 1829, concerned about the possible drift of the American houses, Barat asked Duchesne to meet with the local superiors in lower Louisiana and report to her; her response made the practical suggestions that Duchesne increase the use of English in class, avoid the use of the Catholic catechism with Protestant pupils, allow sisters to walk outside the convent grounds, admit mixed-blood and illegitimate converse sis-ters, allow them to wear the same habits as the choir sisters, and teach them writing on Sundays.[130] Ten years later, a visit by Mère Elizabeth Galitzine, newly arrived from France, took up many of the same points. Three long reports detailed weaknesses in the government and organization of the American communities, with specific suggestions for improvement, right down to the clothing worn by orphans while doing the laundry. She found, in particular, that Duchesne was admitting novices "little capable of religious virtue" and who needed far more instruction and supervision, a reflection, perhaps, of the rapidity of vocations under the onslaught of demand. For a former Russian aristocrat like Galitzine, giving the converse sisters special permissions, such as writing on Sundays, would only "foster in them ideas above their station." While avoiding overt criticism of America and Americans (in order not to "wound [their] national pride"), she argued that Sacred Heart sisters should hold up their European houses as models to imitate. Even Galitzine, however, saw the value of adaptation "according to the circumstances, the times, the places, and the individuals; that which is suitable at one moment does not suit at another; it is the spirit of flexibility and tact in the choice of means that brings good results."[131]

Its wide variety of schools, more casual style, American recruitment, and increasing use of English notwithstanding, the Sacred Heart did not Americanize to the same extent as other religious orders with European roots. The Sisters of St. Joseph, for example, did not require its American novices to learn French, cooperated more actively with civic authorities to provide a wide variety of educational and charity services, and often made important decisions without seeking permission from superiors in France, a situation that eventually led to the formal division of the French and American communities in 1860.[132] The Religious of the Sacred Heart, by contrast, remained intimately tied to France in their internal culture and their decision making.[133] Social class, as Patricia Byrne has persuasively argued, was undoubtedly one reason behind this contrast. The Sisters of St. Joseph, drawn from the peasant and lower-middle classes, had less cultural capital to lose than the elite women represented by the Religious of the Sacred Heart. The two orders also came from different monastic traditions. The Sacred Heart sought the spiritual perfection that the enclosed convent symbolized, whereas St. Joseph had from its seventeenth-century origins in rural France emphasized service to the poor in a wide variety of forms without formal cloister. Its historical experience, as well as its constitutions, were more flexible.[134]

Although the Sacred Heart prospered in the United States, it did so by reproducing its successful educational model in new locations, leaving the job of providing services to the masses of Irish and German immigrants that flooded into St. Louis in the 1840s and 1850s to the Sisters of St. Joseph, the Sisters of Charity, and a new wave of religious orders like the Sisters of the Good Shepherd, who came from France in 1849; the Sisters of Mercy, who migrated from Ireland in 1856; and the School Sisters of Notre Dame, who arrived from Bavaria in 1858.[135] On the Missouri frontier, as in nineteenth-century France, the popularity of Catholic religious orders—both in supply and demand—led to an overlapping network of specialized services and functions. Pioneers in 1818, by 1850 the Religious of the Sacred Heart had carved out an established place and mission.

3

"We Shall Need Jesuits to Bring Them to Us"

What, however, about the Indians? Philippine Duchesne's work in the United States, although pioneering in the frontier context, was not all that different from her mission in France: the education of girls—poor as well as rich—in order to create a more stable Catholic society. Her missionary passion, however, was "to civilize the savages" following the model pioneered by Marie de l'Incarnation in seventeenth-century Quebec.[1] Her first contacts with Indians, at the Ursuline convent in New Orleans and on the trip up the Mississippi River, fulfilled her sense of destiny. The Indian baskets she sent back to France from New Orleans "prove that they are capable of reaching a knowledge of God." And the Indians she saw lining the riverbanks were majestic. "The chief and the princesses," she wrote, "were clothed in embroidered habits, on horseback with the men of their entourage, and all of them, seen from afar, did not appear ridiculous in any way, but rather presented an imposing and interesting sight." These noble Indians, she claimed, had been "inconsolable" when the Jesuit mission at Kaskaskia had closed and continued to reject Methodist missionaries because they were not "black robes."[2]

Up close in St. Charles, things looked a little different. "These savages," she lamented, "who remain respectful of priests, why do they not go to them to be instructed, as they go in hordes to ask for whisky to get drunk…? We have the pleasant idea of instructing the docile, innocent savage women, but laziness and drunkenness affect the women as much as the men." In another letter, however, she reported that a "severe law" among Indians required wives to keep husbands when they were drunk:

"The women are veritable slaves; if the household moves, the woman will have three children on her back while the [male] Savage walks freely with his weapon."[3] The rough-and-tumble habits of frontier St. Charles, a center of Indian trade where drink, entertainment, and loose sexual mores ran rampant, Duchesne—like others—found shocking, and much of its corruption she blamed on "the inhabitants, in part mixed-race savages." Only full-blooded Indians "walk equally with whites."[4] But such individuals were in short supply in St. Charles: "[S]ince the expansion of Americans from the East and their wars with the Savages," the Indians stayed away. "God allows certain glimmers of religion to bring conversions now and again," but the "diversity of languages, the enormous distance of the country, [and] the difficulty of the roads make all connection impossible for the moment." Destiny may have carried her all the way to St. Charles, on the very edge of the North American frontier, but "I have not seen any little Indian girls in the month since we settled here," she wrote, clearly disappointed, in October 1818.[5]

Philippine Duchesne arrived in Missouri at just the time when relations between Indians and settlers were undergoing a vast transformation due to the American march west. The original French settlers in St. Louis and environs had developed close relations with the various Indian tribes that inhabited the Mississippi and Missouri river basins, depending on them as partners in the lucrative fur trade that dominated the frontier economy in the eighteenth century. This partnership was reinforced by family and kin ties, as French (or French Canadian) men sired children with Indian women, resulting in a substantial population of high-status biracial individuals who acted as cultural intermediaries between Europeans and Indians.[6] By the beginning of the nineteenth century, this bicultural population began to migrate farther inland, along the Missouri River, pushed out of St. Louis by rising land values and Anglo-American immigrants, and pulled toward the wilderness, where fur trading was still possible. In the next two decades, the game population became further depleted, leaving Indian and French traders scrambling for new items of trade, particularly alcohol, whose abuse increased during a period of economic and social decline. The effects of poverty, drunkenness, and dislocation explained much of the loose and violent behavior Duchesne reported from the streets of St. Charles in 1819. By the 1830s and 1840s, alcoholism and diminishing resources had destroyed or weakened many of the Indian settlements in the Missouri interior that had previously worked cooperatively with French traders.

In this increasingly unstable political, economic, and demographic environment, children of French traders and Indian women continued to occupy a privileged position, mediated in part by their access to European and Catholic culture. Fathers, though usually leaving their offspring with their Indian mothers for their first years, often insisted that they be taken to St. Louis for their education. The Sacred Heart school in St. Charles enrolled some of these mixed-race children, the most prominent of whom was Rosalie Manuel, daughter of Manuel Lisa, one of the wealthiest and most ambitious European traders (of Spanish origin) on the Missouri frontier, and the noble Omaha woman Mitian, whom he wed (polygamously) in 1814 in order to solidify commercial relations with her tribe in an increasingly competitive economic environment.[7] Rosalie Manuel, "fille de Sauvagesse," appears as a signatory to two letters sent by the boarding pupils to Sophie Barat, the first from St. Charles in July 1819 and the second from Florissant in 1820.[8] At the time of her arrival at the school, Rosalie was a mere four years old, an age that Duchesne believed nevertheless was young enough to "prevent the vices that, after that age, overpower [Indians] completely."[9] Although Rosalie appears to have been the only mixed-race boarder at this time—fully integrated with the white daughters of the St. Louis elite, undoubtedly due to her father's high economic status—the paying day school also enrolled a few girls of similar European Indian lineage. Duchesne praised two in an 1824 letter:

> Among our day pupils, two Indian girls have given us the greatest consolation. One of them really has no faults; she longed ardently to follow our vocation but has not yet obtained permission. The other in six months learned to read and write well, and she memorized a great many hymns. She speaks her native language, Spanish, French, and English. She will be prepared for great usefulness even among the white people in her native section of the country, for few of them know how to read. She is very eager to be well instructed in order to be able to baptize all the sick children of her tribe, and she knows exactly how she should do it.[10]

The sisters of the Sacred Heart also had a mixed-race girl as a domestic servant, who "might one day be a nun," and, for a short time, a pupil of mixed Indian and African lineage, whom Duchesne described in the most unflattering terms as "lazy, violent, greedy," leading her to conclude that "blood mixed with that of Indians and blacks forms a race very difficult to lead to virtue."[11] Yet, however willing Duchesne was to educate these mixed-race girls, they did not fulfill her desires regarding Indian education. Despite the similarity of their locale to that of Marie de l'Incarnation, complete with French Canadian immigrants, she wrote to France in 1819, "if our Sisters see us surrounded by Savage girls, they are much mistaken." "Like Marie de l'Incarnation," Duchesne wrote, "we need Jesuits to bring them to us."[12]

The promised Jesuits arrived in 1823 through the efforts of Bishop Dubourg, who recruited them directly from the White Marsh novitiate in Maryland, which housed a group of Belgian Jesuits, recent immigrants not yet acculturated to America. At the end of May 1823 seven novices, two priests, and three lay brothers (all in their twenties) along with three slave couples arrived in Florissant, where they were housed on a farm owned by the bishop and greeted warmly by the neighboring Sisters of the Sacred Heart, who took it upon themselves to provide the new arrivals with a myriad of housekeeping services, as well as money, food, and supplies.[13] Although Duchesne immediately proclaimed herself thrilled with the acquisition of Father Charles Van Quickenborne, the Jesuit superior, as a confessor, their two strong personalities quickly clashed. "I have found a master Father," she wrote to Sophie Barat. "I no longer do what I wish. Still he is not content, he would like a more interior life, more details of the account that one gives of one's soul, and you know that I am not lengthy."[14]

At issue, however, was more than the length of Duchesne's confessions. When they disagreed over material—and often minor—issues such as the carpet in the sanctuary or the hiring of outside help, Van Quickenborne used his authority as her confessor to withhold access to the sacraments.[15] In one standoff regarding the Sacred Heart chapel, Van Quickenborne threatened to remove the altar that Duchesne had donated; she countered by reclaiming the tabernacle, which belonged to her; he subsequently denied her absolution on the Feast of the Sacred Heart, and she had to feign illness to disguise her absence at Mass. Not until a week later was the dispute resolved and Duchesne returned to the sacraments.[16] On another occasion, he denied her communion at the altar rail in the parish church. According to another nun, "Mother Duchesne with unaltered countenance stood up and returned to her place. Despite this treatment, he and Reverend Mother Duchesne were on the best of terms. She and her daughters were used to his oddities and did not mind them."[17] It seems doubtful that she did not mind these public humiliations—denial of the sacraments was a harsh sanction for a Catholic nun— but in her own writings, she excused Van Quickenborne's methods as normal for a strict spiritual director. Writing about Mère Octavie Berthold, whose facial scar Van Quickenborne frequently ridiculed, Duchesne wrote, "He has worked a great deal on this soul and with success. He guides her by renunciation, detachment, and humility. We are all very happy under such direction."[18]

In 1827, however, she asked Bishop Rosati for a confessor who was both "not too young" and not a Jesuit because "if we are directly dependent on the superior, he often hampers our operations." "I myself," she pointed out, "had trouble with the first one, who rarely gave absolution, and the second, who did not like to give Communion outside of Mass."[19] Duchesne was not the only individual to have difficulties with Van Quickenborne, who was infamous among his fellow Jesuits and superiors for his severity and his gloomy disposition.[20] However, gender roles in the Catholic church played an important role in their relationship. Although she was ostensibly his equal (local superior of the Sacred Heart community as he was local superior of the Jesuit one), more experienced and older than he, and generous provider of extra funds and services—often at great hardship to the Sacred Heart sisters—his control over her spiritual life made her his dependent.

Van Quickenborne and the Jesuit community were also Duchesne's entrée to the Indians. The diocese of St. Louis, which separated from New Orleans in 1827, extended all the way to the Pacific Ocean, and Catholics estimated its Indian population at 165,000 souls divided into more than fifty tribes. Van Quickenborne arrived in Missouri with a reputation for missionary zeal—he and Father Joseph Timmermans were responsible for 485 baptisms in Maryland between December 1819 and April 1823 alone—and a strong interest in Indian evangelization.[21] Duchesne saw Jesuit corporate organization and their historical experience with Indians as essential to the conversion project because "at the time of Marie de l'Incarnation, the Jesuits, scattered everywhere, gathered the children together, soothed the parents, interpreted their varied languages…These works surpass what detached missionaries can do." She also wrote admiringly of the government support given to Catholic missionaries in California under the Spanish regime.[22] In fact, Bishop Dubourg had brought Jesuits to Missouri in part with funds promised by the U.S. government for work among Indian tribes in the West. Initially funded at six hundred dollars for three missionaries to travel to tribal settlements, Dubourg bargained it up to eight hundred dollars for four missionaries running a boarding school for Indian boys at the Jesuit novitiate in Florissant, at least until the Jesuits were ready to move farther west.[23] The promised financial support came from the "civilization fund" of ten thousand dollars per year, which Congress established in 1819 in order to teach Indians agriculture and literacy, which would, in its view, assimilate them to white American behavioral and work habits. Both Protestant and Catholic missionaries used the opportunity to solicit government funding for their Christianizing efforts, arguing that only through conversion could Indians become fully integrated into the American nation. The government, in turn, became dependent on church personnel to carry out their Indian education project, in which evangelization and "civilization" became two sides of the same coin. By 1824, the number of Indian schools had jumped from three to thirty-two, serving 916 children.[24]

Under the incentive of government funding, Van Quickenborne developed a plan—mostly unrealized—to educate Indian boys at the seminary in Florissant, marry them off to Indian girls educated by the Sacred Heart sisters, and then resettle them in new Indian villages established on lands granted by the United States west of Missouri, where they and others would "be brought together to live under laws made for them by the government, practice farming and live after the manner of civilized nations." The government would provide the farm, equipment, and stock and would fund the missionaries, who would live among them. "For why educate youths in our Seminary," Van Quickenborne wrote, "if after two or three years they must return to their tribesmen, who are still sunk in barbarism?"[25] The educated, converted Indians would inspire others by their example, while missionaries would proselytize among their tribes. By 1829 he envisaged buying a six-thousand-acre parcel of land in Missouri that could be divided among 240 families in twenty-five-acre lots, centered around a church and presbytery, with Catholic instruction for all. Encouraged by General William Clark, former explorer and now superintendent of Indian affairs in St. Louis, and buoyed by a promising meeting with President Andrew Jackson in 1829, Van Quickenborne imagined "another Paraguay," evoking the successful seventeenth-century Jesuit colony for Indians in South America.[26] Not only did permanent Indian-Catholic settlements provide more scope for conversion than roving Indian tribes, but they also confirmed the Euro-American assumption that settled agricultural communities were more virtuous, literally more civilized, than a seminomadic hunting lifestyle, a view that had characterized Jesuit thinking about Indians since their first settlements in seventeenth-century New France. "In order to convert them," he wrote, "it would first be necessary to make them into men, to give them laws.... It is necessary to change their customs and their way of life, which are directly opposed to the maxims of the Gospel."[27]

The Jesuit Indian school for boys was opened in Florissant in May 1824 with two Sac boys, joined by eight from the Iowa tribe shortly thereafter; the school grew to enroll about thirty Indian boys, including four sons of chiefs. Its purpose was to train Indian boys in Euro-American norms of behavior, convert them to Catholicism, and teach them "the mechanical arts such as are suitable for their condition."[28] In order to enable them to form Catholic households once adults, Van Quickenborne quickly proposed that the Religious of the Sacred Heart open a parallel boarding school for Indian girls, who would become marriage partners for the boys. Philippine Duchesne, not surprisingly, reacted enthusiastically to this project, as it allowed her to evangelize and teach Indian girls without sacrificing cloister. Van Quickenborne brought her "two little frightened Indian girls" in April 1825, joined by about ten others soon after.[29] Unlike the handful of high-status, mixed-race girls previously enrolled in the Florissant school, these girls were full-blooded Indians who were instructed separately from the other boarders and the day pupils. Duchesne did not take care of them personally but left the job to two English-speaking sisters, who slept with them in a separate building, where the girls' buffalo skins were rolled up to make classroom space during the day. However, she visited them daily, and when one of the girls became ill, she became "the object of Mother Duchesne's special care and solicitude for some two months" until she died "a happy death" in her arms. According to parish records, Duchesne also acted as godmother to three Indian girls.[30]

Although the curriculum of the Indian school was in theory the same as that of the day school, Duchesne quickly decided that since the progress of the Indian girls "could not be great, at least we try with some to make up for it by inspiring in them the benefits of the love of work." Besides religious instruction, this consisted primarily of teaching the Indian girls needlework and farm labor: "We leave to her [the sister in charge of the Indian girls] the active occupations," she wrote Sophie Barat, "these children not being in a state to stand a sedentary life."[31] Likewise, the Indian boys next door spent six hours a day working in the fields, a practice the Jesuits justified through the need to accustom them to agricultural work, considered low-status work by hunting tribes but necessary to the American plan of settling them on fixed lands. Acculturation to Euro-American behavioral norms and work discipline were the most important pedagogical imperatives in both schools. "We opened a school for Indian and half Indian boys," wrote one of the Jesuit brothers. "They were taught to wear clothes, to eat with knives and forks, to say their prayers in English and to work in the fields."[32] Spinning, weaving, sewing, knitting, and other forms of textile work, as well as the barnyard chores taught to the Indian girls, were the feminine equivalent of tilling fields and chopping firewood and were all skills that future farmwives would be expected to possess.

By 1831, however, both the boys' and the girls' Indian schools in Florissant suffered from declining enrollments, forcing their closure, and government support for proposed Catholic settlements in the West had been replaced by a policy of removal. The Florissant Jesuit seminary became, rather than a flourishing Indian academy, the starting point for missions west into Indian territory. This work was considered all the more pressing because of competition with Protestant missionaries, who had taken many of the posts that Van Quickenborne had assumed would go to Jesuits.[33] Beginning in 1827, he made three trips to the Osage Indians, who had requested Catholic missionaries from Bishop Dubourg. Among these Indians, Van Quickenborne said Mass, gave out medals and crucifixes, baptized some converts, and tried to interest them in a more permanent settlement of missionaries.

Finally in 1836, the Jesuits opened a mission in the Kickapoo village located at the confluence of the Missouri River and Salt Creek, not far from Fort Leavenworth, Kansas. Van Quickenborne and two other priests built a Catholic school, which soon enrolled about twenty boys despite the tribe's protests that they already had a Methodist missionary school. Now that game was becoming depleted and hunting more difficult, Van Quickenborne hoped that the Indians would "begin therefore to disperse themselves in the countryside and live in the manner of our European peasants."[34] The Jesuits used this mission as a base in order to make excursions among neighboring Indian tribes, where they also attempted to make converts, sometimes more successfully than among the Kickapoo themselves. Father Verhaegen, who succeeded Van Quickenborne, reported that the adult Indians were hard to convert due to "excessive drink," undoubtedly aggravated by an American settlement just across the Missouri River.[35] The Kickapoo school, whose enrollment declined, lost its government subsidy of $500 per year in 1840. Following the departure of a group of the most interested tribesmen and their families even farther west, the mission closed.

In these remote missionary projects in the late 1820s and 1830s, Philippine Duchesne participated only vicariously, avidly following the progress of her Jesuit neighbors and other Catholic missionaries to the Indians, fretting about Protestant competition, talking about Indians with her pupils, and dedicating prayers, Masses, and acts of mortification for Indian conversion. When Van Quickenborne baptized a group of Osage children in 1827, "the principal ornament" above the makeshift altar "was a pretty banner of Madame Duchesne's, holding a beautiful engraving of the blessed Virgin, embroidered by the young ladies of the Sacred Heart pensionnat." In 1832, she enthusiastically reported "the arrival of some savages whom no one in St. Louis could understand. They came from west of the Rocky Mountains, near the Pacific Ocean, a distance of 600 leagues, to learn how the Whitemen pray.... The difficulties of such a long trip and the hardships of living among such poverty-stricken people may hinder missionaries from going to them."[36]

Despite her intense interest during this period, Duchesne had her hands full with the establishment of the Sacred Heart academies in Grand Coteau and St. Louis, as well as with greater recruitment to the society. More significantly, however, there was no precedent for a nun traveling into Indian territory, even in the company of priests. For real conversion, she admitted, "one would need to live in their midst. So far, no women have risked this." Nevertheless, Van Quickenborne's plan of purchasing land in Missouri "in order to attract savage families, marry there their own pupils, train them to culture, to good morals, to Religion" was the kind of mission in which she thought Sophie Barat would allow her to take part. "I do not think that it would be reckless or imprudent," she wrote in 1829, "to be among those who finally performed the long-desired work that brought us to America." Van Quickenborne himself imagined a role for nuns as teachers of girls, "as in Canada," in such a settlement.[37] In 1833, when her cousin suggested she might return to Ste-Marie-d'en-Haut to retire, Duchesne wrote definitively, "My desire has always been to die among the savages," though she admitted that up to then it had been a "pipe dream." "I am not saintly enough," she concluded, "to attract a school of savages; we find closer to us types of white savages who live without faith and without religion in a mortal indifference."[38] Sophie Barat was also discouraging about a permanent settlement of Sacred Heart sisters among the Indians, though her instructions to Duchesne suggested that it would not be impossible: "You would need two to three solid subjects, somewhat older, who knew English.... You would have no financial resources. I see nothing but difficulties and would not dare to give my approval. Speak of it to me again should you find this establishment possible. Tell me who is the bishop of this small tribe and what would be the material and spiritual resources."[39]

Philippine Duchesne's frustrations in reaching the Indians resulted in part from changing conditions on the frontier. She had the misfortune to arrive in North America at just the moment that U.S. policy shifted definitively toward Indian removal rather than Indian assimilation. Although Thomas Jefferson had first hoped that Indians could be completely assimilated into white society, Indian resistance, especially during the War of 1812, led him to propose resettling them in the vast lands of the Louisiana Purchase, an idea drawn from a long British and American tradition of "Indian country." In 1816, nearly five thousand Indians lived within what would become the state of Missouri but would soon be displaced, not without violence, by tribes moving in from the east. The Osage tribe, one of the largest, had virtually disappeared from Missouri by the early 1830s. In 1830, under the presidency of Andrew Jackson, whose reputation had been made fighting Indians on the frontier, the Removal Act authorized the exchange of Indian lands for those west of the Mississippi. More important perhaps, continued westward expansion of white Americans put continual pressure on Indian lands and Indian ways of life. The new state of Missouri renounced its long tradition of intercultural mixing and trading with repeated insistence that Indians, including mixed-race individuals, be moved outside of the state to make more room for white settlers and their slaves, effectively shifting the frontier to the western borders of the state.[40]

In her letters, Duchesne showed an appreciation for these realities. The government bought Indian land, she reported to Sophie Barat, and then pushed the Indians into "too small a space and not having enough space for hunting, which serves as their only means of subsistence, these amassed tribes make war and destroy each other insensibly." Declining enrollments in the Indian schools, she realized, resulted from parents' reclaiming their children before moving west.[41] She also read the reports published in the *Annales de l'Association de la Propagation de la Foi* by Catholic missionaries, many of whom, of course, she knew personally, that traced the same movement. The "vanishing American" became an icon of this period in both France and the United States, exemplified by bestsellers such as *The Last of the Mohicans* (1826), as well as countless lesser-known novels, essays, and speeches that mourned the disappearance of the Indians—or at least mythologized versions of them—from the American landscape.[42] Historian Brian Dippie argues that the widespread idea that Indians were fated to disappear rationalized and effaced the policy that engineered that very disappearance. The debate about Indian removal and extinction was simultaneously a debate about the possibility of Indian acculturation. Though many commentators viewed Indians through the lens of the "noble savage," they also cited alcohol abuse and intertribal warfare as signs that Indians could not adapt to "civilization" and therefore had to be quarantined for their own benefit as much as for whites.[43] Others simply wanted them out of the path of Manifest

Destiny. "The policy of the government," Duchesne wrote, "is to chase all the savages out of the states. It buys their lands and pushes them into other uninhabited land. The chiefs say: 'You are stronger, we must cede to you,' and they withdraw, not without grief."[44] When she finally got an opportunity to work among an Indian tribe, it would be by following them into that "uninhabited land."

The Sugar Creek Mission

That opportunity finally arrived in 1841, twenty-three years after Duchesne set foot in America, when the Jesuits made another attempt to settle among Indians, this time the Potawatomi tribe recently displaced to Kansas. Although they solicited Sacred Heart nuns to join them, Duchesne was initially not among the small group chosen by Elizabeth Galitzine, secretary general, who had just arrived in Missouri to inspect the American houses. Galitzine replaced Duchesne as American superior, a change Duchesne had for years requested out of humility, but one that also necessarily lessened her power. In 1841, at age seventy-two and suffering from ill health (a decline Duchesne herself blamed on going from an active life to "a complete lack of anything to do"[45]), Duchesne was not an obvious choice to make a hazardous journey west into Indian territory. The two Jesuit missionaries, Fathers De Smet and Verhaegen, long familiar with her missionary ambitions and grateful for her unflagging spiritual and financial support, however, insisted that she accompany the younger and more robust Lucile Mathévon, Mary Ann O'Connor, and Louise Amyot, even if they had to "carry her all the way on our shoulders."[46] Duchesne herself had lobbied Barat to undertake the project, assuring her that the mission was "easy" and "without danger." Furthermore, it was "necessary" due to the competition with Protestant missionary wives for the conversion of women and girls, and, finally, "this converted nation" promised great success analogous to the Paraguay missions. As for cloister, she promised, the sisters would not leave the grounds of their establishment except to go to church. Adequate provisions would be guaranteed by the cultivated land around the mission, and the tribe was already partially Christianized.[47] As a first step for women religious to join men in evangelizing among Indians, this opportunity appeared ideal.

Indeed, the Potawatomi Indians were a tribe long known to French Catholic missionaries, whose first contacts came in the seventeenth century in their original homeland in the lower Michigan peninsula, where Jesuit priest Claude Allouez founded the mission of St. Francis Xavier near Green Bay (Wisconsin) in 1669, baptizing about four hundred Potawatomi by 1672.[48] Over the course of the next century and a half, the Potawatomi expanded south and east, with villages on the future sites of Grand Rapids, Milwaukee, Chicago, and South Bend, Indiana, while negotiating shifts in power from the French to the British. They adapted to European incursions into their territories by adopting certain European technologies (horses, firearms, manufactured clothing, axes, and hoes) and by reorienting their economies toward fur trapping in order to trade with Europeans. Indeed, the Potawatomi were prominent in the creation of what historian Richard White has termed "the middle ground," intercultural political and economic accommodation between Indian tribes and the French and British empires in the Great Lakes region.[49]

That middle ground did not survive the disappearance of those empires. After American acquisition of the Old Northwest territories, the Potawatomi began losing their lands, even before the Removal Act of 1830. Dispersed over several states and divided among themselves, some Potawatomi disappeared into the northernmost areas of Michigan and Wisconsin, about a third migrated to Canada, and others accepted the offer of the U.S. government for resettlement west of the Mississippi.[50] In September 1833, tribe members met with hard-nosed American negotiators in Chicago to sign a treaty that exchanged their lands east of the Mississippi for five million acres in Missouri, Iowa, and Kansas.[51] The most controversial cession was the Platte country, which the state of Missouri was simultaneously seeking to annex; the government eventually moved these Indians to Council Bluffs, not far from the Jesuit Kickapoo mission. Believing there to be five hundred baptized Catholics among them, De Smet arrived in Council Bluffs in 1838 to find two thousand Potawatomi waiting on the landing, not, however, for the arrival of Catholic missionaries but instead for the cargo his steamboat carried. "Not a single one," he wrote, "seemed to have the slightest knowledge of our arrival among them, and they all showed themselves cold or at least indifferent toward us. Out of some thirty families of French half-breeds only two came to shake hands with us; only a few have been baptized." De Smet worked among these Potawatomi for three years, baptizing 308 individuals and marrying 20, but overall the Jesuits considered the mission a failure, and they abandoned it in 1841 in order to put more resources into their mission at Sugar Creek, Kansas. Here priests had accompanied another band of Potawatomi Indians in 1838, some already baptized Catholics, from the St. Joseph River in Michigan.[52] Unlike the Kickapoo or the Council Bluffs missions, Sugar Creek was showing signs of success from the Catholic point of view: high numbers of converts, fidelity to religious rites, a desire for education, and some government funding to continue their work.

Here Duchesne, with three other Sacred Heart sisters and five Jesuits, arrived in July 1841 after a voyage of four days down the Missouri River and four days overland. When they arrived within twenty miles of the Potawatomi village, after a short rest at the home of a French settler, Indian scouts guided them to a prairie where 260 men on horseback awaited to escort their wagons to the village:

At their head were the resident missionaries and following them two
Indians bearing a red and white flag. They were in gala dress: bright hued
blankets, plumes and moccasins, their hair tied on the top of the head so
as to form a waving tail, the hands and feet strangely tattooed, while large
red circles painted round the eyes gave them a very ferocious appearance.
The newcomers were terrified at such a vision, all save M[other]
Duchesne, who went to meet them with the joy of a mother who has
found a long lost child.[53]

Introduced to the Potawatomi villagers by Father Verhaegen as a woman who had
waited thirty years to instruct them, Philippine Duchesne shook the hands of all
seven hundred men and embraced all the women and children. Despite the length
of her journey and her own poor health, she "did not appear fatigued but rather
showed real enjoyment of this novel and seemingly interminable ceremony."[54]
Indeed, little quelled her enthusiasm for having arrived "in the long desired land"[55]:
neither the discovery that no house was prepared for them, nor the cramped, temporary quarters in an Indian cabin with only outdoor cooking facilities, nor the
constant stream of Indian men and women who silently watched them from the
floor of their cabin, nor even her inability to communicate with most of the natives.
Unlike Marie de l'Incarnation and her Jesuit missionary heroes, Duchesne did not
master languages easily. "The language," she reported to her brother in France, "is
extremely difficult...some words of this barbaric tongue run to ten, nine, eight
syllables, and as yet there is no dictionary, no grammar, and just one book of prayers.
I think I shall never learn such a language."[56]

Unable to speak more than a few words of Potawatomi and non-English-
speaking besides, she left most of the teaching to her more linguistically adept sisters and spent her days in prayer—at least three hours in the morning and another
three in the afternoon, according to most accounts—as well as helping with the
physical care of the Indian girls, particularly those who came to live with the nuns
once they built a larger house. "It was a real pleasure," the chronicler of the Sugar
Creek mission wrote, "for M[other] Duchesne to relieve the little Indian girls of
vermin, to help at the washing, and at all that was hardest and most repugnant to
nature." In the hard winter that followed, she visited the ill and infirm, "aiding them
to die well," and they in turn provided the " 'great queen of the Great Spirit' " with
gifts of eggs or even scalps after warfare. "To have shown horror or repugnance for
such strange spoils," wrote the chronicler, "would have been a mortal offence."[57]
At Sugar Creek, despite her age and infirmities, Duchesne could live a religious life
of prayer and renunciation while participating in the civilizing mission.

Central to that mission was education. In this period of increasing domesticity,
both government agents and missionaries put a new emphasis on the education of

Indian girls as the cornerstone of acculturation. "If the women are made good and industrious housewives," wrote T. Hartley Crawford, commissioner of Indian Affairs, in 1839, "their husbands and sons will find comfortable homes and social enjoyments, which, in any state of society, are essential to morality and thrift. I would therefore advise that the larger proportion of pupils should be female."[58] Catholics, of course, had long believed that religious faith was strengthened through the education of future wives and mothers and that those lessons were best imparted by nuns. As a complement to the Jesuit school for Potawatomi boys, the Sacred Heart sisters opened a school for girls and women, which quickly enrolled about forty to fifty pupils, depending on the season. By September, Duchesne was also reporting that "several chiefs of the small neighboring nations will give us their daughters" if they could board them.[59] In a mixture of English and Potawatomi, the sisters instructed the girls in religion, reading, and writing, teaching them hymns they could sing in church, as well as the Gloria and the Credo in Latin to accompany the Mass. The Jesuits preferred, the sisters reported, that the girls learn their prayers in Indian languages because "that way it would be easier to keep them in their innocence and their simplicity."[60] In addition to teaching them to become faithful Catholics, the sisters also sought to turn them into good housewives, instructing them in sewing, spinning, carding, knitting, washing, cooking, baking, and churning butter, skills that their pupils picked up "with a surprising facility" even if they could "not apply themselves for a long time at the work." At the end of the 1840s government inspectors enthusiastically reported great success in the mastery of these domestic skills.[61]

The critical sign of female Indian assimilation into Euro-American culture, however, besides increasing piety, was the clothing they made and wore, which was evoked as a cultural symbol in nearly every missionary report. According to historian Susan Sleeper-Smith, the Potawatomi Indians had traded in cotton and wool cloth since the eighteenth century, creating distinctive and refined clothing. Yet the Sacred Heart nuns reported that "the first civilized costumes" worn by the Indian pupils "consisted of three or four yards of blue material which they wrapped around themselves and sewed on with homemade thread."[62] At the time of her visit to the Indian mission Elizabeth Galitzine reported that, thanks to the sisters' care, "all the women and girls are properly dressed."[63] Duchesne even contributed some of the money she had solicited from her cousins in France to purchase Europeanstyle clothing to supplement the homemade dresses. To the nuns, clothing was a marker of civilization and safety. "They are civilized savages," Lucile Mathévon assured Sophie Barat about the Potawatomi at Sugar Creek. "[T]hey are dressed like the French; we will be completely safe there."[64]

Overall, the Sacred Heart sisters had a positive impression of their pupils, praising them for intelligence and piety, though noting that they sometimes had little interest in the subjects and skills that made up the school curriculum, a disinterest that they usually characterized as laziness and occasionally as cultural difference. When the school first opened, they reported, "the little Indian girls showed no willingness for the subjection of school life, and every morning it was necessary to capture them, a feat performed by the Jesuit Fathers, who had to drag them along by their clothes." Nonetheless, "quick to realize the benefit granted them, they soon went readily to their classes."[65] Whatever their motives for attending, the school, in fact, had no shortage of Potawatomi pupils throughout the decade the Sacred Heart sisters were active in Sugar Creek. Philippine Duchesne reported that the Jesuits advised them to "overlook many things in the Indian girls and gain their affection by every means possible...one must use methods entirely different from those used with white children," a comment that was at once condescending and aware of cultural difference.[66] Duchesne frequently characterized the Potawatomi as lazy and marked their progress toward "civilization" by their willingness to work longer and harder.

Like most Euro-American observers of Indian culture, the men and women religious at Sugar Creek also applied their own gender standards to the Potawatomi, not only trying to teach women domestic skills but also criticizing the men for their lack of activity outside hunting (almost impossible in the game-poor lands of eastern Kansas) and seeking to turn them into farmers. Unlike the men, "the women were not quite so idle," the sisters reported.[67] Despite the poor quality of the land around Sugar Creek, the Jesuits organized the Indian men into working guilds, with overseers who led them to the fields, taught them farming techniques, and led them in prayer.[68] "Elsewhere," wrote Jesuit Father Hoecken in 1839, "field work falls on men since they are stronger; here, the women are charged with it"; once a week he gave agricultural lessons to the Potawatomi men to "reestablish order thus reversed."[69] In this world already turned upside down by gender, the Sacred Heart sisters reported racial confusion as well. Their black slave, Edmund, who accompanied them to Sugar Creek, "is here a very important man. He is almost as respected as we are. He teaches the savages the craft of carpentry....The Indians are almost as black as he, of a gentle nature, [and] are now dressed very decently."[70]

Above all the Potawatomi Indians at Sugar Creek were distinguished by their receptivity to Catholicism, especially in contrast to their tribespeople in other villages in the area. "The Catholics," Duchesne wrote, "form a village separated from the pagans who honor above all the devil in order to keep him from harming them. The Catholics have among themselves neither drunkenness nor dance nor gambling. We see every Sunday about a hundred at the holy table; at Christmas, four hundred take the sacraments."[71] In embracing Catholicism, the Potawatomi gave up the superstition and idolatry that had characterized their past beliefs and reformed dangerous behaviors such as drinking alcohol. By the missionaries' enthusiastic accounts, the religious practice of these Indians was exemplary, characterized by regular attendance at morning Mass and evening prayer, enthusiastic participation in hymn singing, and faithful adherence to the sacraments. "On Saturdays," Duchesne wrote her brother, "the priest scarcely leaves the confessional."[72] The pious example of the majority encouraged additional baptisms, which were held, Duchesne reported, nearly every week. Responsible for inscribing their names in the baptismal register, she herself acted as godmother to at least three adult Indians, two women and one man, whose Christian name of Jean François Régis clearly reflected her own devotion to that saint.[73] She reported that Potawatomi worshippers carried rosaries with them to Mass, and on a single day, more than two hundred received the scapular, a symbolic piece of cloth adorned with an image of the sacred heart, which they wore over their shoulders as a sign of divine grace and a protection against evil.[74]

More than one missionary, Duchesne included, compared the fervor and simplicity of these Indians to that of the early Christians. "Our good Pottowattomies [sic]," wrote one of the Jesuit missionaries about the Sugar Creek celebration of Corpus Christi day in 1843, attended in great numbers and with great ceremony, "so often designated by the contemptuous appellation of 'savages,' seem to understand far better than most of those who lay the highest claims to Christianity, Catholicism, and civilization, the earnest invitation of the Church on this day, to show love and gratitude for the inestimable favour conferred upon mankind." The Potawatomi, wrote another Jesuit, "are the only true Christians among the natives," and to prove the link between piety and survival, he also claimed they were also the only Indian tribe whose population had increased rather than declined. By 1847, the Jesuits reported thirteen hundred practicing Catholics at Sugar Creek, "accustomed to sober, industrious habits, emulating the white man in the various duties and exercises of a civilized life."[75] The Sugar Creek example also appeared, to Catholic missionaries at least, to demonstrate the superiority of their religious message and methods over those of competing Protestants. The superintendent of Indian Affairs had declared, Duchesne wrote proudly in 1844, "that the fathers had succeeded with [the Potawatomi] more than all the Methodists who swarm everywhere.... Catholics are necessary to civilize the savages." By 1848, when the Sugar Creek mission was closed, half of the Potawatomi population in Kansas was Catholic.[76]

What indeed were the factors behind this apparent, and unusual, success? The Jesuits—and by extension the Sacred Heart sisters—described the Sugar Creek mission as a revival of their work among the Potawatomi in Michigan and Wisconsin, where the descendents of the tribespeople first converted in the seventeenth and eighteenth centuries had retained memories and allegiances to Catholic personnel and doctrine. Indeed, the Jesuits operated a mission along the St. Joseph River in southwest Michigan continuously from 1689 until their suppression in 1763 and reopened it in 1822. Those tribal traditions were reinforced by French Catholic missionaries in the 1830s who worked among various Potawatomi bands near Lake Michigan, some of whom accompanied them west into Kansas. In 1831, Father Stephen Badin, a missionary priest living with a small group of Potawatomi Indians in Illinois reported that they were honest, industrious, sober, and pious—"innocent souls," he said, who participated in the soul of the church before they became members of its body—and sympathized with their plight at the hands of a government that was buying up their land "for a trifle." Furthermore, Potawatomi tribesmen told him that they had "kept the custom of praying, like the black robe who was once in St. Joseph, had instructed our ancestors."[77] This theme occurs frequently in Duchesne's letters as well.

The ancestral memory may well have been more mythical than real. According to Potawatomi historian James A. Clifton, the records of the Jesuit mission that operated from 1680 until 1759 near Fort St. Joseph, Michigan, show that the priests—few in number—mainly served French-speaking *métis* and that full-blooded Potawatomi converts were relatively infrequent.[78] Those who did convert assimilated Christian concepts into traditional Potawatomi religious beliefs. When the Jesuits returned to Michigan in 1822, they found a Potawatomi preacher named Menomini who had merged Catholic and Potawatomi beliefs and practices into a new ecclesiastical cult.[79] Beginning in the 1820s, however, when Potawatomi society faced multiple crises, most obviously American pressure on their lands and culture, conversion to Catholicism was used as a defensive strategy, all the more appealing because Catholic missionaries, unlike Protestants, disapproved of the removal policy and worked toward assimilation. Baptist missionary Isaac McCoy, for example, was an important advocate of removal of the Potawatomi from the Great Lakes region to Kansas, imagining a racially segregated state of detribalized Indians.[80] The three Catholic priests who worked among the Potawatomi in the 1830s, on the other hand, tried unsuccessfully to convince the American government to allow the Potawatomi to stay on their lands.[81] Conversion to Catholicism also evoked an earlier historical period when the Potawatomi had far more power. One converted tribe leader, Leopold Pokagon, successfully resisted removal by using his Catholicism, as well as education, property holding, and abstinence from drink to prove to U.S. officials that his band was "civilized" and therefore worthy of staying in Michigan. His conversion, though sincere, was, in his eyes, a way of leading and protecting his people.[82] From the point of view of the Jesuits, his return to the fold was a return to the glory days of North American evangelization and proof that their missionary efforts were not in vain.

The Sugar Creek mission fulfilled many of the same functions. Competition among Catholic, Baptist, and Methodist missionaries in Kansas for the souls of Potawatomi Indians living in settlements around Sugar Creek and the nearby Osage

River had material consequences in the form of government grants and educational funds, which fueled an interdenominational struggle that lasted until the missions were closed in the late 1840s.[83] To the Jesuits, a flourishing Catholic Potawatomi community was an important symbol of success that put them back in the missionary game and provided them with resources for expansion.[84] From here, De Smet and others launched missions among Indians in the Rocky Mountains and the Oregon territory. The Sugar Creek Potawatomi, in turn, by embracing Catholicism, received protection and services available to them through missionary agents.

James A. Clifton argues, furthermore, that, like the Catholic Potawatomi converts in earlier centuries, this population included a "majority" of French-speaking, mixed-blood Indians (a legacy of the close ties and frequent intermarriage between the French and the Potawatomi during the seventeenth and eighteenth centuries), whose background and socialization patterns were not that different from those of the Belgian and French Jesuits—or of the Sacred Heart sisters—who worked among them.[85] According to Clifton, American Indian policy, by singling out Indians for special education efforts, "actually helped convert a large number of French-speaking *métis* into legal 'Indians' " in both Catholic and Protestant mission schools. These culturally and biologically mixed individuals, many of whom joined the migration west, were counted as Potawatomi by government and religious agents and "generally considered by them to be exemplary Indians" even while rejected by parts of the tribe resisting assimilation.[86] In the upheavals of the first half of the nineteenth century, U.S. agents and Euro-American missionaries found it easier to deal with these cultural middlemen than to seek consensus among a dispersed and divided Potawatomi tribe, which enhanced the power of these individuals.[87]

The Sacred Heart sisters did not distinguish between full- and mixed-blood Potawatomi at Sugar Creek, though Duchesne occasionally refers to *métis* individuals in her letters. In 1842, for example, she labeled the neighboring Osage Indians as "very barbarous" but added, "[H]owever, since there are many mixed bloods among them, Father Aelen went there and was well received by the great chief…he baptized thirty."[88] When the Sacred Heart sisters arrived at Sugar Creek, Joseph Napoleon Bourassa, the individual who presented Duchesne to his tribespeople, was a *métis* married to a Potawatomi woman. He was bicultural, as well as biracial, leveraging some legal training he had received while a teacher in Kentucky to successfully reclaim a house built by a white trader on Potawatomi land in Kansas. Individuals like Bourassa lived in an ever-shifting space between cultures—refused an annuity due to him from the U.S. government in 1831 because he was dressed " 'as the Whites,' " yet rejected by full-blooded tribespeople living just sixteen miles away at Pottawatomie Creek.[89] The group of Potawatomi Indians living at Sugar Creek came, in fact, from those parts of the tribe who had assimilated to French culture and Catholicism most thoroughly over the previous decades; those at Pottawatomie Creek had resisted acculturation, a cultural divide within the tribe that peaked in the decade between 1837 and 1847.[90]

For those Potawatomi already familiar with French Catholic culture, conversion to Catholicism was one available strategy to cope with the immense cultural, political, social, and legal dislocations in Potawatomi life during the first half of the nineteenth century. Baptism and participation in Catholic ritual at Sugar Creek provided access to a powerful community experience and opportunities for Indian leadership. Many missionary accounts state that when Jesuit priests were absent, and sometimes even when they were not, Indian men replaced them in leading prayers and preaching sermons. Not only did many speak "with great assurance and many gestures," at least three individuals were marked with "extraordinary grace," including one woman who "was instructed by Our Lady herself." Duchesne reported in a letter to her sister that, invited to give a sermon, "the Indian . . . finishes his discourse with the air of an experienced orator."[91] The Jesuits and the Sacred Heart sisters also introduced a number of religious confraternities into the Sugar Creek community, which allowed for the reinforcement of Catholic practice and belief. Many Potawatomi traditions, such as respect for family and elders, feast days, and fasting, were easily integrated into Catholic practice. Philippine Duchesne, for example, took regular walks in the Sugar Creek cemetery, an act that could have been interpreted among Potawatomi witnesses as expressing the same reverence for the dead as they practiced themselves.[92] Furthermore, many devotional practices of Catholics, such as singing, ritual body movement, and the veneration of ritual objects such as crosses, rosaries, and scapulars had parallels in traditional Potawatomi worship. The sacrament of penance mirrored ritual actions for restoration to the community after the violation of taboos. Even the Catholic Mass, centerpiece of Sugar Creek religious life, could have evoked the Potawatomi practice of eating to gain spiritual strength. In addition, the hours that Philippine Duchesne spent on her knees in prayer—an act of much fascination and admiration at Sugar Creek—resonated in a culture that venerated "physical prowess and performative actions that were meant to strengthen the body and spirit."[93] Methodist missionaries, who made little headway among the Potawatomi, claimed scornfully that the Indians were merely exchanging one form of idolatrous worship for another: "Catholicism requires no surrender of superstitions, propensities; she only proposes new objects for their gratification. The transition therefore from paganism to popery is easy."[94]

Both Protestant and Catholic missionaries at Sugar Creek were eager to win converts, and neither imagined a Christian faith that was somehow blended with traditional Potawatomi beliefs. Catholics, however, do appear to have been more adept at using points of cultural contact as an entry to Catholic faith and practice. Baptist missionaries were particularly active among the Potawatomi, yet notably unsuccessful. Unlike Catholics, Baptists made little effort to learn about Potawatomi culture or make accommodations to it, preferring instead to rely on the transformative power of scripture. Missionary Isaac McCoy wrote in 1840, for example, "We had always deemed it sufficient to preach to them [the Indians] the plain truths of the Gospel, and had always found that, in the light of the lamp of life, the trifling character of their ceremonies became so glaring that they were deserted."[95] Yet despite this focus on scripture, the Baptists translated only a few portions of the Bible into Potawatomi. The Catholics at Sugar Creek, on the other hand, developed a range of religious and educational materials in Potawatomi for use in school and church. Catholic missionaries also appeared to make more of an effort to understand Potawatomi culture and traditions. In 1845, for example, Jesuit missionary Christian Hoecken accompanied Potawatomi men on a hunting trip that lasted more than three weeks.[96] Approaching the objects of conversion through their own language and culture was a long-established Jesuit practice that is often cited by historians as a more successful strategy than the less accommodating Protestant approach.[97] In the competition for Christian conversions at Sugar Creek, this pattern appears to have been repeated. The Potawatomi Indians, in particular, had a long history as middlemen and cultural brokers from which they could draw in adapting to conversion pressures. Undoubtedly, they interpreted Catholicism on their own terms and in ways different from those imagined by Catholic missionaries. An individual like Philippine Duchesne, however, viewed their actions through her own cultural lens, seeing and reporting only Catholic practice as she understood it.

The Sugar Creek mission lasted until 1848, when it was moved ninety miles farther west to St. Mary's, Kansas, along the Kaw River. Here the Catholic Potawatomi joined their tribespeople resettled from Council Bluffs, Iowa, where white immigrants had found them, once again, impediments to settlement.[98] The last part of the tribe to sign the new treaty for removal, the Sugar Creek residents were urged to do so by the Jesuit missionaries, themselves attracted by increased financial support promised by the U.S. government.[99] At St. Mary's, the Jesuits and the Sacred Heart sisters re-created the mission infrastructure they had built at Sugar Creek, including schools for both boys and girls, this time boarding, as well as day, as the Indians in the new reservation were more dispersed. They did so, however, without Philippine Duchesne, who had left Sugar Creek in July 1842, just a year after she had arrived, due to failing health. In early 1841, anticipating the long-awaited fulfillment of her missionary ambition, she had reported a "sort of physical resurrection" and after a few months at Sugar Creek was writing about the possibility of traveling to De Smet's new Catholic missions in the Rockies, where she had heard from Indians one could live to more than one hundred.[100] After a hard winter, however, her growing physical weakness alarmed both Elizabeth Galitzine, who visited Sugar Creek in March, and the Jesuit missionaries, who engineered her return to St. Charles in July. She returned to vicarious missionary work: following the accounts of missionaries through letters and published reports, visiting with DeSmet and other Jesuits as they passed through St. Charles, and offering prayers and Masses for the success of their endeavors. In one of her last letters to Sophie Barat, some six months before her death, she reported proudly that the St. Mary's boarding school had more than sixty pupils and proposed that the establishment support a novitiate for Indian girls wishing to continue mission work. "Must holy individuals," she argued, "be deprived of religious life because they have savage blood?"[101]

A Frenchwoman in America

In the last decade of her life, Duchesne was increasingly isolated from active work not only by her own physical weakness but also by the rapid pace of change on the Missouri frontier. Having never mastered spoken English, she found herself unable to teach since "all our children speak English, few French, and I cannot even give religious lessons to the two black women in our service or the little poor children."[102] This acknowledgment showed both Duchesne's limitations as a missionary as well as changes in Missouri since her arrival two decades earlier. The largest group of immigrants after 1848 consisted of Germans, who made up one-third of St. Louis's rapidly growing population in 1850 and, according to Duchesne, now formed the majority of pupils in the free school.[103] Although she participated in the housekeeping and gardening chores when able—insisting on making her bed and sweeping her own room and showing a particular interest in the French plants—she spent her free time sewing quilts and vestments, especially for De Smet and other missionaries. Cloistered again at St. Charles, she also turned toward her own spiritual perfection, attending multiple Masses a day, and practicing the kinds of physical austerities that had characterized her entire religious life, from eating poor food to sleeping under a single sheet without a fire in the winter. "She searches," wrote another Sacred Heart nun to Sophie Barat, "for means of suffering." Her role in the community was now one of inspiration and emulation. "[W]e regard her," wrote Sister Emilie St-Cyr, one of the first American recruits and now superior at St. Charles, "as the relic of the house,"[104] and the veneration in which she was held nurtured an aura of sanctity that would only grow stronger after her death on 18 November 1852.

Despite thirty-four years residence in the United States, Philippine Duchesne died, as she had lived, a Frenchwoman. Her experience on the American frontier was conditioned by an almost mythic view of New France that she shared with many of her compatriots in the first half of the nineteenth century. Although the French migrated to the United States in far smaller numbers than other Europeans, political reversals at home, as well as the opening up of regular shipping and trade after the end of the Napoleonic wars, resulted in a small surge of migrants, who joined those who had fled during the Revolution from metropolitan France or Haiti. In addition to these permanent immigrants, historian Harry Liebersohn describes the nostalgia of French elite travelers after 1815, who imagined "a New France that had but recently flourished."[105] To a Catholic like Duchesne, the nostalgia manifested itself largely through references to past missionary experience, especially her unwavering belief that American Indians retained an ancestral commitment to the Catholic faith and that Catholics in turn, especially French Catholics, had an evangelizing responsibility toward them, no matter who controlled the American West. The ancestral memory she so often attributed to Indians really belonged to Catholics like her. However, her sympathy for Indian displacement—if for no other reason than that it hampered her mission—put her at odds with the U.S. government, which was determined to solve the Indian "problem" by moving them as far west as necessary.

In the settler society where she did most of her work, Duchesne also went against many of the prevailing tendencies of American society in the first half of the nineteenth century. She was a Catholic evangelist during the Protestant Great Awakening, willing to convert by subterfuge if necessary. During a period of increasing emphasis on marriage and motherhood, she was not only celibate but a leader independent, by and large, of patriarchal authority, despite the nominal oversight of her bishop. She valued class distinction more than racial difference, keeping both nuns and pupils distinguished by social class, even while experimenting, however tentatively, with educating blacks. Yet her disapproval of Americans' democratic and commercial values, manifested in her scorn for the material wealth and egalitarian customs of many of her pupils and their parents, did not prevent her from creating successful educational institutions for young women on the frontier that perpetrated French values, ideas, language, and spiritual traditions, part of a cultural empire that replaced the lost political empire of the seventeenth and eighteenth centuries.[106]

Duchesne also represents a pivotal moment in the development of American Catholicism, in which European traditions of community and authority faced American notions of individualism and democracy.[107] The Sacred Heart sisters, much more so than other contemporaneous European women's religious orders who migrated to America, remained in touch with their French roots, institutional and spiritual, even as the personnel became increasingly Americanized. The schools they established in Missouri were on the forefront of a nineteenth-century Catholic revival that transplanted certain European devotional practices across the Atlantic, chief among them the veneration of the sacred heart. Among Indian tribes, the evangelization by Sacred Heart sisters drew both from the seventeenth-century missionary tradition and foreshadowed the Indian boarding school, the dominant vehicle for native acculturation by the second half of the nineteenth century.

Philippine Duchesne's experiences as a Frenchwoman in America reflect not only her position between the Old World and the New but also her geographical location. Historians like Peter Kastor and Stephen Aron have recently pointed out the importance of understanding both upper and lower Louisiana as places of cultural mixing and contestation.[108] Whether one terms this location as a "frontier" or a "borderland," Duchesne arrived just as Missouri was making a definitive transformation from a site where individuals from mixed national, ethnic, and racial backgrounds interacted to one dominated by American laws, migrants, and culture.[109] Duchesne both participated in and resisted this transformation. The Sacred Heart schools that she founded functioned as incubators for a consolidated elite made up of girls from old European settler (and, early on, even mixed-race Euro-Indian) families and the new American powerbrokers, like the Clarks and the Bentons, in the region.[110] However, as Missouri became a state increasingly identified with slave labor, she resisted American notions about racial difference. And in clinging to the seventeenth-century model of French and Indian accommodation, she sought to re-create the kind of "middle ground" that French settlers had forged in "Louisiane" long before she arrived.

However much regret she sometimes expressed for the lost cloister of her youth, Philippine Duchesne's most salient personal characteristic was flexibility in the service of a fixed goal—which she defined as salvation—that she demonstrated from the moment she refused to leave Ste-Marie-d'en-Haut to make the respectable bourgeois marriage expected by her family. Kneeling in the Visitation chapel on 10 September 1788 to take the habit as a novice, she committed herself to a life within its walls but adapted remarkably rapidly to the changing conditions around her when that enclosed world burst open. The French Revolution, which so many Catholics, especially nuns, lamented for its destruction of centuries-old monastic institutions, in fact unleashed a great wave of creativity in women's religious life, of which Philippine Duchesne and the Society of the Sacred Heart were only one example. Though she kept many elements of Visitation spirituality, the Revolution freed her, literally, from physical enclosure to practice a different kind of apostolic life, for which she helped determine the rules as she went along. Without it, it is difficult to imagine how she would have ended up buried on the banks of the Missouri River rather than those of the Isère.

Or is it? A Visitation convent opened in Kaskaskia, Illinois, in 1832 and in St. Louis proper ten years later, founded by nuns from Maryland. Duchesne was certainly aware of their existence—among other reasons because they were competitors for the same pupils—and she makes scattered references in her letters to the Visitation sisters in Georgetown, whose circulars she received in 1823.[111] Did she ever imagine herself as a Visitation sister, not in Grenoble, but in St. Louis? Without direct evidence, it is, of course, impossible to know. But if so, she never expressed regret for the unusual path her religious life had taken, preferring to see her entry into the Sacred Heart and her missionary travels as the workings of providence, which brought a new wave of French Catholic nuns to the very heart of the New World, as they had once brought Marie de l'Incarnation to its edges two centuries before.

PART II

Saving Souls
Emilie de Vialar

4

Rehearsal in Algeria

Emilie de Vialar "disobeys [me] with a rare ease and a hopeless tenacity," wrote the exasperated bishop of Algiers, Mgr Dupuch, in 1841 about the superior general of the Soeurs de St-Joseph de l'Apparition, a recently founded religious order that provided educational, charitable, and health care services in the new French colony of Algeria. "She has been from the very beginning," he continued, "extremely tiresome and irritating, especially regarding spiritual matters."[1] Yet public opinion in Algeria scarcely backed him up. As Dupuch maneuvered to expel Vialar and her sisters, both European and indigenous residents of Algiers signed petitions asking that they stay. Muslim leader Moustapha Ben Mohamed, muphti maleki, declared to the pope, "Mme Emilie Vialar is a virtuous woman." Five years earlier, soon after Vialar's departure for Algeria, her hometown friend Eugénie de Guérin had pronounced, "She will be the Teresa [of Avila] of our century."[2] Disobedient, virtuous, saintly: Emilie de Vialar was not a woman about whom either her critics or her supporters equivocated.

Dupuch's statement—and the responding petitions—were part of a campaign to force Vialar and her religious sisters out of the new French colony in Algeria, where she had arrived in 1835 and he three years later, in 1838. The two strong-willed individuals soon clashed, disagreeing about the extent of episcopal authority over the founder of her own religious order and about the priorities of the Catholic church in a Muslim land now governed under the French flag. By 1842, as a woman and an upstart, Vialar had lost this battle and was forced to abandon her Algerian establishments, which provided education, charity, and health care to

European settlers and native inhabitants alike. The experience she gained there, however, allowed her to expand her fledgling missionary order first into Tunisia and then to the eastern Mediterranean, where both the Catholic church and the French state were trying to establish a foothold in the crumbling Ottoman Empire. In these lands, she was successful in extending Catholic influence and the role of Catholic women missionaries. Her work, however, also revealed the tensions between church and state jockeying for position in the changing political landscape of North Africa and the Middle East.

Key to the success of Vialar's sisters and their rapid expansion was the public and official perception of their work as discrete, useful, and apolitical, which depended in turn on Vialar's ability to negotiate power with clerics and laypeople alike. To both, sisters like hers were ultimately too valuable to ignore, inaugurating a new period of French missionary activity that focused on service to women and children, symbols of the domesticating mission at home and abroad. Unlike the expansion of the Religious of the Sacred Heart to the United States, where the hardships of frontier life discouraged many French vocations (though not American ones), Vialar recruited enthusiastic young Frenchwomen into an active religious order that eschewed the traditions of cloister for travel and settlement among unfamiliar peoples in unfamiliar lands. They were joined by Catholic women from settler populations, chiefly in Tunisia and Malta. At the time of her death in 1856, Vialar oversaw a religious order that had expanded throughout the Mediterranean basin, and she was far more powerful than most bishops. Dupuch, the erstwhile bishop of Algiers, for his part, died disgraced and penniless the same year.

The "Teresa of Our Century"

Emilie de Vialar was privileged from birth. Born in 1797 in the wine-growing town of Gaillac, midway between Toulouse and Albi, both her parents came from old established local families. Her mother, Antoinette de Portal, was the younger daughter of Baron Antoine de Portal, who trained as a physician in Montpellier and established a lucrative Parisian practice before the Revolution. During the Napoleonic period, he treated Pope Pius VII during his exile in Fontainebleau. At the Restoration, he became court physician to Louis XVIII and Charles X. Her father, Jacques-Augustin Vialar, son of a judge, came into his inheritance at age twenty-three and never exercised a profession, living instead off his investments and serving in local government.[3] During the Revolution, when his family emigrated to London, he stayed behind as a member of the municipal council in Gaillac. Yet when the couple were married in 1794, they chose a priest who had refused to take the loyalty oath.[4] In 1826, then a widower (Antoinette de Portal died in childbirth in 1810, when Emilie was thirteen), Jacques-Augustin Vialar successfully petitioned for his own noble title (becoming "de" Vialar) on the basis of the role his family had played in the region, its devotion to the monarchy, and his status as the father to the three only grandchildren of Baron de Portal. According to his petition, he also possessed 590,000 francs in capital and 28,000 francs in annual revenue.[5] The real money in the family, however, belonged to his father-in-law. At the time of his death, in July 1832, Baron de Portal left half his fortune of several million francs to his childless older daughter, Mme de Lamourié, and the remaining half to his three Vialar grandchildren, of whom Emilie was the second oldest and the only girl.[6]

The inheritance changed Emilie de Vialar's life. At the age of thirteen, she had been sent to the elite Parisian convent of the Abbaye-aux-Bois, run by the Congrégation de Notre Dame, a Catholic Reformation order that had been enclosed by papal bull in 1628. Two years later, after her first communion and the death of her mother, she returned to Gaillac to keep house for her widowed father, who expected her to make an appropriate marriage. Instead, according to her own retrospective account, she had experienced a spiritual awakening at the age of eighteen that convinced her that her calling was outside of marriage.[7] She turned to charity work, nursing poor patients in their homes and attracting beggars to the back terrace in search of handouts, to the irritation of her father, who disapproved of his daughter's religious turn. For twenty years, Vialar lived a modest life at home, socialized as little as possible, attended church frequently, continued her charity projects, and dressed the part of an aspiring religious: dark dress, simple cross, plain hairdo.[8] In 1826, during a visit to Paris to see her aunt, she complained of the demands of sociability: "I try to lead in Paris the same sort of life as at Gaillac, going to church as much as possible and ordinarily I go twice a day; nevertheless I am often hindered because I cannot go to St. Sulpice [church] during the hours of services because of our dinner, which is at the same time, so that I never hear any of the evening sermons." Nevertheless, in her time in Paris, Vialar made the rounds of various Paris churches to hear well-known preachers. She also visited its hospitals, whose administrators were friends and acquaintances of her grandfather and whose nurses belonged to the religious order of the Filles de la Charité.[9]

When she received her inheritance in 1832, she wasted no time putting her legacy to use. Her friend Eugénie de Guérin, a local woman of letters, predicted, "Here is Emilie de Vialar in all the embarrassment of her fortune.... We will soon have a convent in Gaillac." Indeed, by December, Vialar had bought a house near the Gaillac parish church of St-Pierre to house a convent, school, and hospital.[10] At Christmas she was joined by four other young women, three friends and her former maid, who took vows the following March on the feast of St. Joseph. By her own account, written to the pope in 1839, this was a project she had planned for more than ten years. At her father's home, she left a letter explaining her definitive departure for the new convent, although she also—like a dutiful daughter—offered to visit him each day. Nevertheless, he did not speak to her for months. "It is said that [the convent] is not well approved by the family," wrote Eugénie de Guérin, "but [Vialar] believes it is from God, which consoles her."[11]

The purpose of the new religious order, which Vialar named the Soeurs de St-Joseph de l'Apparition after an inspirational painting she had seen announcing the incarnation of the son of God to Joseph,[12] was the education of poor children, as well as health care and "miscellaneous works of charity," which included the distribution of food and other alms. Eventually the sisters operated several schools for different classes of girls, ran a pharmacy, made home visits to the ill, and provided spiritual and material aid to Gaillac's prisoners.[13] These services were all typical of the new types of active religious orders founded in the post-Revolutionary period. Like many other female founders, Vialar worked in collaboration with her parish priest and longtime spiritual director, Abbé Mercier. She, Mercier, and a local Jesuit priest collaborated on the first rules for the order, approved by Archbishop de Gualy of Albi in 1835.[14] Like most contemporaneous religious orders, the Soeurs de St-Joseph admitted both choir sisters, who came with dowries and education, for the higher-status tasks, like teaching, as well as poorer and less-educated women as converse sisters, strong enough to care physically for the sick and do the heavier work around the convent. Although the sisters worked for their own spiritual perfection through daily attendance at Mass, the practice of religious exercises, and silence within the convent, their primary road to salvation came through active service to others. In this, they necessarily mixed with the inhabitants of Gaillac in their daily activities. Although the rules specified that men should not enter their rooms unless absolutely necessary, the convent was far from enclosed. The new sisters left to work among the poor, and Vialar especially was engaged in a whirlwind of administrative activity to establish her new order: writing her aunt for seeds that would supply the convent garden with healing herbs, reviewing textbooks for use in the schools, and negotiating with the town for a new parcel of land facing her convent, as well as the dead-end street, which divided the two lots.[15] "Emilie builds and unbuilds," wrote a bemused Eugénie de Guérin. "[I]t is the work of Penelope.... You cannot count the number of vocations that this convent has awakened." Indeed, by June 1833, not six months after its founding, the Soeurs de St-Joseph de l'Apparition had grown to twenty-six members.[16] It continued to grow steadily, attesting to the attraction of active religious life among the young women of Gaillac.

The rapid growth of this order speaks not only to Vialar's energy and initiative but also to the utility of the new, active, religious congregation in a France desperately in need of welfare services. Gaillac in 1831 had 7,725 inhabitants (which grew to 8,199 in 1836), the majority of whom were farmworkers, with a substantial minority of artisans. In the early 1830s, more than eight hundred of these were indigent—three hundred of them over seventy years of age—and eighty children under the age of ten begged on the streets. Gaillac's welfare office [*bureau de bienfaisance*] in 1831 had only nine hundred to two thousand francs in annual funds, which far from covered the needs of these impoverished residents. Flu and smallpox epidemics in 1832 and 1834 caused almost five hundred deaths, pointing up the need for increased nursing, pharmacy, and medical services. In March 1832 riots broke out over the high cost of wheat.[17] "In the wink of an eye," wrote Eugénie de Guérin, "there were three thousand men in the town square. Two women, accused of raising the price of wheat, were in the hands of these angry rioters, who led them to the river without [Mayor] Rigal, who came to save them." Two years later, a small number of starving and desperate men formed the "gang of Mina" that terrorized Gaillac, stealing from residents in their homes, including the convent of the Soeurs de St-Joseph. The government sent four hundred troops, and the gang's leader was executed in 1835.[18]

Under these difficult circumstances, the need for expanded charitable services to secure public peace and order was obvious. Emilie de Vialar's interest in philanthropy was matched by that of her contemporary Joseph Rigal, who became mayor after the Revolution of 1830. Unlike Vialar, who promoted private and Christian charity, however, Rigal sought a more comprehensive, municipal solution that would centralize donations and relief, modeled on the urban charity of large cities such as Bordeaux and Strasbourg. In this project he largely failed, but he did throw his support behind the expansion of public instruction in Gaillac, where few children attended school in 1830 and one-third of the local conscripts were illiterate. After 1833, the municipal council made primary school free of charge for boys and allocated one-sixth of the town budget to fund it.[19] Although there were no public schools for girls in Gaillac until 1867, from the time of their founding, the Soeurs de St-Joseph provided (separate) schools for both wealthy and poor girls, which greatly expanded their educational opportunities, previously limited to three small private schools.[20] "The classes are teeming with pupils," stated Eugénie de Guérin in late 1833.[21] The same could be said of the sisters' pharmacy and soup kitchen.

Vialar's initiatives, unlike those of the municipality, had the advantage of being bankrolled by her considerable fortune, but Gaillac was also undergoing something of a religious revival after the ravages of the Revolution, which had seen the Eglise St-Michel become a temple of Reason and the altar of the Eglise St-Pierre moved to the town square (rechristened Place de la Liberté) to serve as the altar of the fatherland. In 1795, however, the town's inhabitants requested the reopening of the churches. In 1798, a year after Vialar's birth, the townspeople renewed a vow they had made to St-François-Xavier a century earlier when hail and ice had ruined the wine harvest. The restoration of Gaillac's churches was financed by its most prominent families, and Baron de Portal contributed a relic of the bones of St. Peter the Apostle in 1807.

Most significant of all, perhaps, missionaries came to Gaillac several times, the first when Vialar was eight years old. After another mission preached in 1816, her former grade-school teacher, a woman who had been elected to personify the goddess of Reason in 1793, reconverted to Catholicism. These internal missions, which characterized Restoration Catholicism, were akin to revival meetings in their ability to captivate crowds and produce spiritual awakenings.[22] In 1829, two prominent Jesuit preachers came to Gaillac on the first Sunday of Lent, preaching and celebrating communion for a period of several days. By the fourth and last Mass, according to the Catholic periodical *L'Ami de la religion*, nearly the entire town attended, requiring one and a half hours for two priests to distribute communion. A crowd, "imposing by its number and its reverence," then followed the clerics to Place du Grand-Faubourg to install a large mission cross, paid for by parish subscription, at the foot of which the accomplished orator Abbé Guyon "preached fidelity, peace, and union." Vialar and her friends attended this mission; more than a year later Eugénie de Guérin was still humming its opening hymn.[23] During the Revolution of 1830, anticlericals tried to tear down the mission cross (succeeding only in destroying the monarchical fleur-de-lys in front of it) and continued to agitate for its removal after the change in administrations; a compromise solution engineered by Mayor Rigal to move it to the town cemetery lost by two votes. At the Fête Dieu celebration in 1832, anticlericals disrupted the procession at the mission cross by singing rival anthems. Elite Gaillac society in the 1830s was divided into two political factions of "blancs" and "tricolores," the former representing supporters of throne and altar and the latter liberal reform. Yet Vialar identified with the tricolors and was therefore on the side of reform.[24]

The rapid entry of dozens of young women into the Soeurs de St-Joseph after 1832 reflected the revival of Catholicism in Gaillac. Despite the high status of its founder and the acknowledged virtue and utility of its charitable enterprises, however, the local elite reacted unfavorably to the new initiative, at least at first. There was only one other religious order active in the town, the Soeurs de la Charité de Nevers, who had run Gaillac's hospital and orphanage before the Revolution and were reconstituted in 1802.[25] In 1832, five sisters cared for the sick at Hospice St-André and accepted abandoned children anonymously through a revolving window. To their superior, Emilie de Vialar's father complained, "I would have understood if my daughter had entered, for example, the Order of Nevers, with the special clause that after her probationary period, she would have been sent back to Gaillac, [as] Superior of the convent that she would have founded with her money, but wanting to found a new Institute, this is beyond me."[26] This criticism is telling. Vialar's father objected less to his daughter's religious vocation than to its form. Under the Old Regime, which shaped his understanding of religious life, there were appropriate convents for spiritually inclined daughters of the elite, and Jacques-

Augustin Vialar might have been more easily reconciled to one of these, though like most parents of his time, especially a widower, he would have been reluctant to part with an only daughter. What was unsettling about his daughter's ambition was the novelty of her enterprise even though it was more promising for his personal comfort, especially if Emilie made good on her promise to visit daily. Unreconciled to her new ambition, however, Jacques-Augustin Vialar remained estranged from his daughter until 1838, when his son Augustin brokered a reconciliation.[27]

Her father's anxiety was shared by his social circle. Eugénie de Guérin reported the general state of feeling in Gaillac after only a month:

> Here is Emilie already at the head of a small colony of saints. Zoé Maruéjouls said goodbye to the world on Friday, to her father, to her mother; she is totally absorbed by God and by Emilie. For the rest, we gossip happily about these poor postulants, we find them too young, too beautiful to live exposed outdoors, we would like to see them sheltered by a wall. "Cloister yourselves, put yourselves behind a grille," is what we say to them everywhere in a low voice, then aloud, "It's very good."…We don't give more than three years of life to the order of St. Emilie, because, we say, it needs at its head another head than hers, a grey head at least and then a little less vivacious.[28]

Not only did Vialar's youth and exuberance count against her, but an uncloistered community dominated by the daughters of the elite defied the community's expectations. Until the nineteenth century, women religious who worked among the poor and the sick were drawn almost exclusively from the lower classes, as the example of Vincent de Paul's Filles de la Charité proved. Organized in the seventeenth century, these sisters were preceded by an association of upper-class Dames de la Charité, who distributed alms and medicine among the rural poor. When de Paul discovered that these elite women were reluctant to undertake the hard and unpleasant physical work of nursing, he recruited the Filles de la Charité from the peasantry to act as their auxiliaries. In order to get around the papal requirement that religious orders of women be cloistered (which would have inhibited home care), he steadfastly denied that his "daughters" were a religious order at all, dressing them in conservative, secular clothes and requiring only annual, renewable vows.[29] By the time of the Revolution, these—and smaller, locally based orders like them—had shaped the public imagination of charitable sisters: uncloistered but also of modest origins and habits, almost invisible in their daily work.

Upper-class women like Emilie de Vialar and her friends entered upper-class orders like the Visitation, where Philippine Duchesne began her religious career, or the Congrégation de Notre Dame, whose sisters educated Vialar in their fashionable

Paris pensionnat. Despite the existence of two classes of sisters in Vialar's order, their uncloistered status and the nature of their daily work marked them all as lower class. Even their habits (black wool dresses, white mantle and bonnet) came under fire as too fashionable for proper nuns. The normally supportive Guérin noted critically, "I don't like either the mantle or the bonnet; a religious habit should not have any worldly airs." The gold cross worn by the choir sisters (the converse sisters wore silver) was also considered too ostentatious.[30]

Local criticism and gossip kept up for well over a year, as Guérin noted in regular bulletins to her friend Louise de Bayne, casting herself as one of Vialar's sole defenders: "St. Teresa [of Avila] was also criticized, disapproved of, condemned by the world and even by the saints, but God made her work complete. I compare Emilie to her and I defend her against all those who attack her."[31] Only in August 1834, almost two years after the founding of the new religious order did she report a softening of public opinion: "We speak much less about this holy house and we finally start to view it favorably. We see that it will be an immense good for the poor and for education."[32] In fact, religious orders like that of Emilie de Vialar were becoming more common in the 1830s, and cloistered orders were in an overall decline, never having recovered from the destruction of the Revolution. As elsewhere in France, apostolic sisters began to expand in this region. In Villefranche de Rouergue, north of Gaillac, Emilie de Rodat, ten years older than Emilie de Vialar, founded the Religieuses de la Sainte Famille in 1816. In Oulias, the Soeurs de St-Joseph de Lyon founded a local house in 1829; in Valence, the Soeurs du Sacré-Coeur were founded, also in 1829; in Albi, the Dames du Bon Sauveur arrived from Caen to open a house for people who were deaf and mute and those who were mentally ill; and in nearby Castres, Emilie de Villeneuve founded the Soeurs de l'Immaculée Conception in 1836.[33] Nearby villages, beginning with St-Affrique in 1839, requested that the Soeurs de St-Joseph establish houses in their communities to offer the same services as in Gaillac. By this time, seven years after its founding, the order had grown to eighty members. However shocking the good people of Gaillac may have found her, Emilie de Vialar had hit upon a winning formula that satisfied the active spirituality of young Frenchwomen, as well as the social needs of the French population.

The Religious Reconquest of Algeria

Her ambitions, however, did not end in Gaillac. In 1835 she and three Soeurs de St-Joseph sailed across the Mediterranean to Algiers at the invitation of its municipal council to provide nursing services in the new French colony. This new establishment, which began Vialar's missionary vocation, had not been anticipated when she founded her order three years earlier but resulted from family connections. Her oldest brother, Augustin de Vialar, had resigned from his government position as a royal prosecutor at the time of the Revolution of 1830, not wishing to serve the new king, Louis-Philippe, and planned a journey to North Africa. En route to Egypt, he stopped in newly conquered Algiers and decided to settle there instead, renting a house in Algiers and purchasing farmland on the Plain of Mitidja despite the danger posed by rebellious Algerians. Back in Gaillac, Eugénie de Guérin saw the same initiative in Augustin as in his sister: "[He] travels the world and the seas, he is going to colonize Algiers, clear the deserts and soon become emperor of the Bedouins. Oh! They are founders in that family."[34]

Like many other early French settlers, Augustin dreamed of an Algeria transformed by agriculture. "I believed I glimpsed the time when this beautiful land, this magnificent gift of Providence still today sterile," he wrote in 1835, "would be made fruitful through work."[35] In addition to indigenous labor, he imported thirty peasants from his native Languedoc to work on his Algerian estates. Elected president of the Société Coloniale, Augustin de Vialar was among a group of Frenchmen who argued for the permanent occupation and settlement of Algeria by the French, by no means certain in the first decade after conquest. The violent resistance put up by Algerians did not dissuade him from believing that the French could replicate "the rich and powerful colonies" that Europeans had founded in North America. During his time in Algeria, he claimed in 1835, "no French farmer had been a victim of the hostility of the Arabs."[36] Four years later, the forces of Abd el-Kader, the leader of the Algerian rebellion, attacked the French colonists on the Plain of Mitidja, though Vialar's estates were spared.

In the meantime, he had also made a reputation as a man of charity by restoring a Muslim shrine near his estates, sponsoring a free vaccination clinic at the town hall in Douera, and opening a small hospital in Boufarik in May 1835 to treat local Algerians. Although the initial personnel for the hospital were secular, Augustin de Vialar, supported by the municipal council of Algiers, called on his sister to provide nuns from her new order to expand its staff.[37] Emilie de Vialar and three nuns arrived in Algiers in August 1835 to find the city overwhelmed by a cholera epidemic. Instead of going to the hospital in Boufarik, they remained in Algiers, three sisters working in the civil hospital and the fourth in a special hospital established for Jewish residents, among whom the epidemic was the most deadly. By mid-September, the French administration reported 2,714 cases of cholera, of whom 1,534 died.[38] Among the survivors were the four Soeurs de St-Joseph, whose nursing skill and devotion had proven their utility to Europeans and natives alike.

Once the immediate health crisis had abated, Emilie de Vialar threw her energy and her fortune into the establishment of Catholic good works in the new French colony. In 1833, Algeria counted 7,812 Catholic civilians; by 1836, that number had

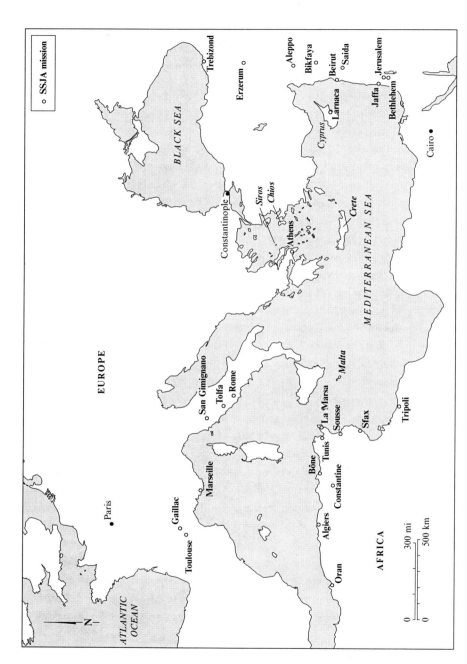

Mediterranean Basin missions during the lifetime of Emilie de Vialar

grown to 14,561; and by 1838, it was 20,000 and climbing.[39] Vialar's initial mission was to provide services for these Catholic residents, many of whom were poor and not French and whose religious faith and practice, regardless of nationality, were considered superficial by both church and state.[40] In Algiers, the Soeurs de St-Joseph opened, in quick succession, an infirmary and a pharmacy, three girls' primary schools (boarding, paying, and free), a *salle d'asile* (nursery school) to serve working parents, an orphanage, and a refuge for prostitutes. Their schools were rapidly crowded with pupils: At least 150 children had enrolled in the nursery school by 1838, and several hundred girls attended the primary schools. In 1837, the Soeurs de St-Joseph permanently took over the staffing of the six-hundred-bed hospital, previously carried out by male nurses, as well as the prison service. According to Vialar's description, their house in Algiers also functioned as an ad-hoc asylum for individuals in all kinds of need or trouble, from soldiers needing new clothes to abandoned wives to foreigners in distress.[41]

The French occupiers believed—or hoped—that regular religious and charitable institutions like these would deepen faith and improve morals—in short, turn Algeria from an outlaw colony run by soldiers into a settler colony populated by church-going, law-abiding residents. In these various charitable enterprises, the sisters not only provided Christian care and instruction but, as Frenchwomen, also helped assimilate a European multinational population to French norms. In 1840, the non-French European population of Algiers (more than half Spanish, followed by Italians, English, and Germans) numbered 7,954 individuals, to the French population of 7,316.[42] Their establishments followed the path of French conquest, as the French opened up new territories and the colonial population increased. In 1837, the French administration invited Vialar to open an establishment in Bône that would provide both educational and medical services; nearly identical requests from Constantine and Oran followed in 1839. Although Vialar recruited more sisters—three dozen were soon at work in Algiers alone—there never seemed to be enough for the multiplying requests. Overwhelmed with work, small wonder that Vialar wrote the following to her cousin in 1837: "[T]he days are always too short for me; besides the visits that I have to receive or make, my personal affairs, the administration of my house, the direction of my Sisters, I must see to our classes, the number of Sisters that I have here being insufficient."[43]

Although their services were initially directed toward European settlers, Vialar reported that the Soeurs de St-Joseph also proved popular with the indigenous Jewish and Muslim populations. "Jews, Christians, and Muslims," wrote Vialar with evident pride, "come without exception to knock on our door."[44] The Soeurs de St-Joseph handed out food to the poor and took in abandoned wives and children of all religious persuasions. The free schools and the orphanage accepted Jewish and Muslim girls, though few of the latter enrolled. Most important, perhaps, they offered medical services without distinction of religion. Vialar identified the Jewish population in Algiers as particularly in need of medical care due to their inadequate diet and impoverished living conditions; by her assessment, neither they nor Muslims had much medical knowledge.[45] In their infirmary, the sisters quickly attracted up to one hundred patients a day, plus a gaggle of spectators drawn by the unusual sight of women religious binding up the wounds of Algerian men. According to Vialar, both Kabyles from the Atlas mountains and Arabs from the plains brought their sick to be treated by the Soeurs de St-Joseph and invited them to establish similar services among their populations. In Constantine, the Muslim municipal council wanted to open a Muslim hospice run by the Soeurs de St-Joseph.[46] According to her own account, she even received an invitation, unfulfilled, to establish a hospital among the desert tribes in Biskra. The sisters also went into private homes to nurse patients, "our sex allowing us to gain admittance among Moorish women who, most often, do not receive any care during their illnesses."[47]

Besides supplying valued charity and health services to the native population, many of whose traditional sources of assistance had been weakened or destroyed by French occupation, the willingness of many sisters (though not Vialar herself) to learn Arabic undoubtedly facilitated their acceptance by the Algerians. Although the voices of Muslim Algerians themselves are largely absent from these accounts, suggesting we should be cautious about their accuracy, Vialar's letters and reports from other clerics in Algeria paint a picture of welcoming and curious natives eager to interact with the sisters. The Arabs, Vialar reported, greeted the sisters in the streets with the title "Bléa-Orti," meaning "bonnes soeurs" and "the Muslim women that I had known during my last stay ... saw me again with joy and reproached me for having quit them to return to France." In Constantine, where Vialar healed the chief of the desert tribes, Cheik-el-Arab, she said he told her, "If an Arab makes the slightest insult to the cross that you wear, I will sever his head instantly."[48] The vicar general of Constantine, Abbé Suchet, claimed that the sisters were routinely referred to as "marabouts" or "saints" and were invited as guests of honor into Arab homes.[49] Whether or not this view of the sisters was widespread, clerics active in Algeria certainly believed that they had enhanced the prestige of Christianity among Arabs.

From the point of view of French officials, the services provided by the Soeurs de St-Joseph extended the "civilizing" role of France and proved the benevolence of its rule, which justified military conquest and continued occupation. As early as 1832, before pacification was complete and the future status of Algeria decided, the French occupiers drew up plans to provide health care and education in the nascent colony. In part, they proposed these initiatives in order to attract a larger settler population, such as a plan to bring in midwives, who could offer services not furnished by army doctors. Officials argued that the midwives could also assist indigenous women in childbirth, as well as give courses in a classroom equipped with instruments and mannequins of a mother and fetus. They also proposed opening a branch of the Société de Charité Maternelle, the French association dedicated to helping indigent mothers, which would help moralize the population in view of their "eventual prosperity."[50]

Schools, likewise, would extend French culture, especially if indigenous children were taught the French language. The French characterized most Muslim schools—available only for boys—as mere laboratories for religious training, focused almost entirely on the memorization of the Koran.[51] Both health care and schools, furthermore, in the view of French officials, contrasted scientific and "enlightened" ideas with religious superstition, making them cultural projects that went beyond the simple delivery of medical care and language lessons.[52] Using Catholic nuns to carry out some of these projects therefore carried a certain risk, in which officials had to weigh their availability, affordability, and dedication against their obvious religious devotion, not always as "enlightened" as officials might have hoped, as well as possibly inflammatory to Muslims and Jews. In 1839, for example, a small controversy erupted concerning the appropriateness of having the Soeurs de St-Joseph staff the civil hospital, which served individuals of all faiths. The government had originally employed civilian nurses, all men, who, some argued, were dishonest and often drunk. Hard to recruit, they were accused of neglecting and abandoning patients. The sisters, on the other hand, according to most commentators, provided regular and devoted care at a low cost. Nonetheless, "to plant the cross" in the hospital invited the suspicion, if not the reality, of proselytizing. Yet after the cholera epidemic, the Muslim members of the council had voted to keep the sisters—"The crescent voting for the cross!" one French official enthused[53]— and they stayed. Still, religious activity in the hospital, undoubtedly because ill and dying patients were considered particularly susceptible to conversion pressure, remained an area of concern for French authorities worried about Muslim religious sensibilities.

The Diocese of Julia Caesarea

From 1835 until the end of 1838, the Soeurs de St-Joseph were among the few representatives of the Catholic church resident in Algeria. The army employed its own chaplains, but at the time of conquest civil religious authority was initially conferred on four Arabic-speaking members of the Lazarists (Congrégation de la Mission), a French order with long missionary experience in the Mediterranean basin.[54] The French administration initially assumed that this solution would allow it to appoint and replace priests as it saw fit, under the supervision of an apostolic prefect, whom the king could revoke if necessary. The Holy See, on the other hand,

saw the head of the Algerian church as dependent on Propaganda Fide, the arm of
the church responsible for missionary activity throughout the world. When in 1833
Propaganda Fide replaced the government's hand-picked apostolic prefect (whose
conduct had become scandalous) with its own candidate, the French deprived the
new incumbent of salary and room and board and began exploring the possibility
of establishing a new French diocese in Algeria.[55]

From the French point of view, there were both pros and cons to such a move.
It had the advantage of putting a new bishop under the umbrella of the concordat,
a disadvantage to Rome that Pope Gregory XVI only reluctantly accepted. The
establishment of a diocese and the appointment of a bishop would also allow for a
more regular and stable religious organization appropriate for the growing number
of French settlers, as well as put priests assigned to Algeria—who were either over-
zealous or badly behaved in the eyes of the military administration—under episcopal control. On the other hand, the religious budget, adequate for an apostolic
prefect, would have to be quadrupled for a bishop and his retinue. Even more wor-
risome was the potential independence of an Algerian bishop, who, concordat or
not, could not be pressured as easily as mere missionaries. "A high ecclesiastical
functionary," wrote Maréchal Valée to the minister of war, "would undoubtedly
acquire an influence that could sometimes become awkward, and the proselytizing
spirit directed by a prince of the church, irremovable from his see, could alienate
the natives even more from us and increase the separation that exists between the
two peoples."[56] In the end, however, the government decided that French prestige
demanded the establishment of an Algerian diocese, proclaimed, after negotiation
with the Holy See, by papal bull on 9 August 1838.[57] Whatever doubts Rome might
have had regarding the new diocese appeared to have disappeared by the summer
of 1838, when the Holy See considered giving Valée a papal decoration for his work
on behalf of the Catholic religion in Algeria.[58] On receiving the newly appointed
bishop in Rome, Gregory XVI exclaimed, "God be praised; the African church is
coming back to life. I hold next to my heart the successor of Saint Augustine." The
name of the new diocese, Julia Caesarea, reflected the belief that Algiers was located
on the site of Julius Caesar's Mauritania.[59]

Paris and Rome were in agreement that such a sensitive position required an
individual who possessed "profound piety, high prudence, and exquisite tact," as the
papal nuncio to Paris put it.[60] In the new bishop, former vicar general of Bordeaux,
Mgr Antoine-Adolphe Dupuch, they thought they had found their man. Church
officials praised his activist work in Bordeaux, where he had established educational
and charitable institutions despite the presence of a significant Protestant elite.[61]
On his appointment, Dupuch traveled first to Pavia, Italy, where he accepted the
relic of St. Augustine for "return" to North Africa, then to Rome for the pope's
blessing. He arrived in Algiers on New Year's Eve 1838 to great pomp, processing

from the docks through two lines of French troops, where he was met at the cathedral by the civil and military authorities, magistrates, foreign consuls, and Protestant, Jewish, and Muslim clerics. In lieu of church bells, his arrival was accompanied by cannon fire.[62]

Dupuch embarked immediately on a vigorous campaign of diocese building, literally and figuratively. Needing a cathedral in Algiers, the French administration converted a mosque in the center of the European quarter that had belonged to the minority Turkish Hanefi sect, which was moved to a smaller mosque until then occupied by the army. This transformation was part of a larger project to rebuild the lower city of Algiers, next to the harbor, in order to house and parade French military troops and create structures for French administration. To do so, the French took over public and private buildings for other uses, razing them when, for example, they wanted to create a large public square in front of the dey's former palace. Although the minaret of the al-Sayyida mosque was demolished in this first wave of rebuilding, authorities balked at tearing down the mosque itself because they were afraid of disturbing the Muslims' religious sensibilities.[63] Appropriating mosques, however, rather than erecting new buildings, was the preferred method of opening Catholic churches throughout the colony. Muslims, church and government officials claimed, preferred that their mosques be turned into Catholic churches rather than army depots or other secular buildings.[64] However, the new cathedral of St-Philippe would also stand as a visible symbol of French power. "In raising the cross on its high minaret," wrote Valée, "we give to all a new proof that the takeover of Algiers by France is definitive." Inside the mosque-turned-cathedral, already in the form of a cross "by a remarkable coincidence," as Valée put it, Dupuch surrounded the inscriptions from the Koran with gold letters reading "*Jesus Christus heri, hodie et in secula*" [Jesus Christ yesterday, today, and forever] and turned the niche designed for the imam to chant prayers into a chapel dedicated to Mary.[65] His episcopal residence was located in the former palace reserved for provincial beys visiting Algiers, while the private mosque of the Ottoman dey became the hospital chapel. In Constantine, Dupuch chose "the most beautiful mosque for the most beautiful Catholic church of the colony." In Blidah, when the French soldiers occupied the city, they raised an enormous cross on the minaret of the city mosque, followed by a Mass held inside "for the first time in centuries."[66]

Simultaneous with the transformation of mosques, church officials sought to reclaim ancient Christian sites. In April 1839, Dupuch took a tour of his new diocese, accompanied by several clerics and five members of the Soeurs de St-Joseph de l'Apparition, including Emilie de Vialar. Although the journey was miserable—high winds and torrential rains impeded their travel—all seemed worthwhile when the little band arrived outside the Algerian city of Annaba, recently rebaptized the French city of Bône, at the abandoned Roman site of Hippo, once inhabited by St. Augustine

(354–430), bishop of Hippo Regius. Here the Soeurs de St-Joseph picked flowers for the makeshift altar among the ruins, where Dupuch said Mass. On it he also placed a "remain of the holy Pontiff [Augustine], which was given to me by the holy Father, the first returned to this dear land after 1,410 years."[67] He immediately opened a subscription to build a basilica to hold the relic, reputedly Augustine's elbow.[68]

When the French established a military garrison in Philippeville, Dupuch wrote back to France, evoking the "immense ruins of Russicada...of Roman construction"; in Announah, he found "an antique Christian temple...still decorated with its cross," where he could pray at the spot where martyrs had suffered in 359; in Douéra, he began the construction of a church "not far from the seven palm trees, as described in Scripture."[69] Abbé Suchet, the vicar general in Constantine, asked the bishop to appeal to the king to save the ruins of an ancient chapel built by Emperor Constantine himself. It was not simply a piece of architecture, he argued, "but the only remains of our beautiful and ancient heritage in these countries...these stones...will protest continually against the usurpation by Islam of the ancient Christian faith."[70] The church's interest in reclaiming its archeological heritage in North Africa supported the French view of themselves as the heirs to the Roman empire. In this reading of history, the French were merely restoring Christian rule to North Africa after its unjust expropriation by Muslims over fifteen centuries.[71]

Accompanying the (re)establishment of Catholic spaces was that of Catholic institutions. In a remarkably short time, the diocese of Algiers reproduced the infrastructure of a typical French diocese. In the pages of the *Annales de la Propagation de la Foi*, read by missionary supporters and donors back home in France, Dupuch not only reported his travels throughout the colony but also catalogued new Catholic establishments: churches, schools, orphanages, lay societies, hospitals. In 1843, he bragged that he would soon have more than fifty churches or chapels, a seminary, a clerical school for boys, an orphanage, nearly 400 lay members and three branches of the Dames de la Charité, sixteen schools and other houses run by 75 nuns, as well as 72 religious brothers and 66 priests to serve a population of 50,000 civilian Catholics in the diocese, plus 80,000 French soldiers.[72]

Wherever the French extended their conquests in Algeria, Dupuch made sure church institutions followed, making the most of his symbolic power. Not only did he claim that the European residents were clamoring for new religious establishments, but he also made every effort to show the effects of Catholic display on Muslims as well. When he arrived in Constantine, he reported, "I was received there and celebrated as a friend, a father, a true Bishop. The natives formed part of my guard and my escort; their chiefs flocked around me, brought me presents,...gave me a burnoose of honor, attended all the religious ceremonies." In Blidah, where the soldiers placed the cross on the former mosque, "six Arabs carried it," and "for the first time in centuries, the *Exaudiat*, the *Laudate Dominum omnes gentes*, the accents of the prophets and the martyrs rang out."[73] In Dupuch's telling, the Arabs were props on the great stage set for the triumphal return of Christianity to North Africa. On his return to Bône in 1843, Dupuch lauded the "marvelous effects of the return of the relics of St. Augustine," and, on the feast day of St. Monica, Augustine's mother, he consecrated a women's charitable society.[74]

The Bishop vs. the Superior General

The charitable institutions undertaken by Emilie de Vialar and the Soeurs de St-Joseph dovetailed nicely with Dupuch's projects. Vialar, too, had followed the French army into new colonial spaces. Initially, Dupuch called the sisters resident in Algeria his "dear and tireless auxiliaries"[75] and facilitated their expansion to Constantine and Bône. Together Vialar and Dupuch founded a double orphanage in Algiers, with Dupuch providing the financing and Vialar the personnel. However, the first signs of trouble emerged just before its opening in December 1839, when Dupuch discovered that Vialar had also opened an establishment in Oran without his knowledge. He complained to her that he had to learn about it from the news-paper and, more generally, that "I don't have any idea what happens in your various houses; subjects leave, arrive, go away, are assigned, moved, moved yet again without my having any notion; the Sisters are allowed little by little to forget the spirit of their Institute, in going out alone, going out much too late."[76] Among the specific complaints he lodged was that the Soeurs de St-Joseph had little religious formation and no government authorization and that Vialar resisted his attempts to bring other, longer established, female religious orders to work in Algeria. Most critically, however, Vialar refused to acknowledge his authority over her, considering herself ecclesiastically dependent on the archbishop of Albi, in whose diocese her home-town of Gaillac was located.[77] Dupuch also contended that he had the right to modify the rules of the order, as well as to issue orders to individual sisters, which Vialar saw as undermining her authority as superior general. Her complaints about him were soon equally strident—"Monseigneur Dupuch is a natural in never renouncing a wish that he has expressed"—and her determination equally strong. "If I must die the victim of an unjust persecution, I am ready to sacrifice myself," she wrote in 1840, "because my vocation has been recognized as certain."[78] Once engaged, the battle between these two self-confident religious, about the same age, one a bishop, the other the founder and superior general of a rapidly expanding order, dominated both their lives, as well as those of their subordinates for the next three years, until the Soeurs de St-Joseph left Algeria in early 1843.

In this dispute, turf played a large role. Not only did Vialar precede Dupuch to Algeria, but she also had her own financial resources and network of contacts within the French administration and colonial society. In the four years before his arrival, furthermore, the absence of ecclesiastical authority in the nascent colony allowed Vialar unusual scope for initiative; the regularization of church structures after 1838, coupled with Dupuch's domineering personality, almost guaranteed conflict. It is hard to ignore Dupuch's incessant use of the first-person pronoun in his reports back to France—"already I have a very flourishing girls' school [and] a nursery school with one hundred little children"[79]—about establishments that Vialar had founded long before he arrived. One of Dupuch's strategies upon arrival, in fact, was to break the monopoly that the Soeurs de St-Joseph had over Algerian charitable institutions by importing rival religious orders from France. These nuns, unlike the Soeurs de St-Joseph, without contacts or experience in Algeria, would be forced to rely on him as their benefactor and intermediary. To keep any one religious order from dominating, he proposed that each of the three Algerian provinces house a different group, simultaneously reducing Vialar's field of action to her Algiers establishments alone.[80] These maneuvers, which infuriated Vialar, caused some bad feeling among Dupuch's new protégées as well. When the Soeurs de St-Joseph called on the newly arrived Soeurs de la Doctrine Chrétienne in June 1841, their superior apologized that in coming to Algeria "they had not expected to replace anyone" because they did not like to compete with "other establishments who devote themselves to the same works as ours."[81] The new sisters were also more expensive, which annoyed the French administration. Emilie de Vialar, independently wealthy, had subsidized most of her projects herself.

Dupuch also stated a desire to bring religious orders into Algeria that had been in existence for a longer period of time and whose training was more extensive and more regular. One of his most persistent complaints about Vialar was that she trained her novices too rapidly and with too little attention to the norms of religious life. Although Vialar denied this vehemently and Dupuch undoubtedly exaggerated his case, there was probably some truth to the accusation. Founded in 1832 and arriving in Algeria in 1835, the Soeurs de St-Joseph expanded rapidly in response to demand, numbering sixty sisters in Algeria alone by the time of Dupuch's arrival in 1839. Only in 1843 would Vialar make a concerted effort to develop more extensive written rules, particularly regarding the novitiate.[82] In the meantime, she recruited and placed sisters as quickly as possible. Dupuch wanted to take over the training of the Algerian novices, as well as rewrite the constitutions Vialar had developed in 1835 in Gaillac and had had approved by her local bishop, Mgr de Gualy, of the diocese of Albi. Although de Gualy offered to release Vialar from her obligations to him and she toyed with the idea of downgrading her order into an association of faithful laywomen, Vialar was loathe to give up her powers of recruitment, training, and placement to any bishop. What Vialar was attempting to create was a centralized religious order, or *congrégation*, in which she was ecclesiastically independent of bishops in the dioceses where members were active. Men's *congré-gations* on this model, such as the Jesuits or the Lazarists, had existed since the sixteenth century; only after the French Revolution did this become the dominant model for women, and they were slowly accepted. In Algeria, as in Gaillac, however successful the model, uncloistered, upper-class nuns operating independently still caused consternation, and the scope of Vialar's ambition and authority undoubtedly threatened Dupuch.

In her power struggle with Dupuch, Vialar was able to exploit a jurisdictional uncertainty in canon law as to the clerical supervision of women religious belonging to a centralized religious order active in more than one diocese. When each religious house was self-governing, the standard pattern in the Old Regime, the male superior general was usually the local bishop. After the Revolution, however, when new centralized religious orders such as Vialar's might have houses in multiple dioceses, the administrative role of the respective bishops was less clear. Now simultaneously dependent on the archbishop of Albi and the bishop of Algiers, Vialar not surprisingly preferred the distant and supportive superior to the demanding and difficult one on her doorstep. Her suspicion, probably not unfounded, was that Dupuch's goal was to co-opt her order and "to make of it a new institution that would put us under his complete dependence and allow him to give himself the title of founder." Above all, she prized unity, which she feared would be broken if the communities in Algeria obeyed rules different from those in France. "There is not a religious community in France," she declared to the government, "who would accept such conditions without signing its own death certificate."[83]

This conflict was also rooted in gender authority in the Catholic church, which allowed Dupuch to apply the ultimate weapon available to a priest but not a nun: denial of the sacraments. In February 1840 Dupuch threatened to suspend any diocesan cleric who approved, supported, or favored Vialar by words or actions. Some priests went further and harassed the Soeurs de St-Joseph, accusing them of schism and heresy by remaining loyal to Vialar, sometimes refusing them absolution. For nine months, from mid-1841 until Easter 1842, Dupuch deprived the sisters of confessors and therefore of Holy Communion, inspiring first "fear" and then "indignation" among Vialar's disciples in Algeria.[84] With only a single exception, they remained loyal to her during the entire crisis, refusing to defect to the bishop, standing up to disapproving clergy, continuing to recruit new members, and going about their work as usual despite the threat of closure of their establishments. According to Vialar, Dupuch sought to discredit them by portraying them as "women without a rule and perhaps without honor and of erroneous faith," in short as unregulated, scandalous, and heretical women. The gender hierarchy was also made clear by one of his parish priests, who asked the nuns "if they believed that God had withdrawn his light and grace from Monseigneur to give them to a woman"? Vialar herself was characterized as an "appalling woman" who was "intriguing" with her money and influence in order to eliminate the bishop of Algiers and replace him with an apostolic prefect of her choice.[85]

One way out of the impasse was to appeal to Rome, where Vialar journeyed in late 1840 in order to acquire papal approbation of her statutes, which would have freed her from dependence on diocesan bishops altogether. Confident in the rightness of her cause, she mobilized her network of well-connected family and friends. In Paris, her aunt paid a call on the papal nuncio and reminded him that Vialar had a supporter in Queen Marie-Amélie.[86] Her brother provided her with a letter of introduction to the French ambassador to the Holy See, a former colleague on the Conseil d'Etat in Paris. His wife presented Vialar to Cardinal Lambruschini, the papal secretary of state, who arranged a friendly audience with the pope, after which she made the rounds of influential cardinals to press her case. "The approval of our constitutions is at present certain," she wrote confidently in January 1841, expecting the whole affair to be wrapped up in a month or two.[87] A year later, she was still in Rome, still well received but increasingly frustrated, especially as conditions worsened for her sisters in Algeria. Dupuch's arrival in Rome in February 1842 only strengthened her resolve, especially after she heard the rumor that Dupuch was slandering the sisters by calling them "public women" and herself "an ambitious woman" whose "pride produced real disasters."[88]

Although Vialar did receive redress for the specific issue of restoring confessors to the Algerian sisters, her eighteen-month stay fell short of its ultimate objective. In May 1842 the pope finally issued a laudatory decree in favor of the Soeurs de St-Joseph but failed to approve their constitutions. The report, prepared by Père Rozaven, was far more critical than the official statement of praise ultimately issued by the pope. It cited a variety of issues that traditionally concerned conservative Roman prelates regarding the behavior and activity of women religious. Since the Soeurs de St-Joseph did not observe cloister and did not take perpetual vows, he maintained that they were not entitled to the privileges of full-fledged *religieuses*, which would have included exception from dependence on diocesan bishops. Open to the world, they were susceptible to the kind of "disorder" that might demand episcopal intervention. On the other hand, the female superior general, according to these rules, Rozaven noted, had almost "unlimited powers." He also objected to the practice of centralizing financial control in her hands, with receipts from one establishment used to subsidize another, as well as the provisions made to allow missionary sisters to vote absentee in congregational elections. Finally, the habit of the Soeurs de St-Joseph was "not religious enough," with special mention of their "too worldly" bonnet rather than the traditional veil.[89]

These criticisms reflected tensions within the Holy See as to the status of women religious like Vialar, who were in the process of inventing a new form of religious life in the early nineteenth century. Papal approval in the past had been bestowed only on cloistered orders of nuns, and as Frenchwomen in particular broke the mold, the Catholic church found itself reluctant to allow the new active *congrégations* and their strong-minded leaders the same privileges, much less one that was less than ten years old and whose founder had shown, in Rozaven's words, "insubordination" toward both civil and religious authority.[90] The pope, wrote another observer from Rome, could not "sanction the resistance of a nun to episcopal authority," wishing "above all that Mme Vialar would obey." Yet Dupuch's poor reputation in Algeria was also well known in Rome, where the Holy See regarded him badly for his tendency toward self-aggrandizement, whereas Vialar was well connected and her works admired. "In this situation the pope and the Congregation [of Bishops and Regulars] hesitate, deliberate, and don't know what side to take," wrote the same individual, torn between "seeming to sanction a refusal of obedience" and "forcing her to bend before a will that they themselves had described as capricious and arbitrary." Instead, they delayed, hoping that either Dupuch or Vialar would leave Algeria of their own accord.[91] When this did not happen, issuing a laudatory decree that praised Vialar's works but stopped short of changing her ecclesiastical status was a useful compromise. However, although Vialar realized that the decree was an unusual step in itself and a public reproach to Dupuch—and in public she spun the decision for all it was worth—it did not settle her Algerian future.

The Problem of Muslim Conversion

As the standoff between Vialar and Dupuch escalated, public opinion in Algeria remained solidly on her side. Thanks to her brother, Augustin, Vialar could draw on the support of many influential French colonists in Algeria, who lobbied on her behalf. In Algiers, Vialar herself reported in January 1840 that she had seen Maréchal Valée once and visited his daughter nearly every day. In 1841 Soeur Emilie Julien reported that the sisters were sure of the protection of the mayor of Algiers, Baron Hubert.[92] Threatened with removal from Algeria, the sisters found testimonials in their favor flooding in. "Their works are the most touching, the most effective of Christian morality," declared a petition signed by more than two hundred European inhabitants, including most of the colonial elite. Other colonial officials, including the director of the interior in Algeria, Count Guyot, added individual statements of support. More surprising perhaps was a petition signed by 140 Muslim notables, who expressed their gratitude for the sisters' work with the sick:

These women avow a true friendship and a sincere pity for all those who suffer and are ill, no matter what religion the unfortunate ones belong to. They do not cease to visit them, and whenever they can commit an act of charity, they never stay away. They are not loath to provide aid during serious illnesses such as cholera and in general those which terrorize human beings...we see in the organization of the society of these women, a true source of good deeds.

"Mme Emilie Vialar," added Moustapha Ben Mohamed, muphti maleki, "is a virtuous woman."[93]

The apparent support of Muslim inhabitants for the work of the Soeurs de St-Joseph was undoubtedly the most significant factor in their favor. From the very beginning of French colonization, officials worried about the effect of the implantation of Catholicism among a Muslim population that was consistently characterized as "fanatical" on religious issues.[94] The specter of an Algerian "holy war," triggered by religious "fanaticism" hung over the first decade of French rule. "Every missionary who disembarks in Algiers," wrote the newspaper Le Commerce, "does more in favor of the power of Abdel Kader than a regiment added to his forces."[95] At the same time, the French did not want to be seen as irreligious or lacking in respect for religion. Abd-el Kader, the leader of the Muslim military resistance against French rule, was also quoted as not believing that the French were Christians because they had no priests or churches; otherwise, he said, "[W]e would be the best of friends because the Koran, our holy book, orders us to live in peace with Christians."[96] In 1839 Valée wrote hopefully back to Paris that, through the appointment of a bishop, "we will succeed in convincing the Muslims that religious sentiment is not completely extinguished among us." Yet, the first quality Algeria needed in a bishop, Valée also wrote, "is a pious tolerance" because "fanaticism is one of the most powerful arms that is employed against us."[97]

To many French officials, the view that Muslims possessed unnaturally strong religious beliefs did not justify so much the implantation of purely secular French rule as a redefinition of Catholicism as a "tolerant," nonproselytizing faith that promoted universal values. "If it is true that monuments testify to the power of peoples," editorialized the Moniteur algérien as early as 1832, "the moment has arrived to show the Muslims, without danger, that we also possess a sublime religion that we take pride in professing because, more than any other, it teaches charity, it preaches union, it commands tolerance, it prescribes prayer, it demands respect for sworn faith, [and] finally it looks on hospitality as a pious duty."[98] The French government, one Algeria booster wrote, showed its dedication to religious liberty by erecting not only Catholic institutions but a Protestant church as well. Furthermore, by moving public ceremonies into private space, the French showed that Christianity and Islam could live in peace.[99] French rule, the minister of war went so far as to suggest, could provide a model of tolerance in which "the sound of the bells and the hymns of the Roman church blend happily with the voice of the crier who calls [Muslims] to prayer from the top of the minaret," provided that neither Muslims nor priests upset the balance.[100] The more secure the French felt in their rule, however, the fewer objections they made regarding Catholic appropriation or even destruction of Muslim symbols. "The events that have occurred since last November have radically altered the general situation," the minister of war wrote in mid-1840, authorizing the demolition of Muslim baths in order to expand the Algiers cathedral.[101]

Although the establishment of a diocese in Algeria was also a sign of increasing French confidence that their Algerian rule was permanent, the high profile that Dupuch adopted caused concern among military and civilian leaders. Compared to Vialar and her sisters, Dupuch made few friends in Algeria. Within six months of his arrival, a military official reported that "there is already in the army an entire vocabulary of words and jokes by him or about him." About the grand outdoor procession he organized for Corpus Christi in 1839, the same official wrote, "He wastes no time in this country and I fear that he lacks prudence in his enterprises...especially in regards to the natives," bringing a quick admonishment from Paris not to allow religious ceremonies to become "an object of insult by Christians" toward Muslims "in a country where religious fanaticism often brings weapons to hand."[102] Events reinforced this fear, as the war with Abd el-Kader resumed in November 1839 with Muslim attacks against French settlers on the plain of Mitidja. In 1841, during General Bugeaud's offensive against Abd el-Kader, Dupuch, believing he had special responsibility for Algerian-French relations, initiated an exchange of prisoners, angering both the French military administration and the Soeurs de St-Joseph, into whose care eighty-nine men and women were delivered, lodged, "pell-mell," in the Ste-Croix chapel in Algiers. His claim to have effected fifteen Muslim conversions frightened Algerian parents enough to scuttle a French plan to create a *collège arabe* in Paris to educate elite Algerians.[103] At the offices of the Propagation de la Foi in France, officials became increasingly concerned about his mismanagement of the funds they sent him for good works.[104] Although French authorities became impatient with how often his religious enthusiasm escaped their control, Dupuch's clerical enemies in Algeria denounced him to the Holy See as a Gallican, a charge Vialar echoed in Rome.[105]

Most frustrated by the question of conversion, on which the French government maintained a firm ban, Dupuch complained to the pope that French Catholics could freely become Muslims, but he could minister only to Catholics.[106] A young Louis Veuillot, serving as secretary to General Bugeaud in Algeria, wrote in response to the government's criticism of Dupuch's outdoor Masses: "If you fear wounding

Muslims so much, remove your flag, your navy, your army and go away because it is there that you wound them." The Muslims, he claimed, found the ceremonies "beautiful" and "touching."[107] In Algeria, Catholics like Veuillot and Dupuch were more interested in the possibility of converting Arabs than in bringing the often religiously lax settlers and soldiers back into the fold. Unable to approach the subject directly, Dupuch used church institutions, personnel, and ceremonies to order and display Catholic power and dogma in the hopes of spontaneous conversion. Soon after his arrival, he claimed a convert in the wife of the former bey of Constantine, a Genoese woman named Aïcha, who had been sold into slavery as a baby and who was rebaptized Marie-Antoinette and given into Vialar's custody for religious instruction.[108] With the French governor of Constantine, he arranged for Muslim children raised in the newly established Catholic orphanage to be able to convert as adults if they so desired.[109] The province of Constantine was where Dupuch and his vicar general, Abbé Suchet, reported the warmest welcome among Arabs (awakening their most fervent hopes for conversion), stimulated perhaps by the willingness of the native aristocracy to collaborate with the French as Abd el-Kader threatened their power by preaching a holy war against the invaders.[110]

In contrast to Dupuch, Vialar's approach to conversion was much more discreet. "We have recognized that here," she wrote to the pope, "any dramatic conversion would be inopportune, that it would distance many Europeans from us and would forever close the ear of the natives."[111] Outwardly, the sisters contented themselves with the establishment of good works, the practice of which ensured their salvation, and possibly touched or informed those they served as well. By simply being present during the religious instruction given to Catholic girls, Vialar wrote that she hoped that their Jewish and Muslim classmates would be touched by divine grace "to taste the truth of the Gospels."[112] In Constantine, Abbé Suchet reported that, besieged by curious locals, the sisters handed out small religious statues and medals, especially to Arab women, and answered their questions about Christianity and their own lives as Catholic nuns. "They never leave," he wrote,

> without these poor Moslems asking to kiss *Sinaïssa Allah* (or the Christ that the nuns wear on their chests). It is truly surprising, the veneration and confidence that they have inspired in the city and in the entire province, as the sick of faraway tribes also come to be cared for by them. Their presence here will produce, I am sure, a prodigious effect and hasten radically the civilization, if not the conversion, of these poor peoples.

The undoubtedly somewhat exaggerated admiration he describes was itself, he argued, a method of "pacifying" Algeria through "the moral effect of tender charity," following the model of Christ himself.[113] At the very least, the demonstration of skill and devotion by religious women would increase admiration for and decrease hostility toward the Catholic church. Moreover, among a devout population, the Soeurs de St-Joseph may well have been useful cultural intermediaries by combining material and practical aid with religious symbols and gestures.[114]

However, if Vialar wrote to the pope that "We seek *first* to make loved and respected our religion" [emphasis mine], she ended the sentence with "it is only in the greatest secrecy that we will be able to accomplish conversions."[115] Through their monopoly on health care, the Soeurs de St-Joseph had an opportunity to offer Christian salvation at the moment of illness and death through the sacrament of baptism. Vialar reported that during the cholera epidemic that brought them to Algeria in 1835 the sisters had not only brought lapsed Catholics back into the fold but had also converted several Protestants and baptized an adult of unspecified religious origin. After they had established a permanent presence in the colony, they also instructed and baptized "a Negress" whose illness brought her to their house and reconverted a Christian woman, "another Negress," who had served in a Muslim household. A third individual, "a Moor covered in wounds," to whom the sisters had offered asylum, also converted and wore a "Christ on his chest" even among Muslims, but his residence with the sisters "sheltered him from insults." More generally, without specifying any numbers, Vialar claimed that "adult Moors and Jews on their deathbeds or in health received holy baptism by the intermediary of the sisters."[116]

But the real success in deathbed conversions lay elsewhere. In the same report, addressed to the pope, Vialar stated that "above all divine Providence has even placed us to obtain at death's door, the salvation of a great number of children."[117] Vialar was referring here to the practice of baptizing non-Christian children at the point of death—*in extremis*—rather than leaving them, from the Catholic point of view, in eternal limbo. By canon law, all baptized Catholics could baptize another individual in immediate danger of death if a priest was not available. Adults had to express a desire for baptism; there was no such requirement for children, although the age of consent was ambiguous. The baptism of the dying, especially children, had been a focus of missionary work since the Jesuits entered New France in the seventeenth century; in the nineteenth century, the Holy Childhood Association (l'Oeuvre de la Sainte Enfance) encouraged the baptism of dying Chinese infants.[118] The most notorious case of unauthorized baptism in the nineteenth century was that of a Jewish child, Edgardo Mortara, whose alleged baptism by a family maid resulted in his removal from his parents and incarceration in a Roman orphanage.[119]

Vialar and her sisters, therefore, were participating in a common Catholic evangelizing activity, with the critical difference that in the lands where they worked, they kept it secret from all but church authorities. Years after the fact, Vialar's successor as superior general, Emilie Julien, claimed that during the cholera epidemic the sisters had secretly baptized six hundred Muslim or Jewish children before their death, scarcely the kind of religious neutrality promised to non-Christians and presumably unknown to their Jewish and Muslim supporters.[120] Abbé Banvoy, missionary in Bône, reported to Propaganda Fide that the Soeurs de St-Joseph had permission from the Archbishop of Albi to baptize children in danger of dying until they were eleven years old, though he preferred that they stopped at age seven.[121] Abbé Montera, missionary in Algiers, for his part, viewed the nuns as essential to this work since he shared the common European view that Muslim families were impregnable to outsiders. "Access to Muslim homes," he wrote in a confidential report to Propaganda Fide, "is forbidden to everyone, and their domestic secrets are impenetrable. Only the holy sisters of charity enjoy the privilege of being welcomed in their houses." Sought out in cases of illness, the Soeurs de St-Joseph used not only their medical skills but also "the spirit of religion" as "a balm" in treating Muslim patients, and they effected baptisms when possible. However, he was careful to assure Rome, they "acted with maximum prudence and circumspection since, if the secret was disclosed, they would lose their reputation and the influence they have with the dying." They would also lose their standing with the French administration, which "would view this unfavorably and highly disapprove of it."[122] What Dupuch did in the open air—to the alarm of the French authorities—the Soeurs de St-Joseph did behind the closed doors of Muslim homes—without their knowledge.

For this reason, the Soeurs de St-Joseph—or other nuns like them—were an integral part of the Catholic mission in Algeria. Without the sisters' ministry, as one priest told Vialar, "we can do nothing with the natives," reversing the usual roles so that "the priests, in this regard, can be nothing but their auxiliaries."[123] This theme was taken up by the Abbé Suchet, vicar general in Constantine, who wrote long elegies to the work of the Soeurs de St-Joseph. They were his entrée into Muslim homes as the aide major of the sisters. Inspired by their example, he took up the study of practical medicine "like a sister of charity,…going like them to visit [patients] at home." Careful to restore gender order, however, he specified that when he "penetrated the interior of all these Arab houses, closed up until then to all men…I am received and feted even more than the sisters of charity because they know that the French *marabout* is much above them."[124]

Yet key to Suchet's narrative is the contrast between the humble French nun and the decadent Muslim elite. This is his description of the reception given to a soeur de St-Joseph in one Arab household:

> They assemble all the slaves, all the children, the entire family. All give
> cries of joy; the husband and the wife each take her by one hand that
> they kiss with respect; the children kiss her arms, and the slaves the hem
> of her robe: she is conducted in triumph like this to the most beautiful

rooms of the house. They pile up cushions on which they make her sit and there she receives a kind of worship: they give her the most exquisite delicacies; they offer her the most sweet-smelling oils. The poor nun, completely embarrassed, refuses all. Then the admiration is at its height; they say to her: *But you are therefore Marabouta* (a saint).

In Suchet's telling, the humility of the Christian nun contrasts vividly with the sumptuousness of the forbidden Muslim interior and triumphs over it. After the outdoor Mass and games held on the feast day of St. Philip, the Soeurs de St-Joseph crowned the victors, producing, again, a telling contrast. "Nothing," Suchet wrote, "was stranger or more touching at the same time to see these black, copper, or white Africans kneel before the French nuns and receive on top of their heads, them, these fierce children of the desert, crowns from the timid and trembling hand of the humble sisters of charity." In another instance, he described a meeting between "the most learned and spiritual woman of the region" and the Soeurs de St-Joseph, in which "both of them were amazed and enthusiastic," even more so because "these poor Muslim women, as you know, can never see anyone." Like many French clerics, Suchet emphasized the invisibility of Muslim women, seldom seen on the streets and, if so, with "the face enveloped in a white cloth" so that "one barely saw their eyes." This cloister contrasted with the visible activity of the nuns, far from enclosed. The clinics opened by the Soeurs de St-Joseph were also spectacles of their own, as patients and curious onlookers crowded into formerly Muslim spaces—"the hall of the great council of the *ulemas* and the *muftis*" in Constantine—to watch the sisters at work.[125]

Committed to her faith, Vialar walked a narrow line in her evangelization efforts in Algeria. Occasionally, as in the Mass celebrated on the ruins of Hippo or the feast day described by Suchet, the Soeurs de St-Joseph were willing to participate in public ceremonies that marked the territory as French and Christian, but they, unlike Dupuch, did not initiate such ostentatious displays of Catholicism. As women religious, they could not transform mosques into churches or organize processions on church holidays. However, they were not less committed to evangelization than was Dupuch. As Christian women visible in the streets of Algerian cities and in their clinics, schools, and asylums, they relied on good works to demonstrate their faith. This more private arena for action, however, had a silver lining unavailable to male clerics in that it allowed the sisters an opportunity to save souls, as they saw it, through the baptism of dying children inside Muslim homes. These acts remained unknown to the children's parents, to the population at large, and to the French authorities, surfacing only in documents intended for clerics who shared their priorities. This discretion undoubtedly facilitated their rapid expansion in Algeria and was one of the reasons Emilie de Vialar was able to stage such a fierce resistance to Dupuch's attempt to displace and control her.

In the end, however, the colony proved too small for their dueling personalities. Without Roman approval of her constitutions, Vialar turned toward the French government in Algeria for support, arguing that the establishments she had founded relied on at least a "tacit" contract, which the authorities could not break without serious cause. She also specifically cited the petitions of support signed by indigenous Algerians.[126] Although Vialar's establishments in Algeria were legally constituted, she did not have official authorization for her congregation in France—not unusual for a religious order less than ten years old—which made her vulnerable. In Paris, the minister of war was eager to stay out of the quarrel between Vialar and Dupuch but admitted in May that, without authorization, "the conduct to follow by my department is entirely mapped out." He acquiesced to Dupuch's request to replace the Soeurs de St-Joseph with the Filles de la Charité (a congregation with a long official history in France) and instructed the governor general in Algeria to cooperate. To avoid a public outcry, however, he recommended not closing the three establishments in Constantine, Bône, and Algiers simultaneously but over a period of several months.[127] On the ground, however, emotions remained high. Dupuch ordered the Constantine establishment closed on the first of July, threatening the local superior that, if the sisters did not leave for Algiers on the boat at the end of the month, he would excommunicate them.[128] To replace the Soeurs de St-Joseph, Dupuch brought in the Filles de la Charité, the Soeurs de la Doctrine Chrétienne de Nancy, and the Soeurs du Bon-Pasteur. An 1844 circular of the last congregation referred to Dupuch as "a second Moses" and "a heroic man" and stated, "Monseigneur comes to see us every week since we have lived in Elbiar and goes through the least details with the liveliest interest."[129] Finally Dupuch had the admiring sisters he could guide.

With the pope now refusing to interfere in a French government matter, Vialar turned her attention to receiving material restitution for the establishments she was forced to abandon, refusing to believe the official reassurances that she would be recompensed. "It is cruel to say it," she wrote to her brother, "but Mgr Dupuch should arouse our mistrust, absolutely like that of a skillful thief who is looking to fleece you. He wants to have my house, as one wishes to have a well-located shop that is well stocked, in order to place the new sisters without having to pay a *sou* for it." She planned instead to sell her house to the city, "and with the price they give me, I will organize my affairs."[130] Nonetheless, the government, now forced to allocate 20,000 francs annually to pay for replacement sisters, reimbursed her for only 4,800 francs. Financially, Vialar took a heavy blow, having sunk at least a third of her personal wealth, or 100,000 francs, into the Algerian establishments.[131] Emotionally, the Algerian departure was almost as devastating. When the Soeurs de St-Joseph turned over control of the Algiers hospital to the Filles de la Charité, one of them wrote, "It was not however without spilling tears and looking behind them that our first Mothers left the hospital.... They would have preferred to die in the breach. But He for whom they battled reserved them for other combats."[132]

If she lost the battle, however, Emilie de Vialar won the war. In 1845, Dupuch resigned as bishop of Algiers in disgrace. Fleeing his many creditors, his departure from Algeria was facilitated by none other than Augustin de Vialar, Emilie's brother. From Paris, her aunt triumphantly passed along the news of the "great disorder in his affairs and the enormous sums for which he is pursued" and volunteered to see whether she could help reestablish Vialar in Algeria now that her nemesis had departed.[133] Dupuch himself wrote to Vialar soon after his departure as if the two had never been in conflict, expressing his desire to see his "dear daughters" again in Rome. "Perhaps," he asked, "I will run into you again on one of my new voyages?" In 1853 he was still writing about his "vivid interest" in her "admirable works." The minister of religious affairs passed the hat among his fellow bishops and the Algerian clergy for donations to liquidate Dupuch's debts until Napoleon III finally granted a 220,000-franc credit in 1852.[134] In and out of exile, Dupuch died in 1856, having supposedly written a letter, which she destroyed, begging forgiveness from Emilie de Vialar.[135] In Algeria two decades later, another bishop, Charles Lavigerie (1867–92), took up Dupuch's themes of restored Christian glory in North Africa and once again encouraged active proselytizing among Muslims.[136]

For Emilie de Vialar, the Algerian experience both whetted her appetite for missionary work in non-Christian lands and provided important lessons for the future. Without the coincidence of her brother's entry into Algeria shortly after France's conquest, she might not have become a missionary at all. But after eight years in North Africa, she saw the future of her order as a Mediterranean one. The dispute with Dupuch alerted her to the sometimes difficult position of women religious working among other Catholic clerics in overseas missions. However, it also strengthened her resolve and the solidarity among her sisters. Women religious might have been at a disadvantage when faced with intransigent bishops, but at the same time they occupied a new and important role in working with indigenous populations whose families and homes had in the past been closed to male missionaries. In Algeria, Vialar created a model—based on education, nursing, and charity, as well as secret baptism—for sustaining mission activity in a region where the proselytization of non-Christians was forbidden. Forced out of Algeria, she took this model with her to other lands in the Ottoman Empire.

5

Refuge in Tunisia and Malta

Depressed and impoverished, Emilie de Vialar left Algeria in March 1843. But three years earlier, as her dispute with Dupuch heated up and now committed to missionary work, she had opened a house in Tunis that could support those in Algiers, as well as "intimidate" Dupuch, as she put it to the pope in 1841. A year later, she revised its utility as an establishment "that could open a door to new works, if I am forced to leave Algeria."[1] The presence of some Tunisian boarders in her school in Bône had alerted her to the need for European educational establishments in Tunis, where she learned there were also no hospitals or pharmacies. Her work in Algeria had also whetted her appetite for working among North Africans. "Tunis," she wrote to the archbishop of Albi, "is a city as significant as Marseilles, and it is an infidel city: this is what attracts me with joy."[2] In Tunis, Vialar opened two schools (one with tuition, one without), a dispensary, and a hospital, all staffed by five sisters, one of whom also made home visits to the sick. As in Algeria, Vialar initially financed the new foundation herself, although her funds were much reduced; by 1844, the Oeuvre de la Propagation de la Foi, the Catholic fund-raising organization in Lyon, was providing an annual subsidy of two thousand francs. The hospital also received private donations, in part thanks to fund-raising efforts of the French consul and his wife, who acted as Vialar's sponsors in Tunisia and who saw charitable works run by French nuns as raising the profile of France vis-à-vis other European nations, chiefly Britain and the Italian states.[3] All of these missionary objectives—social welfare, education, national prestige—distinguished the work of the Soeurs de St-Joseph from past missionary orders in the region—all male—whose primary goal was ransoming Christian captives to prevent them from converting to Islam.[4] It also marked the increasing power of Europeans in Tunisia, especially after the French negotiated a new commercial treaty in 1830 that allowed them free rein to open new consulates and direct commercial relations with Tunisian manufacturers.[5]

Most important of all, however, Vialar benefited from the patronage of Ahmad Bey, the new ruler of the regency of Tunis, son of a Catholic Sardinian woman who had been captured as a child and married to Ahmad Bey's father after converting to Islam. This maternal legacy may explain his interest in Catholicism, which he manifested on a state visit to France, touring churches in Avignon, as well as a correspondence with the pope between 1847 and 1851.[6] Sponsorship of projects like Vialar's also represented an opportunity to modernize his country in order to prevent closer Ottoman oversight on the one hand and increased European control on the other.[7] The French conquest and occupation of Algeria had reshuffled power alignments in the southern Mediterranean, and Ahmad Bey, who succeeded his father in 1837 and died in 1855 (just one year before Vialar), used internal reform and careful diplomacy as a means of keeping his independence from both the Ottoman Turks, who had recently reestablished direct control in Tripoli on Tunisia's southeastern border, and France, now the established power to the west. He reorganized the army on European lines, ended the slave trade and slavery, and expanded economic privileges for Europeans in Tunisia. On the outskirts of Tunis he built a great palace, La Mohammedia, on the model of Versailles. In 1846, in the wake of rumors of an Ottoman invasion, he made a state visit to France, designed to scare the Turks and force the court of Louis-Philippe to acknowledge him as an independent and equal sovereign.[8]

Within Tunisia, the turn toward the West increased the power of the European communities, which demanded and received more economic and legal privileges, while jockeying among themselves for dominance. The European population also grew in numbers and social diversity. In 1830, about two to three thousand Europeans, mainly from old established trading and merchant families, were resident in Tunis; in 1860, the European population numbered more than ten thousand, many of them poor—and in the view of the elites—unruly immigrants from southern Europe and the Mediterranean islands. Italians, especially Sardinians and Sicilians, made up the largest group, followed by Maltese, Greeks, French, and small numbers of English, Austrians, and Spanish.[9] Europeans, who were not allowed to own property and retained their original nationality (under the protection of the foreign consuls), lived in the lower part of the medina, segregated from the majority Muslim population and the indigenous Jewish community.

Vialar, however, received permission from Ahmad Bey to establish a house, rented by the state, in the Muslim quarter of Tunis on rue Sîdî Saber in May 1842, where she opened a pharmacy and an outpatient clinic. The following year, she added a small hospital, named after St-Louis, consisting of two rooms and six beds. This initiative, as historian Anne-Marie Planel has pointed out, fulfilled three simultaneous functions: It boosted the profile of France, promoted Catholic charity, and demonstrated Ahmad Bey's commitment to European-style progress. Julia Clancy-Smith argues that another motivation was to control the new, poor, and socially undesirable European migrants, who fell outside of the jurisdiction of the beylical state and whose numbers overran the resources of the foreign consuls, who were nominally charged with their welfare.[10] In this, Ahmad Bey differed little from the French elites, who sought similar social control by nuns over marginal French populations at home. Admission to the hospital appears to have been limited to Europeans who could provide a certificate from their consul or some other "trustworthy person,"[11] but in the clinic the nursing sisters treated individuals of all faiths under the supervision of one of Tunis's two doctors, one French, one Maltese. That the inhabitants of Tunis found this establishment useful was reflected in the financial contributions made not only by European Catholics but also by Greeks, Protestants, and Jews, as well as by the bey himself on occasion. In 1848 he allowed the hospital to move to a former barracks on rue Zénédia, where the number of beds doubled, and the original site was dedicated solely to outpatient services. According to the Abbé Bourgade, in 1851, the clinic served up to eighty Arabs every day. The Soeurs de St-Joseph also made home visits to ill patients. All health services were free of charge.[12] Like the Abbé Suchet in Constantine, Bourgade emphasized the Muslim patients' gratitude: "Relieved of their wounds, these Arabs leave blessing the daughters of charity [Soeurs de St-Joseph], who inspire so much zeal and devotion. This is very good, they say, often while pointing to the cross of the sister; it is like Mohammed." "This," he concluded, "is the way to follow in order to arrive at the heart of man."[13]

Whether or not Tunisian patients indeed compared their nurses to Mohammed, the Soeurs de St-Joseph provided much-needed health services. Jean Ganiage has calculated that for the European population in mid-nineteenth-century Tunis, only 647 out of every 1,000 children reached the age of five, a level of child mortality roughly equal to that of France a century earlier. In addition, Tunis suffered from frequent epidemics of smallpox and typhus, which were likely to strike adults, as well as children. Sanitation was bad, especially in the poor European quarter, and few doctors were available to the general population, the best serving the bey or other elites.[14] Under these circumstances, trained nurses were invaluable. Cholera, which struck Europe for the first time in the nineteenth century and which neither European nor North African doctors understood, first arrived in Tunis in 1849–50, carried from Algeria by travelers and soldiers. All those who could afford it fled the city, leaving its poorest inhabitants vulnerable to the disease. In Tunis, just under 17,000 individuals were affected, and 7,600 succumbed out of a population of approximately 150,000 (for a death rate of 5 percent and a rate of illness about double that).[15] The Soeurs de St-Joseph, who had previous experience with cholera in Algeria, closed their schools in order to devote their entire staff to nursing the sick; the last victim was a twenty-two-year-old sister.[16] This display of selflessness facilitated their acceptance by elites and commoners alike.

As Vialar opened other establishments in Tunisia (Sousse, 1842; Sfax, 1852; La Goulette, 1855), health care services were always included. In Sousse, for example, the mission was led by Soeur Joséphine Daffis, who, in her fifty-four years in residence was, according to a church historian, "a nurse, pharmacist, doctor, dentist, even surgeon, exercising these diverse talents among the Arabs, the Jews, the Christians, men, women." Daffis, the heiress of a prominent Toulouse family and who had previously served in Algeria, was written up in the *Gazette du Languedoc* in 1850 as capable of amputations; the doctor who wrote the article had instructed her in the use of chloroform and left her a supply.[17] With skills like these, small wonder that Emilie de Vialar wrote to her brother that her sisters had "the confidence of the people."[18] In a larger sense, the Soeurs de St-Joseph participated in the shift from Arabic to European medical practice that occurred in the nineteenth century, accelerated by epidemic disease and the bey's interest in modernization, and which eventually became a rationale for French colonization at the end of the century.

The schools opened by the Soeurs de St-Joseph proved equally popular, although, as in Algeria, the pupils were European and Christian (with a few Jewish girls) rather than Tunisian and Muslim. However, this was a rapidly growing population, thanks to the migration of southern Europeans in the early nineteenth century. The public school in Tunis began with only 25 pupils (15 Italian girls and 10 Maltese) in 1840; in 1844 Vialar reported to the Propagation de la Foi that they enrolled 120 pupils, 80 of them free of charge. "We gather in our classes a great number of Christian children," she wrote, "who are entirely ignorant of their religion...it is not rare to see a certain number of young people abandon the title of Christian to become Muslims."[19] In fact, in the decades before Vialar's arrival, the lines between faiths sometimes blurred as Christians and Muslims participated in common religious rituals such as the pilgrimage of Notre Dame de Trapani in La Goulette, especially popular among Muslim women.[20] Although missionaries were encouraged by Muslim and Jewish veneration of Christian symbols, they feared the spiritual trafficking might also go the other way, especially as becoming Muslim in Tunisia provided far more material and legal advantages than did Christianity. To prevent this kind of religious defection, children enrolled in St-Joseph schools were given a solid Catholic education. According to another cleric, some of the Jewish girls also "became pious by hearing the catechism recited and hymns sung." By 1855, in all of their Tunisian schools, the Soeurs de St-Joseph instructed over 300 children.[21] Some of these establishments started off and remained extremely poor, especially when the majority of their funding depended on the donations of local inhabitants. In Sousse, for example, the sisters were first lodged at the home of the French vice consul until he raised the money to rent a modest house. From 1842 to 1862 the sisters moved four times and used the same room as a refectory, dormitory, and parlor; the children were packed into narrow stuffy rooms until a new, permanent house was built in 1864. In Sfax, they were also initially housed with the vice consul until they moved to a small, uncomfortable house in the Christian quarter; the donations they received were not sufficient to buy all the furniture they needed.[22]

On the other end of the social spectrum, Vialar also opened a secondary school for the daughters of Tunisia's European elite, who might otherwise have sent their daughters to France or Italy for their education. This initiative was supported by Giuseppe Raffo, who donated a large house in the seaside suburb of La Marsa (where the Tunisian and European elite socialized), paid the costs of staffing the school, and transferred his five daughters and seven nieces from the Sacred Heart school in Paris.[23] Tunisian born of European parents, Raffo became the brother-in-law of Mustafa Bey, Ahmad's father, and served him as interpreter and secretary, while profiting handsomely from fishing and export monopolies. When Ahmad Bey became regent, Raffo became an informal minister of foreign affairs whose ear was essential for European consuls seeking increased influence with the bey.[24] A Sardinian subject and a Christian, Raffo leveraged that influence on behalf of the Catholic community on numerous occasions, and Vialar benefited from his patronage.[25] As a result, Vialar was especially conscious that the La Marsa school had to meet high educational levels—the model she cited was that of the Society of the Sacred Heart—and chose as director Soeur Camille, "a very distinguished subject." Meeting the challenge could "ensure in the future the stability of our works in the Regency." This stability would result not only from the school fees the Soeurs de St-Joseph could collect from these elite pupils but also from the "nucleus of educated Sisters" such an establishment would nurture.[26]

If Raffo provided an entrée into Tunisian politics and society, Vialar's most important clerical collaborator in Tunisia was the Abbé François Bourgade, her spiritual director and close friend. They had already bonded in Algeria, where in 1838 Bourgade, ordained a priest only two years earlier, traveled on his own initiative to work among French soldiers and civilians and also became chaplain to the Soeurs de St-Joseph. When he took Vialar's side in the conflict with Dupuch, confessing and providing communion to the sisters when no other priest in Algeria would, the bishop relieved him of his official positions. In early 1841 Bourgade secretly followed Vialar to Tunis, where, at her behest, the French consul named him the chaplain of the new royal chapel in Carthage, opened in 1842.[27] While Vialar was in Rome to gain approval of her constitutions, he became her main epistolary confidant, a correspondence that resumed whenever Vialar was absent from Tunisia. In 1846, for example, while on a visit to her ill father in Gaillac, she regretted not having the time to write him every day. Such close spiritual and emotional relationships between religious women and male clerics were not uncommon in the nineteenth century.[28] In this case, besides their shared mission, Vialar was especially attracted to Bourgade's spirituality, which was inspired by the eighteenth-century founder of the Redemptorist order, Alphonsus di Liguori, who had just been canonized in 1839. This theology emphasized frequent confession—Bourgade confessed the Tunisia sisters weekly—but generous absolution. Both Bourgade and Vialar were also inspired by Liguori's work among the down-and-out in Naples, a population similar to the poor Italians and other Mediterranean peoples who had washed up on the shores of Tunisia.[29] Bourgade became Vialar's spiritual director, as well as her partner and protégé. More generally, however, she also wrote him about the day-to-day administration of her order, and as his main patron, she also sought to advance his interests in ways large and small, whether by consulting with the Pères de Ste-Croix about the possibility of providing teachers for Bourgade's schools in Tunisia or collecting subscriptions for his books or sending him a new cassock and the material for a frock coat from Paris.[30]

In Tunisia, Vialar and Bourgade worked together on building Catholic institutions that served not only European Catholics but also indigenous Jews and Muslims. Bourgade helped establish the curriculum at her first school in Tunis and examined its pupils. In March 1841 he wrote enthusiastically to Propagation de la Foi that some Jewish girls had enrolled and that Muslim parents had asked that their daughters be included if Vialar would establish a separate class for them.[31] In 1842, on his own initiative, with his own money, and in partnership with Pompeo Sulema, a Jewish refugee from Livorno, Bourgade founded a secondary school for boys of all nations and faiths, directed by a school committee that included representatives from each faith and each nationality.[32] Named (despite its interconfessional character) Collège St-Louis, this school offered local boys instruction in French, Italian, Arabic, Greek, Latin, calligraphy, history, natural history, physics, geography, mathematics, bookkeeping, commercial statistics, business practices, logic, and rhetoric. A small free school was attached for working-class boys, as well as a nursery school staffed at first by the Soeurs de St-Joseph and a Jewish woman, later by the sisters alone. By 1851, the three schools together had a total of 180 pupils, half of whom were Muslims or Jews.[33] "We receive in our establishments young Tunisians," wrote Bourgade, "without distinction of nationality and religion, and prepare them thus, by the beneficial effect of education, by the example of Christian morals, this social fusion, safeguard of their common interests. They are not to our eyes, either Muslims nor Jews, but equally dear children on whom we lavish our paternal care." Until the Revolution of 1848, Bourgade's school was funded by the French king, as well as by private fund-raising he conducted in France.[34]

Bourgade's vision was one of active engagement with Islam and Muslims in order to persuade them intellectually of the superiority of Catholicism. Unlike most Catholic clergy active in North Africa, he had learned Arabic and read the Koran. In addition to his clerical and educational work, he collaborated with two local Tunisians on a bimonthly newspaper in Arabic and installed a small printing press at the Collège St-Louis as a means of publishing books that would explain Christianity to Arabs. Three of these were his own, published in 1847, 1852, and 1855 in French, followed by partial or complete translations in Arabic.[35] As he wrote to Napoleon III in 1855, even if it were impossible to convert Muslims immediately, "it would be salutary and easy to bring them closer to the Gospel...speaking to their hearts by charitable works is not enough; we need more, to speak to their mind, and for this three things are necessary: learn their language, have an in-depth understanding of their theology, and debate with them."[36] The charity practiced by the Soeurs de St-Joseph was the first step but not the last; instead, the Muslims would be conquered by reason.

Of these three publications, the first, *Soirées de Carthage*, was most influenced by Bourgade's association with Emilie de Vialar. In it, Bourgade imagines a dialogue between an Islamic mufti and a "Soeur de la Charité" who had just treated his wife. The two participants bless each other and attribute the wife's improvement to God, thereby demonstrating common religious ground. But the conversation then turns to the relative positions of Catholic and Muslim women, with the mufti asking how the sister was able to leave her homeland and her parents and expose herself to the dangers of the sea in order to live among strangers. If it is a dowry preventing her marriage, he offers to provide one. The sister responds that she is married to God and asks in turn, "How are women educated here? What do you do to cultivate her intelligence? Nothing. What do you do to ennoble her heart and guide her sentiments? Nothing. What religious principles do you give her? She is attracted to virtue but never to the mosque." His children, she charges, spend the first ten years of their lives with their mother, but she cannot teach them. In contrast, in France, the woman "is an angel in the house...the man is the head that directs, the arm that protects; the woman the soul that invigorates and consoles." The mufti responds to this affirmation of the importance of wives and mothers in the home with a simple, "C'est beau!" [It's beautiful!][37]

Next, the two discussants take up the question of Muslim divorce, which the imaginary sister condemns because it undermines women's security in the household and goes against (Christian) scripture. Finally, the sister reaches her theological limits, informing the mufti that she is "only a simple woman; I know enough to behave and to teach children, but I am not a doctor [of theology] for debating." She recommends he approach a "Christian marabout."[38] In subsequent dialogues between this mufti and an Islamic cadi, the two regret that the "toubibas (medicine women)" who have come from France are not Muslim but also conclude that Muslims degrade and enslave women while Christians ennoble and respect them. The Christian practice, they think, is more in keeping with the will of God, citing both scriptural and Koranic passages regarding women. When a priest joins the imaginary conversation, they move on to the reasons for celibacy among Catholic clergy and compliment him that he "knows the Koran as we do," certainly a plea for cross-religious understanding.[39]

It is hard to imagine that the idealized conversations in this volume represent real debates between Muslims and Christians in Tunisia, but it is significant that Bourgade envisioned the role of women in general and Catholic nuns in particular, as both common and contested ground for religious dialogue. His stated goal of bringing Muslims closer to the Gospel, which informed all his work in Tunisia, included assimilating Muslims to European views of women's roles, which reflected the growing influence of domestic ideology. His belief in the universal applicability of Christianity was reconfigured in terms of new gender norms. Women, including Muslim women, could take the lead in bringing their families to religious truth. Although nuns like Vialar, as celibate women, stood outside the domestic model, in Bourgade's dialogues, they defended it vigorously. Simultaneously, in a seeming paradox, they represented women who left home and braved dangers to engage intellectually on equal terms with Muslim (if not Christian) men.

Bourgade's and Vialar's interest in dialogue, however, did not deter either one from engaging, as in Algeria, in the secret baptism of children in danger of dying. In 1842, Bourgade sent a list of 115 baptisms effected between 5 May and 18 December to Propaganda Fide, with the following note: "This enclosure must not be inserted in any public document." Sixty-eight of the children were Muslim, and the remainder Jewish; the total included fifty-five girls and sixty boys. All trace of their Muslim or Jewish origins was erased, as only their baptismal names were recorded, all proceeded by Saint or Sainte. The quality of the handwriting suggests that Bourgade did not compile the list himself; more likely it was the work of a Soeur de St-Joseph.[40] In 1856 Emilie de Vialar summarized sixteen years in Tunisia: "[T]he work par excellence is that which our sisters exercise with such success; I speak of the Baptism of Infidels at the moment of their death. This work must remain in the greatest secrecy because of the Arab Infidels and the Jews, whose confidence we would lose. It is a fact that a single sister baptized in one year more than 1,000 children in Tunis, and with the aid of her companions, she can surpass this number annually."[41] Sisters in establishments opened in other Tunisian cities also participated in these baptisms; the multitalented Soeur Joséphine Daffis in Sousse, for example, also baptized "several thousand" Jewish or Muslim children.[42] There is no hint in the records that these baptisms became public knowledge—presumably all of the children did indeed die—or otherwise threatened the sisters' work. As in Algeria, it was their work in health care, particularly home visits, that allowed them access to these children; by comparison, their educational work was limited largely to Christians and a few Jews.

Vialar's close collaboration with Bourgade in Tunisia occasionally landed her in the crossfire of local church politics. The shared Catholic project of redefining North Africa as Roman and Catholic was crosscut by national rivalries that dated from the Old Regime. These rivalries only intensified as the European population grew in Tunisia. Because of Ottoman treaties that recognized the king of France as the protector of Latin missions in the Ottoman Empire, which, nominally at least, included Tunisia, French consuls were in charge of Catholic missionaries there, a role only intermittently recognized by Rome and often resented by missionaries of other nationalities, chiefly Italian.[43] France, for its part, sought to use this privilege as a way of increasing its influence in Tunisia, even though the French community was numerically much smaller than the Italian or the Maltese, whose interests were protected by Protestant Britain.

Early in the century, French Romantics like Chateaubriand rediscovered France's links to Carthage not only as ancient Christian territory but also as the site of the death of Louis IX (St. Louis) in 1270 during the eighth crusade.[44] In 1830, after the signing of a treaty between France and Tunisia, the bey ceded a piece of land on the ancient site for the construction of a religious monument in honor of Louis, and in 1840–41 King Louis-Philippe ordered the addition of a domed chapel designed in a Gothic style to honor his ancestor and namesake. Positioned at the top of a hill, on the presumed spot of the camp of St. Louis, it was easily visible from the surrounding countryside. Vialar and the Soeurs de St-Joseph attended its inauguration, resplendent with French military personnel and symbols, just as they had participated in the Mass on the ruins of Hippo when St. Augustine's relic was "returned" to Algeria. In 1842, at Vialar's recommendation, Abbé Bourgade was appointed its chaplain.[45] However, the Italian Capuchin order quickly complained to Rome that this appointment meant that it would lose the ecclesiastical business—baptisms, marriages, and funerals—of French citizens in Tunis.[46]

Beyond national rivalries, Bourgade's liberal Catholicism and his confidence in interfaith dialogue sat uneasily with the rest of the clerical establishment in Tunis. When the Holy See upgraded Tunis to an apostolic vicariate in 1843, it appointed an Italian Capuchin, Mgr Fedèle Sutter, who quickly clashed with Bourgade over authority and finances. They also disagreed on dialogue with Muslims (though they agreed on the necessity of *in extremis* baptism), Sutter viewing them as mere infidels, whose conversion was impossible for political reasons, while Bourgade sought connections between Islam and Christianity.[47] Sutter also criticized his administration of the Collège St-Louis, whose funds, he charged, Bourgade mismanaged and whose students he neglected because he was "always absorbed in his meditations of Carthage." Furthermore, educating young Catholics with Jews, who themselves had close contacts with Muslims, "from whom they learn oriental vices," was dangerous to their purity.[48]

Vialar also received a letter from Sutter's chancellor and Bourgade's enemy, Père Anselme d'Arcs, who reproached her for instructing children in a "Jewish house," which he claimed was forbidden by church law. These complaints resulted in Propaganda Fide withdrawing its funding from Bourgade's school in 1854 to support Sutter's new, homogenously Catholic school in Tunis, run by the Frères des Ecoles chrétiennes.[49] In 1856, the festering situation came to a head, and Vialar complained that Anselme d'Arcs had sought to "trouble the conscience" of several Soeurs de St-Joseph serving in Tunisia by telling them that the rules of the order (and subsequently their vows) were not valid and by starting a rumor that other nuns were arriving to replace them.[50] Reminiscent of her troubles in Algeria, Vialar responded in characteristic fashion by contacting the French foreign minister, who wrote to the consul in Tunis and to the ambassador to the Holy See in Rome; she herself wrote to Cardinal Ferretti, claiming that "the Reverend Father Anselme includes us in his antipathy against Monsieur l'Abbé Bourgade." The "systematic hostility" ceased at least overtly after the French consul wrote that the apostolic vicar should have no doubt as to "the effective protection that the French government would give to the order of St. Joseph" if it was again persecuted.[51] In 1852 and 1855 Vialar collaborated with the Capuchins in opening houses in Sfax and La Goulette, where the Catholics expanded their services to the growing European communities. Two years after Vialar's death, however, in 1858, Bourgade's papal authorization was revoked, and he departed from Tunis, leaving the administration of the Collège St-Louis to his Jewish partner, Pompeo Sulema.[52]

For forty years the Soeurs de St-Joseph were the only female missionaries in Tunisia until the French established their protectorate in 1880. Indeed, Tunisia provided unusual freedom for Vialar and her sisters to build a missionary infrastructure of hospitals, clinics, and schools, which served a wide swath of the local population, both settler and native, from the daughters of consuls to Tunisian elites to poor southern European migrants to indigenous Arabs. As in Algeria, the key to their success was their focus on good works and their discretion in proselytizing. However, unlike in Algeria, the lines of clerical authority were blurred by missionary rivalries and overlapping spheres of influence, which allowed a maverick priest like Bourgade and an independent woman like Vialar room to maneuver. No jealous bishop was able to appropriate Vialar's work and push her out. She also had the support of the civil authority in the person of Ahmad Bey, who saw opportunities for consolidating his power and stabilizing his state in the work of a group of

Catholic nuns. Vialar, here as elsewhere, showed an enormous talent for networking among both the European and the Tunisian elites. For the rest of her life—and beyond—Tunisia would remain one of the centers of missionary activity that demonstrated the ability of the Soeurs de St-Joseph not only to survive but also to flourish in a Muslim land.

The Maltese Connection

In 1845, during one of her frequent trips across the Mediterranean, Vialar made an unexpected stop on the island of Malta, where her ship from Tunis to Rome had been blown off course. The detour proved providential. Scattered references in her letters suggest that Vialar had already contemplated establishing a mission in Malta, but she did not take any serious steps until she found herself marooned there in the summer of 1845. Ill and exhausted from the aftereffects of the Algerian expulsion, the hard work of setting up shop in Tunis, and financial problems in Gaillac, Vialar spent eight months recovering her health. Shortly before she left, she wrote her aunt enthusiastically, "[Y]ou have no idea of the beauty of the climate of this island. Since the end of the summer, it is like the most beautiful month of May in the south of France, no rain, even less cold."[53] But as home to a devout Catholic population now under British rule, Malta provided advantages beyond its temperate climate. By mid-July Vialar had opened a French-style boarding school in a large house donated by a wealthy supporter and situated by the sea. Within its first nine days it enrolled seventeen boarders, including the daughters of the consul of Tripoli, the daughter of a British government official, the nieces of the island's principal banker, and the daughters of two prominent British doctors. Heads turned, according to Soeur Emilie Julien, when the girls, uniformed in white dresses with blue sashes and blue hat ribbons, entered the local church for the first time, and the priest recommended the school to the congregation.[54] This elite—and well-dressed—clientele ensured the financial success of the enterprise as well; Vialar estimated that the receipts from the boarding school would rise to ten or twelve thousand francs in a short time. Food and clothing were cheaper than in Gaillac. The boarding school offered classes in Italian, French, and English, and Vialar's not-so-secret goal was to "ward off" the establishment of a Sacred Heart academy, which would have competed for pupils. In the capital city of Valletta, Vialar opened a day school, which had enrolled over one hundred pupils by late August, some of them "the richest of the island."[55] The school also provided separate classes for poorer girls. Within a few months, the Sacred Heart sisters had decided not to come, Vialar's health was noticeably better, and she noted that "my Sisters work hard, but at least their work is accompanied by a remuneration that will put us at ease."[56]

Judging from their rapid popularity, the schools established by the Soeurs de St-Joseph in Malta filled a growing need among Maltese Catholics. Until 1798, Malta had been governed by the Knights of St. John, who provided public charitable services from health care to education.[57] Their defeat by Napoleon, who suppressed convents and expelled foreign priests, and the subsequent transfer of Malta to British rule left a charitable vacuum. The Catholic establishment was especially concerned with not allowing British Protestants to fill this gap, even though the British authorities scrupulously respected the role of Catholicism on the island in order to garner the loyalty of its inhabitants.[58] Nonetheless, Catholic clerics, who were trying to extract additional funds from Propagation de la Foi, pointed in alarm to the "enormous sums" spent by Protestants, as well as the support of "a Protestant government, with a Protestant bishop, numerous and always growing Protestant clergy." The Soeurs de St-Joseph in particular were essential because they "diverted Catholic girls from Protestant schools that they attended in great peril to their faith" and enrolled Protestant pupils, who received a Catholic education. Catholicism in Malta also held the potential to contribute to Catholic missions throughout the Mediterranean.[59] Indeed, in 1815, the evangelical Protestant Church Missionary Society had opened a Mediterranean center of operations in Malta, which distributed Bibles and Christian tracts in the languages of the Ottoman Empire.[60] Malta could become, its clerics believed, a rival "center of Catholic action" and a "nursery of missionaries" due to the enterprising nature of its inhabitants. In fact, despite the exaggerated fears of Catholic prelates in Malta, the church became stronger during the period of British rule.[61]

Vialar herself noted on arrival that "in a country eminently Catholic, uncloistered sisters are a true necessity for instruction as well as charity."[62] However, she was equally quick to grasp that the "eminently Catholic" country also produced religious vocations that allowed for rapid expansion not only in Malta itself but also throughout the mission territory of the Soeurs de St-Joseph. As quickly as their schools gained pupils, the Soeurs de St-Joseph also attracted new novices. By late July, they had already enrolled five potential members "capable of helping us with the classes, and without the help of two of them from very good English families, it would have been impossible to do our work, at least without taking on an English teacher, who would have cost us 1,200 francs per year."[63] Maltese sisters brought in money and valuable skills to the order. "We find here," Vialar wrote enthusiastically in August 1845, "a very large number of individuals called to the religious life, well skilled in needlework, speaking for the most part several languages, and of such a great piety that, at this moment, our house, composed of a majority of postulants, resembles a religious house that has existed for many years."[64] As might be expected, the flourishing schools themselves provided numerous recruits.

Nonetheless, the Maltese establishments turned out to be more than simply self-perpetuating houses. From the very beginning, Vialar saw the potential of the sisters recruited in the "brilliant pensionnat" to staff missions abroad.[65] Maltese sisters were placed in North Africa and, beginning in 1846, in Greece and the Middle East. Besides their availability and their piety, their language abilities made them valuable. The native language in Malta was a Semitic language that facilitated the acquisition of Arabic, and most of the sisters also spoke or learned Italian, French, and English. When Soeur Emilie Julien arrived in Beirut in 1847, she wrote to Vialar that the Maltese sisters "are perfectly able to make themselves understood by the natives."[66] Vialar sent Maltese sisters all over the Mediterranean, and Malta itself, located strategically between its western and eastern halves, became an informal administrative center for the congregation, where Vialar also brought French sisters on their way to more distant missions and those needing the recuperative benefits of Malta's climate and sea air. "I am happy to find myself in Malta," Vialar wrote in December 1845. "[F]rom this center I can organize the foreign houses." A year later, after a five-week stay in Rome, she spent ten days in Malta, where she brought all of the French sisters "who were without work and at my charge in Gaillac.... In the space of twenty days, I had distributed them all in the various missions founded by the bishops in Syria, Beirut, the island of Chios, and the island of Cephalonia, and finally in Indochina, at Moulmein." She herself traveled on to Athens and then established a mission at Siros before returning to Malta.[67] From 1854 to 1856 the Soeurs de St-Joseph opened and operated a hospital for soldiers recuperating from the Crimean War, which also served the purpose of training the sisters in nursing and pharmacy.[68]

The diaspora of Maltese Soeurs de St-Joseph around the Mediterranean basin reflected the more general patterns of Maltese emigration in the nineteenth century. With one of the highest population densities in Europe, as well as internal crises ranging from epidemics to economic downturn to drought, Malta had a high level of outmigration, resulting in almost 15 percent of the Maltese population living abroad in the mid-nineteenth century. Due to proximity, established trading routes, and the availability of inexpensive transport, their favored destination was North Africa, particularly Algeria and Tunisia, with smaller numbers in the eastern Mediterranean.[69] In Tunisia alone they formed 60 percent of the European population. For those same reasons, the return migration rates were also high. Maltese migrants moved back and forth between their small islands and the North African coast as work opportunities and economic need dictated. Unlike the highly trained sisters, most of the emigrants were poor, unskilled, and illiterate and were characterized as "Christian Arabs" or "African" because of the Semitic language they spoke, the darker color of their skin, and their dress.[70] These attributes allowed for better integration with the indigenous Tunisian population, although the elite Europeans saw them as socially undesirable. In Tunisia, they were among the patients and pupils of the Soeurs de St-Joseph, as they would be in later missions around the Mediterranean. In 1854, for example, Vialar informed the Abbé

Bourgade that she was sending a Maltese sister to teach a special class for Maltese girls in Sfax. The largest group of Catholics in Athens, where the Soeurs de St-Joseph established a house in 1856, was also Maltese.[71] Yet the Maltese not only were devout Catholics but also benefited from British consular protection wherever they settled. More than other migrants from southern Europe, they served as intermediaries between European and North African culture.

At the same time, the Soeurs de St-Joseph were themselves part of the midcentury migratory wave, as Vialar moved members around the Mediterranean—from France, Italy, and Malta to Algeria, then Tunisia, and points east. Most sisters continued to be recruited in France, where the Soeurs de St-Joseph had several houses in the region around Gaillac. In 1853, however, to increase recruitment possibilities, Vialar agreed to the opening of a house at Trémorel in distant Brittany, a province known for its Catholic piety. The foundation was successful enough to warrant the opening of a novitiate there shortly thereafter, and Breton nuns joined those from the southwest in staffing missions abroad. Between 1842 and 1853 she also opened three houses in Italy, the first one in Rome, precipitated by her long stay during the Dupuch crisis. In 1844 the Soeurs de St-Joseph were asked by the government of Tuscany to work in the woman's prison at San Gimignano (later transferred to Amborgiana), and in 1853 Vialar founded a new establishment in Tolfa, in the mountains northwest of Rome, where Roman sisters could escape the city without long voyages. Vialar established these Italian houses not only with an eye toward politics—close to the protection of the Holy See, on which "all her future depended"—but also because recruiting Italian sisters added value, especially language skills, to her overall missionary enterprise. "The congregation made great sacrifices for the Rome house," an early chronicler wrote, "but it is indispensable to our dear Missions."[72] As uncloistered sisters on the French model, the Soeurs de St-Joseph could provide services that cloistered Italian nuns could not.

The houses Vialar established in Tunisia and Malta were essential links in her missionary enterprise because they served as intermediate stops and training stations. French and Italian sisters were likely to spend time in Malta or Tunisia before being sent to more distant missions. Almost every letter Vialar exchanged with Abbé Bourgade after she left Tunis contained details of personnel movements similar to the following: "I am sending to Sousse an excellent Italian teacher, Soeur Caroline; she writes very well, knows Arabic. If her health improves, she would do well for Tunis, well brought up, speaking French and reading it, skillful in needlework." Seven years later, the same sister returned to France for three months of pharmacy training and was then placed in Tolfa, Italy.[73] In 1854, at the request of the French consul in Tripoli, who had previously served in Tunis, she sent two sisters from Tunisia to open two paying classes in a rented house, one for French-speaking girls, the other for Italian speakers, as well as a free school to serve the largely Maltese

Catholic population.[74] As nuns were transferred from Tunisia or Malta to Tripoli or the Middle East, others were sent to take their place, which resulted in a stable community in Tunisia of about ten to twelve sisters until Vialar's death in 1856.[75] Pierre Soumille has calculated that 100 Soeurs de St-Joseph passed through Tunisia between 1840 and 1900, of whom 61 were French (34 from the southwest or the Massif Central, 21 from Brittany, and 6 from other regions), 21 Italian, 6 Maltese, 2 born in Tunisia of Maltese parents, and the remaining 6 from missions in Tripoli, Syria, and Greece.[76] As the nineteenth-century equivalent of a modern CEO, Vialar spent a great deal of her time and energy on the placement of sisters throughout her growing missionary empire, and in this enterprise Tunis occupied a special place: "I take care of Tunis as the apple of my eye because the infidel countries are those which occupy my attention. A young lady has joined us, provisionally, a perfect subject, 27 years old, rather well off and in control of her fortune, skillful in needle-work, especially in embroidery, knowing flower arrangement, intelligent [*bonne tête*], well behaved; I intend her for Tunis."[77]

The multinational character of the sisters serving in Tunisia, however, was sub-ordinate to Vialar's vision for her order. In 1845 she replaced the superior in Tunis because "she walked a false road that resulted in making the Tunis establishment foreign to the spirit of the Congregation, *a purely Italian establishment* [emphasis hers]. I have called from Tuscany a Sister who will do much better than she in Tunis."[78] Soeurs de St-Joseph were first and foremost part of a religious order and only secondarily members of national states, as Vialar was quick to remind them. The multinational character of the order made them especially effective in serving the mixed European communities around the Mediterranean and allowed them access to states not yet under European domination. Small in numbers compared to ordinary migrants, these nuns also served as cultural intermediaries between Europe and Africa, as well as between European elites and poor European migrants. As single women, however, they broke with the usual migratory pattern of single men and families. As active nuns, they spread a new religious model of uncloistered sisters dedicated to good works that Frenchwomen pioneered but that proved popular among individuals of other nationalities as well.

Problems at Home

In 1840, when the rules of the Soeurs de St-Joseph were rewritten, the congregation defined itself primarily as a missionary one: "The particular spirit of this congrega-tion is to exercise works of charity in infidel countries."[79] Although the sisters provided the usual array of charitable services—schools, pharmacies, soup kitchens—in their French communities, as they did abroad, the main purpose of the French houses was to provide sisters for foreign missions. Vialar could ill afford to ignore the health of her establishments and novitiates in France, which provided the majority of recruits and funding for her congregation, and she traveled constantly, not just to Gaillac but also to see to her order's interests in Paris and Rome. Nonetheless, the period following the expulsion from Algeria was personally and professionally difficult. Within four years, she lost three important individuals in her life: first, Mgr de Gualy, the steadfast archbishop of Albi, who died in 1842; then, in 1845, the Gaillac curé, Abbé Mercier, who had helped her found the congregation; and finally, her father, now reconciled to his daughter's vocation, who died in 1846. The new archbishop and the local priest were less supportive than their predecessors. From Tunis, "on the advice of her confessor" (that is, Bourgade), Vialar composed an account of her spiritual awakening and vocation because "letters from France informed me that some people were spreading the rumor to the new Archbishop of Albi that I was a woman who loved traveling around and who was wasting her time and her fortune."[80]

The fortune was being wasted, however, by three individuals in whom she had put her trust: Soeur Pauline Gineste, superior in Gaillac (and one of the original four members of the congregation), the new chaplain there, and a local businessman charged with handling the congregation's temporal affairs. When she returned to Gaillac in 1846 to nurse her father through his final illness, Vialar discovered that Gineste had run up huge debts. This financial scandal caused long legal complications, a split with Gineste, and the departure of eleven sisters from the congregation; it also set tongues wagging—again—in Gaillac, where some of the debt was held by friends and acquaintances. More seriously, it left Vialar in dire financial straits. Vialar had expanded in Algeria with little concern for a more uncertain financial future. By 1840, she found herself borrowing money in Algeria and France to expand the Algerian establishments, loans that became difficult to pay back once the government confiscated her houses after the dispute with Dupuch. The houses in Tunisia and Malta became self-supporting, but the discovery of new debt in Gaillac dealt a heavy financial blow. Vialar immediately reduced the personnel in Gaillac to four sisters and three postulants, just enough to keep up the charity works there, and sent the others overseas. Despite five years of litigation in the Toulouse courts, she never recovered her money, and the bulk of her father's inheritance went to paying off debt.[81] Vialar's personal fortune was gone, and for the rest of her life, she worried continually about income and expenses, adding chief financial officer to her duties.

In early 1847, unable to tolerate the bad feeling in Gaillac and the lack of support from the archbishop of Albi, Vialar moved the *maison mère* to Toulouse, where she set about establishing a school and a novitiate. But starting over in Toulouse proved difficult. Still beset with financial problems—for a while Tunis was supporting Toulouse—she lost a large part of her paying clientele following the revolutions of 1848, when upper-class parents withdrew their daughters to cloister them safely in the countryside. She also felt herself surrounded by detractors, both clerical and lay, as gossip from home followed her thirty-five miles west to Toulouse. "My enemies in Gaillac," she wrote to Bourgade, "like starving wolves seek to fleece me to annihilation.... They write ceaselessly, letter upon letter, to our Superior." Perhaps because of these letters, she did not get along with her new chaplain, whom she described as "making me suffer for eight months true moral tortures" as a result of her refusing to acquiesce to his government of her order. He, she charged, saw her sisters as mere "daughters of the parish, like the Sisters of Charity," rather than the vanguard of a multinational organization. Her letters to Bourgade took on the tones of a martyr: "My various enemies fight me to the death on moral questions; they agitate in all directions as if their prey was going to escape them."[82]

Finally, in 1852, Vialar decided that Toulouse could not provide her with the necessary clerical support, financial means, or new novices that her congregation required and moved the *maison mère* once again, this time to Marseilles. Although much farther away from her Languedoc roots, this port city had great advantages. The local bishop, Mgr de Mazenod, was friendly and supportive. "I am with him as with Mgr de Gualy, archbishop of Albi," Vialar wrote in relief.[83] Their compatibility stemmed in part from a shared interest in missionary activities, as Mazenod was the founder of the "Pères Oblats" (Missionnaires Oblats de Marie Immaculée), a missionary congregation founded in 1826 that had sent priests to British Columbia, Ceylon, and Natal. To Mazenod, the Soeurs de St-Joseph served as a female complement to his society, and he proposed dispatching them to locations where he had already placed male missionaries. However, he also did not interfere in the internal workings of Vialar's congregation, which kept their relationship stable.

Since most of the Soeurs de St-Joseph traveling abroad embarked or disembarked in Marseilles, having the motherhouse there also saved time and money. Most important, in Marseilles, Vialar found it easy to recruit new sisters and pupils wealthy enough to bankroll the cost of the novitiate, the poor classes, and the medical facilities she opened. She distributed one thousand copies of the school's prospectus but also relied on local word-of-mouth networks from influential individuals who had benefited from the sisters' care. In 1854 she reported enthusiastically that she had found "a rich demoiselle who will give at her entry [into the congregation] enough to buy the house that we occupy."[84] Dowries now had to make up for the lost fortune, and Vialar rejected a candidate in 1854 because she could not "maintain the postulants and novices without a pension." At the same time, however, she refused another individual "because we need as much intelligence as possible" for foreign missions; weaker candidates could enter purely French congregations.[85]

During this period, Vialar was also preoccupied with the formal authorization of her congregation. Having failed to obtain papal authorization in 1842, she renewed her attempt to get authorization from the French government, the lack of which had played a critical role in her expulsion from Algeria. Since Vialar had not founded her religious order before 1825, she needed a specific law of authorization by the French legislature (previously authorization took only a royal decree). Throughout 1843 Vialar collected testimonials to her work in France and abroad and traveled to Paris to lobby for this authorization. Despite friends in high places—she was joined in the capital by the French ambassador to the Holy See—she failed to obtain it, which was not uncommon for religious orders under the July Monarchy. Although her order continued its work as before and continued to expand, lack of authorization gave her less flexibility in acquiring property, which had to be held in the names of individual sisters rather than the order as a corporate entity. Legal authorization would also strengthen her hand against recalcitrant clerics, allow her (after 1850) to place sisters in French schools without a teaching credential (the *brevet*), and ensure that the order would continue after her death.

In the 1850s, Vialar took up the cause again, this time under the more religiously sympathetic Second Empire. One sticking point was agreement on the statutes, finally resolved by having the Soeurs de St-Joseph de l'Apparition adopt the already authorized statutes of the Soeurs de St-Joseph de Cluny, the missionary order founded by Anne-Marie Javouhey, because of the two orders' similarity in mission and structure. "There is only the Congregation of the Soeurs de St Joseph de Cluny," wrote Vialar, "that is composed like mine, that is, governed by a Supérieure Générale under the jurisdiction of Bishops, and that goes formally abroad." Vialar wrote to Javouhey to request a copy of her statutes and was pleased to find that they were short and similar to her own. Using these, the Soeurs de St-Joseph de l'Apparition were recognized as a legal religious order by imperial decree on 17 October 1855, but Vialar wrote to Soeur Françoise Pezet that "the current statutes will not change in any way."[86] Their relationship with Rome and with diocesan bishops also remained in place. In 1862, six years after Vialar's death, a new set of statutes also specified that the superior general of the congregation was dependent on the Congregation of Bishops and Regulars in Rome, to which regular reports should be sent, although "the houses of the Soeurs de S. Joseph rest under the jurisdiction of the respective Bishops.... No house will be founded in a diocese without the agreement of the Bishop, whose desires relative to the placement and movement of subjects we will also try to satisfy."[87] The fracas in Algeria, or even the lesser problems with the archbishops of Albi or Toulouse, never repeated themselves.

During both the aftermath of the Algerian conflict and expulsion and the troubles at home in France, Vialar's ability to build her religious order depended largely on the institutions she developed in Tunisia and Malta. Tunisia was a Muslim-majority kingdom with a sympathetic indigenous leader; Malta was a devoutly Catholic island under the control of a rival European power. They were linked by the continuous back-and-forth migration of the Maltese, who could be found in cities all around the Mediterranean, particularly in North Africa and the Middle East, becoming clients almost everywhere the Soeurs de St-Joseph settled. In Malta they provided new recruits and important financial resources. Equally important, however, was the patronage of the Tunisian bey, who saw Vialar's mission as providing important new services that could perhaps stave off European control of his state. With his support and in the absence of strong Catholic authority in the form of a bishop, Vialar's works flourished, providing her with the institutional basis to expand farther east into more complex regions of the Ottoman Empire.

6

Expansion in the Ottoman Empire

Even while the French houses were in crisis, Vialar continued to found foreign missions. As a woman with an established network of contacts and a track record in missionary work, she received various proposals; part of her job as superior general consisted of weighing and responding to these offers for the overall good of the congregation. When she opened the Italian houses, Vialar guessed—incorrectly, as it turned out—that they might "open the doors" of "all the little Italian states, then that of Sardinia and the Austrian states."[1] But she was alert to new possibilities, most of which came from clerics stationed in mission territory—anyone from a bishop to a parish priest—who knew her personally or by reputation. Requests also came from the foreign, especially French, consuls, who were transferred from post to post, as in the case of a new foundation in Tripoli, but pure happenstance could also be a factor. In 1846, in Malta, Vialar met a brother of the Oblats de Marie of Turin, who also ran a mission in Moulmein, Burma. Their superior general requested six to eight nuns who could teach and nurse, including some who could do so in English. Vialar sent six sisters, mostly Maltese, in 1846.[2] Eight years later, when the bishop of Perth requested Soeurs de St-Joseph to educate young Catholic girls in Fremantle, Vialar sent four French sisters, the superior a mere twenty-five years old, who studied English from grammar books on the long sea voyage.[3]

Most of all, though, by the mid-1840s the Soeurs de St-Joseph were recognized as having a certain expertise with populations in the Mediterranean basin, and their largest missionary expansion came in the Ottoman Empire, beginning in Larnaca, Cyprus, in 1844. In these places they leveraged the experience they had gained in Algeria and Tunisia in an even more complicated political and religious environment. Although often neglected by historians more interested in formal French colonies, France's interests in the Ottoman Empire in the mid-nineteenth century were extensive. After about 1840, French commercial ties, political interests, and missionary expansion in the Middle Eastern territories of the Ottoman Empire increased. For much of the century, France's cultural policy in the Middle East was largely sustained through the work of Catholic missionaries, who were supported by lay Catholics back home. Missionaries, government officials felt, were especially effective in promoting the French language through schooling.[4] Catholics, for their part, saw the Middle East as potential ground for evangelization, at least among the Christian communities, both indigenous and foreign. Women missionaries who could not only open schools but also provide charity and health care were key to this new strategy, pioneered by the Filles de la Charité, who arrived in Constantinople in 1839 and quickly established themselves in the main cities of the Ottoman Empire.[5] Five years later, the Soeurs de St-Joseph followed, first to Greece, newly independent, and then to the Ottoman Empire proper, from the Greek isles to Lebanon, Jerusalem, and Armenia. In all of these places, their interests and those of the French state both coincided and competed in ways more complex than in previous mission sites.

Proselytizing among "Schismatics"

In 1846, Vialar traveled to Athens where she was hosted by the Sardinian consul and his wife, old acquaintances from Algeria, who accompanied her to the island of Siros in the Aegean Sea, where the bishop had requested four sisters to establish schools for girls. Here Vialar also found another clerical kindred spirit in the person of Pierre Privilegio, the parish priest of the church of St-Sébastien. Like Abbé Bourgade in Tunisia, he became an important, if more intermittent, correspondent and spiritual guide in the years that followed, especially as her troubles in France mounted. Remembering "the encouragements that I received from you during my short stay [on Siros]," she apologized in 1852, "I see you, despite my apparent negligence in writing, as the most constant friend of my feeble person."[6] Three more Greek missions followed: on the island of Chios, just off the Turkish coast, in 1848; in Canea, Crete, in 1852; and in Athens in 1856. Vialar did not visit these—indeed, Siros would be the farthest east she would ever travel—but from France she oversaw their foundations and placed appropriate sisters. The expansion of her order was a complex administrative task that showcased her considerable managerial skills, honed through previous successes—and failures. It is impossible to consider her life in these later years as distinct from the institution she had built and continued to guide.

The Catholic missionary effort in Greece was spurred by a number of factors, both religious and political. The Greek war of independence from the Ottoman Empire had renewed Western European interest in Greece, both as an object of Romantic imaginings and as a diplomatic prize in the Balkans. In France, the image of Greece was shaped by Chateaubriand's *Itinéraire de Paris à Jérusalem* (1811), which portrayed the Greeks as slaves among the ruins of their ancient civilization, overseen by oppressive Turks. In the second edition, Chateaubriand included a special "Note sur la Grèce" (1825), which accused French Christians of neglect in having "abandoned to all their sorrows four million Christians," "your Greek Orthodox brothers," who are "forced to embrace Islam."[7] A year earlier at the Salon de 1824, the Romantic painter Delacroix had exhibited the painting *Scènes des massacres de Scio*, which portrayed the Turkish massacre of the Greek inhabitants of Chios in 1822, one of the most notorious episodes of the war of Greek liberation. The painting inflamed public opinion in France, and Louis XVIII bought it for the national collection at the Louvre. Through the interpretive frame provided by writers and artists like Chateaubriand and Delacroix, many French viewed the Greek war of independence against the Ottoman Empire as the liberation movement of an oppressed Christian people against an infidel enemy. When Greece finally gained its independence in 1832, after an eleven-year war, many Europeans interpreted it not only as a recovery of the roots of their own civilization but also as a besieged Christian outpost in hostile Turkish waters. France, Britain, and Russia were also fierce diplomatic rivals for influence and power in the region, as the "Eastern question" moved to the forefront of European affairs. Since Britain had been instrumental in the peace process and gained control over the Ionian islands, France had an interest in a strong and independent Greek nation, supporting (unsuccessfully), for example, the transfer of Crete to Greek hands. In 1846, the French also opened the Ecole française d'Athènes on the model of the successful Ecole française de Rome in order to best the British in cultural influence.[8]

In this context, Catholic missionaries could also work to recover Greece for the West, and French missionaries in particular could extend French influence and culture. Although the Greeks were popularly viewed as lost Christian brothers, they were, from the viewpoint of the Catholic church, also "schismatics" who had strayed from the true faith almost a thousand years earlier to found the Orthodox church. In fact, Catholic evangelization in the new Greece, whether independent or still under Ottoman control, was, as elsewhere in the Mediterranean world, difficult. Greek identity had long been defined by allegiance to the Greek Orthodox church, which in turn supported the fight for independence, producing martyrs in slain priests, monks, and bishops. During the war, Catholics often distanced themselves from the rebels, increasing tensions between the two churches. The Greek constitution of 1844 made the Greek Orthodox church the official state religion and outlawed proselytization by other religious faiths. Despite this apparent ascendency, however, the Greek Orthodox church found itself on the defensive in the new state. Church powers were severely curtailed by the new secular constitution, which, similar to the French concordat of 1801, allowed the state to appoint bishops and priests, pay salaries, and administer church property. Immediately after independence, the Greek government had closed two-thirds of the new nation's monasteries and convents and seized their assets in order to fund a new system of state schools.[9]

In this atmosphere, Catholic missionary initiatives were badly received. In Athens, the Greek government closed the school of the Soeurs de St-Joseph for three years after an Orthodox woman converted to Catholicism in their chapel. When it reopened, they were allowed to enroll only Catholic girls, turning away almost two hundred Greek Orthodox applicants.[10] Since the Catholic population of Athens numbered only about one thousand, this prohibition limited their potential clientele and, with it, their income and impact.

Given these realities on the ground, Vialar was most successful on the Aegean island of Siros, which was the strongest bastion of Latin Christianity in Greece, home to a significant Catholic population since the Fourth Crusade in the thirteenth century. In 1700, the island counted more than six thousand Catholics and 61 regular and secular clergy; the Orthodox population numbered only seven families and one priest.[11] During the Greek war of independence, the Catholic residents of Siros remained neutral, preferring to remain under the known protection of the Ottoman Empire rather than throw their lot in with Greek Orthodox compatriots. The war brought numerous refugees, however, especially after the massacres on Chios, followed by fifteen hundred Greek soldiers, which altered the political and religious status quo. The treaty that ended the war assigned all of the Aegean islands except Chios to Greece, resulting in a complaint from the residents of the island of Siros that they would be forced "to change our religion in order to live with people so intolerant."[12]

Siros, however, flourished as an important Greek trading center during the mid-nineteenth century, and new migrants increased the Catholic population. Out of the approximately eight thousand Catholics within the borders of the new Greek state, five thousand lived on Siros. When Vialar traveled there in 1846, she established a small boarding school, as well as a large free school that enrolled approximately 150 girls. The Soeurs de St-Joseph were aided by two Catholic lay assistants who taught the Greek language. As late as 1855, no equivalent school existed for boys, who attended Greek Orthodox schools.[13] Local clergy also worried about the influence of Protestants on the island, and Vialar considered it something of a coup when she recruited the two converted daughters of a Protestant minister to the Soeurs de St-Joseph. "The subjects are worth more than their dowry," she wrote enthusiastically to Abbé Privilegio, agreeing with him that, with their language skills, including Greek, they could be sent to open a house in Athens.[14]

In Chios, Crete, and Cyprus, by contrast, the Soeurs de St-Joseph worked among a majority Greek population still under Ottoman control. The independent Greek state contained only about a quarter of all Greeks; most of the remainder lived in the Ottoman Empire.[15] During the Greek war of independence, Greeks on Cyprus and Chios rebelled in favor of joining a united Greece, resulting in violent repression, including the massacres in Chios immortalized in the Delacroix painting. The rebuilding of Catholic institutions on these islands, as well as on Crete, where the Greek Catholic population was small, began in earnest in the 1840s. The chief missionary on the island of Cyprus was Abbé Brunoni, a native son, sent by Rome in 1830 and who later became archbishop of Constantinople. An active cleric, he quickly reestablished three Catholic churches and a chapel and worked with the French consul to return the Maronites on the island and their churches to Catholic oversight after three centuries "under the arbitrary jurisdiction of the Greek bishops." In 1843, on the recommendation of officials at Propagation de la Foi, he met Emilie de Vialar in France. She sent four sisters to Larnaca the following year to open a school and health facilities. Reflecting the new clerical preference for women missionaries over men, these sisters, he thought, would be more effective than priests in "uprooting through education certain erroneous beliefs" among the Catholic population, who, he lamented, had become indifferent to their religion due to the freedom accorded on the island to all faiths and "the social relations that exist between their members."[16] Upon arrival, the sisters immediately began their nursing duties, quickly attracting a clientele from neighboring villages. Within two months, Brunoni reported they had treated five hundred patients of all nationalities and faiths and had opened a small hospital.

Vialar also drew up a prospectus for a school that shows that the educational project here was ambitious and inclusive. The prospectus emphasized that children of all social levels and ethnic and religious backgrounds were allowed to enroll. Translated into Greek and Italian, Brunoni circulated it widely, including among Orthodox Greek families, because, in his words, "the main objective is Charity without distinction of religion."[17] When the school opened in January 1845, it was immediately overenrolled at ninety-one pupils, including the daughters of the French consul. Although a girls' school, the sisters also accepted boys under the age of eight due to the "current needs of the country." Pupils who had paid three francs per month in tuition, however, were educated in a separate class from those who had paid nothing. Non-Catholics were allowed to arrive at school a half hour later than Catholic girls in order to skip the morning Mass, and the school curriculum did not list catechism or Bible history among its subjects.[18]

At the beginning of 1846 an enrollment census listed thirty-nine girls and six-teen boys, ranging in age from one to fourteen. Eighteen of the girls and three of the boys were paying pupils, including two boarders, and the rest attended free of charge. The fathers' professions encompassed a wide range of socioeconomic levels, including consular officials, a doctor, a professor of classical Greek, merchants and tradesmen, a silk worker, a tailor, and a fisherman; the last names were of Italian, Slavic, and Greek origin. The school provided instruction in Greek to poor children and "a complete education in French to boarders and day pupils of the wealthy class."[19] The curriculum was divided into two parts: domestic instruction, including cooking, embroidery, mending, and other needlework, and "intellectual" instruction, including reading, writing, arithmetic, French, Italian, history, and geography.[20] Classes were held for four hours in the morning and three in the afternoon under continual supervision of at least one nun. Pupils were to be accompanied to and from school by a servant or family member and dress unostentatiously. By November of the same year, Brunoni was trumpeting the success of the school not just in terms of numbers of pupils but also in the improved "reserve and modesty" of the girls, as well as greater obedience toward their parents.[21]

Brunoni urged the opening of a boarding school, as well as the day classes, arguing that "a young girl living always under the supervision of the *braves soeurs* acquires an assuredly more careful education than those of the day pupils." These pupils from the "best families" would also pay more and start with some elementary knowledge.[22] In order to expand the school to accommodate boarders, plans pro-ceeded to build a larger establishment, which met with the usual fund-raising chal-lenges and some opposition from local Greeks and Turks, presumably threatened by the rapid expansion of Catholic institutions. Nonetheless, the first stone of a new convent was laid in 1846, and the building was completed and opened in 1848. The new establishment consisted of approximately twenty rooms, including a chapel, sacristy, dispensary, pharmacy, kitchen, and schoolroom, as well as living quarters for the nuns and for boarding pupils. The school flourished, reporting twenty-five boarders, fifteen half-boarders, and more than sixty day pupils in 1857, all super-vised and taught by four Soeurs de St-Joseph.[23] By providing various levels of edu-cation and supervision to different clienteles and promising religiously neutral instruction, Vialar had tapped into a market for girls' education that eclipsed the small Catholic population in Cyprus.

The establishment of the Soeurs de St-Joseph on Chios in 1848 and Crete in 1852 followed similar lines, though with fewer resources. In Chios, where the local Catholic population was 416 (to about 80,000 Orthodox and 1,650 Muslims), the local bishop wrote personally to Vialar after twenty-four Catholic fathers signed a petition requesting a school for their daughters. Vialar sent three French sisters and one Italian, two of them from Cyprus.[24] In Chania, Crete, the Soeurs de St-Joseph were invited by the Capuchin fathers, who donated a building. Vialar sent two sisters, but within two years the numbers of pupils justified the addition of two more. French, Italian, Maltese, German, Greek, and Jewish girls learned French, as well as needlework, music, and drawing.[25]

In both places however, funding remained a significant issue. Crete was expensive and Catholic families—unlike in Malta or Tunisia—poor. By 1855, due to the deaths of a number of Catholic benefactors who had helped subsidize their rent, the sisters had acquired a five-hundred-franc debt and needed a larger and more convenient house. The bishop of Chios wrote in alarm to Propagation de la Foi in Lyon that the local rumor was that the sisters were considering leaving the island because of lack of funds. The bishop himself scarcely lived in luxury, sharing a building with two other priests and a boys' school; his revenues barely maintained the cathedral, much less other diocesan expenses. Even in Athens the four Soeurs de St-Joseph whom Vialar had sent in 1856 lived initially in quarters they compared to a stable in Bethlehem, with only olives and fish to eat and ten francs in their pockets.[26] Although Vialar never closed a Greek house, the sisters' survival depended precariously on private charity and the fund-raising abilities of the local clerics.

Besides money, the most pressing problem was the contested position of the Catholic church in a majority Greek Orthodox community overseen by Ottoman Muslim authority. Although Vialar and her sisters had experience negotiating the boundaries of Islam, Judaism, and Catholicism, balancing another religious faith complicated their work. Unlike Algeria, Greece was not under French control; unlike Tunisia, they did not have the patronage of the ruler; unlike Malta, there was not a large, devout, Catholic population. Secrecy about certain activities became paramount. When the Soeurs de St-Joseph arrived in Chios, the bishop blessed the foundation of their new chapel, well hidden within the convent, and placed the first stone himself in great secrecy, as the Turks did not allow chapels to be built. The bishop complained to Turkish authorities that the Catholic population, despite being faithful subjects of the empire, were persecuted by the Greeks.[27] In Chania (Crete), where the Muslim population outnumbered the Orthodox and both vastly outnumbered Catholics, on the other hand, the Turkish governor, "seeing the great good done by the hospital and the school for girls," as the local Capuchin put it, donated a piece of land next to the church to expand these institutions. The governor presumably did not know about the "holy baptism, administered furtively by these good *Suore di San Giuseppe*." Fifteen years among the Turks, the Capuchin admitted, "has taught me that one sister of charity can do more good among them than one hundred of the most ardent [male] missionaries."[28] The Soeurs de St-Joseph who arrived in Cyprus in 1845 had traveled via Rome, where they received a plenary indulgence from the pope to baptize individuals at the point of death. They could use this tool more effectively, the report to Propagation de la Foi ingeniously argued, had they more funds to provide more alms to the Turks, which would get them into more homes.[29]

Intertwined with the question of religious influence was that of national patronage. French consuls in the region saw the establishment of French sisters above all as an opportunity to promote their national interests. "France," read one report from Athens, "is visibly the instrument which God is using to bring into the Fold our dissident brothers, and for the conversions of the infidels." In Crete, Catholic agents appealed to the French ambassador in Constantinople for help in rebuilding the Catholic church, where, finally, "the French flag was planted on the ruins of our old church," which was rebuilt with French money.[30] During the Crimean War, French soldiers stopped to provision in Chania, where a collection was taken up to build a hospital in which the Soeurs de St-Joseph could take care of the ill and wounded. In Chios, even a Spanish Capuchin made a nationalist appeal to the French Propagation de la Foi, arguing that funding a new "French" church would add "luster" to the French nation. The bishop of Siros and Athens complained about the "fatal future" of Catholicism because of increased Russian promotion of Orthodoxy after independence.[31]

Display of French-sponsored Catholicism, along with political support from French consuls, was one important tool the French could use to combat this trend. When they arrived in Cyprus, for example, the Soeurs de St-Joseph were welcomed with great official enthusiasm among the French and European community, as one of the sisters reported:

> The French consul, in full dress uniform, that is, with his decorations, top hat, etc., followed by all the foreign consuls and the city notables, came to find us in order to take us to the Mass, in great pomp; we had five officials in red robes and their lances, always in front, who dispersed the crowd that the bad weather had not kept from going out.... It is impossible to tell you how good the French consul and the other gentlemen are to us.... Wherever we pass, we are greeted with "Welcome! You are angels sent by Heaven!"[32]

Vialar herself wrote proudly about the Fête Dieu celebration at the Athens school: "For the first time one saw coming out of the house sixty young girls dressed in white and veiled, carrying a white banner embroidered by the Sisters with the image of the Holy Virgin; all the Greeks rushed to see this procession and were thrilled by it!" It received special compliments from the French and English consuls.[33] Clearly display was important to the sisters, as well as to French officials, as it provided a visible measure of their success and reinforced their belief that their religious symbols could be universally embraced.

The missions that Vialar established in Greece had the consolation of bringing Catholic institutions to a small Catholic population that had been neglected for centuries. At times, they also served a broader public of Greek Orthodox and Muslims in their clinics and schools. Without a powerful state patron, they were bolstered by the support of French diplomats, but they relied above all on a local network of clerics and elites. The sisters' activities both reinforced and undermined lines of religion, nationality, ethnicity, and class. In their schools they provided education—albeit a segregated one—to both rich and poor. If the Soeurs de St-Joseph offered upper-class girls the cachet of a French education, they also taught poorer children in Italian and Greek. Here, as elsewhere, they provided apparently religiously neutral good works that might bring respect for Catholicism in a region with a strong Christian tradition of its own. Under the façade of neutrality, however, they engaged in secret acts of evangelization, from building chapels to baptizing dying children.

To Jerusalem

In January 1847, Vialar sent her most trusted disciple, Soeur Emilie Julien, to open a house in Beirut, marking the entry of the Soeurs de St-Joseph into the Middle East. The school in Beirut, long sought by local Catholic officials, was, in fact, an easy distance from the sisters' mission in Larnaca, Cyprus, established three years earlier. Julien wrote back enthusiastically to Vialar that the house was "delicious"; the French consul general had welcomed them with a "patriotic amiability"; and that, although there were few paying pupils, the city could furnish two to three thousand poor children. "I hope," she concluded, "that when you come to Syria, you will be satisfied."[34] Enmeshed in her financial and religious problems at home, Vialar never did travel to Beirut, but from Toulouse and then Marseilles she orchestrated the expansion of her order into the Middle East. She was not alone. In the mid-nineteenth century, this region was a veritable hive of missionary and protoimperial activity as Catholics, Protestants, and Orthodox vied for increased influence and European nation-states scrambled to establish footholds in the weakening Ottoman Empire. As the head of a missionary order that recruited increasingly from outside France and saw itself as representing universal Catholicism, Vialar had to negotiate carefully between the shoals of church and state.

In Lebanon, the introduction of the Soeurs de St-Joseph was the beginning of renewed French influence in the region, one node in a web of interlinked private and public French institutions that continued for the rest of the century and foreshadowed the French mandate after World War I.[35] Since the seventeenth century, the French had seen themselves as the protectors of Maronite Christians, some two hundred thousand strong, who followed the authority of the pope. In the 1840s they helped defend the Maronites militarily and brokered a peace deal between Maronites and Druzes.[36] In gratitude the Maronite patriarch encouraged more French missionaries. At his death in 1845, the French consul in Beirut praised him for his close attachment to France and his "courageous and intelligent fight against the evangelicals."[37] The one hundred pupils enrolled in Beirut were Maronite Christians, described by the sisters as ignorant, yet docile and intelligent. The educational project here was clearly designed to assimilate these girls to French culture and standards of behavior. "I managed to get them not to speak Arabic," wrote a young novice, "and after two weeks, one could already read passably in French." Julien's assessment was harsher, calling them "veritable savages," a state that she blamed on the "little education that mothers give here to their children." Within a month, however, the girls had learned to obey the classroom rules, and "their little hands got used to European needlework." The school soon doubled as a sewing workshop, where the pupils mended clothes sent by "the good ladies of Beirut," many of whom came to admire "the progress of our dear children." Showing some interest in local conditions, however, Julien argued that learning to sew would give the girls a marketable skill.[38]

Within a few months of establishing this school, however, the Soeurs de St-Joseph were forced to turn it over to the Filles de la Charité, who had first been given permission to set up a mission in Beirut and who had powerful advocates in the form of their male partners, the Lazarists, long established in the region. Julien reported that they did not speak Arabic and were seen as government agents who ruled by "fear."[39] This kind of intracongregational rivalry was new to the Soeurs de St-Joseph, a rude introduction to the complicated religious and imperial politics of the Middle East. "I suppose," Julien wrote to Abbé Bourgade, "that you know that this is nothing but a political objective by France, which is looking to expand its influence by means of the Sisters of St-Vincent [Filles de la Charité] and the Lazarists."[40] Although we only have Julien's word for it, in this particular case the Soeurs de St-Joseph were apparently considered less French than their rivals. The arrival of the Filles de la Charité forced them to find another base of operations in Lebanon, preferably one that gave the two rival religious orders enough space. Planning to go to Zahle in the Beqaa valley, where there was a welcoming missionary priest, they stopped in Bikfaya, where the inhabitants appealed to them to stay. The religious devotion in Bikfaya soon captivated them. "How happy you would be, my dear Mother," Julien wrote to Vialar, "to see the faith that animates the Maronites of Bikfaya! Consider that the fathers and mothers confess every week and receive communion Fridays and Sundays; these good people seem to me to resemble the first faithful of the Church....I confess to you naively that I take an extreme pleasure in making our poor cook discuss the life of Jesus Christ or the

Holy Virgin or the Apostles; her responses enchant me and at the same time she teaches me Arabic." Within a month, they had seventy day pupils and four boarders, two of whom expressed a wish to become nuns. Bikfaya, in fact, held promise as a future novitiate, providing Arabic-speaking sisters for the order.[41] Vialar, however, had different plans for her Middle Eastern personnel: a new establishment in Jerusalem, a project that she had been working on since 1842. However, she kept this information secret until the last moment "because we have enemies so relentless against our work," a reference perhaps to the recent rivalry with the Filles de la Charité.[42] Finally, on 14 August 1848, at dawn, Emilie Julien and two other Soeurs de St-Joseph entered Jerusalem, the first Catholic community of nuns to arrive in the city in the modern era.

In accepting an invitation to establish a mission in Jerusalem, Vialar plunged her order into the complex, midcentury religious politics of the Holy Land. In many ways, this period was a favorable one for Christians in the Middle East. During the Egyptian occupation of Syria from 1831 to 1840, local Christians were given increased equality with Muslim inhabitants. With an eye to conciliatory gestures toward Europe, Ibrahim Pasha, the Egyptian commander-in-chief in Syria and son of Muhammad Ali, the Egyptian governor, worked to increase security and religious toleration, opening up Damascus and Jerusalem for the first time to foreign and diplomatic residents, relaxing rules on the repair and building of churches and convents, and forbidding taxes on Christian visitors to the Holy Land. After direct Turkish rule was restored in 1840 with the help of Britain, Russia, Prussia, and Austria, the new sultan worked to modernize the region and continued policies favorable to European Christians. Foreign consuls and merchants proliferated all over the region, jealously guarding their privileges and interfering in local affairs, raising the Muslims' suspicion that the European powers were building the groundwork for eventual occupation.[43]

Increasing numbers of Christian pilgrims and tourists also traveled to the Holy Land in this period, spurred by a religious revival in Europe, the rise of biblical scholarship, and renewed interest in the conversion of Jews. In France, Napoleon's invasion of Egypt and Syria had reminded the French of the present-day reality of the Holy Land, and Chateaubriand's writings romanticized it, painting a picture of persecuted Christian clerics keeping the faith alive in the land of Jesus's birth, abandoned by Christians since the Crusades.[44] As a result of the improved conditions after 1831, religious orders began to return to the region, beginning with the Jesuits to Syria in 1833, followed by the Lazarists and the Filles de la Charité. The Soeurs de St-Joseph de l'Apparition were part of this missionary revival in Palestine, which brought twelve missionary orders by 1885, of which ten were French.[45]

However, Palestine was also the site of intense rivalries that cut across national states, religious faiths, Christian denominations, and Catholic interest groups.

Traditionally, Catholic interests in the Ottoman Empire were represented by the French government, which had been given oversight over all Catholics in accordance with treaties with the Ottoman Empire in 1569. The Franciscan order, primarily Italian and Spanish priests, had been custodians of the Christian holy places since 1217. In October 1847, however, the Catholic Church, seeking a higher profile in the region that might bring indigenous Christian churches under Roman authority, reestablished the post of Latin patriarch of Jerusalem, appointing a young but accomplished cleric from Genoa, Joseph Valerga, who had previous experience in Mesopotamia. In so doing, it transferred the powers that had belonged to the Franciscan order to the new patriarch—to the ire of the Franciscans, who had expected that one of their own would be appointed patriarch.[46] Although the new French consul in Jerusalem and the French ambassador to the Holy See were not great supporters of the local Franciscans, both opposed the new post, fearing that a non-French patriarch would try to decrease the influence of the French religious protectorate. Instead they argued for an increase in French missionaries, including the Soeurs de St-Joseph, who, "being French and only living here through us and under our uncontested and exclusive protectorate, would not be able to invoke, in any way, the protectorate of a foreign power." French officials were also protective of France's symbolic privileges at the Sunday Mass in Jerusalem, which included an *exaudiat* for the French king, favored seating for the French consul, and a special role for him during the service.[47]

Despite all the diplomatic ink spilled over these seemingly minor issues of precedence and recognition, the arrival of Valerga in January 1848 nonetheless marked a new visibility for the Catholic church in the Holy Land. Local Muslims, Jews, and Christians lined the streets of Jerusalem to watch the new patriarch, accompanied by sixty Franciscan priests and escorted by the Turkish army, parade to the Franciscan convent church to give his first sermon and deliver a papal blessing.[48] Although only about four thousand Latin Catholics (few of them French nationals) fell under Valerga's mandate, he soon embarked on an energetic campaign of philanthropic works from schools to hospitals that made use of the stream of Catholic missionaries, mainly French, now arriving in the Middle East. Like Chateaubriand, he invoked the history of the Crusades to justify Catholic expansion.[49]

This increasing activity of the Catholic church, however, came up against other Christian denominations in the Holy Land, also expanding under national patronage. No fewer than eleven Protestant missionary groups interested in proselytizing in the Middle East were founded between 1795 and 1824.[50] The return of the Jews to Palestine was supported by British Protestant evangelicals, who saw it as the fulfillment of biblical prophecy; such interests were well represented in the circles around Lord Palmerston, British foreign secretary and then prime minister.[51] An Anglican bishop was appointed to Jerusalem in 1841 under the joint patronage of Britain and Prussia.

In 1850, the Ottoman Empire approved Protestants as a *millet*, or community with religious rights, which provided some protection for individuals converting to Protestantism. Both Russian and Greek Orthodox clergy also became more active in the region, and by 1853 Greek Orthodox priests in Jerusalem had opened a seminary and had plans for a printing press. Russia reaffirmed its support of the four Orthodox patriarchs of Constantinople, Antioch, Jerusalem, and Alexandria, reinforcing its role as protector of Orthodox interests in the Middle East.[52]

As European powers jockeyed for position in the Ottoman Empire, in other words, protection of Christian minorities was one tool to extend their influence, and the consular corps jealously guarded against potential slights and embarrassments. France feared that even Catholic powers like Spain and Austria were undermining traditional French interests in the Holy Land, trying to place Catholic nationals under consular protection rather than under the French umbrella, as guaranteed by the sixteenth-century treaties.[53] In turn, conflicts among Christian denominations, many of which went back centuries, became matters of state. By 1853, the religious rivalries among the great powers, fought largely over symbols and institutions, acted as a trigger for the Crimean War, as the French and the Russians disputed claims as guardians of the Christian holy places.[54]

In their charitable work in Jerusalem, the Soeurs de St-Joseph were caught in the crossfire. Nowhere was this more true than in the disputes over the new Catholic hospital, which employed the sisters as nurses and pharmacists. Health care in the city was divided by nationality and religious denomination, an English hospital having been founded in 1844, a Jewish hospital in the same year, and a German hospital in 1851. The Austrians sought to increase their influence by expanding the hospital run by the Franciscan order. In 1851 the French consul, concerned about the growing influence of the Austrians, and Valerga, eager to extend his authority at the expense of the Franciscans, joined together to found a new Catholic hospital, under the spiritual protection of St. Louis and the temporal protection (and financing) of the French government. From the beginning, however, Valerga and the consul disagreed on just how French the hospital should be, the patriarch emphasizing the importance of the display of Christian charity to Muslims, and the consul noting its impact on "our political influence in the Levant."[55] Once opened, Valerga treated the hospital as a Catholic institution that was dependent on him and by extension the Holy See and financed by a variety of Catholic sources. French diplomats complained bitterly that the sign he placed on the hospital merely read "Ospedale Cattolico," even though it was routinely referred to as "the French hospital because of its origins and because of the French nationality of the sisters who serve there." Yet not all of the Soeurs de St-Joseph, at the hospital or elsewhere in the city, were French. The same diplomatic broadside complained that "it is a Maltese sister whom he has placed at the head of the schools of Jerusalem."[56]

To Vialar, however, the nationality of the individuals she assigned to key posts was irrelevant to the order's mission, which was the expansion of the Catholic faith. In fact, she was a strong supporter of Valerga, who told her that he counted more on the schools run by her sisters than the Franciscan fathers for the "preservation of the faith." With their access to natives as pupils and patients, the highest Catholic authority in the Holy Land now argued that Catholic nuns could do more good than the custodians of the most important Christian sites. In order to remain in his good graces, when Valerga visited Paris, Vialar pulled strings to ensure that he did not lodge with the Lazarists, who were promoting the interests of the Filles de la Charité over her sisters in the Middle East. In Jerusalem, Emilie Julien emphasized the need for keeping "harmony between the two camps" of Franciscans and the Latin patriarch. Vialar reaffirmed her confidence in Julien's "great gentleness and tact" by giving her the title of provincial, with jurisdiction over Chios, Cyprus, and Syria.[57]

Under Valerga's patronage, Julien's direction, and Vialar's encouragement from France, the Soeurs de St-Joseph expanded quickly in Palestine and Syria, establishing missions in Jaffa in 1849, in Bethlehem and Saida in 1853, and in Aleppo in 1856. In addition to their hospital work, the Soeurs de St-Joseph in Jerusalem established a school for indigenous children that enrolled 125 pupils in its first two years, including a handful of boarders and orphans.[58] By 1852, the mission was successful enough that they were pleading with Valerga to find them more space in order to accommodate all of the children, build an on-site chapel, and add a garden or courtyard. They also especially wanted to expand in order to provide lodging for wealthy European women pilgrims, who were now beginning to travel to Jerusalem in greater numbers and who might become donors. Finally, in 1853, Valerga was able to buy a plot of land contiguous to their existing building in order to expand their establishment.[59]

The value of the sisters was, as elsewhere, in training girls to become good mothers, preferably good Christian mothers, according to European norms. Married at twelve to fourteen years of age, girls, Julien reported, were expected only to "know how to make an Arab shirt."[60] In schools run by the sisters, girls not only learned to sew but also acquired basic academic subjects, mainly in Italian, and some French. "Their native Arabic," reported pilgrim Louis Enault, "is only permitted during recess." He also noted some hostility toward the sisters by the local community, who sometimes withdrew their daughters from the school. The sisters' practice of providing asylum to prostitutes or "young girls [fleeing] the shameful bonds of polygamy" also riled up the locals, especially since the sisters were suspected of encouraging religious vocations. At the same time, however, they garnered goodwill because of their willingness to attend the sick during outbreaks of fever and cholera.[61]

Despite their success, however, the Soeurs de St-Joseph had considerably more competition in the Middle East than they had experienced elsewhere. The mission opened by the sisters in Saida was conceived as a "dike against the ravages of Protestantism" by Mgr Brunoni, with whom Vialar had worked to establish the missions on Cyprus. The opening of the school there exceeded expectations, enrolling on the first day more than 200 Catholic pupils and 50 Muslims in a town of 1,500 Catholics, 3,000 Muslims, and several hundred Orthodox. Brunoni also reported with satisfaction that the Soeurs de St-Joseph had "extracted" about a dozen young girls who had been "seduced" by Armenian Protestants. Although the smallest in size, the seventy-pupil school at Jaffa was characterized by Valerga as the "most flourishing" because it enrolled "little and big girls, Latins, Maronites, Greeks, Melechites, Jews, and even Muslims," whose parents often left them until age 16 or 18 rather than pulling them out at age 12. By 1853, the establishment had produced one novice, whose "example will exercise a happy influence over her young companions and will kindle new vocations to religious life."[62]

The school in Bethlehem, with a more substantial Catholic population, enrolled 150 to 180 girls during the school day, as well as some of their mothers after hours. Here in the birthplace of Christianity, however, Valerga fretted about Protestant missionaries, who had also opened up a school and pharmacy and were trying to "insinuate themselves in the minds of the simple and the ignorant" by handing out money. Catholic good works, on the other hand, "are a language, a special virtue to open the eyes of heretics in the middle of whom our vocation calls us to live."[63] In France, Vialar worried in turn about pleasing Valerga, who had invited the Dames de Nazareth to establish a mission in their namesake city. "He has great zeal for the works of our sisters in Jerusalem," she wrote to Soeur Céleste Peyre, "which compensates for the loss that we endured in not going to Nazareth.... Let's console ourselves besides in remembering that Monseigneur wants to extend our works in the environs of Jerusalem." "Jerusalem," she reminded her in another letter, "is envied by all the Congregations."[64]

In their charitable work in the Middle East, the Soeurs de St-Joseph maintained the balance between religious neutrality and evangelization that they had honed in Algeria, Tunisia, and Greece. The Jerusalem school was inclusive, enrolling pupils of mixed religious and ethnic heritage. "Our classes would make you die of laughter, dear Mother," wrote Soeur Emilie Julien to Vialar. "[T]hey enroll Latins, Greeks, Copts, schismatics, and Turks. Several days ago, we were offered some Jewish girls, but I have not seen them come even though I gave my consent." Turks, Julien reported to Abbé Bourgade, "come to see us; we also go to them, and they receive us warmly. We enjoy general esteem." Nonetheless, she also acknowledged the need for discretion in religious matters because "Jerusalem is captive of Constantinople."[65] In 1854, Valerga reported more than eight thousand free consultations given at the Jerusalem hospital, as well as untold numbers of home visits by the sisters. "During these visits," he added, "the nuns opened the door to Heaven to ninety-one children in danger of death....The most absolute silence must be kept on this particular point."[66] The Ottoman Empire prohibited the conversion of Muslims, and Jews in Jerusalem who accepted Christian charity lost access to charitable funds distributed by rabbis and could no longer be buried in a Jewish cemetery. Nonetheless, Valerga reported nineteen conversions to Catholicism in Jerusalem during 1852, as well as two new Soeurs de St-Joseph.[67]

One strategy that the Soeurs de St-Joseph used in order to allay the fears of Muslim parents was to segregate the Muslim pupils. In Saida, Soeur Emilie Julien reported that they "were in one class, separated from the Catholics; they learned how to sew and do needlework; they made less progress in reading and writing." Despite the segregation, the girls were nonetheless exposed to Catholic practice and dogma:

> Our Muslim pupils learn with happiness our religious songs, as well as our prayers, which displeases intensely the Muslim mothers. When these children returned to their families in the evening, they sang the litanies of the holy Virgin and our beautiful French hymns in her honor. These fanatical women forced their husbands to withdraw their children from the Christian schools. Nonetheless, these children have not lost the fruit of almost two years of Catholic education; they are distinguished even today among all the Muslim women by a stamp of Christian civility, and they maintain a great sympathy for the Sisters and for Christians in general.[68]

Emilie Julien anticipated "the immense good they could do among Turks and Jews" once they began offering nursing care: "How many baptisms will we have the opportunity to perform at death's door!"[69] If the sisters' outward roles were as educators and nurses, they never forgot their fundamental responsibility to bring salvation through Christian practice and baptism.

Beyond the Holy Land but still in the Ottoman Empire, Vialar established two missions in Armenia, one at Trebizond in 1852 and another at Erzurum in 1855. Like the missions in Lebanon, these establishments brought her sisters in contact with an indigenous Christian church that the Holy See was eager to claim for its own. The Armenian national church had been independent from that of Rome or Constantinople since its origins, but an Armenian Catholic church was formalized in 1742. An Armenian Catholic *millet* was established in 1829, and Pope Pius IX established bishoprics in Trebizond and Erzurum, among other Armenian centers, in 1850.[70] A port city on the Black Sea, Trebizond had been the home of Capuchin missionaries since 1661, when they were expelled from nearby Georgia by the

Russian emperor. After 1845, the Capuchin superior received the powers of an apostolic prefect from Rome, and in 1851 Père Philippe de Bologne asked Vialar to send three sisters to Trebizond, five days by steamboat from the order's mission in Chios.[71] Three years later, at the request of the French consul in the inland town of Erzurum, Vialar established a second Armenian mission.

These missions, because they were in Christian territory, appeared to offer larger numbers of potential converts. When Vialar appointed her trusted associate, Soeur Gabrielle Coeur de Roy, as local superior in Trebizond, she informed her that "it is a very important foundation in the interests of the salvation of souls and the glory of God; there are 40,000 souls there and never have Sisters been established." She also allowed two young women from Constantinople to enter the order and complete their novitiate there, sending them several catechisms and *La parfaite religieuse* by St. Alphonsus Liguori. By 1852, the mission had attracted a dozen new novices.[72] Vialar was also heartened by the presence in Trebizond of a doctor whom she had known in Tunis, who could train the sisters in nursing, for which Vialar also sent instructional materials from France. Nothing was more important than nuns who could learn new skills and new languages, as she wrote to Soeur Eugénie Laurez: "Nothing could please me more than that you learn the Turkish language...how I thank God for the care that you have taken to educate yourself."[73]

As in the Holy Land, the French government saw the expansion of Catholic missions run by French personnel as an opportunity to extend national influence. The French consul in Trebizond argued that if the mission "is protected by France, it will also be completely French in sentiment." Since the "Armenian heresy" was dying through "indifference, ignorance, and the immorality of its leaders," the consul advocated investing money to rebuild a larger church and open a school in Trebizond and smaller establishments in other Armenian centers. These initiatives would also prevent the Austrian government from opening more missions under its protection.[74] In the inland mountain town of Erzurum, the problem was "American Protestant missionaries who try to deflect, to their profit, part of the people of this region and succeed much more by the help of their money than by the influence of their doctrines." Establishing a mission run by French sisters would also "augment the legitimate influence that France exercises over the spirit of the Christian populations in these lands."[75] Protestant conversion among Armenians was indeed growing in midcentury, facilitated by Protestant encouragement for local clergy and autonomous congregations.

The French consul also valued women religious because of their access to Armenian homes. Although much of the Armenian population was nominally Christian, and some even Catholic, he had no hesitation in characterizing it as "fanatical" and "hostile to the propagation of Religion and of the Civilization of the Nations of Europe." Catholic clergy ran up against "the antagonism of Native

Priests, under whose exclusive and despotic denomination the population is placed."
In this region, even Christians, he reported, had taken on Muslim habits of female
sequestration where European men, "under permanent suspicion," could not enter.
Nevertheless, Catholic nuns could overcome this "distrust" and "repulsion" through
"Christian charity." "Progressively," he predicted, "the Soeurs de St-Joseph will succeed in making themselves welcomed and even loved by the wives of the most
important Armenians. The little girls will be confided to their enlightened care, and
later they will manage to persuade these families to send their young boys to the
free school of the Capuchin fathers."[76] In Trebizond, the sisters opened a one-room
school for girls of all social classes (until the complaints of the better-off parents
forced them to open a second, paying school) but added extra hours of instruction
for their mothers, whose religious ignorance was matched only by their lack of
"order, cleanliness, and economy." As a result, they claimed, the mothers learned to
take better care of their houses, as well as participate in the sacraments.[77]

In all of their missions, the Soeurs de St-Joseph saw girls as the key to a
Catholic future; here they attempted to influence grown women as well. The
Soeurs de St-Joseph also provided health care, most notably during a smallpox
epidemic that ran through the Circassian population, who had arrived in Trebizond
as refugees in 1854. According to convent records, Soeur Gabrielle Coeur de Roy,
with one of the novices as an interpreter, "went all around the contaminated neighborhoods and provided care, aid, and consolation to the sick," as well as ensuring
that, through baptism, "at least four hundred children went to heaven to rejoice
with their little brothers and sisters."[78] In Erzurum, the sisters arrived immediately
after the Russian invasions during the Crimean War. The region also experienced
harsh winters and frequent earthquakes, during which the sisters gave asylum to
the wounded and displaced.[79]

Vialar's missions in Ottoman territory, from the Greek islands to distant
Armenia, shared a number of important characteristics. The range of services
offered by the sisters drew from a standard repertoire of education and health care,
with occasional deviations into disaster relief or pilgrim lodging. Outwardly at
least, they were as inclusive as possible, making their educational and medical services available to individuals of all ethnicities and religions. However, neither
schooling nor health care came without strings attached. In schoolrooms, they
attempted to displace indigenous languages with European ones, usually French
or Italian, and impose a European curriculum and European-style codes of
behavior. When they could get away with it, they also taught girls Catholic hymns
and prayers. Above all, they tried to mold girls into women who had, at the very
least, a respect for Catholicism. They enthusiastically embraced their nursing
work, aware that it gave them clandestine means for evangelization through the
well-practiced skill of baptizing dying children. As (mainly) French members of a

transnational church, the Soeurs de St-Joseph balanced loyalties to church and state and exploited the resources of both to their advantage. Vialar, however, was not inclined to promote an exclusively French agenda in the region, increasingly envisioning her order as multinational in the service of a universal church. As she had in Algeria, Tunisia, and Malta, Vialar built a network of contacts and supporters, but these were more likely Europeans than native—mainly clerics but also consuls and European elites. She also had to contend with more competition both within her church and outside of it—the Holy Land especially was a rich religious prize coveted by many missionary groups, just as it was a political prize coveted by European nation-states.

A Different Kind of Missionary

In December 1855, eight months before her death at age fifty-nine of a strangulated hernia acquired decades earlier, Vialar founded her last mission, sending four of her nuns to Aleppo at the request of her old associate, Père Brunoni, now apostolic delegate in Syria. "She said a tender goodbye," the official register reads, "because they went far away into the unknown and left the country for the first time. They were very young."[80] The journey proved particularly difficult for the intrepid nuns. A storm on the Mediterranean nearly sank their ship, and they could not dock at Jaffa for two days. After stops in Beirut and Alexandretta (Iskenderun), they traveled overland to Aleppo by mule, where they foiled two mugging attempts and one sister fell into a ditch during a snowfall. When they finally arrived at the Franciscan monastery, "there was a great commotion among the Christian population. The consuls came to see the Sisters; all the Franciscan Fathers, the town notables, the few French, and Italians with their wives hastened to satisfy their curiosity more than their courtesy."[81] In February 1856 they opened a small school that provided instruction in Arabic and French; by 1858, they had more than two hundred pupils in a new school opened with the consent of the "Oriental bishops."[82] As elsewhere, the Soeurs de St-Joseph in Aleppo offered free health care and medicine. This operation followed what was by now a well-established pattern for the Soeurs de St-Joseph: initial hardship, guarded welcome by the community, the establishment of educational and medical services, and rapid expansion. That it had become routine in the two decades since Vialar's initial foray into Algeria was a measure of not only her personal initiative and dogged determination but also the changing landscape of missionary work in the early nineteenth century.

Vialar and her sisters exemplify the entry of active, apostolic women into the missionary field in ways not previously seen. Instead of their gender serving as a handicap, as it had for Philippine Duchesne's long-delayed mission to the Indians, it provided distinct advantages. In this order, there were no concerns about cloister. Vialar and her sisters traveled all over the Mediterranean basin by ship, mule, or any other form of local transport—and even beyond to places like Burma and Australia—without hesitation. The initial concerns of the residents of Gaillac when their upper-class daughters joined Vialar in her audacious experiment disappeared once the order demonstrated its success. Vialar had no trouble recruiting new members, especially as she opened up entry to Catholic women outside of the Gaillac region and even outside of France. Between 1845 and 1859, 21 percent of their membership was non-French, largely Italian and Maltese but also Tunisian, Lebanese, and Armenian. This development only accelerated in the decades after Vialar's death.[83] Once they arrived in a foreign mission, the Soeurs de St-Joseph were visible in the streets as they bustled about visiting patients and establishing schools and clinics. Vialar herself, as well as her most trusted lieutenants, worked and socialized with male clerics, French and other European officials, and local elites. If we are to believe the grandiose claims of European clerics, they were even guests of honor in Muslim homes, where they were treated like minor deities venerated for their sanctity. Instead of being peripheral to missionary efforts, they moved to their very center.

Access to Muslim (as well as Christian and Jewish) homes was, in fact, one of the important advantages of inviting women missionaries into a region previously only open to male clerics. Women and children were now seen as the key players in evangelization because home and family were identified as the locus of spiritual and cultural life. Muslim homes, in particular, were seen as impenetrable by any outsiders besides women, giving both Protestant and Catholic missionary women a special role. Anglican women, for example, founded the Church of England Zenana Missionary Society to work inside *zenanas*, or the secluded areas in Indian households.[84] Similarly, Catholic priests sought out women missionaries as intermediaries with local populations who distrusted male clerics' physical and spiritual access to the household. This reluctance was particularly widespread in the traditional societies of the Mediterranean basin and helped to fuel the expansion of the missions of the Soeurs de St-Joseph. Freed from enclosure themselves, the Catholic sisters entered the homes of cloistered Muslim and other indigenous women, usually as healers. That role, furthermore, gave them opportunities to reach individuals at their most vulnerable, when they might be most open to spiritual alternatives.

Vialar's religious discretion, on view from the first days in Algeria, was a significant factor in her success. She was able to expand rapidly into regions dominated by Muslims because she was perceived as religiously neutral, interested in providing services and alleviating suffering rather than gaining Catholic converts. Her salvation—and that of her sisters—did not depend on results but on effort, on good works rather than on conversion, which meant that she was free to concentrate on building institutions like schools and clinics rather than preaching or proselytizing. Serving others was her ostensible and immediate goal. Vialar nurtured a reputation for tolerance and cross-cultural understanding—as we can see, for example, in her opposition to Dupuch in Algeria and her work with Bourgade in Tunisia—that became an essential part of the identity of the Soeurs de St-Joseph to this day. However, Vialar's religious calling was fundamentally shaped by the accident of the original locale of her missionary work—following her brother into Algeria, which then opened doors elsewhere around the Mediterranean—which required this kind of tolerance in order to survive and prosper. Had she developed her missions in another part of the world, where open evangelization was allowed, the Soeurs de St-Joseph de l'Apparition might have developed a different reputation and identity altogether.

But as a missionary, was Vialar playing a double game? The religious neutrality and inclusiveness she cultivated was also in some measure a façade behind which remained the ultimate goal of the spread of Catholic Christianity. At times her good works appear as merely strategies to a greater end. However dedicated the Soeurs de St-Joseph were to instructing the ignorant and alleviating the suffering of the sick and dying, their own testimony, as well as those of other Catholic clerics, make it clear that their ultimate objective was to save souls through baptism and conversion. Because they worked in regions where the open acknowledgement of this goal would have resulted in their expulsion, they resorted to subterfuge and secrecy in ways that make us doubt the sincerity of their religious neutrality. They also did not challenge the theology of the nineteenth-century Catholic church, which dictated that the only path to salvation was through Catholic conversion and adherence to Catholic doctrine and sacraments.

Nothing encapsulates the sisters' dilemma between service and evangelization more than the secret baptism of dying children. Too young, from the Catholic point of view, to chose their own fate, these children were unhesitingly freed by the sisters from eternal limbo. From their point of view, this action was a merciful by-product of their nursing expertise. Within the confines of the church, they counted up those baptisms as an essential measure of their success, bragging about their numbers and anticipating future results. Since the conversion of adults was virtually impossible, it is clear that their target audience was children and that they practiced secret baptism whenever and wherever they could. Yet Vialar and her sisters were also finely attuned to the political dangers of baptism and thus kept this work unknown to parents, local authorities, and even secular French or European officials, who did not share their evangelical objectives. For lack of any evidence to the contrary, we can only assume that none of their baptisms became public; if any of these children survived, the sisters appear not to have made any further attempts to bring them into the Catholic fold. Nonetheless, the Soeurs de

St-Joseph themselves were greatly empowered by their ability to baptize these children. Although baptism was a traditional goal of Catholic missionaries, it had always been the exclusive prerogative of priests. That women religious in the Mediterranean region were now more successful than male priests in the single most essential sacrament in the Catholic faith represented a spiritual world turned upside down.

Vialar also practiced a neutrality among national rivals that sometimes frustrated her French sponsors. The expansion of the Soeurs de St-Joseph in North Africa, Greece, and the Middle East coincided with the slow decline of the Ottoman Empire, which provided new political opportunities for European nation-states. Due to historical ties to the empire, as well as sheer great-power survival, France believed it had much to gain in this region. It saw missionaries of French origin as potential tools of influence and expansion who might mark a territory as French. Not until the late nineteenth century, however, would French Catholic missionaries redefine themselves as national agents.[85] Vialar, though identifying herself as a Frenchwoman and willing to rely on French political protection when offered, in no way saw her work as limited by nationality. Not only did she actively recruit sisters of many national origins into her order, but she also worked with clerical and lay intermediaries without concern for nationality. She often took advantage of muddled power relations to extend her own personal empire. When challenged, she resisted attempts to define her project as a French one. The essence of her faith was its universality. The good works of the Soeurs de St-Joseph, as a religious order with its origins in France, might redound to the benefit of the French nation, but such identification could not be taken for granted outside of a formal French colony like Algeria. Although French officials around the Mediterranean often welcomed Vialar's work as auxiliary to their own efforts, when they had a choice of religious orders, as in the Holy Land, they also appeared downright suspicious of its multinational characteristics. As an extranational figure, Emilie de Vialar in some ways defied the emerging colonial and national paradigm that would dominate the late nineteenth and early twentieth centuries.

Nevertheless, as a French-based religious order steeped in European cultural norms, Vialar and her sisters acted as imperial agents of a sort. The educational and medical institutions that they founded displaced indigenous forms of schooling and health care. Vialar was party to a modernization project in the Ottoman Empire that assumed the superiority of European culture. In Algeria, it was a product of outright conquest and domination. In Tunisia, it was facilitated by a bey eager to ensure the integrity of his kingdom during a period of rapidly changing power relationships through European-style reform. In Greece, the sisters entered at the end of a liberation movement that brought Greeks back into the European family, and in the Ottoman Empire they acted as agents of increased European influence and prestige.

All over the Mediterranean, they assimilated an impoverished southern European migrant population—popularly considered more "African" than "European"—to European norms. Their schools, clinics, and hospitals were essential components of the "civilizing mission" that preceded formal imperial structures.

Most significant of all, Vialar's role as head of this expanding religious order exemplifies the opportunities that the revolution in women's religious life provided. She began her life with the advantages of birth and fortune, but most of her success was due to her ability to exploit changing gender notions in the Catholic church, although not always without conflict. Beginning with a father who disapproved of her vocation and continuing with a bishop who sought to rein in her independence, Vialar fought against patriarchy at home and in the church. She spent her inheritance as she pleased, raised more money when she needed it, and kept a large organization financially afloat. Because she offered services that both church and state, as well as foreign powers and local communities, valued, she was able to negotiate terms and overcome setbacks. She was an expert networker who cultivated friends in powerful places and cooperated with male clerics who shared her vision. Venerated by her sisters, she was both a leader and a role model.

Emilie de Vialar represented a new kind of religious woman, more daring and less bound by tradition than Philippine Duchesne. Like Duchesne, she used the resources—familial and financial—at her disposal to fulfill her religious vision. Unlike Duchesne, however, she came of age not under the Old Regime monastic structure of enclosed convents dedicated to prayer but during the period of church reconstruction after the ravages of the Revolution. The same religious energy that allowed Duchesne to travel to America allowed Vialar to imagine a different kind of religious life, one that allowed single women, dedicated to God and wearing simple habits and even "worldly bonnets," the freedom to engage in direct charitable acts both in France and overseas. The initial resistance to this model, first in Gaillac and then in Algeria, reflects its transitional nature. Vialar governed her order and jousted with bishops and politicians apparently undaunted by her status as a woman, buoyed instead by her social status and her steadfast belief in the rightness of her actions, which she defended, in the words of Bishop Dupuch, "with a rare ease and a hopeless tenacity."

PART III

Missionary Utopias
Anne-Marie Javouhey

7

French Origins and African Experiments

In November 1798 Anne Javouhey, age nineteen, wrote her father that she had "promised God to devote myself entirely to the service of the ill and the instruction of girls." Solemnly enough, she had made this vow during a midnight Mass celebrated by a renegade priest in the home of her elder brother, Etienne, on the anniversary of her baptism. It was scarcely welcome news to her father, Balthasar, a prosperous Burgundian peasant, who had already denied permission for his daughter to take up a religious life. "All your refusals," the same letter began, "do not discourage me."[1] However, her father had prudence on his side. The content of the vow—active service to others—suggested that young Anne Javouhey wished to join a religious order dedicated to good works. But how? A mere eight years since the Revolutionary government had outlawed all religious vows and closed all convents and monasteries, such opportunities were nonexistent. In Grenoble, Philippine Duchesne would not move back into the old Visitation convent for three more years, and it would be six before she joined forces with Sophie Barat in the Society of the Sacred Heart. In Gaillac, Emilie de Vialar was one year old. Before the Revolution, a peasant girl with religious sensibilities like Javouhey's might have joined a religious association such as the Filles de la Charité, whose uncloistered sisters dedicated their lives to nursing, teaching, and charity. However, the Filles de la Charité, disbanded during the Revolution, would not be reauthorized for another two years and then only to provide nursing services, not to reestablish communal life.

Furthermore, her father knew that a daughter dedicated to good works outside of a formal religious structure would be a financial drain for a large peasant family of four daughters and two sons. However dramatic his daughter's religious gesture (and her subsequent attempts to fulfill it), Balthasar Javouhey was sensible enough to resist. Almost every letter Anne Javouhey wrote to him in the first decade after her vow apologizes for the harsh words they had exchanged and the trouble she had caused him. Despite her tone of filial respect, however, she did not give an inch, framing her vocation as "the Will of God, whether or not it suits."[2] Balthasar was fighting a losing battle with his determined daughter, who was inventing a form of religious life just as France was emerging from the spiritual chaos of the Revolution and whose charisma and vision spread to her siblings. On 12 May 1807 not only Anne but also the other three Javouhey daughters, Pierrette, Marie-Françoise, and Claudine, took vows as Soeurs de St-Joseph, becoming Mères Anne-Marie, Marie-Thérèse, Marie-Joseph, and Rosalie, respectively. The youngest, Claudine-turned-Rosalie was only seventeen years old. Anne-Marie, unsurprisingly, became superior general. With all four daughters now in religious habit and Catholic orders gradually springing back to life in the wake of Napoleon's concordat, Balthasar threw in the towel and bought them a former convent, now nationalized property of the state, in the nearby town of Cluny for 12,800 francs.[3] Through sheer force of personality, the Soeurs de St-Joseph de Cluny were born.

In her lifetime, Javouhey created an extraordinarily successful religious order. Yet both Javouhey's life and her work were full of contradictions. Although the sisters serving in France always outnumbered those overseas, Javouhey's religious order became identified as the female missionary order par excellence, the institution to which the French government most commonly turned to staff schools and hospitals in old and new colonies (except Algeria). After her first trip to Africa in 1822, Javouhey herself became convinced that her God-given mission was to evangelize among Africans wherever in the French empire they might be found, from Senegal to the Caribbean to French Guiana. In the established settler colonies she had to work within the confines of slave society, yet in the wilds of Guiana she let loose her desire to create the perfect Christian community, run by Catholic nuns and populated by displaced Africans. Although a faithful Catholic, Javouhey had much in common with the Romantic socialists and utopians of her era, seeking harmony and perfection through communal living. She developed ideas about race that, on the one hand, affirmed the essential equality of all human beings under God but, on the other, assumed that Africans should emulate French Catholic peasants. Coming of age in the religious violence of the Revolution and fearful of republicanism, Javouhey nevertheless became one of the rare Catholic advocates of abolitionism, basing her beliefs not on liberal human rights principles but on religious grounds of equality and perfectibility. Because of these views Javouhey was intensely disliked by the colonial settlers whose world she destabilized yet admired by colonial officials, who found in her a partner in expanding France's civilizing mission abroad. Most male clerics tried—unsuccessfully—to reign in her independence and power, but her sisters followed her to the ends of the earth. Most of all, the energy, determination, and confidence in her own vision that she showed in her relationship with her father followed her in her dealings with officials, clerics, sisters, friends, and enemies for the rest of her career.

Finding a Vocation

Born in 1779 in a rural commune in Burgundy, Anne Javouhey had an adolescence marked by the religious upheaval of the French Revolution. Faithful Catholics before the Revolution, the Javouhey family remained so after 1789 even though Balthasar served as a municipal councilor and therefore was expected to enforce the new religious legislation. His wife, Claudine, taught her children the catechism and gave aid to priests who had refused to take the oath to the Civil Constitution of the Clergy.[4] As a teenager, Anne participated actively in the underground church, accompanying nonjuring priests from farm to farm, acting as a lookout during clandestine Masses, and hiding altar linens and ornaments from pillaging crowds. In 1796 she began giving catechismal instruction to the village children, changing locales frequently to avoid suspicion. Decades later, from French Guiana, she wrote to one of her sisters about that time when "we were so fervent, so happy."[5] Deeply affected by the priests she met and helped, the de-Christianization campaign in France during the Revolution appeared to have had the opposite effect on her, strengthening her faith through oppression and resistance. In this, Javouhey, along with her mother and her sisters, followed a pattern typical of many women and girls, especially after the fall of Robespierre in 1794, when popular Catholicism staged a revival. Both Olwen Hufton and Suzanne Desan have described the active role women took in defending Catholic property, restarting Catholic worship, and supporting renegade priests.[6] Through female activism, a grassroots church—however controversial and politicized—predated the formal resurrection of the institutional church through Napoleon's concordat with the pope in 1801. Out of such lay action also came new religious orders and associations dedicated to the re-Christianization of France and service to others that would mark the religious landscape of nineteenth-century France.

Though energetic, resourceful, and determined, Javouhey did not immediately find her niche in this shifting spiritual environment. In 1800, two years after the private vow Javouhey made in her brother's house, she appeared to have found a religious home in the newly created Soeurs de la Charité, founded in 1799 in

Besançon by Jeanne-Antide Thouret, a former Fille de la Charité. This active order responded to the religious and charitable vacuum in late revolutionary France by enrolling pious women who wished to nurse the sick, help the poor, and teach the illiterate, exactly the kind of work Javouhey had vowed to undertake. Javouhey was the fifth woman to join the new association. Although at first she described the mother house in Besançon as "a paradise on earth," two months after moving there she left the order without taking vows.[7] In 1807 she wrote that God had made it clear "in a completely extraordinary but certain manner" that this life was not her vocation. Hagiographic tradition within the order attributes this statement to a dream in which she was surrounded by children of all races and promised protection by Teresa of Avila.[8] It is not hard to imagine, however, that the headstrong Javouhey chafed under the religious discipline imposed by Thouret, whose main activity at this time was training her new novices.[9] Javouhey's stay there, though short, did provide her, however, with a model for an active religious life.

Javouhey did little better as "Soeur Justine" three years later, in 1803, when she briefly joined a reconstituted Trappist (or Cistercian) contemplative community in Villarvolard, Switzerland, at the invitation of former Trappist monk Dom Augustin de Lestrange. Exiled by the Revolution, in its aftermath Lestrange sought to reestablish religious life in France, making contact with like-minded individuals and inspiring them with his vision and charisma. (Fresh from a missionary trip to America, Lestrange's experiences also had a strong impact on Philippine Duchesne when he visited the Grenoble convent in 1806.) Although the political climate was unfavorable to contemplative monastic orders like the Trappists, he thought it might be possible to establish subsidiary orders of religious men and women following a modified Trappist rule, who would undertake active work such as teaching and thereby raise a new generation faithful to the church. In Javouhey, Lestrange saw a potential disciple and partner. Equally enthusiastic, Javouhey sent him (unsuccessfully) to get her father's backing and made a private vow of obedience to him. In 1803, she arrived at the Swiss monastery with her brother Pierre, who also wished to enter. Lestrange sensibly sent Pierre back since he was still subject to French military conscription.[10] After two or three months, Javouhey also left the monastery—disenchanted, one assumes, with the contemplative life—to return to Burgundy.

But her collaboration with Lestrange continued. "I have found a location where one could open a good Establishment for orphans," he wrote to her in 1806. "[F]ind me half a dozen fervent sisters."[11] Like Javouhey, these women would spend a few months receiving training in a Trappist monastery and then return to France to do good works. To this concept Javouhey added the idea that the quasi-Trappist order should consist of both male and female branches because "from time to time" she met "young men who wish to follow the same rule as we do."[12] Although male orders like the Trappists sometimes spun off female branches, it was highly unusual for a woman to propose initiating an order for men. Nonetheless, the first statutes of the "association formed in Châlon under the name of the Society of St. Joseph" in 1806 specified that "it is formed of two societies, one of men and the other of women."[13] When the climate appeared more favorable to formal Trappist reestablishment under Napoleon, however, Lestrange and Javouhey amiably parted ways, and the men's branch was dropped.[14] The rules of the Soeurs de St-Joseph, however, bore traces of their Trappist influence until 1810, with religious services beginning at four-thirty in the morning and requiring the daily recitation of the Salve Regina "à la Trappe."[15]

At the same time that Javouhey was trying to find an appropriate structure for her religious life, she was experimenting with the good works that formed its raison d'être. These consisted primarily of opening schools for poor children in neighboring villages, where Javouhey and a few companions taught them the catechism, rudimentary literacy, and some manual skills. They also prepared the children for their first communion and took in orphans. Only one of the first schools that Javouhey opened in small neighboring villages in Burgundy lasted very long. Napoleonic France had few educational options for peasant children and few resources to sustain them. For girls especially, most municipalities were reluctant to consecrate any public funds; Javouhey and her companions lived off of local charity or the small school fees paid by parents. In one location they tried to supplement their meager income with spinning and the manufacture of muslin. In those early years, Javouhey often found herself in debt, unable to purchase even the most essential foodstuffs, and had to appeal to her father for relief.[16] Most of the schools were opened in former church buildings, usually closed convents. In other cases, Javouhey prevailed on her father to rent or purchase a building, which he did grudgingly. Except for her own sisters, her teaching companions were also ephemeral, consisting of local pious girls attracted no doubt by Javouhey's energy and charisma but also likely to abandon her when the going got tough. About one, Javouhey wrote to Lestrange, "I think that we cannot count on her for the moment; she has a swelled head, but it is not her fault, it is perhaps me."[17] Just as Javouhey was refining her teaching skills in these early schools, she was also learning how to lead.

Javouhey represented a new generation of Catholics, especially women, who sought to rebuild the church from the ground up. These initiatives were not always welcome to the more cautious hierarchy. "Mgr de Fontages [the bishop of Autun] said to me," reminisced a local priest about the origins of the Soeurs de St-Joseph de Cluny, "there they go, these young people, captured by their imagination. I cannot accommodate their demands." Javouhey's response, he claimed, was "I cannot abandon my project; the very holy Virgin orders me to go forward."[18] Intrepid, Javouhey drew on a network of clerical contacts in the region but also did not hesitate to contact clergy she did not know. "Arriving in Autun," she wrote, "and having no acquaintances, I went to the church; I asked the first priest who showed up if he would pass along a letter to Monseigneur [the bishop]; he told me that he would do so with pleasure."[19] In 1805, Javouhey was buoyed by a brief audience with Pope Pius VII as he passed through the region on his return to Italy after the coronation of Napoleon. The new bishop of Autun (the uncooperative one having died in early 1806) provided a religious rule and clerical oversight, allowing Javouhey to receive government authorization for her nascent congregation. In December 1806, while on a military campaign in Prussia, Napoleon signed an imperial decree that established the Soeurs de St-Joseph de Cluny as a religious congregation of women dedicated to good works. Although Napoleon's policy toward the reestablishment of religious orders in France was cautious, he saw utility in active orders that could provide educational, nursing, and charitable services. He also hoped that the French church, bound now to the state by the concordat of 1801, could provide the basis of social order and allegiance to his own regime. In this new climate, emerging religious orders like the Soeurs de St-Joseph, which promised to take up useful work and owed their very existence to the Napoleonic regime, gained approval.

The Soeurs de St-Joseph de Cluny were, to an unusual extent, a family affair. Anne-Marie Javouhey's three younger sisters, Pierrette (Mère Marie-Thérèse), Marie-Françoise (Mère Marie-Joseph), and Claudine (Mère Rosalie) took the habit with her in May 1806, along with five other unrelated young women. In the girls' school she opened in Châlon in 1806, her brother Pierre opened a companion school for boys. Although Pierre never took orders, eventually marrying, his daughter Thérèse joined the Soeurs de St-Joseph as Mère Marie-Thérèse, as did another niece (daughter of the elder Javouhey son, Etienne), who became Mère Clothilde and one of the mainstays of the congregation. Two daughters of Javouhey cousins also joined the order. In a reversal of gender roles where the female relatives usually followed the male, Pierre Javouhey accompanied Anne-Marie Javouhey first to Senegal and later to French Guiana, as did cousins (once removed) Louis and Léopold Javouhey. Javouhey actively sought to find auxiliary posts for her male relatives, which provided her with familial allies wherever she went and gave them work and privileges. "My cousin," she wrote from Senegal in 1822, "has just been named surveyor, a very nice position for him."[20]

When the Soeurs de St-Joseph entered colonial work, this family network became one of its key assets. While Anne-Marie Javouhey lived in French Guiana for years on end, Marie-Joseph ran the congregation in Paris, Marie-Thérèse oversaw the establishments in the Caribbean, and Rosalie those in Bourbon and Senegal. Although the founding members of female religious orders were often close—one thinks of Sophie Barat and Philippine Duchesne or Emilie de Vialar and Emilie Julien—four women who were sisters in blood, as well as religion, made for a particularly united front. This unusual solidarity at the top made the Soeurs de St-Joseph an especially independent female religious order and accounted, in part, for its success.

Colonial Habits

Nothing in the foundation of the Soeurs de St-Joseph de Cluny suggested a future as a missionary or colonial religious order, notwithstanding Javouhey's alleged dream while a novice in Besançon. Instead, at their inception the Soeurs de St-Joseph de Cluny can be understood as one of several small, local, active female religious orders springing up in France in the aftermath of the revolutionary religious upheaval. Like many such orders, they benefited both from a steady demand for their services and from a ready supply of pious young women eager to join up. They grew slowly in their first decade, numbering only fifteen members in 1816. After the Restoration and the entry into colonial work, however, their membership exploded. In 1825, the Soeurs de St-Joseph had 122 members, of whom 71 were serving in France and 51 in the colonies; in 1852, the year after Javouhey's death, the total membership was 1,218, of whom 342 served abroad and 876 in France.[21]

As these figures show, although their colonial missions shaped the order's identity, never did the number of sisters serving abroad outnumber those resident in France. In important ways, the Soeurs de St-Joseph remained true to their origins, providing educational and charity services in communities throughout France and developing a subsidiary specialty in treating people with mental illnesses in "maisons des aliénés," opening the first such house with five hundred beds in Rouen in 1825. During the first year Rosalie Javouhey spent struggling to survive in Senegal, Anne-Marie opened seven new houses in France.[22] The French establishments were also spread over a surprisingly large area beyond Javouhey's native Burgundy, from Bailleul in the north to Carcassonne and Limoux in the south, making the order national rather than regional. Javouhey took care also to establish houses in the port cities to facilitate the travel of nuns overseas. Throughout France, the houses of the Soeurs de St-Joseph also served as recruitment centers for the order, including the overseas missions. Like Vialar's Soeurs de St-Joseph de l'Apparition, the French base remained essential to the success of the Soeurs de St-Joseph de Cluny.

The entry of the Soeurs de St-Joseph de Cluny into missionary work resulted from Javouhey's initiative in seizing new opportunities. Unlike Duchesne or Vialar, Javouhey had neither an independent source of wealth (beyond the financial largesse of her father, who was not very wealthy) nor influential contacts in aristocratic or clerical circles. In fact, she showed her independence from Catholic opinion, as well as her openness to new ideas, by utilizing the mutual method in education when she opened a school in Paris in 1815. Championing the so-called Protestant and constitutional mutual method distanced Javouhey from conservative Catholic clerics.[23] Still, the success of the school and the Paris beachhead, however precarious (the Soeurs de St-Joseph had seven addresses in six years), brought Javouhey a certain notoriety in government circles. Interested parties made their way to the Paris school to observe her experiment and meet the dynamic superior general. One of these visits, by a wealthy and influential Bourbon (now Réunion) settler, Philippe Desbassayns, led to an invitation to open a mission there.[24] Javouhey, alert to new and exciting possibilities to expand her field of action, aggressively pursued this opportunity, making direct contact with colonial and government officials without informing her bishop. The rest of her career would be characterized by a steady correspondence and collaboration on colonial matters with officials high and low in successive French regimes. Her success depended in part on her ability to leverage these contacts and to negotiate on behalf of her order on equal terms. In turn, her direct contacts with French government officials reinforced her distance from episcopal supervision and gave her an independent power base. "Our friends in the two ministries," she wrote in 1827, referring to the colonial ministry and the religious affairs ministry, "are still the same and, if possible, better than ever; they are my temporal directors."[25]

The timing of the entry into colonial work mirrored the Restoration government's renewed concern with the state of France's empire, which was at a particularly low ebb. Canada had been lost at the conclusion of the Seven Years' War in 1763; St-Domingue had revolted and become the independent nation of Haiti in 1804; Napoleon Bonaparte had sold Louisiana to the United States immediately after, and the European empire had fallen in 1814. France overseas was now represented by the tiny North American islands of St-Pierre and Miquelon, the still productive Caribbean islands of Guadeloupe and Martinique, the languishing colony of Guiana in South America, the Indian Ocean island of Bourbon, and a handful of trading posts in India and on the west coast of Africa, including the two Senegalese islands of Gorée and St-Louis. All of these colonies, with the exception of St-Pierre and Miquelon, and the Indian ports, relied on slave labor, although the British insistence after 1817 that the French stop the Atlantic slave trade complicated economic recovery.

Nonetheless, for reasons of national pride, as well as national wealth, the Restoration government sought to make the best of what it had by launching new initiatives overseas, especially ones that would encourage French investment and settlement. The infrastructure provided by women religious—primarily hospitals and schools—were part of this new vision. As a youthful and expanding religious order with a dynamic and innovative leader, the Soeurs de St-Joseph de Cluny displaced the Old Regime order of the Soeurs de St-Paul de Chartres, which

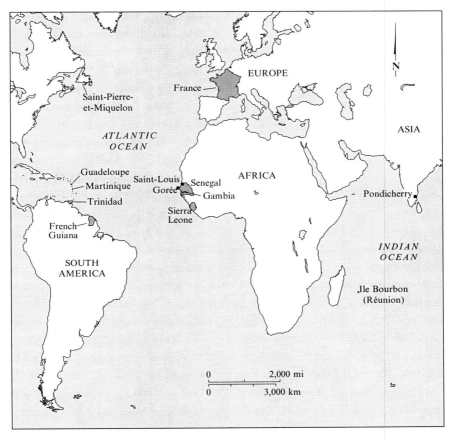

Atlantic and Indian Ocean missions during the lifetime of Anne-Marie Javouhey

had provided hospital services in French colonies before 1789.[26] By 1825 the Soeurs de St-Joseph de Cluny had become France's official female colonial order, contracted to provide public hospital and educational services. They had sixteen religious in Bourbon, thirteen in Senegal, eight in French Guiana, eight in Guadeloupe, six in Martinique, and three in the French trading post at Pondicherry, India, as well as a novitiate in the northern French city of Bailleul, specifically designated for the training of colonial nuns.[27] In 1826, they sent sisters to St-Pierre and Miquelon and in 1836 to Trinidad. When the apostolic prefect of Martinique traveled to France to recruit Ursulines, Javouhey reported proudly that he was told that "a sole congregation was approved for the colonies, the Congrégation de Saint-Joseph de Cluny."[28]

For Javouhey, the expansion into colonial work was a heaven-sent opportunity and not only for the potential good she and her sisters might do among French settlers and colonial subjects overseas. In contracting with the French colonial ministry to provide women religious for missions abroad, Javouhey could also put her order on a firm financial footing, which would allow it to prosper and expand. In exchange for providing the requisite number of sisters to serve in a colonial mission, the colonial ministry paid an annual salary for each nun plus a one-time payment that covered the trousseau, traveling costs within France, food and lodging in the port of embarkation, and the ship's passage. Housing and furniture in the colony were usually provided as well. In 1822, Javouhey negotiated an increase in salary in Bourbon from 1,000 to 1,200 francs for ordinary nuns and from 1,200 to 1,500 francs for the local superior; this was double what the Soeurs de St-Paul de Chartres had been offered in 1816.[29] "The Congregation of St-Joseph is at your service," wrote Javouhey to the minister of the interior in 1818, after insisting that half the salaries be paid directly to the mother house and requesting extra funds for schoolbooks and the establishment of a chapel in Bourbon.[30]

Although the Soeurs de St-Joseph lived in relative poverty in the colonies where they were established and used most of their income to fund their works, central financing allowed Javouhey to transfer funds where needed and to pay for the training of new sisters in France. In 1826, for example, she reported that, at a moment when "I didn't have fifty francs," a letter came from Senegal enclosing three thousand francs, part of which she promptly disbursed to various French houses in need of funds and the rest she used to make a payment on a house for ill and infirm sisters.[31] The colonial missions also provided goods, from fine woods (Guiana) to coffee (Bourbon), which were sent back to the French houses. As superior general of the congregation, Javouhey also retained control over the choice of personnel to send overseas, a task that occupied much of her time and energy, as evidenced by its frequent mention in her letters. She was also the sole interlocutor with the government. By the time the Soeurs de St-Joseph revised their statutes in 1827, the colonial mission was front and center, specifying the centralized nature of the congregation, in which the French houses and the colonial missions came under the same central administration and authority, that is to say, Javouhey and her council.[32]

These rules were adopted in part because of a schism that emerged in the Bourbon colony in 1824, when Javouhey elevated the younger (but better educated and more dynamic) Soeur Bathilde over the more experienced Soeur Thaïs, who refused to accept the decision.[33] Her noncompliance split not only the Soeurs de St-Joseph resident on the island but also local officials and local clergy and diminished the reputation of the congregation. In order to reassert her authority, Javouhey sent six new sisters to replace those who had followed Soeur Thaïs, as well as her sister Rosalie Javouhey to bring peace back into the community. While the new arrivals and the nuns loyal to Javouhey waited long months first for Rosalie and then for Javouhey's instructions and authorizations to arrive in the distant colony, the local priests denied them the sacraments and spread the rumor that the Soeurs de St-Joseph were not a properly constituted religious order and its members not real nuns. Eventually, worried by the effects of the scandal on the island's inhabitants, the colonial minister ordered the dissidents home to France.[34]

However, the incident had shown how fragile a religious order spread over three continents with infrequent and unreliable communications could be. Although the nuns owed their obedience to Javouhey as their superior general, there were other claims on their loyalty, from local superiors who considered a particular colony their fiefdom to local officials and clergy who had legal and spiritual powers over them. "The Bourbon affair," Javouhey wrote once it was all over, "has enlightened us as to the need to move subjects around from time to time." She was especially alert to the manipulation of local clergy, writing Rosalie, "Study the rule, see what it demands and what it defends; follow it to the letter.... Have you not noticed as I have, how dangerous it is to associate too much with priests? The malicious ones take advantage of everything [and] the devil benefits not less. I ask you with clasped hands, my heart full of grief, not to see them except at the altar and the confessional."[35] In another case, in Martinique, a schism was averted when the local superior refused the demand of the apostolic prefect, the highest clerical authority in the colony, to abandon the Soeurs de St-Joseph to join a community of Ursulines he wished to reestablish.[36] Javouhey's hard work in establishing colonial missions would be lost if she had to fear this kind of attrition. However, even more important, the essence of the new kind of religious order developed by women like Javouhey in the nineteenth century was its centralized structure, which she was prepared to defend at all costs, even with her members spread throughout the world. "That the sisters in France and those in the colonies are absolutely alike in everything," she insisted in 1825, "color, shape of habits, manner of wearing them...I am going to establish the same order throughout the congregation."[37]

For the young nuns venturing into colonial spaces, both the journey and the destination presented certain ambiguities and tensions with their religious status. Although the dominant model of female religious life in nineteenth-century France became one of active engagement with the world, the concept of enclosure continued to play a number of roles in the work of the Soeurs de St-Joseph de Cluny. Embarking on colonial missions in the early nineteenth century, these nuns had no clear models for their behavior either as women religious or as white women in French colonies. Their rules prescribed distance from the world as the best means of protecting their virtue and modesty. Javouhey sent them abroad in groups of at least three, not allowing a single nun to travel alone because she "objected to the inconveniences and the dangers" such an individual would face.[38] The novelty of young women traveling on a ship—often for months on end—where all of the crew and most of the passengers were secular men, produced a certain amount of anxiety. Soeur Marie-Joseph Varin, in charge of the small community on the very first voyage to Bourbon, wrote to Javouhey that the nuns had seldom left their room aboard ship, "even though it was small and we suffered much from the heat and bad air...[but] it was better to suffer than to expose ourselves; never did we go out except all four together....It is undoubtedly a very boring life to be shut in a small room, but I can tell you that never did any young men permit themselves to joke with us." Yet when the ship made a stop in Rio de Janeiro (a route to the Indian Ocean dictated by the Atlantic winds), they stayed in a cloistered convent, where Varin found it "funny to speak through a grille."[39]

What substituted for cloister was a strict adherence to the rules of the order down to the smallest detail. "In all countries, in all types of work, [the rules] will direct you and keep you from all error," exhorted Javouhey in a letter to the sisters in Bourbon, identifying the monastic virtues of renunciation, self-sacrifice, charity, obedience, humility, and poverty as those "for all climates, all countries."[40] Following the rules provided uniformity and unity to the congregation over the vast distances that separated members from one another and from the French motherhouse. It also provided them with guidelines of behavior that ensured their virtue and chastity. "If it enters into your duties to have conversations with men, whoever they are, God will help you...but never seek conversations with young priests under the pretext of instructing yourselves: it is a temptation of the devil," wrote Javouhey to her young members. Likewise, "particular friendships" were to be avoided "like the plague," as was "associating with the world." "I cannot protect you enough against [the world's] traps and its seduction, above all in the countries where you live," began her exhortations against too much socialization. Although Javouhey recognized that the work of the congregation required mixing with local inhabitants, she specified that the parlor, where visitors could be received, should be empty as often as possible and visits made only for reasons of "great need" or "great charity." In another letter, she specified that a particular Soeur Clémence and "all the chatterboxes like her...never, never, never go out for visits, walks, or, even less, errands."[41]

Other evidence suggests, however, that this separation from the outside world was far from strictly followed, especially in impoverished and improvised colonial establishments. Even Javouhey herself recognized that "we are not nuns according to the Council of Trent; we are nuns according to our zeal for religion and the laws of the Church today...we do not leave ordinary life."[42] In describing the sisters' crowded lodgings in St-Louis, Senegal, the local French apostolic prefect complained that "the two doors of the court are always open and people are continually coming in...consequently [the sisters] are forced to receive visits from all sorts of people, military and otherwise, without being able to evade them." In 1824 Soeur Victoire, assigned to the hospital in St-Louis, ran off with the pharmacist. In Bourbon Rosalie Javouhey reported that a certain Soeur Véronique had former pupils following her in the streets "kissing her as if she were a relic," from which she drew the lesson that the sisters "should never familiarize themselves in this manner with the pupils in their classes."[43] This example also suggests, however, that true enclosure was virtually impossible given the nature of the educational and health care work that the Soeurs de St-Joseph took on. Only in established colonies, such as Guadeloupe and Martinique, with a larger population of French settlers, could they open boarding schools for young girls; in these semicloistered environments they could protect their own virtue and that of their pupils. In slave colonies, a certain distance from local society also protected the Soeurs de St-Joseph from the corrupting nature of plantation life.

Travel overseas in this period was physically, as well as spiritually, hazardous. Of the first thirty sisters sent to St-Louis, Senegal, more than half died under the age of forty. The causes of death included typhoid, yellow and other fevers, liver and intestinal illnesses, consumption, an accidental fall, and two drownings; only one sister died of old age.[44] In 1818, the Soeurs de St-Paul de Chartres pulled two of their sisters from Martinique "after the awful dangers that our poor sisters experienced on the sea at the peril of their lives," a clue perhaps to the reason this religious order ceded much of its missionary work to the Soeurs de St-Joseph.[45] Even among the younger and hardier Soeurs de St-Joseph, however, some of the nuns could not tolerate the tropical climate in the colonies or found the work there too fatiguing. There were also natural disasters to contend with, such as the hurricane in 1825, which killed the superior of the house in Guadeloupe and wounded two sisters.[46] Although the order became more experienced at missionary work, the dangers did not noticeably diminish over time. A young nun returning from Senegal in 1831 drowned when her ship sank while entering the Gironde River in France; reportedly she refused a sailor's offer to save her if she renounced her religious state. In 1849, the eight nuns traveling to Cayenne, French Guiana, reported to Javouhey that on the seventh day of their forty-eight-day journey, three sailors died of cholera, and five of their trunks disappeared. "We have made a great sacrifice in leaving Cluny and all our dear mothers," they wrote. In 1852, a father inquired after his daughter, who had been sent to Pondicherry ten years earlier; he was eager for news because "I am an old man about to descend into my tomb."[47] Families were far away, traveling conditions long and perilous, and local conditions unfamiliar and uncertain. Becoming a missionary sister took both a sense of adventure and strong religious conviction.

Apprenticeship in West Africa

In March 1822, Anne-Marie Javouhey herself traveled twenty-six days, twelve of them seasick, to St-Louis, Senegal, where she joined her sister Rosalie, who had arrived in

1819 with five Soeurs de St-Joseph, and her brother Pierre. The journey itself was not without its dangers; only six years earlier the French frigate *Medusa*, carrying the new governor of Senegal, had shipwrecked north of St-Louis on an uncharted reef. The survivors were left to trek overland through the desert or succumb to murder and cannibalism on the raft immortalized in Géricault's famous painting of 1819 and in a tell-all book by one of the survivors, already in its fifth edition by 1821.[48] In St-Louis, although the Soeurs de St-Joseph lived in more comfort than many of the island's inhabitants, Rosalie's letters had prepared her for the difficulties of the mission there: lack of priests and therefore sacraments (in 1820, the Soeurs de St-Joseph took Easter communion on 27 August), no church, exhaustion, too few beds and too many deaths in their hospital, and the seeming indifference of the local population. Although the Soeurs de St-Joseph were undoubtedly improving the quality of health care, they had failed to maintain a school. "If you knew how difficult it is to tame and train these poor blacks," Rosalie wrote to her niece. "[It is] even more [difficult] to instruct or enlighten them. In the eight months that we've been here we've not reached those who surround us in the slightest way." "I admire [your project]," she wrote several months later to Anne-Marie, "but it is more the work of God than that of men. I urge you to renounce it."[49]

None of these warnings had the least effect on her older sister. Arriving in Senegal—her first trip outside of the metropole—Anne-Marie Javouhey marveled at her new surroundings:

> [The] population is enormous for the territory; there are as many and even more people on all the streets than in Paris on the rue St-Honoré....They all seem to me in mourning because their skin is black. I feel a great need to work for their happiness....I am going to start with very little, but the well-founded expectation of success upholds my courage and will help me overcome the obstacles.[50]

The statement shows Javouhey's naiveté about other races and cultures, even if associating black skin with mourning was less derogatory than the traditional European association of blackness with evil or depravity.[51] What is most striking is her certainty that her mission would succeed. Three years earlier, when the plans for her voyage had first been laid, she proclaimed her confidence that "God would keep us from all dangers" because "the motive is so good."[52]

For the two years that Javouhey lived in West Africa, she was a whirlwind of activity, improving the hospital, setting up schools, starting a mission on Gorée, acquiring a farm in the interior, and traveling south to Gambia and Sierra Leone. "My dear mother bustles around," wrote Rosalie in admiration. "[W]e had great need of her presence and the help of our sisters to reform various things and create other useful ones."[53] Although Javouhey made numerous stops in Senegal in later years, particularly on the way back and forth from France to South America and the Caribbean, she never lived there again. Nonetheless, this first *séjour* abroad proved formative as it was Javouhey's introduction to the contested problems of race and slavery in the French empire and shaped much of her future work.

The French presence in West Africa after 1817 consisted of two trading posts, one on the island of St-Louis, located where the Atlantic meets the Senegal River, and another approximately two hundred miles southwest, on the island of Gorée, facing the present site of Dakar. Both had just been returned to France after a period of British rule during the Napoleonic Wars.[54] Although the French had used both islands as trading and military posts since the seventeenth century, neither had a very large settler population. Because European men often formed temporary liaisons with African women, however, both colonies had a population of mixed-race individuals, usually referred to as *habitants*, who served as cultural and commercial intermediaries between Europeans and Africans. The remainder of the population was African, either free (19 percent in Gorée in 1823) or slave (81 percent in Gorée in 1823).[55] On the two islands, resident slaves were held almost exclusively by Africans or mixed-race individuals, not Europeans, and were treated relatively well. They were employed primarily as sailors, artisans, and domestic servants and could also be rented out, usually to French government officials, merchants, and ships' captains, for additional income.[56]

Beginning in the late seventeenth century both islands also served as export ports for the Atlantic slave trade, which dominated their economy.[57] Slaves were captured in the interior, marched west, sold to French slave traders, and shipped from the ports. Since the exported slaves were more likely to be men, women slaves outnumbered men in the port towns.[58] Although Britain imposed the abolition of the slave trade on France after the Congress of Vienna, the French failed to enforce this during the Restoration period; between 1814 and 1831, at least 482 French slave ships sailed to West Africa to load human cargo.[59] Besides slaves, the major export item was gum arabic (a vegetable resin extracted from gum trees by slave gangs), a key ingredient in textile manufacturing. During the French Revolution, the monopolies of the Old Regime trading companies were replaced by competition between various French commercial firms, whose employees stayed longer in the colony and sought to make their firms profitable rather than benefiting personally from clandestine trading. The new French settlers were less dependent, therefore, on African middlemen (and women).[60] When the two colonies were returned to France, the French were eager to exploit their wealth and local resources—and that of their hinterlands—as a first step toward rebuilding their empire.

The decision to invite women religious into the French outposts in West Africa was symptomatic of this new approach to colonization in the early nineteenth century, focusing on settlement, as well as a new appreciation for the role of women in the "civilizing" process. Both settlement and "civilizing" demanded a sanitary and educational infrastructure that the Soeurs de St-Joseph could provide through hospitals and schools. One of Rosalie Javouhey's first initiatives in the St-Louis hospital was the washing of linens with hot water and soap. The nuns had relatively little medical training, and they suffered from a persistent lack of medications, but unlike previous lay nurses, they provided care without requiring private fees or bribes.[61] They also provided better organization and regular meals. In 1821, the French governor laid the foundation stone for a new hospital on the north end of the island, where it would have room to grow; the following year he established a "conseil de santé" [health committee]. By 1829, the hospital in St-Louis had 155 beds, staffed by seven Soeurs de St-Joseph. According to the colonial administration, however, the "able hands" of the nursing sisters in the hospitals would also provide an "excellent means of influence over the population." For the nuns themselves, of course, nursing the ill and dying was an opportune moment to bring them closer to God and the Christian faith. Javouhey herself saw religion as "the base of all the good and great institutions," essential to the civilizing mission.[62] In a colony that suffered from a shortage of priests, women religious could serve as clerical auxiliaries.[63]

Even more than health care, education provided a vehicle for French acculturation. Unlike in the other slave colonies, such as Martinique, Guadeloupe, Bourbon, or French Guiana, French policy toward Africans in Senegal at this time was assimilationist, and access to education was one method of creating a French-speaking African elite who could serve as clerks, administrators, and even soldiers.[64] But as mothers, women were also now targets of colonial interest and activity. In 1821, a year before Javouhey arrived in Senegal, the government saw little need for more than two priests (one in St-Louis and one in Gorée), considering the small number of resident Christians and "their absolute lack of zeal." According to one official document, the most important project in St-Louis was instead to reopen the girls' school because "it is by means of the coming generation that one must proceed; in Senegal education is entirely at home; mothers are extremely ignorant and lazy; they have none of our habits and do not even speak French; train the mothers [because] in matters of morals women make opinion and opinion makes the law." The new governor of Senegal, who became Javouhey's close collaborator and ally, Baron Roger, argued that the "blacks and mulattos of St-Louis were as much strangers to us as the Turks....The richest women, even though daughters of Frenchmen, neither speak nor understand our language." "All these improvements," he wrote to Javouhey, "could come out of a good girls' school....By this means only can we rectify morals and put this population in contact with our customs and laws."[65] The role of educated mothers was now recognized as key to acculturation efforts in the colonies, just as it was in the metropole.

Javouhey was enthusiastic about improving the educational facilities in Senegal. In St-Louis, a small school for mixed-race and African boys based on the mutual method had existed since 1817, founded by Jean Dard, a former pupil in Anne-Marie Javouhey's school in Autun and a classmate of Rosalie Javouhey. But there had been no schools for girls ever since a small school annexed to the hospital had failed for lack of pupils. Since the small population of Europeans did not include many women and children, the majority of the pupils in the schools established by the sisters were the mixed-race daughters of European men and African women. When Javouhey visited her congregation's new mission in Gorée in May 1822, she reported that the school already had sixty-two "signares," or mixed-race girls, "almost white," she specified, most of whom did not know how to write despite being 20 to 25 years old. Fortunately, she added, "they showed the greatest desire to learn." By the end of 1822, the girls' school in St-Louis had enrolled one hundred girls, as well as sixty-four young women aged 20 to 27.[66]

In both Gorée and St-Louis, these signares were among the most influential of the islands' inhabitants and served as cultural brokers between the French and the Senegalese. During their time in Senegal, European men often formed households with African or Eurafrican women by engaging in Wolof marriage rites that were not valid in France, termed by the French "mariage à la mode du pays," or customary marriage. The advantages of these arrangements for European men were that they provided regular sex, domestic stability, more comfortable housing, better food and medical care, and integration into the local community.[67] Given the high mortality rates among Europeans in Senegal, men with local wives had a much better chance of survival. During the Old Regime, the men, restrained by the commercial monopolies enforced by the companies they worked for, traded clandestinely through their wives. The women in turn used their connections with European men to build up wealth through trade and property that they could transmit to their children. In addition, signares and their domestic slaves, also mainly female, took on the work of provisioning and caring for slaves destined for transatlantic export, as well as the many Africans who protected and transported slave cargo and manned slave ships.[68] By the eve of the French Revolution, Gorée had fifty large brick or stone houses inhabited by signare households, up from just six in 1772, and women were significant property owners of both land and slaves.[69] As the permanent residents of Senegal and the necessary interlocutors with Senegalese culture and society, the signares' relationships with European men gave them more freedom than other local women, and when their husbands returned to France, they were free to remarry. Although signares adopted some features of European life, their households remained fundamentally African in customs, organization, and language.[70] In short, signare households traditionally served to assimilate Frenchmen to African society and customs in a form beneficial to both sides.

The assimilationist project of the post-Revolutionary period, however, ran in the other direction. Now the goal of the French administration was to assimilate

Africans—or at least a mixed-race elite—to French culture and customs. The education offered by the Soeurs de St-Joseph promised to turn Eurafrican girls into young women instructed in the French language, history, geography, domestic arts, and the Catholic faith. The large number of pupils they enrolled suggested that the signares saw the advantages of a French-centered curriculum in a period when the French were reasserting their control over the colony. Javouhey reported a warm welcome when she arrived in Gorée in 1822. "All the good signares came to offer me their services," she wrote. "I found them charming; they brought their young ladies from the following day, we have already sixty-four in class." One of them rented her a house that faced the sea and doubled as a school. Given the high enrollments, Javouhey wrote back to France for more teachers and teaching supplies, especially catechisms and textbooks in French grammar, history, geography, and religious history.[71] Their curriculum in this school was very similar to the one they offered girls in France, although because the vast majority of mixed-race girls in Senegal were Wolof-speaking, they faced greater pedagogical challenges. As late as the 1840s, French officials complained that the pupils in their schools had a weak understanding of French, making the "results of the lessons often uncertain." One proposed solution was a boarding school in order to "more easily form French morals, ideas, and habits."[72] The Soeurs de St-Joseph opened one in 1847.

To Javouhey and the other Soeurs de St-Joseph, these schools also provided an opportunity to deepen the faith of this influential and nominally Catholic population. Catholic baptism was widely practiced among the mixed-race population as a ceremony of inclusion in the Eurafrican community, and there is some evidence of a flourishing Catholic parish on Gorée (the more Christian of the two locales) before the Revolution. Yet, by the early nineteenth century, actual Catholic practice was virtually nonexistent. Besides baptism, there was little adherence to other Catholic rites such as marriage or funerals. In part, this resulted from a severe shortage of priests willing to serve in Senegal and their extremely limited tenure and language skills. However, most Africans appear to have assimilated Catholic ceremonies to local ones—baptism for Wolof naming rites, for example—and drew on multiple religious traditions when appropriate.[73] Adopting Christianity provided access to a hybrid identity rather than an exclusive faith.

Catholic marriage was a particular stumbling block. The entire social structure of the signares was based on the fact that their marriages followed African tradition, which provided them with social and financial legitimacy but were not legal according to French law, which made Frenchmen—some of whom had wives back in France or planned to marry when they returned home—more likely to marry them. After the restoration of French rule on the islands, however, both missionaries, for moral reasons, and the French state, for legal ones, became more interested in regularizing and legitimizing these marriages. In 1818, only a single Christian marriage had taken place in St-Louis; between 1820 and 1828 there were twelve; and between 1830 and 1840, thirty-two. In 1853 the Abbé Boilat (himself the son of a customary marriage) reported proudly that "families today are very appropriately composed, and morality alone is in style," attributing the change to the effects of the Gospel.[74] In Senegal, the French civil code regarding marriage, which limited the property rights of African wives and their (illegitimate) children, was applied in 1830.[75] Those signares whose relationships were not regularized by French marriage became little more than concubines, especially as trade monopolies were broken, destroying the underground economy for personal profit, which served as the rationale for the partnership between European men and African women.[76] The new focus on domesticity for women, as well as a shift in power from the household to the public sphere, also lessened the dominance of the signares, especially in trade. Assimilating this elite community of women to French language, faith, and culture, therefore, diminished their power and threatened the fluid nature of Eurafrican identity in Gorée and St-Louis.[77] Attending the Soeurs de St-Joseph school opened up access to French culture but also trapped African women in its gender assumptions regarding marriage and domesticity.

Teaching, acculturating, and deepening the faith of mixed-race girls did not exhaust the opportunities Javouhey imagined for Africa. Once she arrived in Africa, evangelizing among Africans appeared to her more promising than among Europeans, whom she found "very bad subjects who did not want to hear about religion," not even at the moment of death, whereas the blacks were "good, simple...it would not be difficult to convince them by example."[78] The moral superiority of black Africans, whom she viewed as innocent, compared to what she saw as decadent and depraved colonists, was a frequent motif in her writings. After about a year's residence in Senegal, she set out a plan for a school for black girls she thought the congregation could open. She imagined an enrollment of two dozen girls from six different African provinces, aged eight to ten, who would remain in the school until they reached the age of twenty. Three converse (or lower-class) sisters would look after these girls "like true mothers," and the house would be built "in the greatest simplicity, but with a closed courtyard and good walls."[79]

In 1826, the congregation did open a boarding school with a French Catholic curriculum for African girls in St-Louis.[80] Segregated from the school for French and mixed-race girls, this school admitted free black girls (or mixed-race orphans) between the ages of six and eleven for a period of four years, during which they were not allowed to leave or see their parents except in the presence of a nun. The girls were given lessons in reading, writing, arithmetic, and religion, as well as instruction in housekeeping and domestic skills. Prayers were said at the appropriate times each day, and the girls attended Mass on Sundays and holidays. The only language allowed was French. Some concessions to indigenous customs were made in the form of clothing (bare legs and feet allowed for the first three years), food (wild boar and couscous), and bedding (floor mats), but otherwise the goal of the school was complete acculturation into the religion, language, and customs of France without integration into the French school. The lower-class status of the school was marked by the time in the school day devoted to domestic duties like cleaning, laundry, sewing, cooking, and gardening. These girls, much like their peasant counterparts in France, were being trained primarily as housewives and laborers, assimilated to French norms but not encouraged to rise above their station. Perhaps unsurprisingly, the school failed to attract many pupils, and in 1832 local French administrators thought its cost not worth the effort and withdrew their funding. In St-Louis, the Soeurs de St-Joseph accepted some black girls into their regular school but segregated them into a separate class; in Gorée, the admission of blacks took place only after the abolition of slavery in 1848.[81] In theory, slaves with Christian masters were also Christian; in reality, no missionary, even Javouhey, reached the slave population in any substantial numbers before the abolition of slavery in 1848.

A barely acknowledged issue was that many African girls—unlike the mixed-race daughters of signares—were likely to be Muslim and less amenable to Catholic evangelization. In fact, on the subject of Islam, Javouhey's letters from Senegal are curiously silent. Only two exceptions stand out. On a visit downriver from St-Louis in 1822, she spoke of an encounter with Muslim cowherds, who asked her why she did not pray with them. "I took advantage of these circumstances," she wrote, "to speak with them of our holy religion." She nonetheless admired these Muslims, whose habits of prayer she praised and whose life she characterized as "in harmony with that of the Old Testament patriarchs... if something happens to them, it is God who wanted it; they do not complain. They have nothing to themselves and share their bread with their fellow men. Yes, I do say, these people will be the condemnation of Christians!" Yet she also found them fanatical, ignorant, and prone to illusions in part because of their "good faith," which made them prey "to one superstition after another." Good examples, she thought, might "bring them gently to truth," especially the children. A second comment on African Islam can be found in her description of the African boarding school. "I see [it] as a great good for religion if we succeed in this establishment," she explained. "[W]ithout it we will never be able to make [our] religion known to blacks; we must distance them from the marabouts, separate them from the crowd in order to enlighten them and give them a taste of religion and the advantages that it brings."[82]

These references are the only times that she acknowledges the competition of Islam, which was undergoing both a geographic expansion and a religious revival in the late eighteenth and early nineteenth centuries. Muslim leaders were beginning to insist on more orthodoxy from their subjects, embarking on jihads to spread the faith, and religious brotherhoods deepened it.[83] There was already a long Islamic tradition in West Africa, centered in Mauritania, of which St-Louis formed the outer fringe. In fact, St-Louis housed a significant Muslim neighborhood on the south end of the island. The expansion of Islam also resulted from French policies, which accelerated its spread by giving Muslim chiefs more authority over tribal peoples, as well as by the growing perception among Africans themselves that the social and political dislocations that they were experiencing would be best served through a new religion. In this case, Islam, already an African religion, better preserved their customs and institutions. Both increased Muslim assertiveness and French assimilation policy seem to have hardened the lines between the (large) Muslim and the (small) Christian populations in Senegal, in contrast to more negotiated identities in earlier periods.[84] According to Laure Bernard, an admirer and contemporary of Javouhey, Muslims in Senegal did not voluntarily engage in religious discussions with her. Only one young Arab, she reported, accepted Javouhey's invitation to read several passages of the Gospels and the Koran side by side, concluding, however, that the Koran was the superior text. Also according to Bernard, Javouhey was informed by Florence, her young African companion, that Muslim marabouts told slaves that conversion to Christianity would perpetuate their captivity in the afterlife. Although David Boilat, a Senegalese priest sponsored by Javouhey, argued that the Catholic missionary benefited from the prestige associated with the Muslim marabout as a man of God, Koranic schools for both boys and girls also competed with missionary schools.[85] In large part, Javouhey acted as if these impediments did not exist, although they undoubtedly help explain why Catholic evangelization in Senegal, including hers, was not more successful.

Colonizing Africa

In addition to the urban establishments in St-Louis and Gorée, Javouhey also hankered after a mission based on the small-scale farming familiar to her from her own peasant upbringing. In Dagana, 120 miles upriver from St-Louis, she planned an agricultural settlement farmed by Africans on a nine-hundred-acre concession from the French government. Her ability to acquire this land resulted from her friendship with Senegal's new governor, Jacques-François Roger, previously legal counsel for the Soeurs de St-Joseph, who had arrived in Senegal in 1819 and become governor in 1821, thanks in part to Javouhey's support.[86] Politically progressive, Wolof-speaking, ambitious, and extremely energetic, Roger was a new kind of French colonial administrator who had more in common with late nineteenth-century governors like Faidherbe than with his contemporaries.[87] His ambition for Senegal was to open up to agriculture the entire Senegal River valley, where he had already established a small cotton plantation. Roger's goals were foremost capitalist and commercial; he thought the French were vegetating in the port cities, especially after the abolition of the slave trade in 1815, and needed to bring larger parts of the interior under control and cultivation. He was supported in these schemes by the new colonial minister, the marquis of Clermont-Tonnerre, who sought a substitute for the lost colonial revenues in Saint-Domingue, now an independent (and hostile) Haiti. By opening up Africa itself to large-scale colonial crops, Roger hoped to obviate the need for either the slave trade or the brutal form of slavery practiced in the Caribbean, a way, according to historian Christopher Miller, to "forget" Haiti.[88] Roger's predecessor as governor, Julien Schmaltz, who had arrived in 1816, had begun the process of exploring and mapping the lands adjacent to the Senegal River and proposed cultivating cotton, sugar cane, and indigo. He had also signed a treaty with the local Waalo ruler that ceded land in return for an annual fee of more than ten thousand francs and promised military protection against neighboring states.[89]

Under Roger, land concessions were offered to inhabitants of St-Louis and Gorée, soldiers at the end of their tours of duty, and French immigrants who could invest at least five thousand francs. The government contracted to provide initial tools, livestock, building materials, and munitions and contributed to the sinking of wells and the building of irrigation canals. The French also established three additional forts along the river to protect against invasion and provided land concessions to native chiefs in the region in exchange for their cooperation.[90] To objections regarding the unhealthiness of the climate for Europeans, Roger pointed to the longevity of the Soeurs de St-Joseph in Senegal. Saint-Simonian in spirit if not in name, he imported specialists in agriculture, botany, chemistry, and engineering from France and established a farm at Richard-Toll to serve as an agricultural laboratory. In the space of just a few years, he had experimented with a great variety of European and tropical plants, including peanuts (later to become one of Senegal's main exports), before settling on cotton and indigo (as the most promising for trade) and sweet potatoes, melons, mangoes, and rice (for internal consumption). In St-Louis, he built a factory to process indigo and imported a cotton gin. By September 1822, there were fifteen concessions under cultivation along the river, including the one owned by Javouhey. Eschewing the language of Caribbean slavery, he refused to call these new farms plantations, preferring "gardens."[91]

In turning Senegal into a model agricultural colony, however, Roger also believed that he was contributing to its "civilization" by improving the material lives of Africans and introducing a European work ethic. In this way, the exploitation of the Senegal River valley would "serve both our fatherland and humanity."[92] It was in the moral benefits of farming that his vision coincided with that of Javouhey. "We will establish there," she wrote in 1822, dreaming about her Dagana plantation, "a village of good Christians…the sugar cane will be big, the orange and lemon trees will bear fruit, the houses will be well built, our herd will have multiplied, and all this will have been done in common with new farmers who will be regarded as the people of God."[93] In late summer 1822 Javouhey took the two-day steamboat journey upriver and spent six weeks on her new plantation. She wrote enthusiastically about the land, the new cabins, and the cattle; the last, she reported, had cost them only forty francs each, and some were fatter than those in France. At Dagana, Javouhey also described multiple interactions with Africans, including the Muslims, whom she compared to Old Testament patriarchs. The parlor in the sisters' house, where they received "the princes and the kings who visit us often," was also often full of local women, who were drawn by the novelty of the congregation's mirror. Their husbands, however, could not believe that Javouhey was "a woman and so active; that it was I who directed the workers; they praise me interminably."[94] Javouhey had big plans for her plantation. Long concerned with the future of the children who populated the congregation's orphanages in France, she thought some of them could immigrate to Dagana. She also imagined two establishments there (one for boys and another for girls) for the instruction of black youth. This idea, she argued, was "naturally attached to the great project of civilizing Africa, to make of them an agricultural people, hardworking and above all, honest and Christian." As "a nursery of honest men and good Christians," Dagana was to Javouhey a potential site of cultivation in a double sense.[95]

The Achilles heel of the French fantasy of agricultural expansion in the Senegal River valley was the lack of an available labor force in a region depopulated by ecological changes, war, and the slave trade. By and large the African chiefs reneged on their treaty obligations to provide labor, and African laborers did not flock to work on the French plantations. "It is precisely this habit that the blacks have of working for themselves," Roger wrote, exasperated, in 1820, "that creates the problem of using them for our cultivation." Unable to imagine that the local Africans had interests separate from those of France, he complained about their independence, their "whims," their chiefs' lack of authority, and their unwillingness to give up farming their own lands in the hope of earning more working for Europeans. The only solution, he concluded, was to make European products indispensable so that they would work for money. Javouhey also noted the "singular" facts that the Africans around Dagana did not use money and that they "only looked to feed and dress themselves and have no foresight for tomorrow."[96]

After considering a few fanciful possibilities, like importing workers from the Canary Islands or reimporting them from the Caribbean, Roger decided to solve the apparent labor shortage by developing a sort of indentured servitude, *engagement à temps*, which bound former slaves to work on the plantations for a period of seven years if they had been seized from slave ships or fourteen years if they had been purchased in the interior. Two hundred free men of color who had been arrested for political crimes—that is, for demanding abolition and enfranchisement—were also deported from Martinique as part of this labor force.[97] This temporary form of slavery was rationalized as a method of spreading European "civilization" through the agency of former *engagés*, who would return to their home villages with new work habits and farming skills, a sort of "apprenticeship in freedom."[98]

Although Roger considered himself an abolitionist and took pains to assure the *engagés* that they were neither slaves nor captives and would be fully free at the end of their term of engagement, the very existence of a system of forced labor blurred the lines between slavery and freedom in ways that facilitated the continuation of a clandestine slave trade.[99] In Javouhey's plans for the Dagana plantation, however, she designated three thousand francs per year to pay the African workers rather than engaging indentured servants. While in Senegal, she also bought and freed six African slaves, aged nine through twenty-five, five of whom were *engagés à temps*.[100] Her neighbors along the Senegal river, however, did make use of the new system, as Roger had intended,; in the sixty plantations (more than twelve hundred hectares) that existed in 1826, three hundred (or one-fifth) of the fifteen hundred Africans employed as farmworkers, were *engagés*. An 1831 law made it illegal to bring captives to St-Louis or Gorée unless they were *engagés*, although many were undoubtedly simply treated as slaves. The number of these indentured servants in Senegal as a whole peaked at more than twenty-five hundred in 1839 and then declined; new engagements were outlawed as of 1844, four years before the abolition of slavery in the French colonies.[101]

The agricultural experiment in the Senegal River valley ultimately failed. Besides the labor shortage, the region experienced incursions from neighboring African states, which were afraid of French expansion in the interior. Local Waalo residents resented the large French land concessions, which they did not believe gave the French outright ownership, and began a systematic campaign of destroying property. The infusion of new investors into this region also threatened the revenues of the traditional slave and gum traders, who had long enjoyed a monopoly on doing business with the French. Finally, and perhaps most important, the crop yields were disappointing.[102] Roger wrote to Javouhey in 1825, after she had returned to France, that the gum crop was completely wiped out due to drought (which, he also reported, the local residents attributed to the arrival of the Europeans) but that cotton was providing "a satisfying little harvest and that next year will work wonders."[103] The following year, he requested repatriation to France due to the toll on his health of eight years' residence in Senegal. On his return he declared optimistically that "colonization had been founded" in Senegal.[104] However, from 1822 to 1825, the colony had exported fewer than fifty thousand kilos of cotton, and the expenses of supporting agriculture in Senegal were 1.25 million francs against 188,000 francs in returns. Many of the technical experts left the colony when Roger did, and plantation owners began abandoning their holdings. By 1831, the July Monarchy had removed the funds for Senegalese agriculture from the budget, and in 1835 the fruit trees at Richard-Toll were cut down.[105] The French government put its resources back into the more profitable gum trade, to be replaced by peanuts in the 1840s. St-Louis continued to expand but did so as the hub of a river empire based on commerce rather than agriculture. Javouhey's lands at Dagana seem to have been abandoned after the dry winter of 1825 and the death of her cousin in the same year.[106] Her collaboration with Roger, however, who became a French deputy under the July Monarchy, would continue as she further developed her interests in slave education and emancipation.

Javouhey's interest in West Africa extended beyond the French possessions there. In 1823, she traveled south, first to Ste-Marie (Bathurst to the English) on Banjul (St. Mary's) Island in Gambia and then to Freetown, Sierra Leone, at the invitation of Governor Charles MacCarthy, who asked her to organize hospitals in both places. Javouhey went not only without official permission but in direct opposition to a request from the French interior minister to return to France, where, he judged, her order needed her. Javouhey herself justified her trip to set up new establishments in British territory as "a guarantee for the others in Africa, in case of a rupture between the French and English governments."[107] Although France and Britain were rivals on the west coast of Africa, the French commander in Senegal argued that her "zeal" and "charity" "could only make the Catholic religion and the French name loved abroad." MacCarthy, for his part, wrote to Roger that Javouhey's success disproved the "absurd assertion" that Africans were "incapable of being civilized." Reminding Roger that he had spent two years in Senegal (during the British occupation), MacCarthy assured him that "our cause is the same."[108] MacCarthy was, in fact, the son of a French army officer and a woman of Irish descent and had fled France in 1791 to take up arms with the British. First sent to recruit in Acadia (Nova Scotia), he was posted to St-Louis in 1812, where he contracted a customary marriage with a signare, with whom he had a son, before being transferred to Freetown.[109] This background, personal, as well as political, undoubtedly made him more comfortable with inviting Catholic nuns to work in a British colony; at any rate, Protestant missionaries did not typically undertake hospital work, and Javouhey had gained a reputation for results in West Africa.

In both Gambia and Sierra Leone, Javouhey found the hospitals in terrible shape and bustled about to improve them. In Gambia, the European patients slept on straw mattresses, and the African ones on mats, and each patient was responsible for cooking his raw meat "in his own manner." "What disorder results!" Javouhey complained.[110] The hospital in Sierra Leone was overcome by yellow fever patients, from whom Javouhey contracted the disease herself, becoming seriously ill for months. Before she fell ill, however, she cleaned and provisioned the hospital and applied the fever remedies (mustard baths, blisters, quinine tonic) that she had learned from the doctor in St-Louis. However, the main advantage the Soeurs de

St-Joseph brought as nurses was not medical knowledge but organization. One nun, she wrote MacCarthy in a proposal to take over the administration of the Sierra Leone hospital, could serve as pharmacist, as well as assist the doctor, bandage wounds, distribute meals and medicine at fixed hours, change bed linens, and generally oversee the care of the patients and the cleaning of the rooms. A second nun would be in charge of the kitchen and the laundry (assisted by African women for the heavy work), including the marketing and the supervision of servants. This description demonstrates that what Javouhey offered, much like and much earlier than Florence Nightingale in the 1850s, was a professionalization of hospital nursing, carried out by disinterested yet compassionate women, as opposed to care by individuals whom she characterized as "lack[ing] order, attention, and, I argue, compassion for the sick."[111]

Her travels south also gave Javouhey ideas for new projects. At the dilapidated French trading post of Albreda along the Gambia River, she marveled at the quality of the soil, the variety of vegetation, and the size of the fruit. "If all this was well cultivated," she fantasized, "what advantage could one not gain!" Roger, she hoped, would take a trip south to see the potential.[112] Even more significant, both Gambia and Sierra Leone presented new possibilities for educating African youth. Since the British abolition of the slave trade in 1807, Africans—many of whom were women and children—who were seized from illegal slave ships had been returned to British possessions on the west coast of Africa. In Ste-Marie, among the five hundred girls and one thousand boys separated from their parents, Javouhey proposed selecting fifty between the ages of eight and ten to educate; she had even identified an unused infirmary with enclosed courtyards and large gardens in which to establish this orphanage. She thought about bringing a dozen African girls to Senegal to start a new establishment in which they might "find as much response as among the Whites, perhaps more." In Freetown she found "magnificent churches" and a community, unlike St-Louis or Gorée, dominated by Christians, chiefly evangelical Protestants, who "sang hymns" in religious services as early as five in the morning and as late as nine in the evening, as well as a sizeable Catholic community, although temporarily without a priest.[113]

In Sierra Leone Javouhey also had her first exposure to the potential of African Christian villages. Freetown had been initially founded by British abolitionists and settled by black emigrants from Nova Scotia—Loyalist refugees from the Revolutionary War—who had already converted to Christianity in North America. Since 1807, it had become an important center for the suppression of the slave trade along the west coast of Africa. Slave ships of all nationalities captured by the British were sent to Sierra Leone, where their cargo of captured slaves was released.[114] Now absorbing tens of thousands of Africans of mixed nationalities seized from those slave ships, Governor MacCarthy had come up with a plan to replace the improvised and ramshackle settlements around Freetown with orderly parishes run by Protestant missionaries.[115] Thirteen such villages, centered around a church and school and combining civil and religious authority, were functioning during Javouhey's visit. It is not hard to imagine that this initiative informed her later experiment in Mana. Although there is no evidence she visited the villages, perhaps she discussed them with MacCarthy during her long convalescence from yellow fever in his country house. The mission villages around Freetown—built in European style, well provisioned with European goods, and peopled with African converts—encapsulated the potential of slave emancipation under Christian patronage. Like Javouhey and Roger, MacCarthy saw Christian conversion and assimilation to European culture and civilization as going hand in hand.[116]

The African Seminary

When Javouhey left Senegal in 1824, it had become clear to her that the most promising way of evangelizing in Africa was to develop an indigenous clergy who had the language skills, the native habits, and the resistance to disease to live among the local population. At this time, this was a radical idea among clerics and laypeople alike. To form such a clergy, she proposed that the Soeurs de St-Joseph open a school in France for African children, who would be encouraged to become priests or nuns at the end of their studies. Even if they did not choose to enter the religious state, they could return to Africa as schoolteachers and role models. The school would be located in the novitiate in Bailleul, in northern France, and their chaplain would be charged with supervising the education of the boys.[117] Such a project had support in France. The vicar general of Beauvais, in whose diocese the school was located, evoked the image of some of these African boys' becoming "missionary priests, apostles" and even fantasized about "the extraordinary spectacle of a hierarchy completely composed of blacks who from the altar boy to the pontiff piously fulfill their ministry." An African pope was a remarkable vision for a nineteenth-century cleric. Several years later, the curé of Fontainebleau offered her land in his parish and compared her to past Catholic heroes like François Xavier, Bartolomé de Las Casas, and Vincent de Paul. "You will have trained," he enthused, "a new people."[118] In Senegal, she also had the support of Baron Roger, though he debated whether an African normal school should be located in France or in Africa. In France, he feared, pupils would become too Europeanized, unable on their return to Senegal to sleep on the ground, eat couscous, or tolerate the climate. In Africa, however, they might remain too attached to African habits, unable to absorb the lessons imparted to them by their European teachers. An establishment in Senegal would also be expensive to establish and maintain since the teachers would have to be imported from France. On balance, he, too, preferred a French school, which would result in the "moral and intellectual improvement of the population of our colony" and "extend our influence over commerce and civilization in this part of Africa."[119]

Javouhey succeeded in recruiting ten African children (seven boys, three girls) to send to France in April 1825 and ten more (all boys) in May 1827, aged seven to fifteen. About half, like David Boilat, son of a French sailor and a signare, were of mixed race; two of the boys, including Arsène Fridoil, had English fathers. One boy was a liberated slave, and the three girls belonged to the colonial government. The two Moussa brothers were sons of the African cantor at the church in St-Louis, who presided over hymn-singing services in the absence of a priest. The most prominent of the pupils was Amand Mamoudou Sy, the Muslim son of the king of Boundou, in the interior, who was being held in St-Louis as a hostage. The school took in three additional boys: a Galibi Indian boy from French Guiana, a former Senegalese slave rescued by the sisters, and a Haitian native resident in France; they had arrived in 1824, 1828, and 1829, respectively.[120] Javouhey also brought back with her from Africa a young Fouta girl named Florence, a former slave rescued by Rosalie Javouhey. Even as a child of nine or ten, Florence had become Javouhey's constant companion in Senegal, serving as interpreter throughout West Africa and nursing Javouhey back to health when she caught yellow fever in Sierra Leone. In France, Florence became a romantic figure, evoking for those who met her the cruelties of slavery and the potential of Africans. "Endowed with a lively intelligence, pious, educated, her talents and her physique embodied the delightful creation of Mme de Duras," wrote Javouhey supporter Laure Bernard after Florence's death, referring to the fictional heroine of a best-selling tragic novel about a Senegalese girl rescued from slavery and raised in France. "Happier than Ourika," Bernard continued, "Florence had a destiny to fulfill, her fervent soul accepted it with enthusiasm, but death came to surprise her while she dreamed of a new destiny for her compatriots."[121]

Though these numbers, twenty-four pupils in all, fell far short of her original plan—Javouhey had hoped to add at least five pupils to the school every year—she followed the children's fortunes closely even as she traveled around the Atlantic, bringing news of them to their families whenever she stopped in Senegal. Eleven of the children, including Florence, were baptized in France, some with Javouhey as godmother, although she required that they receive appropriate instruction and seek baptism voluntarily. "Diola is converted," she reported in 1825, referring to one of the girls. "I took her to her godmother the other day."[122] Javouhey repeatedly declared her satisfaction with the experiment and was especially proud of Florence, who was enrolled in the boarding school that the Soeurs de St-Joseph had established for more advanced girls—all the others French, some young Javouhey relatives.

Javouhey reported, "Florence makes rapid progress in all subjects: piety, religion, artistic accomplishments; everything is easy for her. In music, she is stronger than Soeur Clothilde. They say that she knows as much in four months than the third-year pupils; she will make a good nun." One day, Javouhey hoped, Florence would become her secretary. She added her cousin's young sons, Jules and Auguste Javouhey, to the group of boys, "with no distinction," and worried that she could not find a good drawing instructor for them. Above all, she admonished her sister to keep the boys' teacher happy because "one day these children will work for the glory of God in the colonies."[123]

In France, however, the children succumbed to homesickness and illness, primarily tuberculosis, which resulted in the deaths of thirteen between 1827 and 1834, all as teenagers. After the first few deaths, in 1829, Javouhey transferred the children to a house in Limoux (Aude), in the south, where she hoped they would find the climate more congenial. Here also she added a garden to train in agriculture those children who were neither pious nor adept in their studies.[124] But the children continued to fall ill, exacerbated no doubt by communal living. The death of Florence at age seventeen in September 1831 hit Javouhey especially hard. "It is very painful," she wrote in 1834, "to see all these children die without knowing where their illness comes from."[125] The high mortality also alarmed their parents in Senegal, nine of whom lobbied the governor of Senegal for the return of their (eleven) children. In 1834 Pierre Moussa, cantor at the church in St-Louis, answering the charge that in recalling his son home he was depriving the church of a "servant," wrote, "I am religious, but I find that my child is far too young to say that his vocation is to become a priest....I fulfill my Christian duties and I have a clear conscience." "I beg of you, with all my family," he added "to restore our child to us." The parents of Charles Caty pleaded, "[Y]ou would render a service in returning him to Senegal as soon as possible and console a no longer young father and mother who wish to have their child [home] before the end of their lives." Five of the children also asked to return home, but four, Jean-Pierre Moussa, Charles Caty, Arsène Fridoil, and Amand Mamoudou Sy, petitioned the ministry to stay "in France, where we are as happy as we will ever be elsewhere" and where they could finish their education.[126] Of these four, Caty died in 1833, and Mamoudou Sy in 1834, but Moussa and Fridoil survived. Of the original group of twenty-four children, thirteen died, six returned safely to Senegal, and two went to French Guiana (one of the girls followed Javouhey to Cayenne in 1828, and the Haitian boy became head gardener in Mana in 1838); only three became priests.[127] In sheer numbers, Javouhey's grand experiment was a failure.

The three priests—David Boilat, Arsène Fridoil, and Jean-Pierre Moussa—nevertheless represented the first Senegalese clergy ever ordained. Boilat and Fridoil were the light-skinned sons of mixed-race women and European men, and Moussa had two African parents. They received their seminary education first in Carcassonne and then at the Séminaire du Saint Esprit, the institution responsible for training French colonial clergy, and were ordained in 1840 to great fanfare. They said their first Mass for the Soeurs de St-Joseph, and soon after, Moussa, assisted by the other two, celebrated a Mass for King Louis-Philippe and Queen Marie-Amélie, supporters of Javouhey's colonial projects. In 1841, after fifteen years' absence, Moussa arrived home in St-Louis to a hero's welcome, where he celebrated Mass, assisted by his aging father, and was appointed interim priest.[128] Javouhey wanted to bring the other two priests to her new settlement in Mana, where she could continue to guide them.[129] Roger argued instead that they should stay in France, where he had helped them receive funding for further education, including Arabic. "Having put them in contact with the most advanced civilization," he wrote her, "having expanded their spirit and their views to drive them back immediately into the desert…having prepared them to receive the rank of Doctor in Theology, in order to prevent them from achieving this goal, it's a thoughtlessness, a contradiction, a fault, to which I, myself, cannot be an accomplice." Instead, he thought the presence of black priests in France would help the cause of abolition. The superior of the Séminaire du Saint-Esprit argued that they could do more good in Africa than in Mana, where the population was already accustomed to white priests.[130] Perhaps under his influence, Boilat and Fridoil also chose to return to Senegal, where Boilat helped found a new boys' *collège* in St-Louis (where Moussa became a teacher), and Fridoil became a curé in Gorée.

Although all three were much better educated and more intelligent than the average colonial priest, they all ran into trouble, undoubtedly made worse by the great expectations they embodied. Inexperienced, as Javouhey had feared, they had no protectors in Senegal to help them navigate the petty politics of the little colony, and the apostolic prefect who arrived in 1843 had only contempt for indigenous priests. Although Senegalese natives, they suffered from ill health. When Boilat and Fridoil cooperated with the colonial governor in setting up the new, advanced boys' school, education being a subject close to their hearts, they encountered the hostility of the Frères de Ploërmel, who ran the colony's only other boys' school, which was now losing pupils to the new venture. When the school failed, the two Senegalese priests were blamed, accused of moral laxity and financial mismangement.[131] But as indigenous priests, their efforts to improve orthodoxy—by firmly condemning the practice of customary marriage (Boilat and Fridoil were both the children of such marriages), for example—were especially ill received. Anti-Muslim, they also failed to appreciate the extent of the Islamic revival. On the other hand, Moussa was condemned for his taste in African music, for giving European parishioners too harsh penitences, and for teaching the catechism to slaves (in Wolof no less). Boilat also claimed that Fridoil's conversions of African women, which gave them "more morality," "displeased the crowd of libertines come from overseas." Fridoil's support for abolition and his work among emancipated slaves after 1848 also alarmed the colonists and the mixed-race elite.[132]

Too European for the Africans and too African for the Europeans, the three priests occupied a liminal status in their former home. Accused of alcoholism and scandalous conduct, Moussa was sent to a seminary in Bordeaux for retraining, only to return to Africa within a few months, first to Dakar and then to Bathurst as a parish priest; he left for Haiti in 1853 (two years after Javouhey's death) and died there excommunicated and embittered in 1860. In 1846, Javouhey called the rumors about him "atrocious slanders" and identified his enemies as "ours," recommending him to the patronage of Queen Marie-Amélie.[133] Both Fridoil and Boilat were fired from the Collège de St-Louis, Fridoil completely in debt from his attempts to keep the school afloat, and both chose to return again to France in 1853, two years after Javouhey's death. Fridoil died on the voyage. Thanks to the intervention of the bishop of Meaux, an admirer of Javouhey, however, Boilat became a parish priest in France, where he remained until his death in 1901.[134] In 1853, he published a detailed and nuanced ethnographic study of Senegal, *Esquisses sénégalaises* [Senegalese Sketches], the first by an African author and illustrator. In it we hear echoes of Javouhey's assimilationist beliefs in his desire to make the Senegalese both French and Catholic through evangelization and education.[135]

However problematic the careers of these three priests, Javouhey's initiative in training them suggested the possibility of an indigenous African clergy that would take over the work of evangelizing Africa. What mattered here was the principle rather than the execution. Long before other Catholics, including François Libermann, who is usually credited with the idea, saw the potential of an African clergy, Javouhey had already effected the ordination of three African priests.[136] When she arrived in Mana, French Guiana, in 1826, she envisioned creating a male religious order made up in part of African clergy, the Frères de St-Joseph, that would parallel the Soeurs de St-Joseph de Cluny. In subsequent years, she imagined training black clergy on a larger scale, and in 1844, she wrote confidently that within six months she would be going to Rome to start the process to found a "black seminary" in Mana and one in Senegal, a project, like others, that never materialized.[137] Claude Langlois argues that, in "intervening directly in the sacerdotal terrain," Javouhey crossed a gender line in the French church by identifying and educating future clergy.[138] In viewing Africans as potential sisters, brothers, and priests, however, Javouhey not only reinforced her own sense of equality within the church but also accorded them the same status.

Anne-Marie Javouhey had more ideas than lasting results in West Africa. The Soeurs de St-Joseph provided the only hospital services in the colony and certainly improved the quality of health care. In Gorée and St-Louis, the schools founded by the sisters for settler and mixed-race girls grew and lasted, which undoubtedly helped secure French influence in the colony. However, the boarding school for black girls, with which Javouhey hoped to reach a new generation of Africans, floundered. Black girls, when later admitted to the regular schools run by the congregation, were kept apart in separate classes, a segregation based as much on social class as on racial difference.[139] The Soeurs de St-Joseph did not appear to convert many Africans to Catholicism, particularly among the large Muslim population. The Dagana plantation did not survive the French abandonment of large-scale agriculture in the Senegal River valley. Although Javouhey did not participate in it, neither did she speak out, publicly or privately, against either the slave trade or the new systems of *engagement à temps* during her time in Senegal.[140] Her experiment with educating Africans in France was a demographic failure, and the consecration of three African priests proved to be more important in theory than in practice.

Nonetheless, if we examine Javouhey's experience in Senegal as part of her entire religious career, we can see how formative a period it was. Thinking about her return to France, Javouhey wrote to her sister Marie-Joseph: "How I love Africa! I will not say goodbye to Africa; I will return to continue the great work that God in his mercy appears to have confided in us." To Rosalie she wrote, "Tell me, I beg of you, could I do in France the quarter of what I do in Africa?" Finally, on her return to Paris, she wrote to Rosalie again: "The time that I spent in Africa strengthened me in the resolution to consecrate my existence to the care of an abused and unhappy people.... Only religion can give solid principles without danger, because its laws, its dogmas attack not only the crude exterior vices, but change the heart, destroy evil at its root. Do you want to civilize Africa? Start by establishing religion there.... The youth seem to me to merit all your solicitude."[141] Now convinced that her mission was among Africans, some of the many ideas Javouhey nurtured in Africa she would apply among Africans elsewhere, primarily in French Guiana.

8

The Mana Colony

In 1827, Javouhey conceived of a new colonial project somewhat on the lines of the failed Dagana plantation in Senegal but across the Atlantic in the French colony of Guiana. Although the Soeurs de St-Joseph now ran establishments in all the French colonies, including a school in Cayenne, Javouhey felt hamstrung by the requirements of settler society. Only in a self-sufficient religious community uncorrupted by worldly contact did she see a possibility for the true regeneration of society in harmony with God. Increasingly, she sought an opportunity, in the words of her cousin, "to found a town where she could assemble a population she raised and that would develop under her care."[1] The location of this new settlement was at the westernmost fringe of French territory, along the Mana River, not far from the Maroni River, which formed the border between French Guiana and Dutch Guiana (now Surinam). Isolation was ensured by the 220 kilometers between Mana and the capital city of Cayenne, the absence of roads after Kourou (160 kilometers from Mana), and the Atlantic winds, which made a return sea voyage to Cayenne take more than a month (the trip *from* Cayenne took three days). To the west were scattered settlements of runaway slaves (maroons) living beside the Maroni river, and behind Mana stretched the Amazon forests, inhabited only by peaceful Amerindian tribes. Although Javouhey asked the government for a land grant, transportation to Guiana, building and maintenance labor, and the initial equipment and supplies, as well as continued support for eighteen months, the new colony was to be left entirely independent in matters of governance and economic livelihood. The Soeurs de

St-Joseph—including Javouhey herself—would act as teachers, nurses, administrators, and an additional workforce on the land. She recruited thirty-six sisters to accompany her, thirty of whom were "converse" sisters dedicated to manual labor, specifying that they should be between nineteen and twenty-four years of age, good workers, in good health, and of good character. During harvest time, even Javouhey herself took to the fields.[2]

The remaining colonists were to be French peasant men or women who were "accustomed to the fatigues and privations of a simple and rustic life."[3] In return for a three-to-five-year engagement, they each received four hundred hectares of land, cleared at government expense; travel expenses; food rations, clothing, and other expenses for eighteen months; farm equipment, plants, seeds, and livestock.

French Guiana

The government also provided a chaplain, two doctors, and a hospital and was responsible for the building and maintenance of houses, roads, dikes, and canals. During the period of their engagement, the participants were expected to work for the collective; after their term had expired, they could remain on the land or leave; either way, they had a right to a proportional share of all that was produced at Mana. Most were farmers, but Javouhey also recruited artisans in order to make the settlement self-sufficient. Forty-one Frenchmen, five wives, and ten children accompanied the Soeurs de St-Joseph to Mana in August 1828, for a total of ninety-eight colonists.[4]

Javouhey's real goal, however, was to prepare the land for the settlement of French orphans. The Soeurs de St-Joseph, of course, tended to orphans in France, and sending them to Mana was intended in part as a solution to a social problem at home. Javouhey also saw orphans as more easily molded to a lifestyle that emphasized hard work and religious devotion, especially in an isolated locale such as Mana. Orphaned boys were intended for a life on the land; orphaned girls as their wives or as religious sisters. They could be found either in orphanages for abandoned children run by the French government or among the poor relatives of the converse sisters. The children would learn farming and animal husbandry under the supervision of the sisters and the French settlers. Javouhey envisioned four villages eventually at Mana, each one housing one thousand orphans. The children, she thought, would be especially helpful in tending goats and chickens.[5]

Javouhey's ambitions for Mana dovetailed nicely with the interests of the French government. Seeking to rebuild their empire, officials hoped that French Guiana could be developed as a profitable territory that would, in the words of a government report, "compensate us for the colonial possessions we have lost."[6] Based on a plantation economy, Guiana in 1819 consisted of 13,309 slaves, 1,698 free individuals of color, and a mere 987 white settlers. Since the abolition of the slave trade in 1817 made importation of new African labor difficult, the colonial ministry focused on the need to attract European farmers to Guiana.[7] Rather than large-scale plantations, these new colonization schemes rested on agricultural communities of individual peasant farmers. One of these early plans proposed settling as many as 100,000 individuals over a period of twelve years, reduced to 2,400 farmers, 4,400 military conscripts, and 4,200 foundlings in later drafts. In the event, fewer than two hundred individuals, including two Soeurs de St-Joseph as nurses, migrated in 1822 to form a colony named "Nouvelle Angoulême" on the banks of the Mana river. It failed for lack of leadership and the poor conduct of the settlers, largely due to drunkenness. The government withdrew funding, and the settlers dispersed. A few years later, the captain of the Mana military post received government approval and money to recruit migrants from his home region in the Jura. Three families, totaling twenty-seven individuals, formed the vanguard of this new settlement.

After initial success, this experiment also faltered, and the colonists were sent back to France.[8]

Javouhey's project for the same site appeared to officials to reduce the costs and simplify the administration of such a settlement. At 80,000 francs, her proposal left 130,000 francs in the Mana budget to provide support until 1830, after which time, officials hoped, the colony would be self-supporting.[9] Even more important, Javouhey appeared to provide the vision and drive needed to make a settlement succeed. "Steady" and "persevering," "capable of triumphing over obstacles," in the words of officials, Javouhey would inspire the colonists to work harder and to unite around a common goal. In short, this renewed attempt at colonization was "conceived in a completely different spirit."[10] Indeed, no sooner had Javouhey arrived than she fired off a list of requests to the governor of French Guiana: more livestock, the formation of the immigrants into a militia (to replace the military fort), and the transfer of the black leper hospital from the Iles du Salut to a spot six leagues from Mana, where the sisters undertook the care of the lepers, a self-sacrificing job that earned them much goodwill.[11]

At Mana, Javouhey was clearly in her element. Although her first reaction to the abandoned settlement was to lament the "disorder" of "this poor colony," putting it into order provided an outlet for her considerable organizational energy. "We arrived here four months ago," she wrote to a sister back in France, "[but] you would believe it four years if you saw the establishment. Everything marches along with a firm step toward good order." Describing her daily activities, she rhapsodized:

> I visit [the artisan workshops] four times a day and sometimes even
> more. I begin with the woodworkers and the cabinet makers; I pass by
> the wood turners; I enter into the shop of the clog-makers, which leads
> me to the cobblers; I visit the carpenters at the same time as the pit
> sawyers; I go to the forge, then to the locksmiths and the boilermakers.
> When I have visited all the mechanical arts, I return to visit the farmers;
> there I find my center; first I go see the gardeners, and after having seen
> the work of the men, I rest near the sisters' field, which is the equal to
> that of the men; it is with the sisters that I weed and plant beans and
> manioc; I sow rice, corn, etc., etc., while singing hymns, telling stories,
> laughing with all my strength, sorry that our poor sisters in France do
> not share our happiness.[12]

Her letters were equally enthusiastic regarding the land, the livestock, and the provisions the government had purchased for them. In her report to Governor Jubelin, she outlined at least a dozen possible crops, including bananas, rice, corn, tobacco, coffee, and indigo. Javouhey described Mana as a veritable garden of Eden: "The fish are abundant in our rivers: the other day, I was seated in a boat [and] a beautiful carp jumped on me....We throw the rice on the muddy ground, with no cultivation, and it becomes tall like me."[13] Beyond the joys of country living, Javouhey found great satisfaction in the communal life she was building. "It will be a little religious town," she wrote, "in which all the inhabitants eat the same food, live like the children of the same family. The entire society rises at the same hour, prays at the same time, performs all its actions according to the rule. Isn't it edifying to see the men fulfill their [religious] duties so well! Sometimes I am so happy, it seems like a dream." The Mana community, she claimed, resembled that of the ancient patriarchs, especially after their herds of cattle grew to three hundred. She called all the male inhabitants "brother" and proposed (unsuccessfully) that the Trappists open a house for men at Mana.[14] Her leadership skills were clearly important to the survival of the colony. When she left for several months to visit the St-Joseph establishments on Martinique and Guadeloupe, the governor reported that progress at Mana faltered, improving only on her return.[15]

Yet despite her formidable energy and relentless optimism, Javouhey had no better luck than her predecessors in establishing a permanent settlement of Europeans at Mana. Despite her descriptions of Mana as an agricultural paradise on earth, one of her own sisters described the first two years as "the time of misery and the greatest poverty."[16] Nor did the Mana immigrants meet her expectations. A small number of young men deserted the settlement for Martinique soon after arrival. The next hint of trouble appeared in a letter dated June 1829, when Javouhey wrote, "Little by little the flock is purged of bad subjects." Nine residents, in fact, had left in 1829 due to "unhappiness," and four had died.[17] Three years after her arrival, she was disillusioned with the quality of residents she had attracted. "Few," she wrote, "have shown the courage and devotion necessary to such undertakings: Half left halfway [through their engagement] and those who have stayed only want to live as Europeans" and "fear the least appearance of suffering." Her booster, Laure Bernard, claimed that the immigrants were afraid of the thick forests surrounding Mana and the Indian tribes who lived there.[18]

Other sources suggest that the quasi-monastic life at Mana (the daily communal Mass was held at five-thirty in the morning) and its extreme isolation from other settlements, including prohibitions on trade and commerce, discouraged French settlers. Few of them appear to have bought in to the concept of a communal utopia, especially one where the initial establishment was so difficult. Some resented the unusual authority the government had granted Javouhey in running the colony. Those who had taken up residence in Mana, wrote the governor after his inspection of 1829, preferred to "establish themselves individually than stay in association." He also did not see how the colony was to grow since most of the unmarried women were nuns, leaving no European marriage partners for the single men. Out of the original fifty-six colonists in 1828, by 1832 five had died, eight had left for other parts of Guiana, and twenty-nine had returned to France, leaving only fourteen. Including the Soeurs de St-Joseph, the entire community had been reduced by about half, from ninety-eight settlers in 1828 to forty-six in 1832.[19] Those who remained were not farmers but artisans, and Javouhey turned to exporting wood to Martinique to make ends meet. The orphans never materialized, in part because the government had already spent almost two hundred thousand francs on Mana and was reluctant to spend more.[20] Mana was far from becoming the self-sufficient farming community of Frenchmen and women that colonial officials had envisioned.

Evangelizing Africans

Javouhey, however, still retained great faith in the agricultural and spiritual potential of Mana with the right workers. To keep her colony afloat, she turned to the concept of establishing a settlement primarily for Africans. Part of the ongoing debate about settling Guiana was the question of whether Europeans were well suited for the climate and the type of farming undertaken there. Over the two centuries that the French had already controlled Guiana, few Europeans had migrated voluntarily, and mortality rates from malaria and various fever diseases were high.[21] The repeated failures of settlement plans in Mana and elsewhere in Guiana suggested to many observers that climate and mortality were important disincentives. In 1824, 15 percent of the whites in Mana died from illness, as compared to 2 percent of the black population, implying that Africans could better withstand the environment.[22] Governor Jubelin, on the other hand, found the deaths of a mere five white colonists (one of whom drowned, one of whom arrived with a chest illness, and three of whom died of sunstroke) in Javouhey's colony encouraging. However, he also believed that, in tropical countries, white farmers could not survive without the assistance of black workers. To help clear the land and drain the swamps he had already provided Javouhey with a small workforce of black slaves "habituated to difficult work" and already "acclimated."[23] To these she added about twenty rescued runaway slaves from Brazil and Surinam and a dozen slaves whom she had purchased from inhumane owners for forty thousand francs of her own money. "She did not hesitate," Jubelin reported, "to include in her acquisitions several fugitive blacks who were sent back from Surinam and other individuals with bad reputations." The Africans proved to be harder workers than the French settlers, but Javouhey also had evangelical goals in mind, intending to "make them into good Christians."[24] By 1832, Mana was no longer a majority white settlement but one with equal numbers of Europeans and Africans.[25]

To make this transformation definitive, in 1835 Javouhey contracted with the government to populate Mana with 477 Africans (227 men and 250 women) who had been transported to Guiana after being seized from illegal slave ships. The Africans, who had been housed in government workshops *(ateliers du roi)* in Cayenne since 1831, were moved to Mana in seven groups between March 1836 and April 1837.[26] Of these, 405 were indentured; the remaining 72 were children born after the abolition of the slave trade. One source suggests that the majority were Bagous and Congos. Javouhey described them as "coming from various nations" with "no other bonds except those of slavery."[27] The government also contracted to pay the Soeurs de St-Joseph two hundred francs for the upkeep of each African and twenty-five thousand francs in annual salaries for the nuns at Mana.[28] Three of the white colonists remained in Mana, two of them employed as woodcutters; there was also a doctor and his family and a resident priest. Javouhey's cousin Louis immigrated with his family to serve first as construction foreman and later as town registrar. By 1836, however, Mana had become a colony with a majority African population (more than five hundred blacks to about two dozen whites), where the celibate Javouhey described herself "as a mother in the middle of her large family" and her charges as "her new children."[29]

This reinvention of Mana as a site of moralization and gradual emancipation of African slaves under the direction of the Soeurs de St-Joseph de Cluny gave Javouhey a captive population to evangelize and train.[30] It also provided a useful service for the new July Monarchy, which had come to power in 1830. Having taken a more activist role in enforcing the prohibition of the slave trade than the Restoration government, which looked the other way while slave ships sailed from Nantes and other French ports, it was nevertheless unsure what to do with the Africans it seized on the high seas.[31] Officials feared that returning them to Africa would risk their recapture yet that freeing them in the slave colonies might serve as a dangerous catalyst to slave rebellion, a fear shared by plantation owners. Instead, they distributed them between the slave colonies under seven-year terms of indenture *(engagements)*, following the system that had been developed by Roger in Senegal, hoping that gradual emancipation would buy them some time.[32]

Javouhey's proposal to cloister the almost five hundred individuals held in Guiana under religious rule at Mana seemed both a safe and a responsible solution, especially as she promised to educate them in anticipation of their liberation. Her interest in Africans was well known and well regarded in the colonial ministry, as well as in the Tuileries Palace, where, on a return trip to France, Javouhey lobbied personally for her new project with the king and queen. The king's sister donated a sum of money, with which Javouhey purchased six young slave girls, as well as a boy and his mother in Senegal, emancipated them, and transported them across the Atlantic.[33] In Guiana, the governor praised her success in transforming the Africans she had purchased or rescued, whom he characterized as "notoriously the worst subjects of the colony, most recaptured prisoners or former runaways," into "honest, peaceful, and hardworking" residents of Mana.[34]

To most French colonists resident in Guiana, however, Mana as a home for former slaves was useful only to the extent that its distance isolated free and semi-free blacks from contact with the slaves who guaranteed their livelihood. Otherwise, they considered the Mana settlement a dangerous social and economic experiment, warning that the new Mana residents would quickly establish contact with the maroon rebels from Surinam camped along the Maroni river and create "another enemy at our doors."[35] This particular fear appeared to have little foundation as the great slave rebellions in Surinam between 1764 and 1776 had not touched Guiana, and French runaway slaves had made little contact with their Dutch counterparts.[36] However, French settlers had long depended on slavery as the labor force that made Guiana a viable colony. Although the slave system resembled that of the Caribbean islands, Guiana was a much poorer colony, where many fewer slaves were available.[37] Even at the height of the slave trade, few ships bothered to make the journey. In the eighteenth century, due to the direction of the Atlantic winds, four out of ten ships missed the landing at Cayenne even when within sight of the port, and the trip from the Antilles could take up to two months (the outward journey took about six days). The difficulties of importation raised the price of slaves and diminished their quality. Runaway slaves could easily take refuge in the dense forests, and the colony did not have the manpower to recapture them.[38] Slaves in Guiana, therefore, were kept in somewhat better physical and material condition than their counterparts in St-Domingue, Guadeloupe, or Martinique because they were less easily replaced. Yet, as in these colonies, disease, malnourishment, and lack of medical care kept mortality rates high and birthrates low, further endangering the future of the slave labor force.[39] Under these conditions, the colonists were hostile to any suggestion of a change in the status quo. Furthermore, successful slave rebellion in St-Domingue during the French Revolution and the British abolition of slavery in 1834 made them nervous about the future of their way of life. Javouhey's Mana experiment not only raised the specter of slave emancipation but also diverted funds and labor from their plantations without a clear economic benefit to themselves. At best, Mana would become an economic competitor and pave the way for definitive slave emancipation; at worst, it would gobble up scarce investment monies from Paris and incite slave rebellion.

Furthermore, the Mana settlement put administrative control in the hands of a woman, who, the colonial clergy continually complained, considered herself more powerful than even the priest assigned to Mana. In fact, she was. In addition to choosing the nuns who were sent as missionaries to Mana in her role as superior general of her order, Javouhey had civilian powers there that included the appointment of any administrators (whom she recruited among members of her own family) and medical personnel, the organization of a police force if necessary, a trade monopoly, and the ability to authorize new construction and crops and grant permission for blacks to leave the colony. She rejected the offer of anxious French authorities to place a military post at Mana, arguing that she would not need armed forces to govern the individuals under her care because, she claimed, "religion, morality suffice."[40] Likewise, she refused even a resident government agent, who might become the "real chief of the establishment." The civilizing process, she argued, required "unity of power and method." "The establishment of Mana," she wrote in 1838, "is a big family where maternal authority is the only one that has been employed until now and appears to have sufficed."[41]

Although she could call on the governor of Guiana if necessary, her authority flowed directly from the colonial ministry in Paris, which also provided the funds for personnel and materials. It affirmed that Javouhey had full support to choose the "system of education and discipline that she judges the most appropriate to the civilization of blacks." According to the colonial minister, Javouhey made the complete isolation of her colony "an absolute condition." No one, she insisted, could come to Mana without her permission, including merchants, "which prevents intrigues from penetrating there." The colonial minister acquiesced by outlawing the use of the Mana river to Guiana ships in 1835.[42] Javouhey's ability to fulfill her vision at Mana derived directly from the confidence she enjoyed in Paris, where she received the powers and funds she needed to make her colony successful. Officials there were more willing to support progressive experiments than were local elites, whose interests were threatened more directly by both the substance and the symbolism of Javouhey's colony. "Their hate," she wrote in 1839, "increases with our success."[43]

The Mana Model

At Mana, work, order, and religious devotion were the organizing principles. The main project of the colony was agriculture, but it had little in common with the plantation economy in other parts of Guiana, South America, or the Caribbean, where slaves produced large quantities of sugar, coffee, and cotton.[44] Instead, like French peasants, most African inhabitants cultivated a variety of crops on a small scale. Moreover, although Javouhey implied that she and her sisters were providing instruction in farming, many of the crops grown at Mana—manioc, rice, bananas— would have been familiar to individuals native to the west coast of Africa. To agriculture, Javouhey added training in French artisanal trades from shoemaking to carpentry to baking bread. Physically, the colony, Javouhey wrote, "resembles a pretty village in France; all is symmetrical, the streets are wide, the houses simple but well lined up."[45] By 1838, fifty hectares were farmed on behalf of the community, and another fifty divided into eighty-five plots for individual households, each bordered by a well or a canal. Eventually, 180 cabins were built on three streets. The common buildings included a church, the convent (with dormitories, refectory, common rooms, and laundry), the hospital, a general store, a warehouse, a workshop and forge, a presbytery for the priest, and a brick house for the surgeon.[46]

Mana's economic organization was similar to that of a seigneurial domain. Javouhey, in her double role as superior of a religious community and colonial administrator, oversaw everything from prayers to crops. Unfreed residents spent approximately five hours a day, three days a week on an assigned task for the community, usually agricultural in nature; the rest of their time they could farm personal plots of land, a division of labor that Baron Roger recommended to Javouhey as making use of "their natural self-interest." The newly freed hired themselves out two days a week to Javouhey in exchange for rations and three francs a week, and she noted that they worked harder after liberation "because we pay them more."[47] In exchange for their labor the African residents also received food, lodging, clothing, instruction, and medical care. Childcare was provided by the sisters, who also ran the school. The entire community began its day at five-thirty in the morning with prayer, hymns, and catechism. Following the monastic model, the rest of the day was strictly divided into periods of work, meals, recreation, and religious instruction, the latter occupying up to three hours a day. According to Soeur Philémon Poulachon, who lived in Guiana from 1839 until 1890, two hundred Africans "listened with religious attention" to a sister who instructed them on "the state of mind necessary to the reception of the sacraments and the obligations that they were going to contract on becoming Christians."[48] Unsurprisingly, the Soeurs de St-Joseph especially encouraged baptisms; the first ceremony took place in 1836 with eighty individuals.

Javouhey put great stock in the formation of Christian households as a means to moralization, so much so that at one point she proposed buying and importing (and later emancipating) about thirty additional Senegalese women to serve as marriage partners for the excess male population at Mana.[49] She also personally vetted requests to marry, discussing the proposal with the young woman, arranging a meeting between the parties, and, if all went well, setting the date. Once married, the couple was rewarded with new clothes and small plots of land for household use. "Each household," Javouhey reported, "occupies an individual cabin, clean, solid, well ventilated, with a sturdy iron-framed door and windows." Until they were married, however, men and women lived in separate lodgings, and the women and children were cloistered with the sisters "night and day," mixing with men only for work, church services, and religious instruction.[50] These precautions, Javouhey argued, as well as the isolation of the Mana colony, ensured that the Mana residents were protected from the "vicious habits to which they were so unfortunately previously inclined." Above all, they had no opportunity to pick up irreligious and immoral habits from others. "Bad examples," she wrote in the same report, "kill societies."[51]

The first liberation of blacks, which took place in 1838, was celebrated with great pomp. These 185 individuals included those whose terms of engagement had begun in 1831, as well as the slaves that Javouhey had acquired earlier. After Mass was celebrated, the governor of Guiana pronounced their liberation and handed each one a certificate of emancipation. Javouhey, for her part, provided new shoes for each newly freed individual, "an emblem of his new condition as a free man," according to her nephew, the right to wear shoes.[52] More substantially, they also received plots of land "to care for and make fruitful." "In becoming free," Javouhey wrote, "they become owners." Nonetheless, Javouhey did not imagine that the newly liberated were ready to venture out on their own. "The liberated," she wrote in a report to the colonial minister,

> are too new in civilization to be able to do without the instructions
> that must direct them in their new life. The barely formed social and
> familial ties cannot have acquired the strength that holds together
> societies…the newly freed, after having caught a glimpse of the dawn
> of civilization, would fall again into the shadows of the savage life.[53]

"We will keep them near us for at least two years," she wrote Baron Roger, "to see how they conduct themselves, then to the extent that their plantations grow, they will build new houses on their land three leagues from Mana." Her mission, she wrote on another occasion, was to "settle them on the soil." As the black residents built their cabins and "furnished them equal to ours," Javouhey interpreted the acquisition of household and other goods, "fishing boats and especially parasols" as signs of progress because "all these objects can only belong to free people."[54]

The premise of the entire Mana establishment was that quasi-religious enclosure provided the best opportunity for the regeneration of society, especially that of blacks, whom "everyone on earth seems to doom to an eternal degradation." Placed in "a single establishment, under a single authority…and isolated from all foreign contact," Javouhey argued, the Mana inhabitants could be taught "the love of work and escape from laziness," which would allow them "to act like free men, that is, to maintain themselves in peace and good order."[55] During her thirteen-year sojourn in Guiana, Javouhey lauded the tranquility of the Mana "forests" as preferable to "society," suggesting that they could also be a refuge for Catholics persecuted in France. She referred to the "solitude" at Mana as resembling that of "Thébaïde," evoking a desert retreat for the early Christian hermits, a term also used by eighteenth-century writers who advocated a return to nature. On one administrative trip to Cayenne, Javouhey wrote, "I cannot accustom myself any longer to the problems of the world, of business; I am only fit to live in the woods ... [where] it is sweet to serve God without distraction!" And upon a return visit to Paris in 1834, she praised the newly acquired convent, where "no one could penetrate the interior," as providing solitude "as at Mana" while still being "two steps from our affairs."[56] Javouhey herself, as much as she might have expressed a longing for the forests of South America, was a charismatic and engaged leader whose eleven hundred plus letters, worldwide travel, and constant communication with officials contrasted with the isolation she advocated for her colonists. In the virgin lands of Guiana, however, enclosure became the rule for all inhabitants of the Mana colony because isolation provided the possibility of reform according to religious and moral values, which she saw as compromised elsewhere. Although her goal was to "civilize" Africans, she also often expressed a deep suspicion of the civilizing process itself. "The more one acquires civilization," she wrote in 1840, "the more malice grows."[57] To achieve regeneration, Javouhey sought to remove the blacks under her control from the dangers of society.

Men Like Us

Javouhey's ideas about race and abolition matured during her years in Mana. Unlike most Europeans of her time, Javouhey believed in the perfectibility of blacks, provided that they were instructed in Christian beliefs and behavior. Africans, despite their race and color, she argued, were not "totally lacking in those qualities that made men in society" and could, as she saw it, be safely freed. "The Blacks," she wrote, "are not deaf either to the voice of morality and religion, nor to that of civilization; sons of a common father, they are men like us."[58] All peoples, in her view, were created equal in God's eyes. When the slaves in the French empire were liberated in 1848, she wrote, "These are creatures who have a soul as we do; they did not ask for life, God gave it to them, it is about time that we make them acquainted with their Creator, who has prepared for them the same rewards in eternity."[59] Unlike clerics who supported slavery, Javouhey did not believe that racial equality had to wait for eternity. With the right training, Africans were capable of achieving European levels of civilization in this lifetime. The key, in her view, to the redemption of Africans was transforming them into men and women "like us" by converting them to Catholicism and training them in European values and work habits in settings designed to mimic prosperous and pious French country villages.

Nonetheless, she was also a strong believer in gradual emancipation given the conditions in which African slaves had been held. The experience of slavery itself had eliminated a sense of discipline among the newly liberated, who "thought that their status as free men would give them the ability to live without any worries, without any work." Not only had slavery not provided any incentive to develop work habits, but "need, fear, dependence had made [slaves] cold and selfish." "Not having anyone to share his sorrows and his joys," she wrote of the slave,

> separated early from his father and mother to be sold to another master...To what end would it have served him to attach himself to places and people? He knew well that his existence did not depend on himself and that he had to sacrifice everything to the order or caprice of the person who had paid for him.

Raised in such a system, the former slave had no sense of "conduct or wise habits" that he could maintain "in the middle of cities."[60] At the moment of the liberation of the first group of slaves at the Mana colony, Javouhey wrote of "a dispossessed race, pulled down to the rank of brutes, whose intelligence was denied."[61] Still, those individuals had made tremendous progress under her tutelage. The success, in her view, of the Mana colony proved that "their race, their color, is not totally deprived of those qualities that make man social. From that, one can therefore judge that the emancipation of the slaves is not impractical." The only question, she concluded, was the best way to do it.[62]

Of course, such a view came laden with baggage that implied inferiority: "I like Blacks much better: they are good, simple...they imitate easily what they see Whites do."[63] The supposed imitative qualities of blacks was problematic, of course, if whites provided bad examples, but it also held out hope for their improvement if they were properly educated. Javouhey's frequent references to the Africans under her control as children reinforced dependency and tutelage. Their progress did not always meet her expectations: "[T]heir intelligence develops slowly; pride and foolishness come along faster...they will carry the vices of slavery for a long time." She did not think that slaves should be freed until they were twenty-three years of age. Yet by 1845, she lauded the qualities of Mana residents by comparing them favorably with French peasants: "There are few villages in France that, in every respect, present as satisfying a material and moral situation."[64]

Javouhey was driven by a Christian conception of obedience to God and society in which blacks had to be inculcated before they were ready for "civilization." "We live," she wrote, "in a century of selfishness and independence; everything leads to this devastating torrent; we need great grace to protect ourselves from it and moreover a continual attention over ourselves." Under the guidance of the Soeurs de St-Joseph de Cluny, however, the former slave would learn the love of work and of others, as well as "submission: not that painful obedience that is only compelled by brutal force, but that gentle and filial obedience that is obtained by benevolence and conviction."[65] Freedom was not an absolute value but one subordinate to one's status as a Christian.[66] In fact, in 1843 she petitioned the French government to emancipate two Mana residents, a husband and wife aged twenty-two and twenty-one, respectively, ahead of schedule because of their "deference, submission, and integrity" since their arrival in the colony.[67] Much to the concern of colonial officials, she eschewed the use of force to keep order, refusing to allow a police force or corporal punishment, relying instead on moral suasion. "The free man," she wrote, "is distinguished from the slave by virtue."[68] To her, the good order of the Mana colony, which saw no outbreaks of rebellion or violence and little attrition among freed blacks, proved the rightness of both her cause and her methods. In 1845, she informed the colonial ministry that "order and tranquility are maintained...without gendarmes, without soldiers, without the use of repressive or punitive means."[69]

Although Javouhey sometimes expressed frustration at the slow assimilation of black adults, she had great hopes for the next generation. Her view of children suggested that she believed in a Lockean premise of a "blank slate" rather than innate racial characteristics that could never be overcome. Children of African descent, having been educated in European work habits, "which are a necessity, a condition of life for civilized people," would grow up to become productive members of society. Then, she proclaimed, far from the French inhabitants of Cayenne having to fear the Mana settlers, "the question would be reversed."[70] In order to achieve this goal, the children in Mana (who numbered 230 by 1842) attended the school run by the sisters, where, in addition to religion and basic literacy and numeracy skills, they were given work training consisting of needlework and sewing for girls and farming and artisanal trades for boys.[71]

However, Javouhey's plans to educate children did not stop with those already resident in Mana. In 1841, Javouhey unsuccessfully lobbied the colonial ministry to buy and transfer to her care the entire population of slave children in Guiana aged three to fourteen, some two to three thousand individuals, in whom "rested all hope of the future," in order to prepare them for emancipation. At Mana, she would create "a vast asylum...in which we would educate the children ourselves...removed from the stupid direction of their mother and father, sheltered from the cradle from all bad domestic influences, kept with care from all bad examples and from their own propensities."[72] Once again, isolation and enclosure provided the best possibility of raising children untainted by immorality and vice:

> Oh! what I would give to see raised in the middle of the Guiana forests,
> as in the womb of nature alone, supported on one side by religion, on the
> other by morality and the love of work, this population of children, led
> by piety and gentleness, animated with the desire to do good, strong
> against seduction and vice, who could show to the world that

Christianity alone is capable of producing the great effects of civilization
that philanthropy only dreams of in its impotence![73]

Given time, training, and the right setting, she implied, anyone could become virtuous; without it, even whites were not immune to vice. "Our family," she wrote in
1838, "is composed of seven hundred people easier to lead than twenty white colonists."[74] In fact, she clearly preferred to evangelize among populations like children
or Africans, whom she saw as uncorrupted by society. Although her writings give
no evidence that she had read Rousseau or other Romantic philosophers, in these
sentiments, Javouhey's language is similar to that of contemporary thinking about
both the innocence of children and the uncorrupted state of nature.

Rather than secular philosophy, Javouhey's most important reference point for
Mana was undoubtedly the seventeenth-century South American "reductions"
established by the Jesuits to evangelize Indians. In a letter sent soon after her arrival
in Mana in September 1828, Javouhey wrote, "I hope that we will make a new
Paraguay where the Lord will be served, loved, and glorified." Six years later, when
she transformed Mana into "an asylum to place Negros who are destined for freedom, to instruct them, to direct them for five or seven years, before making them
completely free," she claimed to be "following the example of Paraguay."[75] Although
she does not mention them, Jesuit missions for Indians also flourished in Guiana
itself during the first half of the eighteenth century, disappearing after the Jesuit
expulsion from France in 1763. However, the Jesuit reductions in Paraguay became
the best known of all the early modern "mission states" because they were the most
successful in commanding Indian loyalty and the most independent from state
structures of political power.[76] In the reductions, the Jesuits protected Indians from
enslavement while attempting to Christianize them.

The Jesuit reductions operated as a source of inspiration but not as a blueprint.
Although the reductions were far larger in population than Javouhey's Mana colony,
the two projects had in common a desire to provide to a vulnerable population
sanctuary from the brutality of other Europeans in a self-sufficient settlement run
according to European religious and cultural norms. The daily schedules, which
were derived from monastic models, the enclosure of women, communal property,
and the emphasis on settled agriculture were also common features. However, the
Jesuits in Guiana, while opposing the enslavement of Indians, had owned Africans,
in whose culture they saw little redemptive value.[77] Javouhey, on the other hand,
made only limited attempts to convert several hundred Indians who lived not far
from Mana and with whom the colony had frequent contact, declaring her attempts
"fruitless."[78] In choosing to evangelize among Africans but not among Indians,
Javouhey showed her independence from the Jesuit model even while invoking it.
Instead, she followed her own sense of destiny. In adapting the Jesuit heritage,

however, Javouhey was also actively claiming it for a female religious order in unprecedented fashion. In establishing her own small-scale colony in Guiana, Javouhey was making a bold claim for the potential of women's governance within the Catholic church.

Mana's size, location, and organization also drew from contemporary utopian experiments of the 1820s and 1830s. From the very first, when Mana was intended as a white colony, Javouhey envisioned one where the residents eschewed private ownership and worked together for a common good. "The system of these establishments," the project proposal stated, "should be in the associational spirit of institutions created recently in England and the United States of America. All would be in common: work, methods of provision, food supplies, products for members, no private property of any kind in the colony."[79] Like Javouhey, many Romantic socialists also envisioned the new world as a better location for utopian experimentation than the old.[80] Among the many proposals submitted to the French colonial ministry for developing Guiana was one by Charles Fourier.[81] Furthermore, many contemporary Romantic socialists also sought to create heaven on earth through a rejuvenated Christianity.[82] There is nothing in historian Jonathan Beecher's description of Romantic socialism as a movement that "wanted a society bound by ties of love and affective solidarity," "based on cooperation rather than competition," and "organized around this common good" that would have been unfamiliar to Javouhey, probably because the Romantic socialists cast their ideals in largely religious language.[83]

But there were also differences with the utopias imagined or created by socialists of various stripes. Javouhey did not question the theology or the authority of the contemporary Catholic church, even if in Mana she distanced herself from clerical oversight and claimed a direct relationship with God. She reinforced traditional family units and traditional sexual morality, which some, though by no means all, Romantic socialists questioned. Despite the communal nature of production, Javouhey retained the ability of the Soeurs de St-Joseph to make a profit through the sale of crops, woods, and other natural resources at Mana, a feature usually eschewed in utopian ideal communities (though less so in the real-world communes they established). Although both Javouhey and many Romantic socialists were attracted by their understanding of early Christian communities, Javouhey's vision was one of self-denial and self-effacement based on the monastic model, whereas many socialists focused on a shared community of goods and the individual fulfillment of its residents.[84] Javouhey's interest in slaves and abolition also distinguished her from most Romantic socialists. Although most condemned slavery, its practice and France's colonial empire remained peripheral to their concerns; chattel slavery for many was merely an advanced form of capitalist wage slavery, destined to disappear as part of the same transformation in economic relations.[85]

Finally, despite the prominence of women in some utopian socialist circles, unlike any other such settlement, utopian or Christian, Mana was run by a woman.

The closer contemporary parallel was probably with missionary settlements established for free blacks in Africa and the Caribbean. In Mana's second incarnation, as a colony for displaced Africans, French officials proposed that in time it could be used as a sort of model training settlement for slaves awaiting freedom while simultaneously increasing Guiana's prosperity. "It is the Liberia of the Americans," the minister of marine and colonies was reported to have declared to the governor of Guiana. "[S]oon slavery will be banished entirely and this new free-town will be populated not only with freed slaves of the Antilles, but undoubtedly with ransomed Africans. It is to this establishment, perhaps, that Guiana today deprived of manpower...will one day owe its prosperity" in a "new colonial society, born of free labor." Laure Bernard predicted that Mana would go beyond being "a place of asylum and reward," like Sierra Leone or Liberia, by becoming "a place of regeneration," where birthrates would rise and racial hostility would decline, ensuring the "future prosperity of French colonies."[86] Liberia and Sierra Leone were obvious parallels to Mana in that they provided asylum for former slaves largely under religious auspices. Both originated as places of settlement for slaves recaptured from slave ships, as well as sites of return migration for North American blacks. Liberia was promoted largely by the Quakers and other evangelical Protestants in a period of social reform and religious awakening.[87] Javouhey, of course, had visited Sierra Leone in 1823 and thus had firsthand knowledge of the villages established there by Protestant missionaries.

Despite their theological differences, Javouhey might have also found herself at home among the Baptist missionaries who created free villages for blacks in Jamaica. Indeed, neither the familial metaphors nor the village setting of Mana were exclusive to Javouhey's Catholicism. Catherine Hall has shown how, among British Protestant missionaries, "black inferiority was further encoded in the language of the family," where "blacks were...children who must be led to freedom." In Jamaica, missionaries created villages centered around church and school for nineteen thousand freed slaves, who were encouraged to imitate English domestic family life, "a more ordered England in the Caribbean." Like them, Javouhey created a colonial site, as Hall puts it, "for acting out white visions of how black people should live."[88] The paradox of that vision was that it was one of the few of its time to acknowledge the ability of blacks to assimilate to European norms and to work actively toward that end.

Under the right circumstances, Javouhey, too, believed that black Africans, as well as white religious sisters like herself, could create the perfect Christian society in the form of an ideal French village. Skin color, in her view, was no obstacle to the realization of this utopia. In 1835, after five years' residence in Mana, she wrote to her sister Rosalie, "I will make a great number, our fellow creatures, happy even if they have black skin."[89] This comment encapsulates both Javouhey's willingness to believe in the essential equality of blacks as "fellow creatures" and her conviction of her rightness to lead them. As such, it also shows an inherent tension between her belief in white cultural superiority and the equality of all peoples, a substantial gray area that George Fredrickson has called "culturalism" rather than "racism."[90] Although Javouhey's letters, as in this example, sometimes suggest that blacks could become equal to whites in spite of, rather than regardless of, their skin color, she clearly did not subscribe to the emerging notion of the primacy of biological difference. By becoming Christian, blacks could overcome their differences. Living in a period when ideas about racial difference were still in flux, Javouhey was able to discount skin color but not adherence to African beliefs or customs, which would have negated her faith in the superiority of Catholic Christianity in its European incarnation as the only route to eternal salvation.[91]

Religious Utopia or Economic Monopoly?

How successful was Javouhey's radical experiment? On one measure, all commentators agreed: Mana had avoided the high death and low birth rates typical of slave societies, including the rest of Guiana.[92] This demographic edge was attributed to the age and gender structure of the population, the lighter workload at Mana than on other plantations, the medical care provided (including a birthing hospital), and the somewhat healthier climate.[93] On the issue of moralization, many colonial officials also gave Javouhey credit. Christian baptisms, marriages, and legitimacy rates all exceeded those among people of color elsewhere in Guiana.[94] By 1838, when the first group of Africans was liberated, outside assessments of Mana agreed that religious instruction had achieved results. In his inspection, the governor of Guiana argued that "the most constant gentleness" had improved most of the young people and even produced "respectful submission" among the older men. Those gains resulted not only from the work of the sisters but also from the fact that Mana's isolation kept its residents away from "the free blacks of Cayenne, who are almost all devoted to indolence and vagrancy." Even the freed blacks at Mana, by contrast, rose at half past five in the morning for prayer and then went to work. Cloistering unmarried women with the sisters "had entirely changed the habits of this population."[95] Officials were relieved that most former slaves accepted the offer to stay on lands in or near Mana and did not desert the colony to return to Cayenne, where they might present a security risk. The few who left had returned, proving that they had developed a "love of the land," which was also interpreted as moral improvement. In 1841, the governor reported that most Mana inhabitants attended

Mass, properly dressed. They had begun to desire more comfort, as measured in better furniture for their cabins, which were built along straight and well-aligned streets. These were all signs, in his view, of civilization.[96]

Over time, however, as Mana came under other kinds of scrutiny, its moralizing effects also came under question, as critics charged that these were merely superficial. Marriage, in particular, had long been considered a marker of assimilation by both missionaries and officials, who were frustrated by the low number of legitimate couples among the slave population.[97] However, Javouhey's critics cast doubt on the validity of marriages when unmarried women were sequestered with the sisters. "In order to get out of prison," the colonial council suggested, "it is entirely possible that young women decide to get married without having the calling." Contrary to earlier reports, these skeptics claimed that only women went to church, that many fewer children attended school than were officially enrolled, and that little real progress had been made at Mana. Even the buildings, praised in some reports, were described as rundown in others.[98] Any examples of "civilized" behavior were attributed to the time the blacks had spent in government workshops in Cayenne before their transfer to Mana rather than the Christian lessons of the sisters. "One finds in Mana the innate habits of the African black," an 1846 report stated, "more or less modified by a poorly understood civilization." Some argued that a group of women, however saintly, could not provide the discipline that governing blacks required, claiming that "the population of Mana becomes turbulent and quarrelsome."[99]

Others criticized the "dictatorial power" that Javouhey held, seeing it as dangerous to good order and unnatural in a woman.[100] The large amounts of government money that Javouhey managed without financial accountability and her penchant for entrusting the recordkeeping and police enforcement of the colony to her cousin and his family—whose competence some doubted—also came under new scrutiny. The extent of Javouhey's personal authority in Mana, in fact, made even her admirers increasingly concerned about whether the improvements at Mana would outlive her tenure. "The vigor of her intelligence," wrote Governor Charmasson in 1842, "might make us forget that she is not young—and that few women are capable of governing the legacy that she will leave to the congregation." After she returned to France in 1843, one critic charged that "African morals and customs were almost entirely substituted for the religious principles by which one had hoped to bring [the blacks] to civilization."[101]

Of course, if any of these accusations were true, it is likely that what colonial officials and elites perceived as superficial adherence to Christian rituals and European customs was instead the persistence of African cultural practices. There exist no direct records of life at Mana as experienced by the black residents themselves. Only once does Javouhey refer to the indigenous culture of Africans, declaring herself happy to "make them talk, to make them tell stories of their country."[102] Otherwise, she seemed convinced that they were empty vessels in which French Catholic culture could be poured. In religious matters, slaves elsewhere in Guiana appeared to have merely assimilated Catholic beliefs to African ones, but priests, religious education, and sacramental practice were rare on most plantations.[103] By contrast, Africans in Mana had access to regular sacraments and an intense religious education, which would suggest that the practice of Catholicism became more orthodox there. Over time, however, liberated blacks, the majority of whom were born in Africa, formed a village of their own a few miles distant from the main settlement and the church, which might have allowed them some freedom to live and worship in their own fashion. A (hostile) government report from 1854 claimed that, because Mana residents were transported as a group rather than individually, they had "at base always stayed African above all" and would return to the "cult of fetishes" if left to themselves.[104] At the very least, it is doubtful that Africans at Mana understood or practiced Catholicism in the same way as did peasants in France.[105] Colonial officials sometimes complained that, in religious matters, Mana residents merely parroted the lessons they had learned, which suggests that they were at least adept at telling Europeans what they wanted to hear.

It was the economic organization of Mana, however, that received the harshest criticism from outsiders. The Soeurs de St-Joseph had a monopoly on the commercialization of crops, livestock, and forests, as well as provisioning Mana through a single store. No outside ships docked there without their permission. As early as 1839, however, these commercial arrangements began receiving increased scrutiny from officials. The residents themselves, the officials reported, complained that they could not get to Cayenne to market their products or purchase goods themselves, forcing them to deal only with the sisters, who bought low and sold high. The order made its money on their "double monopoly," as well as the generous government subsidies that underwrote Mana.[106] Hence, they had no reason—and perhaps, officials suggested, as women, not enough knowledge—to undertake the large-scale agricultural production that would make the colony truly profitable. Instead, Mana was made up of "small producers, planters of manioc, farmers of rice, work that took no trouble, no labor."[107] Although Javouhey's letters continued to laud the fertility of the soil and the abundance of the crops at Mana, officials argued that the land was underutilized. In 1841, the governor contrasted the output of a state workshop *(atelier d'esclaves)*, in which the same number of slaves produced 138,000 francs' worth of sugar cane in a year, with Mana, where "revenue is absorbed by expenses."[108] The sisters, critics charged, harvested the valuable woods bordering the settlement to build a new church but did not think to develop them as export commodities (a charge that was certainly untrue, as Javouhey had sold woods from the Mana settlement since its foundation but only to the profit of her order).[109] The colonial government redefined Mana as a failed experiment because it enriched the Soeurs de St-Joseph de Cluny without adding to Guiana's prosperity. In 1843, the governor no longer saw the need for "the luxury of a religious order and all its expensive apparatus." "What a loss for French Guiana," he wrote, to have moved five hundred potential state workers to Mana when they could have been put to work building roads and canals instead.[110]

According to this new analysis, Mana's economic structure also prevented its residents from developing the work habits that only a free-enterprise economy could sustain. Whatever moral advantages Javouhey's regime might have produced were undercut, in the view of these capitalists, by the bad example of its monopoly. Lacking incentive to produce because they could not make a profit, the blacks fell back on their "natural tendency, which is laziness," preferring to hunt or fish rather than work the soil. The residents might be, as the governor wrote in 1841, "infinitely happier than those of the workshops, first because they are free...and second place, because they only work when they want," but they lacked the work discipline that characterized a truly "civilized" society. Even the trappings of European material life—cabins, furniture, clothes—that were usually cited as signs of improvement were sometimes redefined as signs of "luxury" rather than "utility."[111] Industry and agriculture, not religion and morals, were the true basis of civilization.

The very isolation of the colony, which at its inception was considered the best way to train Africans in European practices of discipline and order, was reinterpreted as its fatal flaw. Without increased communication with other parts of the colony and the free trade that would follow, critics contended that the Mana inhabitants would never rise above "primitive man" no matter how many church services they attended. In fact, they had backslid and were "no more advanced than the Indians neighboring the village of Mana."[112] Although a few officials worried that opening up Mana might present some risks in terms of increased desertion or an upsurge in criminal behavior, by the mid-1840s, the consensus had become that breaking Mana's isolation was necessary to the economic health of Guiana and the continued moral improvement of its residents. Capitalist imperatives and rhetoric trumped the utopian language of a mere decade earlier. In part this shift in attitudes was due to the increasing likelihood of slave emancipation in the French empire in the near future. Colonial officials saw Mana, one of the few places in Guiana with a concentrated free black population, as an experiment in free labor whose success (or failure) might guide the future. That its residents practiced only subsistence agriculture alarmed them.

The debate about production, from Javouhey's perspective, missed the point. Her goal had never been to produce in large quantities, and the combination of individual household plots and religious commons achieved her vision of a self-supporting religious commune. If anything, she was disappointed that the freed blacks at Mana preferred to farm their own plots rather than "seeing the advantages of a common enterprise," a failing she attributed to "their jealous and selfish character."[113] But even more frustrating was the attitude of the French officials. "The colonial administration," she wrote, "is and must be a slave to numbers; it desires a mathematical exactitude that a work of charity includes with difficulty."[114] The economic model of the slave plantation, however profitable, was one she consciously rejected as immoral and inhumane (as did, unsurprisingly, the blacks resident at Mana). As the head of a rapidly expanding religious order, however, she sought to balance revenues and needs throughout her organization to maximize its overall impact. She sought maximum government support for her overseas missions, which, in her view, contributed to France's colonial enterprise; Mana was no exception. She had no compunction about applying any profits the order made there elsewhere, such as transferring fifty-five hundred francs from Guiana to subsidize its establishment in Brest in 1828.[115] This kind of financial transfer remained common throughout Javouhey's tenure in Mana. Nor was she without business acumen, as when she applied to the colonial ministry in 1839 to sell goods from Mana in the Antilles or neighboring foreign colonies, where her profits would be higher than in Cayenne.[116] When necessary, she even chartered her own ships. Daughter of a peasant, she also had a shrewd eye for good land and livestock. But ultimately the value of Mana—or any other mission run by the sisters— was not the money it made but the good it did. That good, Javouhey argued repeatedly, derived expressly from its closure to the outside world, in which economic matters was irrelevant. "We will live like the ancient hermits of [the desert]," she wrote when Mana was first established. "[W]e will no longer be familiar with money; we will find under the soil all the needs of life."[117]

In January 1847, however, responding to multiple complaints and changing priorities, the unique regime of Mana as a closed settlement run by the Soeurs de St-Joseph de Cluny came to an end when the government brought it under direct colonial control. Most significantly, it was gradually opened to outside trade and investment (although with restrictions to protect the presumably gullible residents from fraud) with a view toward developing large-scale agriculture. Fearing that the port might become a center of contraband trade, permission was still required to land there.[118] The sisters—without Javouhey, who had returned to France in 1843—remained as educators and nurses but not as administrators or commercial agents. The government put some thought into who should govern Mana, favoring an individual who would develop the colony rather than simply reap its profits himself. One of the candidates was even a Monsieur Ursleur, a member of "the old class of color," an artisan who had become a landowner. In the end, however, the officials chose a young Frenchman, Eugène Mélinon, who had been attracted to Guiana several years earlier because of his training in botanical studies; not part of the old colonial elite, he was more likely to pursue reform.[119] He immediately introduced a new land system with a stronger emphasis on private property, resulting in the temporary desertion of a group of Africans to farm farther upriver, basing their claim on promises they said Javouhey had made to them. This minor rebellion ended when the government sent a ship with an extra detachment of soldiers and removed the ringleaders to Cayenne. The Soeurs de St-Joseph, the ship captain reported, while not encouraging resistance, "watched these latest developments with a sentiment mixed with pleasure."[120]

In the wake of this incident, Mélinon proposed bringing more European settlers to Mana—Irish immigrants or married soldiers in their last year of duty perhaps—in order to provide examples of "civilization" and private ownership. He also saw possibilities in "civilizing" nearby Indians, whom he believed more rapid learners than blacks. He also invited the Frères de Plöermel, a male teaching order that was rapidly expanding into colonial settings, to establish a school for boys "to balance the influence" of the Soeurs de St-Joseph.[121] One sister, resident in Mana for eighteen years, reported to Javouhey that the black residents no longer had hospital privileges, forcing the nurses to visit them in their cabins. She was also bothered by the numerous soldiers now loitering about the settlement.[122] Symbolically, officials removed the picket fence put up by Javouhey when she arrived in 1828 to mark off the order's domain.[123]

For the better part of two decades, however, Javouhey was given an unusual opportunity, as a woman and a nun, to head a unique experiment in the annals of French empire, one that sought to solve on a small scale the difficult and contested problem of African slavery. To the debate, Javouhey added a working model of a free (or semifree) African community that met the French criteria for stability and order. It is hard to imagine, however, its larger applicability. One of the paradoxes of the Mana settlement was that, although Javouhey's ambitions for it were limitless—she saw it as a new paradigm for emancipation while also hoping it would become a training ground for all the slave children of Guiana—its very existence depended on isolation and enclosure, which were not easily replicated elsewhere.

Javouhey's ability to establish such an unusual settlement depended not on her relations in the colony, which were hostile, but on the support she received from Paris, which desperately sought a way to make Guiana into a profitable colony while simultaneously reducing its dependence on slavery. Their views on how best to do this shifted like the notorious Guiana winds, while Javouhey's vision remained steady, borrowing from sources as diverse as Catholic universality, Jesuit reductions, utopian socialism, and abolitionist theory. Although she drew from the Catholic missionary tradition in seeking to form an ideal Christian community, she did not work among the indigenous or settler populations, as was usually the case, but instead with individuals specially imported to this remote spot, drawing on the model of contemporary utopian communities. Yet Mana did not promise equality to all residents but instead bound them in a hierarchy of Christian obedience to Javouhey, through which they were offered the possibility of freedom from the bonds of slavery. To achieve this, Javouhey saw no other solution than isolating them at the edges of empire, where they remained uncorrupted by the very French civilization they were supposed to emulate.

9

Catholics and Abolitionists

In the wilds of South America, Javouhey forged a new identity, overstepping the boundaries of expected behavior for a woman and a nun. But within the Catholic church this independence from clerical authority raised alarm bells. During her second sojourn in Mana and on her return to France in 1843, Javouhey's life was increasingly dominated by a conflict with the bishop of Autun, in whose diocese the order's motherhouse of Cluny was located. Until 1829, she had had cordial relations with the resident bishops of Autun, who left her alone to pursue her missionary ambitions. The appointment of a young and ambitious bishop, Mgr d'Héricourt, however, began a long power struggle over the extent of her authority and the limits of her independence. The "Autun affair," as it became known to the order, was a conflict, like many others between female superiors general and bishops in nineteenth-century France, rooted in ambiguous jurisdiction and authority resulting from the new centralized religious order that French nuns were pioneering. Present in many French dioceses both at home and abroad, the Soeurs de St-Joseph de Cluny fell under the purview of numerous bishops, among whom the bishop of Autun claimed particular rights since the order was headquartered in Cluny. Bishops like Héricourt were reluctant to cede power and authority to women religious in general, but a woman like Javouhey—independent in mind and action and with progressive ideas regarding slavery and abolition—was almost guaranteed to ruffle ecclesiastical feathers.

The Autun Affair

The central point of contention between Javouhey and Héricourt was over the secular administration of the Soeurs de St-Joseph. As supérieure générale, feminine, she claimed the right to run the worldly affairs of her order—opening houses, placing sisters, traveling freely, and so forth—without episcopal interference. But in 1835 Héricourt claimed for himself the role of supérieur général, masculine, a position that was normally limited to oversight in spiritual matters. As part of his bid for extended authority, Héricourt prepared a document of twenty-four articles that he proposed to substitute for the order's 1827 statutes, effectively hijacking its governance. Specifically, the new articles allowed Héricourt to decide on the admission of novices, administer the order's financial resources, and approve the personnel appointments made by Javouhey, as well as any decisions regarding new establishments. He also wanted to consolidate the order's novitiates in Cluny, require Javouhey to take up permanent residence there, and limit her travels abroad by requiring that she obtain specific authorization from him for each trip. Without his explicit permission, he claimed, an overseas voyage was tantamount to her resignation.[1] In short, he wanted to control the training of the Soeurs de St-Joseph, as well as dictate the movements and activities of their leader. Although he promised Javouhey that the colonial missions could continue, his reforms not only curtailed her power but also threatened to reduce the Soeurs de St-Joseph to a regionally based organization without the national and international profile that Javouhey had spent decades building.

In 1835, under considerable ecclesiastical pressure and anxious to return to Mana, where the experiment in evangelizing Africans was about to begin, Javouhey signed the document. "He begged, implored, to engage me to do it," she wrote afterward. "[N]ot succeeding, he ordered me. I was alone, I signed." Immediately regretting this step and supported by the nuns who made up her general council, she refused to sign a second time, when the bishop submitted the articles for approval to the ministries of religious affairs and colonies. Her position, which she maintained unwaveringly for the next decade, now became that "our congregation should be governed by the supérieure générale, aided by the Council in all that is temporal administration....Monseigneur forced us to sign that which he did not have the right to demand."[2] Héricourt immediately refused her permission to return to Mana, a decision that Javouhey successfully appealed to the government, who issued her travel orders. In retaliation, Héricourt prevailed upon the archbishop of Paris to close the order's Paris chapel, forcing the sisters resident there to take the sacraments elsewhere. "It is a sad revenge," Javouhey wrote, "to punish innocents to satisfy offended pride! I will not worry about this; I put my confidence in God." Claiming that only the statutes of 1827, which vested secular power in the supérieure générale, that is, Javouhey herself, and her council, were valid, she was determined to resist. "It is this unity that makes us strong," she argued. "[I]t exists in our rule, so it shall be in our hearts and in our spirit."[3]

On her side in this dispute, Javouhey had two significant sources of support. First, the members of her order joined her in denouncing Héricourt's actions as untenable, according to their reading of the rules. The head of the order, the local superiors of the French houses wrote to her in 1835, had to be elected by the chapter: "No bishop, whatever the respect that we bear for him, can declare himself our superior general."[4] Repeated attempts by Héricourt and his clerical supporters, especially after Javouhey returned to Guiana in 1836, to get the sisters to agree to the change in statutes, failed. On the eve of her own departure, Javouhey recalled her sister Marie-Thérèse Javouhey from Martinique to reinforce the family presence in France. Everywhere Héricourt turned, as Claude Langlois has put it, he ran into another Javouhey sister, niece, or cousin who refused to cede to his pressure. To her youngest sister, Rosalie, head of the order in Bourbon and on the front lines in Cluny after the death of Marie-Thérèse in 1840, Anne-Marie wrote, "[Y]ou have been my support; I will be yours."[5] But the rank-and-file Soeurs de St-Joseph remained loyal as well. In 1845, when Javouhey discovered that the chaplain at the Cluny novitiate, under orders from Héricourt, was counseling novices in the confessional that she was "in revolt" from the bishop's authority, she traveled there personally to plead her case, leaving individuals free to follow her to Paris or leave the order. Her charisma bested the spiritual threats of a bishop. Out of eighty postulants and novices, only eleven decided to leave. As one wrote, "I am attached to her [Javouhey] heart and soul, persuaded that in following her, I am on the path that conducts me to [eternal] Life."[6]

Javouhey's second area of support derived from her friends in high places. At the time of the Revolution of 1830, Javouhey—undoubtedly reliving her memories of religious persecution during the Revolution of 1789—reacted in alarm and made contingency plans to flee from France to Spain and from the French colonies to British or Dutch Guiana. Nonetheless, she quickly adjusted to the new regime, extending her governmental contacts to the court of the new Orléans monarchs, who became strong supporters of her colonial projects. In December 1835, on the eve of her second departure for Guiana and after the Autun affair had begun, Javouhey went nearly every day to the Tuileries Palace to meet with the king, culminating in a royal Mass for the success of her Mana experiment. In the course of a trip to the Americas in 1838, his son, the Prince de Joinville, made a detour to visit Javouhey at Mana, as well as to tour the nearby leper colony, gathering information, he said, to report to his mother. Two years later, the three Senegalese priests celebrated Mass in the royal presence. In 1843, when the Autun affair was far from settled, Javouhey reported that the queen had visited their Paris boarding school twice in one week in order to visit a relative who was enrolled there.[7] Clearly, Javouhey's ecclesiastical status did not worry the royal family. Nor did it worry the government. In 1835, the colonial minister, eager to see the Mana experiment launched, saw no reason that church disputes should get in his way, arguing that the 1827 statutes had seemed to work quite well and that with them the congregation could "continue its services to the colonies in the same spirit and with the same means as in the past." In addition, her old friend Baron Roger, now a French deputy with increasing influence in a liberal monarchy, told her to "count on me" to provide support for Javouhey's sisters in France.[8] Javouhey's continued ability to open houses and missions abroad and to collect government stipends allowed her to continue her work despite Héricourt's disapproval. When the Autun affair took on new intensity in 1845 after Javouhey's return to France, she reported proudly that "Nothing escapes the surveillance of our friends; the highly placed individuals who guide the affair assure us that we have nothing to fear."[9]

In turn, Mgr d'Héricourt fought back through ecclesiastical channels. He attempted to close the Cluny novitiate and send the novices back to their families. He told the novices that they were risking their salvation by entering an order whose members were in "open revolt against bishops and against the church." Most significantly, he worked hard to rally other bishops to his cause, sending letters to those in dioceses where the Soeurs de St-Joseph worked.[10] He needed their cooperation in enforcing bans outside of his jurisdiction, but he also appealed to clerical solidarity in the face of an errant nun. "Episcopal authority sticks together," he wrote to the bishop of Beauvais, "and more than ever we have to stay united." Perfect cooperation among bishops, he argued as late as 1847 (a year after the dispute had nominally been settled), could cut off recruitment and therefore bring Javouhey into compliance.[11] Monseigneur Affre, first as vicar general and then as archbishop of Paris (where he was embroiled in a very similar dispute over authority with Sophie Barat, superior general of the Religious of the Sacred Heart), assured Héricourt of his full support, banning Mass and confessions in the order's Paris chapel.[12] The bishop of Beauvais, whose diocese housed the large St-Joseph novitiate at Bailleul, initially agreed to close it in favor of that of Cluny. "All for you, all with you, nothing without you. That is my motto," he wrote.[13]

Although the bishop of Autun sought cooperation in order to reinforce his authority, the affair also threatened schism within the order, as local bishops and apostolic prefects used the opportunity to assume the same privileges that Héricourt demanded in France. In Bourbon, for example, the apostolic prefect claimed the power to direct both the spiritual and the temporal affairs of the Soeurs de St-Joseph on the island, moving them around and directing their establishments in the same way as he did with diocesan clergy. Javouhey was equally annoyed, however, by the bishop of Trinidad, who, "without the participation of the bishop of Autun," gave the habit to some young postulants in his diocese without her knowledge. "It appears," she complained, "that he does not fear Mgr d'Autun, but should he fear me? And can't he warn me in little more regular manner than by a scrap of news-paper that he only sent once everything was over?"[14] Javouhey ceded control of her order to no bishop, even friendly ones.

The dispute followed Javouhey to Guiana, where she had to face the hostility of the apostolic prefect, Abbé Guillier, who took up Héricourt's campaign to force Javouhey to submit to the new rules. In a series of letters to the bishop of Autun and a report to Rome, he outlined his case. First, she could not be trusted. "Javouhey is for me an enigma and a very embarrassing figure," he wrote to the bishop of Autun. "[O]ne cannot count on what she says, as opposed to her conduct. She makes state-ments and retracts them according to what suits her."[15] He called the orthodoxy of her faith into question, alleging that she had received several hundred copies of the New Testament translated into "vernacular language" and had used a "course of education of the Jew Levi" until it was forbidden by the church. He also accused her "enterprise," that is, Mana, of being "a speculative affair" in which she was allowing herself to be "an instrument of an abolitionist society" in order to make a profit and pay her debts in France. She had, he insinuated, lied to the original, white colonists at Mana, and he questioned what had happened to the balance of the government grant she had received at that time. Echoing the views of the local elites, who objected to the trading monopoly at Mana, he repeatedly accused her of substi-tuting economic greed for religious piety and neglecting the religious instruction of the Soeurs de St-Joseph, who were "occupied from morning to night by mercantile speculations" and were reduced to mere "store girls." Those nuns, he charged, were admitted too easily because Javouhey was more interested in expanding her order than in religious training. "It has happened," he reported to Rome, "to admit some who postulated, took the habit, did their novitiate and their profession the same day." Religious rules, he charged, were not followed at Mana, especially those regarding enclosure.[16] This view was echoed by Abbé Lafond, the priest resident in Mana in 1836, who reported to the bishop of Autun that Javouhey broke monastic rules every day, including prayer, silence, and meditation. "I recognize nothing Christian in her," he concluded.[17]

Guillier, who had lived in Guiana since 1818, was particularly scornful of Javouhey's abolitionist leanings. She was more interested in "the philanthropic ideas of the day" than in heading a religious order, he charged:

> The project of the abolitionists, of which she is the agent, is obviously a
> deception and a chimera. One cannot improvise the civilization of
> Africans any more than the majority of children, and I do not conceive

how that woman, who has a head of sense and reason, was able to let
herself be fooled and throw herself headlong into the dreams of the
utopians of the day.

If the Jesuits had failed to emancipate African slaves systematically in South America,
Guillier argued, "utopians" like Javouhey certainly could not succeed.[18] Most important of all, however, Javouhey refused to submit to his authority: "She does not
recognize laws or rules or authority; she wants to be entirely independent in order
to *come to the aid of humanity*" [Guillier's emphasis]. Guillier was especially irate
that Javouhey "absolutely" refused to write a letter of resignation as superior general of the Soeurs de St-Joseph "at my dictation." "You wear, I said to her, a habit
that supposes you a member of a religious order," he fulminated. "[E]ven more, you
pretend to be its superior general, but there is no religious congregation without an
ecclesiastical superior, what is yours? It is not the Bishop of Autun, she said, and
I will never recognize him as such."[19]

Because of Javouhey's "duplicity" and "Machiavellian conduct," Guillier denied
her (and the other sisters at Mana) the sacraments for almost two years (from
October 1841 to June 1843), a not inconsequential sanction for a sixty-something
Catholic nun living in the tropics.[20] Nonetheless, Javouhey downplayed the ban,
even denying that she minded being publicly refused communion in a Cayenne
church. "This time of trial," she reportedly said, "was for me the happiest of my life;
seeing myself as it were excommunicated because it was forbidden to all priests to
give me absolution, I went walking by myself in the great virgin forests of Mana and
there I said to God, 'I have nothing more than you, Lord, this is why I have come to
throw myself in your arms and beg you not to abandon your child.'"[21] According to
another Soeur de St-Joseph, she decided to return to France to face Héricourt when
"she heard a voice from heaven that told her not to resist any longer."[22] Nonetheless,
before her departure, she launched an unsuccessful campaign for the colonial
ministry to appoint a separate apostolic prefect for Mana, one who would be
independent from that of the rest of Guiana.

Javouhey's relationship with many colonial priests, especially those assigned to
Mana, had long been difficult. Few embraced Javouhey's ideas about African capacity
for civilization; instead, they prudently respected the wishes of plantation owners by
not overemphasizing black equality with whites before God. Religion, in their view,
was a means of keeping slaves submissive, not emancipating them.[23] Guiana, even
more than other French colonies, was a very unattractive posting, one that even
Guillier himself called "a type of exile, which demands from those who come to fulfill these jobs great self-denial and painful sacrifices."[24] The result was few clergy, and
of poor quality. In 1837, the governor of French Guiana described the two he encountered at Mana as "little worthy of fulfilling the important functions that have been

conferred on them." Even more telling, perhaps, "the more ardent one, the younger, suffers with impatience the supremacy of the Superior general; he wants to share authority with her and not be charged simply with the direction of consciences and the morals of penitents; the other, somber, self-seeking, fanatical by calculation or by weakness, wanted the Superior general to augment his fees." The first had already left, and the other planned to do so within a few months.[25] Mana provided neither a life of ease nor much scope for priestly initiative, as Javouhey saw their work as auxiliary to hers. Often Mana did not have a resident priest at all, which perhaps was one reason that Javouhey could view her deprivation of the sacraments with equanimity. She certainly had more scope for action without the nagging presence of men who did not share her vision and whom she did not generally consider qualified for missionary work. Of one, she wrote, "He is a holy priest, but a very nasty man," and succeeded in getting him sent back to France.[26] However, the short tenure of priests at Mana lent credence to the view of Guillier and other clerics that religious life there was unregulated, verging on the unorthodox. And for priests to take orders from a nun was an inversion of the natural order within the Catholic church. The archbishop of Paris specifically cited her frequent complaints about colonial priests to the colonial ministry as evidence of her insubordination.[27]

Javouhey, in fact, went beyond complaints in imagining that she could establish an order of priests, the Pères de St-Joseph, who would solve the problem of scarce and incompetent colonial clergy. "In Senegal," she wrote in frustration in 1834, "there has not been a priest for eighteen months, none at Gorée; in St-Pierre-et-Miquelon, one who is crazy…at Mana three priests in three months.…In Martinique, where the [SJC] house donates three thousand francs in salary, it has trouble finding a mediocre one." Under these conditions, Javouhey proposed a plan that even she acknowledged as "daring," of establishing a seminary in Limoux (where she was also training the African priests) and a second one at Mana, where, she claimed, "the Holy See will establish an abbé who could train priests for the colony."[28] She anticipated that the Mana seminary would, like the one in Limoux, train black men, as well as white, and it fueled her desire to settle the three Senegalese priests in Mana rather than in Senegal.[29] She wrote Guillier that, although this new order of priests would follow a spiritual rule similar to that of the Jesuits, the statutes of the Soeurs de St-Joseph could serve as a model in temporal matters.[30] In floating this idea, Javouhey remained consistent with her own vision—she had wanted a companion male order since her Trappist days—but stepped over a clear gender line in the church, where no male religious order had ever been founded by a woman, though the reverse was not uncommon. That such an order would also train black priests only added fuel to the fire.

The hostility that Javouhey provoked in Héricourt, Guillier, and other male clerics fueled the narrower and more legalistic struggle over the rules. Most agreed that she was a woman with unusual talents and a forceful character. Nevertheless, as the bishop of Beauvais wrote, "I wish to see in Madame Javouhey more obedience, more religious spirit, less confidence in her ideas, less eagerness to admit [novices] and found [establishments] and more care to regularizing and improving." Although "capable," "active," and "enterprising," according to the archbishop of Paris, she was not "religious enough" and lacked "devotion," "patience," and "submission," all qualities appropriate to the religious state, particularly among women.[31] Her inability to bend to male ecclesiastical authority and her propensity to justify her independence by direct divine inspiration clearly rattled most of the clerics with whom she came in contact. She needed to be "regulated," as Héricourt reminded the colonial minister in vain. He criticized her specifically for opening houses without permission and keeping congregational property in the name of various family members, a strategy that clearly increased her independence. "The great difficulty," Héricourt wrote in 1835, "will be to sort out the colonial regime and to ensure the return of revenues."[32]

Control of novices and novitiates was also a particular flashpoint. The bishop of Autun sought to limit the congregation's novitiates to a single one, located in his diocese, in order to increase his supervision. When the archbishop of Paris refused to allow Javouhey to move the Cluny novitiate to Paris, she decamped to Fontainebleau. In a letter to Héricourt in 1841, she specifically refused to cede her authority to open up novitiates in the colonies. Within France, she denied that a single novitiate was enough because the order "is too large and not rich enough to meet travel expenses from one end of France to another." If Héricourt "continues to torment us, we will transport the Cluny novitiate elsewhere."[33] However, critics claimed that novices were admitted too easily and with too little training, a charge that was likely true, given the rapid expansion of the order and the great demand for its services. During the long dispute with the bishop of Autun, Javouhey circumvented many normal procedures in admitting novices that would have required his acquiescence, on occasion allowing nuns to take vows from her rather than a priest or bishop.[34] In making the personnel decisions herself, however, Javouhey not only provided enough sisters to meet demand but also molded a dedicated and loyal membership.

On her return to France in 1843 Javouhey began to turn the tide of clerical opinion in her favor, convincing the archbishop to reopen the Paris chapel and enlisting the papal nuncio in her cause. She also imagined opening a second novitiate in Compiègne, "a great edifice that will contain two to three hundred people," as well as one in Karaikal, India, just south of Pondicherry, where the sisters had a mission.[35] She even considered—but rejected—the idea of leaving the diocese of Autun altogether despite the sentimental ties attached to the Cluny headquarters and its use as a recruiting ground for novices. After a meeting with Héricourt in July 1844—the first he had deigned to grant her or any of her sisters since the dispute had begun—she declared herself optimistic about a reconciliation of sorts: "I do not say that Mgr d'Autun is converted, but he is caught in his nets, he cannot untangle himself." But, she warned, "Be modest, make ourselves small to soothe the pride of our enemies."[36] Nonetheless, hostilities with Héricourt flared up again a year later when she discovered his attempt to turn the Cluny novices against her, as well as his publication of antagonistic reports regarding her position and conduct. The arrival in France of Guillier, whom she discovered had circulated an equally hostile document in government circles for three years, only intensified her concern. "I had," she wrote to Rosalie and Clothilde Javouhey, "several moments of worry on the subject of the colonies because the bishop of Autun has done everything to undermine the trust of the ministers of the Navy [and Colonies] and of Religious Affairs... [ellipses hers], but the relationship is reestablished."[37]

In 1846, three years after her return to France, Javouhey finally established a fragile peace with the bishop of Autun, based on the 1827 statutes, in which she agreed to a single novitiate at Cluny, which gave him "a special authority...more extensive than that of each bishop over the communities of sisters who reside in different dioceses." She refused, however, to live permanently in Cluny since her business affairs were in Paris; for foreign travel she promised to consult him.[38] At age sixty-seven, this last concession probably weighed less heavily on her than it had earlier in her life; indeed, Javouhey never left France again. Brokered by a third party, the agreement was "a model of obscurity," which was undoubtedly its intention.[39] Yet the conflict continued to simmer. In March 1849 the archbishop of Orléans, with the permission of the papal nuncio, admitted ten Soeurs de St-Joseph based in Paris to the novitiate, and six months later the new archbishop of Paris, Mgr Sibour, approved the opening of a novitiate—one large enough to house two to three hundred individuals—in Paris. "We are saved from disaster," wrote Javouhey in triumph, noting that she also had the support of the papal nuncio. Héricourt, for his part, denounced the new novitiate as a means for Javouhey to "elude, as she has always done, Episcopal Authority."[40]

From now on, although the Soeurs de St-Joseph retained a base in Cluny, the Paris house became its main center. "The archbishop of Paris," wrote Javouhey, "gives us all the necessary approvals for the principal novitiate and the free exercise of our rules." Taking no chances, however, Javouhey requested that he formalize his "personal authorization" with "an official act" that she could use "in case of need" to establish "the legitimacy of our position in Paris." The bishop of Autun, she declared, still "believes that the congregation belongs to him" and "wishes that I [would] disappear from the congregation."[41] To his claims that she was no longer supérieure générale because elections had not been held at the appropriate time, she denied that the rules applied to her: "It seems to me obvious that this measure in the statutes and constitutions is only applicable to superiors general to come, to those who are not founders.... But the Founder is the superior by her very quality of Founder, which she can never lose.... No man can remove this quality for the reason that no man gave it to her; God only can revoke it."[42] Not even the deaths of Javouhey and Héricourt, within days of each other, in 1851, completely ended the dispute. In 1852, the vicar general of the diocese of Autun complained that the Soeurs de St-Joseph had opened an unauthorized novitiate in Basse-Terre, Guadeloupe, and charged that many nuns were received into the order without episcopal knowledge or approval.[43]

The similarity between Emilie de Vialar's conflict with the bishop of Algiers and that of Javouhey and the bishop of Autun was not lost on either woman. Although Vialar's correspondence with Javouhey no longer exists, Javouhey mentioned Vialar several times in her own letters and wrote directly to her on at least one occasion. "I thank God," Javouhey admitted, "not to be in Algiers; Mgr d'Autun is a sheep in comparison." Javouhey also felt, probably correctly, that she was in a stronger position than Vialar since she had officially approved statutes with which to defend her autonomy. Fundamentally, however, Javouhey judged the rightness of Vialar's cause, like her own, by its intrinsic spiritual value: "If it is the work of God, she has nothing to fear from the malice of men."[44] Like Vialar, Javouhey considered traveling to Rome to ask the pope to appoint an ecclesiastical supérieur général, which would free her from dependence on any diocesan bishop, claiming that then she could "die in peace."[45] But she did not have Vialar's contacts in Rome, and, to make her order acceptable to the Holy See, she would have undoubtedly needed to compromise on other issues, such as enclosure. "All the nuns in Rome being cloistered," warned a French priest, "they are not used to seeing nuns in the streets, and this could produce a bad effect." One of the priests assigned to Mana suggested that the Soeurs de St-Joseph leave their order for one in which they could live as "true nuns."[46]

Just what made up a "true nun" was, in fact, one of the contested definitions in this conflict. Traditionally, a Catholic nun lived enclosed and devoted the majority of her time to prayer and contemplation. Although the active nun devoted to good works was becoming the dominant model during the nineteenth century, as an activist nun who bowed to no man, Javouhey tested the limits of this innovation. In considering the question of whether Rome could adjudicate the dispute, Héricourt denied that the Soeurs de St-Joseph de Cluny were among "truly religious congregations like the Sacred Heart or Picpus"; instead, "the Javouhey family is an enterprise, a speculation, it would elude the decisions of Rome, as it has mine."[47] Only in 1854, three years after Javouhey's death, did the Congregation of Bishops and Regulars in Rome issue a decree on behalf of the Soeurs de St-Joseph de Cluny, acknowledging its canonical status as an order dependent on the Holy See. It declared that, as "individual sisters," the superior general and the members of the council would depend on the bishop of Autun, but in those matters relative to the congregation, they would have the "freedom to act according to the Rule,... turning in extraordinary cases" to the Holy See itself.[48] Still somewhat murky in its division of episcopal and papal powers (it was not specified just what constituted an "extraordinary case"), this decree occupied an intermediate position between becoming a full papal order (like the Religious of the Sacred Heart) and the simple statement of praise obtained by Vialar in her similar conflict. The form of the centralized, active, female religious order continued to bedevil the theologians in Rome as it did bishops in France.

Abolishing Slavery

Some of the hostility that Javouhey experienced from French and colonial clerics was directly related to her support of the abolition of slavery in the French empire. She was, however, as a Catholic and a woman, an unusual figure in the French anti-slavery movement in the early nineteenth century. Unlike its British counterpart, it was neither a mass movement nor one rooted in religious enthusiasm.[49] Although French slaves had been emancipated in 1794 under the French Republic in reaction to armed revolt in the valuable sugar colony of St-Domingue (later Haiti), Napoleon restored slavery in 1802.[50] Opposition to the slave trade mounted in the 1820s, and the first association formed to take up the abolitionist cause after the Revolution was the Société de la morale chrétienne, founded in 1821, whose membership rosters included most of the liberal opposition to the Restoration monarchy, including the duc d'Orléans, who acceded to the throne in 1830 as King Louis-Philippe.[51] Although about one-third of the society was Protestant (compared to less than 2 percent representation in the French population), its members were not evangelicals in the British mold. Like Javouhey, they believed that slaves had to be prepared for freedom through education, but, unlike her, most of them derived that belief from liberal principles regarding universal rights rather than religious conceptions of the equality of individuals under God. They also favored gradual emancipation for purely practical reasons since such a strategy could dampen the potential economic and political dislocation that might follow an abrupt emancipation. After the Revolution of 1830 in France and the emancipation of slaves in the British Empire in 1834, French reformers founded a new antislavery society, the Société française pour l'abolition de l'esclavage. Never topping one hundred individuals, the members came from the same governing elite: liberal, universalist, disproportionately Protestant, and, of course, male.

Javouhey's connection with these groups was Baron Roger, her close friend and now a liberal deputy from the Loiret, as well as one of the most consistent proponents of abolition. Roger saw Javouhey's work as ammunition for the antislavery cause. "Consider that 250,000 slaves wait in a way for the result of your experiment," he wrote at the time of the first liberation of slaves in Mana in 1838. "You work for all of them as much as for the Blacks of Mana." Two years later, predicting an "inevitable" and "even imminent" liberation, he asked her to provide "proof" that blacks would work not only for their own survival but also for a "moderate salary." "What are their needs, their tastes, their desires?" he asked. "Since they have been established in a village, how in their conduct and inclinations do they differ from our peasants in France?" Javouhey, he believed, could provide evidence that black slaves could pass "to the state of liberty" without "falling back into the savage state." The Senegalese priests were proof of an even higher civilizing potential: "[T]he presence of these African priests serves the cause of emancipation very usefully in Paris. Do you not see that they are a perpetual and living protest against the slavery of blacks? That under their cassocks, it is emancipation itself that walks in the streets of Paris!"[52] Profiles of the three priests and a eulogy to Florence were published in the *Revue des Colonies* and *L'Ami de la religion*, while the Société pour l'abolition de l'esclavage distributed an engraving illustrating Moussa's first Mass in Senegal.[53]

In turn, Javouhey asked Roger to lobby the members of the emancipation commission to support her proposal to educate the slave children of Guiana. He introduced her to the duc de Broglie, president of the abolitionist society. Javouhey was also acquainted with Alphonse de Lamartine, French deputy and Romantic poet, who invited her to speak before the society after she was attacked in the press for her antislavery views. Lamartine believed that Catholicism could form the basis of a reformed and progressive society, and he supported the gradual emancipation of slaves, promoting a ten-year preparation period in 1838.[54] She was also known to Victor Schoelcher, the most prominent of France's abolitionists, who published an antislavery sermon by one of the Senegalese priests. Like Javouhey, Schoelcher argued that slavery itself rather than racial difference had caused the inferiority of blacks, and like her he supported gradual emancipation—until 1840, when he lost faith in the willingness of plantation owners to educate their slaves.[55]

Within the Catholic church, Javouhey's ideas about race most closely resembled those of the Abbé Grégoire, a former revolutionary bishop, who became the most prominent (and notorious) Catholic abolitionist until his death in 1831. Although there is no evidence that Javouhey was acquainted with him, or even with his writings, both shared a belief in racial equality via universal Catholicism. Grégoire's opposition to racial prejudice, as Alyssa Sepinwall Goldstein has argued, "was founded on the premise that oppressed groups, once they had escaped their oppression, would abandon their cultural—and even racial—particularity."[56] Conversion to Catholicism would, in time, efface all cultural differences and make racial difference irrelevant. What this really meant, of course, was that, through Catholicism, all peoples could acculturate to European standards and values. Like Javouhey, Grégoire universalized French Catholic culture as the goal to which peoples of all races should aspire, and he saw blacks in particular as blank slates on which European civilization could be written once the bad influences of the French colonists had been removed. He also believed in the need for a complete renewal of colonial clergy to Europeanize blacks.[57] Grégoire's pariah status in the French Catholic church, however, due to his political activities during the Revolutionary and Napoleonic regimes, prevented him from mobilizing French Catholic opinion in favor of abolition. He expressed his views through writing rather than practical action and, unlike Javouhey, remained steeped in the experiences and ideas of the French Revolution.

Both Grégoire and Javouhey were atypical of Catholic clerical opinion on race and assimilation, at least until the 1840s. From the first European foundations in the sixteenth century, Catholic missionaries active in the Caribbean islands and in Latin America were much more interested in converting native Indians than African slaves and were often slaveholders themselves. Seventeenth-century French missionaries participated in the formation of racial discourse that justified the enslavement of Africans as a New World workforce. Because the French Code Noir, first promulgated in 1685 (though poorly enforced), required baptism and the religious education of slaves, most theologians justified slavery as a means to Christian salvation, an idea that had first been approved by Pope Nicholas V in 1454.[58] Colonial clergy before the 1840s were few in number, conservative in outlook, and hostile to new initiatives in the colonies; by and large, as in Guiana, they ministered only to French settlers who opposed emancipation.[59] Although most did not participate personally in the plantation economy, as had missionaries under the Old Regime, some did own slaves as servants. In 1822 Abbé Guillier, Javouhey's future adversary in Guiana, accepted a gift on behalf of his order of a plantation that included ten slaves and urged the purchase of more. In Bourbon, priests participated in the agricultural and commercial life of the colony, including the owning of slaves.[60] As late as 1846, the superior general of the seminary of the Saint-Esprit, which trained colonial priests, justified the pro-slavery teachings of his institution as consistent with the theology of the Catholic church. "They told us at the seminary," one priest wrote, "the slaves are not unhappy; what is miserable and degrading in their condition, custom has made so natural for them that they seem not even to perceive it or wish for better."[61] At best, the colonial clergy urged for better, more Christian treatment of slaves by masters rather than an overturning of the institution itself. At home, the metropolitan clergy were not notably more favorable. On the eve of emancipation, in 1847, only 10 percent of the French Catholic clergy signed a petition calling for the immediate abolition of slavery.[62]

Yet, despite the lack of interest among the Catholic clergy regarding abolition, Javouhey was at the vanguard of a grassroots clerical campaign for "moralization" that led the Catholic church into a more active missionary stance. These individuals did not come from the established hierarchy of colonial priests but from a new generation of religious activists. Influenced both by the religious upheavals of the French Revolution, which proved that the faith had to be actively defended, and the social Catholicism of the early nineteenth century, these clerics, mostly members of religious orders founded after the Revolution, based their actions on their own religious experience, valuing piety over theology.[63] They sought to make Christianity universal through the active evangelization of new populations. Their efforts matured in the 1840s, simultaneous with the growing abolitionist campaign, and began slowly to change views within the church. The Frères de l'Instruction chrétienne de Ploërmel, a Breton teaching order for boys under the direction of Jean-Marie de la Mennais, who joined the Soeurs de St-Joseph in colonial work in 1837, took an antislavery position. Likewise, the Congrégation du Sacré-Coeur de Marie, founded by François Libermann and Frédéric LeVavasseur in the 1830s as a missionary order destined for the Caribbean and Africa, argued for gradual emancipation. In 1848, it merged with the Congrégation du Saint-Esprit, the chief supplier of priests for the colonies.

In the 1830s and 1840s, some members of the secular clergy who worked directly with blacks showed increased interest in the moralization campaign as well, publishing negative accounts of the colonial system and the conditions in which slaves were held.[64] For example, Abbé Monnet extended his mission to slaves in Bourbon soon after his arrival in 1840, echoing Javouhey in his opinion that only the negligence and indifference of whites was holding back blacks from becoming Christians. The Abbé Dugoujon, one of the most radical abolitionist priests, who denounced slavery based on his experiences in the Antilles, addressed the letters in his book to "our friends," the three Senegalese priests sponsored by Javouhey.[65] The speed with which these new religious orders, including the Soeurs de St-Joseph de Cluny, grew showed that, at a grassroots level, young Catholics had a considerable desire to evangelize among non-European populations. Javouhey and her sisters, however, were among the only women, Catholic or otherwise, active in the cause of emancipation.[66]

A changed attitude also finally came from the top. After centuries of justifying slavery and the slave trade as consistent with Catholic teachings and even necessary to guarantee the Christian conversion of Africans, in 1839 Pope Gregory XVI (previously head of Propaganda Fide) issued a papal bull condemning the slave trade. To enslave "Indians, Blacks, or other such peoples," the pope exhorted, treated them "as if they were not humans but rather mere animals." Furthermore, neither lay Catholics nor clerics were permitted to defend the slave trade. In the document, these directives were preceded by a history of Catholic antislavery efforts that linked the disappearance of slavery to the expansion of faith.[67] Hence, the bull also implicitly promoted increased evangelization efforts. The following year Gregory XVI issued an encyclical on missionary activity, and one in 1845 recommended the development of an indigenous clergy.

The 1839 bull against the slave trade launched an abolitionist campaign in the religious press, particularly Louis Veuillot's *L'Univers*, as well as a flurry of books by reformist colonial clergy that described slave conditions and promoted the Christianization of slaves in view of eventual emancipation.[68] The director of the St-Esprit seminary, Abbé Hardy, for example, published a book in 1838 that promoted Christian instruction for slaves and supported progressive liberation rather than sudden emancipation, as the British empire experienced in 1834. The apostolic prefects in the four French slave colonies opened a competition to write a special catechism for blacks. And in 1846–47, at a clerical retreat in Paris, abolitionist Cyrille C. A. Bissette enrolled hundreds of Catholic priests and three bishops in a petition campaign for emancipation.[69] Although most historians have seen Catholics as marginal to the abolition movement in France, in a recent dissertation Troy Feay argues that both Catholic activists and Catholic rhetoric were key to the shared campaign of slave moralization that developed during the July Monarchy.[70] Javouhey's work among slaves in the French empire was part of this effort and provided a working model of gradual emancipation for the fledgling French anti-slavery movement during the July Monarchy.

The Moralization Campaign

In this climate, Javouhey found a more willing audience for her views, as the French government used missionary networks in a renewed campaign to prepare slaves for eventual emancipation. Even unbelievers like Victor Schoelcher relied strongly upon the missionary work of both the Soeurs de St-Joseph de Cluny and the Frères des Ecoles chrétiennes de Ploërmel to prepare for emancipation in the colonies. In 1840, a royal decree requiring French colonial clergy to provide religious instruction to slaves and to admit slave children to free schools provided new opportunities for these religious orders to expand their ministry beyond the French settler community. Anticipating an eventual end to slavery, the French government saw the "moralization" campaign as essential to an orderly emancipation whenever it might take place. Guadeloupe, Martinique, Bourbon, and Guiana still counted approximately a quarter million slaves in the period between 1830 and 1848.[71] Colonial clergy were now explicitly charged with weekly catechism lessons for slave children and monthly visits to plantations. Previously, they had been responsible for the religious education of slaves, but with only thirty-two priests for 130,000 slaves in a colony like Guadeloupe and a budget barely adequate for the maintenance of churches, this responsibility had remained completely hypothetical. Only eighty-eight priests in total served the four slave colonies, fewer than one cleric for every four thousand people.[72] The new decree provided an additional 400,000 francs to increase the number of clergy and to build additional churches in the four slave colonies and 200,000 francs for the extension of primary education to slave children over the age of four, of which Javouhey was able to secure 90,000 francs to fund twenty additional Soeurs de St-Joseph. As the colonial minister wrote her in 1839, the government's objective was nothing less than a "social transformation" in "the not too distant future." Furthermore, in 1844 he argued that teaching the catechism to slave women in particular would have "an immense influence over the moralization of slaves in general."[73]

Social transformation, of course, was Javouhey's forte, and the new campaign—and money—provided her with new opportunities for black evangelization beyond Mana. By the 1840s, the Soeurs de St-Joseph had already established flourishing educational establishments in the slave colonies, but by and large, outside of Mana they served a white settler elite. As such, these schools competed with boarding schools in France to which settler families might otherwise send their daughters and had to offer the same advantages in curriculum and training. When Javouhey first visited the *pensionnat royal* in St-Pierre, Martinique, in 1829, she praised it as "this fine establishment that cedes nothing to the best houses of education in France." "Everything is brought together here," she wrote, "piety, wisdom, science, modesty, good behavior." These elite colonial schools also brought in substantial funds—in 1829, Javouhey estimated the profits of the Martinique school at 40,000 francs and of that in Guadeloupe as 10,000 francs—money that could be used to subsidize other works at home or abroad.[74] Because of the value these schools provided, Javouhey was careful to provide them with high-quality teachers and extra amenities. In 1834, for example, she sent a music teacher to the Antilles and upgraded the training given to teaching sisters to include foreign languages, adding that the "Ladies of the Sacred Heart have promised to initiate us into all their secrets." These improvements helped to double the enrollment at the boarding school in Guadeloupe, housed on a former plantation outside of Basse-Terre known as "Petit Versailles."[75] Both the colonial ministry and the colonial governors, in turn, saw the education offered by the sisters as increasing the piety, the "useful knowledge," and the "agreeable talents that a woman called to live in the world needs." The first superior of the new boarding school in Martinique, however, echoed a common trope about settler girls, complaining that at age ten they already had "a fickleness, a dissipation contrary to modesty." Whatever the inborn vices of these girls, the nuns hoped to reform them through the strict enclosure and rules of the convent. All pupils, even those whose families lived in town, were required to board, and visits were allowed only once a week and under the supervision of a nun.[76] For fear of losing their white pupils, however, the Soeurs de St-Joseph did not enroll girls of color.

In Bourbon and Cayenne, where settlers were poorer, schools were more permeable. In 1818, Soeur Marie-Joseph Varin reported to Javouhey from Bourbon that few girls were full-time boarders, compared to a slightly larger group of "half boarders," and a much larger group of day pupils, sixty of whom were educated free of charge. She attributed this situation to both the poverty of the inhabitants and the attachment parents had to their children. From the very beginning, the sisters in Bourbon enrolled free girls of color; in St-Paul, the king's representative even allowed that they had more scholarly aptitude than the white girls. In subsequent years, however, administrators warned against too much education for free blacks because it might upset the "balance" between the two groups, and they saw religious lessons like those imparted by the Soeurs de St-Joseph as improving relations between slaves and masters.[77] Since paying pupils, however, were important to the financial stability of the order in Bourbon, when Rosalie Javouhey arrived on the island in 1825, she added drawing and music lessons at the school in St-Denis to appeal to a certain class of parent. Twenty years later, the Soeurs de St-Joseph refused to give up their paying classes, still essential to their balance sheet, even with increased demand for free schools.[78] In Cayenne, according to Javouhey, "the colony is so poor, so hard up, that the parents cannot make any sacrifice; everything depends on us." In the school, she specified that "the day classes of color are well separated." Two classes served the daughters of white settlers, and a third, free girls of color. An attempt in 1834, however, to separate legitimate and illegitimate girls— a proxy for race, as was commonly done in the Antilles—failed due to community pressure. When she first arrived in Guiana in 1830, Javouhey expressed a keen interest in educating mixed-race girls, claiming that "they are difficult to raise, but they have great means," suggesting that finding funds to support the Cayenne school was nearly as important as expanding her pedagogical mission.[79]

Although the Soeurs de St-Joseph also educated some mixed-race and black girls in free classes or nursery schools attached to the more prestigious settler schools in the slave colonies, the extra funds provided by the government after 1840 gave Javouhey an opportunity to expand these efforts. With money to pay additional personnel and a renewed sense of mission, she was able to open more schools and more classes in existing schools and thereby to provide a basic education to poor free girls of color, as well as a handful of slave girls, segregated by class and race. The nuns also provided catechism classes for adult women and *associations de persévérance* for girls after their First Communion. Evidence suggests that the new primary schools for free blacks were popular with parents. In response to demand, in Guadeloupe, Javouhey authorized the opening of seven schools in the three years between 1842 and 1845.[80]

Whatever the meaning of these schools to their clients—and we have no sources to tell us—to the nuns their overriding purpose was Christianization. Although most of the slaves in these four colonies were baptized Catholics, few practiced other sacraments, and many mixed Christian practices with indigenous African ones. "We do not need great science," Javouhey wrote, "but much piety, good will, religious instruction, so that they love the catechism, in order to win souls for God." The nuns who were sent to work in these establishments also had less training. However, in 1847, Javouhey opened a new boarding school in Martinique, where "honest girls, without distinction of color, according to the intentions of the government," could be enrolled.[81] Although "honest" undoubtedly meant legitimate, usually a code for race, such a school opened up the possibility of advanced education for a few mixed-race or black girls, provided they could pay the tuition.

Slave education was a particularly knotty problem. Even though the Soeurs de St-Joseph had entered a growth phase in the 1840s, it was hard to imagine that they could provide the necessary personnel to educate the large numbers of slave children in the slave colonies. In Martinique, local superior Soeur Onésime Lefèvre estimated that, if they opened a school in each town, they would need at least an additional hundred nuns, for which there was no money nor enough personnel.[82] Many slave-owners refused to send slave children to school, preferring they work instead. In 1845, the Soeurs de St-Joseph de Cluny still had no slave pupils on either Martinique or Guadeloupe among the approximately seven hundred girls they educated. In catechism classes run by the church in Martinique, only about a third of the participants were slaves, a much lower proportion than their representation in the general population.[83] Besides the slaveowners' reluctance to obey the new law, this imbalance resulted from logistical problems. Slaves living in towns had access to the new free schools opened there, but most of the slaves lived on plantations. The governor of Guadeloupe estimated the number of slave children living on plantations at between 15,000 and 18,000 children aged four to fourteen. In 1844, a government report estimated that religious instruction had been introduced on only slightly more than half of the thirty-six hundred plantations in the slave colonies, more, proportionately, in Martinique and Guiana than in Guadeloupe and Bourbon.[84]

Javouhey was also reluctant to send teaching sisters to isolated plantations. As she wrote the colonial minister in 1844 regarding educational efforts in Bourbon, "It would be improper for nuns, like male missionaries or even brothers, to go catechize, isolated, on individual plantations." Instead, she defended the "free classes" at schools in town, open to "all poor families no matter what their position and their color," as well as the special catechism classes on Sundays and holidays open to all slave girls and women over the age of ten.[85] In 1846, however, the French government provided additional funding for educational efforts on plantations. In response, Javouhey answered a request from the richest landowner in Martinique,

Augustin Pécoul, to furnish two sisters to open a school serving 120 children on his and neighboring plantations. Pécoul, who had also invited the Frères de Ploërmel as catechists, expressed confidence that if more colonists like him took the initiative for reform, they could cease to "tremble" at the idea of emancipation. A year later, a similar request came from a plantation owner named Kayser on Guadeloupe. The conditions of this foundation specified that the sisters were to eat by themselves and that they would be able to attend mass on Sundays and holidays.[86] However, Soeur Onésime Lefèvre in Martinique still expressed concern that the distance from town, the bad roads, and the hot climate would make travel to religious services difficult. She preferred that nuns live in groups of three, close enough to town to walk, avoiding daily contact with plantation owners or representatives. Even the governor of Martinique agreed that the nuns should avoid dependence on the plantation, but he was willing to pay for the experiment.[87]

Admitting children from other plantations, which might compromise the good order of the Pécoul plantation, and putting young children of both sexes in the same classroom, which Lefèvre believed carried "the vice of illegitimate birth," were also controversial measures. By April 1848, however, she reported to Javouhey that the schools on the plantation had been "a success that we had not counted on." In addition to teaching children, the sisters provided evening prayer and religious instruction to adults on the plantation. The same month Pécoul sent a letter to the "citizen minister" of colonies asking for funds to bring the sisters to a second plantation he owned at Bassepointe. Nonetheless, the project of opening schools on plantations was abandoned at the end of 1849, after one of the sisters assigned to the Pécoul plantation defected from the order, and the government increased its requests for teachers in towns.[88]

Although the government appeared satisfied with the work of the Soeurs de St-Joseph in the slave colonies, praising their ability to improve morals and "the love of family," the colonial elite were hostile to the new schools. "The letters from Martinique and from Guadeloupe," wrote Javouhey in 1846, "are not friendly; they believe that it is I who made the laws regarding the abolition of slavery and the mixing of colors." She believed that their concern was unwarranted: "Everywhere we find that instruction makes Negroes gentler, more submissive to their masters."[89] The expansion of the Soeurs de St-Joseph into racially mixed education led to increased conflict with French settlers, especially in Martinique and Guadeloupe, where plantation owners were a significant economic force. As the colonial economies weakened because of a decline in demand for cane sugar, planters upheld the existing system of slave labor more tenaciously than ever. A short-lived uprising of free blacks in Martinique in 1833, the same year as slave emancipation in the British empire, had badly frightened the white settlers. In the 1840s, despite the new policy emanating from the metropole, the colonists tore up the edicts requiring slave education and blocked the clergy from entering the plantations. Even the poorer whites withdrew their children from the free schools to prevent their mixing with children of color, and the local officials recommended segregated schooling.[90]

Under these conditions, Lefèvre, more cautious than Javouhey, objected to expanding education to girls of color for fear that the white families would withdraw their daughters and hence the financial support that underwrote the entire mission. "You know," she wrote Javouhey in 1846, "that in the colonies we are enemies of innovation…as for the admission of children of color among the whites, they will not ever submit; the white families withdraw their children and the others give us very few…there is no possible reasoning on this question." She warned of a "violent crisis" in the boarding school and proposed that, since their building was "immense," she could "arrange things in a way to spare everyone." Furthermore, she objected to Javouhey's plan for a separate school for colored girls because "the class of color has not yet acquired enough affluence to sustain a *pensionnat*." Only in July 1848 did the boarding school in Guadeloupe begin, cautiously, to admit girls of color. Its superior, Soeur Léonce Tristant, wrote Javouhey that only about forty white pupils were left in the school due to "the great misery.…Providence seems to want to replace them with pupils of color,…[so] we have taken the big step."[91]

Indeed, it could be argued that local superiors like Lefèvre and Tristant were only being prudent given the financial reliance of the Soeurs de St-Joseph on the daughters of white settlers, but the practice of racial segregation in Guadeloupe and Martinique had already provoked Victor Schoelcher to denounce the Soeurs de St-Joseph de Cluny in his book *Des colonies françaises: Abolition immédiate de l'esclavage*, published in 1842. In 1849, after emancipation had revolutionized Caribbean society, Schoelcher complained to Javouhey that Lefèvre was dragging her feet by refusing to enroll illegitimate girls in the order's flagship boarding school, which he saw as a pretext for racism: "I ask you, you whose spirit is right and just, Is this not still hate hidden under an appearance of morality? Are children responsible for the faults of their parents?" (By contrast, Schoelcher praised the "excellent sisters of Gorée and St-Louis.")[92] During the moralization campaign, the Soeurs de St-Joseph in the Antilles tolerated more racial segregation than did, for example, the Frères de Ploërmel, who refused to separate black and white children in their schools. Philippe Delisle argues that the difference can be attributed to the longer period that the sisters had been in the colony, as well as Javouhey's practice of allowing considerable authority to local superiors like Lefèvre, despite her own championing of the abolitionist cause.[93] Although this analysis has merit, Javouhey herself also understood the importance of the funds brought in by the prestigious Caribbean establishments, which allowed her to experiment elsewhere. She, too, was willing to compromise here for the sake of her greater mission.

With little fanfare, however, Javouhey was breaking with tradition to admit mixed-race and black women as Soeurs de St-Joseph. She had promoted the idea of black Soeurs de St-Joseph ever since she had brought Florence and her companions from Senegal but had run into obstacles ranging from lack of vocations to parental resistance to the expense of sending novices to France.[94] In 1846, however, Javouhey wrote to the local superior in Bourbon that "we are going to have a novitiate in Trinidad for girls of color, black and mulatto. The superiors and novice mistresses will be French...our statutes will be for them as for us; the missionaries will occupy themselves with the instruction of the poor people of the countryside, the care of the sick, [and] will teach them to work."[95]

The first sister of color was Soeur Marie-Joseph, born in Norfolk, Virginia, and in the service of the wife of the governor of Martinique, who brought her to Javouhey in France in 1845. When the local superior in Cayenne identified another promising candidate, Javouhey recommended she be sent first to Martinique and then to Trinidad for training.[96] It is notable that she chose to launch this initiative in an English colony (although one with a substantial Catholic population), where slavery had already been abolished. Furthermore, she specified that she had the support of both the bishop of Trinidad and the papal nuncio in Paris.[97] Indeed, Victor Schoelcher, getting wind of a transfer of a black novice from Martinique to Trinidad, accused Lefèvre, "imbued with the prejudices of her confraternity," of hiding the novice because her skin color would scandalize white settlers.[98] Given the racial climate in the Antilles and the few pupils of color in the boarding schools (the most likely site of recruitment), however, it is not surprising that Javouhey did not look for new novices there. The Frères de Ploërmel had similar problems integrating black members in the Antilles.[99] Nonetheless, she did extend the experiment—tentatively—to French colonies. In 1848, she wrote the local superior in Bourbon, "In all the colonial houses, we need to have several black sisters" as "associated sisters" [religieuses agrégées]. But she left it to the local superior to "examine before God if the thing is doable." In 1850, she repeated, "[T]ry to find black nuns to help you because we need classes for blacks." "In all our houses in the Antilles, we receive them like the others," she claimed.[100] The admission of sisters of color to the order promised to help solve the problem of personnel for the new missions, although the black sisters wore a habit that was slightly different from that of the French sisters, signifying, perhaps, their second-class status.[101]

"On the Edge of a Volcano": The Revolution of 1848

Slavery was formally abolished in the French empire on 27 April 1848 as a by-product of the Revolution of 1848, which began in February of that year as a popular uprising. The new provisional government of the Second Republic included many important abolitionists, and Victor Schoelcher, the chief advocate of immediate emancipation, used the opportunity provided by the change in regime to push through abolition over the protests of colonial elites.[102] In many ways, the granting of freedom to slaves vindicated Javouhey's views on the potential of blacks. But even though abolitionist opinion in the late 1840s shifted, she had never been a partisan of immediate emancipation. Like most Catholics who had lived through the 1789 Revolution, she was wary of revolutionary enthusiasm and the disorder it provoked. "All the republicans," she wrote, "are not saints. The first days were very difficult...[ellipses hers] only the word 'republic' with choruses of Ça ira, alas! We didn't know what to say!" Yet, like other Catholics of the time, she rejoiced in the surprising unity between revolutionaries and clerics: "But one, more aware than the others, began to cry, long live our Lord Jesus Christ! Long live M. le curé...[ellipses hers] it did us good; many cried the same: we want religion, liberty for all, no more slaves."[103] She even saw potential for a reawakening of faith. "I have the greatest confidence," she wrote to her sister, "that [the revolution] will result in great good for everyone, the prophecies will come true, this will reanimate faith that seems asleep." By May, however, she "trembled" that the "Communist spirit" would result in the banishment of religion, and during the June Days, the Soeurs de St-Joseph, partisans of order, provided soup to the mobile guards tasked with putting down revolution. Javouhey also hoped to care for several hundred children abandoned by the "Paris war," a reprise of her longstanding interest in orphans.[104]

Despite Javouhey's view of the Revolution from the front lines, however, she understood that the implications for the colonies were even more significant. First and foremost, she sought to safeguard the order's missions in an unstable situation. "We are on the edge of a volcano," she wrote Soeur Onésime Lefèvre in Martinique. "[S]how yourselves completely devoted to the Blacks; it's our lifeline."[105] Even as critics like Schoelcher clamored for the removal of nuns like Lefèvre, whom they perceived as hostile to black freedom, Javouhey encouraged her to open additional classes for blacks and to accept pupils of color in the boarding school, although, she conceded, "I do not tell you to look for them." A year later, she declared her pleasure with Lefèvre for having followed her instructions and enrolled girls of color. To the local superior in Guadeloupe, Javouhey suggested that she "encourage the colonists to support the government" in the abolition of slavery and "show yourselves completely devoted to the education of slaves."[106] To the request that she remove nuns who were perceived as less favorable to blacks, Javouhey answered that "if, after my recommendations, they had anything to complain about, I would recall them." Javouhey counted on her reputation for devotion to blacks to keep the colonial missions intact. "Without Mana," she wrote, "they would have passed into other hands." She also worked to keep her government contacts in place even though "we change naval ministers like we change shirts." Indeed, in July, she reported information that Baron Roger had "delivered to me himself, although very secretly, on the subject of the measures taken for the colonial schools."[107]

That information was hopeful for Javouhey and her order. The Second Republic decreed that free primary schools should be established in all communes, including those overseas. By late March the government had already requested fifty additional nuns, to be divided among all the colonies, reducing salaries by a third in order to pay for additional personnel. In April Lefèvre reported that their schools in Martinique were overcrowded in all locations, many of them with slave children.[108] Throughout the colonies, the demand for new schools opened by missionaries increased rapidly. By 1850, the Soeurs de St-Joseph were operating eighteen schools with more than two thousand pupils in Martinique, fifteen schools with eighteen hundred pupils in Guadeloupe, and ten schools in Bourbon, now patriotically renamed Réunion.[109] Emancipation opened up clear opportunities for expansion, which Javouhey eagerly embraced.

Yet, supplying enough personnel remained a key problem. Until her death in 1851, Javouhey was engaged in a continual effort to recruit and train more nuns to send abroad despite having doubled the size of her order since her return to France in 1843.[110] An idea floated by the government to open a novitiate in Martinique in order to reduce transportation costs failed for lack of local vocations.[111] Javouhey instead bought a large convent in Paris in early 1849 at great expense to serve as both a second novitiate (after Cluny) and a place for colonial sisters to rest and restore their health after tours abroad. Yet, although the new establishment housed three hundred nuns, new colonial sisters could not be created overnight despite the pressing demands of the colonial ministry. "It takes time to instruct them," Javouhey conceded. "[T]hey should have at least two years; we can scarcely give them one, as the needs are so pressing; the rest comes in the practice of their duty."[112] But in the expansion of her order, Javouhey saw the hand of providence in the events of 1848. "France is so guilty," she wrote, "that God has transferred his spurned graces to savage countries, and the Soeurs Saint-Joseph are perhaps chosen for this noble mission." At age sixty-eight, she even fantasized about traveling to Guiana and the Caribbean to reorganize the missions herself. "If I had one hundred years to live," she wrote in 1850, "I would ask to spend them in the colonies."[113]

What worried Javouhey was the violence that accompanied slave emancipation. Of the four slave colonies, those in the Antilles provided more cause for concern than the others. In Martinique, news that the Second Republic had proclaimed emancipation precipitated slave riots that caused the governor to proclaim immediate emancipation on May 23—before the official decree arrived in the colony. His counterpart in Guadeloupe followed suit on May 27. Some of this violence was directed toward the Soeurs de St-Joseph. In August, Javouhey reported that "they told us that the Blacks were so set against the superior [in Guadeloupe] that they threatened to burn the house." In Guiana and Réunion, however, the slaves were freed according to the government's timetable, August 10 for Guiana and December 20 for Réunion. Cayenne, Javouhey wrote, "is very tranquil, it will be our best colony."[114] Javouhey also worried about what would happen to the colonists if they did not receive government compensation for their slaves, which had implications for her revenue-producing schools, which supported the poorer missions. "The colonists will be ruined, the colonies long ill," she wrote. "God knows what all this will become, what we will earn." Yet she also welcomed the opportunity to get back to basics: "The spirit of poverty, the vanity of riches, it is that we must understand and will give us peace, rest."[115] The poorer houses, she thought, better withstood the new pressures than the flashier and wealthier establishments.

In the colonies, the great fear was that the former slaves would leave the plantations in search of more independent or more lucrative work elsewhere, a fear Javouhey shared. "Have the Blacks gone back to work?" she asked the local superior in Guiana in August 1848. "[W]ithout that the colony will be lost." Mana, she thought, could serve as an example of a well-regulated settlement where the residents stayed on the land.[116] Indeed, there almost all of the former slaves stayed put. Most already had what many newly freed Guianese slaves appeared to want: a small plot of land they could cultivate for their own family. "Mana is today perhaps the only area that provides an ensemble of regular work," reported a local official to the colonial minister in 1850.[117] Elsewhere in Guiana, the sugar plantations had lost more than half of their laborers by the end of 1850, workers choosing instead to cultivate personal plots with subsistence crops. Even in Mana, an attempt to grow coffee failed in part because "the inhabitants of Mana much preferred to cultivate their isolated plots where they were freer," even if they could produce more than three times as much value by working on a common crop.[118] The attempt by Mélinon in the late 1840s to strengthen the sense of private ownership among the Mana residents appeared to have backfired. Left to their own devices, officials claimed they worked three times less than laborers in other parts of the colony. In 1849, the government granted a concession at Mana to the sugar company of Frères Bare, who wanted to use black labor for sugar monoculture. Officials continued to lament, however, both the seeming unwillingness of black residents to hire out their labor and the cost of maintaining the colony.[119]

In February 1852, the French government—now the more conservative and labor unfriendly Second Empire—passed legislation that required workers in the Antilles and Guiana to possess a *livret de travail* or an act of engagement, among other legal measures to encourage former slaves to get back to work. In Guadeloupe, the governor taxed land where neither sugar nor coffee was cultivated. By 1850, many former slaves had returned to their former villages or plantations to work the land in both Guadeloupe and Martinique, and in the next three decades, planters recruited indentured laborers from India.[120] On the two islands, the sugar industry recovered and even innovated during the Second Empire. In Guiana, however, the lack of workers led to declining levels of production after a surge in the first half of the nineteenth century.[121] Without slavery and the plantation economy it supported, the colony became even less economically viable. The slow collapse of the economy after abolition led the French government to designate Guiana as a penal colony in 1851, the year of Javouhey's death.[122] Although Mana continued as a free town proud of its distinctive heritage, Javouhey's vision of a free black peasantry in Guiana ultimately failed.

One solution to creating a more stable society in the former slave colonies was expanding religious authority. Additional clergy were assigned to the colonies, and Martinique, Guadeloupe, and Réunion were upgraded to bishoprics.[123] As the revolutionary moment passed, clergy were seen as necessary brakes on social and economic transformation. Religion, in short, could help manage the transition to freedom by pacifying the former slaves and encouraging them to work. Claude Prudhomme argues that the civil and clerical authorities in Réunion became allies in promoting order and tranquility on the island and that clerics who preached democracy or equality were expelled from the colony.[124] Similar forces were at work in the other former slave colonies. In Guadeloupe, for example, hostile colonists forced the recall of the Abbé Dugoujon, an ardent abolitionist appointed as apostolic prefect by Schoelcher in 1848. In Guiana, Javouhey wanted to place her sisters on the plantations to urge the blacks to work because "they would listen to nuns at least as much as priests."[125]

These forces were also at work in Senegal, which did not figure in the moralization campaign or the debates over the slave question in the 1840s. The two colonies held only about six thousand slaves in total, most employed in domestic and artisanal work, and very few were held by Europeans. However, the abolition of slavery on 23 August engendered protests from signares and other *habitant* slaveholders, especially in St-Louis, and hastened their decline as a social and economic group.[126] French officials in the 1840s and 1850s saw the expansion of missionary education as a way of increasing French influence in the colony, even if many Senegalese natives were Muslim rather than Christian. "Until this day," a government report read, "Senegal has stayed exclusively African: the black natives, the majority of women of color, are complete strangers to the French language.... France has dominated them but not instructed them." To combat the "immoral habits" of the "maternal roof" of the signares, the governor recommended opening boarding facilities, a change that would require doubling the number of teaching sisters.[127] In 1847, the Soeurs de St-Joseph opened a special class in St-Louis for recently baptized "young *négresses*" on Saturdays, and by 1850 they had a class with seventeen Muslim pupils, whose parents were promised religiously neutral education. Three years later, a special commission asked them to open a class for young black girls in the Gorée school so that they could profit "from the benefits of public instruction." By 1858, they enrolled approximately 120 to 130 black pupils in Gorée, segregated from the European and mixed-race pupils not only by race but also by class, language, and religion.[128]

If the Revolution of 1848 opened up new opportunities for religious orders like the Soeurs de St-Joseph de Cluny to minister to people of color, it also turned them into auxiliaries of the state in teaching habits of order and deference to colonial populations. Although the Second Empire was very supportive of the development and expansion of female religious orders, one could argue that, after Javouhey's death in 1851, the most creative period of the Soeurs de St-Joseph ended.[129] Javouhey herself spent much of the last decade of her life building the institutional structure that would outlive her. "I pass part of my life in a carriage," she wrote of her constant journeys between St-Joseph houses in France, where her sisters were also in great demand. "The clergy who were against us look to make us useful," she boasted in 1850. "[E]very parish priest would like the Soeurs de St-Joseph for his parish. We will surround Paris with great and small houses that do great good among young people, and then will bring us postulants who are poor but excellent." Money was always in short supply; she lamented that only one-fifth of all novices were able to pay their way. More than forty years after she had founded her order, she also had to figure out what to do with the sisters who were now too old to work.[130]

But where France planted the flag, the Soeurs de St-Joseph followed. In 1844, Javouhey opened a mission in Tahiti, in 1846 on the islands off the coast of Madagascar, and in 1847 in the Marquesas Islands, where, she claimed, the people were "more savage than at Mana." "When I die," she wrote in one of her last letters, Tahiti "is the first colony I will visit."[131] Indeed, Javouhey is so closely associated with the expansion of the French empire that she is the only woman whose name is engraved on the side of the former French colonial museum in Paris (now the Cité nationale de l'histoire de l'immigration), built in 1931.[132]

A Great Man

On 4 March 1849, the black men in Mana, now invested with full citizenship rights, voted for the first time to send a representative to the new republican National Assembly in Paris. Out of 140 votes, a slim majority of 73 voted for the white candidate, Vidal de Lingendes; the remaining 67 for the candidate of color, Jouannet, who won in Guiana as a whole with 3,420 votes to 601, evoking the worst fears of the French settlers. Only 201 of Vidal de Lingendes' votes came from nonwhites, and a third of those votes came from Mana. Elsewhere in Guiana, the key to Jouannet's landslide victory was the black voters' fear that slavery might be reestablished.[133] Without knowing any details about the election campaign in Mana, it appears—superficially at least—that the residents there were less suspicious of whites or less fearful that they would be reenslaved than other Guianese of African descent. The alarmed colonial officials certainly saw it as one of the few bright spots in an otherwise dismal electoral landscape. Despite the "unrest that the elections sowed in Mana as everywhere," one reported to Paris two months later, "there at least one can note in other respects a satisfactory state of affairs, a compact population attached to the soil."[134]

Yet certain sources claim that neither Vidal de Lingendes nor Jouannet was the first choice of the Mana voters, who instead insisted on casting their votes for Anne-Marie Javouhey. "Vainly," one biographer writes, "did one tell them that women could not form part of political assemblies." Upon finally understanding the gender realities of French politics, the voters supposedly stated, " 'If we cannot name our Dear Mother, name whom you like, it's all the same to us.' " Another source claims that they then refused to vote altogether.[135] Like first-time voters all over France in 1849, the inhabitants of Mana apparently preferred to send a familiar candidate to the National Assembly, throwing their support behind the local notable. Yet Javouhey was not running for anything, nor, of course, as a woman, could she even cast a vote herself. But as a woman and a nun, Javouhey, even more than most other heads of female religious orders, confounded both her admirers and her critics, including the voters at Mana.

Throughout her career, commentators found her independence and power troubling in a nun and wished for more womanly submission. From Guiana, Guillier questioned whether "her enterprise could be the work of a woman, much less a nun," implying that it was both unfeminine and beyond her capacity. The bishop of Beauvais complained about "her whims," a fairly traditional criticism of female leadership and competence. The *Journal du Havre*, a proslavery newspaper, asked rhetorically, "Can we conceive that in France the colonization of Mana will be seriously entrusted to a woman?"[136] To explain her hold on the African population in Mana, some commentators, including Javouhey herself, used maternal imagery, an easily available metaphor. Not only was Javouhey the "mother" of her congregation, but the Mana residents were also conceptualized as children. In this way, the authority that Javouhey exercised at Mana, despite her celibate status, was neutralized as appropriately feminine.

Nonetheless, it is striking how often observers reached for masculine language to describe a woman who did not seem to fit into traditional gender categories. Most would have agreed with the governor of French Guiana, who reported himself "obliged to recognize in Madame Javouhey a woman of superior intelligence," as well as one who "does not like to submit herself to rules, even those that she herself has imposed." Her cousin Léopold Javouhey commented on her "virile soul and a singular force of will," as well as her physical stamina. Javouhey, he reported, "led in Mana a very active existence, even a very difficult one. She walked the distance from her establishment in Cayenne (220 kilometers) through savannahs and woods, following the paths of redskins, intersected by creeks and great waterways, spending nights in rundown cabins."[137] The image of nuns fending for themselves in the Amazonian wilderness was unusual enough to excite public comment. "It is therefore Sister Javouhey," reported the *Gazette des Tribunaux*, "or in her absence her young companions, who direct independently the work of Mana, and one sees these pious vestal virgins, with their blue robes and their white veils, rowing Indian canoes on the waters or wielding axes in the forests of Guiana."[138] Amazonian women in this example were more than metaphorical. A hostile article published in *Le Temps* in 1836 even evoked a fantastical future for Mana, in which Javouhey, "a woman of intelligence and resolution," would found a dynasty of sisters who would reign over the colony and eventually the continent: "Within ten years, Sister Javouhey will send directly to Europe, from her ports in Mana, ships of 150 to 200 tons, which she may have built herself, loaded with sugar, cocoa, coffee, annatto, etc....[In the future] a sister Javouhey V or VI...will hold the scepter of political balance in South America." As if gender transgression were not bad enough, the article also imagined that Europeans, Africans, and Amerindians would intermarry and breed a new race of intermediate skin colors.[139]

However, King Louis-Philippe pronounced the definitive judgment on Javouhey after she described her plans for Mana "with such a range, such a precision of thought and such strength of reason," by allegedly exclaiming, "Madame Javouhey! Mais c'est un grand homme!" [But she's a great man!] Long before it was picked up by biographers, the epitaph appears in the report prepared by the Holy See on the Soeurs de St-Joseph a mere three years after Javouhey's death.[140] A similar story circulated about her entry into Paris during the Revolution of 1848, which claimed that the crowds allowed her safe passage with the cry, "It's General Javouhey! Oh, that woman is a great man" [C'est un grand homme que celle-là].[141] In a world of separate spheres, for better or worse, Javouhey was considered an exception, an honorary man. When cited by her admirers, of course, characterizing her as exceptional meant that fundamental gender conceptions did not have to be revised. When cited by her enemies, Javouhey's apparent transgression of gender boundaries proved her inherent perfidy.[142]

What did Javouhey herself think of these masculine comparisons? Despite her extensive association with slavery and abolition, she seems never to have invoked the comparison of women's lack of rights (which, for example, deprived her of a vote in 1848) with the institution of slavery, an analogy that became commonplace among women's rights advocates after the seventeenth century.[143] This may have been because the slavery analogy was most commonly made in reference to women's subordination in marriage, an issue of little relevance to a Catholic nun. Nor did she show any interest in the fledgling women's rights advocates in the 1830s and 1840s, even during the Revolution of 1848, when she was in residence in Paris. There, women like Eugénie Niboyet, Jeanne Deroin, Suzanne Voilquin, and Elisa Lemonnier demanded equal rights for women in political clubs and in the press.[144]

For all her insistence on her own independence and authority, Javouhey appeared little interested in overturning women's accepted role in society, happy instead to promote domesticity in the schools operated by the Soeurs de St-Joseph within and without France. In keeping with the emerging domestic ideology of the early nineteenth century, women, she believed, were key to the family, and the family was key to moralization and Christianization. African women could play this same role in society if their education and upbringing were put into European hands, specifically those of the sisters. Until then, black children were better raised by nuns than their own parents, which suggests that motherhood was less a biological function than a cultural one in which even celibate women like Javouhey could participate.

If women's roles in the greater society were essentially unchanged, women religious now bore a larger responsibility for the propagation of the Gospel. About a new mission on one of the islands off the Madagascar coast Javouhey wrote, "Already the [male] missionaries are established there; they wait for the sisters like the Messiah, they say that they can do nothing without women; it is women who make good and evil."[145] Nuns who traveled to far-flung missions therefore required some of the same characteristics that Javouhey herself embodied. Those characteristics were both masculine and feminine. From Senegal she stated firmly that novices were not to be trained as "little women" [femmelettes] but as individuals of "courage" and "good will." In addition, the nun who was to replace her in Mana needed both "a more masculine virtue" and "a more robust humility" in order to "endure the burdens inseparable from my position." In a letter to the nuns who had traveled halfway around the world to evangelize in Oceania, she wrote, "[Male] missionaries know how to die, soldiers know how to die, are nuns not capable of such a devotion for God!" After this call to arms, however, the letter continued, "How can you preach? By your good conduct, your sweetness and your charity. Keep to your duty, my dear daughters, avoid the world," followed by several sentences of advice for remaining quasi-enclosed from outsiders, even priests.[146] The rewards for nuns who transgressed gender boundaries were reserved for the afterlife; in this life, Javouhey preached a code of conduct that she herself did not practice.

In her celibate status, as well as her position of leadership, Javouhey claimed power that was unavailable to her otherwise, but she did not claim it on behalf of all women or even all religious women. Instead, she acted individually to transform the world around her. In this, she shared a sensibility with the Romantics and uto-pians of the early nineteenth century, who also sought solutions in individual action. Most radically, she acted on behalf of individuals of a different race, culture, and religion, although her goal was to transform their culture and religion into hers, thereby, in her view, making their race irrelevant. In this way, she also expanded the reach of the Catholic church in ways that became standard later in the century and formed the basis of an overseas Catholic empire that lasts to this day.

Conclusion

In July 1850, Anne-Marie Javouhey wrote Emilie de Vialar expressing her gratitude for Vialar's recent letter and regretting that she was not able to visit with her during her last trip to Toulouse, but she hoped such a meeting would not be far off: "I propose to pass through Toulouse and to stay a day to see you; it would be a joy to talk with you." She also invited Vialar to visit her in Paris.[1] Did the two women ever carry out this plan to meet and discuss their common interests and problems? Unfortunately, there exists no record of such a meeting, and if it indeed took place, we would of course have no transcript of their conversation. But even the tantalizing suggestion of such a tête-à-tête between these two independent, charismatic, and strong-willed women reminds us of how much they had in common. Neither one ever referred to Philippine Duchesne in their correspondence (nor she to them)—though they were both well aware of the model and the competition the Religious of the Sacred Heart provided—but if we throw her into the mix, as this book has done, we can compose a portrait of the early nineteenth-century missionary nun that takes us from a cloistered convent in Old Regime Grenoble to an Indian village in North America to schools and clinics in the Ottoman empire to a semiautonomous colony on the edge of the Amazon forest, among many other places.

These paths would have been unimaginable the day in 1788 that Duchesne became a Visitation novice, but they determined the course of the missionary work of the nineteenth-century Catholic church, as well as some of the byways of French imperialism. What made those paths possible? Or, asked another way, how did these women live the lives they did? It is clear that all three exercised far more power and practiced more autonomy than did any laywoman of their era. From what sources did their power and autonomy spring?

First, all three women had faith. They had a deep and abiding belief, of course, in God and the universal application of Catholicism to all peoples in all places and at all times. They trusted in "providence" to guide their decisions and explained both successes and setbacks in terms of divine will. Although this book emphasizes other issues over spirituality, there is no way of understanding them that excludes those beliefs, which formed the very basis of their life's work. But all three women also had remarkable faith in their own abilities. Sometimes this self-confidence was hidden in language of self-abnegation and humility, especially in the case of Philippine Duchesne, who continually expressed her unworthiness to head up the Sacred Heart mission in North America, all the while demonstrating her undeniable competence at doing just that. Surprisingly, though, these women often expressed their confidence forthrightly, claiming with certainty that they were following the path God had laid for them. When confronted with obstacles, they showed very little self doubt and instead invoked the rightness of their cause. That they would do so when faced with secular or non-Catholic opponents could perhaps be understood as a difference in worldview, another chapter in a long-running battle between clerics and anticlericals or Catholics and non-Catholics. To do so when faced with the determined opposition of a Bishop Dupuch or Héricault or even the minor remonstrances of a Father Van Quickenborne was another level of confidence altogether. These priests had real spiritual and institutional power over these women, and yet they fought back, certain that God was speaking to them and not to these men, who outranked them in the patriarchal hierarchy of the Catholic church. In all three cases, they seem to have first practiced this filial disobedience on their birth fathers, who opposed their vocations, before confronting their spiritual fathers.

Their extraordinary confidence appears to have come from a number of different sources beyond sheer strength of personality. As founders or founding members of female religious orders, Duchesne, Vialar, and Javouhey inherited a powerful institutional structure that had given autonomy to Catholic women for centuries. These women believed they had a sacred responsibility to uphold the charism and rules of those orders even in disputes with members of their own church, allowing them to overcome their general acceptance of patriarchy within that same church.[2] The new structure of the religious orders that emerged after the French Revolution—centralized, in active contact with the outside world—provided even more resources for demonstrating this autonomy. A woman who provided spiritual and temporal leadership to hundreds, if not thousands, of other women dedicated to the same cause had loyal troops at her back. In the disputes with clerics and bishops described in this book, few sisters deserted the cause of their mother superior. The nineteenth-century transition from a French-centered national church to the ultramontane church ruled from Rome also provided a complex nexus of power relations that women religious like Vialar and Javouhey in particular exploited in order to outflank local bishops. With the rules regarding women religious in such rapid evolution, there was room for maneuver and expanded power. Over the course of the nineteenth century, the Catholic church was remade by these women, who, although unable to practice the sacraments, became, nonetheless, important ministers and evangelists of the faith.

At the same time, all three women also had access to resources, contacts, and networks outside of the church that provided essential support. Family money allowed them to acquire the real estate—the convents in Grenoble, Gaillac, and Cluny—that accompanied their initial foundations. Duchesne and Vialar counted on family fortunes to greater or lesser degrees for the rest of their lives. To make up for her more modest familial resources, Javouhey created an autonomous financial base by contracting with the French government to provide services throughout the colonies, a business relationship that was independent of her status within the church. All three also relied on family contacts and networks in their missionary expansion—Vialar's initial establishment in Algiers at the behest of her brother is one obvious example—but none more so than Anne-Marie Javouhey, whose three sisters and two nieces followed her into religion and provided the backbone of her order. Far from disappearing into convents where they had little contact with their birth families, these women stayed close to them, both emotionally and materially, even as they traveled the world.

Networks of sympathetic clerics also facilitated their work overseas. For every Dupuch or Héricourt, there was also a DeSmet or a Bourgade. But these women were also successful in enlisting lay allies in their cause, even individuals who did not share their religious faith. Baron Roger, Javouhey's greatest lay partner and friend, was only nominally Catholic. The St. Louis Protestant elite sent their daughters to Duchesne's schools, and Vialar ingratiated herself with Muslim notables from the signatories to the Algiers petition to the bey of Tunisia himself. These individuals provided them with networks of power outside of the Catholic church that made their expansion into new territories possible. All three clearly made these friends on the basis of substantial personal charisma. However, they also offered valuable services, whether to frontier parents seeking education for their daughters, or Ottoman rulers seeking to modernize their states, or French officials attempting to stabilize their colonial holdings. For both church and state, the energy and resources that these missionary women and their followers offered were too necessary to suppress, even at the risk of granting more power and autonomy to women.

Besides demonstrating consistent leadership skills and an ability to network, Duchesne, Vialar, and Javouhey all showed themselves remarkably adaptable to changing circumstances. None of the three began her religious life with missionary work as a calling. Duchesne did not even start hers in an active religious order. Her ability to reimagine her religious life and purpose in the aftermath of the spiritual chaos of the French Revolution and then to turn it outward, from Grenoble to St. Louis, demonstrated a surprising flexibility in an individual who began her religious life confined in a convent as a contemplative nun. Vialar jumped at unexpected opportunities, from an invitation to Algiers to the accidental marooning of her ship in Malta, all the while also carefully plotting certain moves such as opening a mission in Jerusalem. Javouhey defined her order as a missionary one only when the material and spiritual benefits of such a move became obvious and her calling as among Africans only after she herself had lived among them. Over time, all three carved out a particular missionary space and profile, but to a certain extent those characteristics developed because of contingent and accidental historical factors that could not have been anticipated at the beginning of their careers. The flexibility they showed, however, was fundamental to their success.

Despite many similarities, there were also clear differences in the life paths of these women. Of the three, Duchesne was the least daring. In part, this caution derived from her status as a subordinate to Sophie Barat, the founder of the Religious of the Sacred Heart. Although Duchesne operated fairly autonomously in North America, she did not have quite the same power as Vialar or Javouhey, for whom their orders during their lifetimes were virtual extensions of themselves. Most of all, however, the difference was generational. Duchesne was the most marked by women's religious life of the Old Regime and the only one of the three to experience it firsthand. Despite her remarkable adaptability, there were certain features of that life that she never completely left behind, particularly an attachment to spiritual mortification and to cloister. There is no evidence to suggest that either Vialar or Javouhey made themselves suffer, physically or spiritually, in the ways that Duchesne sometimes did. Although all three interpreted setbacks as tests from God, only she actively practiced mortification.

The problem of enclosure haunted all three women in one way or another, especially in their relationships with male clerics (or even Gaillac gossips) who criticized their business acumen, their independent decision making, their freedom to travel, and even the style of their habits. But Duchesne actively sought a compromise between the missionary lifestyle to which she felt herself called and the principles of enclosure, which she saw as essential to her religious life. The cloistered Marie de l'Incarnation, who converted Indian girls and women in the seventeenth-century Canadian wilderness, remained her missionary role model. Coming of age during or after the French Revolution, Vialar and Javouhey simply ignored the principle of cloister, which would have made their missionary ambitions impossible. When they evoked past missionaries, these were more likely to be male, like the Jesuits of Paraguay, whose movements were not curtailed by enclosure. Of the three women,

Duchesne was also the one most deferential to male clerical authority, choosing to work around the obstacles of patriarchy rather than confront them directly. In the contrast of Duchesne's life to the other two, we see the very evolution of women's religious life from cloistered to active and from limited missionary experience in North America to the expansion of women missionaries throughout the world.

Most significantly, the missionary effort of these three women differed dramatically because of the different characteristics of the sites in which they worked, their relationship to the local power structures, and the perceived nature of the indigenous inhabitants. Duchesne worked in a region far from formal French power structures, where the very notion of a French empire was nostalgic rather than real. In a borderland between past Indian, French, Spanish, and now American empires, she witnessed the transition from a multicultural and multiracial environment to a race-segregated national state. Vialar operated within the borders of the Ottoman multinational empire, which was rapidly falling prey to increased European encroachment, whether violent and direct as in the military occupation of Algeria or subtle and gradual as in the increased meddling of European consuls and clerics in sites around the Mediterranean. The glue that held this empire together was in large part the dominance of Islam, which all missionary and imperial efforts had to accommodate. Javouhey worked almost exclusively in formal French colonies that were at the center of efforts to revive France's past imperial glory. But almost all of those colonies relied on enslaved Africans as their labor force in an age when the end of slavery appeared increasingly imminent.

In all three places, women were now considered essential to the missionary process, but their freedom to proselytize—always their most important goal—differed markedly. Duchesne had to tread carefully to accommodate the sensibilities of the local Protestants, and her dream of working among Indians was substantially delayed by the transformation of U.S. policy from assimilation to removal. Vialar had the least freedom to effect Catholic conversion—limited to the Christian community. Both she and Duchesne relied on secret baptism, whether it was of dying Muslim children or Protestant schoolgirls, as their ultimate weapon in the battle for souls. Javouhey had the most scope for initiative in this respect—the conversion of Africans was seen as an important tool in colonial transformation—to the extent that she was given a colony of her own and five hundred Africans on whom to experiment. Still, her belief in the inherent equality of Africans often flew in the face of colonial interests, which garnered her opposition and limited her impact.

The problem of the conversion of indigenous peoples, with which all three women struggled, was also rooted in their views of the state of "civilization" of these peoples. Duchesne interpreted the past history of Native Americans with Catholic missionaries as one in which their descendants craved a revival of those missions. Once missionaries had returned, she imagined that they would embrace not only

Catholicism but also the European culture that went with it. Javouhey imagined Africans as empty vessels, without culture or civilization, in which she could pour French Catholic dogma complete with the peasant structures of her country childhood, a vision that animated Mana. Among other blind spots, this view led her to significantly discount the competition of an expanding Islam in West Africa. Only the Orthodox, Jewish, and Muslim residents of the Ottoman Empire—all peoples following monotheistic faiths—were accorded the notion that they already possessed cultures and civilizations of their own, albeit ones that Vialar, like other Catholics of her time, dismissed as "schismatic," "heretical," and "infidel," respectively. However, it was this slightly more generous view of the state of civilization in the Ottoman empire, when coupled with the power relationships that forbade open evangelization, that shaped Vialar's mission, just as Duchesne's understanding of the Indians' supposed ancestral memory shaped hers, and Javouhey's vision of Africans as blank slates shaped hers.

Indeed, it appears that the process of converting natives was by and large unsuccessful in all three cases, at least in the short term. Duchesne wrote enthusiastically about the Catholic practice of the Potawatomi, but her interpretation differed markedly from the assessment of scholars who see this "conversion" as an adaptive strategy among a bicultural population undergoing significant cultural and territorial dislocation. Javouhey also believed that in the isolated confines of Mana she had created an African Catholic population—a view alternately accepted and rejected by outside observers, depending on their agendas—but, like Duchesne, she ignored the extent to which these non-Europeans blended Catholic dogma and practice with their own cultural and religious traditions, a syncretism that was common in the African church.[3] Outside of Mana, although some black and mixed-race schoolgirls may have learned their catechism, it is unclear whether these lessons resulted in lifelong Catholic practice. Moreover, given the difficult conversion environment of the Ottoman empire, to evaluate Vialar's success one would have to believe, as she did, that the baptism of dying children sent them to heaven. Those children did not grow up to found Christian families.

What these women missionaries may have accomplished—although evidence is not plentiful here, either—was to make the existing Catholic population more Catholic. Indeed, to French officials, clerics, and elites, one of the most important roles of women missionaries was domesticating a fractious European settler population. In North America that mission took the form of providing a solid spiritual education to Catholic girls with the hopes that it might not only strengthen their faith in a majority Protestant nation but spill over onto Protestants as well. Duchesne's most lasting achievement was the network of successful girls' schools she created, from convent academies for elites to day schools offering basic education to poorer girls. In so doing, she not only spread the Catholic faith but also successfully adapted a French educational model to the American frontier. In missions around the Mediterranean, Vialar provided medical and educational services to a multinational population of southern European migrants, who were receptive to Catholic messages and practices. Religion bound them together as a community, and the sisters helped make their Catholicism more orthodox. And in Africa and the French slave colonies, Javouhey ministered to an expanding French settler population, as well as mixed-race elites whose adherence to Catholicism reflected their high status. Here Catholicism reinforced a new imperial vision in which France could exploit its colonial holdings through a settled population of French families rather than the rogue actions of traders and soldiers.

In these ways, it is possible to see Duchesne, Vialar, and Javouhey as French imperial agents. Their goals and those of the French government clearly did not always coincide. Since their first priority was Christian evangelization, they often pursued it regardless of national affiliation, and they rarely expressed patriotic sentiments in regard to their work or even their own nationality. Duchesne and Vialar actively recruited local Catholic women into their orders—indeed, without local recruitment the Religious of the Sacred Heart would not have survived in America—and sought to deemphasize national origins within the order and in its missions. They collaborated with individuals of many different nationalities. They also sometimes took positions directly opposed to the interests of their own governments, as did Javouhey in supporting the abolition of slavery.

All that said, however, the Catholic culture that these women promoted was *French* Catholic culture, whether reflected in the curriculum of a Missouri convent school or in the carefully laid-out village grid of Mana. Although all three women saw Catholicism as a universal faith, they did not separate its practice from French forms of devotion. Potawatomi Indians at Sugar Creek and Africans in Mana, for example, were considered successful converts to the extent that they practiced Catholicism in ways that Duchesne or Javouhey recognized as "normal" but that were, in fact, deeply embedded in European and French spiritual traditions. In establishing schools and clinics that served a broader population than Catholics, all three introduced—and sought to assimilate—non-Europeans or marginal Europeans to French standards of schooling and health care. Rarely did one of these women reflect on alternative, indigenous educational or medical practices (except perhaps to dismiss them) or consider what their new models might be replacing. On an everyday basis they both demonstrated and extended the practice of European cultural norms. They also made it possible, even if unconsciously, for France to position itself as an exporter of "civilization" as represented by the "progress" in education and medicine that these women missionaries represented. That these women were clearly self-sacrificing, to the point of dying of cholera while nursing its victims, only made the argument that much more persuasive.

At the same time, some indigenous rulers, like Ahmad Bey of Tunisia, sought out the Europeanizing features of Catholic missions as a conscious strategy to prevent more direct control. J.P. Daughton has shown that the French missionary—although not necessarily in complete sync with government objectives—became a more conscious contributor to the French imperial project under the Third Republic.[4] These three women only began to embody that model, but wherever they established missions, they did help spread French and European cultural norms. In so doing, we can see them as the forerunners or perhaps the enablers of empire.

Missionaries appear to have outlived empire or at least the idea of empire. While no Western power will admit to pursuing imperial objectives in the early twenty-first century, Mother Teresa—a nun of Albanian origin, whose sisters work among the poorest of the poor in India—was acclaimed as a saint within hours of her death, and her canonization is on the fast track in Rome. Even non-Catholics perceive her as the epitome of neutral and generous self-sacrifice.[5] In a counterexample, when four Rwandan nuns implicated in the genocide there fled to Belgium, a Belgian court put them on trial for crimes against humanity, while more prominent criminals escaped justice.[6] In the Middle East, American Christian evangelicals have taken up Israel's cause because they believe it signals the coming resurrection of Jesus Christ. With the U.S. invasion of Iraq, many of these same evangelical groups also perceived an opening for outreach to Muslims that would combine material aid with proselytization. One group, World Concern, has said that its volunteers would care for anyone, regardless of religion, but that " 'we do seek appropriate ways to communicate the love of Christ in both word and deed.' "[7] Their attempts to walk a fine line between service and evangelization in these regions is strongly reminiscent of that which bedeviled Emilie de Vialar.

Nowhere is the missionary legacy more visible than in the international composition of Catholic missionary orders today. Although European female religious orders whose work is confined to their home countries are in demographic freefall, missionary orders have held their own thanks to an influx of young women from developing countries where Catholicism now flourishes. Whereas the numbers of Catholic nuns in Europe and North America have declined in the last three decades, they have increased in Africa, Asia, and Latin America in part because conditions that underlay their expansion in nineteenth-century Europe—lack of welfare and educational services, as well as low female educational levels and restricted opportunities for women—now characterize the third world more than the first.[8] The Soeurs de St-Joseph de Cluny currently operate only 93 European houses but 319 in Asia, Africa, the Americas, and Oceania. In 2006 more than two-thirds of their members (2,026 out of 2,890) worked outside Europe, a reversal of their proportions at the time of Javouhey's death in 1851. By 2005, the French membership of the

Soeurs de St-Joseph de l'Apparition had dropped to 13.88 percent, with 57 percent of their houses located outside of Europe in eighteen different countries, including Burma, which housed the largest group of sisters (141 out of 886). All of the newest members (postulants, novices, and "temporary" professed sisters, 150 in total) come from outside of Europe, except for five residing in Italy and one in Romania. In 2006, more than half the members of the Society of the Sacred Heart worked outside of Europe, and in 2008 the membership was divided almost evenly between Europeans (almost half Spanish) and non-Europeans; French membership has dropped to 5.5 percent. The American members make up the second largest group at 12.34 percent of the total membership.[9]

More than 80 percent of the world's Catholics now live in developing nations. When Benedict XVI traveled to Africa in March 2009, he visited a continent that counts 158 million Catholics, estimated to grow to 230 million, or one-sixth of Catholics worldwide by 2025. Nigeria houses the world's largest Catholic seminary, and African priests minister to Catholics in Europe and the United States.[10] Before and during the last papal election, commentators openly speculated that it was only a matter of time before the Catholic church elected its first non-European pope.[11] When that moment comes, he could be considered the spiritual heir of Javouhey's three Senegalese priests.

The final irony of the three life stories presented in this book may be that if Philippine Duchesne, Emilie de Vialar, and Anne-Marie Javouhey made little headway in converting non-Europeans during their lifetimes, they would rejoice to see how "universal" their Catholic vision, as well as the orders they founded, have now become.

Notes

Abbreviations

AAE-Paris	Archives des Affaires Etrangères, Paris
AAE-Nantes	Archives des Affaires Etrangères, Nantes
AAES	Archivio Affari Ecclesiastici Straordinari, Rome
AAPF	*Annales de la Propagation de la Foi*
ADI	Archives Départementales de l'Isère, Grenoble
ADT	Archives Départementales du Tarn, Albi
AMG	Archives Municipales de Grenoble
AM-Gaillac	Archives Municipales de Gaillac
AN	Archives Nationales, Paris
ANS	Archives Nationales du Sénégal
AOM	Archives d'Outre Mer, Aix-en-Provence
APF	Archives de la Propagation de la Foi, Lyon
ASJA	Archives des Soeurs de St-Joseph de l'Apparition, Paris
ASJA-Gaillac	Archives des Soeurs de St-Joseph de l'Apparition–Gaillac
ASJC	Archives des Soeurs de St-Joseph de Cluny, Paris
ASV	Archivio Segreto Vaticano, Rome
BDC	Madeleine-Sophie Barat and Philippine Duchesne, *Correspondance: Texte des manuscrits originaux présenté avec une introduction, des notes, et un index analytique* (Rome: Religious of the Sacred Heart of Jesus, 1988–99)

MHS   Missouri Historical Society
Prop. Fide   Archivio della Propaganda Fide, Rome
RSCJ-Rome   Archives of the Society of the Sacred Heart, Rome
RSCJ–St. Louis Archives of the Society of the Sacred Heart, St. Louis
SHAT   Service Historique de l'Armée de Terre, Vincennes

INTRODUCTION

1. A handful of other female religious orders entered missionary work in the 1840s, but, with the exception of the Filles de la Charité, who expanded rapidly in this decade, most limited themselves to a few destinations until after 1850.

2. Technically, the term "nun" is reserved for women religious who live in cloister, and apostolic women religious who live in the world are called "sisters," but following common English usage, I use the two terms interchangeably. Likewise, I use "order" and "congregation" interchangeably.

3. On the pressure to cloister, as well as Vincent de Paul's success in getting around it, see Rapley, *Dévotes*. On the early history of the Filles de la Charité, see Dinan, *Women and Poor Relief in Seventeenth-Century France*.

4. The doyen of all work on the new female apostolic orders in nineteenth-century France is Claude Langlois, whose *Le catholicisme au féminin* remains the most comprehensive work on the subject.

5. For a discussion of discourses about convents and nuns in the eighteenth century, see Choudhury, *Convents and Nuns in Eighteenth-Century French Politics and Culture*. To understand how far off discourse was from reality, see Rapley, *Social History*.

6. This viewpoint was not limited to France. In 1781 Joseph II of Austria embarked on a campaign to suppress contemplative convents. See McNamara, *Sisters in Arms*, 553–54.

7. French nuns reacted differently to this crisis, and some continued to keep their vows secretly, often in small communities. The Filles de la Charité, who adopted lay habits, kept 210 of their 430 establishments open during the Terror. (Seven of their members were also executed during this period.) See Dinan, *Women and Poor Relief*, 143–44.

8. On women's religious revival during the Revolution, see Hufton, *Women and the Limits of Citizenship*, chap. 3, and Desan, *Reclaiming the Sacred*.

9. The Filles de la Charité were recognized by Napoleon in 1801 (Dinan, *Women and Poor Relief*, 144). The reconstituted St-Joseph sisters were not the same congregation as the St-Joseph de Cluny and St-Joseph de l'Apparition congregations subsequently founded by Javouhey and Vialar, respectively.

10. Langlois puts hospital sisters in yet a third category, for whom six out of ten remained in 1808. Langlois, *Le catholicisme au féminin*, 79. For an account of the difficulties in reestablishing cloistered convents, see McNamara, *Sisters in Arms*, 565–70.

11. Later in the century similar challenges faced nuns in other European countries. Legislation outlawing or modifying cloistered orders was passed in Spain in 1820, in Portugal in 1834, in Italy in 1860, and in Germany in 1873 and was attempted in Britain in 1871 and Austria in 1874. McNamara, *Sisters in Arms*, 570.

12. Ibid., 566.

13. All statistical data are taken from Langlois, *Le catholicisme au féminin*, 74–75, 78, 203, 205, 307–8, 314.

14. On Lutheran deaconnesses, see Baubérot, "Protestant Woman," 202–5. Martha Vicinus discusses the revival of Anglican sisterhoods in Victorian England in her book *Independent Women*, chap. 2.

15. See Gill, *Nightingales*, and Vicinus, *Independent Women*, chap. 3.

16. Margaret Susan Thompson asserts that she has found "gender-defined confrontations between women and men" in all but one of 175 American religious communities that she has researched. Thompson, "Women, Feminism, and the New Religious History," 142.

17. This flexibility was diminished after the rulings of the First Vatican Council in 1869–70, which sought more uniformity in the statutes and increased oversight of female religious orders. McNamara, *Sisters in Arms*, 609.

18. Thompson, "Women, Feminism, and the New Religious History," 143.

19. Mack, "Religion, Feminism, and the Problem of Agency," 155–56.

20. Ibid., 160–61. Recently, French religious historians have disputed the relationship between the nineteenth-century religious revival and antimodernity. See, for example, Harris, *Lourdes*, and Jonas, *France and the Cult of the Sacred Heart*.

21. The term "empire" to designate French overseas possessions both before and after the Revolution is in itself problematic, and I use it here for the sake of simplicity. The French empire from 1804 to 1815 referred to European possessions. Many historians would deny that an overseas French empire existed before the late nineteenth century, and some not even then. See Banks, *Chasing Empire across the Sea*, 6–9, for a discussion of this issue in the first French empire, and Andrew and Kanya-Forstner, "Centre and Periphery in the Making of the Second French Colonial Empire, 1815–1920," in the second.

22. It is obviously impossible to cite all of the important works on the first and second French empires. Works on specific locations germane to this study are cited in individual sections. For general histories of French empire, see Meyer et al., *Histoire de la France colonial*; Cornevin and Cornevin, *La France et les français*; Manceron, *Marianne et les colonies*; Ferro, *Le livre noir du colonialisme*; Quinn, *French Overseas Empire*; and Aldrich, *Greater France*.

23. For a discussion of the "gaps" in French imperial historiography in the nineteenth century, see Daughton, "When Argentina Was 'French,' " esp. 832–37.

24. Dufourcq, "Etude de l'établissement des congrégations," 620–22, 634–35. On the Ursulines of New Orleans, see Clark, *Masterless Mistresses*. Tangi Villerbu has called for a new Catholic history of the American West in "Faire l'histoire catholique de l'ouest américain."

25. Rogers, *From the Salon to the Schoolroom*, 244–52. For an example of the far-reaching influence of a religious order of French origin, the Sisters of St. Joseph of Carondelet (originally St. Joseph of Lyon), see Coburn and Smith, *Spirited Lives*. On a similar phenomenon in Britain, see O'Brien, "French Nuns in Nineteenth-Century England."

26. Chateaubriand's Natchez cycle (*Atala* and *René*) went through many editions; James Fenimore Cooper's *Last of the Mohicans* was immediately translated into French in 1826. Liebersohn, *Aristocratic Encounters*, 75–78. See also Royot, *Divided Loyalties*.

27. Liebersohn, *Aristocratic Encounters*, 65.

28. See Guarneri, *Utopian Alternative*.

29. On Haiti as a site of French memory in the nineteenth century, see Miller, *French Atlantic Triangle*, chap. 10, and Trouillot, *Silencing the Past*, chap. 3.

30. Edward Said argues that the French occupation of Egypt was a pivotal moment in modern Orientalism. *Orientalism*, 42–43.

31. Daughton, *Empire Divided*.

32. Hefner, *Conversion to Christianity*, 6.

33. The secular version also had, of course, roots in the Enlightenment and the French Revolution. On the civilizing mission under the Third Republic, see Conklin, *Mission to Civilize*.

34. Porter, *Religion versus Empire?*

35. The phrase comes from the title of John Barker's essay, "Where the Missionary Frontier Ran Ahead of Empire," in Etherington, *Missions and Empire*, 86–106.

36. On this issue in a Protestant context, see Robert Eric Frykenberg, "Christian Missions and the Raj," in Etherington, *Missions and Empire*, 107–31.

37. Cox, *Imperial Fault Lines*, 6.

38. On French missions during the early modern period, see Deslandres, *Croire et faire croire*.

39. On Restoration missions inside France, see Sevrin, *Les missions religieuses en France sous la Restauration*; Kroen, *Politics and Theater*; and Riasanovsky, "Trumpets of Jericho."

40. Jean-Claude Baumont, "La renaissance de l'idée missionnaire en France au début du XIXe siècle," in *Les reveils missionnaires*, ed. Duboscq and Latreille, 204–5.

41. Ibid., 212. See also Drevet, "Laïques de France et missions catholiques au XIXe siècle." For further statistics, as well as background and analysis of its representations of empire after 1870, see Daughton, *Empire Divided*, chaps. 1 and 8.

42. On the background of this association and its work in China, see Harrison, "'Penny for the Little Chinese.'"

43. Philippe Boutry, "Le mouvement vers Rome et le renouveau missionnaire," in *Histoire de la France religieuse*, vol. 3, ed. Le Goff and Rémond, 445–46.

44. On the disproportionate influence of Lyonnais missionary orders, see Essertel, *L'aventure missionnaire lyonnaise, 1815–1962*.

45. For much of the nineteenth century Protestant missionary discourse accorded women no role in missionary work beyond that of a missionary's wife. See Valentine Cunningham, "'God and Nature Intended You for a Missionary's Wife': Mary Hill, Jane Eyre, and Other Missionary Women in the 1840s," in *Women and Missions*, ed. Bowie and Kirkwood, 85–105.

46. On women missionaries in the early modern period in general, see Deslandres, *Croire et faire croire*, chaps. 13 and 14. On women missionaries to Canada, see Choquette, "'Ces Amazones du Grand Dieu.'" Works on Marie de l'Incarnation are cited in chapter 1. On the Ursulines of New Orleans, see Clark, *Masterless Mistresses*. There has been no scholarly work on the Soeurs de St-Paul de Chartres. In the Spanish New World, convents were established, but they were cloistered convents that did not take on responsibility for evangelization in any form.

47. Women missionaries, like all baptized Catholics, could baptize children in danger of dying. This issue, which became especially relevant in Muslim lands, is fully discussed in part 2.

48. Cholvy, *Être chrétien en France au XIXe siècle*, 136.

49. Historians of Protestant missions now believe that the number of women in missionary work has been underestimated, largely because many women missionaries did not have formal roles but were often adjuncts to their missionary husbands. However, single laywomen had trouble breaking into missionary work until the second half of the nineteenth century. See Semple, *Missionary Women*, and Midgley, *Feminism and Empire*, chap. 4.

50. Huber and Lutkehaus, eds., "Introduction," *Gendered Missions*, 12. See also Thorne, *Congregational Missions*, chap. 4.

51. Clancy-Smith and Gouda, *Domesticating the Empire*. On the problem of integrating women into the study of French empire from a pedagogical perspective, see Lorcin, "Teaching Women and Gender in France d'Outre-Mer."

52. McClintock, *Imperial Leather*, 36.

53. Jeffrey Cox identifies three "master narratives" in missionary history: marginality, complicity with imperialist goals ("Saidian"), and providentialist ("progress toward a multiracial Christian community"). Cox, *Imperial Fault Lines*, 7–13.

54. See Margadant, "Introduction: Constructing Selves in Historical Perspective," in *New Biography*, 1–32. See also two recent collective biographies of French women authors: Allen, *Poignant Relations*, and Walton, *Eve's Proud Descendants*.

55. Scott, *Only Paradoxes to Offer*, 16.

56. Ibid., 15.

57. Lepore, "Historians Who Love Too Much," 133.

58. The most significant biographies include Callan, *Philippine Duchesne*; Mooney, *Philippine Duchesne*; Peyret, *Sainte Philippine Duchesne*; Darbon, *Emilie de Vialar*; Picard, *Une vierge française*; Testas, *La vie militante*; Cavasino, *Emilie de Vialar*; Delaplace, *La R. M. Javouhey*; Goyau, *Un grand "homme"*; and Lecuir-Nemo, *Anne-Marie Javouhey*.

59. Berthier and Sigaut, *Anne-Marie Javouhey*.

60. Lecuir-Nemo, *Anne-Marie Javouhey*. Javouhey has also been featured in recent historical work on religious missions in the Antilles and the slavery question. See especially Delisle, *Renouveau missionnaire; Histoire religieuse; Catholicisme, esclavage, et acculturation*; and Feay, "Mission to Moralize." I have benefited from the insights of all of these historians, who are cited where appropriate.

61. Duchesne's correspondence with Sophie Barat was published by the Religious of the Sacred Heart: Barat and Duchesne, *Correspondance*. It is also available in English translation. There is also a published collection of the letters of the early RSCJ to the United States: Paisant, ed., *Philippine Duchesne et ses compagnes*. Javouhey's letters are also available in a commercial edition: *Lettres, 1798–1851*. A number of Emilie de Vialar's letters can be found in Darbon, *Emilie de Vialar*, and extended quotations in Cavasino, *Emilie de Vialar*.

CHAPTER 1

1. The vesture record can be found in AMG, GG 203, Vêture, 10 September 1788. The details of the ceremony itself are drawn from Duchesne's personal copy of *Coustumier*

et Directoire pour les Soeurs religieuses de la Visitation de Sainte Marie, and two secondary sources: Reynes, *Couvents de femmes*, 56–61, 70, and Duvignacq-Glessgen, *L'Ordre de la Visitation*, 110–11.

2. I do not mean to imply that the Grenoble Visitation convent or any other Old Regime convent was immune from change, only that living in an enclosed space according to a religious rule allowed for a certain predictability. For a discussion of the tension between regularity and change over time, see Rapley, *Social History*.

3. Devos, *Vie religieuse féminine*, 37; Duvignacq-Glessgen, *L'Ordre de la Visitation*, 118–19, 125–27.

4. Dreyfus, *Sainte Marie*, 71–73.

5. Reynes, *Couvents des femmes*, 67–68; Devos, *Vie religieuse féminine*, 26–27.

6. For more on dowry requirements and class origins, see Chartier, Compère, and Julia, *L'éducation en France du XVIe au XVIIIe siècle*, 235; Dominique Dinet, "Les entrées en religion à la Visitation (XVIIe et XVIIIe siècles)," in *Visitation et Visitandines*, ed. Dompnier and Julia, 186–87. Converse or domestic sisters, who provided the manual labor for the convent, came, of course, from a much lower social group, as did the soeurs tourières, who only took annual vows and ran errands in the community.

7. Dreyfus, *Sainte Marie*, 91.

8. Figure based on a study of 403 Visitation nuns who died between 1667 and 1767, cited in Chartier, *L'éducation en France*, 236.

9. The need for compromise on this issue and the founders' original intentions is a matter of some debate. Visitation nuns were originally allowed some contact with the outside world, and some historians have speculated that Francis de Sales and Jeanne de Chantal intended a sort of mixed active and contemplative order when they began in 1610; by the time of the 1618 constitutions, however, full clausura had been imposed. See Rapley, *Dévotes*, 34–41; Devos, *Vie religieuse féminine*, 21–27, 33–34; Laurent Lecomte, "Jeanne de Chantal 'Maître d'ouvrage' de son ordre," in *Visitation et Visitandines*, ed. Dompnier and Julia, 96.

10. Duchesne did have two paternal aunts, Soeurs Françoise-Melanie and Claire-Euphrosine Duchesne, who were Visitation sisters in the convent in Romans.

11. Pilot, *Eglise*, 17.

12. Dreyfus, *Sainte Marie*, 34–36, 70–71, 91. See also plans of the convent in ADI, 23 H 59.

13. ADI, 23 H 63, Livre du couvent de Ste Marie d'en Haut de Grenoble. ADI, 23 H 70, arrest du conseil d'état du roi, 14 March 1778. On the investment strategies and financial pressures on convents, especially in the eighteenth century see Rapley, *Social History*, chap. 2.

14. Philippine Duchesne was the second child and second daughter born to Pierre and Rose Duchesne, but their first daughter died as an infant. They had four other surviving daughters: Amélie, Charlotte-Euphroyne, Adélaïde-Hélène, and Mélanie, of whom the first three married, and the fourth became a Visitation nun after the Revolution. They also had a son, Antoine-Louis-Hippolyte, who eventually studied law and served in politics. The Périer cousins, all younger than Philippine Duchesne, included Elisabeth Joséphine (with whom she would correspond all her life), Augustin-Charles, Antoine-Scipion,

Casimir-Pierre, Camille-Joseph, and Alphonse. Including children who died young, the two families produced twenty children in twenty years. For details on her family tree, see ADI, 2 E 384, and Wolff, *Les Périer*.

15. ADI, 2 E 384, Note de Pierre Duchesne: Relevé du produit de mon cabinet depuis 1769; Peyret, *Sainte Philippine Duchesne*, 18; Wolff, *Les Périer*, 9, 13, 15, 20; Chomel, ed., *Les débuts de la Révolution française*, 108.

16. Peyret, *Sainte Philippine Duchesne*, 19.

17. RSCJ-Rome, CVII, 2 D, Box 3, Notes sur la Mère Duchesne.

18. Dominique Dinet estimates that 20–25 percent of families initially opposed their daughters' entrance into the Visitation order. "Les entrées en religion," in *Visitation et Visitadines*, ed. Dompnier and Julia, 191. See also Rapley, *Social History*, chapter 9, on the reasons behind vocations, and Choudhury, *Convents and Nuns*, chap. 4, on the myth of the forced vocation in French culture and literature.

19. This decline is measured by a decrease in religious legacies in wills and the closing of several Catholic charitable establishments. Norberg, *Rich and Poor in Grenoble*, 244–47; Bligny, ed., *Le diocese de Grenoble*, 158.

20. ADI, 23 H 52, Examen de Professions, 20 March 1775–6 October 1787.

21. Most biographers agree that it was because of the uncertainty created by the Revolution that Pierre Duchesne did not allow his daughter to take her permanent vows as scheduled in September 1789; instead, she remained a novice in the community.

22. Philippe Bourdin argues that Visitation communities in particular resisted disbanding because they saw themselves as an exemplary order in piety and practice. "Visitation et Révolution," in Dompnier and Julia, *Visitation et Visitandines*, 238. On the proactive response of nuns to French revolutionary policy, see Choudhury, *Convents and Nuns*, chap. 6.

23. AMG, LL 229, Etat et Déclaration des Dames de Ste-Marie-d'en-Haut, 1 February 1791; Elections des Supérieure et Econome des Religieuses Ste-Marie-d'en-Haut, 7 February 1791. Undoubtedly due to her status as a novice, Philippine Duchesne does not appear in these records, although she was resident in the convent at this time.

24. AMG, LL 1, Registre des délibérations du corps municipales de la ville de Grenoble, 9 July 1791. Other convent chapels were closed to the public at the same time. The percentage of refractory priests in Grenoble was relatively small compared to other regions of France, where about 55 percent of the clergy and nearly all of the bishops refused the oath. Timothy Tackett calculates juring priests as 87 percent in March 1791, 81 percent by June 1791, and 70 percent by September 1792. Tackett, *Religion, Revolution, and Regional Culture*, 332. Bligny, *Le diocèse de Grenoble*, 173, gives the number of straight refusals as about fifty priests out of five hundred between January and March 1791. The bishop of Grenoble also refused the oath. Throughout France, however, almost all nuns refused to take the sacraments from juring clergy and many were active in hiding refractory priests and in facilitating their continued ministry to the faithful.

25. Considered less compromising than the oath of the Civil Constitution of the Clergy (among other reasons because Pope Pius VI had never condemned it) and in desperate financial straits, most former nuns swore the Liberté-Egalité oath. Those who did not were sometimes brought before the Tribunal Révolutionnaire. Dinet, "Les entrées en

religion," in Dompnier and Julia, *Visitation et Visitandines*, 480, finds that most Visitation nuns retracted the oath once it became safe to do so.

26. Boussoulade, *Moniales et hospitalières*, 131.

27. Bourdin, "Visitation et Révolution," in *Visitation et Visitandines*, ed. Dompnier and Julia, 229, 249.

28. Thibert, ed., *I Leave You My Heart*. This memoir is translated from a circular letter informing other Visitation houses of the safe arrival of the relic (which was owned by the Lyon convent) and the nuns in Italy.

29. Ibid., 122.

30. Gauchat, *Journal d'une Visitandine*.

31. Ibid., 9–10.

32. RSCJ–St. Louis, Series XIII: Duchesne Collection, Box 1, Packet 1, Histoire de Ste Marie d'en haut devenue le 13 Decembre 1804 la seconde maison de la Société (Grenoble) par la Mère Philippine Duchesne, [1818–19].

33. ADI, 2 E 384, lettre de Mélanie Duchesne à sa soeur Charlotte-Euphrosyne, 16 July 1797.

34. Quoted in Callan, *Philippine Duchesne*, 56.

35. Quoted in Ibid., 57.

36. Quotations from Mme Jouve, Duchesne's cousin, RSCJ-Rome, CVII, 2 D, Box 3, Notes sur la Mère Duchesne.

37. Dreyfus, *Sainte Marie*, 95–96, 102, 108–9. AMG, LL 210, Commune de Grenoble, no. 19, 20 Prairial, An III. ADI, L 667, Etat des détenus dans la maison de Ste Marie d'en Haut, 27 April 1793–10 July 1793.

38. Leflaive, "Philippine Duchesne et Sainte-Marie-d'en-Haut," 46.

39. On charity in Grenoble during the Revolution, see Norberg, *Rich and Poor*, chapter 11.

40. Two churches in Grenoble were returned to regular use in 1795, although with the requirement that they avoid all exterior signs of worship. Chomel, *Histoire de Grenoble*, 241.

41. Bligny, *Le diocèse de Grenoble*, 183. AMG, LL 228, Extrait du procès-verbal de l'administration centrale du Département de l'Isère.

42. RSCJ–St. Louis, "Histoire de Ste Marie d'en Haut."

43. In her own autobiographical account, she credits this idea to her six-year-old niece, who accompanied her, her younger sister, and some other former nuns to the now abandoned convent on Pentecost Sunday in 1801 and proclaimed that she would go to school and take her First Communion on the site. RSCJ–St. Louis, "Histoire de Ste Marie d'en Haut." This moment is prominent in the mythology of the Religious of the Sacred Heart.

44. For more details on the Duchesne and Périer families, see Callan, *Philippine Duchesne*, 47, 71–72; ADI, 2 E 384, Duchesne; Wolff, *Les Périer*, 61–63.

45. By 1804 (An 12), those repairs had cost 6,360 francs. ADI, 1 Q 411. Dreyfus, *Sainte Marie*, 113–14. RSCJ, "Histoire de Ste Marie d'en Haut."

46. All of the quotations in this paragraph and the next are Duchesne's own, from RSCJ–St. Louis, "Histoire de Ste Marie d'en Haut."

47. ADI, 7 V 3/12, A Monsieur le Préfet du Département de l'Isère and Copie des Status des Soeurs de la Visitation. These statutes were in fact quite similar to those of the newly

established Religieuses du Sacré-Coeur. Thérèse de Murinais was not among the signatories.

48. ADI, 7 V 3/12, Visitandines to Minister of the Interior, 21 July 1814. AN, F19, 6335, Visitandines to King Louis XVIII, 1 November 1814.

49. AN, F19, 6335, Philippine Duchesne, Sophie Barat, Josephine Bigeu to Minister of the Interior, 7 January 1816. ADI, 7 V 3/12 and AN, F19, 6335, Questions et réponses relativement à la petition des Dames de la Visitation de Grenoble, 8 November 1814. In 1824, a new Visitation congregation on a different site was founded in Grenoble by Claude Simone. Bligny, *Le diocèse de Grenoble*, 194.

50. See Kilroy, *Madeleine Sophie Barat*, 26–43, for a more detailed account of the origins of the Society of the Sacred Heart.

51. RSCJ–St. Louis, "Histoire de Ste Marie d'en Haut." RSCJ-Rome, CVII, 2, D, Box 1, "De la Vocation de Bienheureuse R. Philippine Duchesne pour les Missions d'après le récit de Sainte Madeleine Sophie; Extrait de Journal du Noviciat de Kientzheim," 12 September 1852.

52. Pilot, *Eglise*, 26. The Napoleonic decree of authorization can be found in ADI, 7 V 3/9, and AN, F 19, 6335.

53. Langlois, *Le catholicisme au féminin*, 80–86.

54. RSCJ–St. Louis, "Histoire de Ste Marie d'en Haut." RSCJ-Rome, "De la Vocation de Bienheureuse R. Philippine Duchesne pour les Missions."

55. Barat and Duchesne, *Correspondance* [hereafter BDC], vol. 3, letter 236, 9 May 1828. Barat frequently claimed that it was not her intention to found an order of "Jesuitesses," but as the analysis of Jeanne de Charry shows, the Society of the Sacred Heart modeled many of its constitutions on those of the Jesuits. De Charry, *Histoire des Constitutions*, vol. 1, *Exposé historique*, 91–98.

56. The phrase is that of Langlois, *Le catholicisme au féminin*, 85.

57. De Charry, *Histoire des constitutions*, 43–45, 99–108, 155, 161.

58. BDC, vol. 2.2, letter 212, 2 September 1826. For a discussion of the issues surrounding cloister and the negotiations with the Holy See, see Kilroy, *Madeleine Sophie Barat*, 169–74, and de Charry, *Histoire des constitutions*, 509–10.

59. RSCJ–St. Louis, "Histoire de Ste Marie d'en Haut." Dreyfus, *Sainte Marie*, 119. RSCJ-Rome, CVII, 2 D, Box 3, "Notes données par la Rde Mère Aloysia Jouve, Vicaire du Centre, nièce de la Vénérée Mère Duchesne," 23 August 1909.

60. BDC, vol. 1, letter 10, March 1806; letter 17, 9 February 1807; letter 21, 15 July 1807.

61. Marilyn Masse, "La Visitation et la dévotion au Sacré-Coeur," in *Visitation et Visitandines*, ed. Dompnier and Julia, 461–82, traces the origins and diffusion of the cult of the Sacred Heart in the Visitation order.

62. Hamon, *Histoire de la Dévotion*, vol. 4, *Luttes indécises*, 228, 291–93.

63. Jonas, *France and the Cult of the Sacred Heart*, 97.

64. Kilroy, *Madeleine Sophie Barat*, 27–29.

65. Jonas, *France and the Cult of the Sacred Heart*, 126, 131–33.

66. Ibid., 126–28.

67. Duchesne took a vow to honor St. François Régis with a Mass on his feast day if she returned to Ste-Marie-d'en-Haut and dedicated a shrine to him in the Florissant, Missouri, convent "in order to obtain his protection over our mission in America."

RSCJ–St. Louis, Series IV, D (Florissant), circular letter of St. Ferdinand, 1 January 1836. RSCJ-Rome, CVII, 2 D, Box 2, "Voeu à St François Régis," 16 June 1817.

68. BDC, vol. 2.1, letter 83, January or February 1818.

69. *Histoire chronologique des fondations de tout l'ordre de la Visitation de Sainte Marie* (1693).

70. RSCJ–St. Louis, "Histoire de Ste Marie d'en Haut."

71. Dreyfus, *Sainte Marie*, 119. RSCJ-Rome, CVII, 2 D, Box 3, "Notes données par la Rde Mère Aloysia Jouve, Vicaire du Centre, nièce de la Vénérée Mère Duchesne," 23 August 1909.

72. BDC, vol. 1, letter 12, 4 April 1806. On the influence of Lestrange, see Laffay, *Dom Augustin de Lestrange*, 325–26.

73. RSCJ–St. Louis, Series XIII: Callan Collection; Box 4, Duchesne to Mme de Mauduit, February 1818. She had also read letters sent by a Grenoble missionary in China and the accounts of religion in China by a Lyonnais cleric. Paisant, *Philippine Duchesne et ses compagnes*, 24.

74. BDC, vol. 1, letters 38 and 55, 3 July 1810 and 29 August 1811. RSCJ–St. Louis, Series XIII: Callan Collection; Box 4, Duchesne to Euphrosine Jouve, 4 August 1816.

75. RSCJ-Rome, "De la Vocation de Bienheureuse R. Philippine Duchesne pour les Missions."

76. Chateaubriand, *Génie*, vol. 4, 232.

77. On these works, see Liebersohn, *Aristocratic Encounters*, 41–60.

78. Comby, *Deux mille ans d'évangélisation*, 203.

79. Dolan, *American Catholic Experience*, 33.

80. Besides Dubourg, the others were Benoît Joseph Flager (Bardstown-Louisville, 1810–50), Jean Lefebvre de Cheverus (Boston, 1810–23), Antoine Maréchal (Baltimore, 1817–28), M. Portier (Mobile, 1825–59), Jean Dubois (New York, 1826–42), Gabriel Bruté de Remur (Indianapolis-Vincennes, 1834–39), Antoine Blanc (New Orleans, 1835–61), Mathias Loras (Dubuque, 1837–58), Jean Chauche (Nachez, 1841–52), Jean-Marie Odin (Galveston-Houston, 1847–61), Jean Bazin (Indianapolis-Vincennes, 1847–48), and Maurice de Saint-Palais (Indianapolis-Vincennes, 1849–59).

81. Chateaubriand, *Génie*, 219–20.

82. There is much historical literature on Marie de l'Incarnation. Recent scholarly works include Deroy-Pineau, *Marie de l'Incarnation*; Davis, *Women on the Margins*; Bruneau, *Women Mystics Confront the Modern World*; and Deroy-Pineau, ed., *Marie Guyard de l'Incarnation*, each of which has complete bibliographies of both primary and secondary works.

83. RSCJ–St. Louis, Series XIII: Callan Collection, Box 8, PD to Mère Brangier, St. Jacques, Canada, 19 December 1851.

84. See, for example, the 29 August 1818 letter from Father Perreau, the confessor to the Paris RSCJ, to Duchesne, in BDC, vol. 2.1. The Visitation convent library in Grenoble contained the Jesuit Relations and likely also a life or writings of Marie de l'Incarnation. Dreyfus, *Sainte Marie*, 112.

85. Davis, *Women on the Margins*, 94–95.

86. Greer, *Mohawk Saint*, 8–9, 81–83. See also Blackburn, *Harvest of Souls*, 61–67.

87. BDC, vol. 1, letter 31, 12 March 1809.

88. The biographical details regarding Dubourg are taken from Annabelle M. Melville's thorough two-volume work, *Louis William DuBourg*. In 1816 Dubourg chose to make his residence in St. Louis rather than in New Orleans because of conflicts there with Father Antonio Sedilla, Capuchin monk and longtime vicar general, who had strong local support. For both religious and political reasons, there had been no resident bishop in Louisiana since 1802. The region had been under the control of the bishop of Quebec until 1762 and the bishop of Cuba until 1793, when Louisiana and the Floridas were established as a separate diocese.

89. This authority included admitting postulants, novices, and nuns taking their initial vows, as well as rejecting or expelling members, acquiring property, modifying the habit (within certain fixed parameters), making changes in individual houses, giving alms to the poor, and breaking cloister to teach school or hear Mass. Normally, these actions would require permission from the superior general in France. BDC, vol. 2.1, letter 82, 7 February 1818.

90. Quotations from RSCJ–St. Louis, Series XIII: Callan Collection: Box 9, "Relation du départ de la petite colonie pour s'établir en Louisiane," 16 February 1818; Box 4, PD to Madame de Rollin (cousin), 29 August 1817 and n.d. (ca. January 1818); PD to community at Ste-Marie-d'en-Haut, February 1818; PD to Madame Jouve, 1 February 1818.

CHAPTER 2

1. On the New Orleans Ursulines, see Clark, *Masterless Mistresses*, and Kastor, *Nation's Crucible*, 216–17.

2. Paisant, *Les années pionnières*, PD to Sophie Barat, letter 15, 20 February 1818; PD to Mme de Mauduit, letter 27, 2 June 1818.

3. Ibid., PD to pensionnaires de Paris et de Grenoble, letter 29, 3 June 1818.

4. Ibid., Eugénie Audé, Octavie Berthold, etc., to RSCJ in France, letter 28, 3 June 1818.

5. Ibid., PD to Thérèse Maillucheau, letter 42 bis, 29 August 1818.

6. On French settlement in the upper Mississippi valley, see Ekberg, *French Roots*; Foley, *Genesis*; and Aron, *American Confluence*.

7. RSCJ–St. Louis, Series IV, M (St. Charles), "Copie abregée du journal commencé à St. Charles et continué à St. Ferdinand et à St. Louis, pour la Société du Sacré-Coeur," 3 January 1819, p. 5.

8. Paisant, *Les années pionnières*, PD to Sophie Barat, letter 33, 22 June 1818.

9. BDC, vol. 2.1, letter 98, 9 July 1818; letter 105, 8 October 1818.

10. Foley, *Genesis*, 80, 237, 244.

11. Paisant, *Les années pionnières*, PD to Mme Jouve, letter 41, 29 August 1818; PD to Père Barat, letter 43, 29 August 1818.

12. These views are expressed in letters to Sophie Barat on 12 September 1818 (letter 103), 8 October 1818 (letter 104), and 15 February 1819 (letter 109), BDC, vol. 2.1.

13. RSCJ–St. Louis, Series IV, M (St. Charles), "Copie abregée du journal," 3 January 1819, pp. 7–8. RSCJ–St. Louis, Series XIII: Callan Collection, Box 1, PD to Louis Barat, 7 March 1821.

14. Paisant, *Les années pionnières*, PD to Monsieur or Madame Barat, letter 73, 3 March 1820. RSCJ–St. Louis, Series XIII: Callan Collection, Box 1, PD to Louis Barat, 7 March 1821.

15. BDC, vol. 2.2, letter 187, 10 June 1824; letter 203, 27 December 1825.

16. AAPF, vol. 3, 574, lettre de Mgr Rosati à S. Alt. Em. Mgr le cardinal Grand-Aumônier, 1 February 1829.

17. RSCJ–St. Louis, Series IV, M (St. Charles), "Copie abregée du journal," 1 November 1824, 48.

18. BDC, vol. 2.1, letter 130, 29 August 1820.

19. BDC, vol. 2.1, letter 138, 24 June 1821. RSCJ–St. Louis, Series IV, M (St. Charles), "Copie abregée du journal," 1 November 1824, p. 48. RSCJ–St. Louis, Series XIII, Callan Collection, Box 4, PD to Mme Jouve, 4 April 1829.

20. BDC, SB to PD, vol. 2.1, letter 118, 27 September 1819; letter 113, 9 July 1819.

21. RSCJ–St. Louis, Series IV, M (St. Charles), "Copie abregée du journal," 21 November 1819, p. 16.

22. Kilroy, *Madeleine Sophie Barat*, 174.

23. Dolan, *American Catholic Experience*, 121.

24. BDC, vol. 2.1, letter 121, 1 December 1819. The issue of episcopal control over women's religious orders came up again in 1843, when Bishop Rosati claimed that only orders with simple vows, those that could be modified by the local bishop, were enforceable in the United States. Corbett, *In Her Place*, 50. This may have been the reason behind Elizabeth Galitzine's injunction to the American Sacred Heart sisters to ask his advice with "an extreme reserve" and not to allow him to think that they needed his permission since "the authority of our Mother General would be weakened." RSCJ-Rome, CIII, Box 4, "Notes de la Mère de Galitzine sur l'Amérique" (n.d., ca. 1840–43).

25. BDC, SB to PD, vol. 2.1, letter 146, 23 November 1821. Growth of the society in France was rapid in the 1820s, and it opened new houses in Italy and Belgium as well. Kilroy, *Madeleine Sophie Barat*, 155. During Duchesne's lifetime, only seventy-two Sacred Heart sisters migrated from France to America. RSCJ-Rome, CIII, Box 4, "Missionaries Sent to North America during Her Lifetime by Madeleine Sophie Barat."

26. RSCJ–St. Louis, Series XIII, Callan Collection, Box 4, PD to novices, 11 October 1829. Paisant, *Les années pionnières*, Lucile Mathévon to SB, letter 120, 8 February 1822.

27. BDC, vol. 2.1, letter 131, 30 October 1820; letter 136, May 1821.

28. BDC, vol. 2.1, letter 114, 29 July 1819; letter 108, 25 January 1819.

29. Dubourg, however, endorsed only the single rank for new recruits, foreseeing no change in status for the two French converse sisters. BDC, vol. 2.1, letter 121, 1 December 1819. RSCJ–St. Louis, Series XIII, Callan Collection, Box 1, PD to Louis Barat, 2 January 1820.

30. BDC, vol. 2.1, letter 121, 1 December 1819; SB to PD, letter 128, 24 May 1820.

31. BDC, vol. 2.1, letter 106, November 1818.

32. Paisant, *Les années pionnières*, PD to SB, letter 109, 17 December 1821.

33. BDC, vol. 2.1, letter 94, 7 June 1818.

34. The Ursulines were among the few religious orders in the New World who evangelized among African slaves in an urban setting. See Clark, *Masterless Mistresses*, esp. chap. 2.

35. Foley, *Genesis*, 238, 254–55, 293–95.

36. RSCJ–St. Louis, Series XIII, Callan Collection, Box 4, PD to Madame de Rollin, 27 August 1820. BDC, vol. 2.2, letter 164, 1 December 1822.

37. They owned eight slaves in 1833. Mooney, *Philippine Duchesne*, 132.

38. BDC, letter 215, vol. 2.2, 25 November 1826, and note by Jeanne de Charry. RSCJ–St. Louis, Series XIII, Callan Collection, Box 1, PD to Bishop Rosati, 1 July 1827; Box 4, PD to Mme de Rollin, 17 March 1839. RSCJ–St. Louis, Series IV, M (St. Charles), "Copie abregée du journal," 1 March 1831, p. 86.

39. RSCJ–St. Louis, Series IV, K (Potawatomi Mission), "Notes sur nos Foundations de Sauvages de Sugar Creek et St. Mary's," Lucile Mathévon to Elizabeth Galitzine, August 1841.

40. Ekberg, *French Roots*, 146–47. Foley, *Genesis*, 101. Morrissey, *As One Sent*, 165–66.

41. Although Dubourg's principal biographer, Annabelle M. Melville, does not consider his attitudes toward slavery or people of color in any detail, Gould and Nolan, eds., *No Cross, No Crown*, xxix–xxx, argue that his Saint-Domingue background and his work in Baltimore gave him an interest in race issues that manifested itself in the recruitment of Sister Ste. Marthe Fontière to undertake the education of black women in New Orleans at the request of the Ursulines.

42. Paisant, *Les années pionnières*, journal de la Maison de Florissant, letter 177, March–December 1823.

43. Davis, *History of Black Catholics*, 37–39, 42–43. Ewens, *Role of the Nun*, 67–68, argues that the financial pressures of women's religious orders in America practically required that they own slaves in lieu of using peasants, servants, or lay sisters; those orders that eschewed slavery did not survive.

44. This is the argument made by Randy J. Sparks, for Catholics in Mississippi, both a slaveholding culture and one dominated by evangelical Protestants. *Religion in Mississippi*, 202–17. See also McGreevy, *Catholicism and American Freedom*, chap. 2, and Morrow, *Persons of Color*, 8.

45. Fredrickson, *Black Image in the White Mind*, 321.

46. Charles Lemarié, "Notes sur les missionnaires français aux Etats-Unis, depuis la guerre d'indépendance jusque vers 1880," in *Les reveils missionnaires*, ed. Duboscq and Latreille, 230. On the Code Noir in Louisiana, see Ekberg, *French Roots*, 147–49, and Foley, *Genesis*, 114–16.

47. Davis, *Black Catholics*, 35.

48. On the Oblate Sisters of Providence, see Morrow, *Persons of Color*.

49. On the role of the Ursulines in promoting Catholicism among the black and colored population of New Orleans, especially women, see Clark, " 'By All the Conduct of Their Lives,' " and Clark and Gould, "Feminine Face of Afro-Catholicism."

50. Although the Sacred Heart archives have no written record of this, they did sometimes provide religious instruction for women of color, and the training seems likely. See Gould and Nolan, eds., *No Cross, No Crown*, xxxii–xxxivn23, 205; and also Davis, *Henriette Delille*, 62–63.

51. Paisant, *Les anneés pionnières*, PD to Père Varin, letter 30, 4 June 1818; Dubourg to SB, letter 68, 30 October 1819.

52. BDC, vol. 2.1, SB to PD, letter 124, 11 April 1820.

53. Ibid., letter 107, 5 November 1818; letter 109, 15 February 1819; Monsieur Perreau, confessor to Paris house to PD, 29 August 1818.

54. RSCJ–St. Louis, Series XIII, Callan Collection, Box 1, PD to Bishop Rosati, 11 April 1831.

55. Besides the two orders of black women religious cited earlier, the Kentucky Sisters of Loretto, founded by Father Charles Nerinckx, a Belgian priest, in 1824 briefly admitted three former black pupils as novices "in a special community with a habit and a rule slightly different from that of the Sisters of Loretto." It did not survive Nerinckx's departure from Kentucky. In New Orleans, two attempts to form integrated orders failed before Henriette Delille founded the Sisters of the Holy Family for women of color only. Davis, *Black Catholics*, 98. Morrow, *Persons of Color*, 117–18.

56. Paisant, *Les anneés pionnières*, PD to SB, letter 48, 8 October 1818; Dubourg to SB, letter 49, 25 November 1818; Dubourg to SB, letter 68, 30 October 1819.

57. Ibid., Octavie Berthold to SB, letter 74 bis, 19 March 1820. BDC, vol. 2.2, letter 152, 28 February 1822.

58. Paisant, *Les anneés pionnières*, Eugénie Audé to SB, letter 35, 5 July 1818.

59. Ibid., PD to Josephine Bigeu, letter 59, 25 April 1819; PD to SB, letter 56, 15 February 1819; PD to SB, letter 48, 8 October 1818; PD to SB, letter 60, 29 July 1819.

60. BDC, vol. 3, letter 252, 18 May 1829. Paisant, *Les anneés pionnières*, PD to SB, letter 40, 30 October 1820.

61. RSCJ–St. Louis, Series IV, M (St. Charles), "Copie abregée du journal," 82, 25 May 1830. BDC, vol. 2.2, letter 165, 4 January 1823.

62. Paisant, *Les anneés pionnières*, PD to SB, letter 69, 15 November 1819.

63. Ibid., Journal de la petite maison Florissant du Sacré-Coeur du Missouri, letter 64, 28 September 1819. RSCJ–St. Louis, Series IV, N (St. Louis City House), "Convent of the Ladies of the Sacred Heart at St. Louis, Missouri, Madame Duchesne, Superior," *Catholic Almanac*, 1833.

64. Paisant, *Les anneés pionnières*, PD to Mme Henriette Girard (for SB), letter 44, 31 August 1818; PD to Thérèse Maillucheau, letter 63 bis, 26 September 1819.

65. RSCJ–St. Louis, Series IV, N (St. Louis City House), "Convent of the Ladies of the Sacred Heart," *Catholic Almanac*, 1833.

66. O'Brien, "French Nuns in Nineteenth-century England," 160.

67. In 1830, 3,000 of St. Louis's 3,500 Catholics were French speaking. Morrissey, *As One Sent*, 277.

68. Rogers, *From the Salon to the Schoolroom*, 244–52.

69. Beadie and Tolley, *Chartered Schools*, 3.

70. Baumgarten, "Education and Democracy," 175.

71. BDC, vol. 2.1, letter 144, 7 October 1821. In the United States, the assignment of classes to particular teachers was often also a function of language skills; English speakers were necessary for the lower-class pupils, whereas the boarding pupils were usually fluent in French.

72. BDC, vol. 2.1, letter 98, 9 July 1818.

73. BDC, vol. 2.1, letter 106, November 1818; vol. 3, letter 328, 5 June 1846. Paisant, *Les anneés pionnières*, PD to Père Varin, letter 30, 4 June 1818.

74. Foley, *Genesis*, 111–12, 278–80.

75. Corbett, *In Her Place*, 56.

76. Baumgarten, "Education and Democracy," 176.

77. BDC, vol. 3, letter 217, 1 March 1827.

78. Ibid., letter 252, 18 May 1829; SB to PD, letter 265, vol. 3, 9 May 1830.

79. RSCJ–St. Louis, Series XIII, Callan Collection, Box 4, PD to Mme de Mauduit, 2 June 1818.

80. RSCJ–St. Louis, Series XIII, Callan Collection, Box 8, PD to Eugénie de Gramont, 2 January 1824.

81. Paisant, *Les années pionnières*, PD to Mère Deshayes, letter 82, 29 August 1820.

82. BDC, vol. 2.2, letter 164, 1 December 1822; vol. 2.1, letter 135, 12 April 1821.

83. Paisant, *Les années pionnières*, PD to Mme de Rollin, letter 80, 27 August 1820.

84. Baumgarten, "Education and Democracy," 172.

85. BDC, vol. 3, letter 328, 5 June 1846.

86. Oates, "Catholic Female Academies," 121–22.

87. Baumgarten, "Education and Democracy," 182ff.

88. There is a large literature on domesticity in both the European and the American contexts. For the United States, see Cott, *Bonds of Womanhood*. For France, see Bonnie Smith, *Ladies of the Leisure Class*.

89. RSCJ–St. Louis, Series IV, N (St. Louis City House), "Convent of the Ladies of the Sacred Heart," *Catholic Almanac*, 1833.

90. MHS, Lane Collection, Mère Xavier for PD to William Carr Lane, 10 April 1828. This letter was composed in English.

91. RSCJ-Rome, CIII, Box 4, "Notes de la Mère de Galitzine sur l'Amérique," n.d. (ca. 1840–43).

92. Baumgarten, "Education and Democracy," 187–88. On conflicts between parents and children over Catholic conversion in France, see Ford, "Private Lives and Public Order."

93. Foley, *Genesis*, 271–74. On the growth of evangelical Protestantism in the South, see Sparks, *Religion in Mississippi*, and Heyrman, *Southern Cross*.

94. RSCJ–St. Louis, Series IV, M (St. Charles), "Détails sur la fondation de la Maison de St. Charles, Mo., commencée le 10 Octobre 1828." BDC, vol. 3, letter 333, 18 August 1851.

95. Corbett, *In Her Place*, 43–44.

96. RSCJ–St. Louis, Series IV, M (St. Charles), "Copie abregée du journal," 28 August 1834. On the Charlestown riots, see Franchot, *Roads to Rome*, 137–45, and Schultz, *Fire and Roses*.

97. RSCJ–St. Louis, Series XIII; Callan Collection; Box 4, PD to Mme Teissière, 20 December 1835 (English translation). The newspapers to which she referred were probably *The Protestant*, which began publication in 1830, and the *St. Louis Observer*, published by Eli Lovejoy.

98. Anti-nun literature was common in this period, particularly books purporting to tell the "true" stories of convents and convent schools. See Franchot, *Roads to Rome*, chaps. 6 and 7. On the Sisters of St. Joseph, see Coburn and Smith, *Spirited Lives*, 42–43. On hostility toward Catholics in general, see Billington, *Protestant Crusade*.

99. BDC, vol. 2.2, letter 153, 6 March 1822; letter 157, 24 June 1822; letter 158, 19 July 1822.

100. BDC, vol. 3, PD to Paris community, letter 229, 7 October 1827. RSCJ–St. Louis, Series XIII, Callan Collection, Box 1, PD to Rosati, 3 October 1827.

101. Paisant, *Les années pionnières*, PD to Mme Louise de Vidaud, letter 89, 10 April 1821.

102. From *Plea for the West*, quoted in Coburn and Smith, *Spirited Lives*, 98. See also Billington, *Protestant Crusade*, chap. 5.

103. Joseph G. Mannard, "Converts in Convents": 79, 81, 86. His case study does not include the Religious of the Sacred Heart.

104. Coburn and Smith, *Spirited Lives*, 162; Hoffman, *Woman's "True" Profession*, 4. See also Kaufman, *Women Teachers on the Frontier*; and Solomon, *In the Company of Educated Women*. These books, however, give little to no attention to Catholic teachers and schools.

105. Quoted in Corbett, *In Her Place*, 42. This school became Lindenwood Female College in 1853 and is Lindenwood University today.

106. In her pathbreaking biography of Catharine Beecher, Kathryn Kish Sklar states that Beecher "was the first to envision teaching as a profession dominated by—indeed exclusively belonging to—women." Clearly, Sklar is forgetting Catholic nuns, who had already developed this model by the 1830s. Sklar, *Catharine Beecher*.

107. Paisant, *Les années pionnières*, Lucile Mathévon to SB, letter 125, 20 June 1822.

108. BDC, vol. 2.1, letter 132, 18 February 1821.

109. Paisant, *Les années pionnières*, Lucile Mathévon to Mère Thérèse Maillucheau, letter 143, 23 November 1822.

110. Ibid., SB to PD, letter 51, 9 November 1818.

111. Quoted in Garraghan, *Jesuits*, vol. 1, 201.

112. Paisant, *Les années pionnières*, Lucile Mathévon to SB, letter 157, 10 March 1823.

113. BDC, vol. 2.1, letter 108, 21 January 1819.

114. Paisant, *Les années pionnières*, Sister Xavier [Anna] Murphy to SB, letter 164, 2 March 1823; journal de Soeur Xavier, letter 166, 6 April 1823.

115. Gould and Dolan, eds., *No Cross, No Crown*, 10.

116. Charles Van Quickenborne, S.J., to Bishop Rosati, September 1834, quoted in Garraghan, *Jesuits*, vol. 1, 215–16. BDC, vol. 3, letter 234, 23 March 1828.

117. The Sisters of St. Joseph, who opened an elementary school for free black children in 1845 in downtown St. Louis, were forced to close it the following year due to hostility from the white community. Coburn and Smith, *Spirited Lives*, 53–54.

118. BDC, vol. 2.1, letter 94, 7 June 1818; Monsieur Perreau to PD, vol. 2.1, 29 August 1818; see also vol. 3, letter 261, 20 January 1830.

119. BDC, vol. 3, PD to Paris community, letter 229, 7 October 1827.

120. BDC, vol. 2.1, letter 120, 15 November 1819; RSCJ–St. Louis, Series XIII, Callan Collection, Box 1, PD to Rosati, 1 December 1822. Paisant, *Les années pionnières*, Mgr Dubourg to SB, letter 68, 30 October 1819.

121. BDC, vol. 2.2, letter 168, 20 May 1823; letter 183, 19 February 1824.

122. Corbett, *In Her Place*, 37. They merged formally with the Daughters of Charity in 1845.

123. BDC, vol. 3, letter 300, April 1834.

124. Corbett, *In Her Place*, 70–71. RSCJ–St. Louis, Series XIII, Callan Collection, Box 8, PD to Eugénie de Gramont, November 1834.

125. APF, Fonds Paris, F 128, Etat du Diocèse de St-Louis, December 1839; Joseph Rosati, bishop of St. Louis, to Conseil central, 1 July 1840.

126. Callan, *Society*, 783.

127. By 1850, the enrollment figures for the various types of schools in North America were as follows: 907 in convent academies, 330 in free schools, 68 in schools for blacks or Indians, and 55 in orphanages. Ibid., 783.

128. To Duchesne's dismay, the Sacred Heart closed Ste-Marie-d'en-Haut in 1833 due to financial difficulties. The city of Grenoble rented it out as a school for the next fifteen years (nine of them funded by Duchesne's cousin, Mme de Rollin). The Ursulines acquired it in 1851 and stayed there until 1904. Today it houses the Musée Dauphinois.

129. Baumgarten, "Education and Democracy," 171–92.

130. Kilroy, *Madeleine Sophie Barat*, 229–30.

131. RSCJ-Rome, CIII, Box 4, "Notes pour les Supérieures seules," n.d. (ca. 1840–43); "Notes de la Mère de Galitzine sur l'Amérique," n.d. (ca. 1840–43).

132. Byrne, "Sisters of St. Joseph," 252–59. On the split with France, see also Coburn and Smith, *Spirited Lives*, 57–62, and on the general problem of the adaptation of European rules to the American context for religious orders, see Ewens, *Role of the Nun*, 69–71, 92–97.

133. Susan O'Brien discusses the same phenomenon in the RSCJ schools in England. O'Brien, "French Nuns in Nineteenth-Century England," 159.

134. Byrne, "Sisters of St. Joseph," 270–71. On the origins of the Sisters of St. Joseph in France, see Vacher, *Des "régulières" dans le siècle*.

135. Corbett, *In Her Place*, 67–70, 72. The number of Catholic nuns in the United States increased from approximately 200 in 1822 to 88,773 in 1920. For an overview, see Eileen Mary Brewer, *Nuns and the Education of American Catholic Women*.

CHAPTER 3

1. "Sauvage" is the term Duchesne uses most consistently in her correspondence to refer to native Americans. She most likely used it in the sense established by seventeenth-century Jesuit missionaries to New France to define individuals who lived outside of civilization or domestic life, as understood by Europeans. It was derogatory insofar as it delineated a state inferior to that of white Europeans and Americans. See Blackburn, *Harvest of Souls*, 45–46.

2. BDC, vol. 2.1, letter 95, 22 June 1818; letter 101, 22 August 1818. RSCJ–St. Louis, Series IV, M (St-Charles), "Copie abregée du journal," 5, 3 January 1819; PD to Thérèse Maillucheau, Series XIII, Callan Collection, Box 8, 29 August 1818. See Sleeper-Smith, *Indian Women and French Men*, chap. 2, on the importance of Kaskaskia as an Indian village, as well as a French-Catholic settlement.

3. BDC, vol. 2.1, letter 106, November 1818. Paisant, *Les années pionnières*, PD to mères, soeurs, et élèves de la Société du Sacré-Coeur, letter 52, 20 November 1818.

4. BDC, vol. 2.1, letter 109, 15 February 1819.

5. Paisant, *Les années pionnières*, PD to Thérèse Mailucheau, letter 54, 16 December 1818. BDC, vol. 2.1, letter 104, 8 October 1818.

6. Thorne, *Many Hands of My Relations*, chap. 2.

7. Ibid., 129–31.

8. Paisant, *Les années pionnières*, Les pensionnaires de Saint-Charles à la Mère Barat, letter 60 (pièce jointe), 29 July 1819; les élèves de Florissant à Mère Barat, after letter 74, 1820. See also Callan, *Philippine Duchesne*, 762n12. Interestingly, Rosalie is identified by her father's first name rather than his surname.

9. Paisant, *Les années pionnières*, PD to Mme de Rollin, letter 61, 1819. Duchesne is speaking of Indian girls in general, not Rosalie Manuel in particular, in this passage. The need to isolate Indian girls from their families comes up frequently in her letters.

10. RSCJ–St. Louis, PD to Eugénie de Gramont, Series XIII, Callan Collection, Box 82 January 1824.

11. Paisant, *Les années pionnières*, PD to "mes Mères, Soeurs et élèves de la Société du Sacré-Coeur," letter 52, 20 November 1818; PD to Louise de Vidaud, letter 89, 10 April 1821.

12. Ibid., PD to SB, letter 56, 15 February 1819; PD to Thérèse Mailucheau, letter 54, 16 December 1818.

13. Melville, *Louis William DuBourg*, vol. 2, 627–37; Garraghan, *Jesuits*, vol. 1, 55–78.

14. BDC, vol. 2.2, letter 175, 25 September 1823.

15. Mooney, *Philippine Duchesne*, 158–60.

16. RSCJ–St. Louis, Series XIII, Callan Collection, Box 5, notes de la Révérende Mère Jouve concernant la Vie de notre vénérée Mère Duchesne, n.d.

17. RSCJ–St. Louis, Series XIII, Callan Collection, Box 5, Mother Shannon's reminiscences of Mother Duchesne, n.d.

18. BDC, vol. 2.2, letter 191, 22 November 1824.

19. RSCJ–St. Louis, Series XIII, Callan Collection, Box 1, PD to Rosati, 3 October 1827.

20. Garraghan, *Jesuits*, vol. 1, 27, 384. Morrissey, *As One Sent*, 279–80.

21. *AAPF*, "Mission du Missouri," 563, July 1832. Garraghan, *Jesuits*, vol. 1, 27. On the missionary vision of Jesuits and other Catholics, see Tangi Villerbu, *La conquete de l'Ouest: Le récit français de la nation américaine au XIXe siècle* (Rennes: Presses Universitaires de Rennes, 2007), 178–88.

22. BDC, vol. 2.1, letter 114, 29 July 1819; vol. 2.2, letter 163, 30 October 1822.

23. Garraghan, *Jesuits*, vol. 1, 47–55, 157. The actual amount of monies received, approximately $3,100, never covered the cost of the school, which was more than $10,000.

24. Dippie, *Vanishing American*, 10. Bowden, *American Indians and Christian Missions*, 167. Prucha, *Great Father*, 152.

25. Van Quickenborne to Superior General Fortis, 29 June 1824, quoted in Garraghan, *Jesuits*, vol. 1, 174.

26. Van Quickenborne to Dzierozynski, 29 April 1825, quoted in Garraghan, *Jesuits*, vol. 1, 171. For a full description of the Van Quickenborne's plan, see 170–75. Dippie, *Vanishing American*, 51, outlines a similar (unfulfilled) plan of a Christian colony of Indians developed by Baptist missionary Isaac McCoy in 1823.

27. *AAPF*, vol. 4, "Lettre du R. P. Charles Van Quicken Born [*sic*], de la compagnie de Jésus, au R. P. Ros…de la même compagnie," 588, 10 March 1829. Blackburn, *Harvest of Souls*, chap. 3, has a full discussion of this theology. See also Prucha, *Great Father*, 136; Dippie, *Vanishing American*, 42; and Pearce, *Savagism and Civilization*, 73.

28. Van Quickenborne to Secretary of War John Calhoun, 21 November 1824, quoted in Garraghan, *Jesuits*, vol. 1, 153.

29. Quoted in Garraghan, *Jesuits*, vol. 1, 157.

30. RSCJ–St. Louis, Series XIII, Callan Collection, Box 5, reminiscences of Mother Shannon, 1875; Series IV, D (Florissant), baptismal records (typescript), St. Ferdinand's church.

31. RSCJ–St. Louis, Series XIII, Callan Collection, Box 1, PD to Rosati, 1 July 1827. BDC, vol. 2.2, letter 197, 23 April 1825.

32. *Reminiscences of Peter De Meyer*, 1867, quoted in Garraghan, *Jesuits*, vol. 1, 164.

33. Garraghan, *Jesuits*, vol. 1, 171–72.

34. *AAPF*, vol. 10, "Lettre du R. P. Van-Quickenborne à un autre Père de la même Société," 133, 4 October 1836.

35. *AAPF*, vol. 11, "Lettre du P. Verhaegen, de la Compagnie de Jésus," 469, 20 June 1838.

36. *AAPF*, vol. 3, "Lettre de M. Vanquickenborne, à madame Xavier, supérieure des Dames du Sacré-Coeur," 513, 6 November 1827. RSCJ–St. Louis, Series XIII, Callan Collection, Box 1, PD to Bishop Dubourg, 29 January 1832.

37. RSCJ–St. Louis, Series XIII, Callan Collection, Box 4, PD to Madame de Rollin, 1 January 1827; Box 1, PD to Père Perreau, 10 November 1829. *AAPF*, vol. 10, "Lettre du R. P. Van-Quickenborne à un autre Père de la même Société," 146, 4 October 1836.

38. RSCJ–St. Louis, Series XIII, Callan Collection, Box 4, PD to Madame de Rollin, 23 June 1833.

39. BDC, vol. 3, SB to PD, letter 293, 16 October 1833.

40. Dippie, *Vanishing American*, 48–50, 57, 68. Prucha, *Great Father*, 136–44, 206. Foley, *Genesis*, 247–48. Aron, *American Confluence*, 210, 216. On Jacksonian policy in particular, see Satz, *American Indian Policy*.

41. BDC, vol. 2.2, letter 208, 15 June 1826. RSCJ–St. Louis, Series XIII, Callan Collection, Box 4, PD to Madame de Rollin, 1 January 1827.

42. Dippie, *Vanishing American*, 12–15, 21–25. French readers in America could also read the pro-Indian reports in *Le Courrier des Etats-Unis*, a French newspaper published in the United States. See Liebersohn, *Aristocratic Encounters*, 75–78.

43. Dippie, *Vanishing American*, 13, 21, 24, 40, 60–61. Satz, *American Indian Policy*, 253. Governor William Clark of Missouri, for example, facilitated Indian removals from the state but rationalized them as a way of protecting Indians from the corruption of frontier society. Aron, *American Confluence*, 228.

44. BDC, vol. 2.2, letter 203, 27 December 1825.

45. Ibid., vol. 3, letter 321, 15 January 1841.

46. RSCJ–St. Louis, Series IV, K (Potawatomi Mission), "Notes sur nos Fondations de Sauvages de Sugar Creek et St. Mary's," 2.

47. BDC, vol. 3, letter 321, 15 January 1841; letter 323, 18 May 1841. Duchesne seems unaware of another French religious order, the Sisters of the Holy Cross, who were

providing education to the Pokagon Potawatomi, who had remained behind in the environs of South Bend, Indiana, beginning in the 1840s. See Sleeper-Smith, *Indian Women and French Men*, 109–11.

48. Edmunds, *Potawatomis*, 8–9.

49. White, *Middle Ground*, 35.

50. Prucha, *Great Father*, 248–52. See also Clifton, *Prairie People*, 296–311. Sleeper-Smith, *Indian Women and French Men*, chaps. 6–8, argues that more Potawatomi remained in the Old Northwest than historians have assumed, either by negotiating for the rights of Catholic Indians to stay on their lands, by constructing themselves as white ("hiding in plain sight"), or by exploiting marginally profitable lands like marshes and swamps that white settlers did not want.

51. Altogether, tribespeople signed thirty-nine treaties with the U.S. government between 1789 and 1837, including one in 1795 that sold the Americans six square miles of land at the mouth of the Chicago River. Prucha, *Great Father*, 248–53. See also Edmunds, *Potawatomis*, chap. 10.

52. The remaining Potawatomi in Iowa were themselves moved to Kansas in 1848. Garraghan, *Jesuits*, vol. 1, 443–46. On the migration of the Potawatomi to Sugar Creek, located near contemporary Centerville in Linn County, Kansas, see Garraghan, *Jesuits*, vol. 2, 180–96.

53. RSCJ–St. Louis, Series IV, K (Potawatomi Mission), "Account of the Foundation among the Pottowatamies."

54. Ibid.

55. BDC, vol. 3, letter 324, 21 July 1841.

56. RSCJ–St. Louis, Series XIII, Callan Collection, Box 4, PD to Hypolite Duchesne, 12 September 1841.

57. RSCJ–St. Louis, Series IV, K (Potawatomi Mission), "Account."

58. Quoted in Prucha, *Great Father*, 288.

59. BDC, vol. 3, letter 326, 22 September 1841. By 1843, the RSCJ was boarding six Indian pupils.

60. RSCJ–St. Louis, Series IV, K (Potawatomi Mission), "Notes sur nos Fondations de Sauvages de Sugar Creek et St. Mary's" (by Catherine Tardieu); copy of letter from Lucile Mathévon to Mère Galitzin, August 1841, 6.

61. RSCJ–St. Louis, Series IV, K (Potawatomi Mission), "Notes sur nos Fondation de Sauvages"; copy of letter from Lucile Mathévon to Mère Galitzine, August 1841, 9. Garraghan, *Jesuits*, vol. 2, 208.

62. Sleeper-Smith, *Indian Women and French Men*, 125–30. RSCJ–St. Louis, Series IV, K (Potawatomi Mission), "Account."

63. APF, Fonds Paris, F 128, "Extrait d'une lettre de Madame de Galitzine, Provinciale des maisons des Dames du Sacré Coeur en Amérique," 18 January 1843.

64. RSCJ-Rome, C-IV, Dossier 1, Sugar Creek, Lucile Mathévon to Sophie Barat, 26 April 1841.

65. RSCJ–St. Louis, Series IV, K (Potawatomi Mission), "Account."

66. BDC, vol. 3, letter 327, 28 February 1842.

67. RSCJ–St. Louis, Series IV, K (Potawatomi Mission), "Account."

68. Garraghan, *Jesuits*, vol. 2, 216. As in the comments about clothing, the missionaries ignored the Potwatomis' own agricultural tradition. See Sleeper-Smith, *Indian Women and French Men*, chap. 5.

69. *AAPF*, vol. 13, lettre du père Hoecken, missionnaire de la compagnie de Jésus près des Pottowatomies, à un père général de la même compagnie, 27 December 1839, 61.

70. RSCJ–St. Louis, Series IV, K (Potawatomi Mission), "Notes sur nos Fondation de Sauvages"; copy of letter from Lucile Mathévon to Mère Galitzine, August 1841, p. 6.

71. RSCJ–St. Louis, Series XIII, Callan Collection, Box 1, PD to Père de la Croix, 20 February 1842.

72. RSCJ–St. Louis, Series XIII, Callan Collection, Box 4, PD to Hypolite Duchesne, 12 September 1841.

73. Garraghan, *Jesuits*, vol. 2, 228–29n87. During the decade in which the mission was established at Sugar Creek, there were 478 adult baptisms and 923 child baptisms. According to the mission registers, the number of baptisms peaked in 1842.

74. RSCJ–St. Louis, Series XIII, Callan Collection, Box 1, PD to Père de la Croix, 20 February 1842. On the significance of the scapular, see Myhre, "Potawatomi Transformation," 374–78.

75. Verheyden, "Corpus-Christi-Day among the Pottowattomies," 251. *AAPF*, vol. 16, "Lettre du P. Thébaud, Missionnaire de la Compagnie de Jésus, au Kentucky, à un de ses Supérieurs," 15 October 1843, 460–61. Father Verreydt, S.J., quoted in Garraghan, *Jesuits*, vol. 2, 226.

76. RSCJ–St. Louis, Series XIII, Callan Collection, Box 1, PD to Père de la Croix, 25 July 1844. About 2,000 non-Catholic Potawatomi Indians also lived nearby, and there were both Methodist and Baptist schools for the Potawatomi in the area. In 1848 the total number of Kansas Potawatomi was recorded as 3,235 individuals. Garraghan, *Jesuits*, vol. 2, 202, 619.

77. *AAPF*, "Lettre de M. Badin, ainé, Missionnaire chez les Poutouatomis," vol. 6, 156–57, 14 January 1831; vol. 4, 547, lettre de M. Badin à M.**, 1 September 1830. On Badin's work among the Potawatomi, see also Garragher, *Jesuits*, vol. 2, 177–80.

78. Clifton, *Pokagons*, 19–21. These records cover the years 1722–61. Edmunds, in *Potawatomies*, 9, cites baptismal figures from Jesuit self-reporting of forty Indians before 1672 and four hundred by 1676; however accurate these numbers may be, the number undoubtedly declined in the eighteenth century, when the number of Jesuit priests available to staff the mission decreased.

79. Clark, "Jesuit Impact," 388.

80. Ibid., 382. See also Robert F. Berkhofer Jr.'s introduction to the reprint edition of McCoy, *History of Baptist Indian Missions*.

81. Myhre, "Potawatomi Transformation," 98–129.

82. Clifton, *Pokagons*, 65–68. Sleeper-Smith, *Indian Women and French Men*, 102–5. Other tribal leaders tried this same strategy, not always successfully. See Edmunds, *Potawatomies*, 264–71, for failed attempts, and Liebersohn, *Aristocratic Encounters*, 80–83, for a similar analysis of Jesuit success with the Salish tribe in Montana.

83. Clifton, *Prairie People*, 315.

84. Before 1836, only three of the fifty-two mission schools for Indians in the United States were Catholic. Garraghan, *Jesuits*, vol. 2, 202.

85. Clifton, *Prairie People*, 316. See also Sleeper-Smith, *Indian Women and French Men*, for a discussion of the importance of mixed-blood communities in facilitating Indian assimilation. Myhre, "Potawatomi Transformation," 157, believes that Clifton's contention that the majority of Catholic Potawatomi were of mixed European Indian blood is exaggerated and puts the number of *métis* at one-fifth to one-fourth. He provides, however, no evidence backing up this figure.

86. Clifton, *Prairie People*, 250–51, 281–82.

87. Clark, "Jesuit Impact," 386.

88. RSCJ–St. Louis, Series XIII, Callan Collection, Box 1, PD to Père de la Croix, 20 February 1842.

89. Jones, "Potawatomi Faces the Problem," quotation on p. 53.

90. Myhre, "Potawatomi Transformation," 32.

91. RSCJ–St. Louis, Series IV, K (Potawatomi Mission), "Account." Quoted in Callan, *Philippine Duchesne*, 654.

92. Myhre, "Potawatomi Transformation," 299, 345, 386. Sleeper-Smith, *Indian Women and French Men*, 103.

93. These spiritual parallels are suggested by Myhre, "Potawatomi Transformation," 347–49, 355, 359, 362, 373. The quotation is found on p. 363.

94. *Twenty-fourth Annual Report of the Board of Missions of the Methodist Episcopal Church*, 1843, 27, cited in Ibid., 2.

95. McCoy, *History of Baptist Indian Missions*, 505.

96. Myhre, "Potawatomi Transformation," 207, 295.

97. The differences between French Catholic and English Protestant missionary practice in colonial North America has been most fully developed by Axtell, *Invasion Within*.

98. These two groups, however, remained separate. On the resettlement of the Potawatomi and the treaty negotiations, see Clifton, *Prairie People*, 329–46.

99. See the report cited in Garraghan, *Jesuits*, vol. 2, 597–98.

100. RSCJ–St. Louis, Series XIII, Callan Collection, Box 8, PD to Elizabeth Galitzine, 7 January 1841; Box 1, PD to Père de la Croix, 24 October 1842; Series IV, K (Potawatomi Mission), "Account."

101. BDC, vol. 3, letter 335, 22 April 1852.

102. RSCJ–St. Louis, Series XIII, Callan Collection, Box 4, PD to Mme de Rollin, 10 April 1837.

103. Aron, *American Confluence*, 202. RSCJ–St. Louis, Series XIII, Callan Collection, Box 4, PD to Mme Jouve, 29 March 1846.

104. RSCJ-Rome, CVII, 2 D, Box 3, "Notes about Mother Duchesne from Sr. Barnwell." RSCJ–St. Louis, Series XIII, Callan Collection, Box 8, Mère Thiéfrey to SB, 19 February 1848. RSCJ-Rome, CIV, Dossier 2, St. Charles, Sr. Emilie St-Cyr, superior to SB, 28 April 1847.

105. One numerical estimate is that thirty thousand Frenchmen and women migrated between 1815 and 1818. Blaufarb, *Bonapartists in the Borderlands*, 19. Liebersohn, *Aristocratic Encounters*, 65.

106. Clark Rubenstine has argued that, from the beginning of French colonization in North America, the presence of Catholic nuns and the education of girls served political, as

well as religious, ends. Rubenstine, "French Colonial Policy and the Education of Women and Minorities."

107. On this issue, see McGreevy, *Catholicism and American Freedom*, and Dolan, *American Catholic Experience*.

108. Kastor, *Nation's Crucible*. Aron, *American Confluence*.

109. For a discussion of the frontier/borderland terminology, see the article published by Adelman and Aron, "From Borderlands to Borders," and the responses to it published in the October issue of the *American Historical Review* (vol. 104, no. 4).

110. I am grateful to Susan E. Grey for this insight.

111. BDC, vol. 2.2, letter 168, 20 May 1823.

CHAPTER 4

1. AN, F 19, 6213, bishop of Algiers to unknown recipient, 18 November 1841.

2. APF, Fonds Lyon, G 6, petition from Moslem inhabitants of Algeria to Pope (French translation from Arabic), 11 October 1841. Eugénie de Guérin, *Lettres à Louise de Bayne*, vol. 2, *(1835–1847)*, 15 April 1836.

3. Testas, *La vie militante*, 7.

4. ASJA, MS Abbé Brunet. Presumably such an individual was not hard to find. Timothy Tackett lists the number of priests in the Gaillac district who had taken the oath of the Civil Constitution of the Clergy as only 39 out of 190, or 21 percent. Tackett, *Religion, Revolution, and Regional Culture*, 359.

5. Auschitzky and Auschitzky, *La Famille maternelle de Maïten Brusaut*.

6. Guérin, *Lettres*, vol. 1, 207, 5 August 1832.

7. ASJA, "Relation des Grâces," 13 May 1848.

8. ASJA, MS Abbé Brunet.

9. ASJA, 1 A 4.3 Vialar to Mlle Pezet (Gaillac), 20 January 1826.

10. Guérin, *Lettres*, vol. 1, 207, 5 August 1832; 232, 4 December 1832. Eugénie de Guérin, eight years younger than Emilie de Vialar, also came from an established local family. She and her brother, Maurice, participated in the Romantic literary revival, largely through Maurice's friendship with Jules Barbey d'Aurevilly. Eugénie de Guérin's *Journal* was first published in 1860, twelve years after her death. Her witty and perceptive observations on Gaillac society in the 1830s come from her letters to her best friend, Louise de Bayne. See also Bannour, *Eugénie de Guérin*.

11. ASJA, "Rapport envoyé par Emilie de Vialar, en Mars 1839, à S. S. Grégoire XVI." ASJA, MS Abbé Brunet. Guérin, *Lettres*, vol. 1, 230, 4 December 1832.

12. The original painting by Detroy is in a museum in Toulouse; Vialar probably saw a copy in the church of St-Jacques de Montauban. Desprats, "Emilie de Vialar (1797–1856) à Gaillac," 95–107.

13. ASJA, "Rapport envoyé." "Registre historique des Etablissements de la Congrégation des Soeurs de St-Joseph de l'Apparition" (Gaillac), 1.

14. *Massilien*, 24.

15. ASJA, "Réglement de la Maison de Gaillac," 15 January 1834. ASJA, 1 A 4.4, Vialar to Mme Lamourié, 12 February 1833; Vialar to Mme d'Aubilli, 6 March 1835; AM Gaillac, 3 T 1, Vialar to mayor and municipal council, Gaillac, 15 November 1833.

16. Guérin, *Lettres*, vol. 1, 279, 14 May 1833. *Massilien*, 20.

17. AM-Gaillac, 5 T 2, Dossier Calvert: Manuscrit Gaillac 1830–48, chap. 4, "La vie sociale," chap. 5, "La vie charitable," chap. 6, "Les principaux événements." ASJA, conference de Jean Calvert, "Gaillac au temps d'Emilie de Vialar."

18. Guérin, *Lettres*, vol. 1, 173, 8 March 1832; 362, 5 February 1834, 14 January 1835.

19. AM-Gaillac, 2 Q 248, "Extinction de la Mendicité: Voies et Moyens," 1838. ASJA, Conference de Jean Calvert, "Gaillac au temps d'Emilie de Vialar." In 1833 France also passed the Guizot law, which mandated a boys' school in every commune.

20. AM-Gaillac, 5 T 1, "Instruction public depuis la Révolution."

21. Guérin, *Lettres*, vol. 1, 332, 20 November 1833.

22. On Restoration missions, see Sevrin, *Les missions religieuses*; Kroen, *Politics and Theater*; and Riasanovsky, "Trumpets of Jericho."

23. *L'Ami de la religion*, 23 May 1829, quoted in Guérin, *Lettres*, vol. 1, 11, 12 March 1830.

24. AM-Gaillac, 5 T 2, dossier Calvert: Manuscrit Gaillac, 1830–48, Chap. II, "La vie politique." ASJA, Conference de Jean Calvert, "Gaillac au temps d'Emilie de Vialar."

25. Founded in 1680, the Soeurs de Charité et Instruction chrétienne de Nevers had about one hundred communities in 1789. After their reestablishment in 1811, they grew to two thousand sisters and 250 communities in 1850. The Lourdes visionary, Bernadette Soubirous, joined the order in 1866.

26. Quoted in Darbon, *Emilie de Vialar*, 27.

27. ASJA, 1 A 4.4, Vialar to Mme de Lamourié, 26 April 1838.

28. Guérin, *Lettres*, vol. 1, 242–43, 25 January 1833.

29. On the early history of the Filles de la Charité, see Rapley, *Dévotes*; Jones, *Charitable Imperative*; and Dinan, *Women and Poor Relief*.

30. Guérin, *Lettres*, vol. 1, 311, 25 August 1833; vol. 1, 392, 5 May 1834. Three years later, however, Guérin poked fun at these kinds of criticisms upon hearing that controversy had erupted over the habit of the new religious order, the Soeurs de l'Immaculeé Conception, founded nearby by Emilie de Villeneuve: "I know their habit; there is something singular about the headpiece. It seems that the head is what is most difficult to calibrate in a religious outfit." Vol. 2, 180, 11 May 1837.

31. Guérin, *Lettres*, vol. 1, 393, 4 May 1834. See also vol. 1, 254, 20 February 1833; vol. 1, 259, 12 March 1833; and vol. 1, 297, 1 July 1833. The archbishop of Albi also compared Vialar to Theresa of Avila when he heard of her plans to go to Algeria. ASJA, 1 A 4.1, archbishop of Albi to Vialar, 19 July 1835.

32. Guérin, *Lettres*, vol. 1, 427, 17 August 1834.

33. See Cavasino, *Emilie de Vialar*, 350–52, for more information on other local congregations, especially those founded by the two "other Emilies."

34. Guérin, *Lettres*, vol. 1, 242, 25 January 1833. In 1837 she reported the visit of Augustin de Vialar, "l'Africain," to Gaillac, accompanied by an Arab prince. Vol. 2, 183, 11 May 1837.

35. [Augustin de] Vialar, *Simples faits*, 8.

36. [Augustin de] Vialar, *Alger*, 4. Vialar, *Simples faits*, 26.

37. AOM, F 80 1647, "Extrait du Procès-verbal de la Séance du Conseil Municipal de la ville d'Alger, en date du 16 juillet 1835."

38. Deaths in Algiers among the Jewish community were estimated at 438 out of a population of 7,000 at the end of August. AOM, F 80 659, intendant civil, French possessions in North Africa, to governor general, 31 August 1835. AOM, F 80 659, "Choléra-Morbus: Bulletin Officiel," 19 September 1835.

39. Teissier, ed., *Histoire des chretiens d'Afrique du nord*, 122.

40. On the poor religious practices of nominal Catholics in Algeria, see the archives of Prop. Fide, Fondo (S.C.), Barbaria, vol. 14, Abbé Collin, apostolic prefect, Algiers, to Cardinal de Pédicini, 30 April 1832; Abbé L. Muller, 1 January 1833; and SHAT, 1 H 54 (1), Maréchal Valée to minister of war, 27 January 1838.

41. ASJA, "Rapport envoyé."

42. Ministère de la Guerre, *Tableau de la situation*.

43. ASJA, 1 A 4.4, Vialar to Mme de Lamourié, 5 April 1837.

44. Quoted in Darbon, *Souvenirs et documents*, 63.

45. ASJA, 1 A 4.1, Vialar to R. P. Becquet, prêtre au Bon Sauveur, Toulouse, 3 June 1836.

46. ASJA, "Copie de la Requête adressée le 25 Juin 1842," 5. ASJA, 1 A 4.1, Vialar to archbishop of Albi, 7 September 1839.

47. ASJA, "Rapport envoyé."

48. ASJA, 1 A 4.4, Vialar to Mme d'Aubilly, 22 April 1836. ASJA, 1 A 4.1, "Rapport adressé au Saint Père," 29 March 1841.

49. Suchet, *Lettres édifiantes*, 24, 40. On the significance of female marabouts in Algerian Islam, see Clancy-Smith, *Rebel and Saint*.

50. AOM, F 80 1648, intendant civil, régence d'Alger to M. le Maréchal, président du conseil, 1 February 1833; F 80 1647, intendant civil, Algeria, to war minister, 25 February 1836.

51. On the role of schools, see the documents in AOM, F 80, 1843, dating as early as 1832. There were a few exceptions to this generalization. See, for example, the statement in Rozet, *Voyage dans la Régence*, vol. 1, 75, that the education of the average Algerian was superior to that in France since the many public Koranic schools resulted in a high level of male literacy.

52. Turin, *Affrontements culturels*, 84.

53. AOM, F 80 1649, "Simple exposé des faits," 10 June 1839. AOM, F 80 1647, intendant civil, Algeria, to minister of war, 21 February 1836. This incident was part of a much more complex dispute about the hospital staffing, in which accusations of negligence and financial mismanagement flew on both sides.

54. AOM, F 80 1625, minister of war to Maréchal Clauzel, governor general of French possessions in North Africa, 16 October 1835. Vincent de Paul, founder of the Congrégation de la Mission, had originally sent Lazarists to minister to enslaved Christians. Two other "redemptionist" orders, the Holy Trinity and Our Lady of Mercy, also had responsibilities for Christian slaves in Algeria in the period of Turkish rule. None were allowed to proselytize among the Muslim populations. See Wolf, *Barbary Coast*, 157–58.

55. Teissier, *Histoire des chrétiens*, 121. See also the archives of Prop. Fide, Fondo (S.C.) Barbaria, vol. 14, 24 May 1833, for the beginning of a series of letters regarding this dispute.

56. SHAT, 1 H 54 (1), Maréchal Valée to minister of war, 27 January 1838.

57. The papal bull was followed by an ordonnance of the French king on 13 October 1838. The new diocese included all of the French possessions in North Africa and was attached to the diocese of Aix-en-Provence. AOM, F 80 1625, ministre secrétaire d'état de la guerre to governor general of Algeria, 12 December 1838. See also the announcement in *Moniteur algérien*, 21 September 1838.

58. Prop. Fide, Fondo (S.C.), Barbaria, vol. 15, Garibaldi, papal nuncio, Paris, to Cardinal Fransoni. This idea was ultimately rejected because the Holy See feared that a papal decoration would make Valée appear too close to Rome, thereby endangering the establishment of the Algerian diocese in the French Chamber of Deputies.

59. Quoted in Teissier, *Histoire des chrétiens*, 122. Julien, *Histoire de l'Algérie contemporaine*, vol. 1, 160.

60. Prop. Fide, Fondo (S.C.), Barbaria, vol. 15, Garibaldi, papal nuncio, Paris, to Cardinal Lambruschini, secretary of state, Holy See, 29 January 1838.

61. Procacci, *Le relazioni diplomatiche*, vol. 3, 363, Abate Garibaldi, internunzio, Paris, to Cardinale Lambruschini, secretario di state, 2 October 1837. Born in 1800 in Bordeaux, Dupuch studied law and then became involved in lay Catholic organizations as a young man until he entered seminary in 1828; he was appointed vicar general in Bordeaux in 1835. See Madeleine Hardy, *Antoine-Adolphe Dupuch*. Written by his great-niece, this biography presents a highly favorable view of Dupuch.

62. Prop. Fide, Fondo (S.C.), Barbaria, vol. 15, pontifical consul, Algiers, to Prop. Fide, 8 January 1839.

63. Çelik, *Urban Forms*, 28. Eventually the mosque was indeed torn down in order to straighten out the side of the plaza. In addition to the planned destruction of religious spaces in Algiers, there was also widespread looting of mosques when French troops entered the city. For a contemporary critique of French actions, see *Procès verbaux et rapports*, 71–73, 333, 400–1. For a historical analysis, see Hamdani, *La vérité*.

64. Whether or not this rationalization was true, the French sources do not record any instances of actual resistance to the appropriation of Muslim property for Catholic use.

65. SHAT, 1 H 58 (1), Maréchal Valée to foreign minister, 14 September 1838. Veuillot, *Les français en Algérie*, 57–58.

66. Suchet, *Lettres édifiantes*, 8. *AAPF*, vol. 13, 361, lettre de Mgr Dupuch, 21 November 1840.

67. *AAPF*, vol. 11, 452, lettre de Mgr Dupuch, 22 April 1839. The ceremony is also described by Suchet, *Lettres édifiantes*, 34.

68. On the transformation of Annaba/Bône and its environs to emphasize the continuity between ancient Rome and imperial France, see Prochaska, *Making Algeria French*, 213–22.

69. *AAPF*, vol. 11, 450, 22 April 1839; vol. 13, 355, 21 November 1840; vol. 13, 80, 15 August 1840. After he left Algeria, Dupuch published a four-volume history of Christian Algeria, *Fastes sacrés de l'Afrique chrétienne*.

70. Suchet, *Lettres édifiantes*, 300–1, 8 February 1840.

71. Thomson, *Barbary and Enlightenment*, 42–44, argues that this view was developed during the Enlightenment. See also Lorcin, "Rome and France in Africa."

72. *AAPF*, vol. 16, 26–27, "Extrait d'une lettre de Mgr Dupuch," 14 September 1843.

73. Ibid., vol. 11, 451, "Lettre de Mgr Dupuch," 22 April 1839; vol. 13, 361, "Lettre de Mgr Dupuch," 21 November 1840.

74. Ibid., vol. 16, 15, "Extrait d'une lettre de Mgr Dupuch," 14 September 1843.

75. Ibid., vol. 11, 447, "Lettre de Mgr Dupuch," 22 April 1839.

76. ASJA, 1 A 4. 2, Dupuch to Vialar, 8 December 1839.

77. AN, F 19 6213, bishop of Algiers to unknown, 18 November 1841.

78. ASJA, 1 A 4.1, Vialar to Mr. Mercier, 11 June 1840; 1 A 4.3, Vialar to Sœur Pauline Gineste, 6 June 1840.

79. *AAPF*, vol. 11, 447, "Lettre de Mgr Dupuch," 22 April 1839.

80. AN, F 19 6213, bishop of Algiers to unknown, 18 November 1841. See also ASJA, 1 A 4.2, Dupuch to Soeur Emilie Julien, 2 May 1841.

81. ASJA, 12 A 3, Soeur Emilie Julien to Vialar, 7 June 1841.

82. ASJA, Vialar to Soeur Victoire Tessonnière, 5 February 1843.

83. ASJA, "Copie de la requête adressée le 25 Juin 1842," 7, 9.

84. ASJA, 1 A 4.2, Dupuch to diocesan clergy, 1 February 1840; 1 A 4.1, "Rapport adressé au Saint Père," 29 March 1841; 1 A 4.3, Soeur Justine Cormary to Vialar, 4 October 1841; 12 A 3, Soeur Emilie Julien to Vialar, 5 August 1841.

85. ASJA, 1 A 4.1, Vialar to Mr. Mercier, 11 June 1840; "Lettre adressée à Monsiegneur de Gualy [archbishop of Albi] (probablement par Mère Emilie Julien)," n.d.; 1 A 4.6, Emilie Julien to Vialar, 1 February 1842.

86. ASJA, 1 A 4.4, Mme de Lamourié to Vialar, 26 April 1840.

87. ASJA, 1 A 4.4, Vialar to Mme de Lamourié, 7 January 1841.

88. ASJA, 1 A 4.1, Vialar to Abbé Bourgade, 8 March 1842.

89. ASJA, "Sommario voto del P. Rozaven Consultore," 6 April 1842. In 1844, Vialar acquiesced to a request by the new archbishop of Albi that the Soeurs de St-Joseph add a veil to their habit. ASJA, 1 A 4.1, Vialar to Abbé Edouard Barthe à St-Affrique, 13 April 1844.

90. ASJA, "Sommario voto del P. Rozaven Consultore," 6 April 1842.

91. SHAT, 1 H 78-01, unsigned letter written from Rome, 17 November 1841.

92. ASJA, 1 A 4.1, Vialar to archbishop of Albi, 10 January 1840; 12 A 3, Soeur Emilie Julien to Vialar, 19 April 1841.

93. Copies of the petitions, dated 11 October 1841, can be found in APF, Fonds Lyon, G 6. Unfortunately, I know nothing about the conditions under which the signatures were solicited and gathered.

94. See Lorcin, *Imperial Identities*, for a discussion of this stereotype in colonial French thought and practice.

95. AOM, F 80 1649, "Simple exposé des faits," 10 June 1839.

96. Quoted in Teissier, *Histoire des chrétiens*, 122. I cannot vouch for the accuracy of the quotation, only that the French believed this was Abd el-Kader's view.

97. SHAT, 1 H 60 (1), Maréchal Valée to foreign minister, 4 January 1839; 1 H 56 (1), Maréchal Valée to foreign minister, 5 May 1838.

98. "Fondation d'une Eglise catholique à Alger, son influence sur les indigènes," *Moniteur algérien*, 14 July 1832, p. 2.

99. Genty de Bussy, *De l'établissement*, vol. 1, 244, 248–49.

100. AOM, F 80 1627, minister of war to governor general, Algiers, 26 September 1838.

101. Ibid., 15 July 1840.

102. SHAT, 1 H 62 (1), colonel d'état major to minister of war, 1 June 1839. AOM, F 80 1627, minister of war to Maréchal Comte Valée, governor general, Algiers, 17 August 1839.

103. Julien, *Histoire de l'Algérie*, vol. 1, 160, 191; ASJA, 12 A 3, Soeur Emilie Julien to Vialar, 13 July 1841 and 20 July 1841. See also SHAT, 1 H 78-01, unsigned letter from Rome, 17 November 1843.

104. APF, Fonds Paris, G 8, président, conseil central de Lyon, to président, conseil central de Paris, 26 March 1844.

105. ASJA, 1 A 3.9, E. Drouelle and Godbourg, pères de Ste. Croix to pope, 20 February 1842. Prop. Fide, Fondo (S.C.), Barbaria, vol. 16, Abbé Bourgade to Cardinal Fransoni, 17 March 1842. ASJA, 1 A 4.1, Vialar to Abbé Bourgade, 31 January 1842.

106. Pioneau, *Vie de Mgr Dupuch*, 355–56.

107. Veuillot, *Les français en Algérie*, 238.

108. *AAPF*, vol. 11, "Lettre de Mgr l'Evêque d'Alger," 646–47, 17 August 1839. Because this individual was European born, her embrace of Christianity was not technically a conversion.

109. Suchet, *Lettres édifiantes*, 245, 15 September 1840.

110. Tournier, *La conquete religieuse*, 72.

111. ASJA, "Rapport envoyé."

112. ASJA, 1 A 4.1, Vialar to R. P. Becquet, prêtre au Bon Sauveur, Toulouse, 4 August 1837.

113. Suchet, *Lettres édifiantes*, 30–31, 60–61, 37.

114. Turin, *Affrontements culturels*, 91, gives an example where a doctor was forced to write a blessing on a piece of paper to assuage the wife of a dying Muslim man. Such gestures would have come naturally to a Catholic nun.

115. ASJA, "Rapport envoyé."

116. ASJA, 1 A 4.1, "Rapport adressé au Saint Père," 29 March 1841.

117. Ibid.

118. Greer, *Mohawk Saint*, 6–7. Harrison, " 'Penny for the Little Chinese,' " 81–82. Canon law on this point had been developed during the eighteenth-century pontificate of Benedict XIV, based on a reading of St. Thomas Aquinas, in relation to the forced baptism of Jews. It covered abandoned children as well. See Caffiero, *Battesimi forzati*, chap. 2.

119. Baptized children were not supposed to be reared by non-Catholics. This case helped launch a campaign for Jewish emancipation. See Kertzer, *Kidnapping of Edgardo Mortara*. Kertzer lays out the ecclesiastical requirements on pp. 33 and 310n2. See also chap. 2, "Forced Baptisms," in his *Popes against the Jews*. Kertzer, however, confines himself to cases in papal lands, where surviving baptized children could be seized and brought up by the church as Catholics. A case with direct implications for France was the Montel affair, which he discusses in "Montel Affair."

120. Prop. Fide, Fondo (S.C.), Barbaria, vol. 18, Soeur Emilie Julien to Cardinal Barnabò, PF, 6 May 1859. This number, if Julien really meant to refer only to the cholera epidemic and not the entire period of residence of the Soeurs de St-Joseph in Algeria, seems unduly high in proportion to the total number of cholera deaths as reported by government officials.

121. Ibid., vol. 15, Abbé Banvoy to PF, 6 July 1838. Banvoy wanted Propaganda Fide to rule on the maximum age of this practice.

122. Ibid., Abbé Montera, Algiers, to PF, 12 January 1838.

123. ASJA, 1 A 4.1, "Rapport adressé au Saint Père," 29 March 1841.

124. Suchet, *Lettres édifiantes*, 59–60, 63.

125. Ibid., 24, 32–33, 36–37, 40, 53–57.

126. ASJA, "Copie de la Requête adressée le 25 Juin 1842," 19–20.

127. AOM, F 80 1625, minister of war to Lieutenant General Bugeaud, governor general of Algeria, 7 January 1842. AAE-Paris, mémoires et documents, France, 2118, minister of war, Algerian Affairs, to foreign minister, 13 May 1842.

128. ASJA, 1 A 4.2, Dupuch to superior, Constantine, 20 July 1842.

129. APF, Fonds Paris, G 8, circulaire, religieuses de la Communauté de Notre-Dame de Charité du Bon-Pasteur d'Alger, 10 January 1844.

130. ASJA, 1 A 4.4, Vialar to Augustin Vialar, 1 August 1842; Vialar to Soeur Pauline Gineste, 25 September 1842.

131. Vialar to governor general of Algeria, 12 January 1843, cited in Darbon, *Souvenirs et documents*, 158.

132. Sœur Euphrasie Maraval, superior, Hôpital Civil d'Alger, ca. November 1842, quoted in Darbon, *Souvenirs et documents*.

133. ASJA, 1 A 4.4, Mme de Lamourié to Vialar, 27 January 1846. Busy with other missions, Vialar did not pursue the idea of returning to Algeria in an official capacity, although she often visited her brother there, especially after the February 1843 death of her sister-in-law, leaving two young motherless nieces.

134. Dupuch to Vialar, 22 July 1846, quoted in Picard, *Une vierge française*, 102. ASJA, 1 A 4.2, Dupuch to Vialar, 3 December 1853. AN, F 19 2486B, minister of justice and religious affairs to bishops of France, June 1846; "Mémoire à l'appui de la manifestation du clergé d'Afrique en faveur de Monseigneur Dupuch, premier et ancien Evêque d'Alger," February 1852; République Française, décret, 1 November 1852.

135. Cavasino, *Emilie de Vialar*, 157.

136. These efforts were poorly received by the French government. On Bishop Lavigerie, see Lorcin, *Imperial Identities*, 177–81.

CHAPTER 5

1. ASJA, 1 A 4.1, "Rapport adressé au Saint Père," 29 March 1841; "Copie de la Requête adressée le 25 Juin 1842," 13.

2. ASJA, 1 A 4.1, Vialar to archbishop of Albi, 20 June 1840.

3. ASJA, 1 A 4.3, Vialar to Soeur Pauline Gineste, 28 January 1844; 1 A 3.9, Lagau, French consul, to Vialar, 14 October 1843.

4. The "ransoming racket" ended in 1816. See Clancy-Smith, *Mediterranean Passages*, 255. I am grateful to the author for sharing this work with me in advance of publication.

5. Gallagher, *Medicine and Power*, 40.

6. Clancy-Smith, *Mediterranean Passages*, 257.

7. The definitive study of Ahmad Bey's reign remains that by Brown, *Tunisia of Ahmad Bey*. Other useful sources include Abun-Nasr, *History of the Maghrib*; Tlili, *Les rapports culturels et idéologiques*; and Sebag, *Tunis*.

8. For an account of the diplomacy surrounding this visit, see Brown, *Tunisia of Ahmad Bey*, 325–34.

9. The French colony ranged from old merchant families to soldiers and technicians invited by Ahmad Bey. Sebag, *Tunis*, 275–76.

10. Planel, "De la nation à la colonie," vol. 2, 462. Clancy-Smith, *Mediterranean Passages*, chap. 7.

11. Prop. Fide, Fondo (S.C.), Barbaria, vol. 16, Bourgade to Cardinal Fransoni, 7 September 1843. Bourgade notes, however, that when certificates were refused, "we passed over these formalities."

12. Planel, "De la nation à la colonie," vol. 2, 460–62. APF, Fonds Lyon, G 124, Bourgade to M. le président du conseil de Paris, 20 June 1851. Clancy-Smith, *Mediterranean Passages*, 273.

13. Bourgade, *Carthage*, 1.

14. Ganiage, *La population européenne*, 30–31, 84–85.

15. Clancy-Smith, *Mediterranean Passages*, 272–273. Gallagher, *Medicine and Power*, 110.

16. ASJA, "Registre historique des établissements de la Congrégation des Soeurs de St-Joseph de l'Apparition depuis la fondation en 1832 jusqu'à nos jours 1898 (Tunis)," 13.

17. Pons, *La nouvelle église*, 223. Cited in Darbon, *Souvenirs et documents*, 251. The original article was dated 16 September 1850.

18. ASJA, 1 A 4.4, Vialar to Augustin de Vialar, 30 August 1843.

19. Figures are from APF, Fonds Lyon, G 124, Vialar to président du conseil, 29 September 1844. Quotation is from G 6, Vialar to directeur, 5 February 1843.

20. Clancy-Smith, *Mediterranean Passages*, 256.

21. APF, Fonds Lyon, G 124, Bourgade to M. le président du conseil de Paris, 20 June 1851. Planel, "De la nation à la colonie," 118.

22. ASJA, "Registre historique (Sousse, Sfax)," 16, 18.

23. Clancy-Smith, *Mediterranean Passages*, 264.

24. Windler, *La diplomatie comme expérience de l'autre*, 425. See also Brown, *Tunisia of Ahmad Bey*, 227–29.

25. Vialar and Raffo had a falling out in 1846, when Raffo began pursuing Soeur Emilie Julien, against her will, romantically. Vialar was particularly concerned about the consequences of such a scandal in an "infidel land," where the "Arabs considered [the sisters] as beings apart, who have renounced everything to serve God." Prop. Fide, Fondo (S.C.), Africa-Malta, 24 January 1846. Subsequent letters in this same series give the details of Raffo's pursuit, which caused Julien to flee to Malta.

26. ASJA, 1 A 4.1, Vialar to Bourgade, 10 August 1842; 1 A 4.4, Vialar to Augustin de Vialar, 14 July 1843.

27. Planel, "De la nation à la colonie," 120. Soumille, "Les multiples activités," 237–39.

28. ASJA, 1 A 4.1, Vialar to Abbé Bourgade, 28 April 1846. See the discussion in Harris, *Lourdes*, 226–36.

29. Planel, "De la nation à la colonie," 127. Clancy-Smith, *Mediterranean Passages*, 270.

30. ASJA, 1 A 4. 1, Vialar to Bourgade, 10 August 1842; 14 May 1847; 1 A 4.2, Vialar to Abbé Bourgade, 18 December 1854.

31. APF, Fonds Lyon, G 124, Bourgade to president, conseil, 21 March 1841. This class for Muslims appears never to have been established.

32. Planel, "De la nation à la colonie," vol. 1, 120–21. ASJA, 1 A 3, Bourgade to Vialar, 17 May 1844.

33. Prop. Fide, Fondo (S.C.), Barbaria, vol. 16, prospectus, Collège St-Louis à Tunis, 1842; vol. 18, Bourgade to Cardinal Fransoni, 26 November 1855. Soumille, "Les multiples activités," 246.

34. Bourgade, *Carthage*, 1. Clancy-Smith, *Mediterranean Passages*, chap. 7.

35. These titles were *Soirées de Carthage, ou Dialogues entre un prêtre catholique, un muphti, et un cadi* (1847); *Le clef du Coran* (1852); and *Passage du Coran à l'Évangile* (1855).

36. AAE-Paris, affaires diverses politiques, secours religieux, 2, "Note remise à S. M. l'Empereur, par l'abbé Bourgade, aumônier de la chapelle impériale de Saint-Louis, à Carthage," 21 October 1955.

37. Bourgade, *Soirées de Carthage*, 7–9, 12–14.

38. Ibid., 14–16.

39. Ibid., 18, 24, 30–31.

40. Prop. Fide, Fondo (S.C.), Barbaria, vol. 16, "Liste des enfants baptisés en cas de mort pendant ces derniers mois à Tunis," 18 December 1842.

41. Prop. Fide, Fondo, (S.C.), Barbaria, vol. 18, Vialar to Cardinal Ferretti, 3 June 1856.

42. ASJA, "Registre historique (Sousse)," 17. See also the entries for Tunis and Sfax.

43. Windler, *La diplomatie*, 178–79.

44. Chateaubriand, *Itinéraire*.

45. Windler, *La diplomatie*, 201–4. Soumille, "Les multiples activités," 241–43.

46. Prop. Fide, Fondo (S.C.), Barbaria, vol. 16, Pietr Paolo da Malta (Capucin) to Cardinal Fransoni, 4 March 1842.

47. Soumille, "Les multiples activités," 247–48.

48. APF, Fonds Lyon, G 124, chancelier vicaria, Tunis, to conseil central, 2 June 1853.

49. ASJA, 1 A 4.1, Vialar to Bourgade, 5 September 1847. Prop. Fide, Fondo (S.C.), Barbaria, vol. 17, Bourgade to Cardinal Fransoni, 18 June 1854.

50. AAE-Nantes, Rome–St. Siège, 575, minister of foreign affairs to French ambassador, Holy See, 16 May 1856. See also Prop. Fide, Fondo (S.C.), Barbaria, vol. 18, letters from Soeurs Marie Delas and Cyprienne Bonnevialle, 11 May 1856, 13 July 1856.

51. ASJA, 1 A 4.6, Vialar to Soeur Céleste Peyre, 18 June 1856. Prop. Fide, Fondo (S.C.), Barbaria, vol. 18, Vialar to Cardinal Ferretti, 3 June 1856. AAE-Nantes, Rome–St. Siège, 575, consul general, Tunis, to minister of foreign affairs, 18 June 1856.

52. Tlili, *Les rapports culturels*, 445. Bourgade never returned to Tunisia and died in 1866.

53. ASJA, 1 A 4.4, Vialar to Mme d'Aubilly, 23 February 1846.

54. ASJA, 12 A 2, Mère Emilie Julien to Soeur Pauline Gineste, 24 July 1845.

55. ASJA, 1 A 4.1, Vialar to Mgr de Jerphanion, archbishop of Albi, 24 August 1845.

56. ASJA, 1 A 4.3, Vialar to Soeur Pauline Gineste, 15 November 1845.

57. Donato, *L'émigration des Maltais*, 33.

58. Protestant missionaries were in fact discouraged, and Catholic religious instruction continued to be given in schools. Koster, *Prelates and Politicians*, 39–41.

59. APF, Fonds Lyon, D 162, "Quelques motifs qui peuvent engager l'oeuvre admirable de la Propagation de la Foi à venir en secours au collège de S Paul à Malte," 23 December 1846; "Extrait d'une lettre du R. P. Esmond de la Compagnie de Jésus," 5 June 1847; Fonds Paris, D 154, "Traduction d'une lettre de Mgr l'Evêque de Malte adressée au Conseil central de Lyon," 18 July 1849.

60. Thomas F. Stransky, "La concurrence des missions chrétiennes en Terre sainte, 1840–1850," in Trimbur and Aaronsohn, eds., *De Bonaparte à Balfour*, 201.

61. APF, Fonds Lyon, D 162, "Quelques motifs qui peuvent engager l'oeuvre admirable de la Propagation de la Foi à venir en secours au collège de S Paul à Malte," 23 December 1846. Kostner, *Prelates and Politicians*, 47.

62. ASJA, 1 A 4.3, Vialar to supérieure, Tunis, 17 June 1845.

63. ASJA, 12 A 2, Mère Emilie Julien to Soeur Pauline Gineste, 24 July 1845.

64. Quoted in Darbon, *Souvenirs et documents*, 204, Vialar to M. Molis, 5 August 1854. Vialar required Maltese novices to pay not only a pension but also a lump sum "according to the position of the family, but never under 1,200 francs."

65. ASJA, 1 A 4.1, Vialar to Mgr de Jerphanion, archbishop of Albi, 24 August 1845.

66. ASJA, 12 A 1, Soeur Emilie Julien to Vialar, 6 August 1847.

67. ASJA, 1 A 4.3, Vialar to Soeur Honorine Piques, 5 December 1845; 1 A 4.4, Vialar to Mme d'Aubilli, 12 December 1846.

68. ASJA, 1 A 4.4, Vialar to Mme d'Aubilly, 2 July 1856; Vialar to Marguerite and Euphémie de Vialar, 3 August 1856. The hospital closed on 15 August 1856.

69. Blouet, *Short History of Malta*, 178. See also Godechot, *Histoire de Malte*, and Vadala, *Les maltais hors de Malte*.

70. Julia Clancy-Smith, "Marginality and Migration: Europe's Social Outcasts in Pre-colonial Tunisia, 1830–81," in Eugene Rogan, ed., *Outside In: On the Margins of the Modern Middle East* (New York: Tauris, 2002), 152, 161. Donato, *L'émigration des maltais*, 29. Andrea L. Smith, "Les maltais en Tunisie à la veille du protectorat: Une population intermédiaire," in *La Tunisie mosaïque*, ed. Alexandropoulos and Cabanel, 115–17.

71. ASJA, 1 A 4.2, Vialar to Bourgade, 18 December 1854. Prop. Fide, Fondo (S.C.) Grecia Arcipelago et Candia, Abbé Privilegio to PF, 26 May 1855.

72. ASJA, 1 A 4.3, Vialar to Soeur Céleste Peyre, 8 September 1853; "Registre historique (Rome)," 65.

73. ASJA, 1 A 4.1, Vialar to Abbé Bourgade, 5 September 1847; 1 A 4.3, Vialar to Soeur Céleste Peyre, 18 January 1854.

74. ASJA, "Registre historique (Tripoli de Barbarie)," 80.

75. Planel, "De la nation à la colonie," 117.

76. Soumille, "Les multiples activités," 342.

77. ASJA, 1 A 4.1, Vialar to Bourgade, 6 October 1848.

78. ASJA, 1 A 4.1, Vialar to Mgr de Jerphanion, archbishop of Albi, 24 August 1845.

79. ASJA, 4 A 1, "Premières Constitutions de 1835 avec les suppressions et additions approuvées par Mgr de Gualy," 16 November 1840.

80. ASJA, Relation des Grâces (begun 27 September 1843).

81. When it was all over, Vialar alleged that Gineste had cost her one hundred thousand francs. ASJA, 1 A 4.3, Vialar (Marseille) to Soeur Céleste Peyre, 28 December 1853.

82. ASJA, 1 A 4.1, Vialar to Bourgade; 1 A 4.2, Vialar to M. Pierre Privilegio, curé de St-Sébastien, Syra, Greece, 30 March 1851; 1 A 4.2, "Rapport qui semble avoir été adressé à Monsieur l'Abbé Bourgade," 4 April 1851; 1 A 4.2, Vialar to Bourgade, 21 February 1850.

83. ASJA, 1 A 4.3, Vialar to Soeur Eugénie Laurez, 11 October 1852.

84. ASJA, 1 A 4.3, Vialar to Soeur Céleste Peyre, 13 June 1854.

85. ASJA, 1 A 4.6, Vialar to Soeur Céleste Peyre, 14 July 1854. The dowry was set at six thousand francs, paid over five years, with an additional three hundred francs in pension for novices. ASJA, 4 A 1, "Premières constitutions de 1835 avec les suppressions et additions approvées par Mgr de Gualy," 16 November 1840.

86. ASJA, 1 A 4.2, Vialar to Bourgade, 28 December 1854; 1 A 4.6, Vialar to Soeur Françoise Pezet, 20 November 1855.

87. ASJA, 2 A 12, Constitutions des Soeurs de S. Joseph de l'Apparition, 25, 1862.

CHAPTER 6

1. Quoted in Darbon, *Souvenirs and documents*, 187, Abbé Picard to Emilie de Vialar, 2 July 1844.

2. Cited in Ibid., 206, père recteur, Oblats de Marie de Turin to Vialar, 9 December 1845.

3. ASJA, "Registre historique (Fremantle, Australie)," 159.

4. On increasing French cultural influence in the Middle East in this period, see Burrows, " '*Mission Civilisatrice.*' "

5. See Curtis, "Charity Begins Abroad."

6. ASJA, 1 A 4.2, Vialar to M. Pierre Privilegio, curé de St-Sébastien, Syra, 10 November 1852.

7. Chateaubriand, *Itinéraire*, 22.

8. Basch, *Le mirage grec*, 45–46.

9. Koliopoulos and Veremis, *Greece*, 142–46. See also Frazee, *Orthodox Church and Independent Greece*.

10. ASJA, "Registre historique (Athènes)," 99.

11. Frazee, *Catholics and Sultans*, 171.

12. Quoted in Ibid., 250.

13. ASJA, "Registre historique (Syra)," 91. APF, Fonds Paris, D 151, Mgr Alberti, évêque de Syra, to président, Oeuvre de la Propagation de la Foi, 18 March 1855.

14. ASJA, 10 C, Privilegio to Vialar, 21 October 1848; 1 A 3.9, Privilegio to Vialar, 15 January 1851; 1 A 4.2, Vialar to Privilegio, curé de St-Sébastien, Syra, 30 May 1851.

15. Koliopoulos and Veremis, *Greece*, 277. They point out that, although Athens had 26,000 inhabitants in 1840, 120,000 Greeks lived in Constantinople.

16. APF, Fonds Lyon, D 146, Brunoni, to président, Conseil central, 5 November 1843; 5 February 1844.

17. Ibid., 20 January 1845.

18. APF, Fonds Lyon, D 146, "Prospetto della Scuola delle Suore dell'Apparizione di San Giuseppe, nell'Isola di Cipro," 12 December 1844.

19. Ibid., "Catalogue des enfans admis dans les classes des Soeurs de Saint-Joseph de l'Apparition, Chypre," 1 January 1846. Prospectus, quoted in Darbon, *Souvenirs et documents*, 192.

20. Ibid., "Prospetto della Scuola," 12 December 1844.

21. Ibid., Brunoni to président, 2 November 1845.

22. Ibid., Brunoni to président, Conseil central, 20 January 1845.

23. Prop. Fide, Fondo (S.C.), Terra Santa e Cipro, vol. 19, "Pianta della Casa delle Suore di S. Giuseppe dell'Apparizione," n.d. [1846]. APF, Fonds Lyon, D 146, "Etat des recettes et dépenses présummées pour l'année 1857."

24. APF, Fonds Lyon, D 145, "Etat des recettes et dépenses présumées pour l'année 1850," 30 December 1849. ASJA, 10 C, petition from Catholic parents, Chios, 5 March 1847. See also APF, Lyon, D 145, 19 January 1847. APF, Fonds Lyon, D 145, Bishop Justiniani to central council, 20 September 1848.

25. ASJA, 10 C, "Rapport concernant l'Ecole française des Soeurs de St-Joseph de l'Apparition à la Canée, Crète," n.d.

26. APF, Fonds Lyon, D 148, R. P. Séraphin de Callinsetta, superior, Capuchins, to président, Conseil central, 26 May 1854, 21 July 1855; D 145, Bishop Justiniani to central council, 9 January 1851; letter from Firmin Guys, Lazarites, Smyrna, 9 July 1852. ASJA, "Registre historique (Athènes)," 99.

27. ASJA, 10 C, "Détails sur la maison de Chio fondée en 1848." Prop. Fide, Fondo (S.C.) Grecia Arcipelago e Candia, Catholic bishop of Chios, to Mgr Rechid Pacha, grand visir, Constantinople, 16 December 1851.

28. APF, Fonds Lyon, D 148, R. P. Séraphin de Callinsetta, superior, Capuchins, to president, conseil central, 24 February 1855, 7 May 1855, 19 January 1856. According to the "Mission des PP Capucins à la Canée, Tableau" of 15 September 1854, the population consisted of 270 Catholics, 5,400 Greek Orthodox ("hérétiques"), and 11,380 Muslims ("infidèles").

29. APF, Fonds Lyon, D 146, "Etat des recettes et dépenses présumées pour l'année 1852."

30. APF, Fonds Paris, D 151, "Etat de recettes et dépenses présumées pour l'année 1856." Prop. Fide, Fondo (S.C.), Grecia Arcipelago e Candia, Vattier de Bourville to Propagation de la Foi, Paris, 10 February 1853.

31. APF, Fonds Lyon, D 148, R. P. Séraphin de Callinsetta, superior, Capuchins, to president, conseil central, 24 February 1855; D 145, Padre Agostino dos Sorso, presidente della Missionne di Cappuccini, 10 December 1852. Fonds Paris, D 151, "Etat des recettes et dépenses présumées pour l'année 1848," 13 December 1847.

32. Soeur Marie-Eugénie Pages to Abbé Balitrand, Gaillac, quoted in Darbon, *Souvenirs et documents*, 192–93.

33. ASJA, 1 A 4.4, Vialar to Mme d'Aubilly, 2 July 1856.

34. Indeed, the city's population quadrupled between 1830 and 1850; increasing numbers of the residents were Christian. Fawaz, *Merchants and Migrants*, 31, 47–48. ASJA, 1 A 4.6, Emilie Julien to Vialar, 14 January 1847.

35. Fawaz, *Merchants and Migrants*, 75–76. See also Thompson, *Colonial Citizens*.

36. Frazee, *Catholics and Sultans*, 277–79. In response, the British championed the Druzes in Lebanon. See Ma'oz, *Ottoman Reform*, 214.

37. AAE-Nantes, Rome–St. Siège, 573, Eugène Poujade, consul general, Beirut, to French ambassador, Rome, 31 May 1845.

38. ASJA, 12 A 1, Soeur Mary, novice to Vialar, 15 March 1847; 1 A 4.6, Julien to Vialar, 26 February 1847, 26 March 1847. ASJA, 12 A 1, Julien to Bourgade, 16 May 1847.

39. ASJA, 12 A 1, Julien to Vialar, 6 August 1847.

40. ASJA, 1 A 4.6, Julien to Bourgade, 5 October 1847.

41. ASJA, 1 A 4.6, Julien to Vialar, 6 April 1848; Julien to Bourgade, 5 October 1847; Julien to Vialar, 16 November 1847.

42. ASJA, 1 A 4.1, Vialar to Bourgade, 5 June 1847.

43. Christians enjoyed more freedoms under Egyptian rule than Ottoman; nonetheless, their status improved markedly compared to what it had been before 1831. Foreign consuls used the protection of Christians as an excuse to interfere in local affairs. For more details, see Ma'oz, *Ottoman Reform*, esp. chaps. 2, 14, 15, 16, and Shepherd, *Zealous Intruders*, chap. 4.

44. Shepherd, *Zealous Intruders*, 16, 26–28. Chateaubriand, *Itinéraire*.

45. For more details on the spread of missionary orders in the Holy Land, see Claude Langlois, "Les congrégations françaises en Terre sainte au XIXe siècle," in *De Bonaparte à Balfour*, ed. Trimbur and Aaronsohn, 219–39.

46. The position itself harkened back to the twelfth century, when Rome had established Latin patriarchs in the crusader kingdoms of Constantinople, Antioch, Jerusalem, and Alexandria. Thomas F. Stransky, "La concurrence des missions chrétiennes en Terre sainte, 1840–1850," in *De Bonaparte à Balfour*, ed. Trimbur and Aaronsohn, 213.

47. AAE-Nantes, Rome–St. Siège, 574, consul general, Jerusalem, to French ambassador, Rome, Holy See, 29 August 1844. See also Stransky, "La concurrence," 212.

48. Wandelburg, *La Palestine*, 142.

49. Stransky, "La concurrence," 217. *AAPF*, vol. 25, lettre de Mgr Valerga, patriarch de Jérusalem, à Messieurs les membres des Conseils centraux de la Propagation de la Foi, 20 January 1853, 203–5.

50. These included the London Missionary Society (founded in 1795), Church Missionary Society (1799), British and Foreign Bible Society (1804), London Society for Promoting Christianity among the Jews (1809), American Board of Commissioners for Foreign Missions (1810), Edinburgh Medical Missionary Society (1814), American Baptist Missionary Board (1814), Missionary Society of Basel (1815), American Bible Society (1816), Society for the Diffusion of Christianity among Jews (1824, Berlin), and Missionary Society of Berlin (1824). The first Protestant missionaries, Bibles in hand, arrived in the Holy Land in 1819. Stransky, "La concurrence," 198, 203.

51. Laurens, *La question de Palestine*, 52. On the attempts of Scottish churches to convert Jews in the Middle East, see Marten, *Attempting to Bring the Gospel Home*.

52. APF, Fonds Paris, E 19, lettre de Mgr Valerga, patriarch de Jérusalem, à Messieurs les membres des Conseils centraux, à Lyon et à Paris, 20 January 1853. Gadille and Zorn, "Le projet missionnaire," 141. See also Stransky, "La concurrence," 208–10.

53. AAE-Nantes, Rome–St. Siège, 574, French ambassador, Rome, Holy See, to Mgr Barnabò, secretary of Propaganda Fide, 19 February 1853; consul, Jerusalem, to foreign minister, 18 February 1855.

54. In 1849 Valerga traveled to Europe to convince the pope and the Catholic monarchs to support a claim by the Franciscans for the return of guardianship of the holy places, which they had lost to Greek Orthodox priests in 1755. Napoleon III championed their cause, submitting a joint request with the governments of Austria, Belgium, Spain, and Sardinia. In 1852 the Ottomans revised the agreement regarding custodianship of the holy places, angering the Russians. Frazee, *Catholics and Sultans*, 306.

55. AAE-Paris, Mémoires et Documents, Turquie, 127, Mgr Valerga, Latin patriarch of Jerusalem, to minister of foreign affairs, 16 December 1851.

56. AAE-Paris, Mémoires et Documents, Turquie, 127, note: Le patriarche latin de Jérusalem, n.d.

57. ASJA, 1 A 4.1, Vialar to Bourgade, 6 December 1849; 1 A 4.6, Julien to Bourgade, 7 July 1849.

58. ASJA, "Registre historique (Jérusalem)," 115.

59. APF, Fonds Lyon, E 20 (P), Julien to Valerga, 27 April 1852. APF, Fonds Paris, E 19, Valerga to président de l'oeuvre, 18 March 1853. On pilgrimages in this period, see Catherine Nicault, "Foi et politique: Les pèlerinages français en Terre sainte (850–1914)," in *De Bonaparte à Balfour*, ed. Trimbur and Aaronsohn.

60. ASJA, 12 A 1, Julien to Bourgade, 9 September 1851.

61. Enault, *La Terre-Sainte*, 204–6.

62. APF, Fonds Paris, E 14, Brunoni to M. Choiselet, 3 February 1854; délégation apostolique de la Syrie, 7 December 1855; E 19, Valerga to président de l'oeuvre, 20 January 1853.

63. APF, Fonds Paris, E 19, Valerga to Membres du Conseil central de Paris, 24 November 1851. See also his letters of 15 March 1853 and 18 March 1853.

64. ASJA, 1 A 4.3, Vialar to Soeur Céleste Peyre, 18 January 1854; 28 December 1853.

65. ASJA, 12 A 1, Julien to Vialar, 10 March 1850; 1 A 4.6, Julien to Bourgade, 7 July 1849.

66. APF, Fonds Paris, E 19, Valerga to président de l'oeuvre, 18 March 1855.

67. He did not say from what religion the nineteen individuals converted. The new sisters were almost surely from the Christian population. APF, Fonds Paris, E 19, Valerga to Messieurs les membres des Conseils centraux, 20 January 1853.

68. Quoted in Darbon, *Souvenirs et documents*, 456.

69. Ibid.

70. Frazee, *Catholics and Sultans*, 256–64. Concerned about this rapid expansion, the Ottoman government did not allow the new bishops to live in their sees.

71. ASJA, 1 A 4.4, Vialar to Augustin de Vialar, 28 June 1851.

72. ASJA, 1 A 4.3, Vialar to Soeur Gabrielle Coeur de Roy, 21 February 1852; Vialar to Soeur Eugénie Laurez, 25 July 1852.

73. ASJA, 1 A 4.3, Vialar to Soeur Gabrielle Coeur de Roy, 9 July 1852; Vialar to Soeur Eugénie Laurez, 25 July 1852.

74. Prop. Fide, Fondo (S.C.), Africa Centrale, vol. 5, C. du Havelt to minister of foreign affairs, France, 8 February 1851.

75. Prop. Fide, Fondo (S.C.), Armeni, vol. 41, French consul, Erzeroum, to foreign minister, Paris, 4 October 1852.

76. ASJA, 20 C, French consul, Erzeroum, to Vialar, 1 February 1853.

77. ASJA, "Registre historique (Trébizonde)," 122; 20 C, Maison diverses: Notes et renseignements utiles: Trébizonde, n.d.

78. ASJA, 20 C, Maison diverses: Notes et renseignements utiles: Trébizonde, n.d.

79. ASJA, "Registre historique (Erzéroum)," 128.

80. ASJA, "Registre historique (Alep)," 129.

81. Darbon, *Souvenirs et documents*, 477–81.

82. ASJA, "Registre historique (Alep)," 129.

83. Langlois, *Le catholicisme au féminin*, 556–57.

84. Woollacott, *Gender and Empire*, 96.

85. See Daughton, *Empire Divided*, esp. chaps. 1 and 8, for a discussion of this transformation.

CHAPTER 7

1. Anne-Marie Javouhey, *Lettres*, no. 1, to Balthasar Javouhey, n.d. [avant 11 novembre 1798].

2. Ibid., no. 5, to her father, 14 February 1802.

3. He made the purchase in 1812, and the Soeurs de St-Joseph added "de Cluny" to their name in order to distinguish themselves from other religious orders named for St. Joseph.

4. In the department of the Côte d'Or, where the Javouheys lived, 62 percent of the parish clergy took the oath in spring 1791 and 58 percent in autumn 1792. This was higher than the national rate of 52.3 percent (in 1791) and about double the rate of the very Catholic Vendée. Tackett, *Religion, Revolution, and Regional Culture*, 41, 320, 360.

5. Lecuir-Nemo, *Anne-Marie Javouhey*, 23–24. Javouhey, *Lettres*, no. 216, to Mère Rosalie Javouhey, 12 July 1830.

6. Hufton, *Women and the Limits of Citizenship*, chap. 3. Desan, *Reclaiming the Sacred*.

7. Javouhey, *Lettres*, no. 4, to her mother and her father, October 1800.

8. There is no contemporaneous specific record of this event, and even the retrospective accounts (which all date after Javouhey's death) suggest that its meaning was unclear to Javouhey at the time. In her letters, Javouhey's only reference to the dream consists of the following statement, made in 1807: "It was nine years ago that the Lord made me understand in a completely extraordinary, but certain, manner that he called me to the condition that I have embraced to teach the poor and raise orphans." Javouhey, *Lettres*, no. 20, to "un chef de bureau du Ministère des Cultes et de l'Instruction publique," 1 November 1807. The footnote added by the editor of her letters claims that this statement alludes to her dream of children of various races, as related in the *Annales historiques de la congrégation*. Rosalie Javouhey also interpreted it in this way in an 1867 circular to the Soeurs de St-Joseph. See *Notice sur la Congrégation*, 8, and Lecuir-Nemo, *Anne-Marie Javouhey*, 33–34.

9. Mezzadri, *Sainte Jeanne-Antide Thouret*, 110–12. Mezzadri, however, attributes Javouhey's departure to her newfound missionary vocation, 114.

10. ASJC, 2 A b 2.2, Dom Augustin de Lestrange to Balthasar Javouhey, 10 August 1803. Due to Pierre Javouhey's attempts to enter the Trappist order, Lestrange later had to defend himself against the charge that he was illegally recruiting in France. Laffay, *Dom Augustin de Lestrange*, 293, 300. Lecuir-Nemo, *Anne-Marie Javouhey*, 37, argues that Pierre's motivation was that he had drawn a bad lottery number and was therefore liable to be drafted. Hufton, *Women and the Limits of Citizenship*, 128–29, suggests that draft dodging was a male form of protest against the revolutionary regime and support for the church.

11. ASJC, 2 A b 5.2, Lestrange to Anne-Marie Javouhey, 20 April 1806.

12. Javouhey, *Lettres*, no. 10, to Dom Augustin de Lestrange, 1 May 1804.

13. ASJC, 2 A b 4.4a, Status de l'Association formée à Châlon sous le nom de Société de St-Joseph.

14. Lestrange was ultimately disappointed, however, as Napoleon abandoned the project of reestablishing the Trappists in France in 1811. Laffay, *Dom Augustin de Lestrange*, 326, 356.

15. ASJC, 2 A b 4.1, Règlement des Soeurs de Saint Joseph de Cluny fait par la fondatrice dans les commencements de l'Institut [ca. 1810].

16. Javouhey, *Lettres*, no. 20, to "un chef de bureau du Ministère des Cultes et de l'Instruction publique," 1 November 1807. Javouhey, *Lettres*, no. 25, to her father and mother, 7 February 1810. Lecuir-Nemo estimates Balthasar Javouhey's fortune at about one hundred thousand francs at the time of his death, having spent about an equal amount to pay off his daughters' debts and buy the Cluny house. Lecuir-Nemo, *Femmes et vocation missionnaire*, vol. 1, 20.

17. Javouhey, *Lettres*, no. 10, to Dom Augustin de Lestrange, 1 May 1804.

18. ASJC, 2 A b 3.2, M. l'Abbé Gally to Mère Rosalie Javouhey, 22 October 1863.

19. Javouhey, *Lettres*, no. 11, to Dom Augustin de Lestrange, August 1805.

20. Ibid., no. 60, to Mère Marie-Joseph Javouhey and Mère Clotilde Javouhey, begun 20 April, finished 22 May, 1822.

21. Lecuir-Nemo, *Anne-Marie Javouhey*, 360–61.

22. ASJC, 3 A, Rosalie Javouhey to Anne-Marie Javouhey, 28 June 1820. On the expansion of the Soeurs de St-Joseph de Cluny in France, see also Lecuir-Nemo, *Anne-Marie Javouhey*, 159–63.

23. For a full discussion, see Curtis, *Educating the Faithful*, 97–98.

24. Prudhomme, *Histoire religieuse*, 48–49, 53–54.

25. Javouhey, *Lettres*, no. 143, to Mère Rosalie Javouhey, 14–15 April 1827.

26. The colonial minister complained that the Soeurs de St-Paul de Chartres could not provide enough members for the colonies; moreover, not all of them had "the required qualities for such a destination." AN, F 19, 6211, minister of the navy and colonies to minister of religious affairs and public instruction, 1 July 1825. The Soeurs de St-Paul de Chartres appear to have made a comeback in the 1830s and 1840s in the Caribbean colonies and French Guiana.

27. AN F 19, 6208, "Etat actuel de la Congrégation de St-Joseph," 1825.

28. Javouhey, *Lettres*, no. 110, to Rosalie Javouhey, 13 September 1825.

29. AN, F 19, 6208, minister of the navy and colonies to minister of interior, 27 August 1816; minister of the navy and colonies to superior general of the Congrégation

des Soeurs de St-Joseph, 25 January 1822. For more details on the financial arrangements between the SJC and the government, see Lecuir-Nemo, *Femmes et vocation missionnaire*, 92–93.

30. AN, F 19, 6212, superior general, Soeurs de St-Joseph de Cluny, to minister of the interior, 20 March 1818.

31. Javouhey, *Lettres*, no. 128, to Mère Clothilde Javouhey, 25 November 1826.

32. The statutes allowed for a "supérieure principale" in each colony, named by the superior general, but that individual could modify statutes for local needs only with the express permission of the superior general; she also had to file a report every six months and accept the personnel decisions of the superior general. *Statuts de la Congrégation* (1827), 11–14.

33. The characterization of the two nuns' abilities was made by Governor Freycinet to the colonial minister, AOM, FM SG Réunion 21 129, 15 January 1823. See also Javouhey's description of Soeur Bathilde's qualities in *Lettres*, no. 89, to Rosalie Javouhey [between 1 and 14 January 1825].

34. Soeur Thaïs entered a Visitation convent in Nantes; one of the sisters entered the Soeurs de St-Joseph de Lyon (a different order altogether); one sister entered a Carmelite convent in Grenoble, one died in Bourbon, one returned to Cluny, and two others returned to the St-Joseph fold when Rosalie Javouhey arrived in Bourbon. ASJC, 2 A d, "Premier départ pour Bourbon." For more information on the Bourbon schism, see Lecuir-Nemo, *Anne-Marie Javouhey*, chap. 5.

35. Javouhey, *Lettres*, no. 102, to Rosalie Javouhey, 10 June 1825; no. 89, to Rosalie Javouhey [between 1 and 14 January 1825].

36. Goyau, *Un grand "homme,"* 94.

37. Javouhey, *Lettres*, no. 105, to Rosalie Javouhey, begun 25 July 1825, finished 5 August.

38. AOM, FM SG Réunion 429 4529, Rapport, Marine, Direction des colonies.

39. ASJC, 2 A d, Marie-Joseph Varin to Anne-Marie Javouhey, 21 November 1817; 29 April 1817.

40. Javouhey, *Lettres*, no. 107, to Mère Rosalie and all the sisters of Bourbon, 29 July 1825.

41. Ibid.; no. 122, to Mère Rosalie Javouhey in Bourbon, 1 May 1826.

42. Javouhey, *Lettres*, no. 110, to Mère Rosalie Javouhey in Bourbon, 13 September 1825.

43. ASJC, 2 A e (2), M. Terrasse, apostolic prefect of Senegal and Gorée, to superior general, 15 July 1819. AOM, FM SG Sénégal X 2 (c), commandant et administrateur du Sénégal to colonial minister, 19 April 1824. ASJC, 2 A d, Mère Rosalie Javouhey to Anne-Marie Javouhey, 5 July 1825.

44. Two causes of death and ages are unknown. ASJC, 2 A e (13), list of early sisters in St-Louis published in *La Voise de Nanette*, no. 6, January 1997.

45. AN, F 19 6210, superior general, Soeurs de St-Paul de Chartres, to minister of the interior, 22 May 1818.

46. Javouhey, *Lettres*, no. 111, to Rosalie Javouhey, 21 September 1825.

47. Ibid., no. 84, to Rosalie Javouhey, 31 October 1824, n. 1. ASJC, 2 A I (5), letter from eight nuns in Cayenne to superior general, 24 December 1849. AN, F 19, 6208, Raffin Goujat to minister of cults, 24 June 1852.

48. See Miles, *Wreck of the Medusa*.

49. ASJC, 3 A M. Ros., Rosalie Javouhey to Mère Clothilde Javouhey, no. 38, 15 January 1820; Rosalie Javouhey to Anne-Marie Javouhey, no. 42, 28 June 1820.

50. Javouhey, *Lettres*, no. 54, to her father, March 1822.

51. Cohen, *French Encounter*, 13–15.

52. Javouhey, *Lettres*, no. 35, to Soeur Marie-Joseph Varin, 21 May 1818.

53. ASJC, 3 A M. Ros., no. 74, Rosalie Javouhey to Clothilde Javouhey, 7 March 1822.

54. Britain also gained control over St-Louis and Gorée in 1758, during the Seven Years' War; Gorée was returned to France in 1763, but St-Louis remained in British hands until 1783. During the Napoleonic wars, Gorée was captured by the British in 1800, and St-Louis in 1809; both were restored in 1817.

55. Mbodj, "Abolition of Slavery," 200.

56. Renault, *L'abolition*, 6.

57. The number of slaves exported—and the impact of the transatlantic slave trade on Africa—is a matter of considerable scholarly debate. The number of 304,330 established by Philip Curtin has been disputed by Boubacar Barry, who estimates it as half a million for the British and French possessions in Senegambia from 1687 to 1810 and 6,000 slaves annually. See Curtin, *Economic Change*, chap. 4, and Barry, *Senegambia*, 62–65. James F. Searing estimates that approximately 200–300 slaves per year were exported from the region between Gorée and St-Louis. Searing, *West African Slavery*, 32–34. By the turn of the nineteenth century, slaves exported from Senegal constituted only 3 percent of the transatlantic trade. Getz, *Slavery and Reform*, 9.

58. Getz, *Slavery and Reform*, 24–26.

59. Klein, *Slavery and Colonial Rule*, 19. For a detailed study of the problems in stopping the French slave trade, see Daget, *La répression de la traite des noirs*.

60. Searing, *West African Slavery*, 163–64.

61. ASJC, 3 A M. Ros., no. 22, Rosalie Javouhey to Anne-Marie Javouhey, 7 April 1819. ANS, 3 E 2, Conseil de gouvernement et d'administration, "Sénace du 19 Juin 1820."

62. Javouhey, *Lettres*, no. 55, to Baron Roger, governor of Senegal, March or April 1822.

63. Between 1758 and 1817 St-Louis did not have a regular priest for fifty-four years and Gorée for thirty years. Knibiehler and Goutalier, *La femme au temps des colonies*, 59.

64. Cohen, *French Encounter*, 122–26. See also Crowder, *Senegal*, 12–13.

65. AOM, FM SG Sénégal II 2, "Notes demandées sur le Sénégal," 1821. ASJC, 2 A e (2), Baron Roger to Anne-Marie Javouhey, 27 April 1821.

66. Javouhey, *Letters*, no. 60, to Mère Marie-Joseph and to Mère Clothilde Javouhey, 22 May 1822. Bouche, *L'enseignement*, 401.

67. Biondi, *Saint-Louis du Sénégal*, 48. Brooks, "*Signares* of Saint-Louis and Gorée," 39–41. Sackur, "Development of Creole Society," 150–51. A description of these marriage rites is given in Boilat, *Esquisses sénégalaises*, 222–26. The issue of concubinage in imperial settings is discussed by Stoler, *Carnal Knowledge and Imperial Power*, 46–51.

68. Searing, *West African Slavery*, 96–97.

69. Sackur, "Development of Creole Society," 138. Brooks, "*Signares* of Saint-Louis and Gorée," 38. Not all signares were this successful; women whose mothers were not signares themselves would have married less eligible Europeans.

70. Sackur, "Development of Creole Society," 154, 279. Brooks, "*Signares* of Saint-Louis and Gorée," 33. Biondi, *Saint-Louis du Sénégal*, 68–69.

71. Javouhey, *Lettres*, no. 63, to Rosalie Javouhey, 25 May 1822; no. 62, to Clothilde Javouhey, 23 May 1822.

72. AOM, FM SG Sénégal X 3 bis, commission to governor, Senegal, 4 September 1841. In *Esquisses Sénégalaises*, 212, although acknowledging that they did not always speak French very well, the Abbé Boilat was more positive, reporting that "the young women are very modest and have good manners; they learn sewing, embroidery, and music."

73. Jones, "Catholic Mission," 325–29. Delcourt, *Histoire religieuse*, 18. Sackur, "Development of Creole Society," 240–41, 249–50, 257.

74. Boilat, *Esquisses Sénégalaises*, 209.

75. Biondi, *Saint-Louis du Sénégal*, 97–98. The law was not made retroactive, so only children born after 1830 were affected. Clergy were still complaining in the 1840s about "marriages à la mode du pays," suggesting that they did not disappear in 1830. AOM, FM SG Sénégal X 3 bis, Colonie du Sénégal: Rapport sur l'enseignement des écoles chrétiennes, 1 July 1846.

76. Searing, *West African Slavery*, 163–64.

77. Sackur, "Development of Creole Society," 290–91.

78. Javouhey, *Lettres*, no. 59, to Mère Clothilde Javouhey, end April/beginning May 1822.

79. Ibid., no. 70, "Etat des dépenses à faire pour une maison composée de vingt-cinq fillettes noires à établir au Sénégal," n.d. [December 1822 or January 1823].

80. The details that follow are taken from ASJC, 2 A e (3), "Arrêté portant établissement à St Louis d'une école de jeunes négresses"; "Instructions provisoires pour l'école des petites négresses de Saint Louis," 15 July 1826.

81. Bouche, *L'enseignement*, 402–3.

82. Javouhey, *Lettres*, no. 65, to Mère Marie-Joseph Javouhey, 6 September 1822; no. 112, to Soeur Agnès Goux, 3 November 1825.

83. Hastings, *Church in Africa*, 190–93. On the Muslim revolutions of the eighteenth century, see Barry, *Senegambia*, chap. 7.

84. Trimingham, *History of Islam in West Africa*, 224–27. Sackur, "Development of Creole Society," 289–90.

85. Bernard, *La Guyane française*, 53–54. Boilat, *Esquisses sénégalaises*, 207, 480–82.

86. Roger had failed three previous times to get a job in the colonies. Finally he was sent to Senegal to direct the new royal plantation at Koïel. On arrival he became the royal prosecutor, and then on a return trip to France he lobbied to become governor. He was the first civilian governor of Senegal and the first to have direct knowledge of the colony before his appointment. He also spoke Wolof and on his return to France in 1829 authored a French-Wolof grammar and dictionary, as well as a book of African fables and a supposedly true slave narrative. Georges Hardy, *La mise en valeur*, 117–19. It is likely that Javouhey recommended him for the post in Senegal, especially as he was accompanied by her cousin and godson, André Boissard. The Dagana land was held in Boissard's name. Lecuir-Nemo, *Anne-Marie Javouhey*, 87–88.

87. Miller, *French Atlantic Triangle*, 250–51. Most of the previous (and succeeding) governors were naval officers waiting for a higher rank or command. Biondi, *Saint-Louis du Sénégal*, 79.

88. Miller, *French Atlantic Triangle*, chap. 10.

89. Barry, *Senegambia*, 138. Schmaltz's tenure in Senegal, however, was not notably successful, marked by a failed attempt to settle two hundred French colonists on Cap Vert (adjacent to Gorée), and he left the colony impoverished.

90. ANS, 3 E 4, "Séance du 15 Mai 1822." Hardy, *La mise en valeur*, 48.

91. Biondi, *Saint-Louis du Sénégal*, 83–86. Barry, *Le royaume du Waalo*, 220–21. Miller, *French Atlantic Triangle*, 253.

92. Quoted in Hardy, *La mise en valeur*, 122.

93. Javouhey, *Lettres*, no. 65, to Mère Marie-Joseph Javouhey, 6 September 1822.

94. Ibid.

95. Ibid., no. 67, to M. de Mauduit, directeur des colonies, 25 November 1822; no. 68, to Rosalie Javouhey, 25 November 1822.

96. AOM, FM SG Sénégal II 2, copie d'une lettre écrite de la Rivière du Sénégal par Mr. J. J. Roger, 12 January 1820. Javouhey, *Lettres*, no. 65 to Mère Marie-Joseph Javouhey, 6 September 1822.

97. Miller, *French Atlantic Triangle*, 255.

98. Zuccarelli, "Le régime des engagés à temps," 420–24. See also Barry, *Le royaume du Waalo*, 231–34.

99. Engagés could be owned by private individuals and were traded in slave markets and not always freed; their children were also often not registered and traded as slaves. The French government also began to use *engagements à temps* in military recruitment. Klein, *Slavery and Colonial Rule*, 25. See also Hardy, *La mise en valeur*, 146; Barry, *Le royaume du Waalo*, 232, and Getz, *Slavery and Reform*, 46–51.

100. Javouhey, *Lettres*, no. 60, to Marie-Joseph Javouhey and Clotilde Javouhey, 20 April 1822–22 May 1822.

101. Presumably this decline also represents the fulfillment of fourteen-year terms of engagement begun in the late 1820s. Mbodj, "Abolition of Slavery in Senegal," 199. Zuccarelli, "Le régime des engagés à temps," 432, 437, 459.

102. Barry, *Senegambia*, 138–39. More details can be found in his *Le royaume du Waalo*, 223–31, 235–36. See also Getz, *Slavery and Reform*, 45–46. Poor crop yields resulted from environmental and ecological changes in the region. Searing, *West African Slavery*, 172.

103. ASJC, 6 A d 2, Baron Roger to Javouhey, 18 November 1825.

104. Quoted in Hardy, *La mise en valeur*, 232.

105. Biondi, *Saint-Louis du Sénégal*, 88–89. Hardy, *La mise en valeur*, 244–45.

106. In 1825, gum accounted for three-quarters of Senegal's export trade. Peanuts were favored when French industrialists decided to use peanut oil as a lubricant. Barry, *Senegambia*, 140–42. Searing, *West African Slavery*, 166–67. Lecuir-Nemo, *Anne-Marie Javouhey*, 125–26.

107. ASJC 2 A e (2), secretary of state and interior to superior general, 27 August 1822. Javouhey, *Lettres*, no. 71, to Mère Rosalie Javouhey, 28 January 1823.

108. AOM, FM SG Sénégal X 2 (c), commandant et administrateur du Sénégal to colonial minister, 10 June 1823; Governor MacCarthy, Sierra Leone to Baron Roger, governor, Senegal, 31 July 1823.

109. Bouquillon and Cornevin, *David Boilat*, 15–16.

110. Javouhey, *Lettres*, no. 71, to Mère Rosalie Javouhey, 28 January 1823.

111. Ibid., no. 73, to Governor MacCarthy [between 22 March and 31 December 1823].

112. Ibid., no. 71, to Mère Rosalie Javouhey, 28 January 1823.

113. Ibid. AOM, FM SG Sénégal X 2 (c), Javouhey to Soeurs de St-Joseph de Cluny, 22 April 1823. Javouhey, *Lettres*, no. 72, to Soeur Euphémie Grousset, 22 March 1823.

114. For the international politics surrounding the treaty of 1818, which allowed this practice, see Daget, *La répression de la traite des noirs*.

115. The population of Freetown went from 1,871 in 1807 to 15,081 in 1822. Sanneh, *Abolitionists Abroad*, 111. The missionaries were mainly provided by the Church Missionary Society (CMS).

116. Fyfe, *History of Sierra Leone*, 128–31. Sanneh, *Abolitionists Abroad*, 113.

117. AOM, FM SG Sénégal X 2 (d), Javouhey to colonial minister, 21 April 1824.

118. AOM, FM SG Sénégal X 2 (d), Abbé Clausel de Conssergues, vicar general, Beauvais, to colonial minister, 22 April 1824; curé, Fontainebleau, to Javouhey, 11 June 1829.

119. AOM, FM SG Sénégal X 2 (e), governor, Senegal, to colonial minister, 24 August 1824.

120. Bouquillon and Cornevin, *David Boilat*, 35. Lecuir-Nemo, *Anne-Marie Javouhey*, 170–72. For a complete list of the children, see Lecuir-Nemo, *Femmes et vocation missionnaire*, 162.

121. Bernard, *La Guyane française*, 56.

122. Javouhey, *Lettres*, no. 120, to Mère Rosalie Javouhey, 23 February 1826. Florence's godmother was the wife of the minister of the navy. Nine had already been baptized in Senegal. Lecuir-Nemo, *Femmes et vocation missionnaire*, 162.

123. Javouhey, *Lettres*, no. 84, to Rosalie Javouhey, 31 October 1824; no. 204, to Mère Clotilde Javouhey, 13 July 1829; no. 176, to Marie-Joseph Javouhey, 21 June 1828; no. 188, to Marie-Joseph Javouhey, 3 and 12 February 1829.

124. ASJC, 2 A d (3), "Notes sur les jeunes Sénégalais," n.d. Javouhey also moved the African school because the bishop of Beauvais objected to its proximity to the SJC novitiate.

125. Javouhey, *Lettres*, no. 250, to Clotilde Javouhey, first days of May 1832; no. 253, to Mère Marie-Joseph Javouhey, 28 May 1832; no. 315, to Clotilde Javouhey, 30 December 1834.

126. AOM, FM SG Sénégal X 2 (e), Pierre Moussa to governor, Senegal, 2 December 1833; FM SG Sénégal X 2 (d), governor, Senegal, to colonial minister, 19 November 1833; Soeur Clothilde Javouhey to colonial minister, 21 August 1832. See also ASJC, 2 A f, four Senegalese children to colonial minister, 16 August 1832.

127. Lecuir-Nemo, *Femmes et vocation missionnaire*, 162.

128. Lecuir-Nemo, *Anne-Marie Javouhey*, 183. Jones, "Catholic Mission," 333.

129. Javouhey, *Lettres*, no. 432, to Baron Roger, 10 August 1840. In letter after letter from French Guiana, she requested that the priests be sent to join her at Mana, where she thought they could do immense good.

130. ASJC, 6 A d 2, Roger to Javouhey, 1 June 1842; 2 A f, "Extraits des lettres de la Chère Mère Marie-Joseph rélatifs aux jeunes Africains," no. 185, 19 June 1838.

131. See Jones, "Catholic Mission," 335–37, for a full account of this episode. See also Boilat, *Esquisses sénégalaises*, 227–43, for his account of the founding of the *collège*.

132. Jones, "Catholic Mission," 337–38. Renault, *L'abolition de l'esclavage*, 7. Boilat, *Esquisses sénégalaises*, 18–19, 232. Lecuir-Nemo, *Anne-Marie Javouhey*, 189.

133. Javouhey, *Lettres*, no. 681, to Soeur Marie-Thérèse Griffaut, 26 April 1846; no. 703, to Rosalie Javouhey, 23 July 1846. His excommunication was lifted shortly before his death, but he did not receive word of it in time.

134. Lecuir-Nemo, *Anne-Marie Javouhey*, 186–87. On Boilat's subsequent career, see Bouquillon and Cornevin, *David Boilat*, chaps. 4–5.

135. Boilat also described a project for agricultural colonization among the Waalo. See esp. Boilat, *Esquisses sénégalaises*, 21, 23, 475–76, and the introduction to the Karthala edition written by Abdoulaye-Bara Diop. Boilat was also the author of a prize-winning Wolof grammar.

136. On Libermann's efforts (and Javouhey as a precursor), see Josef-Theodor Rath, "Libermann: Promoteur du clergé africain (1840–1849)," in Coulon and Brasseur, et al, eds., *Libermann*. When Libermann's missionaries came to Senegal in the late 1840s, Javouhey's African priests considered them rivals, both out of loyalty to the Saint-Esprit seminary, where they had been trained, and out of a preference for a black church that they would lead. Jones, "Catholic Mission," 339.

137. Javouhey, *Lettres*, no. 117, to Mère Rosalie Javouhey, 13 January 1826; no. 553, to Soeur Madeleine Collonge, 25 March 1844. She also outlined a similar project in several letters (nos. 272, 274, 277) in 1833 and 1834.

138. Langlois, "Anne-Marie Javouhey," 138.

139. Bouche, *L'enseignement*, 403.

140. Paule Brasseur, "Le Sénégal et sa lente intégration au mouvement abolitionniste (1815–1830)," in *Rétablissement*, ed. Bénot and Dorigny, 384.

141. Javouhey, *Lettres*, no. 65, to Mère Marie-Joseph Javouhey, 6 September 1822; no. 71, to Mère Rosalie Javouhey, 28 January 1823; no. 86, "à un ministre," 31 October 1824.

CHAPTER 8

1. ASJC, 2 A i (3), "Mana: Renseignements fournis par Auguste Javouhey en 1875 pour 1821–1838." Auguste Javouhey was the son of her cousin Louis Javouhey.

2. Javouhey, *Lettres*, no. 149, to M. Lallemand, curé de Saffres, 17 August 1827. ASJC, 2 A I (3), "Souvenirs de Sr Philémon Poulachon sur la Guyane."

3. ASJC, 2 A i, "Projet d'établissement à former à Mana par les soeurs St-Joseph de Cluny à la Mana," 29 August 1827.

4. AOM, FM SG Guyane 60, "Etat nominatif des soeurs de la congrégation de St-Joseph de Cluny et des colons composant la colonisation de Mana," 17 August 1828 to 15 July 1832.

5. Javouhey, *Lettres*, no. 199, to Mère Marie-Joseph Javouhey, 16 June 1829. AOM, FM SG Guyane 60, "Notes de Madame la Supérieure Génerale," July 1829.

6. This idea was not entirely new. In 1763, in the wake of the loss of France's Canadian possessions, 12,000 French colonists, mainly from Alsace and Lorraine, were

recruited to emigrate to Guiana at considerable cost to the state. Seven thousand died in the first two years, 2,000–3,000 returned to France, and approximately 1,800 remained in Guiana. Mam-Lam-Fouck, *Histoire générale*, 65. See also Lawrence C. Jennings, "Peuplement d'Américains en Guyane: Une colonisation avortée, 1819–1822," in *L'histoire de la Guyane*, ed. Mam-Lam-Fouck and Zonzon, 355–66.

7. Serge Mam-Lam-Fouck, "Apogée, déclin et disparition du système esclavagiste (première moitié du XIXe siècle)," in *Deux siècles d'esclavage*, ed. Bruleaux, Calmont, and Mam-Lam-Fouck, 144, 210, 219, 228–31.

8. The migrants appeared to have been poorly chosen; the members of one family were winemakers, and another family sought to open a cabaret. AOM, FM SG Guyane 61, "Précis sur la colonisation des bords de la Mana (Guyane française)," 20 February 1835, 21, 53–54, 80–81, 85.

9. AOM, FM SG Guyane 60, minister of the navy and colonies to king, Rapport, 22 August 1827.

10. AOM, FM SG Guyane 61, "Précis," 20 February 1835, 90.

11. AOM, FM SG Guyane 60, governor, French Guiana (Baron Freycinet), to minister of the navy and colonies, 24 February 1829. In 1833 the Soeurs de St-Joseph de Cluny took over the leper hospital, where two sisters cared for approximately 125 lepers.

12. Javouhey, *Lettres*, no. 179, to M. Millot, ordonnateur de la Guyane, between 23 and 31 August 1828; no. 185, to Soeur Séraphine Roussot, 18 December 1828.

13. Ibid., no. 206, to M. Jubelin, 13–31 August 1829; no. 204, to Mère Clothilde Javouhey, 13 July 1829.

14. Ibid., no. 183, to Soeur Séraphine Roussot, end of October 1828; no. 204, to Mère Clothilde Javouhey, 13 July 1829.

15. AOM, FM SG Guyane 60, Governor Jubelin to minister of the navy and colonies, 31 December 1829.

16. ASJC, 2 A i (3), "Souvenirs de Sr Philémon Poulachon."

17. ASJC, 2 A i (3), "Mana: Renseignements," 1875. Javouhey, *Lettres*, no. 199, to Mère Marie-Joseph Javouhey, 16 June 1829. AOM, FM SG Guyane 60, Governor Jubelin to minister of the navy and colonies, 31 December 1829.

18. Javouhey, *Lettres*, no. 241, to M. de Saint-Hilaire, directeur des colonies, and no. 243, to M. Jubelin, 22–30 September 1831. Bernard, *La Guyane française*, 61.

19. AOM, FM SG Guyane 60, Governor Jubelin to minister of the navy and colonies, 31 December 1829. AOM, FM SG Guyane 60, "Etat nominatif des soeurs…et colons," 17 August 1828 to 15 July 1832.

20. AOM, FM SG Guyane 60, Governor Jubelin, French Guiana, to minister of the navy and colonies, 10 October 1832; "Précis," 20 February 1835, 104.

21. Marie-Louise Marchant-Thébault, "L'esclavage en Guyane sous l'ancien régime," in *Deux siècles d'esclavage*, ed. Bruleaux, Calmont, and Mam-Lam-Fouck, 13.

22. AOM, FM SG Guyane 61, "Précis," 20 February 1835, 61–62.

23. AOM, FM SG Guyane 60, Governor Jubelin, French Guiana, to minister of the navy and colonies, 10 October 1832; 31 December 1829; unknown to Anne-Marie Javouhey, 23 May 1828.

24. AOM, FM SG Guyane 60, Governor Jubelin, French Guiana, to minister of the navy and colonies, 10 October 1832. Javouhey, *Lettres*, no. 214, to Mère Clotilde Javouhey, 25 June 1830.

25. There were thirty-two of each, including the twenty-nine Soeurs de St-Joseph. AOM, FM SG Guyane 60, Governor Jubelin, French Guiana, to minister of the navy and colonies, 10 October 1832.

26. AOM, FM SG Guyane 61, governor of French Guiana to minister of the navy and colonies, 2 June 1837. On the government workshops, see Pascale Cornuel, "Esclavagisme et engagisme: Le cas de l'atelier colonial de Cayenne (1818–1848)," in *L'histoire de la Guyane*, ed. Mam-Lam-Fouck and Zonzon, 369–89.

27. ASJC, 2 A i (3), "Colonisation de Mana," n.d. Javouhey, *Lettres*, no. 384, to Admiral Duperré, minister of the navy and colonies, 10 April 1838.

28. AOM, FM SG Guyane 61, untitled report from Commission, Département de la Marine, 2 June 1835. Léopold Javouhey estimated the actual payment as 25,000 francs for 477 blacks, or a little more than 52 francs per person. ASJC, 2 A I, "Notes sur quelques essais de colonisation à la Guyane Française," 71. Between 1836 and 1839 the French government spent 237,414 francs on the Mana colony. AOM, FM SG Guyane 61, "Rapport de l'Ordonnateur sur la colonisation des noirs libérés établis sur les bords de la Mana sous la direction de Madame la Supérieure Générale de la Congrégation de St. Joseph de Cluny," 5 October 1839.

29. Javouhey, *Lettres*, no. 369, to Admiral Rosamel, minister of the navy and colonies, 24 August 1836.

30. Mana was not the first abolitionist plan tried in Guiana. In 1785 the Marquis de Lafayette and his wife—a devout Catholic—had also attempted a small-scale abolitionist experiment with about fifty slaves on a plantation they purchased outside of Cayenne. See Willens, "Lafayette's Emancipation Experiment," 222–24.

31. When slave ships were captured, it was common for the slaves to be transferred to public works projects in Senegal or Guiana or simply to "disappear" onto plantations. See Daget, "Abolition of the Slave Trade," 69–71. Guiana received about five thousand slaves from 1817 to 1831 from the clandestine slave trade. Mam-Lam-Fouck, "Apogée," 219. On the new legal measures, see Jennings, *French Anti-Slavery*, 32–33.

32. The French seized a total of about 1,500 Africans, distributed as follows among the four slave colonies: Bourbon 700, Guiana 520, Martinique 250, and Guadeloupe 30. AOM, FM SG Guyane 61, "Rapport: Projet de remettre à Madame la supérieure générale des soeurs de St-Joseph de Cluny les noirs libérés," 20 October 1834.

33. Although Javouhey's intention was to provide these children with a better life, it opened her up to charges of engaging in the illegal slave trade. Lecuir-Nemo, *Anne-Marie Javouhey*, 240.

34. AOM, FM SG Guyane 61, "Notes sur les observations de Mr le Gouverneur de la Guyane au sujet de l'établissement projeté des noirs à la Mana," n.d.

35. AOM, FM SG Guyane 61, "Extrait des délibération du conseil colonial, M. Gibelin," 17 June 1835.

36. Marchand-Thébault, "L'esclavage," 43. The report from the exploration party of 1820 confirmed the lack of danger from Maroni maroons. AOM, FM SG Guyane 61, "Précis," 20 February 1835, 21. For details on the Maroni maroons, see Moomou, *Le monde des Marrons*.

37. Colonists were poorer also and less able to afford slaves. In 1832 only 28 out of 469 white plantation owners owned more than one hundred slaves. Twenty-three of these plantations grew sugar cane. Mam-Lam-Fouck, "Apogée," 145.

38. Marchand-Thébault, "L'esclavage," 16–17, 30–31, 38, 41–42.

39. Mam-Lam-Fouck, "Apogée," 256–57.

40. Javouhey, *Lettres*, no. 380, to Mère Rosalie Javouhey, 23 February 1838. Very rarely using the whip as a disciplinary measure, Javouhey occasionally incarcerated individuals and on at least two occasions turned over justice to a black jury.

41. AOM, FM SG Guyane 61, untitled report from Commission, Département de la Marine, 2 June 1835. Javouhey, *Lettres*, no. 383, "Exposé sur l'état de Mana," first months of 1838.

42. ASJC, 2 A i (1), "Rapport du Ministre de la Marine, M. Duperré, au Roi, sur l'état des esclaves de saisie dans les colonies," 14 August 1835; Admiral Rosamel, minister of the navy and colonies, to governor of French Guyana, September 1835. Javouhey, *Lettres*, no. 380, to Mère Rosalie Javouhey, 23 February 1838.

43. Javouhey, *Lettres*, no. 412, to Soeur Joséphine Tarriot, 30 August 1839.

44. On the slave economy of this period, see Klein, *African Slavery*. For specifics on French Guiana, see Mam-Lam-Fouck, "Apogée."

45. Javouhey, *Lettres*, no. 381, to Mère Clotilde Javouhey, 15 March 1838.

46. Each family also had a plot two leagues upriver. AOM, FM SG Guyane 61, "Rapport de Mr le Gouverneur de la Guyane Française sur l'Etablissement de Mana, Inspection de 1838."

47. ASJC, 6 A d 2, "Lettres addressées à Mère Javouhey," 14 December 1836. AOM, FM SG Guyane 61, "Rapport de Mr le Gouverneur…Inspection de 1838." Javouhey, *Lettres*, no. 389, to Mère Marie-Thérèse Javouhey, 23 October 1838.

48. ASJC, 2 A i (3), "Souvenirs de Sr Philémon Poulachon," n.d.

49. She indeed made a stop in Senegal on her return to Mana in 1835 to effect this plan but managed to procure only a half dozen women among the government population of "engagées," as most were too old. AOM, FM SG Guyane 61, governor of Senegal to minister of the navy and colonies, 1 February 1836.

50. ASJC, 2 A i, Général L. Javouhey, "Notes sur quelques essais de colonisation à la Guyane Française," 74. Javouhey, *Lettres*, no. 384, to Admiral Duperré, minister of the navy and colonies, 10 April 1838; no. 383, "Exposé sur l'état de Mana" [premiers mois de 1838].

51. Javouhey, *Lettres*, no. 383, "Exposé sur l'état de Mana [premiers mois de 1838]."

52. ASJC, 2 A i (3), "Mana: Renseignements," 1875.

53. Javouhey, *Lettres*, no. 429, to Admiral Rosame, minister of the navy and colonies, 25 July 1840.

54. Ibid., no. 382, to Baron Roger, between 15 March and 28 May 1838; no. 441, 1 January 1841; no. 432, 10 August 1840.

55. Ibid., no. 463, to Admiral Duperré, minister of the navy and colonies, 26 June 1841.

56. Ibid., no. 252, to Mère Marie-Joseph Javouhey, 12 May 1832; no. 182, to Mère Marie-Joseph Javouhey, 17 September 1828; no. 259, to Soeur Madeleine Collonge in Senegal, 1 August 1832; no. 311, to Mère Marie-Thérèse Javouhey in Martinique, 9 December 1834.

57. Ibid., no. 421, to Mère Marie-Joseph Javouhey, 1 March 1840.

58. Ibid., no. 384, to Admiral Duperré, 10 April 1838.

59. Ibid., no. 855, vol. 4, 56, to Mère Raphaël Montet, 31 August 1848.

60. Ibid., no. 429, to Admiral Duperré, 25 July 1840.

61. Ibid., no. 384, vol. 2, to Admiral Duperré, 10 April 1838.

62. Ibid., no. 429, vol. 2, to Admiral Rosame, 25 July 1840.

63. Ibid., no. 59, vol. 1, to Mère Clotilde Javouhey, late April or early May 1822.

64. Ibid., no. 423, vol. 2, to Monsieur Gondin, curé de Chabeuil, 23 April 1840. AOM, FM SG Guyane 61, governor, French Guiana (Laurens de Choisy), to minister of marine and colonies, 15 September 1837. Javouhey, *Lettres*, no. 594, vol. 3, to Admiral de Mackau, minister of marine and colonies, 5 March 1845.

65. Javouhey, *Lettres*, no. 317, to Mère Rosalie Javouhey, between 1–19 January 1835; no. 463, to Admiral Duperré, 26 June 1841.

66. Delisle, *Catholicisme, esclavage et acculturation*, 28.

67. Javouhey, *Lettres*, no. 529, to M. Layrle, governor of Guiana, 31 May 1843.

68. Ibid., no. 384, vol. 2, 245, to Admiral Duperré, 10 April 1838.

69. Ibid., no. 594, to Admiral de Mackau, 5 March 1845.

70. Ibid., no. 384, to Admiral Duperré, 10 April 1838.

71. Ibid., no. 489, to Mère Théophile Montet, 25 March 1842; ASJC, 2 A i, "Monographie de l'école primaire des filles de Mana."

72. Javouhey, *Lettres*, no. 448, to M. de Saint-Hilaire, director of colonies, 4 March 1841. In other letters, the ages of the children are specified as five to fifteen.

73. Ibid., no. 463, to Admiral Duperré, 26 June 1841.

74. Ibid., no. 381, to Mère Clothilde Javouhey, 15 March 1838.

75. Ibid., no. 183, to Mère Marie-Joseph Javouhey, 17 September 1828; no. 277, to Mère Rosalie Javouhey, 22 January 1834.

76. Mörner, *Political and Economic Activities*, 199.

77. Marchand-Thébault, "L'esclavage," 46–47, 61–62. On the social structure of the Jesuit reductions among the Guaraní in Paraguay and their cultural impact, see Ganson, *Guaraní under Spanish Rule*.

78. The Indians came to Mana to trade; they also hunted or fished for a fee. Javouhey sometimes acquiesced to requests to serve as godmother for those who wanted their children baptized, and in 1846 two Soeurs de St-Joseph established a permanent base in the Indian village. ASJC, 2 A i (3), "Mana: Renseignements," 1875. AOM, FM SG Guyane 61, "Rapport…Inspection de 1838."

79. ASJC, 2 A i (1), "Projet d'établissement," 29 August 1827.

80. More than one hundred utopian communities were established in the United States before the Civil War. Kumar, *Utopianism*, 73. See also Guarneri, *Utopian Alternative*.

81. However, when his so-called disciple Jules Lechevalier developed a more detailed plan in the 1840s to replace slavery in Guiana with a form of labor based on association, it was widely denounced by abolitionists as a means not to free slaves but to advance the interests of plantation owners through a coercive form of "associative" labor far removed from Fourierist principles. For a full discussion of this plan see Jennings, "Associative Socialism and Slave Emancipation."

82. On these individuals, see Berenson, *Populist Religion*, chap. 2. See also Pilbeam, "Dream Worlds?"

83. Beecher, *Victor Considerant*, 2.

84. I am grateful to Naomi J. Andrews for this insight.

85. For a full survey of utopian socialist views on slavery, see Schmidt, *Abolitionnistes de l'esclavage*, chap. 15.

86. ASJC, 6 A 2 d, from St-Hilaire, maitre des requêtes et directeur des colonies, 8 August 1836. Bernard, *La Guyane française*, 63.

87. On the origins of Liberia, see Clegg, *Price of Liberty*, chaps. 1–3.

88. Hall, "Missionary Stories," 237, 241–44. Hall, *Civilising Subjects*, 136. On Baptists in Jamaica, see also Turner, *Slaves and Missionaries*.

89. Javouhey, *Lettres*, no. 351, vol. 2, to Mère Rosalie Javouhey, 11 October 1835.

90. Fredrickson, *Racism*, 9.

91. Although historians see biological racism as rooted in scientific concepts of the origins of people developed during the Enlightenment, those ideas did not become orthodoxy until much later in the nineteenth century. For a full discussion of this issue, see Cohen, *French Encounter*, chap. 8, and Hannaford, *Race*, chaps. 7 and 8.

92. In the decade between 1838 and 1847, there were 290 births and 150 deaths. Morbidity was also low, estimated at 5 percent (individuals admitted to the hospital), mainly men suffering wounds from cutting wood and women giving birth. AOM, FM SG Guyane 61, compte rendu, n.d.; "Rapport…Inspection de 1838." For a comparative view, see Richard B. Sheridan, "Slave Demography in the British West Indies and the Abolition of the Slave Trade," in *Abolition of the Atlantic Slave Trade*, ed. David Eltis and James Walvin, 259–85.

93. AOM, FM SG Guyane 61, contrôleur colonial to governor, French Guiana, 26 June 1846.

94. In 1845, 68 percent of all adults at Mana were married; 92 percent of the children born between 1838 and 1843 were legitimate. Mam-Lam-Fouck, *La Guyane française*, 181.

95. AOM, FM SG Guyane 61, "Rapport…Inspection de 1838"; chef du bureau du domaine to ordonnateur, 17 April 1838.

96. AOM, FM SG Guyane 61, contrôleur colonial to governor, French Guiana, 26 June 1846; governor of French Guiana to minister of the navy and colonies, 29 October 1841.

97. From 1841 to 1847, this rate was never higher than 1.75 percent despite marriage presents and other incentives given to slaves owned by the government. Mam-Lam-Fouck, "Apogée," 178.

98. AOM, FM SG Guyane 61, "Rapport du conseil colonial de la Guyane Française à S. E. Mr le Ministre de la Marine et des colonies rélativement à l'établissement de la Mana," n.d.

99. AOM, FM SG Guyane 61, governor, French Guiana, to minister of the navy and colonies, 6 October 1843; contrôleur colonial to governor, French Guiana, 26 June 1846; governor, French Guiana, to minister of the navy and colonies, "envoi de tableaux statistiques relatifs à la population de Mana," 5 August 1844.

100. AOM, FM SG Guyane 61, "Rapport du conseil colonial," n.d.

101. ASJC, 2 A i (1), Rapport du Gouverneur Charmasson, 5 December 1842. AOM, FM SG Guyane 61, "Rapport sur l'état de l'esclavage dans la colonie de Surinam et sur le travail libre dans la Guyane anglaise, par M. F. de Caselnau, Extrait, Mana," 22 June 1847.

102. Javouhey, *Lettres*, no. 385, to Mère Marie-Joseph Javouhey, 3 June 1838.

103. Mam-Lam-Fouck, "Apogée," 183–85. For a discussion of the problems of source material and interpretation of the religious life of slaves in Guiana, see: "Réflexions sur les sources du XIXe siècle," in *L'histoire de la Guyane*, ed. Mam-Lam-Fouck and Zonzon, 221–32.

104. AOM, FM SG Guyane 61, "Note statistique sur l'établissement de Mana," 19 November 1854.

105. Delisle, "Colonisation, christianisation et émancipation," 32.

106. AOM, FM SG Guyane 61, "Rapport de l'Ordonnateur sur la colonisation des noirs libérés établis sur les bords de la Mana sous la direction de Madame la Supérieure générale de la Congrégation de St. Joseph de Cluny," 5 October 1839. Similar complaints appear in almost all subsequent government reports.

107. AOM, FM SG Guyane 61, governor, French Guiana, to minister of the navy and colonies, 6 October 1843.

108. Ibid., 29 October 1841.

109. AOM, FM SG Guyane 61, contrôleur colonial to governor, French Guiana, 26 June 1846. On the export value of the woods, see Javouhey, Lettres, no. 376, to Baron Roger, July–December 1837, and no. 387, to Mère Rosalie Javouhey, 17 August 1838.

110. AOM, FM SG Guyane 61, governor, French Guiana, to minister of the navy and colonies, 6 October 1843.

111. AOM, FM SG Guyane 61, Rapport du Conseil colonial de la Guyane française à S. E. Mr le Ministre de la Marine et des colonies rélativement à l'établissement de la Mana," n.d.; governor, French Guiana, to minister of the navy and colonies, 29 October 1841; 6 October 1843.

112. AOM, FM SG Guyane 61, contrôleur colonial to governor, French Guiana, 12 June 1846. The inability of the Indians in Guiana to assimilate to French norms was a longstanding trope in the writings about them. See Hurault, Les Indiens de Guyane française.

113. Javouhey, Lettres, no. 493, to Admiral Duperré, 29 April 1842.

114. Ibid., no. 384, to Admiral Duperré, 10 April 1838.

115. Ibid., no. 186, to Mère Marie-Joseph Javouhey, 31 December 1828.

116. Ibid., no. 408, to minister of the navy and colonies, 20 August 1839.

117. Ibid., no. 184, to Mère Clothilde Javouhey, 14 November 1828.

118. AOM, FM SG Guyane 61, governor, French Guiana, to minister of the navy and colonies, 15 July 1846; contrôleur colonial to governor, French Guiana, 26 June 1846; arrêté concernant l'établissement de Mana, 22 December 1846.

119. AOM, FM SG Guyane 61, governor, French Guiana, to minister of the navy and colonies, 15 July 1846. In 1847, Mélinon married Soeur Juliette, who left the order. AOM, FM SG Guyane 61, Soeur Isabelle, superior, Mana, to Anne-Marie Javouhey, 7 April 1847.

120. AOM, FM SG Guyane 61, "Compte rendu présenté à Monsieur le Gouverneur de la Guyane Française," n.d.; governor, French Guiana, to minister of the navy and colonies, 28 December 1847; H. d'Ellisalde to governor, French Guiana, 21 December 1847.

121. The Frères de Plöermel, founded in 1819 in Brittany, stayed only two years (1845–46), at which time the instruction of boys reverted to the Soeurs de St-Joseph. AOM, FM SG Guyane 61, governor, French Guiana, to minister of the navy and colonies, 28 December 1847; "Compte rendu présenté à M. le Gouverneur de la Guyane Française, sur la situation de la colonie des noirs libérés," n.d. ASJC, 2 A I (3), "Monographie de l'école primaire des filles de Mana," n.d.

122. AOM, FM SG Guyane 61, Soeur Victoire Richard to Anne-Marie Javouhey, 8 April 1847. Soeur Isabelle, the new superior at Mana, reported that only five beds in the

hospital were reserved for blacks. AOM, FM SG Guyane 61, "Rapport à Monsieur le Gouverneur de la Guyane française sur l'Etablissement de Mana," 20 August 1846. Javouhey herself seemed less concerned, arguing that the new regime "will not impede us from doing good." Javouhey, *Lettres*, no. 725, to Soeur Madeleine Collonge, 16 December 1846.

123. AOM, FM SG Guyane 61, governor, French Guiana, to minister of the navy and colonies, 1 December 1847.

CHAPTER 9

1. ASJC, Affaire d'Autun, "Extraits du Décret de Mgr d'Héricourt, évêque d'Autun à la Congrégation des Soeurs de St-Joseph de Cluny," 4 October 1833.

2. Javouhey, *Lettres*, no. 346, to Mère Marie-Thérèse Javouhey, 15 August 1835.

3. Ibid., no. 364, to Mère Théophile Montet, 15 March 1836; no. 486, to Mères Marie-Joseph and Rosalie Javouhey, 14 March 1842.

4. ASJC, Affaire d'Autun, "Lettre collective des Supérieures de Rouen, Asile St-Yon et Collège et de la Supérieure de Darnetal, à la Mère Fondatrice, pour protester contre le changement des Statuts de 1827," 12 July 1835.

5. Langlois, "Anne-Marie Javouhey," 139. Javouhey, *Lettres*, no. 455, to Mère Rosalie Javouhey, 7 April 1841.

6. Javouhey, *Lettres*, no. 640, to Soeur Léonce Tristant, between 15 and 19 December 1845. ASJC, affaire d'Autun, Soeur Theothiste Larfouilloux to Rosalie Javouhey, 15 September 1845.

7. ASJC, Affaire d'Autun, "Note de Soeur Bathilde Laparre relative au comportement de la Fondatrice, avant son départ pour la Guyane en Decembre 1835." Javouhey, *Lettres*, no. 378, to Soeur Onésime Lefèvre, 29 January 1838, note 3; no. 537, to Soeur Madeleine Collonge, 2 October 1843.

8. ASJC, Affaire d'Autun, M. Duperré to bishop of Autun, 12 January 1836. ASJC, 2 A i (3), Baron Roger to Anne-Marie Javouhey, 14 December 1836.

9. Javouhey, *Lettres*, no. 630, to Rosalie Javouhey, 17 November 1845.

10. ASJC, Affaire d'Autun, Rosalie Javouhey to Anne-Marie Javouhey, 22 August 1845. Javouhey, *Lettres*, no. 625, "Circulaire à toutes les religieuses de la congrégation," 25 October 1845.

11. ASJC, Affaire d'Autun, Mgr d'Héricourt to Mgr Gignoux, bishop of Beauvais, 3 August 1844; Mgr Héricourt to a bishop in Italy, 7 January 1847. See also Javouhey, *Lettres*, no. 702, to Mère Rosalie Javouhey, 20 July 1846.

12. Monseigneur Affre inherited this dispute from his predecessor, Mgr de Quelen. See Kilroy, *Madeleine Sophie Barat*, 174, 348, and passim.

13. ASJC, Affaire d'Autun, M. Affre to Anne-Marie Javouhey, 30 October 1835. Mgr Lemercier, bishop of Beauvais, to Mgr d'Héricourt, bishop of Autun, 10 July 1835 and 13 February 1836. Periodic reconciliations sometimes lifted these restrictions, and some bishops, such as that of Quimper, refused to "mix himself up in any affair of this kind." Javouhey, *Lettres*, no. 628, to M. l'abbé Rogeau, curé de Breteuil, 13 November 1845.

14. Janin, *Le clergé colonial*, 376–77. Javouhey, *Lettres*, no. 486, to Mères Marie-Joseph and Rosalie Javouhey, 14 March 1842.

15. ASJC, 4 A c 5, Abbé Guiller to bishop of Autun, 23 November 1840. A member of the Spiritan order of priests, Guiller had arrived in Guiana in 1818 and was apostolic prefect (equivalent to a bishop), as well as curé in Cayenne until his death in 1847.

16. For these accusations, see AAES, Francia, Fasc. 285, no. 482, "Notes sur Mme Javouhey, Supérieure Générale des Soeurs de Saint Joseph, depuis leur établissement dans les colonies," 9 June 1843. ASJC, 4 A c 5, Guiller to bishop of Autun, 23 November 1840; ASJC, 4 A c 5, "Note trouvée jointe aux lettres de Monsieur l'Abbé Guiller sur la Mère Javouhey," n.d.; 2 A I (3), Guiller to Javouhey, 15 August 1844.

17. ASJC, 4 A c 5, Abbé Lafon, missionnaire apostolique, Mana, to bishop of Autun, 10 November 1836.

18. ASJC, 4 A c 5, Guiller to bishop of Autun, 16 January 1840, 5 August 1838.

19. Ibid., 13 March 1842, 7 May 1842.

20. ASJC, 2 A i (3), Guiller, préfet apostolique, to Javouhey, 15 August 1844.

21. Javouhey, Lettres, no. 492, to Mère Marie-Joseph Javouhey, 16 April 1842. ASJC, Affaire d'Autun, Disquisitio 1936, Rome, 86. In a letter to Mère Théophile Montet, however, Javouhey acknowledged the spiritual risk and admitted that she was "cowardly" and "feared the danger" because it had been fifteen months since she had made her last confession. Javouhey, Lettres, no. 523, to Mère Théophile Montet, 7 February 1843.

22. ASJC, 2 A I (3), "Souvenirs de Sr Philémon Poulachon," n.d.

23. Mam-Lam-Fouck, "Apogée," 150.

24. AN, F 19 6210, "Mémoire sur les besoins de la Religion dans la Guiane Française," 1 June 1824.

25. AOM, FM SG Guyane 61, governor, French Guiana, to minister of the navy and colonies, 15 September 1837.

26. Javouhey, Lettres, no. 438, to Soeur Madeleine Collonge, between 1 and 19 October 1840.

27. ASJC, Affaire d'Autun, M. Affre to Mgr d'Héricourt, bishop of Autun, 11 April 1835.

28. Javouhey, Lettres, no. 277, to Mère Rosalie Javouhey, 22 January 1834; no. 316, to Mère Rosalie Javouhey, end of 1834.

29. See references to the "indigenous seminary" in letters no. 285 (to Mère Rosalie Javouhey, 25 May 1834), no. 489 (to Mère Théophile Montet, 25 March 1842), and no. 553 (to Soeur Madeleine Collonge, 25 March 1844). Javouhey, Lettres.

30. Javouhey, Lettres, no. 279, to M. Guiller, 1 February 1834.

31. ASJC, Affaire d'Autun, Mgr Gignoux, bishop of Beauvais, to M. Rogeau, curé de Breteuil, 16 September 1845; M. Affre, vicaire general de Paris, to Mgr Héricourt, 10 March 1835.

32. AOM, FM Généralités 68 (662), bishop of Autun to colonial minister, 7 December 1835. ASJC, Affaire d'Autun, Mgr d'Héricourt, bishop of Autun, to M. Affre, 27 February 1835.

33. Javouhey, Lettres, no. 453, to Mgr d'Héricourt, évêque d'Autun, March 1841; no. 501, to Soeur Balthilde Laparre, 20 June 1842.

34. AN, F 19, 6208, "Notes explicatives sur les inconvénients d'un Noviciat à la Basse-Terre pour la Congrégation des Soeurs de St-Joseph de Cluny, 1852." See also Javouhey, Lettres, no. 617, to Mgr Gignoux, évêque de Beauvais, 2 October 1845. In 1848, the

papal nuncio in Paris allowed Javouhey to give the habit to new nuns who took only annual vows. See no. 800, to Soeur Madeleine Collonge, 12 April 1848.

35. Javouhey, *Lettres*, no. 557, to Soeur Léonce Tristan, 18 April 1844; no. 588, to Mgr Bonnand, évêque de Drusipar, vicaire apostolique de Pondichéry, 3–12 January 1845.

36. Javouhey, *Lettres*, no. 568, to Mère Rosalie Javouhey, 1 July 1844.

37. Ibid., no. 623, to Mère Rosalie Javouhey and Soeur Clothilde Javouhey, 21 October 1845. See also no. 624, to Soeur Madeleine Collonge, 24 October 1845.

38. Ibid., no. 652, to Mgr d'Héricourt, évêque d'Autun, 15 January 1846. The agreement allowed for a second novitiate in theory but only one in reality without, at least, the bishop of Autun's express permission.

39. ASJC, Affaire d'Autun, Mgr Allou de Meaux to Abbé Oudry, 28 February 1846.

40. Javouhey, *Lettres*, no. 898, to Rosalie Javouhey, 21 March 1849; no. 913, to Rosalie Javouhey, 3 October 1849. ASJC, Affaire d'Autun, bishop of Autun, to archbishop of Paris, 6 November 1850.

41. Javouhey, *Lettres*, no. 940, to Soeur Scholastique Delorme, 22 December 1849; no. 947, to Mgr Sibour, archévêque de Paris, end of 1849; no. 1009, to Mère Rosalie Javouhey, 10 April 1850; no. 1098, to M. L'Abbé Caulle, curé du Mesnil-Saint-Firmin, 4 February 1851.

42. Javouhey, *Lettres*, no. 1106, to Mgr Sibour, archbishop of Paris, mid-February 1851.

43. AN, F19 6208, "Notes explicatives sur les inconvénients d'un Noviciat à la Basse-Terre pour la Congrégation des Soeurs de St-Joseph de Cluny," 1852.

44. Javouhey, *Lettres*, no. 489, to Mère Théophile Montet, 25 March 1842.

45. Ibid., no. 988, to Mère Raphaël Montet, 6 March 1850.

46. ASJC, Affaire d'Autun, M. Picard, chanoine honorable, to Soeur Théophile Montet, supérieure de la Maison de St Yon–Rouen, 9 June 1840; 4 A c 5, Abbé Lafon, missionnaire apostolique, Mana, to bishop of Autun, 10 November 1836.

47. ASJC, Affaire d'Autun, Héricourt to bishop in Italy, 7 January 1847.

48. ASV, Congr Vescovi et Regolari, Ist. femm., vol. 1, Consultazione per une congregazione particolare, 43–45, 1853; "Decretum," 8 February 1854.

49. See Seymour Drescher, "Two Variants of Anti-Slavery: Religious Organization and Social Mobilization in Britain and France, 1780–1870," and Serge Daget, "A Model of the French Abolitionist Movement and Its Variations," both in *Anti-Slavery, Religion, and Reform*, ed. Bolt and Drescher, 43–79.

50. Slave revolts in the French Caribbean during the Revolution have become a subject of much scholarly inquiry in the last decade. See especially the work of Laurent Dubois: *Colony of Citizens* and *Avengers of the New World*.

51. These details, and those following, are taken from Jennings, *French Anti-Slavery*. See also Schmidt, *Abolitionnistes*.

52. ASJC, 6 A 2 d, "Lettres addressées à Mère Javouhey," 26 November 1838, 27 January 1840, 4 July 1840, 1 June 1842.

53. Feay, "Mission to Moralize," 113, 260.

54. Javouhey, *Lettres*, no. 465, to Baron Roger, 26 June 1841. Lecuir-Nemo, *Anne-Marie Javouhey*, 372. ASJC, 6 A 2 d, "Lettres addressées à Mère Javouhey," 10 March 1835. Cohen, *French Encounter*, 194. On Lamartine's Catholicism, see Feay, "Mission to Moralize," 79–82.

55. Feay, "Mission to Moralize," 113. Cohen, *French Encounter*, 193, 197. Schoelcher's change toward immediate emancipation occurred with the publication of *Des colonies françaises: Abolition immédiate de l'esclavage* in 1842. On Victor Schoelcher, see Schmidt, *Victor Schoelcher*.

56. Alyssa Goldstein Sepinwall, "Eliminating Race, Eliminating Difference: Blacks, Jews, and the Abbé Grégoire," in *Color of Liberty*, ed. Peabody and Stovall, 33. For a more extended treatment of Grégoire's ideas and career, see her *Abbé Grégoire and the French Revolution*. An older but still useful biography is Necheles, *Abbé Grégoire, 1787–1831*. Many of the tensions in Grégoire's beliefs are also treated in the essays collected in *Abbé Grégoire and His World*, ed. Popkin and Popkin.

57. Alyssa Goldstein Sepinwall, "Exporting the Revolution: Grégoire, Haiti, and the Colonial Laboratory, 1815–1827," in *Abbé Grégoire*, ed. Popkin and Popkin, 65. Necheles, *Abbé Grégoire*, 141.

58. Peabody, " 'Nation Born to Slavery.' " Delisle, "Clergé et esclavage." See also Peabody, "*There Are No Slaves in France*," 19–20.

59. On the colonial clergy during the Restoration and the July Monarchy, see Feay, "Mission to Moralize," 89–99, 125–32, 136–40; Janin, *Le clergé colonial*; Delisle, *Histoire religieuse*, chap. 2; and Brasseur, "Problèmes d'autorité."

60. Delisle, "Clergé et esclavage," 165–66. Prudhomme, *Histoire religieuse*, 77.

61. Maxwell, *Slavery and the Catholic Church*, 111–12. Abbé Dugoujon, *Lettres sur l'esclavage*, 65.

62. Feay, "Mission to Moralize," 56.

63. Ibid., 59–60; see also his discussion of Javouhey, de la Mennais, and Libermann, 316–23.

64. Ibid., 128. Schmidt, *Abolitionnistes*, 164–74.

65. Prudhomme, *Histoire religieuse*, 81. Dugoujon, *Lettres*, 7, 16–17. On the Abbé Dugoujon, see Delisle, "Clergé et esclavage," 169–70.

66. This is in sharp contrast with the British abolitionist campaign, where evangelical women played a significant role. See Midgley, *Women against Slavery*.

67. Gregory XVI, *In Supremo*, cited in Panzer, *Popes and Slavery*, 97–102.

68. Gadille and Zorn, "Le projet missionnaire," 156. See also Schmidt, *Abolitionnistes*, 168–74.

69. [Abbé] J. Hardy, *Liberté et travail*, 471. Drescher, "British Way, French Way: Opinion Building and Revolution in the Second French Slave Emancipation," in *From Slavery to Freedom*, 170.

70. Feay, "Mission to Moralize." Jennings, *French Anti-Slavery*, is typical of the standard view.

71. Jennings, *French Anti-Slavery*, 28.

72. Gautier, *Les soeurs de Solitude*, 139. Jennings, *Anti-slavery*, 111.

73. *Exposé général*, 4, 7. AOM, FM Généralités 68 661, colonial minister to Javouhey, 20 September 1839. ASJC, 2 A d (7), colonial minister to superior general, 2 January 1844.

74. Javouhey, *Lettres*, no. 188, to Mère Marie-Joseph Javouhey, 3 and 12 February 1829; no. 192, to Mère Marie-Joseph Javouhey, 14 March 1829.

75. Ibid., no. 285, to Mère Rosalie Javouhey, 25 May 1834. ASJC, 2 A g (1), "Historique, 1827–52."

76. AOM, FM SG Guadeloupe 113 785, governor, Guadeloupe, to minister of the navy and colonies, 11 March 1824. See also AOM, FM SG Martinique 61 520, Rapport, ministère de la marine et des colonies, 2 December 1825. ASJC, 2 A h 1–4, Soeur Louise Pérard to Mr. Duval (Senlis), 15 February 1827. ASJC, 2 A h (8), Prospectus du pensionnat royal, 1828.

77. ASJC, 2 A d, Soeur Marie-Joseph Varin to Javouhey, 26 June 1818. AOM, FM SG Réunion 35 257, "Note: M. le Commandant et administrateur pour le Roi à Bourbon rend compte de la situation et des progrès de l'instruction publique dans cette colonies," 1 October 1819; FM SG Réunion 429 4525, commandant et administrateur pour le roi, Bourbon, to colonial minister, 6 April 1821; FM SG Réunion 21 129, commandant et administrateur, Freycinet, to "Monseigneur," 19 November 1824.

78. ASJC, 2 A d, Mère Rosalie Javouhey to Javouhey, 5 July 1825. AOM, FM SG Réunion 434 4686, governor, Bourbon, to colonial minister, 15 February 1845.

79. Javouhey, *Lettres*, no. 216, to Mère Rosalie Javouhey, 12 July 1830. Delisle, *Histoire religieuse*, 53. AOM, SG Guyane 144, Copie d'une lettre de Madame la Supérieure générale des dames de St-Joseph de Cluny à M. le gouverneur, 18 March 1836. ASJC, 2 A d, Mère Rosalie Javouhey to Javouhey, 5 July 1825.

80. Delisle, "Congrégations enseignantes," 47.

81. Ibid., 50. Dugoujon, *Lettres*, 73. Javouhey, *Lettres*, no. 648, to Mère Rosalie Javouhey, 2 January 1846; no. 732, to Mère Onésime Lefèvre, 27 February 1847.

82. ASJC, 2 A h 5, Soeur Onésime Lefèvre to Javouhey, 25 August 1846.

83. Ministère de la Marine et des Colonies, *Compte rendu*, 63–83. *Exposé général*, 481.

84. The exact figures were 1,822 plantations with religious instruction and 1,784 without: Martinique (681 with and 280 without), Guadeloupe (574 with and 672 without), Guiana (320 with and 177 without), and Bourbon (274 with and 655 without). *Exposé général*, 90, 127, 145, 162. *Compte rendu*, 93.

85. Javouhey, *Lettres*, no. 556, to Admiral de Mackau, minister of the navy and colonies, 17 April 1844.

86. AOM, FM Généralités 68 661, A. Pécoul to Baron de Mackau, colonial minister, 2 May 1846. Javouhey, *Lettres*, no. 735, to Admiral de Mackau, minister of the navy and colonies, 5 April 1847.

87. AOM, FM Généralités 68 661, Soeur Onésime, supérieure générale, Martinique, 25 February 1847; governor, Martinique, to colonial minister, 10 April 1847.

88. ASJC, 2 A h 5, Soeur Onésime Lefèvre to Javouhey, 19 April 1848. AOM, FM Généralités 68 661, A. Pécoul to colonial minister, 6 April 1848. Javouhey, *Lettres*, no. 974, to Mère Onésime Lefèvre, 15 February 1850. AOM, FM Généralités 68 661, Extraits d'une dépeche ministèrielle, no. 88, 6 February 1850.

89. AOM, FM SG Guadeloupe 149 967, Extrait d'une lettre du gouverneur, 7 August 1844. Javouhey, *Lettres*, no. 708, to Mère Rosalie Javouhey, 21 August 1846; no. 767, to Mère Raphaël Montet, 18 November 1847.

90. Jennings, *Anti-Slavery*, 27, 116–18. Dugoujon, *Lettres sur l'esclavage*, 18–19. See also Feay, "Mission to Moralize," 140–47. *Compte rendu*, 92, 94.

91. ASJC, 2 A h 5, Soeur Onésime Lefèvre to Javouhey, 25 August 1846; 9 July 1846; 2 A g 4, Soeur Léonce Tristant to Javouhey, 3 July 1848.

92. ASJC, 2 A h 6, Victor Schoelcher to Javouhey, 20 April 1849.

93. Delisle, "Congrégations enseignantes," 55–56.

94. For a discussion of some of these issues, see Lecuir-Nemo, *Anne-Marie Javouhey*, 330–31.

95. Javouhey, *Lettres*, no. 667, to Mère Raphaël Montet, 4 March 1846.

96. Ibid., no. 675, to Soeur Madeleine Collonge, beginning of April 1846.

97. Ibid., no. 678, to Mère Onésime Lefèvre, 24 April 1846.

98. Victor Schoelcher, *Histoire de l'esclavage pendant les deux dernières années*, vol. 1, 174–76, in Pago, *Les femmes et la liquidation du système esclavagiste*, appendix 3.

99. Philippe Delisle, "Débats autour de la christianisation des noirs aux Antilles et en Guyane française après l'abolition de l'esclavage (de 1848 aux années 1880)," *Mémoire Spiritaine* 8 (1998): 105.

100. Javouhey, *Lettres*, no. 866, to Mère Raphaël Montet, 18 November 1848; no. 953, to Mère Raphaël Montet, 5 January 1850; no. 1025, to Mère Raphaël Montet, 6 May 1850.

101. For a description of this habit, see Javouhey, *Lettres*, no. 675, to Soeur Madeleine Collonge, beginning of April 1846, note 1.

102. On the abolition of slavery, see Jennings, *French Anti-Slavery*, 273–84; Schmidt, *Abolitionnistes*, 319–37. Both see the Revolution as the decisive event that allowed Schoelcher to push through abolition after the hesitations and half measures of the July Monarchy. Feay argues that the unity between Catholics and Republicans during the early months of the Revolution helped facilitate this process. Feay, "Mission to Moralize," 228–34.

103. Javouhey, *Lettres*, no. 796, to Soeur Léonce Tristant, 24 March 1848.

104. Ibid., no. 795, to Mère Rosalie Javouhey, 22 March 1848; no. 813, to Mère Rosalie Javouhey, 16 May 1848; no. 828, to Mères Rosalie and Clothilde Javouhey, 27 June 1848; no. 834, to Mère Clothilde Javouhey, 15 July 1848.

105. Ibid., no. 791, to Mère Onésime Lefèvre, 14 March 1848.

106. Ibid., no. 790, to Mère Onésime Lefèvre, 12 March 1848, 9 March 1849; no. 793, to Soeur Léonce Tristant, 15 March 1848; no. 819, to Soeur Léonce Tristant, 10 June 1848.

107. Ibid., no. 800, to Soeur Madeleine Collonge, 12 April 1848; no. 840, to Mère Rosalie Javouhey, 29 July 1848; no. 831, to Mère Onésime Lefèvre, 8 July 1848.

108. ASJC, 2 A h, Mère Onésime Lefèvre to Anne-Marie Javouhey, 19 April 1848.

109. Janin, *Le clergé colonial*, 380. Enrollment numbers are not available for Réunion.

110. Javouhey, *Lettres*, no. 745, to Mère Raphaël Montet, 7 June 1847.

111. Delisle, *Renouveau missionnaire*, 272.

112. Javouhey, *Lettres*, no. 1040, to Mère Onésime Lefèvre, 26 August 1850.

113. Ibid., no. 879, to Mère Rosalie Javouhey, 18 January 1849; no. 800, to Soeur Madeleine Collonge, 12 April 1848; no. 984, to Soeur Madeleine Collonge, 28 February 1850.

114. Ibid., no. 844, to Mère Rosalie Javouhey, 7 August 1848; no. 803, to Mère Rosalie Javouhey, 1 May 1848.

115. Ibid., to Mère Clotilde Javouhey, 8 May 1848.

116. Ibid., no. 843, to Soeur Madeleine Collonge, 7 August 1848.

117. Delisle, "Débats," 88–89. AOM, FM SG Guyane 61, commissaire générale de la République Pariset, French Guiana, to minister of the navy and colonies, 4 February 1850.

118. Delisle, *Histoire religieuse*, 145. AOM, FM SG Guyane 61, "Rapport sur l'établissement de Mana et sur le Maroni," 27 November 1850.

119. AOM, FM SG Guyane 61, "Note statistique sur l'Etablissement de Mana," 19 November 1854. Farraudière, *Ecole et société*, 86. AOM, FM SG Guyane 61, governor (Bonan), French Guiana, to minister of the navy and colonies, "Visite de l'établissement de Mana," 24 August 1854.

120. Until 1860 they also introduced Senegalese *engagés* to the Antilles. Blackburn, *Overthrow of Colonial Slavery*, 502–3. Delisle, *Renouveau missionnaire*, 144–45, 147.

121. Klein, *African Slavery*, 111. Mam-Lam-Fouck, "Apogée," 141.

122. On the penal colony, see Toth, *Beyond Papillon*.

123. AN, F 19 6207, "Rapport présenté à Monsieur le Ministre de l'Instruction publique et des Cultes," 5 February 1849. See also Delisle, *Renouveau missionnaire*, 156; Janin, *Le clergé colonial*, 355; and Brasseur, "Problèmes d'autorité," 763.

124. He cites in particular the case of Abbé Joffard. Prudhomme, *Histoire religieuse*, 109–10, 113, 121.

125. Delisle, "Débats," 89–94. Javouhey, *Lettres*, to Soeur Madeleine Collonge, 28 February 1850.

126. Emancipation was limited to those slaves who lived on one of the two islands, and in order to prevent them from becoming overrun with slaves seeking freedom, the French specified that only French citizens on lands belonging to France in 1848 were prohibited from owning slaves. Runaway slaves from neighboring states, unless they could prove they were refugees in a war involving France, were sent back to their owners. On the slave makeup of the two islands, see Searing, *West African Slavery*, 178–83. For a discussion of abolitionist pressures before and after 1848, see Getz, *Slavery and Reform*; Klein, *Slavery*; M'Baye Gueye, "Des affranchissements définitifs à l'émancipation de 1848," in *Les abolitions de l'esclavage de L. F. Sonthonax à V. Schoelcher, 1793, 1794, 1848*, ed. Dorigny, 359–70; and Mbodj, "Abolition of Slavery in Senegal."

127. AOM, FM SG Sénégal X 3 bis, "Rapport sur l'organisation de l'instruction publique au Sénégal," n.d.; governor, Senegal, to colonial minister, 28 December 1844. Boarding became obligatory for children over age seven in 1848. AOM, FM SG Sénégal X 3 bis, arrêté, Conseil d'administration, Sénégal, 31 December 1847.

128. ANS, J 1, "Rapport sur les écoles primaires de la ville de St Louis, Sénégal," 1847. AOM, FM SG Sénégal X 3 bis, "Extrait d'un Mémoire sur la situation du Service administratif: Instruction publique," 31 January 1850. Feay, "Mission to Moralize," 220. ANS, J 1, Commission pour l'examen des écoles to commandant particulier de Gorée, 6 September 1850. Bouche, *L'enseignement*, 417–19.

129. There is little scholarly work on the Soeurs de St-Joseph de Cluny after 1851. One exception is Martin, "Celebrating the Ordinary."

130. Javouhey, *Lettres*, no. 725, to Soeur Madeleine Collonge, 16 December 1846; no. 988, to Mère Raphaël Montet, 6 March 1850; no. 1040, to Mère Onésime Lefèvre, 26 August 1850; no. 1075, to Mère Rosalie Javouhey, 3 or 4 December 1850.

131. Ibid., no. 589, to Soeurs des Iles Marquises, 12 January 1845; no. 1126, to Soeur Régis Fléchel, 28 March 1851. On the SJC in Oceania, see Daughton, *An Empire Divided*, chap. 4.

132. Feay, "Mission to Moralize," 305–6.

133. AOM, FM SG Guyane 15 (B40), "Etat Résumé des votes électoraux de la Guyane Française," 21 March 1849. Mam-Lam-Fouck, *L'esclavage en Guyane*, 28–30.

134. AOM, FM SG Guyane 61, commissaire générale de la République, French Guiana, to minister of the navy and colonies, 6 May 1849.

135. Delaplace, *La R. M. Javouhey*, vol. 2, 343. Groffier, *Héros trop oubliés*, 362. The original source of this anecdote appears to have been Général L. Javouhey, ASJC, "Notes sur quelques essais de colonisation à la Guyane Française," deuxième partie, p. 113.

136. ASJC, Affaire d'Autun, Mgr Lemercier, bishop of Beauvais, to Mgr d'Héricourt, bishop of Autun, 24 February 1835. AOM, FM SG Guyane 60, "Etablissement de la Mana," *Journal du Havre, Commercial et Politique*, no. 2491, 20 January 1832.

137. AOM, FM SG Guyane 61, governor, French Guiana, to minister of the navy and colonies, 29 October 1841. ASJC, 2 A I, Général L. Javouhey, "Notes sur quelques essais de colonisation à la Guyane Française," 19, 34, n.d. Javouhey generally sailed from Cayenne to Mana, but in her letters she does mention one overland trip in 1830. Javouhey, *Lettres*, no. 214, to Mère Clotilde Javouhey, begun 20 April and finished 25 June 1830.

138. AOM, FM SG Guyane 60, "Colonies Françaises: Cour Royale de la Guyane Française," *Gazette des Tribunaux*, no. 1379, 10 January 1830.

139. AOM, FM SG Guyane 61, *Le Temps*, 16 August 1836. The governor of French Guiana condemned the article as the work of Javouhey's enemies and suggested that it was so outrageous that it actually won her support. AOM, FM SG Guyane 61, governor of French Guiana to minister of the navy and colonies, 13 October 1836.

140. Here, however, it is incorrectly attributed to Chateaubriand. ASV, Congr Vescovi et Regolari, Ist. femm., vol. 1, Consultazione per une congregazione particolare, 5, 1853.

141. Delaplace, *La R. M. Javouhey*, vol. 2, 546. Delaplace's source is a "soeur ancienne." There is no corroborating evidence for this story in the archival record.

142. Claude Langlois goes so far as to suggest that it is this reputation of being "beyond the norm" that, unlike for other female heads of religious orders, has denied Javouhey canonization. (She was beatified in 1950.) Langlois, "Anne-Marie Javouhey," 142.

143. On this association, see Offen, "Disrupting the Anglophone Narrative."

144. See Moses, *French Feminism*, chap. 6.

145. Javouhey, *Lettres*, no. 782, to Mère Rosalie Javouhey, 20 January 1848.

146. Ibid., no. 69, to Mère Clotilde Javouhey, 20 November 1822; no. 421, to Mère Marie-Joseph Javouhey, 1 March 1840; no. 716, to Soeur Régis Fléchel, 13 November 1846.

CONCLUSION

1. Javouhey, *Lettres*, no. 1036, to Emilie de Vialar, 13 July 1850. Neither the SJC nor the SJA archives have a copy of Vialar's original letter.

2. Thompson, "Women, Feminism, and the New Religious History," 144.

3. See Sanneh, *West African Christianity*; Hastings, *Church in Africa*.

4. Daughton, *Empire Divided*, chap. 8.

5. For a contrary view, see Hitchens, *Missionary Position*.

6. Richberg, "Rwandan Nuns Jailed in Genocide," *Washington Post* (9 June 2001), A01.

7. Quoted in Caldwell, "Should Christian Missionaries Heed the Call in Iraq?"

8. Ebaugh, "Growth and Decline," 72–73. Steinfels, "Beliefs," *New York Times* (19 September 1998). This imbalance has not halted an overall decline in membership in religious orders worldwide. "Catholic Nuns and Monks Decline."

9. Figures for the Soeurs de St-Joseph de Cluny are from "La Congrégation des Soeurs de Saint-Joseph de Cluny aujourd'hui," http://perso.magic.fr/desarbre/pages/page52.html, and "Congrégation des Soeurs de Saint-Joseph de Cluny dans l'actualité," http://sjcluny.org/web_fr/12_actualite.htm. Figures for the Soeurs de St-Joseph de l'Apparition were kindly provided by Sister Renee Quadros, general secretary. Figures for the Religious of the Sacred Heart were kindly provided by Sister Margaret Phelan, RSCJ archivist.

10. Donadio, "On Africa Trip."

11. Woodard, "Experts Ponder Papal Succession." Donovan, "On Pope's 84th Birthday." Morley, "Hopes for a Third World Pope."

Bibliography

ARCHIVAL COLLECTIONS

Archives Nationales, Paris (AN)

F 19 2486B, Dossier Dupuch et liquidation des dettes, 1841–59

F 19 6207, Evêchés coloniaux, 1848–57

F 19 6208, Colonies: Congrégations religieuses, Congrégation de St-Joseph de Cluny (1818–60)

F 19 6209, Colonies: Guadeloupe, an XII–1868

F 19 6210, Colonies: Guyane-Indes, an XII–1873

F 19 6211, Colonies: Madagascar, Martinique, 1805–1907

F 19 6212, Colonies: Mayette à Tunisie, an XII–1907

F 19 6213, Algérie, organisation du culte catholique, 1819–52

F 19 6240, Notes, correspondance, et rapports concernant les ordres chargés des missions, an XII–1889

F 19 6242, Missions par régions, an XI–1900

F 19 6312, Congrégations religieuses de femmes: Plainte contre la congrégation des Soeurs de St-Joseph de Cluny, 1851

F 19 6335, Congrégations de femmes: Dossiers départementales, Isère

Archives Nationales du Sénégal, Dakar (ANS)

3 E 1, Conseil de Gouvernement et d'Administration, April 1819–November 1819

3 E 2, Conseil de Gouvernement et d'Administration, April 1819–December 1821

3 E 4, Conseil de Gouvernement et d'Administration, 1822

3 E 5, Conseil de Gouvernement et d'Administration, February 1823–November 1824

3 E 10, Conseil de Gouvernement et d'Administration, January 1833–June 1835

3 E 20, Conseil de Gouvernement et d'Administration, December 1847–February 1849

H 6, Santé, organisation et fonctionnement, 1828–46

J 1, Ecoles chrétiennes, 1831–50

Archives d'Outre Mer, Aix-en-Provence (AOM)

F 80 659, Algérie: Choléra, 1830–56

F 80 1562, Algérie: Instruction publique…congrégations enseignantes, 1831–58

F 80 1625–27, Algérie: Culte catholique, 1831–58

F 80 1647, Algérie: Hôpital par localités, 1833–58

F 80 1648–49, Hôpital d'Alger, 1833–58

F 80 1843, Algérie: Instruction primaire; organisation, inspections, rapports, 1835–49

FM Généralités 64 645, Soeurs de St-Joseph de Cluny, envoi dans les différentes colonies, 1816–59

FM Généralités 68 663, Soeurs de St-Joseph de Cluny, abonnement avec la congrégation pour l'entretien au complet du nombre des soeurs nécessaires au service des colonies, 1823–53

FM Généralités 68 661, Soeurs de St-Joseph de Cluny, installation de soeurs de St-Joseph de Cluny sur des habitations; 1er envoi aux Antilles, 1822–50

FM Généralities 68 662, Soeurs de St-Joseph de Cluny: Dossier relatif à la suppression du noviciat de Bailleul, 1835–37

FM Généralités 144 1222, Instruction morale et religieuse des noirs à la Martinique, à la Guadeloupe, à l'île Bourbon, dans la Guyane française, 1842

FM Généralités 259 1778, Instruction publique: Ecole que la congrégation de St-Joseph se propose d'établir à Paris, 1825

FM Généralités 464 2380, Soeurs de St-Joseph de Cluny, correspondance générale, 1821–70

FM SG Guadeloupe 35 311, Instruction publique; Ecoles publiques gratuites, 1840–42

FM SG Guadeloupe 149 967, Mouvements des Soeurs de St-Joseph de Cluny, 1842–46

FM SG Guadeloupe 113 785, Instruction publique: Rapports et correspondance concernant les soeurs de St-Joseph, 1823–47

FM SG Guyane 15 B40, Elections, 1849–50

FM SG Guyane 60–61, Correspondances des gouverneurs relatives à l'enterprise de colonisation agricole de la Mère Javouhey

FM SG Guyane 139 R1, Ecole mixte gratuite, Soeurs de St-Joseph, Sinnamary, 1840–46

FM SG Guyane 144, Soeurs de St-Joseph de Cluny, 1822–46

FM SG Martinique 61 520, Envois en Martinique des Soeurs de St-Joseph de Cluny, 1822–44

FM SG Martinique 97 859, Ecoles primaires de filles, Soeurs de St-Joseph, 1843–62

FM SG Réunion 21 129, Ordres religieux, Soeurs St-Joseph de Cluny, 1823–26

FM SG Réunion 35, Instruction publique, 1819–

FM SG Réunion 429 4525, Soeurs de St-Joseph: Lettres du governeur au ministre, 1817, 1820–31

FM SG Réunion 429 4526–4530, Soeurs de St-Joseph: Lettres (minutes) du ministre au commandant et administrateur, 1816–50

FM SG Réunion 434 4686, Soeurs de St-Joseph, 1841–45

FM, SG Réunion 434 4687, Soeurs de St-Joseph: Moralisation des esclaves, 1846

FM SG Sénégal X 2 (a), Education locale: généralités

FM SG Sénégal X 2 (c), Education locale: Soeurs de St-Joseph de Cluny, 1815–39

FM SG Sénégal X 2 (d–e), Education dans la métropole

FM SG Sénégal X 3 bis, Rapports et correspondance concernant l'enseignment primaire, 1831–82

FM SG Sénégal X 6 (b), Education locale: Soeurs de St-Joseph de Cluny, 1839–54

FM SG Sénégal II 2, Mémoires, Roger, 1821

FM SG Sénégal XIII 19, Essais de colonisation, 1820–26

Archives du Ministère des Affaires Etrangères, Paris (AAE-Paris)

Affaires diverses politiques, Secours religieux, 2, Secours aux Etablissements religieux, 1840–60

Mémoires et documents, France, 2118, Lettre du ministre de la Guerre au ministre des Affaires étrangères au sujet des soeurs de St-Joseph en Algérie, 1842

Mémoires et documents, Turquie, 127, Documents sur Jérusalem; Lettres du Patriarche de Jérusalem; Hôpital de Jérusalem, 1839–60

Archives du Ministère des Affaires Etrangères, Nantes (AAE-Nantes)

Ambassade, Rome-St-Siège, 573, Correspondance du consulat de Beyrouth, 1827–69

Ambassade, Rome-St-Siège, 574, Correspondance des consulats de Jérusalem, Alep, Tripolie de Barbarie, 1818–78

Ambassade, Rome-St-Siège, 575, Correspondance des consulats de Tunis, Alger, Malte, Chypre, Larnaca, Athènes 1816–78

Consulat, Trébizonde, 78, Questions religieuses, 1819–1910

Postes, Jérusalem, 94, Etablissements religieux, Soeurs de Saint-Joseph, 1843–1919

Postes, Jérusalem, 103, Hôpital Saint-Louis à Jérusalem, 1845–1914

Service historique de l'Armée de Terre, Vincennes (SHAT)

1 H 54 (1), Correspondance, Algérie, January–February 1838

1 H 55 (1), Correspondance Algérie, January–April 1838

1 H 56 (1), Correspondance Algérie, May–June 1838

1 H 58 (1), Correspondance Algérie, September–October 1838

1 H 60 (1), Correspondance Algérie, January–February 1839

1 H 62 (1), Correspondance, Algérie, May–June 1839

1 H 78 (1), Correspondance, Algérie, October–November 1841

Archives Départementales de l'Isère, Grenoble (ADI)

2 E 384, Famille Duchesne

23 H 52, Visitation: Vêtures, noviciats, professions. Liste des religieuses à la fin de l'ancien régime, 1758–91

23 H 55, Construction du monastère

23 H 57, Plans du monastère

23 H 59, Plans de l'enclos du couvent

23 H 63, Livre de pensions et rentes dues, 1781–89

23 H 70, Constitutions et reconstitutions de rentes, 1627–1792

L 563, Cultes. Lois, décrets, et instructions, 1789–an XII

L 667, Détenus politiques; état des détenus à Ste-Marie-d'en-Haut, April–July 1793

1 Q 411, Liquidations. Biens du clergé régulier. Ordres de femmes…Visitandines de Grenoble, 1791–1807

7 V 3/9, Cultes. Dames du–Sacré-Coeur, an XIII–19–

7 V 3/12, Cultes. Religieuses de la Visitation, 1806–19–

Archives Départementales du Tarn, Albi (ADT)

3 V 59, Congrégations de femmes enseignantes, Soeurs de St-Joseph de l'Apparition, 1836–1903

Archives Municipales de Grenoble (AMG)

GG 203, Registre des actes de vêture, noviciat, profession et décès du couvent de la Visitation de Ste-Marie-d'en-Haut, 1786–1791

LL 1, 4, 7, 10, Registre des delibérations du corps municipale de la ville de Grenoble, 1790–1792, 1793–an II, an III, an V–an VII

LL 15, Registre particulier pour les requettes et les avis ou réponses du Bureau de la Municipalité, 1792–an VI

LL 210, Biens nationaux. Soumissions de la municipalité de Grenoble pour l'achat des biens nationaux, 1790–an III

LL 228, Instruction publique, an V–an VII

LL 229, Cultes. Déclarations faites par les religieux et religieuses du district de Grenoble, 1790–an VI

Archives Municipales de Gaillac (AM-Gaillac)

3 T 1, Personnalités Gaillacoises: Emilie de Vialar

5 T 1, Dossier Jean Calvet

5 T 2, Dossier Calvet: Manuscrit Gaillac 1830–48

2 Q 248, Associations et sociétés de bienfaisance

Missouri Historical Society, St. Louis (MHS)

Clemens Papers

Schools Papers

Lane Collection

Archives des Soeurs de St-Joseph de l'Apparition, Paris (ASJA)

Registre historique des Etablissements de la Congrégation des Soeurs de St-Joseph de l'Apparition depuis la fondation en 1832 jusqu'à nos jours 1898

1 A 3.9, Lettres de Ste Emilie à et de différentes personnes

1 A 4.6, Lettres de Ste Emilie aux Soeurs et à diverses personnes

1 A 4.3, Lettres de Ste Emilie à ses Soeurs de 1826 à 1856 et à diverses personnes

1 A 4.4, Lettres de Ste Emilie à sa famille

1 A 4.1, Lettres de Ste Emilie aux prêtres

1 A 4.2, Lettres de Ste-Emilie aux prêtres de 1850 à 1856, à Mgr Dupuch, à diverses personnes

2 A 12, Règle de St-Augustin et Constitutions

4 A 1, Esprit de la Congrégation et développement des règles

10 C, Maisons fermées: Grèce

12 A 1, Mère Emilie Julien: Lettres manuscrites et documents officiels

12 A 2, Lettres de Emilie Julien aux soeurs, à Mère Emilie de Vialar, à sa famille

12 A 3, Lettres de Mère Emilie Julien à Mère Emilie de Vialar
20 C, Maisons fermées: Turquie
MS Abbé Brunet, 1880

Archives de Soeurs de St-Joseph de l'Apparition–Gaillac (ASJA-Gaillac)

Conférence de Jean Calvet, "Gaillac au temps d'Emilie de Vialar"

Archives des Soeurs de St-Joseph de Cluny, Paris (ASJC)

2 A b.2, Débuts de la congrégation jusqu'à 1816
2 A c, Histoire de la congrégation
2 A d, Bourbon
2 A e, Sénégal
2 A f, Jeunes Africains
2 A g, Guadeloupe
2 A h, Martinique
2 A i, Mana/Guyane
4 A c 5, Copie des archives de l'évêché d'Autun, Clergé de Cayenne, 1817–45
6 A 2 d, Lettres addressées à Mère Javouhey
Dossier, Affaire d'Autun

Archives of the Religious of the Sacred Heart, St. Louis (RSCJ–St. Louis)

Series IV, D (Florissant), community files
Series IV, K (Potawatomi Mission), community files
Series IV, N (St. Louis City House), community files
Series IV, M (St. Charles), community files
Series XIII: Duchesne Collection, Box 1, Packet 1, Histoire de Ste Marie d'en haut devenue
   le 13 Decembre 1804 la seconde maison de la Société (Grenoble) par la Mère Philippine
   Duchesne
Series XIII: Duchesne Collection, Box 1, Packet 1, Journal de la Maison de Grenoble dite Ste
   Marie d'en Haut, depuis sa fondation le 13 Décembre 1804, jusqu'au 27 Décembre 1813
   par la Mère Philippine Duchesne
Series XIII: Special Collections, Callan Collection, Box 1, Letters written by PD to various
   ecclesiastics in France and the United States.
Series XIII: Special Collections, Callan Collection, Box 4, Letters of PD to her RSCJ nieces
   and other RSCJ; letters of PD to her family
Series XIII, Callan Collection, Box 5, Reminiscences of Mother Shannon about Mother
   Duchesne; notes de la Révérende Mère Jouve concernant la vie de notre vénérée Mère
   Duchesne; notes sur le V. Mère Duchesne par Mère Louise de Vidaud
Series XIII: Special Collections, Callan Collection, Box 7, misc. letters
Series XIII: Special Collections, Callan Collection, Box 8, extracts from letters and
   mementos of Philippine Duchesne; letters to RSCJ
Series XIII: Special Collections, Callan Collection, Box 9, RSCJ data

Archives des Religieuses de Sacré-Coeur, Rome (RSCJ-Rome)

C-III, Box 4, United States, Early History
C-IV, Dossier 1, Closed Houses: St-Ferdinand, Sugar Creek, St. Louis

C-IV, Dossier 2, Existent Houses: St. Charles
C-VII 2, Boxes 1, 2, 3, Duchesne, Life

Archivio Segreto Vaticano, Rome (ASV)

Arch. Nunz. Parigi, Archivio della Nunziatura Apostolica in Parigi
Congr. Vescovi et Regolari, Ist. femm., Congregazione dei Vescovi et Regolari, Istituti
   femminili, vol. 1

Archivio Affari Ecclesiastici Straordinari, Rome (AAES)

Francia, Fasc. 284, no. 475, Algeri
Francia, Fasc. 285, no. 482, Guyana

Archivio della Propaganda Fide, Rome (Prop. Fide)

Fondo (S.C.), Scritture Rifferite nei Congressi:
Africa Centrale
Africa Malta
Armeni
Barberia
Grecia Arcipelago e Candia
Terra Santa e Cipio

Archives de la Propagation de la Foi, Lyon (APF)

Fonds Lyon:
D 145, Chio et Samos, 1833–58
D 146, Chypre, 1841–1918
D 148, Crète, 1840–1924
D 154, Evêché de Syra et Délégation Apostolique de la Grêce, 1829–74
D 162, Malte, 1838–83
E 14, Syrie-Liban, délégation apostolique, 1834–1920
E 20 (P), Jérusalem, Soeurs de St-Joseph de l'Apparition, 1853–1923
F 83, St-Louis, 1822–69
G 6, Alger, 1837–45
G 124, Tunisie I, 1837–78
D 145, Chio, Grèce, 1833–1921
D 151, Grèce-Syra-Rapports, 1838–1921
D 154, Malte, Demandes de secours, 1847–49
E 10, Turquie, Armeniens, 1830–79
E 14, Syrie, Rapports sur les missions, 1833–1921
E 19, Palestine-Jérusalem-Rapports sur les missions, 1838–1920
E 23, Chypre (a) Rapports, 1842–1912
F 128, St-Louis, Rapports, 1835–95
F 161, Etats-Unis–Missions des Jésuites (Missouri), 1841–69
G 7, Carthage (Tunisie), Rapports, 1841–1900
G 8, Algérie-Alger, Rapports, 1842–1918

PRINTED PRIMARY SOURCES

Annales historiques de la Congrégation de Saint-Joseph de Cluny. Solesmes: Imprimerie Saint-Pierre, 1890.

Barat, Madeleine-Sophie, and Philippine Duchesne. *Correspondance: Texte des manuscrits originaux présenté avec une introduction, des notes et un index analytique,* 3 vols. Rome: Religious of the Sacred Heart of Jesus, 1988–99.

Bernard, Laure. *La Guyane française et l'Ordre de Saint-Joseph de Cluny.* Paris: Imprimerie de Ducessois, 1834.

Boilat, David (abbé). *Esquisses sénégalaises.* Paris: Karthala, 1984; orig. ed., 1853.

Bourgade, François (abbé). *Association de Saint Louis ou croisade pacifique ayant pour but de répandre la civilisation parmi les musulmans au moyen d'ouvrages écrits ou traduits en leur langue.* Paris: Firmin Didot Frères, Fils et Cie., n.d.

———. *Carthage (Saint Louis les Protége) Tunis.* Paris: Imprimerie de Vrayet de Surcy, n.d.

———. *La clef du Coran, faisant suite aux Soireés de Carthage.* Paris: Jacques Lecoffre, 1852.

———. *Soirées de Carthage ou dialogues entre un prêtre catholique, un muphti, et un cadi.* Paris: Firmin Didot Frères, 1847.

Chateaubriand, François-Réné. *Génie de Christianisme,* vol. 4, 6th ed. Paris: Le Normant, 1816.

———. *Itinéraire de Paris à Jérusalem.* Paris: P.-H. Krabbe, 1852 (1st ed. 1811).

Conduite des écoles chrétiennes des Soeurs de Saint Joseph, dites de l'Apparition. Gaillac: M. Testan, 1836.

Constitutions et règles de la Société du Sacré Coeur de Jésus. Lyon: J. B. Pélagaud, 1852.

Coustumier et directoire pour les Soeurs religieuses de la Visitation de Sainte Marie. Lyon: Vincent de Coeurfilly, 1638.

Dugoujon, Casimir (abbé). *Lettres sur l'esclavage dans les colonies françaises.* Paris: Pagnerre, 1845.

Dupuch, Antoine-Adolphe (Mgr). *Fastes sacrés de l'Afrique chrétienne,* 4 vols. Bordeaux: Suwerinck, 1850.

Duras, Claire de. *Ourika: An English Translation.* New York: Modern Language Association of America, 1994.

Enault, Louis. *La Terre-Sainte: Voyage des quarante pèlerins de 1853.* Paris: L. Maison, 1854.

Exposé général des résultats du patronage des esclaves dans les colonies françaises. Paris: Imprimerie Royale, 1844.

Gauchat, Gabrielle (soeur). *Journal d'une Vistandine pendant la Terreur ou mémoires de la Soeur Gabrielle Gauchat.* Paris: Mme. Veuve Poussielgue-Rusand, 1855.

Genty de Bussy, M. P. *De l'établissement des Français dans la Régence d'Alger, et des moyens d'en assurer la prospérité,* 2d ed., 2 vols. Paris: Firmin Didot Frères, 1839.

Guérin, Eugénie de. *Lettres à Louise de Bayne,* vol. 1 (1830–1834); vol. 2 (1835–1847). Paris: Librairie Lecoffre, 1924–25.

Guillier (préfet apostolique de la Guyane française). *Simples observations et renseignements exacts sur le Séminaire du Saint-Esprit.* Paris: Séminaire du Saint-Esprit, 1845.

Hardy, J. (abbé). *Liberté et travail, ou moyens d'abolir l'esclavage sans abolir le travail.* Paris: Bailly, 1838.

Histoire chronologique des fondations de tout l'ordre de la Visitation de Sainte Marie. Bibliothèque Mazarine, MS 2439, 1693.

Javouhey, Anne-Marie. *Lettres, 1798–1851*, 4 vols. Paris: Cerf, 1994.

Lauvergne, H. *Histoire de l'expédition d'Afrique en 1830*. Paris: Mme. Ve Béchet, 1831.

Massilien. Beatificationis et Canonizationis. Servae Dei Matris Aemiliae de Vialar, Fondatricis Congregationis S. Joseph Ab Apparitione. Articuli Ad Docendum de Vita et de Virtutibus in Specie. Rome: Guerra e Mirri, 1925.

Michelet, Jules. *Du prêtre, de la femme, de la famille*. Paris: Hachette, 1845.

Ministère de la Guerre. *Tableau de la situation des établissements français dans l'Algérie en 1838*. Paris: Imprimerie Royale, 1839.

———. *Tableau de la situation des établissements français dans l'Algérie en 1840*. Paris: Imprimerie Royale, 1841.

Ministère de la Marine et des Colonies. *Compte rendu au roi de l'emploi des fonds allouées, depuis 1839 pour l'enseignement religieux et élémentaire des noirs*. Paris: Imprimerie Royale, 1846.

Moniteur Algérien: Journal officiel de la colonie (1832–42).

Notice biographique de la T. Rde. M. Rosalie Javouhey, deuxième Supérieure Gle. de la Congrégation de St. Joseph de Cluny. Paris: Victor Janson, 1872.

Notice sur la vie de la R. Mère Marie-Joseph Javouhey, Soeur de Notre Vénérée Mère Fondatrice. Paris: Victor Janson, 1864.

Paisant, Chantal, ed. *Philippine Duchesne et ses compagnes: Les années pionnières (1818–1823): Lettres et journaux des premières missionaires du Sacré-Coeur aux Etats-Unis*. Paris: Cerf, 2001.

Précis sur la colonisation des bords de la Mana, à la Guyane française. Paris: Imprimerie Royale, 1835.

Procacci, Giuliana, ed. *Le relazioni diplomatiche fra lo stato pontificio e la francia*, II Serie: *1830–1848*. Vol. 3, *8 gennaio 1834–31 dicembre 1838*. Rome: Istituto Storico Italiano, 1969.

Procès verbaux et rapports de la commission nommée par le Roi, le 7 juillet 1833, pour aller recueillir en Afrique tous les faits propres à éclairer le gouvernement sur l'état du pays et sur les mesures que réclame son avenir. Paris: Imprimerie Royale, 1834.

"Rapport sur la situation de l'établissement de Mana (Guyane française) en 1847 et 1848." *Revue Coloniale* 4 (February 1850): 65–100.

Règlement des pensionnats et plan d'études de la Société du Sacré-Coeur. Orléans: Alex. Jacob, 1852.

Roger, [Jacques-François]. *Fables sénégalaises, recueillies de l'oulof et mises en vers français*. Paris: Nepveu, 1828.

———. *Kelédor, histoire africaine*. Paris: Nepveu, 1828.

Statuts de la Congrégation des Soeurs de Saint-Joseph de Cluny. Beauvais: Imprimerie d'Ach. Desjardins, 1827.

Statuts de la Congrégation des Soeurs de Saint-Joseph de Cluny. Paris: E. Brunet, 1846.

Suchet, Jacques (abbé). *Lettres édifiantes et curieuses sur l'Algérie*. Tours: Mame et Cie., 1840.

Thibert, Péronne-Marie, ed. *I Leave You My Heart: A Visitandine Chronicle of the French Revolution: Mère Marie-Jéronyme Vérot's Letter of 15 May 1794*. Philadelphia: Saint Joseph's University Press, 2000.

Verheyden, P. J. "Corpus-Christi-Day among the Pottowattomies." *Catholic Cabinet and Chronicle of Religious Intelligence*, vol. 1, no. 4 (August 1843): 251–54.

Veuillot, Louis. *Les français en Algérie*. Tours: Robert Laffont, 1978; orig. ed., 1845.

Vialar (Augustin de). *Alger: Appendice au rapport de M. Passy (Ministère de la Guerre)*. Paris: L.-E. Herhan, 1835.

———. *Simples faits exposés à la réunion algérienne du 14 Avril 1835*. Paris: Firmin Didot Frères, 1835.

Wandelburg, A. Haussmann de (mgr). *La Palestine, la Syrie, et l'Arabie visitées avec Mgr Valerga: Souvenirs de voyages aux missions d'Orient*, vol. 1. Paris: Berche et Tralin, 1886.

SECONDARY SOURCES

Abun-Nasr, Jamil M. *A History of the Maghrib in the Islamic Period*. New York: Cambridge University Press, 1987.

Adams, Christine. *A Taste for Comfort and Status: A Bourgeois Family in Eighteenth-Century France*. University Park: Pennsylvania State University Press, 2000.

Adelman, Jeremy, and Stephen Aron. "From Borderlands to Borders: Empires, Nation-States, and the Peoples in Between in North American History." *American Historical Review*, vol. 104, no. 3 (June 1999): 814–41.

Ahlgren, Gillian T. W. *Teresa of Avila and the Politics of Sanctity*. Ithaca: Cornell University Press, 1996.

Ajayi, J. F. Ade, ed. *General History of Africa*, vol. 6: *Africa in the Nineteenth Century until the 1880s*. Paris: UNESCO, 1989.

Aldrich, Robert. *Greater France: A History of French Overseas Expansion*. New York: St. Martin's, 1996.

Alexandropoulos, Jacques, and Patrick Cabanel, eds. *La Tunisie mosaïque: Diasporas, cosmopolitisme, archéologies de l'identité*. Toulouse: Presses Universitaires du Mirail, 2000.

Allen, James Smith. *Poignant Relations: Three Modern French Women*. Baltimore: Johns Hopkins University Press, 2000.

Andrew, C. M., and A. S. Kanya-Forstner. "Centre and Periphery in the Making of the Second French Colonial Empire, 1815–1920." *Journal of the Imperial and Commonwealth History*, vol. 16, no. 3 (May 1988): 9–34.

Andrews, Naomi J. *Socialism's Muse: Gender in the Intellectual Landscape of French Romantic Socialism*. Lanham, Md.: Lexington Books, 2006.

Argenti, Philip P. *The Religious Minorities of Chios: Jews and Roman Catholics*. Cambridge: Cambridge University Press, 1970.

Aron, Stephen. *American Confluence: The Missouri Frontier from Borderland to Border State*. Bloomington: Indiana University Press, 2006.

Auschitzky, Hubert, and Maïten Auschitzky. *La famille maternelle de Maïten Brusaut, 2e Cahier, t.33, Augustin de Vialar, le Grand Baron*. Bordeaux: N.p., 1999.

———. *La famille maternelle de Maïten Brusaut, 6e Cahier, t. 30, Jacques-Augustin, Baron de Vialar*. Bordeaux: N.p., 1999.

Axtell, James. *The Invasion Within: The Contest of Cultures in Colonial North America*. New York: Oxford University Press, 1985.

Backscheider, Paula R. *Reflections on Biography*. New York: Oxford University Press, 1999.

Banks, Kenneth J. *Chasing Empire across the Sea: Communications and the State in the French Atlantic, 1713–1763*. Montreal: McGill-Queen's University Press, 2002.

Bannour, Wanda. *Eugénie de Guérin ou une chasteté ardente*. Paris: Albin Michel, 1983.

Barry, Boubacar. *Le royaume du Waalo: Le Sénégal avant la conquête*. Paris: Karthala, 1985; orig. ed., 1972.

———. *Senegambia and the Atlantic Slave Trade*. New York: Cambridge University Press, 1998.

———. *La Sénégambie du XVe au XIXe siècle: Traite négrière, Islam, et conquête coloniale*. Paris: L'Harmattan, 1988.

Basch, Sophie. *Le mirage grec: La Grèce moderne devant l'opinion française depuis la création de l'Ecole d'Athènes jusqu'à la guerre civile grecque (1846–1946)*. Athens: Librairie Kauffmann/Editions Hatier, 1995.

Bauberot, Jean. "The Protestant Woman," in *A History of Women in the West*, ed. Geneviève Fraisse and Michelle Perrot, vol. 4, *Emerging Feminism from Revolution to World War*, 198–212. Cambridge, Mass.: Harvard University Press, 1993.

Baumgarten, Nikola. "Education and Democracy in Frontier St. Louis: The Society of the Sacred Heart." *History of Education Quarterly*, vol. 34, no. 2 (Summer 1994): 171–92.

Beadie, Nancy, and Kim Tolley. *Chartered Schools: Two Hundred Years of Independent Academies in the United States, 1727–1925*. New York: Routledge Falmer, 2002.

Beecher, Jonathan. *Victor Considerant and the Rise and Fall of French Romantic Socialism*. Berkeley: University of California Press, 2001.

Bennoune, Mahfoud. *The Making of Contemporary Algeria, 1830–1987: Colonial Upheavals and Post-Independence Development*. New York: Cambridge University Press, 1988.

Bénot, Yves. *La Guyane sous la Révolution ou l'impasse de la révolution pacifique*. Kourou, Guyana: Ibis Rouge, 1997.

———, and Marcel Dorigny, eds. *Rétablissement de l'esclavage dans les colonies françaises: Aux origines de Haïti*. Paris: Maisonneuve et Larose, 2003.

Berenson, Edward. *Populist Religion and Left-Wing Politics in France, 1830–1852*. Princeton: Princeton University Press, 1984.

Berkhofer, Robert F., Jr. *The White Man's Indian: Images of the American Indian from Columbus to the Present*. New York: Vintage, 1978.

Berthier, René, and Marie-Hélène Sigaut. *Anne-Marie Javouhey et le journal d'une femme, apôtre des terres lointaines*. Paris: Univers Media, 1979.

Billington, Ray Allen. *The Protestant Crusade, 1800–1860: A Study of the Origins of American Nativism*. New York: Macmillan, 1938.

Biondi, Jean-Pierre. *Saint-Louis du Sénégal: Mémoires d'un métissage*. Paris: Denoël, 1987.

Blackburn, Carole. *Harvest of Souls: The Jesuit Missions and Colonialism in North America, 1632–1650*. Montreal: McGill-Queen's University Press, 2000.

Blackburn, Robin. *The Overthrow of Colonial Slavery, 1776–1848*. London: Verso, 1988.

Blaufarb, Rafe. *Bonapartists in the Borderlands: French Exiles and Refugees on the Gulf Coast*. Tuscaloosa: University of Alabama Press, 2005.

Bligny, Bernard, ed. *Le diocèse de Grenoble*. Paris: Beauchesne, 1979.

Blouet, Brian. *A Short History of Malta*. New York: Praeger, 1967.

Bolt, Christine, and Seymour Drescher. *Anti-Slavery, Religion, and Reform: Essays in Memory of Roger Anstey.* Hamden, Conn.: Archon, 1980.

Bouche, Denise. *L'enseignement dans les territoires français de l'Afrique occidentale de 1817 à 1920.* Lille: Reproduction des Thèses, Université Lille III, 1975.

Bouquillon, Yvon, and Robert Cornevin. *David Boilat (1814–1901): Le précurseur.* Dakar: Nouvelles Editions Africaines, 1981.

Boussoulade, Jean. *Moniales et hospitalières dans la tourmente révoutionnaire: Les communautés de religieuses de l'ancien diocèse de Paris de 1789–1801.* Paris: Letouzey et Ané, 1962.

Bowden, Henry Warner. *American Indians and Christian Missions: Studies in Cultural Conflict.* Chicago: University of Chicago Press, 1981.

Bowie, Fiona, and Deborah Kirkwood. *Women and Missions: Past and Present: Anthropological and Historical Perceptions.* Providence, R.I.: Berg, 1993.

Brasseur, Paule. "Problèmes d'autorité en matière religieuse: L'érection des diocèses coloniaux (1815–1851)." *Mélanges de l'Ecole Française de Rome,* vol. 104, no. 2 (1992): 737–63.

Brewer, David. *The Greek War of Independence: The Struggle for Freedom from Ottoman Oppression and the Birth of the Modern Greek Nation.* New York: Overlook, 2001.

Brewer, Eileen Mary. *Nuns and the Education of American Catholic Women, 1860–1920.* Chicago: Loyola University Press, 1987.

Briat, Anne-Marie, Janine de La Hogue, André Appel, and Marc Baroli. *Des chemins et des hommes: La France en Algérie (1830–1962).* Hélette: Jean Curutchet, Editions Harriet, 1995.

Brigaud, Félix, and Jean Vast. *Saint-Louis du Sénégal: Ville aux mille visages.* Dakar: Clairafrique, 1987.

Brooks, George E., Jr. "The Signares of Saint-Louis and Gorée: Women Entrepreneurs in Eighteenth-Century Senegal." In *Women in Africa: Studies in Social and Economic Change,* ed. Nancy J. Hafkin and Edna G. Bay, 19–44. Stanford: Stanford University Press, 1976.

Brown, L. Carl. *The Tunisia of Ahmad Bey, 1837–1855.* Princeton: Princeton University Press, 1974.

Bruleaux, Anne-Marie, Régine Calmont, and Serge Mam-Lam-Fouck. *Deux siècles d'esclavage en Guyane française, 1652–1848.* Paris: L'Harmattan, 1986.

Bruneau, Marie-Florine. *Women Mystics Confront the Modern World: Marie de l'Incarnation (1599–1672) and Madame Guyon (1648–1717).* Albany: State University of New York Press, 1998.

Burrows, Mathew. " 'Mission Civilisatrice': French Cultural Policy in the Middle East, 1860–1914." *Historical Journal,* vol. 29, no. 1 (1986): 109–35.

Byrne, Patricia. "Sisters of St. Joseph: The Americanization of a French Tradition." *U.S. Catholic Historian,* vol. 5, no. 3–4 (Summer/Fall 1986): 241–72.

Caffiero, Marina. *Battesimi forzati: Storie di ebrei, cristiani e convertiti nella Roma dei papa.* Rome: Viella, 2004.

Caldwell, Deborah. "Should Christian Missionaries Heed the Call in Iraq?" *New York Times* (6 April 2003), Week in Review, 6.

Callan, Louise. *Philippine Duchesne: Frontier Missionary of the Sacred Heart, 1769–1852.* Westminster, Md.: Newman, 1957.

————. *The Society of the Sacred Heart in North America*. New York: Longmans, Green, 1937.

Carroll, Michael P. "Give Me That Ol' Time Hormonal Religion." *Journal for the Scientific Study of Religion*, vol. 43, no. 2 (2004): 275–78.

"Catholic Nuns and Monks Decline." *BBC News*, http://news.bbc.co.uk/2/hi/europe/7227629.stm (5 February 2008).

Catta, Etienne. *La vie d'un monastère sous l'Ancien Régime: La Visitation Sainte-Marie de Nantes (1630–1792)*. Paris: J. Vrin, 1954.

Cavasino, Agnès. *Emilie de Vialar: Fondatrice, les Soeurs de Saint-Joseph de l'Apparition: Une congrégation missionnaire*. Fontenay-sous-Bois: Congrégation des Soeurs de St-Joseph de l'Apparition, 1987.

Çelik, Zenep. *Urban Forms and Colonial Confrontations: Algiers under French Rule*. Berkeley: University of California Press, 1997.

Charles-Roux, F. *France et chrétiens d'Orient*. Paris: Flammarion, 1939.

Charry, Jeanne de. *Histoire des constitutions de la Société du Sacré-Coeur: Les constitutions définitives et leur approbation par le Saint-Siège*, vol. 1, *Exposé Historique*. Rome: Pontificia Universitas Gregoriana, 1979.

Chartier, Roger, Marie-Madeleine Compère, and Dominique Julia. *L'éducation en France du XVIe au XVIIIe siècle*. Paris: Société d'Edition d'Enseignement Supérieur, 1976.

Chauleau, Liliane. *La vie quotidienne aux Antilles françaises au temps de Victor Schoelcher, XIXe siècle*. Paris: Hachette, 1979.

Cholvy, Gérard. *Être chrétien en France au XIXe siècle, 1790–1914*. Paris: Seuil, 1997.

Chomel, Vital, ed. *Les débuts de la Révolution française en Dauphiné, 1788–1791*. Grenoble: Presses Universitaires de Grenoble, 1988.

————. *Histoire de Grenoble*. Toulouse: Privat, 1976.

Choquette, Leslie. " 'Ces Amazones du Grand Dieu': Women and Mission in Seventeenth-Century Canada." *French Historical Studies*, vol. 17, no. 3 (Spring 1992): 627–55.

Choudhury, Mita. *Convents and Nuns in Eighteenth-Century French Politics and Culture*. Ithaca: Cornell University Press, 2004.

Clancy-Smith, Julia A. *Mediterranean Passages: Migrants and Mobilities in Nineteenth-Century North Africa*. Berkeley: University of California Press, 2010.

————. *Rebel and Saint: Muslim Notables, Populist Protest, Colonial Encounters (Algeria and Tunisia, 1800–1904)*. Berkeley: University of California Press, 1995.

————, and Frances Gouda. *Domesticating the Empire: Race, Gender, and Family Life in French and Dutch Colonialism*. Charlottesville: University Press of Virginia, 1998.

Clark, Emily J. " 'By All the Conduct of Their Lives': A Laywomen's Confraternity in New Orleans, 1730–1744." *William and Mary Quarterly*, vol. 54, no. 4 (October 1997): 769–94.

————. *Masterless Mistresses: The New Orleans Ursulines and the Development of a New World Society, 1727–1824*. Chapel Hill: University of North Carolina Press, 2007.

————. *A New World Community: The New Orleans Ursulines and Colonial Society, 1727–1803*. PhD diss., Tulane University, 1998.

————, and Virginia Meacham Gould. "The Feminine Face of Afro-Catholicism in New Orleans, 1727–1852." *William and Mary Quarterly*, vol. 59, no. 2 (April 2002): 409–48.

Clark, Jerry E. "Jesuit Impact on Potawatomi Acculturation: A Comparison of Two Villages in the Mid-Plains." *Ethnohistory*, vol. 26, no. 4 (Fall 1979): 377–95.

Clegg, Claude A., III. *The Price of Liberty: African Americans and the Making of Liberia.* Chapel Hill: University of North Carolina Press, 2004.

Clifton, James A. *The Pokagons, 1683–1983: Catholic Potawatomi Indians of the St. Joseph River Valley.* Lanham, Md.: University Press of America, 1984.

———. *The Prairie People: Continuity and Change in Potawatomi Indian Culture, 1665–1965.* Lawrence: Regents Press of Kansas, 1977.

Coburn, Carol K., and Martha Smith. *Spirited Lives: How Nuns Shaped Catholic Culture and American Life, 1836–1920.* Chapel Hill: University of North Carolina Press, 1999.

Cohen, William B. *The French Encounter with Africans: White Response to Blacks, 1530–1880.* Bloomington: Indiana University Press, 1980.

Colley, Linda. *The Ordeal of Elizabeth Marsh: A Woman in World History.* New York: Pantheon, 2007.

Comby, Jean. *Deux mille ans d'évangélisation: Histoire de l'expansion chrétienne.* Paris: Declée, 1992.

———, ed. *Diffusion et acculturation du christianisme (XIXe–XXe siècle): Vingt-cinq ans de recherches missiologiques par le CREDIC.* Paris: Karthala, 2005.

La Congrégation de Saint-Joseph de Cluny (Les Ordres religieux). Paris: Letouzey et Ané, 1922.

Conklin, Alice L. *A Mission to Civilize: The Republican Idea of Empire in France and West Africa, 1895–1930.* Stanford: Stanford University Press, 1997.

Corbett, Katharine T. *In Her Place: A Guide to St. Louis Women's History.* St. Louis: Missouri Historical Society Press, 1999.

Cornevin, Robert, and Marianne Cornevin. *La France et les français outre-mer de la première croisade à la fin du Second Empire.* Paris: Tallandier, 1990.

Cott, Nancy F. *The Bonds of Womanhood: "Women's Sphere" in New England, 1780–1835.* New Haven: Yale University Press, 1977.

Coulon, Paul, and Paule Brasseur, et al. *Libermann, 1802–1852: Une pensée et une mystique missionnaires.* Paris: Cerf, 1988.

Cox, Jeffrey. *Imperial Fault Lines: Christianity and Colonial Power in India, 1818–1940.* Stanford: Stanford University Press, 2002.

Crowder, Michael. *Senegal: A Study of French Assimilation Policy.* London: Methuen, 1967.

Curtin, Philip D. *Economic Change in Precolonial Africa: Senegambia in the Era of the Slave Trade.* Madison: University of Wisconsin Press, 1975.

Curtis, Sarah A. "Charity Begins Abroad: The Filles de la Charité in the Ottoman Empire," in *God's Empire: French Missionaries and the Modern World*, ed. J. P. Daughton and Owen White. New York: Oxford University Press, 2012.

———. *Educating the Faithful: Religion, Schooling, and Society in Nineteenth-Century France.* DeKalb: Northern Illinois University Press, 2000.

Curzon, Robert. *Armenia: A Year at Erzeroom and on the Frontiers of Russia, Turkey, and Persia.* London: John Murray, 1854.

Daget, Serge. *La répression de la traite des noirs au XIXe siècle: L'action des croisières françaises sur les côtes occidentales de l'Afrique (1817–1850).* Paris: Karthala, 1997.

———. *La traite des noirs: Bastilles négrières et velléités abolitionnistes*. Paris: Ouest-France Université, 1990.

Darbon, Esprit. *Emilie de Vialar, fondatrice de la Congrégation des Soeurs de Saint-Joseph de l'Apparition: Souvenirs et documents*. Marseille: Oratoire Saint-Léon, 1901.

Daughton, J. P. *An Empire Divided: Religion, Republicanism, and the Making of French Colonialism, 1880–1914*. New York: Oxford University Press, 2006.

———. "When Argentina Was 'French': Rethinking Cultural Politics and European Imperialism in Belle-Epoque Buenos Aires." *Journal of Modern History*, vol. 80 (December 2008): 831–64.

Davis, Cyprian. *Henriette Delille: Servant of Slaves, Witness to the Poor*. New Orleans: Archdiocese of New Orleans, 2004.

———. *The History of Black Catholics in the United States*. New York: Crossroad, 1990.

Davis, David Brion. *The Problem of Slavery in Western Culture*. Ithaca: Cornell University Press, 1966.

Davis, Natalie Zemon. *Women on the Margins: Three Seventeenth-Century Lives*. Cambridge, Mass.: Harvard University Press, 1995.

de Maleissye, Marie-Thérèse, ed. *Femmes en missions: Actes de la XIe session du CREDIC à Saint-Flour (Août 1990)*. Lyon: Editions Lyonnaises d'art et d'histoire, 1991.

Deggs, (Sister) Mary Bernard. *No Cross, No Crown: Black Nuns in Nineteenth-Century New Orleans*, ed. Virginia Meacham and Charles E. Nolan Gould. Bloomington: Indiana University Press, 2001.

Delaplace, F., and Ph. Kieffer. *La Vénérable Mère Anne-Marie Javouhey, fondatrice de la Congrégation de Saint-Joseph de Cluny, 1779–1851*. Paris: Librairie Saint-Paul, 1914.

Delaplace, Père. *La R. M. Javouhey, fondatrice de la Congrégation de Saint-Joseph de Cluny: Histoire de sa vie, des oeuvres et missions de la congrégation*, 2 vols. Paris: Librairie Catholique Internationale, 1885.

Delcourt, Jean. *Histoire religieuse du Sénégal*. Dakar: Editions Clairafrique, 1976.

Delisle, Philippe. *Catholicisme, esclavage et acculturation dans la Caraïbe francophone et en Guyane au XIXe siècle*. Matoury, Guyana: Ibis Rouge, 2006.

———. "Clergé et esclavage aux Antilles et en Guyane françaises: De l'Ancien Régime à 1848." *Mémoire Spiritaine*, vol. 9 (1999): 161–72.

———. "Colonisation, christianisation et émancipation: Les Soeurs de Saint-Joseph de Cluny à Mana (Guyane française), 1828–1846." *Revue Française d'Histoire d'Outre Mer*, vol. 85, no. 320 (1998): 7–32.

———. "Congrégations enseignantes et missions extérieures: L'exemple des Frères de Ploërmel et des Soeurs de Saint-Joseph de Cluny aux Antilles françaises (XIXe siècle)." *Mémoire Spiritaine*, vol. 13 (2001): 41–59.

———. "Eglise et esclavage dans les vieilles colonies françaises au XIXe siècle." *Revue d'Histoire de l'Eglise de France*, vol. 84 (1998): 55–70.

———. *Histoire religieuse des Antilles et de la Guyane françaises: Des chrétientés sous les tropiques? 1815–1911*. Paris: Karthala, 2000.

———. *Renouveau missionnaire et société esclavagiste: La Martinique, 1815–1848*. Paris: Publisud, 1997.

Delumeau, Jean. *Catholicism between Luther and Voltaire: A New View of the Counter-Reformation*. London: Burns and Oates, 1977.

Deroy-Pineau, Françoise. *Marie de l'Incarnation: Marie Guyart, femme d'affaires, mystique, mère de la Nouvelle-France; 1599–1672*. Paris: Robert Laffont, 1989.

———, ed. *Marie Guyard de l'Incarnation: Un destin transocéanique (Tours, 1599–Québec, 1672)*. Paris: L'Harmattan, 2000.

Desan, Suzanne. *Reclaiming the Sacred: Lay Religion and Popular Politics in Revoutionary France*. Ithaca: Cornell University Press, 1990.

Deslandres, Dominique. *Croire et faire croire: Les missions françaises au XVIIe siècle (1600–1650)*. Paris: Fayard, 2003.

Desprat, Bernard. "Emilie de Vialar (1797–1856) à Gaillac." *Revue du Tarn* 165 (Spring 1997): 69–129.

Devens, Carol. *Countering Colonization: Native American Women and Great Lakes Missions, 1630–1900*. Berkeley: University of California Press, 1992.

Devos, Roger. *Vie religieuse féminine et société: L'origine sociale des Visitandines d'Annecy aux XVIIe et XVIIIe siècles*. Annecy: Académie Salésienne, 1973.

Dinan, Susan E. *Women and Poor Relief in Seventeenth-Century France: The Early History of the Daughters of Charity*. Burlington, Vt.: Ashgate, 2006.

Dippie, Brian W. *The Vanishing American: White Attitudes and U.S. Indian Policy*. Lawrence: University Press of Kansas, 1982.

Dolan, Jay P. *The American Catholic Experience: A History from Colonial Times to the Present*. Garden City, N.Y.: Doubleday, 1985.

Dompnier, Bernard, and Dominique Julia, eds. *Visitation et Visitandines aux XVIIe et XVIIIe siècles*. St-Etienne: Publications de l'Université de Saint-Etienne, 2001.

Donadio, Rachel. "On Africa Trip, Pope Will Find Place Where Church Is Surging amid Travail." *New York Times* (16 March 2009), A6.

Donato, Marc. *L'émigration des maltais en Algérie au XIXème siècle*. Montpellier: Editions Africa Nostra, 1985.

Donovan, Jeffrey. "On Pope's 84th Birthday, Succession Talk Looks to Africa." *Radio Free Europe* (18 May 2004).

Dorigny, Marcel, ed. *Les abolitions de l'esclavage de L. F. Sonthonax à V. Schoelcher, 1793, 1794, 1848*. Paris: Editions UNESCO and Presses Universitaires de Vincennes, 1995.

Dornier, François. *La vie des catholiques en Tunisie au fil des ans*. Tunis: Imprimerie Finzi, 2000.

Drescher, Seymour. *From Slavery to Freedom: Comparative Studies in the Rise and Fall of Atlantic Slavery*. New York: New York University Press, 1999.

Drevet, Richard. Laïques de France et missions catholiques au XIXe siècle: L'œuvre de la propagation de la foi, origines et développment lyonnais (1822–1922). Thèse de doctorat, Université Lyon 2, 2002.

Dreyfus, Paul. *Sainte Marie d'en Haut*. Grenoble: Imprimier Allier, 1959.

Dubois, Laurent. *Avengers of the New World: The Story of the Haitian Revolution*. Cambridge, Mass.: Belknap Press of Harvard University Press, 2004.

———. *A Colony of Citizens: Revolution and Slave Emancipation in the French Caribbean, 1787–1804*. Chapel Hill: University of North Carolina Press, 2004.

Duboscq, Guy, and André Latreille, eds. *Les réveils missionnaires en France du Moyen-Age à nos jours (XIIe—XXe siècles): Actes du colloque de Lyon, 29–31 Mai 1980*. Paris: Beauchesne, 1984.

Dufourcq, Elisabeth. *Les congrégations religieuses féminines hors d'Europe de Richelieu à nos jours: Histoire naturelle d'une diaspora*, 4 vols. Paris: Librairie de l'Inde, 1993.

————. "Etude de l'établissement des congrégations religieuses féminines d'origine française dans les Etats-Unis du XIXè siècle comme marqueur de certains modes d'occupation du territoire et de distinction sociale." *Histoire, Economie, et Société*, vol. 11, no. 4 (1992): 619–43.

Duvignacq-Glessgen, Marie-Ange. *L'Ordre de la Visitation à Paris aux XVIIe et XVIIIe siècles*. Paris: Cerf, 1994.

Ebaugh, Helen Rose. "The Growth and Decline of Catholic Religious Orders of Women Worldwide: The Impact of Women's Opportunity Structures." *Journal for the Scientific Study of Religion*, vol. 32, no. 1 (March 1993): 68–75.

Edmunds, R. David. *The Potawatomis: Keepers of the Fire*. Norman: University of Oklahoma Press, 1978.

Ekberg, Carl J. *French Roots in the Illinois Country: The Mississippi Frontier in Colonial Times*. Urbana: University of Illinois Press, 1998.

Eltis, David, and James Walvin. *The Abolition of the Atlantic Slave Trade: Origins and Effects in Europe, Africa, and the Americas*. Madison: University of Wisconsin Press, 1981.

Essertel, Yannick. *L'aventure missionnaire lyonnaise, 1815–1962*. Paris: Cerf, 2001.

Etherington, Norman, ed. *Missions and Empire*. New York: Oxford University Press, 2005.

Ewens, Mary. *The Role of the Nun in Nineteenth-Century America*. New York: Arno, 1978.

Farraudière, Yvette. *Ecole et société en Guyane française: Scolarisation et colonisation*. Paris: L'Harmattan, 1989.

Faury, Jean. *Cléricalisme et anticléricalisme dans le Tarn (1848–1900)*. Toulouse: Service des Publications de l'Université de Toulouse, 1980.

————. "Le Tarn et le Gaillacois au temps des Guérin," in *Lectures Guériniennes*, ed. Claude Gély, 5–12. Montpellier: Publications de la Recherche, Université de Montpellier, 1989.

Fawaz, Leila Tarazi. *Merchants and Migrants in Nineteenth-Century Beirut*. Cambridge, Mass.: Harvard University Press, 1983.

Feay, Troy. Mission to Moralize: Slaves, Africans, and Missionaries in the French Colonies, 1815–1852. PhD diss., University of Notre Dame, 2003.

Ferro, Marc. *Le livre noir du colonialisme, XVIe–XXIe siècle: De l'extermination à la repentance*. Paris: Robert Laffont, 2003.

Flint, John E., ed. *The Cambridge History of Africa*, vol. 5, *From c. 1790 to c. 1870*. London: Cambridge University Press, 1976.

Foley, William E. *The Genesis of Missouri: From Wilderness Outpost to Statehood*. Columbia: University of Missouri Press, 1989.

Ford, Caroline. "Private Lives and Public Order in Restoration France: The Seduction of Emily Loveday." *American Historical Review*, vol. 99, no. 1 (February 1994): 21–43.

Franchot, Jenny. *Roads to Rome: The Antebellum Protestant Encounter with Catholicism*. Berkeley: University of California Press, 1994.

Frazee, Charles A. *Catholics and Sultans: The Church and the Ottoman Empire, 1453–1923*. New York: Cambridge University Press, 1983.

————. *The Orthodox Church and Independent Greece, 1821–1852*. London: Cambridge University Press, 1969.

Fredrickson, George M. *The Black Image in the White Mind: The Debate on Afro-American Character and Destiny, 1817–1914*. New York: Harper and Row, 1971.

———. *Racism: A Short History*. Princeton: Princeton University Press, 2002.

Fuma, Sudel. *L'esclavagisme à La Réunion, 1794–1848*. Paris: L'Harmattan, 1992.

Fyfe, Christopher. *A History of Sierra Leone*. Oxford: Clarendon, 1962.

Gadille, Jacques, and Jean-François Zorn. "Le projet missionnaire," in *Histoire du christianisme*, vol. 11, *Libéralism, industrialisation, expansion européenne (1830–1914)*, 137–68. Paris: Declée, 1995.

Gallagher, Nancy Elizabeth. *Medicine and Power in Tunisia, 1780–1900*. New York: Cambridge University Press, 1983.

Ganiage, Jean. *L'expansion coloniale de la France sous la Troisième République (1871–1914)*. Paris: Payot, 1968.

———. *La population européenne de Tunis au milieu du XIXe siècle*. Paris: Presses Universitaires de France, 1960.

Ganson, Barbara. *The Guaraní under Spanish Rule in the Río de la Plata*. Stanford: Stanford University Press, 2003.

Garraghan, Gilbert J. *The Jesuits of the Middle United States*, 3 vols. New York: America Press, 1938.

Gautier, Arlette. *Les soeurs de Solitude: La condition féminine dans l'esclave aux Antilles du XVIIe au XIXe siècle*. Paris: Edition Caribéennes, 1985.

Getz, Trevor R. *Slavery and Reform in West Africa: Toward Emancipation in Nineteenth-Century Senegal and the Gold Coast*. Athens: Ohio University Press, 2004.

Gibson, Ralph. *A Social History of French Catholicism, 1789–1914*. London: Routledge, 1989.

Gill, Gillian. *Nightingales: The Extraordinary Upbringing and Curious Life of Miss Florence Nightingale*. New York: Ballantine, 2004.

Gislier, Antoine. *L'esclavage aux Antilles françaises (XVIIe–XIXe siècle): Contribution au problème de l'esclavage*. Paris: Karthala, 1981.

Godechot, Jacques. *Histoire de Malte*, 3rd ed. Paris: Presses Universitaires de France, 1981.

Gould, Virginia Meacham, and Charles E. Nolan, eds. *No Cross, No Crown: Black Nuns in Nineteenth-Century New Orleans*. Bloomington: Indiana University Press, 2001.

Goyau, Georges. *Un grand "homme": Mère Javouhey, apôtre des noirs*. Paris: Plon, 1929.

Gray, Richard. *Black Christians and White Missionaries*. New Haven: Yale University Press, 1990.

Greer, Allan. *Mohawk Saint: Catherine Tekekwitha and the Jesuits*. New York: Oxford University Press, 2005.

Groffier, Valérin. *Héros trop oubliés de notre épopée coloniale*. Lille: Desclée, de Brouwer, 1908.

Guarneri, Carl J. *The Utopian Alternative: Fourierism in Nineteenth-century America*. Ithaca: Cornell University Press, 1991.

Guèye, M'baye. "La fin de l'esclavage à Saint-Louis et à Gorée en 1848." *Bulletin de l'I.F.A.N*, Series B, 28, no. 3–4 (1966): 637–62.

Hall, Catherine. *Civilising Subjects: Metropole and Colony in the English Imagination, 1830–1867*. Chicago: University of Chicago Press, 2002.

————. "Missionary Stories: Gender and Ethnicity in England in the 1830s and 1840s," in *White, Male, and Middle-Class: Explorations in Feminism and History*, 205–54. New York: Routledge, 1992.

Hamdani, Amar. *La vérité sur l'expédition d'Alger*. Paris: Balland, 1985.

Hamon, Auguste. *Histoire de la dévotion au Sacré Coeur*, vol. 4, *Luttes indécises*. Paris: Beauchesne, 1931.

Hannaford, Ivan. *Race: The History of an Idea in the West*. Baltimore: Johns Hopkins University Press, 1996.

Hardy, Georges. *La mise en valeur du Sénégal de 1817 à 1854*. Paris: Emile Larose, 1921.

Hardy, Madeleine. *Antoine-Adolphe Dupuch, premier évêque d'Alger (1838–1846): Un pionnier de la mission à l'épreuve du politique*. Paris: Hora Decima, 2006.

Harris, Ruth. *Lourdes: Body and Spirit in the Secular Age*. London: Allen Lane, Penguin, 1999.

Harrison, Henrietta. " 'A Penny for the Little Chinese': The French Holy Childhood Association in China, 1843–1951." *American Historical Review*, vol. 113, no. 1 (February 2008): 72–92.

Hastings, Adrian. *The Church in Africa, 1450–1950*. Oxford: Clarendon, 1994.

Hefner, Robert W., ed. *Conversion to Christianity: Historical and Anthropological Perspectives on a Great Transformation*. Berkeley: University of California Press, 1993.

Henrion, Mathieu Richard Auguste (baron). *Histoire générale des missions catholiques depuis le XIIIe siècle jusqu'à nos jours*, 2 vols. Paris: Gaume Frères, 1847.

Heyrman, Christine Leigh. *Southern Cross: The Beginnings of the Bible Belt*. New York: Knopf, 1997.

Hitchens, Christopher. *The Missionary Position: Mother Teresa in Theory and Practice*. London: Verso, 1995.

Hoffman, Nancy. *Woman's "True" Profession: Voices from the History of Teaching*. Old Westbury, N.Y.: Feminist Press, 1981.

Homberger, Eric, and John Charmley, eds. *The Troubled Face of Biography*. London: Macmillan, 1988.

Huber, Mary Taylor, and Nancy C. Lutkehaus, eds. *Gendered Missions: Women and Men in Missionary Discourse and Practice*. Ann Arbor: University of Michigan Press, 1999.

Hufton, Olwen H. *Women and the Limits of Citizenship in the French Revolution*. Toronto: University of Toronto Press, 1992.

Hurault, Jean. *Les Indiens de Guyane française: Problèmes pratiques d'administration et de contacts de civilisation*. The Hague: Nijhoff, 1963.

Janin, Joseph. *Le clergé colonial de 1815 À 1850*. Toulouse: H. Basuyau, 1935.

Jennings, Lawrence C. "Associative Socialism and Slave Emancipation in French Guiana, 1839–1848." *Revue Française d'Histoire Outre-Mer* 330–31 (1er sem. 2001): 167–88.

————. *French Anti-Slavery: The Movement for the Abolition of Slavery in France, 1802–1848*. New York: Cambridge University Press, 2000.

Johnston, Anna. *Missionary Writing and Empire, 1800–1860*. New York: Cambridge University Press, 2003.

Jonas, Raymond. *France and the Cult of the Sacred Heart: An Epic Tale for Modern Times*. Berkeley: University of California Press, 2000.

Jones, Colin. *The Charitable Imperative: Hospitals and Nursing in Ancien Regime and Revolutionary France*. London: Routledge, 1989.

Jones, D. H. "The Catholic Mission and Some Aspects of Assimilation in Senegal, 1817–1852." *Journal of African History*, vol. 21 (1980): 323–40.

Jones, Dorothy V. "A Potawatomi Faces the Problem of Cultural Change: Joseph N. Bourassa in Kansas." *Kansas Quarterly*, vol. 3, no. 4 (Fall 1971): 47–55.

Julien, Charles-André. *Histoire de l'Algérie contemporaine*, vol. 1, *La conquête et les débuts de la colonisation (1827–1871)*. Paris: Presses Universitaires de France, 1964.

Kastor, Peter J. *The Nation's Crucible: The Louisiana Purchase and the Creation of America*. New Haven: Yale University Press, 2004.

Kaufman, Polly Welts. *Women Teachers on the Frontier*. New Haven: Yale University Press, 1984.

Kertzer, David I. *The Kidnapping of Edgardo Mortara*. New York: Vintage, 1998.

———. "The Montel Affair: Vatican Jewish Policy and French Diplomacy under the July Monarchy." *French Historical Studies*, vol. 25, no. 2 (Spring 2002): 265–93.

———. *The Popes against the Jews: The Vatican's Role in the Rise of Modern Anti-Semitism*. New York: Knopf, 2001.

Kilroy, Phil. *Madeleine Sophie Barat, 1779–1865: A Life*. Cork: Cork University Press, 2000.

Klein, Herbert S. *African Slavery in Latin America and the Caribbean*. New York: Oxford University Press, 1986.

Klein, Martin A. *Slavery and Colonial Rule in French West Africa*. New York: Cambridge University Press, 1998.

———. "Slavery and Emancipation in French West Africa," in *Breaking the Chains: Slavery, Bondage, and Emancipation in Modern Africa and Asia*, ed. Martin A. Klein, 171–96. Madison: University of Wisconsin Press, 1993.

Knibiehler, Yvonne, and Régine Goutalier. *La femme au temps des colonies*. Paris: Stock, 1985.

Koliopoulos, John S., and Thanos M. Veremis. *Greece: The Modern Sequel: From 1831 to the Present*. New York: New York University Press, 2002.

Koster, Adrianus. *Prelates and Politicians in Malta: Changing Power-Balances between Church and State in a Mediterranean Island Fortress (1800–1976)*. Assen, Netherlands: Van Gorcum, 1984.

Koumoulides, John T. A. *Cyprus and the War of Greek Independence, 1821–1829*. Athens: National Centre of Social Research, 1971.

Kroen, Sheryl. *Politics and Theater: The Crisis of Legitimacy in Restoration France, 1815–1830*. Berkeley: University of California Press, 2000.

Krumenacker, Yves. *L'école française de spiritualité: Des mystiques, des fondateurs, des courants et leurs interprètes*. Paris: Cerf, 1998.

Kumar, Krishan. *Utopianism*. Minneapolis: University of Minnesota Press, 1991.

Lacoste, Yves, and André Nouschi. *L'Algérie, passé et présent: Le cadre et les étapes de la constitution de l'Algérie actuelle*. Paris: Editions Sociales, 1960.

Laffay, Augustin-Hervé. *Dom Augustin de Lestrange et l'avenir du monachisme (1754–1827)*. Paris: Cerf, 1998.

Lambert, Alexandre. *Les congrégations de femmes en France de 1825 à 1901*. Paris: Henri Jouve, 1905.

Langlois, Claude. "Anne-Marie Javouhey au miroir de sa correspondance." *Mémoire Spiritaine*, vol. 2 (November 1995): 128–42.

―――. *Le catholicisme au féminin: Les congrégations françaises à supérieure générale au XIXe siècle*. Paris: Cerf, 1984.

Laurens, Henri. *La question de Palestine*, vol. 1, *1799–1922: L'invention de la Terre Sainte*. Paris: Fayard, 1999.

Le Goff, Jacques, and René Rémond, eds. *Histoire de la France religieuse*, vol. 3. Paris: Seuil, 1991.

Lecuir-Nemo, Geneviève. *Anne-Marie Javouhey: Fondatrice de la congrégation des soeurs de Saint-Joseph de Cluny (1779–1851)*. Paris: Karthala, 2001.

―――. *Femmes et vocation missionnaire: Permanence des congrégations féminines au Sénégal de 1819 à 1960: Adaptation ou mutations? Impact et insertion*, 2 vols. Villeneuve d'Ascq: Presses Universitaires du Septentrion, 1997.

Leflaive, Anne. "Philippine Duchesne et Sainte-Marie-d'en-Haut." *Bulletin de l'Académie Delphinale*, vol. 8 (November 1973): 225–32.

Legrain, Michel. "Les esclaves, le mariage et l'Eglise." *Revue de Droit canonique*, vol. 38, no. 3–4 (September–December 1988): 296–329.

Lepore, Jill. "Historians Who Love Too Much: Reflections on Microhistory and Biography." *Journal of American History*, vol. 88, no. 1 (June 2001): 129–44.

Lesourd, Paul. *Histoire des missions catholiques*. Paris: Librairie de l'Arc, 1937.

Liebersohn, Harry. *Aristocratic Encounters: European Travelers and North American Indians*. New York: Cambridge University Press, 1998.

Lorcin, Patricia M. E. *Imperial Identities: Stereotyping, Prejudice, and Race in Colonial Algeria*. London: Tauris, 1995.

―――. "Rome and France in Africa: Recovering Colonial Algeria's Latin Past." *French Historical Studies*, vol. 25, no. 2 (Spring 2002): 295–329.

―――. "Teaching Women and Gender in France d'Outre-Mer: Problems and Strategies." *French Historical Studies*, vol. 27, no. 2 (Spring 2004): 293–310.

Mack, Phyllis. "Religion, Feminism, and the Problem of Agency: Reflections on Eighteenth-Century Quakerism." *Signs*, vol. 29, no. 1 (2003): 149–77.

Mahoney, Irene, ed. *Marie of the Incarnation: Selected Writings*. New York: Paulist Press, 1989.

Mam-Lam-Fouck, Serge. *L'esclavage en Guyane entre l'occultation et la revendication*. Guyana: Ibis Rouge, Presses Universitaires Créoles, 1998.

―――. *La Guyane française au temps de l'esclavage, de l'or, et de la francisation (1802–1946)*. Petit Bourg, Guadeloupe: Ibis Rouge, 1999.

―――. *Histoire générale de la Guyane française: Les grands problèmes guyanais; Permanence et évolution*. Cayenne: Ibis Rouge; Presses Universitaires Créoles, 1996.

―――, and Jacqueline Zonzon, eds. *L'histoire de la Guyane depuis les civilisations amérindiennes*. Matoury, Guyana: Ibis Rouge, 2006.

Manceron, Gilles. *Marianne et les colonies: Une introduction à l'histoire coloniale de la France*. Paris: La Découverte, 2003.

Manuel, Frank E., and Fritzie P. Manuel. *Utopian Thought in the Western World*. Cambridge, Mass.: Belknap Press of Harvard University Press, 1979.

Ma'oz, Moshe. *Ottoman Reform in Syria and Palestine: The Impact of the Tanzimat on Politics and Society*. Oxford: Clarendon, 1969.

Marchand-Thébault, M.-L. "L'esclavage en Guyane française sous l'Ancien Régime." *Revue Française d'Histoire d'Outre-Mer*, vol. 47 (1960): 5–75.

Margadant, Jo Burr, ed. *The New Biography: Performing Femininity in Nineteenth-Century France*. Berkeley: University of California Press, 2000.

Marshall, Joyce, ed. *Word from New France: The Selected Letters of Marie de l'Incarnation*. Toronto: Oxford University Press, 1967.

Marten, Michael. *Attempting to Bring the Gospel Home: Scottish Missions to Palestine, 1839–1917*. London: Tauris Academic Studies, 2006.

Martin, Phyllis. "Celebrating the Ordinary: Church, Empire, and Gender in the Life of Mère Marie-Michelle Dédié (Senegal and Congo, 1882–1931)." *Gender and History*, vol. 16, no. 2 (August 2004): 289–317.

Maxwell, John Francis. *Slavery and the Catholic Church: The History of Catholic Teaching concerning the Moral Legitimacy of the Institution of Slavery*. Chichester: Barry Rose, 1975.

Mbodj, Mohamed. "The Abolition of Slavery in Senegal, 1820–1890: Crisis or the Rise of a New Entrepreneurial Class?" In *Breaking the Chains: Slavery, Bondage, and Emancipation in Modern Africa and Asia*, ed. Martin A. Klein, 197–211. Madison: University of Wisconsin Press, 1993.

McClintock, Anne. *Imperial Leather: Race, Gender, and Sexuality in the Colonial Contest*. New York: Routledge, 1995.

McCoy, Isaac. *History of Baptist Indian Missions*. New York: Johnson Reprint, 1970; orig. ed., 1840.

McGreevy, John T. *Catholicism and American Freedom: A History*. New York: Norton, 2003.

McKevitt, Gerald. "The Art of Conversion: Jesuits and Flatheads in Nineteenth-Century Montana." *U.S. Catholic Historian*, vol. 12, no. 4 (Fall 1994): 49–64.

McManners, John. *Church and Society in Eighteenth-Century France*, 2 vols. Oxford: Clarendon, 1998.

McNamara, Jo Ann Kay. *Sisters in Arms: Catholic Nuns through Two Millennia*. Cambridge, Mass.: Harvard University Press, 1996.

Medwick, Cathleen. *Teresa of Avila: The Progress of a Soul*. New York: Knopf, 1999.

Melville, Annabelle M. *Louis William DuBourg: Bishop of Louisiana and the Floridas, Bishop of Montauban, and Archbishop of Besançon, 1766–1833*. Chicago: Loyola University Press, 1986.

Meyer, Jean, Jean Tarade, Annie Rey-Goldzeiguer, and Jacques Thobie. *Histoire de la France colonial des origines à 1914*. Paris: Armand Colin, 1991.

Mezzadri, Luigi. *Sainte Jeanne-Antide Thouret (1765–1826)*. Paris: Médiaspaul, 1999.

Midgley, Clare. *Feminism and Empire: Women Activists in Imperial Britain, 1790–1865*. New York: Routledge, 2007.

———. *Women against Slavery: The British Campaigns, 1780–1870*. London: Routledge, 1992.

Miles, Jonathan. *The Wreck of the Medusa: The Most Famous Sea Disaster of the Nineteenth Century*. New York: Atlantic Monthly Press, 2007.

Miller, Christopher L. *The French Atlantic Triangle: Literature and Culture of the Slave Trade*. Durham, N.C.: Duke University Press, 2008.

Misner, Barbara. *"Highly Respectable and Accomplished Ladies": Catholic Women Religious in America, 1790–1850*. New York: Garland, 1988.

Monseigneur Valerga, premier patriarche de Jérusalem: Ses derniers jours et sa mort par un prêtre du Patriarcat Latin de Jérusalem. Paris: Henri Plon, 1873.

Moomou, Jean. *Le monde des Marrons du Maroni en Guyane (1772–1860): La naissance d'un peuple; Les Boni.* Cayenne: Ibis Rouge, 2004.

Mooney, Catherine M. *Philippine Duchesne: A Woman with the Poor.* New York: Paulist Press, 1990.

Morley, Jefferson, "Hopes for a Third World Pope." *Washington Post* (5 April 2005).

Morrissey, Thomas. *As One Sent: Peter Kenney, S.J., 1779–1841: His Mission in Ireland and North America.* Dublin: Four Courts, 1996.

Morrow, Diane Batts. *Persons of Color and Religious at the Same Time: The Oblate Sisters of Providence, 1828–1860.* Chapel Hill: University of North Carolina Press, 2002.

Moses, Claire Goldberg. *French Feminism in the Nineteenth Century.* Albany: State University of New York Press, 1984.

Mörner, Magnus. *The Political and Economic Activities of the Jesuits in the La Plata Region: The Hapsburg Era.* Stockholm: Library and Institute of Ibero-American Studies, 1953.

Myhre, Paul O. Potawatomi Transformation: Potawatomi Responses to Catholic and Baptist Mission Strategy and Competition, 1822–1872. PhD diss., Saint Louis University, 1998.

Necheles, Ruth F. *The Abbé Grégoire, 1787–1831: The Odyssey of an Egalitarian.* Westport, Conn.: Greenwood, 1971.

Norberg, Kathryn. *Rich and Poor in Grenoble, 1600–1814.* Berkeley: University of California Press, 1985.

Notice sur la Congrégation des Soeurs de Saint-Joseph de Cluny. Beauvais: Congrégation de St-Joseph de Cluny, 1880.

Oates, Mary J. "Catholic Female Academies on the Frontier." *U.S. Catholic Historian,* vol. 12, no. 4 (Fall 1994): 121–36.

O'Brien, Susan. "French Nuns in Nineteenth-Century England." *Past and Present,* vol. 154 (February 1997): 142–80.

Offen, Karen. "Disrupting the Anglophone Narrative: How (and Why) the Analogy of Marriage with Slavery Provided the Springboard for Women's Rights Demands in France (1640–1848)," in *Women's Rights and Transatlantic Antislavery in the Era of Emancipation,* ed. Kathryn Kish Sklar and James Brewer Stewart. New Haven: Yale University Press, 2007.

———. *European Feminisms, 1700–1950: A Political History.* Stanford: Stanford University Press, 2000.

Pago, Gilbert. *Les femmes et la liquidation du système esclavagiste à la Martinique, 1848 à 1852.* Guyana: Ibis Rouge, 1998.

Panzer, Joel S. *The Popes and Slavery.* New York: Alba House, 1996.

Peabody, Sue. " 'A Nation Born to Slavery': Missionaries and Racial Discourse in Seventeenth-Century French Antilles." *Journal of Social History,* vol. 28 (2004): 113–26.

———. *"There Are No Slaves in France": The Political Culture of Race and Slavery in the Ancien Régime.* New York: Oxford University Press, 1996.

———, and Tyler Stovall, eds. *The Color of Liberty: Histories of Race in France.* Durham, N.C.: Duke University Press, 2003.

Pearce, Roy Harvey. *Savagism and Civilization: A Study of the Indian and the American Mind*. Baltimore: Johns Hopkins University Press, 1965.

Peyret, Raymond. *Sainte Philippine Duchesne (1769–1852): Une française pionnière au Missouri*. Paris: Desclée de Brouwer, 1999.

Picard, Louis (abbé). *Une vierge française: Emilie de Vialar, fondatrice des religieuses Saint-Joseph de l'Apparition*. Paris: Paul Feron-Vrau, 1924.

Pilbeam, Patricia. "Dream Worlds? Religion and the Early Socialists in France." *Historical Journal*, vol. 43, no. 2 (2000): 499–515.

———. *French Socialists before Marx: Workers, Women, and the Social Question in France*. Montreal: McGill-Queen's University Press, 2000.

Pilot, J.-J.-A. *Eglise et ancien couvent de Sainte-Marie-d'en-Haut à Grenoble*. Grenoble: F. Allier Père et Fils, 1869.

Pioneau, E. (abbé). *Vie de Mgr Dupuch, premier évêque d'Alger*. Bordeaux: Paul Chaumas, 1866.

Pirotte, Jean, ed., *Résistances à l'évangélisation: Interprétations historiques et enjeux théologiques*. Paris: Karthala, 2004.

Planel, Anne-Marie. De la nation à la colonie: La commmunauté française de Tunisie au XIXe siècle, 3 vols. Thèse de doctorat, Ecole des Hautes Etudes en Sciences Sociales, 2000.

Plongeron, Bernard, ed. *Pratiques religieuses, mentalités, et spiritualités dans l'Europe revolutionnaire (1770–1820)*. Brepols: Turnhout, 1988.

Pluchon, Pierre, ed. *Histoire des Antilles et de la Guyane*. Paris: Privat, 1982.

Pons, A. *La nouvelle église d'Afrique ou le catholicisme en Algérie, en Tunisie, et au Maroc depuis 1830*. Tunis: Louis Namura, 1930.

Popkin, Jeremy D., and Richard H. Popkin, eds. *The Abbé Grégoire and His World*. Dordrecht: Kluwer Academic, 2000.

Porter, Andrew. *Religion versus Empire? British Protestant Missionaries and Overseas Expansion, 1700–1914*. Manchester: Manchester University Press, 2004.

Prochaska, David. *Making Algeria French: Colonialism in Bône, 1870–1920*. New York: Cambridge University Press, 1990.

Prucha, Francis Paul. *American Indian Policy in the Formative Years: The Indian Trade and Intercourse Acts, 1790–1834*. Lincoln: University of Nebraska Press, 1962.

———. *The Great Father: The United States Government and the American Indians*, 2 vols. Lincoln: University of Nebraska Press, 1984.

Prudhomme, Claude, ed. *Une appropriation du monde: Mission et missions, XIXe–XXe siècles*. Paris: Publisud, 2004.

———. *Histoire religieuse de la Réunion*. Paris: Karthala, 1984.

Quinn, Frederick. *The French Overseas Empire*. Westport, Conn.: Praeger, 2000.

Rapley, Elizabeth. *The Dévotes: Women and Church in Seventeenth-Century France*. Montreal: McGill-Queen's University Press, 1990.

———. *A Social History of the Cloister: Daily Life in the Teaching Monasteries of the Old Regime*. Montreal: McGill-Queen's University Press, 2001.

Renault, François. *L'abolition de l'esclavage au Sénégal: L'attitude de l'administration française, 1848–1905*. Paris: Société française d'Histoire d'Outre-Mer, 1972.

Reynes, Geneviève. *Couvents de femmes: La vie des relgieuses contemplatives dans la France des XVIIe et XVIIIe siècles*. Paris: Fayard, 1987.

Riasanovsky, Maria. The Trumpets of Jericho: Domestic Missions and Religious Revival in France, 1814–1830. PhD diss., Princeton University, 2001.

Richbert, Keith B. "Rwandan Nuns Jailed in Genocide." *Washington Post* (9 June 2001), A01.

Rogers, Rebecca. *From the Salon to the Schoolroom: Educating Bourgeois Girls in Nineteenth-Century France*. University Park: Pennsylvania State University Press, 2005.

Royot, Daniel. *Divided Loyalties in a Doomed Empire: The French in the West from New France to the Lewis and Clark Expedition*. Newark: University of Delaware Press, 2007.

Rozet, Claude-Antoine. *Voyage dans la régence d'Alger ou description du pays occupé par l'armée française en Afrique*, 2 vols. Paris: Arthus Bertrand, 1833.

Rubenstine, Clark. "French Colonial Policy and the Education of Women and Minorities: Louisiana in the Early Eighteenth Century." *History of Education Quarterly*, vol. 32, no. 2 (Summer 1992): 193–211.

Ruedy, John. *Modern Algeria: The Origins and Development of a Nation*. Bloomington: Indiana University Press, 1992.

Ruggieri, Giuseppe, ed. *Eglise et histoire de l'Eglise en Afrique: Actes du colloque de Bologne*. Paris: Beauchesne, 1988.

Sackur, Amanda. The Development of Creole Society and Culture in Saint-Louis and Gorée, 1719–1817. PhD diss., School of Oriental and African Studies, University of London, 1999.

Sadoux, Dominique, and Pierre Gervais. *La vie religieuse: Premières constitutions des religieuses de la Société du Sacré-Coeur: Texte et commentaire*. Paris: Beauchesne, 1986.

Said, Edward. *Orientalism*. New York: Vintage, 1979.

Samb, Djibril, ed. *Gorée et l'esclavage: Actes du séminaire sur "Gorée dans la traite atlantique: Mythes et réalités."* Dakar: IFAN Ch. A. Diop, 1997.

Sanjian, Avedis K. *The Armenian Communities in Syria under Ottoman Dominion*. Cambridge, Mass.: Harvard University Press, 1965.

Sanneh, Lamin. *Abolitionists Abroad: American Blacks and the Making of Modern West Africa*. Cambridge, Mass.: Harvard University Press, 1999.

———. *West African Christianity: The Religious Impact*. London: Hurst, 1983.

Satz, Ronald N. *American Indian Policy in the Jacksonian Era*. Lincoln: University of Nebraska Press, 1975.

Schmidt, Nelly. *Abolitionnistes de l'esclavage et réformateurs des colonies (1820–1851): Analyse et documents*. Paris: Karthala, 2000.

———. *Victor Schoelcher et l'abolition de l'esclavage*. Paris: Fayard, 1994.

Schuler, Monica. "Liberated Africans in Nineteenth-Century Guyana," in *Slavery, Freedom, and Gender: The Dynamics of Caribbean Society*, ed. Brian L. Moore, B. W. Higman, Carl Campbell, and Patrick Bryan, 133–57. Barbados: University of the West Indies Press, 2001.

Scott, Joan Wallach. *Only Paradoxes to Offer: French Feminists and the Rights of Man*. Cambridge, Mass.: Harvard University Press, 1996.

Searing, James F. *West African Slavery and Atlantic Commerce: The Senegal River Valley, 1700–1860*. New York: Cambridge University Press, 1993.

Sebag, Paul. *Tunis: Histoire d'une ville*. Paris: L'Harmattan, 1998.

Semple, Rhonda Anne. *Missionary Women: Gender, Professionalism, and the Victorian Idea of Christian Mission.* Rochester, N.Y.: Boydell, 2003.

Sepinwall, Alyssa Goldstein. *The Abbé Grégoire and the French Revolution: The Making of Modern Universalism.* Berkeley: University of California Press, 2005.

Serrano, Sol, and Alexandrine de la Taille. *Virgenes viajeras: Diarios de religiosas francesas en su ruta a Chile, 1837–1874.* Santiago: Ediciones Universidad Católica de Chile, 2000.

Sevrin, Ernest. *Les missions religieuses en France sous la Restauration, 1815–1830,* 2 vols. Paris: J. Vrin, 1948, 1959.

Shepherd, Naomi. *The Zealous Intruders: The Western Rediscovery of Palestine.* London: Collins, 1987.

Sklar, Kathryn Kish. *Catharine Beecher: A Study in American Domesticity.* New Haven: Yale University Press, 1973.

Slade, Carole. *St. Teresa of Avila: Author of a Heroic Life.* Berkeley: University of California Press, 1995.

Sleeper-Smith, Susan. *Indian Women and French Men: Rethinking Cultural Encounter in the Western Great Lakes.* Amherst: University of Massachusetts Press, 2001.

Smith, Andrea L. *Colonial Memory and Postcolonial Europe: Maltese Settlers in Algeria and France.* Bloomington: Indiana University Press, 2006.

Smith, Bonnie. *Ladies of the Leisure Class: The Bourgeoises of Northern France in the Nineteenth Century.* Princeton: Princeton University Press, 1981.

Solomon, Barbara Miller. *In the Company of Educated Women: A History of Women and Higher Education in America.* New Haven: Yale University Press, 1985.

Soumille, Pierre. "Les multiples activités d'un prêtre français au Maghreb: L'Abbé François Bourgade en Algérie et en Tunisie de 1838 à 1858," in *Histoires d'Outre-Mer: Mélanges en l'honneur de Jean-Louis Miège,* ed. Colette Dubois, Hubert Gerbeau, Yvan Paillard, and Pierre Soumille, vol. 1, 233–72. Aix-en-Provence: Publications de l'Université de Provence, 1992.

Sparks, Randy J. *Religion in Mississippi.* Jackson: University Press of Mississippi for the Mississippi Historical Association, 2001.

Stanley, Brian, ed. *Christian Missions and the Enlightenment.* Grand Rapids, Mich.: Eerdmans, 2001.

Steinfells, Peter. "Beliefs." *New York Times* (19 September 1998).

Stockdale, Nancy L. Gender and Colonialism in Palestine, 1800–1948: Encounters among English, Arab, and Jewish Women. PhD diss., University of California–Santa Barbara, 2000.

Stoler, Ann Laura. *Carnal Knowledge and Imperial Power.* Berkeley: University of California Press, 2002.

Sullivan, Antony Thrall. *Thomas-Robert Bugeaud: France and Algeria, 1784–1849: Politics, Power, and the Good Society.* Hamden, Conn.: Archon, 1983.

Tackett, Timothy. *Religion, Revolution, and Regional Culture in Eighteenth-Century France: The Ecclesiastical Oath of 1791.* Princeton: Princeton University Press, 1986.

Taulier, Frédéric. *Le vrai livre du peuple ou le riche et le pauvre: Histoire et tableau des institutions de bienfaisance et d'instruction primaire de la ville de Grenoble.* Grenoble: Maisonville et Fils et Jordan, 1860.

Teissier, Henri, ed. *Histoire des chrétiens d'Afrique du nord: Libye, Tunisie, Algérie, Maroc.* Paris: Desclée, 1991.

Testas, Pr. *La vie militante de la bienheureuse Mère Emilie de Vialar: Fondatrice de la Congrégation des Soeurs de Saint-Joseph de l'Apparition (1797–1856).* Marseille: Editions Publiroc, 1939.

Thompson, Elizabeth. *Colonial Citizens: Republican Rights, Paternal Privilege, and Gender in French Syria and Lebanon.* New York: Columbia University Press, 2000.

Thompson, Margaret Susan. "Women, Feminism, and the New Religious History: Catholic Sisters as a Case Study," in *Belief and Behavior: Essays in the New Religious History,* ed. Philip R. Vandermeer and Robert P. Swierenga, 136–63. New Brunswick, N.J.: Rutgers University Press, 1991.

Thomson, Ann. *Barbary and Enlightenment: European Attitudes towards the Maghreb in the 18th Century.* Leiden: Brill, 1987.

Thorne, Susan. *Congregational Missions and the Making of an Imperial Culture in Nineteenth-Century England.* Stanford: Stanford University Press, 1999.

Thorne, Tanis C. *The Many Hands of My Relations: French and Indians on the Lower Missouri.* Columbia: University of Missouri Press, 1996.

Tibawi, A. L. *The Modern History of Syria including Lebanon and Palestine.* London: Macmillan, 1969.

Tlili, Béchir. *Les rapports culturels et ideologiques entre l'Orient et l'Occident, en Tunisie, au XIXème siècle (1830–1880).* Tunis: Publications de l'Université de Tunis, 1974.

Toth, Stephen A. *Beyond Papillon: The French Overseas Penal Colonies, 1854–1952.* Lincoln: University of Nebraska Press, 2006.

Tournier, Jules. *La conquête religieuse de l'Algérie, 1830–1845.* Paris: Plon, 1930.

Trimbur, Dominique, and Ran Aaronsohn, eds. *De Bonaparte à Balfour: La France, l'Europe occidentale, et la Palestine, 1799–1917.* Paris: CNRS Editions, 2001.

Trimingham, J. Spencer. *A History of Islam in West Africa.* London: Oxford University Press, 1962.

Trouillot, Michel-Rolph. *Silencing the Past: Power and the Production of History.* Boston: Beacon, 1995.

Turin, Yvonne. *Affrontements culturels dans l'Algérie coloniale: Ecoles, médecines, religions, 1830–1880,* 2d ed. Algiers: Entreprise Nationale du Livre, 1983.

Turner, Mary. *Slaves and Missionaries: The Disintegration of Jamaican Slave Society, 1787–1834.* Urbana: University of Illinois Press, 1982.

Vacher, Marguerite. *Des "régulières" dans le siècle: Les Soeurs de Saint-Joseph du Père Médaile aux XVII et XVIIIe siècles.* Clermont-Ferrand: Adosa, 1991.

Vadala, Ramire. *Les maltais hors de Malte (Etude sur l'émigration maltaise).* Paris: Arthur Rousseau, 1911.

Vandermeer, Philip R., and Robert P. Swierenga, eds. *Belief and Behavior: Essays in the New Religious History.* New Brunswick, N.J.: Rutgers University Press, 1991.

Vicinus, Martha. *Independent Women: Work and Community for Single Women, 1850–1920.* Chicago: University of Chicago Press, 1985.

Villerbu, Tangi. "Faire l'histoire catholique de l'ouest américain: Une terre de missions à réévaluer." *Revue d'Histoire ecclésiastique,* vol. 101 (2006): 117–42.

Walls, Andrew F. *The Missionary Movement in Christian History: Studies in the Transmission of Faith*. Maryknoll, N.Y.: Orbis, 1996.

Walton, Whitney. *Eve's Proud Descendants: Four Women Writers and Republican Politics in Nineteenth-Century France*. Stanford: Stanford University Press, 2000.

Weber, Alison. *Teresa of Avila and the Rhetoric of Femininity*. Princeton: Princeton University Press, 1990.

White, Richard. *The Middle Ground: Indians, Empires, and Republics in the Great Lakes Region, 1650–1815*. New York: Cambridge University Press, 1991.

Willens, Lily. "Lafayette's Emancipation Experiment in French Guiana, 1786–1792," in *Transactions of the Sixth International Congress on the Enlightenment, Brussels, July 1983*, 222–24. Oxford: Voltaire Foundation, 1983.

Windler, Christian. *La diplomatie comme expérience de l'autre: Consuls français au Maghreb (1700–1840)*. Geneva: Droz, 2002.

Wolf, John B. *The Barbary Coast: Algiers under the Turks, 1500–1830*. New York: Norton, 1979.

Wolff, Jacques. *Les Périer: La fortune et les pouvoirs*. Paris: Economica, 1993.

Woodard, Colin. "Experts Ponder Papal Succession." *Christian Science Monitor* (29 July 2002).

Woollacott, Angela. *Gender and Empire*. New York: Palgrave Macmillan, 2006.

Zuccarelli, François. "Le régime des engagés à temps au Sénégal (1817–1848)." *Cahiers d'études africaines*, vol. 2, no. 7 (1962): 420–61.

Index

abolition
  Anne-Marie Javouhey and, 1–3,
    237–38, 243, 251–52
  British and, 11, 202, 216, 243, 247,
    251, 326n66
  French and, 243, 253–54
  French Catholics and, 14, 245, 247
  in French colonies, 255–57,
    318n30
  French scholarship on, 247
  papacy and, 246–47
  Société française pour l'abolition de
    l'esclavage and, 243–44
Affre, Mgr, 236, 323n12
African students in France, 203–5
Ahmad Bey, 1, 132–35, 139–41, 149, 172,
  270
alcohol
  Catholic clerics and, 207
  French settlers in Guiana and, 211
  Indians and, 50, 75–76, 81, 83, 88, 90
  white Americans and, 76, 81
Aleppo, 164, 169
Algeria, 2, 9–10, 12, 101, 109, 111–19,
    121–23, 125, 127–29, 132–34, 140,
    172, 178, 267, 297n51, 297n54
  Société Coloniale and, 109
  See also Algiers; Constantine; Dupuch,
    Mgr Antoine-Adolphe; el-Kader,
    Abd; St-Joseph de l'Apparition,
    Soeurs de; Plain of Mitidja; Vialar,
    Augustin de; Vialar, Emilie de
Algiers, 101, 109, 111–12, 114–17, 121–23, 126,
    265, 297n38, 298n63

L'Ami de la religion, 244
Anglicans, 7, 67, 162, 170, 275n14
Annales de la Propagation de la Foi, 83,
  116
Antilles. See Caribbean
Armenia, 12, 152, 165–68, 170
Aron, Stephen, 96
Athens, 152, 154
Audé, Eugénie, 45, 54, 60
Augustine, Saint, 114–17, 139,
Australia, 13, 170
Austria, 132, 161, 163, 167
  suppression of contemplative
    convents, 274n6
"Autun affair." See d'Héricourt, Mgr;
  Javouhey, Anne-Marie, "Autun
  affair"
Aymot, Louise, 84

Badin, Fr. Stephen, 90
Baltimore, diocese of, 10, 45,
  58–59
baptism, Catholic, 79, 177
  and Code Noir, 57–58, 245
  in Guiana, 218, 226
  and Indians, 89, 92, 293n73,
    293n78
  of Jews, 125, 138–39, 300n118,
    300n119
  of Protestants, 67–68, 267
  secret (in extremis), 125–27, 129,
    138–39, 157–59, 166, 168, 171–72,
    267–68, 300n118, 300n119
  in Senegal, 194, 204

Baptists
  in Jamaica, 225
  and the Middle East, 307n50
  and the Potawatomi, 90, 92–93, 290n26,
    293n76
  in St. Louis, 67
Barat, Louis, 36, 40, 45, 51
Barat, Madeleine Sophie, 6, 36–42, 44–45,
    52–53, 55–56, 58, 64, 70, 72–73, 82, 177,
    182, 236, 266, 281n55
  correspondence with Philippine
    Duchesne, 39, 44, 48, 52–56, 58, 60, 64,
    69–70, 72–73, 78, 81–84, 182, 277n61
  correspondence with other Sacred Heart
    sisters, 77, 87, 94
  dispute with Mgr Affre, 236
Baumgarten, Nikola, 66
Beecher, Catharine, 67–69, 288n106
Beecher, Jonathan, 224
Beecher, Lyman, 68
Benedict XVI, 271
Benton, Sara, 68
Benton, Thomas Hart, 68, 96
Bernard, Laure, 197, 204, 213, 225
Berthold, Octavie, 45, 54, 60, 78
Bethlehem, 164–65
Bigeu, Josephine, 60
biography, 2–4, 17–19
  collective, 1–3, 277n54
  and hagiography, 19, 109
Bissette, Cyrille C. A., 247
blacks
  as "blank slates," 222, 228, 245, 267
  Catholic evangelization of, 246–48
  as Catholic nuns, 58, 203, 205, 253
  as Catholic priests, 203, 205–6, 244, 271
  childishness imputed to, 221–23, 225,
    237–38
  laziness imputed to, 77, 192, 219, 229
  in Missouri, 54–59, 70, 77–78, 83,
    88, 96
  in New Orleans, 47–48, 50, 55–56
  in the United States, 47–48, 54–59, 70,
    77–78, 83, 88
  See also abolition; African students in
    France; Boilat, David; Duchesne,
    Philippine, and blacks; Fridoil, Arsène;
    Javouhey, Anne-Marie, and black nuns
    and priests; Javouhey, Anne-Marie,
    blacks, views of; Javouhey, Anne-Marie,

and slavery; Moussa, Jean-Pierre;
  Sacred Heart, Religious of the, and
  blacks; slave trade; St-Joseph de Cluny,
  Soeurs de, and blacks, racial and class
  segregation in schools of, in Senegal;
  Ursulines, and slaves and free blacks
Blackwell, Elizabeth, 69
Blackwell, Emily, 69
Boilat, David, 195, 197, 204–7, 313n72,
    316n135
  See also blacks, as Catholic priests
Bône (Algeria), 111, 115, 117, 126, 128, 131
Bon Sauveur, Dames du (Caen), 108
Bon Pasteur, Soeurs du, 128
Bourassa, Joseph Napoleon, 91–92
Bourbon, 11, 15–16, 182, 184–89, 192, 236,
    245–47, 249–50, 253, 255, 257, 318n32,
    327n84
Bourgade, Abbé François, 133, 146, 152, 265,
    303n52
  in Tunisia, 135–40
brevet. See credential, teaching
British Empire, 11–13
  abolitionism in, 11, 202, 216, 243, 247, 251,
    326n66
  in the Caribbean, 184
  Catholicism in, 142
  in Greece, 153
  in Malta, 141–42, 144
  and the Middle East, 162, 307n36
  missionaries in, 16, 170, 225, 243
  in North America, 84–85, 147
  Protestantism in, 16, 170, 142
  slavery in, 11, 191, 202, 312n57
  in West Africa, 191, 201–2, 312n54
Broglie, duc de, 244
Brunoni, Abbé, 155–56, 165, 169
Burma, 13, 170, 271

Canada, French, 10–11, 15, 33, 82, 85,
    184, 239
  and Philippine Duchesne, 43–44
  Jesuits in, 48
  See also Saint-Pierre and Miquelon
Cap Vert, 314n89
Capuchins, 139–40, 157–58, 166–68, 283n88
Caribbean, 3, 9, 11, 178, 182, 184, 198, 216–17,
    225, 245
  See also Baptists, in Jamaica; Guadeloupe;
    Martinique

Carmelites, 57

Carondelet, Governor, 63

Catholic Church
    abolition and, 245–47, 257
    bishops' and priests' authority in, 4, 7–8,
        20, 117–21, 127, 129, 233–42
    Catholic Reformation and, 4–5, 7, 17,
        37–8, 103
    and competition with Protestants, 12,
        142
    Congregation of Bishops and Regulars
        of, 242
    "feminization of," 8, 16–17
    and French military, 115–16
    gendered authority in, 119–20, 233–42
    as global and transnational, 13–14
    Holy See, 38, 113–14, 120–21, 139–40, 144,
        148, 162–63, 166, 239, 242–43, 260,
        298n58
    hybrid forms of, 194, 268
    in Nigeria, 271
    and the Ottoman Empire, 102
    and slavery, 238, 245, 247–48
    theology of salvation, 24, 171, 226, 245
    in the twenty-first century, 270–71
    women's aim to rebuild, 5–6, 181
    See also baptism, Catholic; universal
        salvation

Cayenne (Guiana), 42, 209, 215–16, 220, 222,
    226–28, 230–31, 238, 249, 256, 260,
    311n47, 318n30, 324n15, 330n137

Chantal, Jeanne de, 24–25, 35, 278n9

Charité, Filles de la, 38, 103, 177, 274n1
    in Algeria, 128–29
    in Beirut, 160–61, 164
    in Constantinople, 152
    during the French Revolution, 177,
        274n7
    and Napoleon, 274n9
    scope of work of, 4–6
    and social class, 4–5, 38, 107
    uncloistered life of, 4, 38
    in the United States, 72

Charité de Besançon, Soeurs de la, 6,
    179–80

Charité de Nevers, Soeurs de la, 106

Charity, Sisters of, 45, 53, 57, 64, 72, 74, 147

Chateaubriand, François-René de, 14,
    42–43, 139, 153, 161–62, 275n26

child mortality, 133

Chios, 143, 152–58, 164

choir sisters
    in the Society of the Sacred Heart in
        France, 25–26, 29,
    in the Society of the Sacred Heart in
        North America, 54, 63, 73
    in the Soeurs de St-Joseph de
        l'Apparition, 104, 108
    See also converse sisters

cholera, 67, 73, 109, 113, 122, 125–26, 133–34,
    164, 189, 269, 300n120

Chouteau, Emilie, 69

Cistercians. See Trappists

Civil Constitution of the Clergy, oath to. See
    French Revolution

Clancy-Smith, Julia, 133

Clark, William, 67, 80

Clifton, James A., 90–91, 292n50, 294n85

cloister, Catholic
    as a changing norm for nuns, 4–7, 71,
        242, 263
    Emilie de Vialar and, 107, 119–20, 266
    European legislation on, 274n11
    as indispensable for nuns, 44, 242
    Marie de l'Incarnation's vision of, 43,
        266
    nuns' lives outside of, 9, 16, 38, 145, 177
    self-imposed, 31
    and Spanish nuns, 274n11, 276n46
    See also Duchesne, Philippine, and;
        Charité, Filles de la, uncloistered life
        of; Javouhey, Anne-Marie, and;
        St-Joseph de Cluny, Soeurs de, and;
        St-Joseph de l'Apparition, Soeurs de,
        and; Vialar, Emilie de, and

Code Noir, 57–58, 245

Coeur de Roy, Soeur Gabrielle, 167–68

Congress of Vienna, 191

Constantine (Algeria), 111–12, 115–17, 124,
    127–28

consuls, European, 12, 115, 131–33, 135,
    139–41, 144, 151–52, 155–56, 158–64, 167,
    169, 267

converse sisters
    in Africa, 195
    in France, 29, 45, 54–55, 104, 108, 278n6
    in North America, 29, 54–56, 58, 64,
        73–74, 104
    in South America, 195, 210–11
    See also choir sisters

Copts, 165
Council of Trent, 188
Cox, Jeffrey, 14
credential, teaching (*brevet*), 148
Crete, 153, 157–58
Crimean War, 143, 158, 163, 168
Cross, Daughters of the, 57
Crusades, 161–62
cultural intermediaries
    Maltese as, 144
    métis Indians as, 76–77
    Potawatomi Indians as, 85, 91–93
    signares of Senegal as, 193–94
    in West Africa, 204
Cyprus, 151–52, 155–58, 164

Daffis, Soeur Joséphine, 134, 138
Dagana plantation, 197, 200–01, 208–09,
    313n86
Dard, Jean, 193
Daughton, J. P., 13, 270
Davis, Natalie Zemon, 18
Delacroix, Eugène, 153, 155
Delille, Henriette, 58
Desan, Suzanne, 179
De Smet, Fr., 84–85, 91, 93–94, 265
Diderot, Denis, 28
Dippie, Brian, 83
Doctrine Chrétienne, Soeurs de la, 118, 128
Dominican Sisters, 57
Druzes, 160, 307n36
Dubourg, Bishop Louis Guillaume, 43, 45,
    50–54, 56–59, 61, 70, 72, 77, 79, 81,
    283n88, 284n29, 285n41
Duchesne, Philippine
    and American mores, 60–61, 95
    arrival in Louisiana, 47–48
    and baptisms, 68, 92
    Barat, Madeleine Sophie, correspondence
        with, 39, 44, 48, 52–56, 58, 60, 64,
        69–70, 72–73, 78, 81–84, 182, 277n61
    beatification and canonization of, 19
    and Bishop Dubourg, 50–54, 56, 58–59,
        70, 72
    and blacks, 47–48, 55–56, 58–59, 77
    and cloister, 25–26, 28, 31, 38–39, 41,
        44–45, 47, 61, 71, 96, 266
    early life of, 23–24
    educational philosophy of for girls, 61–63
    family of, 23–25, 27–29, 34, 67

and Fr. Van Quickenborne, 78–80, 82
finances of, personal and organizational,
    33–34, 46, 51–52, 78–79
French Revolution and, 26–27, 29
goal of personal salvation, 96, 104, 124
and Indians, 1–2, 27, 41, 43–44, 47–48, 50,
    52, 56–57, 59, 75–77, 80–89, 92–97
and Jesuits, 27, 78–81, 84, 88, 93–94
missionary vision of, 40–42
in Missouri, 50–5
and nostalgia for Old Regime religious
    life, 95, 267
and the Potawatomi, 85–94
and Protestants, 65–68
in the Religious of the Sacred Heart,
    39–41, 45, 51, 64, 177
and Saint François Régis, 33, 41, 70, 89,
    281n67
and the Ursulines, 47
views on social class, 54–56, 64
and the Visitation order, 23–9, 32, 34–36,
    41
vocation of, 25, 39–41
and universal salvation, 43, 48, 68
Duchesne, Pierre-François, 23, 27–29
Dugoujon, Abbé, 246, 257
Dupuch, Mgr Antoine-Adolphe, 101–2,
    114–21, 123–24, 126–29, 131, 135, 144, 171,
    173, 264–65, 298n61
Dutch Guiana. *See* Surinam

education, Catholic
    African students in France, 203–5
    boarding schools in the Caribbean, 189,
        248, 250, 252–54
    boarding schools in France, 4, 25, 31, 34,
        36–38, 236, 248
    boarding schools in the Mediterranean
        basin, 111, 131, 141, 154, 156, 161, 164
    boarding schools in the United
        States, 44, 50–52, 58–68, 71–73, 77,
        79–80, 93–96
    boarding schools in West Africa, 194–96,
        204–5, 208, 257
    in Bourbon, 248–49
    for boys, 33–34, 70, 73, 79–81, 87, 93, 105,
        136, 155–57, 168, 182, 192–93, 203–6, 231,
        296n19, 322n121
    catechism instruction, 61, 64–65, 70, 179,
        181, 194, 206, 247–50

day schools in the Mediterranean basin, 142
day schools in the United States, 51, 70, 72, 77, 80
free schools in Bourbon, 249
free schools in Caribbean, 250–52
free schools in Guiana, 247
free schools in the Mediterranean basin, 111, 131, 136, 144, 154, 168
free schools in North America, 36, 52, 59, 62, 64, 73, 94, 289n127
in Greece, 154
interconfessional, 136–37, 140
el-Kader, Abd, 109, 122–24, 299n96
empire, history of. *See* imperialism, history of
enclosure, for nuns. *See* cloister
engagement à temps, 199–200, 208, 215, 219, 314n101
Enfants de Marie, 58, 61
Enlightenment, 29, 38, 42, 276n33, 298n71
Episcopalians, 67
Erzurum (Ottoman Empire), 166–68
evangelicals, American, 270
evangelization, Catholic, 113, 121–22, 124, 129, 159
and Jews, 161
in Ottoman empire, 152
outlawed in Greece, 154
in Tunisia, 137–38

Feay, Troy, 247, 328n102
Florissant, Mo., 51–2, 55, 60–61, 64–65, 68–71, 77–81, 281
Fourier, Charles, 224, 320n81
Franciscans, 162–64, 169, 308n54
Fredrickson, George, 57, 226
French colonies
in Asia, 2
and British colonialism, 153
scholarship on, 2, 17
in Tahiti, 258
See also Algeria; Bourbon; Gambia; Gorée; Guadeloupe; Guiana; Pondicherry; Mana; Saint-Pierre and Miquelon; Senegal
French Guiana. *See* Guiana
French Revolution, 2, 4–6, 10, 14, 17, 26–33, 35–38, 40–43, 45, 70, 95–96, 102, 105,
108, 177–80, 191, 266, 276n33, 279n21, 279n25, 280n39, 310n10, 328n102
Civil Constitution of the Clergy, oath to, 179, 279n25, 295n4
de-Christianization campaign in France, 6, 179
Fridoil, Arsène, 205–7
See also blacks, as Catholic priests

Gaillac, 102, 104–8, 117, 141, 144, 146–47, 170, 266
Galitzine, Elisabeth, 66, 73–74, 84, 87, 93, 284n24
Gallicanism, 123, 140, 264–65
Gambia, 201–2, 312n57
Gauchet, Gabrielle, 31
gender, history of, 2–4, 8, 17
gender roles
and Arabs, 126–27
in the Catholic Church, 43, 78–79, 119, 173, 207, 239, 261
and confidence, 264
and domesticity, 8–9, 16–17, 51, 138
in Guiana, 226
modernity and, 8–9, 275n
in nineteenth-century France, 2, 8, 28, 137, 182, 259–60
among the Potawatomi, 88
in Senegal, 195
in United States religious communities, 275n16
Good Shepherd, Sisters of, 74
Gorée (Senegal), 11, 190–98, 200, 202, 206–8, 239, 252, 258, 312n54, 312n57, 312n63
Gouges, Olympe de, 8
Gramont, Eugénie de, 65
Grand Coteau (Louisiana), 52, 56, 60, 70–71, 82
Grant, Zilpah, 69
Greek Orthodoxy. *See* Orthodox Christians
Greek war of independence, 12, 153–55
Grégoire, Abbé, 244
Gregory XVI, 56, 114, 246–47
Grenoble, 23–30, 32–34, 36, 39, 70, 279n24, 289n128
Guadeloupe, 9, 11, 184–85, 189, 192, 216, 242, 247–52, 254–57, 318n32, 327n84

Gualy, Archbishop de, 104, 117–19, 126, 131, 146–48
Guaraní Indians (Paraguay), 48, 223
Guérin, Eugénie de, 101, 103–9, 295n10, 296n30
Guiana, 1, 3, 9–12, 178, 184, 186, 192, 211–12, 214–20, 223–26, 228–29, 231, 238, 245, 247, 250, 256, 258–59, 310n26, 316n6, 318n30, 318n32
    See also Mana
Guillier, Abbé, 237–39, 241, 245, 259

hagiography. *See* biography
Haiti, 10–11, 45, 57–58, 95, 198, 204–5, 207, 216, 243
    slave rebellion of, 11, 184, 216
Hall, Catherine, 225
Hamilton, Mathilde and Eulalie, 54
health services
    European practices of, 112, 269
    male nurses, 111, 113
    and mental illnesses, 108, 183
    in Protestant missions, 201
    as rationale for French colonialism, 134
    in West Africa, 201
    See also Charité, Filles de la; Sacred Heart, Religious of the; St-Joseph de l'Apparition, Soeurs de, health services of; St-Joseph de Cluny, Soeurs de, health services of
Hefner, Robert W., 13
d'Héricourt, Mgr, and the "Autun affair," 233–42
Holy Childhood Association (Oeuvre de la Sainte Enfance), 125
Holy Family, Sisters of, 58–59, 70, 286n55
Hufton, Olwen, 179

Illinois, 56
imperialism,
    history of, 2, 4, 17, 20
    "new," 3
India, 170, 257, 270. *See also* Pondicherry
Indians
    and alcohol, 50, 75–76, 81, 83, 88, 90
    Algonquin, 44
    baptism of, 89, 92, 293n73, 293n78
    Huron, 44
    Iroquois, 44
    Kickapoo, 81–82, 85

laziness imputed to, 75, 77, 88
and literacy, 79
métis, 50, 58, 73, 76–77, 80–81, 83, 90–91, 294n85
and missionaries, 1–2, 27, 41, 43–44, 47–48, 50, 52, 56–57, 59, 75–77, 80–89, 90–97, 223
Montagnais, 44
Nipissing, 44
population estimates in American West, 79
and resettlement pressures, 76, 93
See also Bourassa, Joseph Napoleon; Duchesne, Philippine, and Indians; Javouhey, Anne-Marie, and Indians; Mana (Guiana), Indians near; Potawatomi Indians
Indochina, 10, 13, 143
Islam
    in Chios, 156
    Christians' views of, 113, 115–16, 123–24, 137–39, 206
    conversions from, 14, 121–25, 166, 196, 297n54
    conversions to, 132, 134
    in Crete, 157
    in Cyprus, 165
    and Greece, 153, 159
    interfaith projects, 112
    Koranic schools, 113, 197
    Muslim harmony among other monotheists, 122–23, 268
    Muslim homes closed to Christian men, 126–27, 168–170
    in Ottoman empire, as cohesive force, 267
    in West Africa, 196–97, 206, 208, 257, 268

Jackson, Andrew, 80, 83
Javouhey, Anne-Marie
    and agriculture, 197–99, 208, 210–15, 220, 228
    and abolition, 1–3, 237–38, 243, 251–52
    attacked as dishonest, 237
    attacked for independence, 238–41
    "Autun affair," 233–42
    beatification of, 19, 330n142
    and bishop of Trinidad, 237, 253
    and black nuns and priests, 203, 205–6, 239

blacks, views of, 211, 217, 219–22, 225–28, 230, 244, 251, 257, 268
and Catholic clerics, 180–82, 184, 238–40, 264
and civilizing processes, 192, 199, 219–20
and cloister, 215, 220, 223, 266
comic book on, 19
early life of, 177–80
educational goals of, 222
and emancipation of slaves, 201, 208, 219–20, 224, 237–38
and Emilie de Vialar, 148, 242, 263
executive role of, 199, 213, 216–18, 224, 227, 230–34, 254–55, 26–62
and family support, 178, 182–83, 235, 265
and franchise, 259
and government officials, 184, 212–13, 215, 217, 219, 226, 228, 230–31
health of, 201
and health services, 190–92, 202
and the Holy See, 182, 240, 260
and indigenous clergy, 203
and Indians, 223
and Islam, 196, 199
and Jesuits, 238
Mana, communal visions for, 212–15, 217, 219–22, 224, 229–31
masculine imagery for, 1, 259–60
maternal imagery of, 215, 217, 222–23, 259, 261
orthodoxy of challenged, 237
and Pius VII, 182
and royalty, 1, 235–36, 260
and siblings, 180, 182–83, 186, 190
and slavery, 11–12, 14, 208, 224
universal Catholicism of, 195, 207, 213–14, 220–21, 225–26, 231–32, 262
vocation of, 180–82
Javouhey, Balthasar, 177–78, 181
Javouhey, Claudine, 179
Javouhey, Clothilde, 182, 205
Javouhey, Léopold, 182, 260
Javouhey, Louis, 182, 215, 227
Javouhey, Marie-Joseph, 178, 182
Javouhey, Marie-Thérèse, 178, 182, 235
Javouhey, Pierre, 180, 182, 190
Javouhey, Rosalie, 178, 182–83, 186, 188–90, 193, 208, 235, 249
Jefferson, Thomas, 83
Jerusalem, 14, 152–53, 159, 161–66, 266, 307n46

Jesuits, 2, 5, 10–11, 79, 119
and emancipation, 238
in the Middle East, 161
in North America, 10–11, 14–15, 27, 33, 36–44, 48, 56–57, 60, 77–81, 84–85, 87–94, 125, 292n52
orders of nuns, as modeled on, 5, 36–38, 239, 281n55
in South America, 223, 238
"reductions" of, 223, 231, 238
Jews
abductions of Jewish children, 125, 300n119
in Algiers, 109, 111–13, 115, 124–25, 297n38
and Catholic baptism, 125, 138–39, 300n118, 300n119
Christians' conversion goals for, 140, 161, 166, 237, 307n50, 307n51
in Crete, 157
forcible baptism of in Rome, 125
in Jaffa, 165
in Jerusalem, 162–63, 165
"the Jew Levi" in the work of Anne-Marie Javouhey, 237
homes of, nuns' access to, 170
in the Ottoman Empire, 162–63, 165–66, 268
in Tunisia, 132, 134, 136, 140
See also baptism, of Jews; baptism, secret
Jouannet (legislator), 258–59
Joinville, Prince de, and Anne-Marie Javouhey, 235
Julia Caesarea, diocese of, 113–16, 122
Julien, Soeur Emilie, 182–83
in Algeria, 121
and Giuseppe Raffo, 302n25
in Malta, 141
in the Middle East, 143, 159–61, 164–66
as superior general, 125
July Monarchy, 215
and French influence overseas, 9
and religious orders, 148
and Senegal, 200
slavery during, 247, 328n102
See also Louis-Philippe, King
July Revolution. See Revolution of 1830

Kansas, 88–90, 292n52, 293n76. See also Sugar Creek
Kaskaskia, Ill., 48, 56–57, 72, 75, 96

Kastor, Peter, 96
Kentucky, 56–58, 72, 286n55

Lafayette, Marquis de, 318n30
Lamarre, Catherine, 45, 54
Lamartine, Alphonse de, 244
La Mennais, Jean-Marie de, 246
Langlois, Claude, 207, 235, 274n4, 274n10, 281n56, 330n142
Lane, William Carr, 66
Las Casas, Bartholemy de, 203
Layton, Mary, 54
Lazarists. *See* Mission, Congrégation de la
Lebanon 152, 166, 307n36
    French influence in, 159
Lecuir-Nemo, Geneviève, 19
Lefèvre, Soeur Onésime, 250–55
leprosy, 212, 235, 317n11
Lestrange, Dom Augustin de, 43, 310n10, 310n14
    and Philippine Duchesne, 41
    and Anne-Marie Javouhey, 180–81
LeVavasseur, Frédéric, 246
Liberia, 225
    Protestants in, 225
Libermann, François, 246
Liguori, Saint Alphonsus di, 136, 167
literacy
    in Algeria, 112, 297n51
    among Europeans in Tunisia, 143
    female, 4, 38, 59
    in France, 6, 105, 180–81
    among Europeans in Guiana, 222
    among Indians in the United States, 77, 79
    among United States citizens, 59, 63
Loretto, Sisters of, 72, 286n55
Louis, Saint (Louis IX), 133, 139, 163
Louisiana, lower and upper, 96.
    See also Florissant, Mo.; Grand Coteau;
        New Orleans; St. Charles, Mo.;
        St. Louis, Mo.; Sugar Creek, Kans.;
        Ste. Genevieve, Mo.
Louis-Philippe, King, 1, 109, 132, 139, 243
    and Anne-Marie Javouhey, 1, 206, 260
Lutheran deaconesses, 7
Lyon (Bellecour) convent, 30–31
Lyon, Mary, 69

MacCarthy, Charles, 201–3
Mack, Phyllis, 9

Malta, 12, 102, 141–46, 148–49, 157
    outmigration from, 143, 148–49
Mana (Guiana)
    agriculture at, 210–14, 217–20, 228
    and civilizing projects, 219, 225–27
    and emancipation, 216, 219, 225
    engagement à temps at, 215
    as experiment, 225, 229–31, 267
    founding principles of, 217–18
    and the French military, 211–12, 217
    health and illness at, 212, 214, 226
    Indians near, 213
    Javouhey family at, 215–17, 219, 227
    marriage at, 213
    and money, 211, 214, 217–18, 229–30
    residents' dissatisfaction with, 213–14, 216
    and slavery, 211, 214–16
Manteau, Marguerite, 45
Manuel, Rosalie, 77
Marie-Amélie, Queen, 120, 206–7
    and Anne-Marie Javouhey, 236
Marie de l'Incarnation, 15, 43–44, 75, 77, 79, 97, 266, 282n82
Marie-Joseph, Soeur, 253
    See also blacks, as Catholic nuns
Maronites, 155, 159–60, 165
maroons, 209, 216, 318n36
Marquesas Islands, 258
marriage
    Catholic, 194–95
    "customary," 193–95, 312n67
Marseilles, 131, 147
Martinique, 9, 11, 184–85, 187, 189, 192, 199–200, 216, 247, 252, 255–57, 318n32, 327n84
Maryland, 57–58, 64, 79, 96
Mathévon, Lucile, 53, 56, 69, 70, 84, 87
Mauritania, 196
Mazenod, Archbishop de, 147
Mélinon, Eugène, 230–31, 256, 322n119
mental illnesses. *See* health services
Mercier, Abbé, 104, 146
Mercy, Sisters, 74
Methodists, 65, 75, 81, 89–90, 92, 293n76
métis. See Indians; *see also* Potawatomi
    Indians; Bourassa, Joseph Napoleon
microhistory, 18–19
midwives, 112–13
Miller, Christopher, 198
Miquelon. *See* Saint-Pierre and Miquelon

Mission, Congrégation de la (Lazarists), 15, 113, 119, 160–61, 164, 297n54
missionaries
    aim of civilizing colonial populations, 14–16, 112, 124, 267
    American in the Middle East, 167
    British, 139
    competitive nationalism of European, 163
    French Catholic, in Asia, 147
    French Catholic, and Indians, 2, 10–11, 14, 43–45, 48, 51, 58, 79–82, 84–97
    in India, 170
    Italian, 139, 162
    nineteenth-century growth of, 15
    nineteenth-century women as, 16–17
    in Palestine, 12–13, 161–62
    scholarship on, 17
    twentieth- and twenty-first-century, 270
    United States government and, 79–80
    United States Protestant, 51, 167
    See also Charité, Filles de la; Jesuits; Sacred Heart, Religious of the; St-Joseph de l'Apparition, Soeurs de; St-Joseph de Cluny, Soeurs de; St-Paul de Chartres, Soeurs de
missionnaire (term), 15
Missouri (state), 2, 26, 49, 50–53, 55–77, 79–83, 85, 94, 96
    policies for Indians, 291n43
    Protestant elites of, 64, 67, 69, 265, 268
    slavery in, 56–5
Mohamed, Moustapha Ben, 101, 122
Monica, Saint, 117
Monnet, Abbé, 246
Mother Teresa, 270
motherhood
    Catholic, and child-rearing, 87
    as image for nuns' colonial work, 259
    in Islamic world, 137, 160, 164, 166
    Société de Charité Maternelle, 112
    in the United States, 59, 65–66, 69
    in West Africa, 192
    See also Javouhey, Anne-Marie, maternal imagery of
Moussa, Jean-Pierre, 204–7, 244
    See also blacks, as Catholic priests
Mullamphy, John, 64, 72

multilingualism, 112, 142–43, 161
Murinais, Marie-Anne Félicité de, 23, 32, 34–35, 281n47

Napoleon, 11–12, 15, 34
    and religious orders, 35, 37, 179, 181–82, 274n9
    and Malta, 142
    and slavery, 11, 243
National Assembly (Paris), 258
Native Americans. See Indians
needlework, female
    as income source, 30
    of Philippine Duchesne, 40, 81–82
    taught in France, 4, 25
    taught to Indians, 81, 87
    taught in the Mediterranean basin, 156–57, 160, 166
    taught in South America, 222
    taught in the United States, 61–63
    as valuable skill for a nun, 142, 144–45
New Orleans, 10–11, 50–51, 79, 285n41, 285n49
    convents in, 10, 43, 47, 50–51, 54–55, 57–58, 60, 63, 70–71, 75, 283n88, 286n55
    See also Holy Family, Sisters of the, Ursulines
Nightingale, Florence, 7, 202
Notre Dame, Congrégation de 103, 107
nuns, Anglican, 7, 275n14
nuns, Catholic. See baptism, secret; choir sisters; Catholic church, "feminization" of; cloister; converse sisters; Charité, Filles de la; religieuses; Sacred Heart, Religious of the; St-Joseph de l'Apparition, Soeurs de; St-Joseph de Cluny, Soeurs de; St-Joseph de Lyon, Soeurs de; St-Paul de Chartres, Soeurs de; superiors general; Ursulines; Visitation, Order of the
nursery schools, 111, 118, 136, 249
nursing, See health services

Oblate Sisters of Providence, 58
Oblats, Missionnaires de Marie Immaculée (Pères Oblats), 147, 151
O'Connor, Mary Ann, 84
Oregon territory, 91

orphans, 64, 67, 71–72, 74, 106, 111, 116–17,
124, 125, 164, 180–81, 195, 199, 202, 211,
214, 254, 289n127, 309n8
Orthodox Christians, 12, 156–59, 163, 165,
268, 306n28, 308n24
Catholic views of, 153–54, 158, 268
Ottoman Empire, 12, 149, 153–55, 159
and France, 3, 12–13, 102, 139, 152, 162
and Greece, 12
harmony among monotheists of, 122–23,
268
modernization of, 265
prohibitions in against Muslim
conversions, 166, 268
Christians' status in, 163, 268, 307n43,
308n54, 308n70,
in Tripoli, 132
and Tunisia, 132, 139
weakening of, 12–13, 102, 163, 172, 267

Paraguay, 14, 48, 51, 80, 84, 223, 266, 320n77
Pasha, Ibrahim, 161
Paul, Saint Vincent de, 5, 203, 274n3, 297n54
See also Mission, Congrégation de la;
Charité, Filles de la
peasants
European, 81, 285n43
French, 26, 74, 107, 109, 181, 196, 210–11,
217, 221, 228, 244
Javouhey family origins, 177–78, 197, 230
in Mana, 210–11, 213
Pécoul, Augustin, 251
Périer family, 27–28, 33, 278n14
Pius VII, 14, 39, 102, 182
and Anne-Marie Javouhey, 182
Pius IX, 15, 166
Plain of Mitidja, 109, 123
See also Algeria; el-Kader, Abd
Planel, Anne-Marie, 133
Ploërmel, Frères de, 206, 231, 246–47,
251–53, 322n121
Pondicherry, 11, 42, 185, 189, 240
Poor Clares, 45
Porter, Andrew, 14
postmodernism, 17–18
Potawatomi Indians, 1
Bourassa, Joseph Napoleon, 91–93
and Catholicism, 88–92
gender roles of, 87–88
and government agents, 85–87

language of, 86
Menomini, 90
Pokagon, Leopold, 90
religious practices of, 88–89, 92–93
resettlement of, 85
in the seventeenth and eighteenth
centuries, 84–85, 89–90
St. Mary's mission, 93
See also Sugar Creek, Kans.
Presbyterians, 67–69
priests
and Muslim homes, 126–27, 168–170
and Jewish homes, 170
Privilegio, Abbé Pierre, 152, 155
Propaganda Fide, 14, 42, 113–114, 126, 138, 246
Propagation de la Foi, 15, 51, 123, 131, 142, 155
Propagation de la Foi, Filles de, 36
proselytism. See evangelization, Catholic
prostitution, 16, 58, 111, 164
Protestantism
French, 243
Great Awakening, 95
in the Middle East, 162–63
in West Africa, 201–3
See also Anglicans; Baptists; British
Empire, Protestantism in;
Episcopalians; evangelicals, American;
health services, in Protestant missions;
Liberia, Protestants in; Methodists;
nuns, Anglican; Lutheran deaconesses;
Presbyterians; Quakers
Prudhomme, Claude, 257

Quakers
women, 9
in Liberia. 225
Quebec, see Canada, French

racism, biological, 226, 321n91
Raffo, Giuseppe, 135, 302n25
Redemptorist order, 136
Régis, Saint François, 33, 41, 70, 89, 281n67
religieuses (term), 15
Religieuses de la Sainte Famille, 108
religion, history of, 4, 9, 17, 277n53
Restoration government, 42, 184, 215
Réunion. See Bourbon
Revolution of 1830, 106, 215, 235, 243
See also July Monarchy; Louis-Philippe,
King; Restoration government

Revolution of 1848, 137, 146, 253, 258, 260
Revue des Colonies, 244
Richard-Toll plantation, 198, 201
Rigal, Joseph, 105–6
Roger, Baron Jacques-François, 197–98,
    203–4, 206, 215, 218–19, 236, 243–44, 255,
    265, 313n86
Rogers, Rebecca, 62
Romantics, 14, 139, 153, 223–24
    Anne-Marie Javouhey and, 178, 223–24,
        244, 262
    See also Chateaubriand, François-René
        de; Delacroix, Eugène; Guérin, Eugénie
        de; Lamartine, Alphonse de; Rousseau,
        Jean-Jacques
Rosati, Bishop, 56, 59, 68, 78, 284n24
Rousseau, Jean-Jacques, 223
Russian Orthodoxy. *See* Orthodox
    Christians

Sacré-Coeur de Marie, Congrégation du, 246
    See also Saint-Esprit, Congrégation du
Sacré-Coeur, Soeurs du (Valence), 108
Sacred Heart, Religious of the, 2, 6, 27
    as analogous to Jesuits, 27, 37, 281n55
    choir and converse sisters in, 54–56, 58,
        64, 73
    education in the United States, 59–83,
        86–88, 95
    in Grenoble, 23–9, 32, 34–36, 39–41, 45, 51,
        64, 177, 289n128
    and health services, 73
    Pères and Dames de la Foi pseudonym
        of, 40
    and blacks, 55–59, 88
    in the twenty-first century, 271
    and universal salvation, 226
    See also Barat, Madeleine Sophie;
        Duchesne, Philippine.
Saint Charles, Mo. *See* St. Charles, Mo.
Saint-Domingue. *See* Haiti
Saint-Esprit, Congrégation du
    (Spiritains), 15, 206, 245 246, 316n136
Saint Louis of France. *See* Louis, Saint
    (Louis IX)
Saint Louis, Mo. *See* St. Louis
Saint-Pierre and Miquelon, 11, 184–85, 239
Schmaltz, Julien, 198, 314n89
Schoelcher, Victor, 244, 247, 252–54, 257,
    326n55, 328n102

schools, Catholic. *See* education, Catholic
School Sisters of Notre Dame, 74
Scott, Joan Wallach, 18
Second Empire, 2, 148, 256, 258
Second Republic. *See* Revolution of 1848
Senegal, 193–201, 257–58, 312n54
    See also Gorée; St-Louis (Senegal)
Seton, Elizabeth, 45, 53, 72
Seven Years' War, 9, 184, 312
Sibley, Mary Easton, 69
Sierra Leone, 190, 201–2, 204, 225
signares (Senegal), 193–95, 201, 204, 257,
    312n67
    children of, 196, 201, 204, 312n69
Siros, 143, 152, 154, 158
slavery
    in French colonies, 11–13
    and Islam, 197
    outlawed in Tunis, 132
    in West Africa, 191, 193, 196, 199–202, 204,
        206–9, 257
slave trade, 2, 11, 56, 132, 184, 191, 197–200,
    202, 208, 211, 215–16, 243, 246–47,
    312n57, 318n31, 318n33
Sleeper-Smith, Susan, 87
Société de la morale chrétienne, 243
soeurs (term), 15
Soumille, Pierre, 145
Spanish Empire, 50–51, 79, 267, 276n46
    in Tunisia, 132
Spiritains. *See* Saint-Esprit, Congrégation du
St. Charles, Mo., 26, 50–52, 55, 61, 63, 67,
    69–71, 75–77, 93–94
Ste-Croix, Pères de, 136, 151
St-Cyr, Emilie, 94
St-Domingue. *See* Haiti
St. Joseph, Sisters of (Carondelet), 72, 74
St-Joseph de l'Apparition, Soeurs de, 2, 53,
    101
    in Algeria, 108–9, 111–13, 115–29
    in Aleppo, 169
    in Chios, 143, 152–58, 164
    and cloister, 104, 107–08, 120, 170, 266
    in Crete, 152, 155–57
    in Cyprus, 151–52, 155–59, 164–65
    founding of, 104–7
    habits of, 108, 120, 173
    health services of, 108–9, 111–13, 118,
        125–26, 129, 133–34, 143, 151, 155, 163,
        166–69, 171, 269

St-Joseph de l'Apparition, Soeurs de
    (*continued*)
  Italian houses of, 151
  interconfessional work of, 112, 122, 133,
    136, 156, 165
  in Jaffa, 164–65
  in Malta, 141–43, 145–46, 148–49, 157
  rules and statutes of, 145–46, 148
  in Saida (Ottoman), 164–66
  and salvation, 125, 166–67, 170–71
  in Siros (Aegean), 143, 152, 154
  and the Soeurs de St-Joseph de Cluny, 148
  in Tripoli, 145, 151
  in Tunisia, 131–41
  in the twenty-first century, 270–71
  See also Julien, Emilie; Vialar, Emilie de
St-Joseph de Cluny, Soeurs de, 2, 6
  adventurousness of, 189
  archives of, 1
  and blacks, 221–22, 253–54
  in Canada, 185
  in Caribbean, 185, 189
  and cloister, 187–89, 237, 266
  finances of, 181, 183, 186, 212–13, 224,
    228–30, 234, 237, 249, 256, 258
  across France, 183
  education of slaves and, 250, 255
  and French assimilationism, 193–96, 199
  in Guadeloupe, 248–49
  in Guiana, 185
  habits of, 253
  health of, 189–90, 198, 210
  health services of, 190–92, 201–2, 207,
    226, 231
  in Indian Ocean, 185
  and local authorities, 187
  near Madagascar, 258
  in Mana, 208–11, 213–14, 221–22, 230
  in the Marquesas Islands, 258
  in Martinique, 185, 187, 189, 214, 239,
    248–55
  and mental illnesses, 183
  mutual method of education, 183–84
  and Napoleon, 182
  in Oceania, 261
  and priests, 188
  raisons d'être of, 181, 183
  rules of, 186–88, 242–43
  racial and class segregation in schools
    of, 196, 208, 248–49

secular administration of, 234
  in Senegal, 185, 188–90, 195–98, 200–2,
    252
  and the Soeurs de St-Joseph de
    l'Apparition, 148
  in Tahiti, 258
  in the twenty-first century, 270
  See also Javouhey, Anne-Marie
St-Joseph de Lyon, Soeurs de, 108, 311n34
  See also St. Joseph, Sisters of (Carondelet)
St. Louis, Mo., 2, 10–11, 48, 50–51, 56, 60–67,
    69–74, 76–77, 82, 94, 265, 283n88,
    286n67, 288n117
St. Louis, Catholic diocese of, 51–2, 67, 72,
    79
St-Louis (Senegal), 11, 184, 188–93, 195–98,
    200–202, 204–8, 252, 257, 312n54,
    312n57, 312n63
St. Mary's Mission, 93–94
St-Paul de Chartres, Soeurs de, 15, 184–86,
    189, 276n46, 310n26
St-Pierre. *See* Saint-Pierre and Miquelon
St. Sulpice, Eglise, 103
Ste. Genevieve, Mo., 48, 50, 63
Ste-Marie-d'en-Haut, 23, 26, 28–29, 73,
    289n128
Suchet, Abbé, 112, 116, 124, 126–27,
    133
Sugar Creek, Kans., 84–94, 269
  See also Duchesne, Philippine, and the
    Potawatomi; Potawatomi Indians
superiors general
  men as, 119, 234–38, 242
  women as, 32, 34, 37, 117, 128, 233–38, 242,
    263–64
Surinam, 209, 214, 216

Tahiti, 258
Teresa of Avila, Saint, 24, 34, 101, 108, 180
Thouret, Jeanne-Antide, 180
Trappists, 31, 213, 180–81, 310n10, 310n14
  See also de Lestrange, Dom Augustin
Trebizond (Ottoman Empire), 166–68
Trinidad, 185, 253
Trinidad, bishop of, 236–37
Tripoli, 141
  French government's interest in, 152
  Ottomans in, 132
Tristan, Flora, 8
Tristant, Soeur Léonce, 252

Tunisia, 12, 102, 132–41, 143, 148–49
    and Abbé Bourgade, 135–40
    and Emilie de Vialar, 12, 102, 131–41
    See also Ahmad Bey
Tuscany, government of, 144

ultramontanism, 8, 264–65
United States government, 10, 47, 50, 79, 91,
    95, 184
universal salvation, Catholic doctrine of, 7,
    17, 24, 236, 244–46, 264
Ursulines
    and a Boston mob, 67
    in the Caribbean, 185, 187
    in France, 4, 10, 32, 289n128
    in Louisiana, 10, 16, 50–51, 54, 60, 67
    and Native Americans, 27, 44
    and slaves and free blacks, 47–48, 56–58,
    284n34, 285n41

Valée, Maréchal, 114–15, 121–22, 298n58
Valerga, Joseph, 162–66, 308n54
Van Quickenborne, Fr. Charles, 78–82, 264
    and Philippine Duchesne, 78–80, 82
Verhaegen, Fr., 81, 84, 86
Veuillot, Louis, 123–24, 247
Vialar, Augustin de, 107, 109, 120–21, 129
Vialar, Jacques-Augustin de, 102–4, 106–7,
    146
Vialar, Emilie de
    in Algeria, 101–2, 108–9, 111–13, 117–29, 131
    and Anne-Marie Javouhey, 148, 242, 263
    and the archbishops of Albi, 104, 117–19,
    126, 131, 146–48
    attacked as unpatriotic, 172
    beatification of, 19
    brother Augustin and, 107, 109, 120–21,
    129
    canonization of, 19
    and cloister, 104, 107–08, 120, 170, 266
    competitiveness of as educator, 141

    and Dupuch, Mgr, 101–2, 117–21, 123–29,
    131, 135, 144, 146, 171, 173, 264
    early life of, 102–3
    evangelism of, 164, 169, 171–72, 269
    executive role of, 145–46, 151, 159
    father of, 102–4, 106–7, 146
    finances of, personal and
    organizational, 102–3, 106, 109–10,
    117–18, 120, 128, 131, 146–47, 157, 173, 265
    French legislature and, 148
    goal of personal salvation, 170
    and the Holy See, 144, 148
    imperial agency of, 172–73
    and Jesuits, 238
    in Malta, 141–45
    and patriarchy, 173
    reputation for tolerance of, 170–71
    in Tunisia, 12, 102, 131–41
    and universal salvation, 125, 166, 170
Visitation, Order of the, 4, 24–26, 36–40,
    107, 177, 263, 278n2, 278n9, 279n19,
    281n49
    and the French Revolution, 29–32,
    279n22, 279n25
    and missionary work, 41
    and Napoleon, 35
    and Philippine Duchesne, 23, 27–28,
    33–36, 96
    and Ste-Marie-d'en-Haut, 23, 26, 28–29
    in the United States, 65–66, 72, 96
Voilquin, Suzanne, 8, 261

West Africa. *See* Gambia; Gorée; Liberia;
    Senegal; Sierra Leone; St-Louis
Willard, Emma, 69
women's history. *See* gender, history of
World Concern, 270

Xavier, St. Francis, 41–42, 61, 84, 105

yellow fever, 201, 203–4, 208

CPSIA information can be obtained at www.ICGtesting.com
Printed in the USA
LVOW070119240312

274579LV00002B/4/P

9 780199 922840